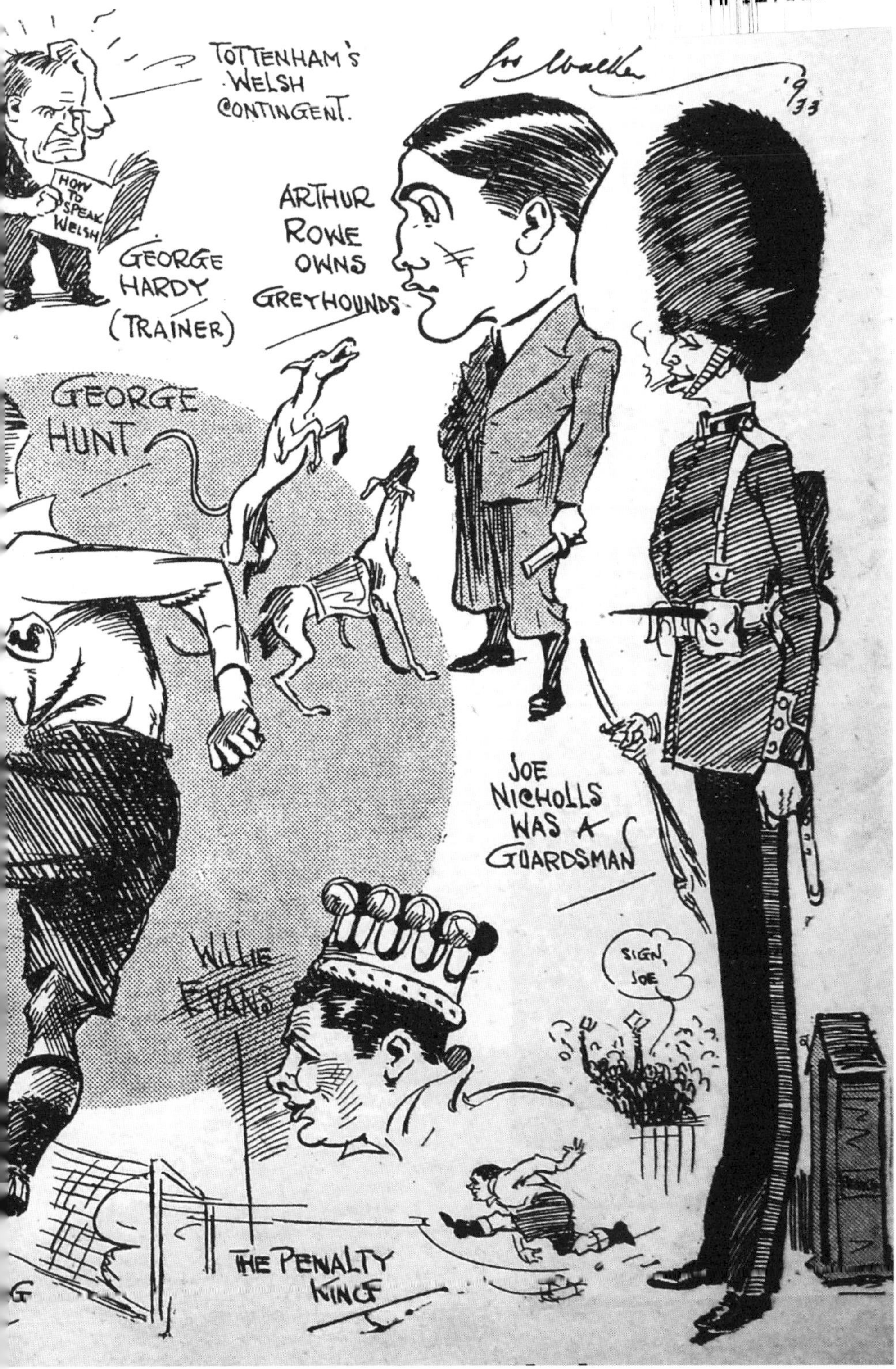
TOTTENHAM'S WELSH CONTINGENT.
HOW TO SPEAK WELSH
GEORGE HARDY (TRAINER)
ARTHUR ROWE OWNS GREYHOUNDS
GEORGE HUNT
JOE NICHOLLS WAS A GUARDSMAN
SIGN, JOE
WILLIE EVANS
THE PENALTY KING

ARTHUR
PUSH-AND-RUN
ROWE

ARTHUR
PUSH-AND-RUN
ROWE

The Inspiration Behind
Spurs, Crystal Palace
and 'Total Football'

Norman Turpin

First published in 2023

© Norman Turpin 2023

This biography would never have seen the light of day were it not for the kindness and hospitality of Graham Rowe (son of Arthur) when permitting me access to his father's copious press cuttings and other memorabilia.

This book is copyright under the Berne Convention. All rights are reserved. Apart from any fair dealing for the purpose of private study, research, criticism or review, as permitted under the Copyright Act, 1956, no part of this publication may be reproduced, stored in a retrieval system, or transmitted, in any form or by any means, electronic, electrical, chemical, mechanical, optical, photocopying, recording or otherwise, without the prior permission of the copyright owner. Enquiries should be sent to the publishers at the undermentioned address:

EMPIRE PUBLICATIONS
1 Newton Street, Manchester M1 1HW

ISBN: 978-1-915616-00-5

Printed and bound in the UK

Contents

	Foreword by Norman Giller	VII
	Preface by the Author	IX
1	**Football at its Best** *The Wave Gathering Momentum*	1
2	**Dreams of White Hart Lane**	
	The Boy Rowe's Path to Success 1906-1929	5
3	**Offside!** *Chapman and the Third Back*	17
4	**Dreams Do Come True 1** *A Spurs First-Teamer 1931-33*	22
5	**Dreams Do Come True 2**	
	Captain of Spurs, Capped for England and…Elastic Tactics! 1933-39	28
6	**Ambassador Rowe** *The Hungarian Connection*	47
7	**Budapest to Chelmsford** *Via World War 2*	57
8	**The Ultimate Dream** *Managing Spurs 1949-50*	75
9	**Push, Run and Succeed** *Rowe: His Methods and Beliefs*	98
10	**'Push-and-Run' Conquers England's Best**	
	Managing Spurs 1950-51	119
11	**Pleasure and Pressure** *Managing Spurs 1951-52*	138
12	**Dreams of Wembley** *Managing Spurs 1952-53*	158

13	**The Hungarian Revolution** ...*and English Decline*	177
14	**Toil and Torment** *Managing Spurs 1953-54*	197
15	**Ignorance and Violence Around Him** *Managing Spurs 1954-55*	214
16	**A Break from the Hotseat** *Goodbye Lane, Hello Selhurst 1955-60*	251
17	**It's Arthur** *A Palace of Dreams 1960-61*	260
18	**A Bold Start then…** *Managing Crystal Palace 1961-63*	284
19	**'Push-and-Run' to 'Kick, Bollock and Bite'** *Crystal Palace 1963-66*	317
20	**Rowe's Ten-Year Pledge Achieved in Nine** *Palace Reach the Promised Land 1966-69*	345
21	**Every Match an Adventure** *Rowe Enjoys Palace's Rise 1969-71*	358
22	**When Others Were Blind** *Forever an Inspiration*	368
	Epilogue	393
	Bibliography and Acknowledgements	395
	Index	401

Foreword

by

Norman Giller

Arthur Rowe would be a leading contender for the mantle of 'Father of Spurs'. The team he led to the League championship in 1950-51 famously played 'push and run' football that was poetry in motion.

In this book, lovingly and meticulously compiled by Norman Turpin, we meet the man behind the manager's mask. Arthur was modest about his achievements and did not seek the spotlight, but the author has dug behind the headlines and discovered a shy hero whose signature football can still be found at the foundation of the current team. The precise, penetrative football is in the Tottenham DNA and Arthur did more than most to introduce and nurture it.

The book has the blessing of Arthur's USA-based son, Graham, who watched his father building the 'Push and Run' Spurs and has quietly extolled his achievements for many years. It is a must-read, not only for Spurs supporters wanting to know the proud history of their club, but also for fans of Crystal Palace, where Arthur later made an impressive impact. 'King Arthur' Rowe deserves this revealing biography.

Norman Giller is a renowned sports historian whose 100-plus books include 20 in harness with Tottenham legend, Jimmy Greaves.

Despite his enormous success, Arthur Rowe's managerial career at Spurs was not always a contented one, but he was certainly admired and loved by those who worked under him. Here he is presented with a clock by Spurs' stars (left to right) Ted Ditchburn, Eddie Baily, Tony Marchi, Mel Hopkins and Ron Burgess.

Preface

'...a side suddenly strings a few passes together, short, quick passes with people moving intelligently to give and take them. It's as if the game suddenly got a little electric shock. The crowd catches its breath, and when it's over everyone claps because it's been a lovely moment.'

ARTHUR ROWE, *FOOTBALL DIGEST MONTHLY* (1974)

In 2017, prior to the final game ever played on the White Hart Lane turf, Daniel Levy, Chairman of Tottenham Hotspur Football Club, said 'It could not be more appropriate that, in what is our last season here, we have seen entertaining, free-flowing football and a return to what has once again been called glory days, such has been the impact of Mauricio [Pochettino] and his team of coaches and players.' Those 'glory days' would never have taken place had Arthur Rowe not led Spurs to the club's first-ever League Championship. Both Rowe and Pochettino preached a swift, short-passing game and, in 2019, Pochettino took Spurs to their first-ever Champions' League Final.

Rowe had been a boy when witnessing his Spurs heroes win the FA Cup and the Charity Shield in 1921. Nearly 30 years would pass before Rowe himself added the next item of silverware to the White Hart Lane trophy cabinet when, for the very first time in the club's history, his Spurs' side captured the Football League Championship itself, and they did it in the greatest style. The previous year's Second Division shield proved to be the first of 14 trophies to arrive at White Hart Lane over the following 24 years, until the end of Rowe protégé Bill Nicholson's reign as manager in 1974. In addition, that spell also saw the Club finish as runners-up in major competitions on three occasions and reach the FA Cup semi-finals twice. This finest period in Spurs' history had been ignited and inspired by Arthur Rowe.

Eleven years after Rowe's greatest-ever 90 minutes as a manager, a nigh-on perfect 7-0 victory over the powerful Newcastle United side of that era, South London paupers Crystal Palace, recently promoted from the Fourth Division, were also hammering in seven goals. Until that point my only personal exposure to professional football had been watching Spurs' great 'Double' side on TV but this was my first-ever visit to Selhurst Park. I looked on unaware that the Palace manager that day had that same year elevated the club from the Fourth to the Third Division, only later learning that the man responsible was the self-same Arthur Rowe, repeating the instant managerial success he had achieved at both Chelmsford City his first club, and his second, Tottenham Hotspur. This he achieved despite experts forecasting that the intricacy of his 'push-and-run' would fail to produce results in the hurly-burly of the lower Leagues.

Ever since that first exposure to Rowe's stimulating breed of football I have been intrigued to learn more about the great man himself: not just of the extraordinary and immediate impact he had on all three clubs he managed, or his playing style (which contrasted drastically to the established English style of the day), but also why he was so respected and admired by those whose path he crossed. Not for him Mourinho's arrogance or the temper tantrums of a Ferguson, Wenger or Allardyce. His upbringing had instilled in him the virtues of common decency, honesty and fair play, along too with a good dose of good humour. At Tottenham, Rowe was never presented with a blank cheque to construct a team of ready-made players, as were his fortunate successors; his triumphs instead achieved on a low budget, yet despite this, he was referred to by leading football correspondent Desmond Hackett as no less than '…the creator of England's finest football.'

Topping English football in 1951 with his awe-inspiring 'push-and-run' Spurs, the British football public's appreciation would have equalled or exceeded that which greeted Pep Guardiola's first Premiership title with Manchester City in 2018. If only Rowe's side could have been witnessed by a similarly large TV audience. At the beginning of this Preface I quote Rowe's description of the spectator's pleasure when exposed to his innovative style of play. This had been his response when asked 20-plus years later if he thought 'push-and-run' was still practised in English football (if only, perhaps, in short bursts). This book will look also into his influence on the great 1950s' Hungarian side which (ironically) turned the spotlight on the flaws remaining in the English game.

Sadly, there is an aspect of tragedy in Rowe's story — his managerial achievements would surely have been greater still had it not been for periods of ill-health and his being hindered at both clubs he managed by individuals who failed to support his innovative approach. These unfortunate associates of his exemplified why English football trailed the rest of the soccer world for far too long, persisting with the long-established trend of muscular, 'hit-and-hope' football. In meeting players who served under Rowe, it is remarkable how they uniformly speak of him with great warmth, lighting-up at the mere mention of his name. He left his mark without screaming into the face of fourth officials, or hurling boots at his players.

Rowe's son Graham, who originally and kindly reviewed a two-page, potted biography of his father that I had written for an aborted book, was the first to suggest I attempt this full-scale biography. I certainly had little need to drum up enthusiasm for the task; after all, this is the life of a unique and inspired individual. I end this preface with a quote by the esteemed Brian Glanville, when marking the occasion of the final match played at the original White Hart Lane in May 2017:

> 'From Arthur Rowe to Harry Kane, there are so many memories of Tottenham's ground.'
>
> BRIAN GLANVILLE, *WORLD SOCCER ONLINE*, MAY 2017

Norman Turpin 2023

1

Football at its Best

THE WAVE GATHERING MOMENTUM

'It's tough to watch your side being beaten, but this was football at its best.'
NEWCASTLE DIRECTOR STAN SEYMOUR AFTER ROWE'S SPURS HAD
DEMOLISHED HIS SECOND-PLACED SIDE 7-0

By Saturday November 18th 1950, Rowe's Second Division champions Tottenham Hotspur, only promoted to the top echelon of English football six months' earlier, had already picked up a healthy 23 from 32 points. With Newcastle United arriving at rainy White Hart Lane that afternoon, an eighth consecutive win would see rookies Spurs leapfrog Newcastle into second place behind leaders Arsenal.

Yet, despite suffering a surprise home defeat the previous weekend, Newcastle had rattled in a phenomenal thirteen goals in their preceding four outings and had lost just one of nine away fixtures. Only Arsenal had conceded fewer goals on their travels. Naturally, therefore, in the build-up to the game, visitors' goalkeeper Jack Fairbrother had told former Arsenal star turned journalist Bernard Joy that he and his colleagues were confident of victory. Included in Newcastle's star-studded line-up were icons such as wing-half and captain Joe Harvey, clever inside-forward Ernie Taylor, England striker Jackie Milburn and lethal Chilean international striker George Robledo. On the other hand Spurs had inexperienced 23-year-old half-back Colin Brittan standing-in for their injured skipper and driving-force Ron Burgess. But Rowe's men would be buoyed by a bumper home crowd of 70,336, which saw many hopeful fans shut-out.

On the sound of the whistle Spurs and Newcastle flew at each other, the home side proving the more threatening with their intense, short-passing game while Newcastle utilised more conventional English tactics, showcasing solo dribbling skills and long passes. Newcastle's tendency to run with the ball allowed Tottenham to drop back and snuff-out many of their attacks. With just five minutes on the clock the ball passed rapidly from Spurs' Colin Brittan to Les Medley, then to creator-in-chief Eddie Baily, before stocky home centre-forward Len Duquemin took possession in midfield, beat a man and passed back to Baily who spotted his left-winger Medley cutting inside and found him with a pass before accelerating outside to collect a return ball. Baily's cross was then struck waist-high, on the run, for inside-right Les Bennett to arrive at speed, diving to nod past 'keeper Fairbrother's right-hand at the near post. It was a goal described by *The London Times* as '… glorious, even extravagant, and it took one's breath away.'

Joe Harvey and his men were already battling desperately to keep Spurs out but could not prevent Spurs increasing their lead after 21 minutes. The swift combination this time was between Baily, Medley, Bennett, Duquemin and then Baily again, who this time collected the ball before beating full-back McMichael and picking his spot. On the half-hour Medley, nominally stationed on the left but now in the inside-right position, took a forward pass from Bennett and, from the edge of the area, sent a shot screaming into the roof of the net. 3-0. Bravely the visitors nearly struck back, Spurs' goalkeeper Ted Ditchburn making a superb goal-line save from Taylor, who stopped to applaud before Spurs headed for the dressing-room with a three-goal advantage. In 45 minutes, White Hart Lane had become 'Red Hot' Lane, with the promise of more fast, inspirational football to come. Spurs' supporters had never had it so good.

Without doubt Newcastle will have discussed striking back early in the second-half so as to regain a foothold in the contest, but instead they were rocked on their heels when Medley scored his second (Spurs' fourth) just three minutes in. On the hour outside-right Sonny Walters picked up number five before coming close again when striking the crossbar, but there was Medley, on hand to complete his hat-trick for number six. With two minutes' remaining Alf Ramsey completed the scoring with Spurs' seventh, this time from the penalty spot. In between Newcastle had emphasised their own strengths, Milburn and Mitchell both striking the woodwork but that afternoon Spurs had carried out one of Arthur Rowe's foremost dictums in perfect fashion: 'Put good football before results,' to which he would add: 'Do this and the results will come.'

And how! The reporter from the *Times* could not contain his admiration and excitement: 'It is hard to imagine a more brilliant exposition of the game than was shown to that vast, swaying assembly, over 70,000 strong, held there spellbound in the rain of a grey November afternoon,' adding, 'This was vintage champagne, something to savour and remember.'

He continued: 'Tottenham, indeed, to use the language of the golfer, were deadly on and around the greens, and that is what counts. But even beyond the important matter of scoring, the quality of their football was sheer joy, demanding an immoderate use of superlatives.' As for Spurs' unfortunate victims that afternoon, the *Times* had every sympathy: '[Newcastle] kept playing football to the bitter end and died like heroes in the cause of something quite out of the ordinary…'.

The majesty of this Spurs performance, especially as it came from a novice First Division side, was emphasised by Newcastle United director Stan Seymour's comments after the game: 'If a film had been taken of the sensational 7-0 victory of Spurs over Newcastle United it could have been used as a world model of how football should be played.'

The sporting Seymour heaped further praise on Rowe's side:

'The greatest team since the war. No team in the world could live with them in this form. It's tough to watch your side being beaten, but this was football at its best. I'd pick the lot for England.'

FOOTBALL AT ITS BEST

Newcastle's Milburn thought Spurs were 'dynamite' while centre-half Frank Brennan said: 'I have always wanted to see football played like this. Spurs are a wonder team.' Bewildered captain Joe Harvey, who at one point in the midst of the action could be seen wearing a baffled grin, came out with a classic comment on the afternoon he had just endured: 'I always got to the ball when it wasn't there.'

An ecstatic *Tottenham & Edmonton Weekly Herald* reporter rhapsodised: 'Spurs have proved beyond all doubt the vast superiority of their new-style soccer…successful application of this style will, I predict, create a revolution in British soccer.' He added: 'Just as clubs found it necessary to discover an answer to [Herbert Chapman's] third-back game, so they will have to remould their ideas to counter Spurs' system. That this will produce a vast improvement in soccer standards is without question. It should give British football the boost it needs to put us back on top of the soccer world.'

Even sidelined Spurs' captain Burgess was overwhelmed. He was easily able to overcome the disappointment of sitting out the game, saying: 'It was the finest exhibition of football I had ever seen, and although I was the Spurs' skipper and thought I knew everything about the team, I sat enthralled, for I realised for the first time why we had won so many matches with our push-and-run style of play.'

Following a typical, seven-pass sequence, Spurs' first of seven goals enters the Newcastle net via the head of Les Bennett (right and below).

Duquemin attempts to round the Newcastle 'keeper.

He continued: 'I was as excited as our most partisan supporters as I watched the close harmony of all departments of the team, the speed and perfection of movement, with the ball always on the move, and even the great Newcastle team were running around almost aimlessly in their efforts to prevent that spate of goals.' Burgess added: 'It was only by becoming a spectator that I realized just how special this side was.'

The Daily Telegraph poetically described how Spurs' attacks '…carried on right through the side, with each man taking the ball in his stride at top pace, for all the world like a wave gathering momentum as it races to the far distant shore.' The architect himself, Arthur Rowe, asked by Jack Milligan of *The Daily Graphic* for his own impressions of his side's performance, replied in typically understated fashion, 'Yes, I think we have a good side.'

Four years' later Hungary would also score seven goals, this time against England in Budapest. When reading the *Times'* football correspondent Geoffrey Green's lyrical summing-up of that superb Hungarian side of 1954 (see below), one can't help but ponder two things, firstly that Green's words might just as well have been applied to Spurs' hammering of Newcastle three years earlier and secondly that Rowe's work inspiring Hungary's own trainee coaches in 1939, most of whom would have 'come of age' in coaching terms by the time their national side was taking 1950s Europe by storm, was no coincidence.

> *'Here was football one could sit and watch until old age finally overcame one. Here was a cultural expression, a game which, even if it was not on this occasion hurtling with sharp conflict, was yet passionate and beautiful in its art. The Hungarian attack, in all its imaginative conception, was like light passing through a prism. It had all the colours of the rainbow and constantly the combination of those colours were changed.'*

2

Dreams of White Hart Lane

THE BOY ROWE'S PATH TO SUCCESS 1906-1929

'The boy was me!'
ARTHUR ROWE'S OWN HANDWRITTEN NOTE ON A PRESS CUTTING PRAISING
AN ANONYMOUS TOTTENHAM YOUTH RECRUIT

Arthur Sydney Rowe, whose vintage champagne football would take English football by storm, was born in South Tottenham's Ferndale Road on September 1st 1906. For one who was to devote so much of his life to Tottenham Hotspur Football Club, it was fortunate he knew nothing of Southern League Spurs' 2-1 defeat to West Ham United taking place just two miles away at White Hart Lane that afternoon.

Arthur's father, Sydney, was a 30-year-old upholsterer, his mother Charlotte ('Lottie'), 29. As a baby Arthur will have been doted on by his 5-year-old sister Daisy Charlotte. Another sister, Violet, followed Arthur and finally came brother Frank, when Arthur was almost 16 and on the cusp of his football career. Mother Lottie's own mother went on to produce a further eight children from a later relationship and when those children were orphaned, one of them, Mary Ann Stringer, moved in with Arthur's parents on their marriage. So as a baby Arthur will have had the loving attentions of an 11-year-old aunt as well as his sister Daisy. At 3-years-old Arthur moved with his family to 80 Thackeray Avenue, half-a-mile from Bruce Grove Station and this small terraced house would remain the family home for around 30 years. At the time of Arthur's birth Tottenham Hotspur Football Club was just two seasons away from entering the Football League. Published that year, *Association Football and the Men Who Made It* (1906) described Spurs as the most popular club in England: 'Did they not play pretty and effective football? Are they not scrupulously fair? Are they not perfectly managed?' Perhaps a description to fit Arthur's own ground-breaking Spurs' side 43 years later.

His own earliest soccer-playing memories involved games played under street lamps. Half-a-century later, writing of the growing use of floodlights in football, Rowe said: 'There will be many who... will identify floodlight football with their earliest days and the back streets of their home-town. Here the lights were the lamp-posts of the kerb's edge, where the pitch was lined by the kerbs themselves. The ball—maybe of rags, or paper, tied to a shape that was near round; the teams—street versus street or group versus group; and full-time [came with] — the

In this family group photo, perhaps taken when Rowe's father was engaged in the First World War, his mother Lottie poses with her eldest child Daisy (back left), Lottie's half-sister Mary Ann (standing, right), Arthur himself and Arthur's younger sister Violet.

breaking of a window or, as most often, the call of bedtime.' He added: 'We soon learned here to have a healthy regard and understanding for the problems of glare and shadow; if you guessed right, you kicked the ball; if not, you kicked the kerb. Simple, and one learned quickly!' Skills were thus developed subliminally during hectic games demanding instant ball control, Rowe explaining: 'The way kids play never changes over the years; they do it instinctively. Pass the ball and run into position to receive it. If you didn't you were out of the game …and you got cold. I only got cold once.' An early inspiration for his greatest gift to football, that which became known as 'push-and-run'.

His father first took Arthur to watch Spurs on his sixth birthday but the 'Lillywhites' would be relegated three years later in the last competitive season before World War I, this despite the appointment as manager of former Newcastle and Scotland half back Peter McWilliam. As a skilled wing-half, who later played a significant role in Rowe's career, he had enjoyed a stellar career with Newcastle where fellow Scot Robert Smyth McColl had substituted Newcastle's direct style with the possession style then played at Queen's Park. Becoming Spurs' manager himself at 31, McWilliam ensured that all his players followed that same philosophy and one who already possessed the technical skills to make it work was 18-year-old Arthur Grimsdell, converted by the manager into a constructive left-half equipped with a powerful shot. Sadly, his changes came too late to save Spurs from relegation but after the hostilities he achieved success simply by asking his men to produce what Rowe later recalled as '…accurate football, well-constructed football'.

The Great War further sparked the rivalry between Spurs and Arsenal which had begun in 1913 when the 'Gunners' moved to North London. It was decided to incorporate two extra clubs in the first post-War First Division season (1919-20) so Spurs' relegation should have been erased from the history books and they should therefore have retained their place as a First Division club after all. Illogically, however, Arsenal instead took their place, this despite their only finishing 5th in Division Two in 1914-15. Nevertheless McWilliam famously led Spurs straight back up and, during the following First Division season, a game against Newcastle would be recalled by 13-year-old Arthur as '...that amazing Boxing Day game...': 'I was one of the many boys who had been passed overhead, over the rails to the edge of the arena itself [on standing-only terraces, small boys otherwise saw little of the action]. I'll never forget the one-and-only Jimmy Dimmock's game that day. He cavorted his way through that Newcastle defence like the great master he was. It tingles to remember!'

Arthur's headmaster at Parkhurst Road School, Mr. E. A. Pope, recalled Arthur as a '...little fair-haired chap of six hanging around the goal-posts, and getting an occasional kick, when the big boys of his school were practising shooting after school hours.' The school, a mere block away from Arthur's Thackeray Road home, appeared to struggle to fill all its 1260 places so he enjoyed the advantage of small class sizes. Interviewed on BBC radio in 1951, Rowe recalled often being caned after skipping classes to watch Spurs' midweek matches. Indeed, he was once punished for 'lack of ambition', having expressed his desire to be an international footballer in an essay on 'What I Would Like to Be'. At around eight years old he turned-out for Parkhurst Road's third XI, this around the time of the outbreak of World War I. Pope recalled Arthur '...running down the right wing, tricking boys much older than himself, and helping his team to win a handsome victory.' Whilst tragedy upon tragedy unfolded in Europe, Arthur progressed on the soccer field, despite describing himself as 'a puny lad'. Rowe enjoyed retelling the story of the earliest footballing advice he received from his father Sydney, 'If your boots are all right for a start, and if you play with your head, you will be a footballer'! Rowe always owed a debt to his father and recalled: 'I would often find my father, on a

In 1920 a 13-year-old Rowe, captain of his Parkhurst Road school team, balances a trophy on his folded arms, and (left) poses for a studio portrait.

Friday night, with my football boots in his hand. He kept the studs right, the uppers well oiled…'.

The *Tottenham & Edmonton Weekly Herald* [referred to hereafter in this book simply as the *Herald*] mentions the right-back and captain Arthur when describing the Tottenham Schools' Football Cup Final on May 14th 1920: 'Rowe shone at the back for Parkhurst, and Nash for Belmont, both boys kicking and tackling with good judgement.' Belmont had already won the League tournament but Rowe's side triumphed 1-0 to take the Cup. The *Herald*, reflecting the times, added: 'It is cheering to see such sparkling school football after the long war period of football inaction.' A year later, from March to May of 1921, Rowe's name began appearing regularly in the local press and, with so many significant matches, Arthur's father must have been very busy caring for those precious boots. Parkhurst Road School was competing strongly in two major tournaments but Arthur was also selected for the Tottenham Schools' side as well as the London Schools' team.

On Thursday, March 10th 1921, Rowe proudly led his Parkhurst Road School team-mates onto the field at none other than White Hart Lane! Parkhurst aimed to retain the Tottenham Schools' Cup against Woodlands Park School. Goalless until fifteen minutes from time, Woodlands then took the lead, but Parkhurst rallied to score twice before the end. Presented with the trophy, the press singled Arthur out: 'Rowe, the captain at centre-half, showed great skill and judgement both in defence and attack.' How thrilled Arthur must have been to win a cup in the stadium of his dreams. 12 years later, fame achieved, he was asked about his switch to centre-half: 'I prefer [the position of centre-half] for two reasons—because you are meeting the ball and [because] you are in the thick of the fight, the centre of all the struggle, all the time.'

A newscutting in Rowe's collection shows Rowe, in dark shirt at the back, during the first (drawn) London Schools' Championship Final against Fulham's Childerley Street Central School in April, 1921. Rowe collected the Dewar Shield following his side's 3-0 win in the replay. This is part of a larger cutting on which Arthur wrote: 'Me in dark shirt — watching.'

Parkhurst Road were also competing to win the Dewar Shield (and thus become the top school side in all London). When beating Millfields Central School of Hackney 4-1, Rowe was credited with 'fine generalship'. To reach the semi-final, Parkhurst had taken a three-goal lead against Islington's undefeated Barnsbury Central School when '…Day accepted a well-judged forward pass from Rowe and netted after running right through.' The score rose to 5-0 when 'Rowe ran through from midfield, eluding the defence, and shot. The goalie saved, but Rowe again sent in from the rebound and scored.' This saw Arthur's team face the strong Central Park School of East Ham in the semi-final at West Ham United's Boleyn Castle Ground (Upton Park). A 'splendid' 2-2 draw meant a replay, Parkhurst, two goals up at half-time, had to settle for 2-2 after 90 minutes and extra time, so a replay was necessary. According to the onlooking Mr Pope, Arthur suffered a painful conclusion to the first game when described as stubbing '…his foot against the ball as it is under an opponent's boot', which forced his toe back, Rowe duly suffering agony as the muscles and bones failed '…to go back into place.' The admiring Mr Pope then continued in the style of a boy's adventure comic of the period: 'Does [Rowe] leave the field? Not he. He stays till the finish, incidentally saving an almost certain goal within two seconds of time.'

But the injury was a serious blow for young Arthur as he therefore missed an England Schoolboys' trial and no further chance presented itself, the only black spot on a perfect few months. Indeed, Arthur withstood the pain to play in the Dewar Shield semi-final replay at White Hart Lane. On this occasion the East Ham school put Parkhurst Road under a lot of pressure: '…Rowe and Thatcher making some fine clearances.' Arthur also contributed to the attack: 'From a free-kick for hands, Rowe scored with a splendid shot, which beat the goalkeeper all the way.' After an equaliser Parkhurst responded and right-winger Mullett struck the winner.

The London Schools' Championship final (with the prize being the Dewar Shield) was played on April 21st 1921, Arthur's school facing Fulham's Childerley Street Central School. A mere two-and-a-half years after cessation of hostilities in the Great War proceeds from programme sales were '…to be devoted to the Parkhurst Road School War Memorial Fund.' Despite the Fulham side being taller and heavier, Parkhurst Road were reported to have '…a decided advantage at centre-half and right-back, where Rowe and Webb showed wonderfully clever form.' Mullett opened the scoring in the first half, only for Childerley Street to equalise and despite extra-time the score remained 1-1, the Fulham school favourites to win the replay a week later. Presumably Fulham's Craven Cottage was unavailable as the replay took place at White Hart Lane, where around 8-10,000 were in attendance. Rowe won the toss and Parkhurst began with sun and wind behind them taking a swift three-goal lead. For the first Arthur had landed his free-kick '…right in front of the goal mouth' where it was headed into his own goal by a defender. In no time a '…fine shot by Rowe was turned into the net by Day,' who then added the third and final goal of the game from a right-wing cross.

Rowe was described as "…the brains of the team, and it was to his skill and generalship—wonderful for so young a lad—that Parkhurst's victory was mainly due. He did the work of two or three men, tackling fearlessly and well, and holding the dangerous Goodrum, so that he had very little rope. He also fed his forwards judicially and accurately, giving them opportunities of which they usually made the most. At the close, Ahl, [Childerley Street's captain], rushed up to Rowe, and was the first to congratulate the Parkhurst captain.' Having led Parkhurst Road School to their finest achievement that season, Arthur received the Shield from Arsenal director Colonel Crisp. It had been 20 years since a Tottenham School had last won the Shield, and, by a quirk of fortune, it had also been 20 years since Spurs had won the FA Cup, the final of which was about to take place.

That busy spring of 1921 also saw Rowe selected to captain Tottenham Boys select side, competing for the Corinthian Shield (contested by London U-15 sides). In the semi-finals Arthur was said to have played 'magnificently' as they defeated West Ham Boys 4-0 at White Hart Lane. In the final against Willesden captain Arthur led Tottenham Boys to a 2-1 victory, so the Corinthian Shield became yet another feather in the Spurs-loving schoolboy's cap. Centre-forward Norman Sidey who, like Rowe, eventually turned professional, had scored to put Tottenham Boys 1-0 ahead at half-time but Willesden scored a breakaway equaliser. Eventually however Hill's accurate shot won Arthur's side the Shield, it having been 19 years since they last achieved it. About ten days later Arthur travelled as reserve as the London Boys side beat Newcastle Boys at St. James' Park. Arthur stands in a team photograph taken on the day, be-suited with tie, his hands behind his back.

Clearly 1921 was the highlight of Arthur's boyhood football life, perhaps exceeding the pleasure he would gain from his later successes in the professional game. At 14 (when compulsory state education finished), he put his schooldays behind him and could begin harbouring serious dreams of professional football with Spurs already interested. But to join the club as an amateur Arthur would have to wait two-and-a-half-years until he turned 17 in September 1923. Meanwhile to ensure his son would have a lifelong career to fall back on if a career in football failed to materialise, father Sidney enrolled Arthur for an upholstery apprenticeship at furniture manufacturer Harris Lebus, where he himself was employed. Clearly upholstery could serve Arthur as a post-football career in those times when few professional footballers (if any) could retire on their earnings from the sport. Harris Lebus was located in Tabernacle Street, Finsbury, and their main client was the famous Maples store (which closed in 1997) on Tottenham Court Road. Arthur's typically draconian apprenticeship contract included the clause: 'No wages will be paid whilst absent through sickness.'

Arthur's sporting achievements were not limited to football, he had also captained both the Parkhurst Road School cricket and swimming teams, winning the Tottenham championship in each sport. Indeed the first medal he ever won was for cricket, while he was also accomplished at track-and-field. In one school sports day his over-12 team won the championship, he himself coming second in the 100 yards, first in the 220 and first in 'Throwing the Cricket Ball'. Academically Arthur (at 13 in December 1919) finished second in his class having totalled 98 from a possible 115 points. Surprisingly he was only adjudged 'Fairly good' for conduct (skiving off to see Spurs play, perhaps?) but in those times behaviour was severely judged. One curious comment in his report read: 'We would like him to try and

Rowe (centre) captains the Tottenham district U-15 boys' select side which won the Corinthian Shield.

"play the game" more in School. He is not always willing and requires "driving." He ought to feel that as a senior boy he can, by example, assist in the government of the School.' Perhaps Arthur was merely shy, or perhaps unwilling to be a 'snitch' but whatever the case, in the midst of his busy sporting spring of 1921, he still excelled in his final exams, graded 'A' in eight of twelve subjects.

Just days before his Parkhurst Road School side won the Dewar Shield, Arthur passed through the turnstiles at Stamford Bridge stadium on what proved to be a hugely significant afternoon for the 14-year-old Tottenham fan to witness McWilliam's Spurs win the FA Cup for the first time in 20 years beating Second Division Wolves 1-0 with a goal from left-winger Jimmy Dimmock. Arthur attended with his father and again recalled being rolled horizontally over the heads of the crowd down to the fence around the pitch (many years later, Rowe would still chuckle at the memory of this in conversation with the BBC's John Motson). Rowe was one of 72,805 spectators that day, another of whom was King George V. Aside from scorer Dimmock, among young Arthur's other heroes that day will have been right-back Tommy Clay, inside-right Jimmy Seed and captain Arthur Grimsdell. It had rained in the morning but, as Arthur travelled across London at lunchtime, the sun came out. But there was then a sudden, violent rainstorm just before kick-off and the players were called from the field. Sitting at pitchside, Arthur too will have suffered a thorough soaking. Eventually the game got under way and Dimmock's winner came early in the second half. The young Arthur will have witnessed the after-match celebrations as the Cup was carried back by 'charabanc' (an open-topped omnibus) from Walham Green and finally up the Seven Sisters Road to White Hart Lane, the Tottenham Town Band following behind, pursued by coach load-after-coach load of Spurs' fans. Witnessing his favourites lifting the FA Cup, Arthur must have been delirious with pride—his heroes now matching his recent personal success. He could scarcely have imagined that his 'Lillywhites' would fail to win another major trophy until he himself was at the helm thirty years later.

Meanwhile Spurs' manager McWilliam had invited Arthur for evening training at White Hart Lane, an event which, he recalled, 'sent his pulses racing'. Years later Arthur recalled meeting heroes including Jimmy Dimmock, Bert Bliss, Tommy Clay, Fanny Walden, Jimmy Cantrell, Jimmy Seed and Charlie Walters. A yellowing press-cutting among Rowe's memorabilia includes a handwritten note at the top, which I'll return to below, but the article itself reports a speech given by a Spurs director named Tom Deacock. He mentions the winning of the Dewar Shield and the '…marvellous football from boys of fourteen or under', who had modelled their style on the Spurs.

I quote the following part in full:

> *'One boy in Tottenham today was the cleverest footballer he had ever seen, and could teach some old pros the tricks of the game. That boy was going to be advised not to play for two years until he got stronger, because if he joined a junior team he would soon get all the football kicked out of him.'*

The note on this cutting was clearly the work of Arthur himself. It simply reads: 'The boy was me!'

The young Arthur had been impressed by certain players and by successful teams, which naturally contributed to the style of football he himself would later promote — he favoured a fast, short-passing game involving all members of a team. A player he particularly admired was Clem Stephenson, star of Herbert Chapman's Championship-winning Huddersfield side. Rowe later recalled: 'Clem Stephenson … fascinated me with his ability to start a flow of cohesive and progressive football as soon as he had possession. I can still see him pushing the ball to a colleague, then following it quickly and at an angle for the return pass and then repeating the move time and again.' Rowe saw how effective that was and thought: 'What if you could get them all playing like that?' As for teams, a later influence were the famous 1928 'Wembley Wizards' when Scotland, with exquisite passing football, trounced England 5-1. The Scots appeared to have either ignored or bypassed the 1925 offside rule change and the resulting negative third back ruse (see Chapter 3), utilising triangular passing between half-back, inside-forward and winger on either side of the field, and, importantly, keeping the ball on the ground. Rowe would himself later employ the triangular system. Of that 1928 Wembley game, Ivan Sharpe mockingly described England's centre-half Tom Wilson thus, 'Wilson's head is a great force when the ball is in the air. He must have wondered whether there *was* any air at Wembley. The ball was never there when Scotland played it.'

By the summer of 1923, and about to turn 17, Rowe had completed Spurs' recommended two years of devotion to developing his physique and increasing his height and began turning out for Athenian Leaguers Cheshunt, one of Tottenham Hotspur's 'nursery' sides. This he continued for around six months. It is not easy to follow Rowe's career in detail at this point but a Mitcham Wanderers match programme dated February 2nd 1924 has Rowe down at right-half in Spurs' 'A' side, while other teams he faced included the likes of Sutton United, Windsor & Eton, Finchley and Grays Athletic. Rowe retained a handwritten note dated Friday, March 13th (1925), signed by then trainer Billy Minter on McWilliam's behalf, requesting Rowe to accompany the Spurs 'A' team as reserve for a game at Oxford. Informing Rowe of the departure time it ends '…bring your boots with

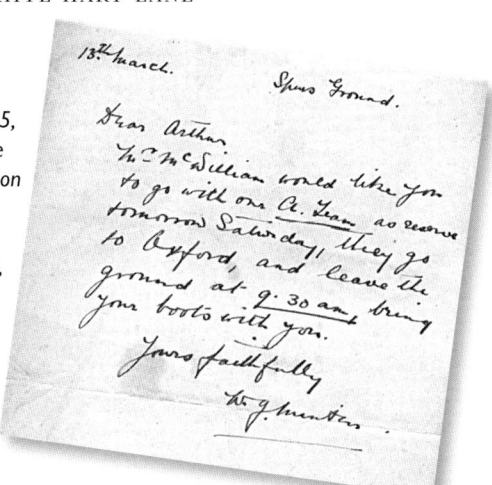

On March 13th 1925, the 18-year-old Rowe received this instruction from Billy Minter, on behalf of Spurs' Manager McWilliam, stating "...bring your boots with you". This was for an 'A' team game at Oxford.

you.' Advertisements in Rowe's mid-1920s match programmes offer such delights as 'Char-A-Banc Trips' and 'The Ducat Football Boot' (with 'rubber sponge toe cushion which covers all toes'), as well as 'Our Noted Blue Serge Suit at 60/-, Made to Your Own Taste', while the players' kit is described in the programmes as including blue 'knickers'.

Spurs' manager McWilliam was soon introducing Rowe to the essential tactic he would himself preach throughout his professional career: that movement on the field was as important for the man *without* the ball as for the man *with* it. McWilliam would also tell his young players to treat the ball as 'their best friend', stroking it rather than belting it, advice Rowe happily absorbed. Arthur would always regret never playing under the Scot for the first-team.

Spurs' first-team was by now declining as ageing players dropped by the wayside, and the club largely depended on home-produced players. Meanwhile rivals Arsenal were frequently investing handsome sums in quality, experienced replacements. By February 1927 a frustrated McWilliam happily accepted almost twice his Spurs' salary to manage Second Division Middlesbrough. He would very willingly have stayed had he been presented with a generous budget for team-rebuilding, or had his annual earnings been increased by a mere £150 per annum (nowhere near the extra £650 he reluctantly accepted at Middlesbrough). Conservative financial thinking, quashing progressive considerations, would become the pattern at Tottenham. In just three months McWilliam proceeded to steer 'The Boro' to promotion. As fortune had it, however, McWilliam's new club went straight back down to Division Two by the end of his first complete season and they were accompanied by... Tottenham Hotspur!

The man who had taken over from McWilliam was trainer Billy Minter, a managerial novice and under him Spurs finished their 1927-28 League programme earlier than most, fifth from bottom and with enough points gained to normally avoid relegation, so they set off to tour Holland but by the time they returned Spurs had dropped into Division Two! Having failed to both keep McWilliam at the club and to adequately replace him, Tottenham now suffered five years of Second Division football before returning to Division One.

Returning to Rowe's progress - in 1923 McWilliam had arranged for Kent League side Northfleet United to serve as a 'nursery' for promising young Spurs' players. This benefitted the Kent club with higher attendances that the quality players attracted whilst saving Spurs around 40% in youth players' wages, as well as League fees, stadium or pitch rent and playing kit. Above all young players acquired competitive match experience. So at 18 in 1925, Rowe began spending his Saturdays playing in North Kent whilst continuing to train at White Hart Lane, thereby keeping up his upholstery apprenticeship. When future Spurs' captain Ron Burgess followed Rowe into the Northfleet side he described the arrangements when returning to London from Saturday games: 'Each lad was supplied with a lunch basket. How we enjoyed those 'banquets' of hot pies, sausage rolls, sandwiches and cake.'

Rowe would later describe what he considered to be the ideal team, which would comprise the physical contribution of the young and the accumulated knowledge of the older players for directing tactics and methods on the field. At Northfleet Arthur played alongside others who would eventually accompany him in the Spurs' first-team, players such as 'Taffy' O'Callaghan and Les Howe, and in his four years Rowe won four Kent Senior Cups and the Kent League Division One Championship (1926).

NORTHFLEET 1925-26 Rowe ironically replaced another Spurs' man at Northfleet who, coincidentally, was named Roe! 'Taffy' O'Callaghan was another newcomer and he and Arthur were destined to spend ten years playing alongside one another. During that summer of 1925 a change to the offside law was introduced and this would play a huge part in Rowe's future. The British response to the change would prove a retrograde step as far as England's standing in world football was concerned (Chapter 13), this despite scoring rates initially rising dramaticallyNorthfleet themselves scored 100 times in just 19 fixtures! But sadly, the free-scoring would inevitably provoke a negative reaction.

In 1925, approaching 19 years of age, Rowe stands at the very end of this line-up of Northfleet players, in front of Club Chairman Joe Lingham.

The highlight of Rowe's initial Northfleet season took place on November 25th 1925 when he played right-half against Division Three South side Queens Park Rangers in the FA Cup first round proper. He left the field after a creditable 2-2 draw with praise ringing in his ears. In the replay on a very muddy Loftus Road pitch, Northfleet enjoyed far more of the attacking play. Rowe's '...constructive methods were a joy to watch' wrote one reporter before adding, however, that once arriving near goal, '...the importance of the occasion paralysed' Northfleet. Nevertheless they kept QPR to a mere 2-0 victory. On top of this landmark game, by season's end Arthur had helped Northfleet to the Kent League Division One title and reached the Kent Senior Cup Final. Their opponents were Folkestone in a game played on neutral territory at Maidstone before 11,000 fans and Northfleet took the trophy for the third year in succession. Rowe had clearly impressed: 'While strong in defence, he is essentially an attacking half. That smashing cross kick of his to the other wing frequently caused consternation in the Folkestone camp.' Rowe's veteran skipper, Northfleet legend Arthur Seccombe, considered the side incorporating Rowe the best in the eight years since the end of World War I and they also won the Kent Senior Shield

1926-27 In Rowe's second season Northfleet again reached the Kent Senior Cup Final, beating Sheppey United on Easter Monday. Arthur, now 20, played despite an injury to his foot incurred just two days before. One report described the terrace fashions of the 1920s, women wearing 'white hose adorned with red embroidery' and village 'lads' with 'Northfleet United' in red lettering on their 'soft' hats, carrying 'huge red rattles'. Meanwhile, the eight ball-boys were 'clad in white'. On the field both sides were said to provide 'clever displays of subtle footwork and combination', the report significantly adding: 'The performance of Rowe and his fellow half-backs was viewed as the principal reason for Northfleet's success.' At an FA Cup defeat of Sittingbourne the reason for Rowe's delayed entry into the Tottenham first-team was perhaps identified. He was reported here to be a 'great little half ...whose work increased in excellence as the afternoon went on.' In his prime at centre-half Rowe only ever reached 5 ft 9 in but here he was described as Northfleet's greatest asset, '...the essence of coolness' and '...with never a suggestion of unfairness or ill-feeling.' Northfleet finally exited the Cup 6-2 away to Third Division Luton Town, and finished runners-up in the Kent League Cup. Rarely on the scoresheet, Rowe struck three times that season.

1927-28 Having now been joined by fellow Spurs Jack Illingworth and Alf Day, the 'Cementers' again reached the Kent Senior Cup Final, aiming for a fifth successive victory, this time against Sittingbourne. An atmospheric match report appears in Paul Harrison's excellent *Images of Sport: Gravesend & Northfleet FC* and to set the scene I quote a little of the descriptive period language from it here. The town of Maidstone was filled by excited fans of both sides as the '...sun broke through and an azure sky displaced the leaden clouds of the forenoon.' 'Hawkers' sold red-and-white rosettes to Northfleet fans and red-and-black ones to the Sittingbourne followers, while transport included the 'horse-and-trap'. Motorised vehicles

At around the time Rowe was putting Northfleet behind him, Rowe's younger brother Frank and sisters Violet (back) and Daisy (front, centre) pose with father Sydney and mother Lottie.

remained such a relatively recent phenomenon that the match reporter was obliged to precede the name of each type with the adjective 'motor', hence the 'hundreds of private motor-cars' competing with 'motor-coaches' and 'motor-cycles'. As kick-off approached '…the firm smooth turf' was '…encircled by thousands eager for the annual struggle to begin.' Right-half Rowe's side were led onto the field by captain Alec Chaplin who, having won the toss, made Sittingbourne play into both the sun and the wind. On this occasion the quality of play, in a close-fought encounter, was poor: 'Science for the most part going by the board in favour of robust kick-and-rush methods.' However the ball swung from end-to-end to please the fans. Rowe's side took an early lead when Sittingbourne's goalkeeper failed to grasp a weak effort which crept over the line. When Rowe tackled Sittingbourne's Cox the ball rolled over the touchline, producing some hilarity: 'A spectator made a lunge at it, lost his balance and capsized. The spectators roared their appreciation of the diversion.' After a Sittingbourne equaliser, two further goals confirmed Northfleet's victory.

On completing his upholstery apprenticeship in May 1928, the now 21-year-old Rowe signed professional forms for Tottenham Hotspur at £4 a week. In 1928-29, however, Rowe was recalled to Northfleet midway through the new season. One must assume this was a disappointment to him but finally, by the summer of 1929, at the 'elderly' age of 22, he could finally devote his talents to the 'Lillywhites', who had finished the previous season in their lowest-ever position (to this day): 12th in Division Two. Considering the immense success he eventually achieved, one can but assume Manager Billy Minter and his successor Percy Smith had perceived Rowe as lacking in height and build. Future Spurs stars such as Les Bennett, Vic Buckingham, Ron Burgess, Ted Ditchburn, Les Medley and Bill Nicholson would also pass through Northfleet and one day play a big role in Rowe's future. By then Northfleet were coached by Jimmy Anderson, who had been employed in various Spurs' roles since as far back as 1908 (indeed, he would in total spend more than 50 years in the service of Tottenham Hotspur).

So, in 1929, Rowe could finally begin his professional playing career with Spurs.

3

Offside!

CHAPMAN AND THE THIRD BACK

'...as sensible as trying to whitewash the ceiling with green paint.'
ARTHUR ROWE'S COMMENT ON ENGLISH SIDES TRYING TO IMITATE HERBERT
CHAPMAN'S ARSENAL WITHOUT PLAYERS OF THE REQUIRED QUALITY

In June 1925, as Rowe progressed at Northfleet, a momentous change was made to the offside law. Before then defending sides regularly stopped attacks by advancing just as the opposing side played the ball forward leaving unwary, advanced opposition attackers stranded offside. Unlike today a player was onside provided he had at least three defending players, usually including the goalkeeper, between him and the goal-line at the moment the ball was played forward. The furthest-advanced defender could, however, easily 'trap' an opponent by moving up just as the ball was about to be played, confident that if he mistimed his move, he still had two defensive colleagues between the ball and goal. Over time the player plotting to enact the 'trap' positioned himself high up the field near the halfway line so that opposing attackers were 'corralled' far from goal (too far to take a shot, for example). When both sides utilised the same tactic play became bunched in the middle third of the pitch and offside stoppages occurred at an average of one every two-to-three minutes.

With boredom increasing and attendances dwindling the offside law was changed so that only two defenders (including the goalkeeper) were required to be between the attacker and the opposing goal-line when the ball was played forward. Under the new law the goalkeeper would usually be the only defender ahead of the attacker for him to be deemed offside at the moment the ball was played forward. Playing the 'offside trap' therefore exposed the 'keeper to more perilous, one-on-one situations. To appreciate the stultifying affects of the game before the law changed, Newcastle United had kept 18 clean sheets from a 42 game season, whilst at the same time they themselves were prevented from scoring on 16 occasions. As the natural human stimulus from witnessing a ball strike the back of the net has been likened to the excitement of ancient Rome when the gladiator's sword was thrust into his opponent, this prevention of goals by trickery rather than skill drove many fans away.

The law change had an instant impact - goals flew in like never before in season 1925/26 as scoring increased by an enormous 40%. The highest goals total in the pre-change season had been 76; in the following season the highest total skyrocketed to Sheffield United's 102. Even the two relegated sides increased their goal tally and, in the second season under the changed law (1926-27) one striker alone, George Camsell, hit 59 of Middlesbrough's 122 goals in the Second Division. Centre-forwards benefitted most - Everton's Dixie Dean topping Camsell's 59 the following season. As more players defeated the trap by being played-in along the wings, their crosses would be met by centre-forwards following up down the middle. This led to more headed goals.

Isaac Newton's Third Law of Motion states 'to every action there is an equal and opposite reaction' and concerned managers now added an extra defender to counter the centre-forward threat. The centre-half responsibility that Arthur Rowe had so personally enjoyed involved both defending *and* attacking. Before the law change the centre-half had been an influential figure, a player who not only defended but hit accurate passes and took opportunities to move up-field with the ball. As Rowe explained: '…you had your centre-half up the field in close contact with your forwards and formed a link…' which produced '…a more collective, closer-knit football…'. After the 1925-26 season teams sacrificed the attacking part of the centre-half's role to man-mark the opposition centre-forward. The responsibility for link play now fell upon one of the inside-forwards who dropped deeper. The huge success of this ploy as developed by Arsenal manager Herbert Chapman quickly led to the tactic becoming omnipresent throughout the Football League and, although effective in the short term, this was to prove hugely detrimental to English football over time. It would take over two decades for a tactical counter-revolution (under Arthur Rowe no less) to undermine it domestically and a little longer still until all the shortcomings of Chapman's formation and tactics were fully appreciated by English football followers.

The insightful opinions of immigrant journalist Willy Meisl, a former player and coach himself and brother of the great Austrian 'Wunderteam' coach Dr Hugo Meisl, are frequently quoted in this book. Willy was a lover of all things British, having fled the rise of Nazism in 1934, and prior to the offside change, had considered the centre-half as '…the most important man on the field.' The ease with which attackers could be played offside with the security of another two defenders between the attacker and goal meant the centre-half could venture forward with confidence. Only the two full-backs were the real, final line of defence in front of the goalkeeper, but following the law change the centre-half would often play just behind the full-backs and, in addition to marking the opposing central striker, became responsible for managing the offside-trap. All changes designed to reduce goalscoring (unless a side had attacking players of Arsenal's quality).

This is where Chapman comes in as it was he who was most credited for introducing the 'third back', although most of the credit should have gone to his vastly experienced inside-forward Charles Buchan who had originated the idea in pre-season. In Arsenal's case the newly designated 'policeman' or 'stopper' centre-half, was Herbert Roberts, who now devoted his entire attention to stopping the opposing centre-forward. Meanwhile a deep-lying inside-forward became the link between defence and attack, a role so significant that Chapman gave it to the

Legendary Arsenal manager Herbert Chapman chatting with the kingpin of his tactic, the supremely talented Alex James.

outstandingly talented (and costly) Alex James. Arsenal thus began their greatest era relying on a counter-attack style. Over time this became more associated with weaker sides confronting stronger ones, putting an emphasis on getting men behind the ball, frustrating a more talented opposition, and, when gaining possession and with opposing players stranded in advanced positions, 'hitting' a target man with a ball played quickly (and long) out of defence, before streaming forward to support him. Chapman's tactic saw goals stemming from defensive positions. His side could spend as much as 80% of their games in negative mode, repelling the opposition before catching them on the break. In the final pre-offside law change season Arsenal had finished 20th but a combination of the law change, the enterprise of Chapman and Buchan and the ever-open coffers of Highbury saw Arsenal rocket to second place a mere 12 months later.

Rowe himself said 'I do not like the idea of the centre-half being solely a third full-back. I would go so far as to suggest that any decent footballer of average build and physical strength could be a successful "third full-back" centre-half.' Meisl echoed Rowe's misgivings on the role change, saying the centre-half '…is now just a stopper, almost immobile and not requiring the skills the pre-offside law change centre-half needed. To mark and tackle a man, to head or kick the ball away is still simple compared with playing football… constructively.' Rowe of course argued he could handle both roles but, over time, he was compelled to accept the third back game in modified form: 'When the Spurs attack, I follow up the forwards, and if the movement demands my return I can generally recover the ground.' Indeed, Arsenal's own David Jack later considered the 1933-34 Spurs' side as an exception to the rule, playing a five-man attack and, in Rowe, utilising a 'roaming centre-half'. Even Arsenal's Buchan said Rowe could play safely out from the back, as he '…had the speed necessary for a quick recovery if the occasion demanded.' Rowe held contradictory views on Chapman, considering the Arsenal manager responsible for much of the negative football which followed the change, but at heart believing him '…a very great man and one I would have liked to know.'

The major long-term problem was that while Chapman's Arsenal side was full of talented individuals, most sides who copied their approach were not. Realising

Chapman's innovation would be mimicked by other clubs, Rowe said: 'They saw [Chapman's] centre-half in action and thought all centre-halves had to be big and strong; players whose major role was merely to put the centre-forward out of the game, but rarely really used the ball. Nobody thought that you might have a centre-half who could do both effectively.' With skill now less essential than height and strength, Rowe pointed out that 'Long, strongly-struck kicks over the centre-half's head were successfully exploited, and the goals began to come — not necessarily by good football, but by a long punt and the determined chaser at centre-forward.' When still employed today, this ploy heavily depends as much on defensive error as the forward's skill.

More than anything Chapman was blessed to have Alex James as his withdrawn inside-forward, a unique talent who could control a hastily cleared ball from his defence, no matter how it arrived, before quickly despatching it to his fast-moving wingers or through the middle into his centre-forward's path. To demonstrate how essential James was, he missed many games in Arsenal's 1933-34 season and the side's goal tally fell dramatically from 118 to 75.

As a result of Arsenal's new tactics, the famous 'W' and 'M' formation became dominant in English football. Only the two wingers and centre-forward remained up front: three men where previously there had been five. An anonymous player's views on the law change were reproduced in Trevor Wignall's *Daily Express* newspaper column in the 1930s, a cutting of which exists in Rowe's own collection which might lead some to assume he himself was the unattributed player concerned, the man who clearly considered the law change had done '...more to ruin the game as a spectacle and to create the modern game of destructive football than any other action could have, or has done.' So, with the entertainment value now reduced to that similarly suffered before the offside change, Rowe rightly considered the cure worse than the original ailment bringing about, as Willy Meisl wrote: '...the slow, but soon unmistakable downslide and deterioration of British football.'

Yet this was the era of Arsenal. Unlike most managerial competitors Chapman had been able to splash huge sums on the likes of inside-forward David Jack (for a fee one-third higher than the highest ever paid at the time), the aforementioned Alex James, speedy wingers Joe Hulme and Cliff Bastin, and the powerful Ted Drake at centre-forward. All were tailor-made to fill specific roles in Chapman's tactical shape. In 1961 Rowe reflected: 'What hope, then, had all the other clubs who tried to imitate the Arsenal pattern? Who could play like James except James? And who could show the icy calm of a Bastin in his finishing — except Bastin? Everybody became imitators without having the right keys to the puzzle, and English football suffered in consequence. All of which was about as sensible as trying to whitewash the ceiling with green paint!'

Without Arsenal's quality, many teams attempted to bridge the gap between defenders and attackers with, as Bernard Joy wrote, '...an enormous kick', adding: 'It was a dreary period of kick-and-rush football with most teams in two separate units [defence and attack] rather than a welded whole.' Some even thought that the pre-1925 game, despite the offside stoppages, offered superior entertainment to that which followed Chapman's innovation.

This all highlights Rowe's greatest achievement — going against the popular grain to return entertainment to the foreground of tactical thinking. Of course, as Chapman countered, 'Pretty football does not pay', but Rowe, Chapman's principal rival as the 20th Century's most innovative English football manager, would never have accepted that.

Even Charles Buchan himself, prime instigator of the Arsenal blueprint, would later call for change after witnessing the 7-1 destruction of England by Hungary in 1954 (see Chapter 13), stating: 'We persist in methods that were very effective when introduced by Arsenal immediately after the change in the offside law was made in 1925.' Those methods were still commonly utilised into the 21st Century, although an influx of technically-minded Continental coaches in the British game is thankfully turning things around. *Match of the Day* cameras no longer spend much time following a football's trajectory through the sky. Hugo Meisl summarised the two post-Chapman approaches to coaching best: 'Mathematically it may be the same if I make it my principle to *receive* [concede] fewer goals than the opponent, or if I *score* more. [But] morally and mentally it makes all the difference in the world. The first is a negative attitude: I am out to spoil; I am destructive. As long as I can stop the other chap from winning, I am a success. I have accomplished my main task. In the second case I am inspired by a positive outlook [as with Rowe]; I want to create something; I am constructive.'

As could have been predicted by the early post-war years the output of goals had withered once again. In the first four seasons the average seasonal goals-per-team dropped from 68 to 61, then to 59 and 56. That last figure relates to season 1949-50, just two goals more than in the pre-offside law change season of 1924-25! And, as will be seen, Rowe's Spurs bucked the trend, scoring no fewer than 81 goals that term.

Not that Chapman's tactics were all to blame; as time went on other factors contributed, including an improvement in goalkeeping technique (Sam Bartram of Charlton, for example, began advancing from goal to cut out through passes or deep crosses). Also it has to be stated that Chapman was an outstanding tactician and hardly to be blamed when spending the money made available to him. Willy Meisl even contended that Chapman would eventually have found a solution to the defensive trend himself had he not died abruptly during the 1933-34 season. Yet while there is a statue of Chapman outside the Emirates Stadium in the 21st Century, there is none of Rowe at the Tottenham Hotspur Stadium...

With a persistent British xenophobic belief in football superiority over other nations, allied to the rigid 'W' and 'M' line-up plus persistent scoffing at play which involved sharp ball control and accurate short passing, English international and club football has played catch-up for most of the 90-plus years since Chapman's 'revolution'.

With one particular, joyous exception that is: the brief, shining moment inspired by that other North London managerial icon, Arthur Sydney Rowe.

4

Dreams Do Come True 1

A SPURS FIRST-TEAMER 1931-33

*'I spread a load of sugar cubes on the table and
tried to trace the passes that led to the goal…'*
ARTHUR ROWE RECALLING A SIGNIFICANT SPURS' PASSING MOVE AT BRADFORD CITY IN
1932, AN INSPIRATION FOR HIS DEVELOPMENT OF 'PUSH-AND-RUN'

Graduating to Spurs' Reserves, Rowe would wait a further 3½ years before his first team debut in season 1931-32. In the three previous seasons the best Spurs had achieved was tenth in Division Two. In early 1929 Spurs boss Billy Minter had signed the prolific former England centre-forward Ted Harper, who had once hit 43 goals in a season and, despite missing more than half the season through injury, he still managed 14 goals. Then, halfway through that season Minter resigned following a nervous breakdown (the first of several managers who succumbed similarly at White Hart Lane). He was replaced by Bury manager Percy Smith, a likeable, intelligent man who had been a prolific goalscorer for Preston and Blackburn Rovers, who took up the reins on the first day of 1930. Rowe will have been delighted to hear that Smith intended to maintain Spurs' passing style.

As back-up to Harper, Smith purchased 20-year-old George Hunt from Third Division Huddersfield. Hunt was a mobile, skilful dribbler with clever feet and a

Rowe (far right) *is clearly engrossed in Manager Percy Smith's tactical demonstration. The other players (left-to-right)* are: *Jimmy Dimmock, Alf Messer, Willie Davies (front), George Cook, Ted Harper (back), Bert Lyons and Bert Hodgkinson.*

DREAMS DO COME TRUE 1: A SPURS FIRST-TEAMER

The official team group for 1931-32. The broad-shouldered Rowe is first player on the left of the middle row. Behind him at far left is ex-Manager Billy Minter and the two be-suited men immediately in front of him are Manager Percy Smith and director Fred Bearman. The prolific scorer Ted Harper is the tallest member of the middle row, in front of towering 'keeper Nicholls, while Harper's ultimate replacement, George Hunt, is fourth from left of the seated players in front. Jimmy Anderson, later to work under Rowe, is far right, back row.

sharp eye for a chance, who could also make a nuisance of himself physically. He would form a close personal relationship with Rowe but, initially, had to wait his turn as Harper struck an extraordinary 36 goals in just 30 matches, a feat only bettered for Spurs by Jimmy Greaves in 1962-63. Had Harper not suffered a serious leg injury in March, Smith may have taken Spurs up at his first attempt.

SEASON 1931-32 So this was how things stood when Arthur Rowe, now 25, finally made his first-team debut at home to Burnley on October 10th 1931. Spurs had just conceded seven goals in two games, so the game also marked the debut of goalkeeper Allan Taylor. Broad-shouldered yet slim, Rowe weighed 11 st. 10 lb on his first team bow and took the field with greased hair combed back and parted with precision. He quickly grasped his delayed opportunity, making the centre-half spot his own for the following four seasons. One reporter wrote of Rowe's debut in the 1-1 draw: 'He tackles hard, positions well, and has sufficient pluck to go up and take a hand in attack now and then. One shot of his after a good dribble was almost the best of the match.' Reading this one wonders why Spurs had been so slow to identify his talent. He was both strong and good in the air, despite being no more than 5ft 9in tall, but did not consider himself an outstanding player.

Much later the distinguished sports barrister Edward Grayson would praise Rowe's ability in the *FA News*, firstly comparing Rowe physically to England international Alf Ramsey: 'Only a fraction of an inch taller than Alf Ramsey in height though more slimly built and more supple in bodily movement, he sprayed his future international forwards, Taffy O'Callaghan, George Hunt, Willie Hall and Willie Evans, plus the uncapped Jimmy McCormick, with the passes they desired:

he underpinned his fellow defenders, and commanded the respect of all the great centre-forwards he opposed, as well as the affection of the fans. Charles Buchan recalled Rowe's centre-half play as 'unobtrusive, quiet and thoroughly efficient', adding, 'he got through his work with such a minimum of fuss that few realized his value to the team.' Perhaps that part-explained Rowe's delay in achieving first-team football. Rowe's direct opponents, such as Dean and Lawton (Everton); Waring and Astley (Villa); Astley and Bowers (Derby County); Camsell and Fenton (Middlesbrough); Gallacher (Chelsea); Gurney (Sunderland) …never took liberties with Arthur's skill; and because of his football talents, and his character, there never was any need to clog.'

Arthur himself rated Camsell the most difficult centre-forward he ever faced: 'Often I was all set to make a tackle, then George would "find" an extra yard and I was beaten.' In Rowe's debut season George Hunt scored 27 goals, and Arthur said at the time: 'For a few yards George Hunt is wonderfully quick, and he takes the ball in rare style, however his fellow forwards may pass to him.' Hunt was also brave, as hard as nails, acrobatic and possessed a strong shot. Another fine player for Spurs that season was George Greenfield, an inside forward who could take-on and beat defenders.

Despite Rowe's efficient debut against Burnley, the recovered Alf Messer returned at Notts County a week later, but a 3-1 defeat saw Smith quickly reinstate Rowe, initiating a 20-game run in the side. The highlight of Arthur's first five matches was a 6-2 November defeat of Swansea Town when Willie Evans, six years younger than Rowe, also made his debut. The 5ft 6in outside-left possessed a powerful shot and celebrated his debut by scoring twice. Arthur had finally tasted victory and in some style. Rowe's sixth first-team appearance saw Spurs beat Port Vale 9-3. Press credit for this went to Spurs' 'young middle men' (Alsford and Rowe) who '…got the ball three times out of four in a tackle and, having got it, insisted on doing something useful.'

Results remained inconsistent but a report on the visit of Oldham on December 19th, a hard-fought 3-2 Spurs victory, stated: 'Rowe is now definitely a success at centre-half', while 'Taffy' O'Callaghan, Rowe's former Northfleet colleague, was described as an enthusiastic, talented player who did not '…suffer with a "swelled head."' Like Willie Evans, inside forward O'Callaghan had worked in the South Wales mines before joining Spurs, top-scoring with 25 in his second season. Spurs began 1932 with a 3-3 draw at home to eventual champions Wolves, a commendable result. Hunt, now a fixture at centre-forward, scored all three. Rowe's first FA Cup tie, at home to First Division Sheffield Wednesday, was a thrilling contest ending 2-2, but Spurs went out in the replay, hardly a disgrace, Wednesday finishing 3rd that season.

A report on a close defeat at Bradford Park Avenue praised Spurs' 'quick, first-time passing' which aroused '…the admiration of the spectators' and Rowe was singled-out for his, 'fine exhibition'. Missing three matches through injury, Arthur returned for the remaining ten matches, the first of which saw right-back Billy Felton make his debut. Smith was building a side fit to challenge for promotion in season 1932-33, a further addition being Rowe's former Reserves' team-mate, goalkeeper

In the opening game of season 1932-33 Rowe takes no chances, clearing left-footed ahead of his goalkeeper Nicholls.

BANG!—Rowe clears the Spurs' goal from a Charlton attack. Nicholls is on the alert for a possible mistake.

SECOND DIVISION
SPURS SET SHARP PACE

Joe Nicholls, who stood no less than 6 feet 4 inches tall and remained first-choice for the next few seasons. His party-trick was to hurl the ball vast distances with accuracy (the fly-kick then being the standard means by which a goalkeeper released the ball). Spurs finally finished season 1931-32 in 8th place, 11 points short of promotion.

SEASON 1932-33 Arthur's second season in the centre of Spurs' defence perfectly commemorated the club's 50th anniversary. Smith had introduced a quick-passing style with which the players struggled to adapt. By October Spurs had dropped into the relegation zone following a promising start to the season that saw a frenetic London derby win over Charlton. Both Rowe and Nicholls garnered praise in the Press: 'NICHOLLS A GREAT GOALKEEPER AND ROWE BEST HALF-BACK.' This 4-1 opening-day victory would have ended much closer were it not for Rowe keeping new Charlton centre-forward Cyril Pearce quiet, despite his 40 strikes during the previous season. Yet Spurs lost 4 of their next 6 games, their only victory a 6-1 trouncing of Manchester United on September 10th. Yet after a 6-2 win at Preston their form was of title-winning calibre. They were playing such speedy and skilful football that they were labelled the 'Greyhounds', the side usually comprising: Nicholls; Felton, Whatley; Colquhoun, ROWE, Meads; Davies (or Howe), O'Callaghan, Hunt, Greenfield (or, later, Hall), Evans.

Spurs' success that season would depend heavily on the 20 League matches (including that win at Preston) ending with a 5-1 win over Oldham Athletic on February 11th. In that period Spurs scored an extraordinary average of over three goals per game. In one of those Rowe faced future Arsenal great Ted Drake, Spurs hammering five goals past Drake's Southampton side without reply. It was clear that Smith had recaptured the short-passing style Minter had cast aside. One report said Rowe '…now appeared as the complete centre-half-back.' The solidity of a Rowe-led defence was making it easy for the front men to damage the opposition.

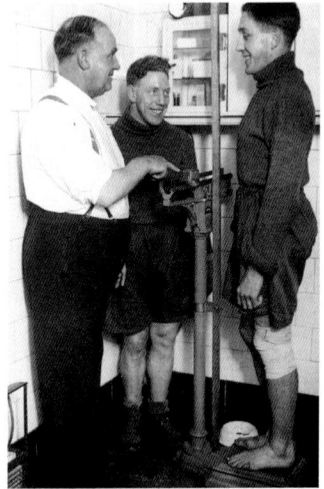

Willie Hall watches in amusement while trainer George Hardy checks Rowe's weight.

A group photo taken around the time of winger Jimmy McCormick's arrival in March 1933. Back: Hunt (36 goals that season), Nicholls, Meads, Rowe. Middle: Evans, Alsford, Felton, Whatley. Front: Hall, Brain, McCormick.

One game proved of particular significance with regard to Rowe's future in the game. Scoreless late-on at Bradford City on November 26th 1932 Spurs players feared the loss of their £2 win bonus when suddenly, just outside his own area, Rowe executed a sharp one-two exchange of passes with Felton. A further four quick, short passes followed before the ball was crossed from the right for Hunt to score, salvaging that bonus. On the train journey back this smooth, rapid-fire passing move became a classic 'Eureka' moment for Rowe, who recalled: 'I spread a load of sugar cubes on the table and tried to trace the passes that led to that goal… I argued that if we could ever plan that kind of move instead of just *hoping* for it to happen we'd score more goals that way.' But his colleagues were not convinced such moves could be planned. Furthermore, as Rowe pointed out, those in charge of running teams in those days '…wanted long, brave balls with forwards chasing and hoping.' However Rowe wanted the Bradford incident repeated. As acclaimed Fleet Street football correspondent David Miller would write, Rowe '…was conscious of the haphazard nature of much of the game, the lack of organized thought. He began to realize that it must be possible to play in a manner that reduced, if only marginally, the element of chance and the unnecessary squandering of possession.'

An idea was born.

On December 3rd the star of a 7-0 victory over Swansea Town was inside-left 'Nobby' Greenfield, one reporter noting: 'I shall long remember the feint with which [Greenfield] sent the defenders running to cover Evans before placing the ball for Hunt to score Tottenham's fifth goal.' Greenfield added two himself. Having been 16th on September 24th, Tottenham were in second place by December.

This was the month when Rowe watched Dr Hugo Meisl's Austrian 'Wunderteam' (18 games unbeaten) lose 4-3 to England. Despite the defeat, Meisl's smooth, accurate passing game delighted Arthur, who will have been particularly impressed by the Austrian coach's rejection of Chapman's 'third back' approach. England's main contribution to the game had been physical strength allied to precision shooting. Rowe fully realised Austria's close defeat had been unlucky but his fellow countrymen ignored this powerful shot across English bows for many years to come (see also Chapter 13).

Three days later Spurs suffered a huge setback in a 2-2 draw against Fulham when the creative Greenfield suffered a leg break so severe that he never fully reclaimed his place in the side. Ironically it was a match recalled more for a humorous incident. Rowe had slid across to stop Fulham's Finch only to concede a penalty. The Fulham penalty-taker, Newton, then struck the ball with such venom against Spurs' goalkeeper Nicholls' face that it bounced back almost to the halfway-line, while Nicholls dropped '…to the ground like a felled ox.' But the serious injury to Greenfield overshadowed all else, Rowe saying that the loss of 'Nobby' was '…a hard blow,' adding: 'It is our job to atone for his absence.' By the time of a Christmas Eve trip to Notts County, Percy Smith had purchased an excellent replacement in the shape of fair-haired 20-year-old Willie Hall. Easily identified due to his stocky stature, Hall would accompany Willie Evans on the left side of the Tottenham attack and quickly became a Spurs' legend, a terrier who could tackle back, dribble, and pass with aplomb.

Three straight wins over Christmas presaged a close defeat at Manchester United but thereafter Spurs lost only one of their 17 remaining matches. With Division One football now on the horizon for 1933-34, Rowe said in a newspaper interview: 'We are a happy lot at White Hart Lane, to which I am strongly attached. Maybe we are not paragons, but we are pals and we try to play football. We cut out the rough stuff, for the directors do not approve of it. Not only so, but fair play is a tradition of the club, and we all try to respond, for the progress of the Spurs is our united purpose.'

To replace an injured O'Callaghan at outside-right, Smith quickly snapped-up Jimmy 'Boy' McCormick from Chesterfield. In a 1-1 draw at Port Vale, Rowe again caught a reporter's eye, 'This player worked tirelessly throughout and initiated many fine attacking movements.' Indeed, Rowe's marshalling of Spurs' defence saw them concede just seven goals in the final nine matches. Ironically, promotion to Division One was only finally achieved after a narrow loss to West Ham. But on the very last day Spurs finally went up in style, beating Notts County 3-1 at a celebrating White Hart Lane, missing the Second Division title by just a solitary point to a Stoke City side that included an 18-year-old winger named Stanley Matthews (of whom, more later). Hunt had hit 36 of Spurs' 96 League goals, much aided by Hall's arrival. Rowe, in common with Felton and Hunt, had missed just one League game and, after his first full season and celebrating with team-mates at Tottenham's Municipal Hall, Rowe will have contemplated the exciting prospect of testing himself against the best of the English game.

'Young' Arthur was finally making up for lost time.

5

Dreams Do Come True 2

CAPTAIN OF SPURS, CAPPED FOR ENGLAND AND… ELASTIC TACTICS! 1933-39

'…a centre-half in a hundred—Arthur Rowe, as solid as any policeman on point duty, who held up three lanes of traffic without a falter.'
JACK ALDRIDGE REPORTING ON PORTSMOUTH V SPURS (JANUARY 5 1937)

So Spurs were back where they belonged, in the English First Division. But would they make a strong impression? Rowe admitted to doubts in the dressing-room. 'There was something approaching fear and trembling in our hearts. the general opinion was that we should not prove good enough for the top class. The players did not quite know where they were; certainly I, personally, wondered what was in store for us.'

SEASON 1933-34 Yet Spurs did get off to a strong start, drawing away to Sheffield United before beating Wolves 4-0 at White Hart Lane, both results achieved with the same eleven which had gained promotion. The advantages to resisting change enhanced the promoted side's team spirit because every player desired to prove himself at the higher level. Rowe later applied this same theory when he himself managed a side to promotion.

On the second Saturday Aston Villa arrived at the Lane and Spurs quickly went two-up. However, after a first half in which Rowe and his fellow defenders kept Villa quiet, the Midlanders pulled it back to 2-2. But Spurs, with Rowe playing exceptionally well, were not to be denied and McCormick set up Hunt for the winner. The return with Wolves two days' later was lost to the only goal of the game, before Spurs won convincingly 3-1 at Leicester, leaving the new boys occupying first place. But this was a mere prelude to a match of singular significance: the first derby with bitter rivals Arsenal in five years taking place at White Hart Lane on September 16th 1933. A match report headlined 'THRILLING STRUGGLE' showcased possibly Rowe's finest-ever performance. In the build-up newspapers anticipated duels between centre-forward Hunt and 'stopper' centre-half Herbie Roberts, and, at the other end, between Rowe and Ray Bowden. Despite the heat, the game drew a record 57,246 to White Hart Lane, with many more shut out. Boos rang out as Arsenal took the field, as Spurs' fans remained embittered by Arsenal's dubious inclusion (at Spurs' expense) in the extended First Division after the war. Played at great speed throughout, the thrills came mainly from Spurs' five front men, despite their average age being just 22 and *The People* newspaper described Spurs '…playing havoc with the schemes and manoeuvres of an experienced, and generally recognised, mechanically perfect organisation.'

Spurs finally took the lead just before half-time, Felton scoring from the spot, but Bowden equalised. Still Arsenal's creative masters, Alex James, David Jack and Cliff Bastin found the going tough against Rowe and his colleagues, who tackled and harassed throughout while, at the other end, Hall was the pick of Spurs' attackers. Eventually, with Spurs tiring, England international Jack began outwitting Rowe, '…who previously had played the greatest game of his career.' But an exhausted Rowe and colleagues held on for the point. George Hunt had a poke at Chapman's methods afterwards: 'We don't mean at Tottenham just to do the fast running stuff: kicking the ball hard and racing helter-skelter after it. Our scheme is to do quick passing and at the same time make fast progress towards our opponent's goal. Mistakes are certain to be made playing this kind of football, but doesn't it fascinate you? It grips me.' Not hard to see why he and Rowe were pals.

'Rowe was an outstanding success who more than once looked like streaking through on his own. He stood for perpetual motion,' wrote one reporter, adding, 'Rowe had some job. His own forwards were greedy for passes, and he [also] had to watch for Bowden and Jack.' Charles Buchan described Rowe as a centre-half who '…often came through with the ball in delightful fashion. He was the complete centre-half.' Another report delighted in Rowe's combat with James. 'Rowe… came nearer to getting into the mind of Alex James than any half back in the country. A man who can do that is good enough to play for England.' At the final whistle James himself went across to congratulate Rowe on his play. It had been a classic contest between two contrasting styles. Afterwards Hunt expressed his significant insight into Rowe the footballer: 'At least a part of the success of my colleague Rowe—and he was very successful in our big match—is due to the extraordinary

These October 1933 caricatures by Jos Walter show various Spurs' personalities of the time, some even engaged in football! Rowe is seen with his greyhounds.

pace which he generates in the course of a few yards. He would beat most of us in a quick sprint either with the ball or without it.' Hunt then challenged Chapman's 'stopper' centre-half approach: 'Haven't we, in [Rowe's] type of centre-half, the real solution of this problem—the player of boundless energy who can work up among his attackers because he is so quick to recover; who can effectively dash even as far as the touch-line when an opponent has broken through.'

Tragically this was the last North London derby witnessed by Chapman. His successor, George Allison, journalist, broadcaster and director, meanwhile wrote a recommendation for Rowe's selection for the forthcoming game between the Football League and the Irish League select teams. Allison considered it essential to decide which type of centre-half was needed, the one '…who supports his forwards or the man who is wedged between the backs.' He continued: 'I had an idea, as I watched Spurs and Arsenal, that I was looking at a man who might fill the bill… this is Rowe, the pivot of the Tottenham team', adding: 'I can assure you, Arsenal players were greatly impressed by [Rowe's] display.'

In heavy conditions Spurs then crashed 3-0 at home to Liverpool, before crossing London to face Chelsea where the great centre-forward Hughie Gallacher was fighting for fitness. This provoked an article making it clear just how capable Rowe had become in a short first-team career: '[For Chelsea] the danger of playing a doubtful Gallacher would be very real, for only a perfectly sound player could hope to hold his own against such a virile, accomplished, hard-tackling pivot as Rowe.' Indeed, Chelsea proceeded to sink without trace, 4-0, a result which proved good preparation for Spurs to greet mighty Sunderland. With Billy Felton unfit, Percy Smith made Rowe captain for the first time. He would also need to keep a watchful eye on his debutant full-back, Fred Channell. As the first local boy to captain the club, even Rowe's successful coin toss was greeted with a cheer. After 30 minutes he received a knock to the head and required three stitches to a cut over his right eye, but one reporter delighted in Tottenham's play: 'Speed, lightning speed;

Another off-field activity Rowe (far left) enjoyed was golfing with Spurs' team-mates, who here include (l to r): Felton, Evans, Whatley, Channell, Hall and McCormick.

in fact, forked lightning. That is what the Tottenham attack must have seemed to the Sunderland defenders. It never seemed to strike in the same place twice. Some of the moves were bewildering in their change of direction…'. In the 18th minute speedy interplay between Evans and Hall had left Hunt free to place his shot wide of 'keeper Jimmy Thorpe. Then, with Spurs on top, Rowe received his injury, missing the final 15 minutes of the first-half. Despite a heavily-bandaged skull, Rowe then, time-and-again, made invaluable interventions. Two more goals finished Sunderland off, a late reply failing to stop Spurs from regaining first place. A week later Spurs toppled Portsmouth 1-0 at Fratton Park.

Around then Rowe demonstrated his concern for the health of soccer in the London *Evening News*: 'I was very much interested to learn that the Football Association had made a new resolve to foster, [both] financially and otherwise, schoolboy football. Whether these efforts will mean that, say in 1940, the supply of good footballers for the leading teams will be equal to the demand remains to be seen. But every little helps.' Rowe then wrote of Spurs' position at the top of the table. 'Speaking for myself, I certainly anticipated that First Division football would be more trying than it has proved.' His reflection on the difference between Second and First Division football was surprising: 'I find myself faced less frequently with the unexpected. The First Division players do the things you think they will do, and consequently it is easier to make up one's mind concerning the proper course of action.' He took the view that it was more difficult to anticipate what was coming in the lower Division because of the greater lack of precision. With tongue-in-cheek (and one imagines a grin on his face) he suggested this might explain his own side's success — that he and his colleagues had developed '…the habit of doing something which is not expected,' thus '…putting their opponents off their stride.'

He then politely responded to suggestions Spurs' success was due to speed alone: 'We are not just a lot of "running-track" experts. Speed alone never won anything worthwhile in football. I should be more pleased if greater reference was made to the skill of the team as a whole. Our success is not in speed. It is in the way skill has been "harnessed" to pace.' A typical demonstration of how Rowe could communicate fluently and concisely. As for that ongoing season, he said '…for the time being we are at least as good as the best.' As for his own playing role, he said: 'I don't go on to the field with hard and fast instructions in my pocket. "Leave it to you", says our manager in effect. And therein must be, so it seems to me, the secret of success in the tactical sense; play according to circumstances. In a word, elastic tactics.' Two Hunt goals in a 4-0 win over Newcastle suggested the step-up from Division Two had not fazed either Hunt or Rowe at all.

Another big landmark soon followed. As Buchan and others had recommended, Arthur was selected for the home international with France on December 12th 1933 played at his beloved White Hart Lane. This was the icing on the cake of what would prove to be Rowe's finest season as a professional footballer. One of two other debutants was team-mate Willie Hall. As for France, a columnist going by the name 'Corinthian' recognised that French football deserved respect. Indeed, the French side included some players who had featured in the 1930 Uruguay World Cup, including forward Émile Veinante (a scorer of a healthy 14 from 24

ARTHUR 'PUSH-AND-RUN' ROWE

Left: *A newspaper cutting announces Rowe's captaining Spurs for the first time, at home to Sunderland on October 7th, 1933.*

Right: *Rowe is photographed at White Hart Lane in the build-up to winning the England cap he proudly wears at far right, following the 4-1 victory over France.*

appearances for France), and full-back Étienne Mattler, who would go on to be one of only five men to appear in the first three World Cup tournaments.

The day of Rowe's big match dawned bright but frosty, the pitch firm and therefore expected to favour the French. Before kick-off a French girl in traditional dress presented a bouquet of white flowers to a surprised English captain Roy Goodall, who was glad when the referee relieved him of it. Once the game got under way the French soon settled down to some '…accurate short passing and clever positioning' but, continued an *Evening Standard* match report, '…they also showed the Continental weakness of not knowing how to finish off clever movements.' This last sentence was printed in bold type, thus emphasising to readers that those pesky foreigners naturally had a weakness! The reporter had hitherto been unaware how inadequate English ball control was, seemingly surprised when obliged to point out that the French '…controlled the lively ball better than the English.' If only the ball had been 'listless'!

As for the action, England centre-forward Camsell scored twice and Manchester City left-winger Eric Brook struck home a free-kick, putting England 3-0 ahead at the break. A match report commended Rowe for breaking up a French attack after poor marking by defensive colleagues. Early in the second-half Hall, receiving from Rowe, beat one man and, feinting to shoot, instead slipped the ball to Brook who crossed for Grosvenor to head home. This completed England's tally, although France did reply before the end.

Hall waited four years for a second cap, but at least he got one, whereas Rowe, despite his performance, was never selected again, but at least remained an England international for the rest of his life. Charles Buchan felt he had failed to take the selectors' eye as he lacked showmanship in his play. Also, of course, thanks to Chapman his attacking style had gone out of fashion. The blinkered mind-set of the English football authorities would become set on utilising a 'stopper' centre-half. At one point during the France game half-back Alf Strange, surprised to find Rowe supporting him during an attack, demanded to know what the debutant thought he was doing coming over to his side of the field, to which Arthur replied: 'I came over to see if you wanted any help'! As a footnote to Arthur's only proud outing in an England shirt, he would later visit the house of a friend to proudly show him the medal awarded for his selection. Arriving home he found the case it was kept in empty. A short while later a workman constructing the new East Stand at White Hart Lane handed the medal to Arthur, saying: 'I thought it might be yours. I found it near Bruce Grove Station' — just eight minutes walk from Rowe's home!

Back in domestic action and, after a 4-1 defeat of Blackburn former Spurs and England star Tommy Clay wrote: 'Rowe's success is chiefly due to uncanny anticipation. He knows the exact moment when to part with the ball, and he senses any danger that may threaten his colleagues.' Suffering some poor results over Christmas Rowe had good reason to recall the game at Villa Park on January 6th, his defence struggling with Villa's double centre-forward ruse (incorporating Astley and Waring). However once captain Rowe called right-half Colquhoun back to perform alongside him as a double centre-half Spurs went on to win spectacularly, 5-1. Spurs' success that afternoon was however overshadowed with the news that the great Herbert Chapman had died at home after a short bout of pneumonia.

Spurs then beat holders Everton 3-0 in the FA Cup third round, Rowe said to have '…repeatedly stopped threatened advances by racing forward and heading away before passes by the Everton forwards could reach their objective.' A controversial encounter followed with the visit of Chelsea and Hughie Gallacher. Even the disciplined, good-natured Rowe becoming involved. From the first whistle Chelsea matched Spurs' delightful passing game with brawn. After a soft penalty was awarded in Hunt's favour, Chelsea tempers rose. Four minutes later Hunt cleverly snapped up a half-chance to make it 2-0. Then, 13 minutes into the second period Rowe and Gallacher clashed in a chase for possession and Rowe, trying to stay on his feet, accidentally ran into Bob McAuley. There followed a suggestion of a kick and a blow after which McAuley was ordered off. Tottenham held on to win a game lyrically described as one '…which dwells in the memory like a nasty blot on a piece of cream-laid writing paper'! McAuley was suspended and the FA

On the morning of the match the Daily Sketch set out the England team as they would line up on the field against France.

Rowe clears from Portsmouth's Jimmy Eason in February 1934. Later in the game, with bandaged head, he shields his 'keeper Joe Nicholls.

stated: 'McAuley is also severely censured for making a false charge against Rowe, of Tottenham Hotspur.'

Spurs then crashed out of the Cup 6-0 at Roker Park. Rowe sported another head bandage after a 0-0 draw with Portsmouth but a Hunt hat-trick against Everton was repeated in a 3-1 victory at Newcastle when the sporting 'Toon' fans cheered Spurs off the field for the quality of their football. With the prolific Hunt netting 13 times in the final 11 fixtures, Spurs achieved a third place finish, commendable for a newly promoted side. Captain Rowe had proved a top-class centre-half and Spurs, with 79 goals (32 from Hunt), had out-scored Chapman's first-placed Arsenal.

FOOTBALL DURING ROWE'S PLAYING DAYS The experience was far removed from today, both fans and players were more likely to be locally born and bred, and, without televised football young fans were less tempted away from their local club. Far fewer females occupied the terraces and hardly any spectators went bare-headed, nor lacked a fag permanently drooping from their lips. Fathers were indeed persuaded by their offspring to invest more in cigarettes as most brands offered collectable cards featuring football stars of the day. Many fans did Saturday morning shifts so arrived at stadiums direct from work clothed in suits and ties, factory overalls, postman or milkman's uniforms with appropriate headgear. Hence the popularity of hot pies in the stadiums. With replica shirts a thing of the future, fans instead sported silk rosettes in the colours of their teams, to accompany home-knitted striped scarves. For economic transport to the ground fans clung to the outside of electric trams such as along High Road, Tottenham. Others would cycle with occupants of houses close to stadiums storing their bikes for the game's duration at threepence a time. Meanwhile, on the field, players' shirts bore no numbers and defensive play was naïve, as exemplified by a 1970s recollection of Rowe's: 'Before the war Stanley Matthews used to do one thing: go outside the full back and get it across. Defenders fell for it every time.' When a defender did win the ball, the usual reaction was to 'give it some leather', getting it as far up-field as possible. In a 1970s interview Arthur recollected his playing days saying that any tactics his team *did* engage in were formulated by the players themselves. As for tactics, Rowe recalled: 'Tactics? The only tactic they had before the War was to get a player who could pass accurately and tell him to hit it over the full backs for someone quick, like Cliff Bastin or Joey Hulme, to run on to. The full backs used to be so unfit that they couldn't turn. They were beaten every time.'

The esteemed *Observer* writer J.A.H. Catton criticised typical training methods of the time: 'Most certainly, ball practice is quite a minor part of a footballer's training in England and team work is supposed to grow as naturally as wild flowers. What fallacies are these!' As Rowe himself recalled: 'We were only allowed to have a ball once a week. In fact the least attention was given to organizing the actual FOOTBALL, which was the most important thing. To economise, equipment was kept to a minimum, training photos showing torn, battered shirts and voluminous, frayed shorts. Meanwhile football boots were padded and rigid as compared to today's soft, slipper-like footwear. In those days it was thought preferable that the boot did not bend and Rowe used just three pairs in 12 years! In all, Arthur was more than a little frustrated with the state of the game, which extended beyond players' onfield needs: 'Everyone accepted their position in those days. The directors travelled first class, the players second.' He was also concerned by the comparatively poor levels of players' pay in those times. By the time his playing days ended he was on around £8 a week in winter and £6 a week in summer which, he emphasised, was relatively good compared, for example, to a carpenter of the time who was lucky to earn £4 a week. But it was in no way sufficient to support a man who could then expect to live another 25-30 years without another trade to fall back on.

As for the standard of refereeing, a press-cutting exists in Rowe's own collection from a column entitled *Trevor Wignall's Daily Sportlight* and is headlined 'Well-Known Player Tells How Soccer has been Spoiled as a Spectacle.' It contains an anonymous footballer's critical opinion of refereeing. Residing in Rowe's very own collection, it is reasonable to assume he himself was that anonymous player. The writer agrees the game has become rougher but shifts the blame from the players onto the referees, allied to the 'great mistake' of the offside rule change in 1925. That Rowe (if it indeed was he) sought anonymity can be appreciated when reading: 'Referees today are, generally speaking, very bad. So few of them have that real knowledge of the game that would enable them to discern the offender and the offended. They do not see the things that happen, simply because they do not know what to look for.' Returning to the change in the offside law, the author writes that 'Before the change defenders could use their brains to stop attacks and didn't need to resort to physical means'. A quintessential Rowe opinion then follows: 'Brain versus brain is far more entertaining than brawn versus brawn at any time, but the wiseheads said the game was slow and dull, so the rule was changed.' The writer addresses his closing remark directly to Wignall: 'Whenever you write of foul play and denounce it, you can be sure of having one admiring reader—the undersigned.' Rowe would later dedicate much time to lecturing referee groups.

SEASON 1934-35 After such a splendid start to life in the First Division there was an air of confidence around White Hart Lane as their second season approached. A similar or better finish was anticipated. The only cloud on the horizon was the Barclays Bank overdraft agreed for the new East Stand. On the opening day of the season the London *Evening News* published an article by Rowe headlined 'THE SPURS WILL PLAY BETTER THIS SEASON'. Recollecting the previous season, Arthur wrote 'If we had lost our opening matches we might have felt that most people were right after all. That we were not good enough. Instead, we went off with a bang, began to tell ourselves that we were equal to the top class, and the sequel you know: we were at the head of the table for a considerable period.' But he forecast that the second season would be more difficult due to the expectation now created, and, tempting fate added, 'I hope we shall not provide a surprise in the wrong direction.' Despite a lack of team strengthening he still confidently asserted: 'If we are as receptive as we think we are, then we should be all the better, as a team, for that season of experience.' Spurs had conceded a substantial 56 goals during their opening season but defensively Rowe felt they had only lacked '…that little bit of experience which enables men to dove-tail; to cover; and turn individual skills into team work. I think the success of the Spurs last season was built on a solid foundation — skill with the ball while working at top speed.'

Indeed, Spurs proceeded to concede just a goal a game in their first six outings, but four games passed before they gained a victory (in fact two, each by 3-1) but on September 22nd classy Aston Villa arrived at the Lane and keeping the ball on the

Rowe shakes hands with Villa captain Danny Blair in September 1934. On the right a nurse reads the latest football news as bedridden Rowe and Willie Hall simultaneously recover from knee surgery that December.

Summer 1935. Arthur marries Amy Lillian Foot, the couple bookended by Spurs' trainer George Hardy and striker George Hunt outside Camberwell Green Registry Office.

ground and with Spurs missing the injured Hunt came away with a 2-0 win. Then the ten games prior to meeting Stoke at home on December 8th included no fewer than five away defeats, including a 5-1 loss to champions Arsenal. Performances were inconsistent and the defence further weakened when the experienced Felton left. Then, during that game with Stoke, a 3-2 win, Rowe incurred a serious knee injury and his season was over. A cartilage operation was required and his playing career suffered a jarring setback. Spurs had lost not only a quality defender but their inspirational captain. Willie Hall had only recently suffered a similar injury so Spurs struggled on without their two international stars. On December 17th 1934 Rowe and Hall were pictured in a nursing home, the matron reading them the latest football news. Spurs conceded an average of nearly three goals per game in the first nine games without their captain. Top scorer Hunt also missed 13 League games during the season and Spurs plummeted swiftly down the table. A 6-0 defeat at Leicester City on March 28th left them propping up the table, a position from which they were unable to escape. Further pain was suffered when Arsenal completed the 'double', 6-0, on the hallowed White Hart Lane turf.

So Spurs plunged back down. If anything measured the contribution of Rowe as player and captain it was this collapse in his absence. Manager Smith had selected no fewer than 36 players during the season and not for the last time it proved difficult for a Spurs manager to adequately invest in new players of sufficient calibre. After one superb initial season at the top Spurs would now remain in the second tier until the second half of the century but Rowe's frustration and sadness as he helplessly watched his side slide back into Division Two were far from his thoughts for at least one day during that summer of 1935 when he married Miss Amy Lilian Foot of Camberwell at Camberwell Green Registry Office. His bride was affectionately known as 'Pom', after a pet Pomeranian dog she had as a child. The wedding was attended by George Hunt and Spurs' trainer George Hardy.

SEASON 1935-36 Despite masterminding promotion, followed by a commendable 3rd place finish in that first Division 1 season, Percy Smith was fired. Conscious of neighbouring Arsenal's success, largely achieved due to copious sums of money spent on the best players available — Smith accused the Tottenham board of making him the scapegoat. He also accused the directors of interference and was not to be the last successful Spurs' manager to suffer a lack of support. It was widely believed the two North London clubs at the time possessed similar wealth, although in Spurs' case they had now landed themselves with that East Stand bank overdraft. The very worst-case scenario had come to pass: Second Division football, a large debt and a drop in income at the turnstiles.

After failed efforts to tempt McWilliam back as manager (he was scouting for Arsenal by then), Crystal Palace boss Jack Tresadern was appointed at the beginning of July. Tresadern had not a single championship or trophy to his name and furthermore, short, sharp passing under his management became a thing of the past, which must have pained Rowe in particular. But Tresadern at least benefitted from the his captain's return for the opening game, a 1-0 defeat at Bradford City, however Arthur then missed the following three games, a win and two defeats, before returning for the draw at Sheffield United in which lanky central striker Johnny Morrison scored. He would go on to hit another fifteen in the next 10 consecutive games. Hunt was, by then, like Rowe, often troubled by injury. By the end of his Spurs' career he had contributed a phenomenal 125 goals in just 185 League games. Meanwhile Rowe stayed fit to serve in a healthy three wins and two draws, before succumbing to injury again, missing a 5-1 win over Burnley and the subsequent nine matches. One of those who filled-in for him was ex-Northfleet debutant Vic Buckingham, nine years Rowe's junior, of whom much more later. After returning to play at Doncaster just before Christmas, Arthur was then ever-present for all but one of the remaining 29 League and Cup matches, helping Spurs to a fifth-placed finish.

During an October 1935 interview Tresadern unsurprisingly stated he didn't believe in a coaching system, on the spurious grounds that English footballers would never, '…cotton on to it… they are not built that way'! He believed more in mixing youngsters with experienced players. At least he did not fail to appreciate his captain's contribution. 'Arthur Rowe, our centre-half, is a great lad for inspiring youngsters when he is on the field'. The interviewer then raised the issue which would remain a consistent concern during both Rowe's spells at Spurs. 'Tottenham appear to be living in the past where transfer fees are concerned. No club will sell a player to Tottenham at Tottenham's price… a club like Tottenham should have a whole house-full of stars.' As later chapters show, Tottenham Hotspur's progress would repeatedly be inhibited by this parsimonious practice for years to come.

Spurs welcomed First Division Huddersfield in the 4th round of the FA Cup on January 25th 1936, five days after the death of King George V (captain Rowe and his players lining-up to respect two minutes' silence before kick-off). As Huddersfield's centre-half Alf Young was said to be on Tresadern's wanted list at the time, no doubt due to Rowe's absences through injury, one sympathetic commentator wrote: 'If only for the sake of the player himself, I hope Rowe has a good game.' Spurs

January 1936. Prior to the 1-0 Cup defeat of Huddersfield, captain Rowe stands at the end of the line (left) as the teams respect two-minutes silence to honour the passing of King George V.

did move on to the 5th round, winning 1-0, before beating relegation-threatened Port Vale 5-1, speedy winger Freddie Sargent scoring one of the five. If Rowe was feeling his injury he was doing well to disguise it as one report described him as '...a great centre-half who blotted the three inside Vale forwards out of the game.'

Bypassing Bradford Park Avenue in the fifth round of the Cup, Spurs were then outclassed 3-1 by Sheffield United in the sixth, nevertheless one reporter wrote: 'My outstanding memory of this glorious stick-in-the-mud cup-tie is of Arthur Rowe, the Spurs' captain and centre-half, in the centre of operations shouting orders like the captain of a floundering ship', adding 'the marvel to me was that in his role of commander he managed to put in so much real work himself.' But Spurs' lack of investment in players was again raised, the reporter highlighting the: '...ominous weaknesses' in the Tottenham side, adding pointedly, 'They were the weaknesses which the directors, ever since the beginning of the season, have promised their supporters they would eradicate and have not done so.' After just three points from the following eight even Spurs' own Handbook criticised the failure to strengthen the side and, the writer added (with some irritation): 'We constantly hear rumours, "the Spurs are interested in a centre half-back." Why a centre-half? Arthur Rowe is, to my football sense, the best player on their books.'

Two victories were then achieved thanks to consecutive hat-tricks from Hunt, but any chance of an immediate return to the First Division nose-dived when Spurs took just two points from six over Easter and finished fifth. Rowe performed his usual centre-half role for the final game, away to Barnsley on May 2nd 1936, but for once his concentration may have been less than total. On that day Rowe's first child, Derek, arrived, and the close-season allowed Rowe to support wife Pom during the couple's introduction to parenthood.

This was the summer of the notorious Berlin Olympics. In the football tournament Great Britain lost to Poland by the odd goal in nine, and, on returning to England, Secretary of the Football Association, Stanley (later Sir Stanley) Rous,

Rowe's colleagues Howe, Sargent (at back) and (in front) Whatley and Phypers, seem to find his solo exercises with a medicine ball amusing.

co-wrote a report criticising the performance of the Great Britain side. Rous and his colleague acknowledged that 'our' play did not compare favourably with other nations who utilised a more attractive, attacking style. These '…old methods, which have for their object attack more than defence,' they wrote, '…proved more effective and certainly more interesting to watch.' But English clubs were not easily persuaded to cast aside Chapman's blueprint. However, the great Austrian coach Hugo Meisl was so encouraged (and more than a little amazed) to witness English soccer authorities at least acknowledging the need to absorb lessons from overseas that he described the FA report as 'remarkable'.

SEASON 1936-37 That August Rowe himself attended an FA instructional course. Soon to turn 30, he was no doubt conscious that injury might curtail his playing career. Ironically, in carrying out one of the course exercises he suffered a back muscle injury. The combination of this and his knee problem proved costly, as although he managed to play in the opening two games of the new season, he proceeded to make a mere 20 appearances during the season. This became a great concern for him: 'As so often,' he said at the time, '…my deputies had been playing in a way which, apparently, the club was not anxious to disturb'. Rowe got off to a good start, *Star* reporter Jack Ingham reporting: 'On [Rowe's] display at West Ham, Tottenham won't need a new centre-half.' Although a late goal led to Spurs' defeat, Tresadern expressed delight with '…the grand form of Arthur Rowe' but injury soon forced him out of the next five games and his return for a 1-0 defeat at Barnsley saw Spurs tumble to 13th.

Rowe's selection for the trip to Burnley in October proved memorable. His immediate opponent was a 17-year-old making his first professional appearance. Just two minutes in, the youngster raced past him and scored. The debutant went on to hit two more in Burnley's 3-1 victory and ultimately received Rowe's accolade as the finest centre-forward he ever faced in his career. Considering Arthur also faced the likes of Dixie Dean, George Camsell and Hughie Gallacher, this was praise indeed. The name of this talented boy was Tommy Lawton and Rowe recommended him to Spurs officials, later joking: 'After all, I had to make some excuse!' Lawton himself recalled '…a wonderful day, made even more wonderful by the thought that I had scored a hat-trick against such a fine centre-half as Arthur Rowe.'

At this juncture Spurs' all-time great Arthur Grimsdell expressed concern at Tresadern's methods, saying the club would not return to Division One unless they reverted to the '…style and method which served them so well in the past.' He added: 'I have always associated the club with the best type of football, and their present position can largely be traced to the abandonment of that ideal.' Grimsdell called Tresadern's style of play '…tearaway football… Speed and dash will always be useful assets but by themselves they lead only to temporary success' but for Rowe, he had nothing but praise. 'This player is a great source of strength to the side, and it is to be hoped that he has no return of the injury that kept him out of the team so long.' As it was, Rowe soon succumbed again.

On a personal level, this was a sad time for the Rowe family. On November 11th 1936, Arthur's mother 'Lottie' passed away aged 59, having for some years suffered from incurable encephalomalacia (cerebral softening). Rowe, frustrated by his injury and often unable to help his colleagues out on the pitch, now grieved for his mother. Without their captain Spurs were marooned in mid-table, but Arthur returned for a 4-0 win at Blackburn Rovers on Christmas Day and before missing a home defeat to Newcastle, Spurs took a further four points from six. Rowe returned for the FA Cup third round tie at First Division Portsmouth and this proved to be Tresadern's finest hour. He played three up front, pulled the inside-forwards back, and concentrated Spurs' attacks on Portsmouth's weaker side. Spurs got on top after ten minutes with a goal from Morrison, who, wrote one reporter, was '…backed-up by a …centre-half in a hundred—Arthur Rowe, as solid as any policeman on point duty, who held up three lines of traffic without a falter.' The victory will have filled Rowe's heart with pride; at Fratton Park that day he must have felt he was back where he belonged: Division One.

Rowe then missed a 3-2 defeat at Bradford Park Avenue, returning for the home fourth round cup tie with Division Two Plymouth Argyle. Four days earlier an 18-year-old Yorkshire-born apprentice had turned professional at White Hart Lane. This was Billy Nicholson, of whom much more later. Against Argyle, McCormick's solitary goal saw Spurs through to a 5th round, 'money-spinning' trip to Everton.

So, on February 20th 1937 Spurs travelled to Goodison Park where Everton were unbeaten in 13 home games. Spurs defended well and knocked the 'Toffees' out of their stride, but Rowe thought the referee '…a little too strict about some offences which were merely the result of two determined players going wholeheartedly for the ball.' It therefore became a dull spectacle until, with 12 minutes left Rowe, who had shut the iconic Dixie Dean out of the game, was adjudged to have fouled the great man in a heading duel. Silence fell over Goodison as Dean shaped to take the spot-kick. Striking it to Jack Hall's left, the 'keeper parried it, but only back to Dean, whose second effort was again pushed away by Hall, this time to Everton's Alex Stevenson, who toe-ended the ball over the bar. With his inherent belief in the significance of luck, Rowe took this triple-miss as a positive sign. Two minutes later

Spurs won a free-kick near halfway and Rowe placed it perfectly, Everton 'keeper Ted Sagar and McCormick challenging for it before McCormick's head, on the turn, just beat Sagar's hands to the ball. Goal! But down went the scorer, knocked out. From nearly conceding a late goal, Spurs, with ten minutes left, were ahead. The hosts piled on the pressure, Hall touching a Cunliffe shot onto the bar but then Joe Mercer sent over a cross which Hall could only help on, Coulter heading home with just two minutes left. Even Mercer considered it a fortunate equaliser. With amusement Rowe reflected afterwards on the irony of both goals being headed by the two shortest players on the pitch, while he himself was described as playing with 'Three-man power' as he kept Dean '…"frozen" to the fringe of the play.'

But Rowe had little time to bask in any glory, the replay taking place two days' later at soggy White Hart Lane. Tommy Lawton, who had caused so many problems for Rowe earlier in the season, had by now joined Everton and lined-up alongside Dean, a nightmare duo for any centre-half to confront. After two minutes Lawton headed home, and on 20 minutes Dean made it 2-0. Then, with Everton expected to build on their lead, Spurs' left-winger Les Miller zipped down the left, crossed, and Morrison scored. So, despite Rowe's description of his side getting a 'real chasing', Everton only led 2-1 at the half. But, on the re-start, Lawton went through and, looking certain to score, was pulled down by Rowe, the referee pointing to the spot but Spurs players pointed to a flag-waving linesman. Rowe, as captain, politely asked the referee if he would consult the linesman. The referee did so and reversed his decision — in the build-up the referee had missed his linesman's flag for a foul throw by Everton's Mercer in his own half.

Morrison then headed an equaliser… but… no! A Spurs' colleague was adjudged to have fouled a defender and soon things turned sour for Rowe's side when Dean side-footed his second, making it 1-3 with little time left. At this point, as Lawton recalled, '…the "Tottenham Roar" started,' and '…the Lilywhites simply poured into attack.' Morrison ran through to score his second: 2-3. Now the 46,972 crowd were roaring Tottenham on. With just four minutes left to play, Buckingham threw-in to Morrison who slipped the ball to inside-right Joe Meek, who beat Sagar with a great finish to equalise. 3-3. With extra-time looming, an exhausted Rowe said to Buckingham 'Boy, I hope there's no extra time!' With two minutes left Miller bypassed Everton right-back Billy Cook, accelerated and crossed. Morrison was there in the middle to meet it with his head for 4-3! At the last gasp, Rowe's Second Division Spurs were through to the FA Cup Quarter-Finals.

Express reporter Stanley Halsey brilliantly illustrated just how heart-stopping those final minutes were. 'So great was the tension when Spurs snatched victory in those last throbbing minutes that I looked down at my programme and found it a crumpled ball of paper in my hand.' Despite the defeat and the painful nature of it, Everton's Joe Mercer always regarded this game as the most thrilling of his career, which totalled more than 430 League games. Of this classic encounter Arthur himself wrote: 'Sheer courage and refusal to accept defeat till that "last whistle" won that game', adding that never had a game been won that '…seemed so inevitably lost.' Mercer atmospherically described the scenes on the White Hart Lane terraces at the end, with hats and programmes being tossed into the air, '…

floating down to earth from the double-decker stand,' resembling 'a snowstorm'. Spurs' fans danced in circles. One well-known reporter had departed before those final amazing minutes to post his match report in time for the presses to run that night, leaving some (in those pre-instant communication days) to wonder what result would be recorded in his paper the following day! Sadly for Spurs they finally went out 3-1 to First Division Preston but it had been a stirring Cup run, second-level Spurs putting two well-established First Division sides out of the competition.

After the Cup exit Rowe would not reappear that season. It appears Tresadern had postponed further treatment for him until the Cup run ended. Arthur's playing career, late to start, was now stuttering to a premature finish. Journalist Stanley Halsey claimed to have received a 'mountain' of letters from Spurs fans asking 'What is going to happen to Arthur Rowe?' 'In every Tottenham local, café, club, wherever Spurs fans gather together, you hear the same rumours being dissected in a search for the truth. Is Rowe going on the transfer list; is he going to become a coach; will his back injury put him out of football forever?' Arthur had begun FA engagements to coach and give lectures, taking his first steps on a coaching or managerial career. One Spurs' director told Halsey he considered him '…a fellow of very good education …who would make a splendid manager or coach.'

Future Championship-winning captain Ron Burgess, then a young groundstaff boy, recalled a practice game around that time when he took a comb from his shorts and began tidying his hair. Rowe was on the opposing side and asked Burgess with a grin if he thought he was a film star, adding: 'Sorry I can't supply you with a mirror, young man!'

Without their captain Spurs won just four of their final 12 fixtures, finishing five places lower than in Tresadern's first season in charge, so Spurs were treading water in their quest for that much-desired return to Division One. Morrison finished with

Rowe holidaying in the late 1930s with sons Graham (in pushchair) and Derek.

a formidable 29 goals in the League plus six in the great FA Cup run, so the classier Hunt was sold to, of all clubs, Arsenal.

SEASON 1937-38 On September 4th 1937 Rowe became a father again when Pom gave birth to second son Graham. Graham has told me of his happy and adventurous childhood, typical for the times, getting into trouble when fishing or collecting birds' eggs. On these occasions his mother would warn him that his father would deal with him once he got home, and Graham admitted his dad had on occasion used a belt on him — no more than was normal during that era of little parental guidance, but one imagines the punishment being as painful for Arthur to apply as for his sons to receive. When Graham finished school at 16 in 1954 his father gave him the perfect advice, that no matter which profession he selected, even if he chose to be a street cleaner, he would expect Graham '…to have the cleanest street in town.'

Meanwhile, in season 1937-38, Rowe would be involved in just 12 games, his knee remaining a problem. By then Tresadern was buying players from lower leagues, further restricting Spurs' ambitions. He appeared in a 2-2 draw in the FA Cup fifth round at Division Two Chesterfield on February 12th as well as the replay four days later, Spurs scraping through to the quarter-finals again. Rowe was said to have closed the centre of the field to the Chesterfield inside forwards and it was only when he limped to the wing near the end that Chesterfield offered any threat. In the last eight Spurs would host Cup-holders Sunderland on March 5th. Arthur ran out for the game in front of what would prove to be the highest-ever attendance at White Hart Lane up until its demolition in 2017: 75,038. With the capacity of today's Tottenham Hotspur Stadium set at 62,850, Rowe can always be recalled as one of eleven Spurs' men who appeared in front of the largest crowd ever for a Spurs home game. Sadly, but perhaps appropriately, it also proved to be the last

Buckingham and Rowe stand guard as 'keeper Hooper punches clear in front of the highest-ever attendance at White Hart Lane. Below: Rowe clears at West Ham.

major encounter he took part in. For the third year in a row Spurs failed to reach the semi-final, going down to a late Sunderland strike. Arthur's final chance of FA Cup success as a player was over.

Arthur returned to face Chesterfield at home, beginning an unbroken spell in the first-team of six games. In a 3-1 victory at Upton Park he was photographed in action, right knee bandaged. Then, a 2-1 defeat at home to promotion challenging Sheffield United on April 15th proved to be Arthur's very last appearance for Tottenham in first-class football. He travelled to the following week's 2-0 defeat at Villa Park but only to stand, be-suited and doleful, in the team group photo taken that afternoon. Without him, Spurs lost four of the five remaining games, finishing fifth, an improvement of just four points on Tresadern's previous season in control and, inevitably, the manager resigned, having never won over the Spurs fans. His chosen replacement, on the other hand, certainly would.

SEASON 1938-39 Re-occupying the hot seat after 11 years away was none other than Peter McWilliam. Arthur, still harbouring faint hopes of continuing his playing career, was delighted to see the return of his hero. In 1952 Rowe would recall McWilliam as a '…much-loved man, [who] brought to Spurs his knowledge, his wisdom, his kindliness and, above all, his love of good football.' Yet, recalled Ron Burgess, the Scot administered very strict rules, believing '…in calling a spade a spade in his broad Scottish brogue, and if a player displeased him, he was not backward in telling him so.' Which leads to an odd story about McWilliam's return related by Deryk Brown in his book *The Tottenham Hotspur Story*. Brown suggests that the initial conversation when McWilliam and Rowe were reunited in 1938 was not encouraging:

'"They tell me you've become a red," said McWilliam to Rowe.

'"I've not changed," replied Rowe.

'"We'll see," said McWilliam, and walked away.'

As it was a time when so many intelligent, educated young people, under the threat of spreading fascism in Europe, were turning to Communism, can one assume that McWilliam was inferring that Rowe held what the Scot deemed as unhealthy political views? Had Arthur exhibited communist sympathies at that time he would have been in very good company as it was then seen by many as the best hope to counter growing fascism in Europe. On the other hand, McWilliam, with views rather right of centre, had perhaps picked-up on Rowe's opinions regarding better pay for footballers at that time (see earlier in this chapter) and the new manager was merely pulling his leg. In an article about eight years' later Rowe criticised how poorly players were remunerated by their clubs: 'It is my personal belief that all clubs would reap fuller rewards if they concentrated on paying the players they sign the most they can afford to pay, rather than the least that they can get the player to sign for!' He added: 'Be as generous as you can afford to be, and above all, be fair! Once players are happy and content that the wages paid are all that can be afforded, then we are well on the way to creating "team spirit."'

Arthur once claimed that when he returned for pre-season training at Spurs in that summer of 1938 he was officially 'written-off' due to his knee injury. But

The attention George Hardy gives Arthur's knee appears to amuse teammates (from left to right) Bill Whatley, Johnny Morrison and Les Howe.

elsewhere he said 'It remains one of my happiest memories that following pre-season practice games Peter told me I was once again to be in the team—and this time, in *his* team, as *his* captain.' Rowe duly took his place in the pre-season photo.

Unfortunately Arthur did not make a single appearance before the end of the year and at 32 he finally closed the door on his playing career. A second 'successful' cartilage operation had only led to thigh muscle wastage so he retired with the satisfaction that his mentor McWilliam had entrusted him with the captaincy, which sweetened the retirement pill somewhat. However no offer of a staff job appears to have been made and he ultimately left the club on a free transfer. Maybe there was simply a lack of suitable roles for him at that particular time. Arthur later claimed McWilliam had both signed him and 'sacked' him, indicating that he felt another role could or should have been found for him at the club. As it was, he found himself, a father of two, with no immediate career options other than upholstery.

His apprenticeship in that trade had so delayed his professional soccer career that his Spurs' first-team career lasted a mere seven seasons. He made 182 League and 19 FA Cup appearances yet never once found the net. He once flippantly excused this as follows: 'They didn't like the centre-half to go too far over the halfway line in those days!'

After Arthur's retirement other players from Spurs' Northfleet nursery side began appearing in the first team, including three future greats: Ron Burgess, Ted Ditchburn and Bill Nicholson. Had it not been for his injury they may have featured alongside him. Spurs finished that final, completed pre-war season in a comfortable seventh place. Ironically the declaration of War in September 1939 was the second occasion when McWilliam's management of Spurs had been interrupted by the onset of hostilities in Europe.

Rowe's career was likewise put on hold.

6

Ambassador Rowe

THE HUNGARIAN CONNECTION

'This trainer must be as intelligent and fine a gentleman as Rowe.
He will be really an Ambassador of English football.'
FROM HUNGARIAN JOURNALIST 'LOTZI' FELEKI'S LETTER TO STANLEY ROUS, OUTLINING
THE HUNGARIAN AUTHORITY'S REQUIREMENTS (20 JULY 1939)

By the time his former Spurs' colleagues had sat around the radio to hear the declaration of war, the unemployed Arthur Rowe had been busy applying for coaching roles. This was no knee-jerk reaction to enforced retirement as a player — he had long been interested in pursuing such a career. As he once recalled: 'Often I would travel miles to take coaching classes with junior and youth clubs. Apart from helping the lads, I wanted to put over my own theories.' Interestingly, he later admitted he had not expected to be a manager: 'I did not think I was big enough, or clever enough to be a manager. But I wanted to stay in the game as a coach.'

Earlier, in 1939, László 'Lotzi' Feleki, a journalist from the Hungarian specialist sport's magazine *Nemzeti* [National] *Sport* (later known as *Nepsport*), was finishing a whole year spent in London studying English football and sending reports back to Hungary. Living close to Highbury Stadium, he had spent most of his time with Arsenal Football Club. But among other coaches Feleki encountered during his time in London were Rowe and the vastly experienced Jimmy Hogan. Both men worked with visiting Hungarians. Many European countries had begun playing soccer some time after its development in Britain and were keen to advance their own soccer progress, hence Feleki's visit. Some prominent British coaches, Hogan in particular, had already worked in Europe, often due to the lack of value placed on coaching by those who ran British football (a malaise prevalent at least up until the late 1950s). Thus the quality of play in nations where British soccer pilgrims worked, developed and improved at a greater pace than back home. Even after World War 2, when the first FA Director of Coaching, Walter Winterbottom, produced a proliferation of qualified coaches, many would work on the Continent due to lack of opportunity at home.

Feleki's reports back to Budapest led the Hungarian Central Committee of Sport to request his help in identifying a British soccer coach to work in Hungary with high school and college students. Coaches in other sports, such as track-and-field, were also sought. No doubt due to Feleki's close relationship with Arsenal, an offer was made to their former centre-forward Jack Lambert, at that time coaching the reserves. Feleki (or possibly the Central Committee of Sport) wanted someone who could coach Chapman's 'third back', counter-attacking style. Lambert initially accepted the offer but then dropped out, so Feleki wrote for help to the Secretary of the Football Association, Stanley Rous, spelling-out the requirement for someone to '…lay down new foundations for Hungarian football.' Thus, in the spring of 1939, Rous recommended Rowe. Incidentally, in similar fashion, in the following decade Rous would suggest another English coach, George Raynor, to the Swedish authorities. Raynor became Sweden's national coach and took them to the final of the World Cup in 1958 although typically, despite this success, he was never offered a prime coaching job in the UK.

Rous, the son of a Suffolk grocer, had organised his own village football team as a schoolboy before becoming a teacher. He also qualified as a referee, eventually officiating at the 1934 FA Cup Final, before being appointed Secretary of the Football Association. In that post he led a crusade to encourage football coaching in England, despite the contempt of many in the game, and published the FA's first coaching manual, 80 years after its founding. Jimmy Hogan was one of the first men Rous approached in 1935 to run a three-day trial coaching course, but he found that Hogan relied too much on practical demonstration, utilising his own skills, and lacked organizational ability. Eventually, Walter Winterbottom got the job, a man who had both played for Manchester United and lectured at Carnegie College. Thereafter Winterbottom successfully ran a second coaching course, put on in 1938, which coincided with Rowe's burgeoning interest in a coaching career (Winterbottom was to become the Football Association Director of Coaching in 1946, the dawn of organised coaching instruction in Britain).

As of April 13th 1939, *Nemzeti Sport* was reporting on an unnamed English coach preparing training sessions. This may have been Lambert before his withdrawal,

A May 1939 Hungarian newspaper reports on Rowe's presentations.

Rowe (fourth from right) works with a group of players in Budapest as journalist László Feleki (on right of enlarged detail) translates by his side.

but is more likely to have been Rowe, planning his coaching programme in advance of his posting to Budapest in May. Arthur duly travelled to Budapest to 'explain' Chapman's 'third-back' game but, as no more than a mere messenger, the third-back tactic will have been presented with less conviction and enthusiasm than had Lambert done it. However, Hungary did adopt the tactic and Nándor Hidegkuti (1953 star for Hungary at Wembley, see Chapter 13) said the third-back system stimulated arguments throughout Hungarian football and György Sárosi, star striker of the pre-war years, someone clearly on the same page as Rowe, '…predicted that the game would lose its beauty and become mere semantics.'

Returning to spring 1939, Rowe would spend four weeks in Budapest from mid-May. Bálint Hóman, then Hungarian Minister of Culture and later prosecuted as partly responsible for sending over half a million Jews to German death camps, had made the visit possible. His initial four-week schedule was to be broken into three weeks of lectures and one week of actual coaching. As he didn't speak Hungarian, Arthur requested Feleki accompany him. Although the sessions were essentially aimed at university and high school pupils, they were also open to coaches, one of whom was none other than future national coach Gusztáv Sebes, who was the same age as Rowe. It was the very same Sebes whose side became the greatest team in the world during the 1950s. Furthermore, the greatest Hungarian footballer of all time, the imperious Ferenc Puskás, then just 12 years' old, also attended — after all, his father was head coach of Budapest club side Kispest, later known as Honvéd, which eventually comprised much of the national team.

Rowe later explained his activities in Hungary: 'My work in the day-time was with the students at the National Physical Training College of Hungary, all training to be sports and physical instructors, but each with his own particular sport to specialise in. As additional students, were a large number of games' teachers who had been brought into Budapest from their various towns and villages especially for this course of football coaching. But more novel and interesting, I thought, were my evening activities. I then attended, in turn, some half-dozen first-class stadiums, where all who were interested were able to join in the coaching. In Budapest at the same time was the famous American hurdles champion, [Robert] Simpson, who was engaged in similar work to mine—athletics coach. These lads wanted the champion's help and advice; they [already] had their own "general" athletics coach. But here was a "specialist", teaching the sport he was a champion exponent of.' On another occasion Arthur recalled: 'In Budapest my coaching was largely with youth groups, with Hungarian coaches in the role of onlookers. My main purpose was to introduce them to English methods and everywhere I went I was enthusiastically received. The only team-coaching that I did was with the players selected to represent Budapest Universities in their forthcoming European international tournament, and the hours that I was with them were among the happiest of the entire trip. In my free time I was able to watch the big clubs in training and also saw a great many of their club matches. In those days Újpest, Ferencváros and Hungária were the leading sides and between them they had many fine players.'

When giving his second session, which was with a group of head coaches, Rowe was accompanied by no less than Dr Károly Dietz, who a year earlier had managed the Hungarian national side to the 1938 World Cup Final (a 4-2 defeat to Italy), and Kálmán Vághy, who would himself become national team coach in 1942. The session covered heading, tackling and using the body in match play, the permitted use of the shoulder '…when the ball is involved' and passing techniques. Clearly the coaches enjoyed and appreciated Rowe's session. Two evenings later he lectured a group of Third Year students at the Hungarian University of Physical Education, covering such things as corner-kicks and ball control using the sole of the foot. The use of the shoulder came up again, Rowe being questioned over its permissibility — Arthur argued it was acceptable providing the arm was not moving. Although hardly the strongest advocate of the over-physical side of the game, being English Rowe had to teach some things which formed part of the 'curriculum' he himself had absorbed during his career.

The following evening Rowe, expressing his pleasure that so many players and coaches were in attendance, once again took the use of the body as the subject of discussion, demonstrating actions then permissible in English football but which would have been deemed a 'foul' by referees of the 'old school' (including those in Hungary). Again, Rowe's opinions proved controversial. He criticised local referees for adjudging the tackling techniques he was teaching (the accepted British style) as foul-play. It clearly remained in the Hungarians' memory that when the Hungarian national side lost 6-2 to England at Highbury three years earlier, the visitors had repeatedly protested that some challenges were unfair. Feleki supported Rowe's opinions, pointing out '…the problem is that the clean, strong and "masculine" style, using the body, is largely missing from Hungarian football. The tackling technique Rowe promotes (in this case, slide tackling) is not against the rules, but simply unfamiliar among the Hungarian players.' Rowe suggested that Hungarian referees judged an action as a foul whether or not the '…target was the ball or the player.'

Despite these differences of opinion over physicality in the game, it is clear that the general perception of Rowe among those he met at these sessions was extremely positive, that they saw him as a very open, honest person, willing to help wherever and whenever he could. He accepted invitations to practically any match, whether they be important adult fixtures or children's games. There was already talk of extending his stay a further week following interest for his services from the Hungarian club Phöbus, founded just three years' earlier and therefore, more than most, open to anything which could improve their approach.

But Rowe then suffered an unfortunate setback. To conclude a session he had organised a practice game, and, despite slippery conditions, he joined-in. At one point he fell, inflaming the knee which had ended his playing career. Taken to a spa, the knee was massaged but he still had to cancel his next session. Having been impressed when witnessing hurdler Simpson, 14 years older than himself, setting a personal example to students, one can imagine Arthur's mortification at being unable to demonstrate his own skills in similar fashion. His disappointment from being unable to continue enjoying the satisfaction of his work was matched by his embarrassment in letting his welcoming hosts down.

The following Wednesday Rowe's comments on a professional game between Phöbus and Elektromos [two clubs who later merged] were reported by the newspaper *Sporthirlap*. Aside from complimenting the quality of the two goalkeepers he again pointed out that physicality which would go unchecked in England was being penalised by Hungarian officials. Of the Hungarian club matches he witnessed, Rowe later said: 'The individual standard was incredibly high wherever I went, but the two [players] that impressed me most were Hungary's international forwards [György] Sárosi and [Gyula] Zsengellér [of Újpest].' Sárosi had been the star of Hungary's World Cup effort the previous year, spending all his career with Ferencváros (who included younger brother Béla) and totalled an extraordinary 351 goals from 383 League games. The truly outstanding Zsengellér had figured at inside-left in the Rest of Europe team beaten 3-0 by England at Highbury in 1938. 'Zsengellér', continued Rowe, '…was so pigeon-toed that it would have been almost impossible for him to play the ball with the inside of the foot, yet his ability with the ball, achieved after many long hours of practice was truly amazing.'

On June 3rd 1939 another article, headlined 'This is How Rowe Teaches', teases the modern-day reader to anticipate confirmation of the often-voiced opinion that it was Rowe who introduced the basics of 'push-and-run' to Hungary (thus

From left-to-right: *Gyorgy Sarosi, Gyula Zsengellér and Gusztáv Sebes (later the coach of the outstanding 1950s' Hungarian national side).*

contributing to the development of the superb Hungarian national side of the 1950s, see Chapter 13). Indeed, in view of that side's much-lauded style, Rowe was said to make the case for midfielders to '…move forward after passing the ball', emphasising that every player should be involved in every moment of a game. On the other hand, Rowe lectured on the need to avoid always passing to a player on the same side of the field, sometimes putting the receiver in a difficult position, encouraging switching the play. As an essential element of his 'push-and-run' theory would be to keep passes short, for greater accuracy and ball retention, then it is difficult to reconcile his proposing long, risky, cross-field passes. But this probably formed part of the fixed curriculum he had been asked to follow, and, in any case, this was only 1939 and there was time enough for Rowe to fully elaborate his ideas before fine-tuning his theories at Spurs. He lectured too on defending corner-kicks and free-kicks (the positioning of defenders and who should pick-up whom), and criticised the Hungarians' tendency to face away from the ball when forming a wall.

The first full week of June 1939 would end his stay in Hungary. He spent it coaching top university players in the style of a coach at a professional English club (good practice for his later career). On June 8th he addressed the University elite team preparing for the University World Championships and, despite his novice status as a coach, some coaches present expressed a wish for Rowe to stay and continue working with their players. In the evening Hungary and Italy were to meet at the Ferencváros stadium and of course everyone present at Rowe's session was excitedly anticipating it. Sadly for Rowe's hosts, Italy triumphed 3-1, and when asked for his opinions Rowe diplomatically said he was disappointed, having wished for a Hungarian victory, but felt the Hungarians had '…defeated themselves.' He felt they had occasionally utilised unnecessarily complicated moves of too many passes ('Keep it Simple' would be a later 'push-and-run' catchphrase of his), comparing their performance with the clean, uncomplicated moves of the Italian side. He also criticised the Hungarian 'keeper for occasionally leaping dramatically to field the ball instead of just catching it. This was Rowe's last recorded activity in Hungary and he was back in England that weekend of June 10th. In terms of his influence on the superb 1950s' Hungarian national side, we know that during his 1939 visit he encountered the following notable Hungarians (and no doubt many others):

Dr Károly Dietz — who had managed Hungary to that defeat against Italy in the 1938 World Cup final.

Béla Guttmann — manager of Újpest, then Hungarian champions, the most famous of Hungarian coaches, best known for taking Benfica to two successive European Cup triumphs in the 1960s.

Lajos Korányi — a defender who played for Ferencváros and Phöbus as well as 40 times for the Hungarian national side (including the 1938 World Cup).

Lajos Lutz — a coach who had played as a midfielder for Újpest and the Hungarian national side.

Professor Ottó Misángyi — of the Main Council of Physical Education.

Ferenc Puskás — almost certainly accompanied by his lifelong friend József Bozsik, the two starring when Hungary demolished England in 1953).

Gusztáv Sebes — future coach of the 'Mighty Magyars' of the 1950s.

KÁLMÁN VÁGHY — Hungarian national coach from 1942.

Arthur will most likely have also met other Hungarian players and coaches of that era, such as BÉLA ANDRASI, GYÖRGY SZEDER, the SÁROSI brothers and GYULA ZSENGELLÉR.

A month after returning to England Arthur received a letter from Feleki with an offer of employment from the Main Council of Physical Education. The offer was to coach a Hungarian club side three days a week, as a '...model of how to train [coach] a team', the sessions to be witnessed by 'would-be' Hungarian coaches.

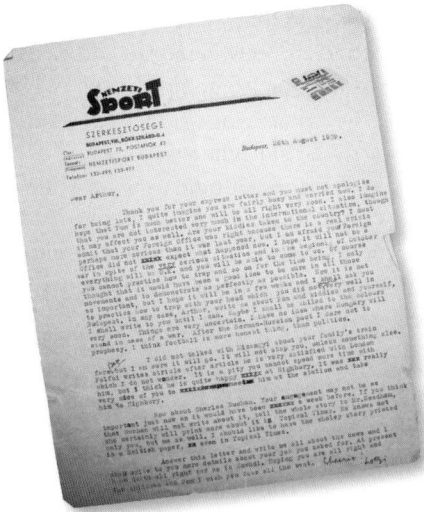

Left: *The letter from 'Lotzi' Feleki (pictured here with wife Szendi) in which he still expressed hope that Rowe would accept the post of coach to the Hungarian national side, despite the approaching war.*

In the role of what was referred to as 'Professor of football in the first Hungarian Trainer Course', Rowe would also lecture coaches. This, emphasised Feleki, '...is really an important job,' explaining that all Hungarian coaches would in future require a certificate to coach and it would be down to Rowe to teach the technical and tactical aspects of the course. The rest of his week would be devoted to youth coaching. The date pencilled-in by Feleki for his return to Budapest was September 1st 1939 'at the latest' and his employment in Hungary was to last one full year. On top of his weekly pay he would receive full lodging for one person and second-class travel expenses. But by far the most significant item mentioned in Feleki's letter was the proposal that during the following spring of 1940 Arthur would prepare the Hungarian national side to compete in that summer's Helsinki Olympics.

Feleki wanted to know what Rowe's 'conditions' would be should he accept the role. One thing Arthur would clearly require was accommodation for wife Pom and his two sons. Considering his minimal coaching experience, the offer to coach a national team demonstrates how significant an impression he had made. In a further attempt to encourage him, Feleki risked offence when suggesting Rowe had insufficient experience to walk into a coaching position in England, so that building a reputation in Hungary would provide a good platform for better opportunities to arise once he eventually returned to England. Feleki: 'One year here I think would be very good for your future at home.'

Interestingly, Feleki's letter indicates Rowe was also coveting journalistic ambitions, possibly as a back-up career should his coaching ambitions fail to come to fruition. This further suggests Arthur had indeed been the 'anonymous' footballer responsible for the article previously quoted in this book which criticised referees. Certainly he would have many further articles published in later life, few, if any, of the standard 'ghosted' variety. Feleki adds '…it would be a good start for your journalistic career' were Rowe to write about his Hungarian coaching experiences for publication in England. Feleki, exhibiting his anxiety, then closes with 'Write me quickly and decide' and indeed, the following day he wrote to Stanley Rous at the FA to facilitate arrangements for Rowe to take up the post.

However, the ensuing three-way correspondence between Feleki, Rowe and Rous make it clear that the likelihood of war was ever-increasing and in his letter to Sir Stanley on July 20th, the Hungarian talks of arranging English football tours, wrote: 'I must say the importance of these tours is bigger than ever now, especially in the present political circumstances, which I think does not need much explanation. I am sure success on the sports field is always better propaganda than the best masterpieces of a Propaganda Ministry.' Feleki then adds his considered opinion that Rowe would be '…good propaganda for Britain from every point of view…', adding: 'I felt that my whole years' work in London was not in vain and neither was Rowe's, as he worked very hard and honestly, as you could see from Dr. Misángyi's letter. I should like to thank you for recommending Rowe to us. He was really very well suited to this role and he certainly strengthened the connection between the English and Hungarian football.' Almost begging Rous to encourage a by-now hesitant Rowe to accept the Hungarian invitation, Feleki ends: 'If we had to choose another man we have to be very careful because in this matter not only football knowledge counts but this trainer must be as intelligent and fine a gentleman as Rowe. He will really be an ambassador of English football.' Feleki wrote to Rowe himself on August 3rd, accepting Arthur's promise of a decision by August 14th. Meanwhile Rous, who Rowe had been unable to see, had mentioned some Foreign Office news to Feleki, most likely concerning the risk of a British subject taking up a post with tensions growing in Europe.

To set the Hungarian political scene at that time, a Hungarian Communist Party had been created following the First World War forming a coalition with the Social Democrats. Nationalisation of industries and land followed, before a former Admiral, Miklós Horthy, formed an army to oppose the government. The Romanian army at one point occupied the capital Budapest and the Communist regime collapsed and Horthy was elected head of state. His was an authoritarian regime and during the 1930s the nation came under the influence of Hitler's Nazi Germany and anti-semitism grew, many Jewish players emigrating from 1938 onwards. Once war had begun it was inevitable that Hungary would join the Tripartite Pact (Germany, Italy and Japan), which duly took place in November 1940. By June 1941 Hungary was aiding Germany's invasion of Russia and by the end of that year Britain declared war on Hungary.

Clearly, during the Hungarian couple's time in England, Rowe and Pom had formed a friendship with Feleki and his wife. Whether true or whether Rowe was preparing excuses to delay acceptance of the offer while the uncertain situation in Hungary developed, Feleki had clearly heard from Rowe that Pom required medical treatment, to which Feleki responded: 'One thing I want to tell you, Arthur. You know I appreciate many things in England. I am considered in Hungary as pro-British [but] …on the other hand I must admit that Hungarian doctors are considered as the best in the world. There are a lot of world-famous surgeons and I think it would be reassuring to have Pom examined by Hungarian professors. And another thing: there are also world-famous medicinal waters for every woman-troubles.' Feleki suggested that a desire to make use of the healing springs would also prove to be an acceptable justification for travel to Hungary, which Pom could state in her passport application.

After having set Rowe up for the job, Feleki was desperate to secure his appointment and his final words (aside from a jocular suggestion that Rowe should apply to be successor to George Allison at Arsenal) indicate how Arthur had been politely responding to his overtures. Feleki repeated the suggestion that he would do better to gain experience in Hungary before attempting to get on the managerial ladder in England: 'Now Arthur dear, I have to finish my letter. Don't worry about me, you can never be a nuisance for me. I know your situation and I understand you. It is still my conviction that this Budapest job would do a lot of good for your future and I don't speak only about *your* future but your whole family. I should be very happy if you succeeded to get a decent job at Millwall, Leicester, or Crystal Palace, but are they really decent and important ones? After one year in Hungary with a lot of articles written about you both in [the] English and Hungarian Press you would be really an important man of English football. This is my deepest conviction.'

There could only one winner in a contest between Rowe exposing himself and his family to untold danger and his acceptance of this first, otherwise very welcome, rung on the coaching ladder. Following a decade of rising tensions a second war seemed inevitable and was finally confirmed when Germany invaded Poland. One imagines that for some weeks Arthur had the Hungarian offer to the back of his mind and continuing correspondence was essentially a mere courtesy to his friend.

On August 26th, a mere eight days before the British declared war on Germany, Feleki sent yet another letter which Rowe may barely have received and read before war had indeed been declared. In it he asks if Arthur's 'kiddies' [Derek and Graham] have been '…taken to the country' (clearly aware of the mass evacuation of British children to the countryside which had begun). He continues: 'I must admit that your Foreign Office was right because there is a real crisis, perhaps more serious than it was last year, but I am afraid your Foreign Office did not expect what happened now. I hope it will not be a war in spite of the very serious situation and in the beginning of October everything will be OK and you will be able to come to us.' He asks Rowe to '…write me about Pom and kiddies and yourself,' before typing: 'I shall write to you until I can', adding, ominously, 'Maybe I shall be called to the colours very soon. Things are very uncertain. I have no idea where Hungary will stand in case of war. After the German-Russian pact [signed three days' earlier, on August 23rd, surprising the world] I dare not to prophesy. I think football is [a] more honest thing, than politics.'

Feleki also responded to Rowe's personal enquiries about he and his wife Szendi's situation: 'At present I am quite all right and so is Szendi. Hoping you are all right and the children and Pom. I wish you four all the best.'

Clearly Arthur couldn't risk the appointment in Hungary but as he said ten years later: 'Had war not broken out I would probably have returned there.' On the occasion of Hungary's gold-medal performance at the 1952 Olympics, he was interviewed about his time in the country. 'I felt I was lucky to have got away before someone blew the whistle on me. I would like to have stayed under different circumstances but it was obvious by then that something was going to happen.' This statement suggests the international situation when Rowe was still working in Budapest had already sufficiently concerned him, but wisely, he had kept his options open, which explains his continuing correspondence with Feleki. Ultimately, the brutal fact was that war dashed Rowe's chance of coaching the Hungarian national side at the 1940 Helsinki Olympics and, by November, Helsinki itself was being bombed by the Russians. By December 1941 the Finnish nation had aligned itself with Nazi Germany and Great Britain had declared war on Hungary. As for Feleki, he would be captured during World War 2, but once the war was over became editor of *Nepsport*. He would also write novels, humourous books and, most significantly, a four-volume biography of Napoleon.

Some years later, in *World Soccer*, Rowe wrote of how he viewed pre-War Hungary: 'In those carefree pre-war days the Hungarian people that I came into contact with were happy, friendly, apparently prosperous, and intensely interested in the game. My impression …was that the Hungarians would certainly rise to the highest class if they could gear their basic skill to greater determination to win matches, for at that time, it seemed, they were content to play merely for personal satisfaction.' In 1970, he reminisced about his time coaching Hungarian university students. He said that he found in the first practice match that the Hungarians '…had much greater skill than here [in England], but their physical application was worse.' Another strong impression on Rowe was seeing '…many youngsters more than content to spend hours playing with the ball in order to perfect their technique.' In 1960 he wrote: 'My own brief experience in Budapest in the summer of 1939 left a very vivid and certain impression that the Hungarians, at least, were players—real players, of high ability or "technique" as they termed it.'

So, in September 1939, the jobless Rowe, as with so many people in Europe at the outset of war, had also to confront how best he could protect and support his young family, this as he awaited the inevitable official demand to submit his services for the war effort. He will have dwelled on the cruel fate of war intervening just when presented with an excellent opportunity, a big step toward further, invaluable coaching experience. How, too, he was turning his back on the very warm and appreciative welcome he would have received back in Budapest.

7

Budapest to Chelmsford

VIA WORLD WAR 2

'Often we played matches only a few miles behind the front lines with the noise of gunfire sometimes tending to drown the sound of the referee's whistle.'
MATT BUSBY REFLECTING ON ARMY REPRESENTATIVE SIDES HE AND ROWE MANAGED AND COACHED DURING WORLD WAR II

'[Chelmsford City's] copy-book football, with the added spice of thrust and purpose, brought the delighted fans to their feet…'.
CHELMSFORD CHRONICLE ON A 7-0 CHELMSFORD CITY VICTORY (NOVEMBER 1948)

Despite the imminence of war, the 1939-40 season started as normal on August 26th 1939, only for Britain to declare war on Germany eight days later. With the threat of bombing raids, allied to the compulsory conscription of all healthy young males not employed in vital occupations, official League football was initially suspended but, three weeks later, football re-started (in regional leagues) as a contribution to raising public morale. Young Ron Burgess's experience was typical. Based in the RAF near Nottingham, he would occasionally guest for both Notts County and Nottingham Forest but also, when convenient, turn out for Spurs.

ROWE: ARMY PHYSICAL TRAINING INSTRUCTOR At the outbreak of war Stanley Rous recommended players and coaches, including the likes of Matt Busby, Stan Cullis, Tommy Lawton, Joe Mercer and Rowe himself, for the Army Physical Training Course at Aldershot. Arthur left no tales of his own army years

Rowe with three Army Physical Training Corps colleagues during World War 2.

but Lawton recalled the Course as the hardest thing he had ever done. Rowe's introduction at Aldershot will have entailed seven weeks of parade-ground drilling, gymnastics and general body-building. When Parliament objected to so many footballers and other athletes being co-opted into the APTC, it was pointed out that in the previous war inexperienced instructors had led to cases of heart problems. Besides, Prime Minister Churchill himself strongly believed in the psychological benefits of men being trained by sporting heroes. Despite rarely being in the line of fire, the duties of APTC instructors were considerable, some were responsible for as many as 2-3,000 men. Joe Mercer had received the rank of Sergeant Instructor by October 1940 and we can assume Arthur received it at around the same time.

ROWE: TEAM MANAGER TO THE ARMY FOOTBALL XI   The role Rowe became most known for was as Team Manager to the Army Football XI and he performed the same role for Combined Services representative sides entertaining the troops in Europe. Rowe recalled, 'We were given a team, a couple of balls, an itinerary, a lorry and a driver, and told to get on with it.' Such tours proved excellent for the morale of watching or participating overseas servicemen, many not knowing if the next day might be their last. As one Commanding Officer put it: 'One soccer party was worth five ENSA shows in battle areas' [ENSA variety shows comprised performances by famous entertainers].

During these tours, Rowe, as trainer or 'Number 2' under Matt Busby, was responsible for a veritable 'Who's Who' of British soccer talent, including the likes of 'keeper Frank Swift (Manchester City and England), half-back Joe Mercer (Everton and England), and strikers Jack Rowley (Manchester United and England) and Tommy Lawton (Everton and England). A Combined Services XI Rowe

Army Team Manager Rowe (far left) *just makes it into this shot of a wartime XI playing in Scotland. Players here include 'keeper Frank Swift, Ted Fenton, Matt Busby and Joe Mercer, while FA chief Stanley Rous is the man in suit and tie.*

took to Belfast included England internationals Raich Carter (Sunderland), Stan Mortensen (Blackpool) and Stanley Matthews (Stoke City). Also taking part was Charlton's George Smith who would cross Rowe's path again later. As Arthur's outlook on life paralleled Busby's the two men formed a good partnership. Rowe once said 'I learned a lot in my Army days about human relationships and the man who confirmed my thinking was Matt Busby. We were sergeants together and we talked a great deal not only about football, but the way life should be lived.' On occasion, the men were not far from danger, playing close to the front lines with gunfire muffling the sound of the referee's whistle.

Taking an FA team to face an RAF representative side at Bristol City's Ashton Gate in January 1944, three stars failed to turn-up with kick-off approaching and, rather than play a man short, Rowe prepared to risk his damaged knee, only for the three to finally show up. This scrambling to put a starting XI together served Arthur well in his first managerial role once war was over. In September 1944, two weeks after the liberation of Paris, he was with the Combined Services XI taking on an Irish side including the great Peter Doherty. Rowe's team overflowed with stars: Swift (Manchester City) in goal, full-backs Laurie Scott (Arsenal and England) and Walley Barnes (Arsenal and Wales), half-backs Archie Macaulay (West Ham United and Scotland), Bernard Joy (Arsenal and England) and Busby, and forwards Matthews, Carter, Lawton, Mortensen and Jimmy Mullen (Wolves and England). Three weeks later in Paris another Services XI beat a French XI 5-0 in front of a 30,000 crowd that included American GIs and local Parisians liberated from German occupation just a month previously. Carter, recalling a 'carnival atmosphere', scored a hat-trick. Others included this time were George Hardwick (Middlesbrough and England), Billy Hughes (Birmingham City and Wales), Frank Soo (Stoke City - another who would reappear in Rowe's life later) and Mercer. Chillingly, the Parc des Princes stadium had only recently been employed by the Germans as a concentration camp for political prisoners.

Rowe's team had to move quickly after the final whistle to face a Belgian representative team at Brussels' Stade Oscar Bossaert the following day. In the hours before kick-off the terraces had to be cleared of mines, the Germans having not long vacated it, and the RAF provided aerial cover for the game as heavy fighting continued only 30 miles away. Rowe's side ran out victors to the tune of 3-0. In March 1945 another strong FA XI returned to Belgium and again played twice in two days, starting with an 8-1 victory in Bruges. Lawton, who rattled-in four goals, recalled that flying over the Belgian countryside in an RAF Dakota they witnessed scenes of devastation but Arthur will have enjoyed the reception the team received from the soldiers stationed there, Lawton likening it to playing in a Cup Final. The following day, in Brussels, the result was close, 3-2 to the FA XI. The players in Rowe's hands this time included 'keeper Bert Williams of Wolves, full-backs Hardwick and Bert Sproston (Manchester City and England), half-backs Busby, Neil Franklin (Stoke City and England) and George Smith, and a forward line of Aubrey Powell (Leeds United and Wales), Mortensen, Lawton, Maurice Edelston (Reading) and Leslie Smith (Brentford and England). Two weeks later the FA XI were in Liège and Rowe may have travelled in one of several Avro Ansons which came close to colliding with a Liberator bomber which had broken down on the runway, climbing rapidly to abort the landing.

Rowe then served as England Team Attendant for the Wales v. England wartime international at Ninian Park, Cardiff on May 5th 1945. England, with Bert Williams in goal, included other 'usual suspects', full-backs Scott and Hardwick, wing-halves George Smith and Mercer, centre-half Franklin and forwards Matthews, Carter and Lawton. Rowe will have enjoyed encountering Spurs' Ron Burgess playing for the Welsh side, which went down 3-2. At the final whistle some of those involved, including Rowe, had to rush back to London to report to the Great Western Railway Hotel in London, in readiness for a tour of Italy starting the following day (the German forces in Italy had finally surrendered on May 2nd so it had only just become safe for footballers and showbiz stars to entertain the British Liberation Army based there).

The tour group was: GOALKEEPERS Swift, Cyril Sidlow (Wolves); FULL-BACKS 'Joe' Bacuzzi, Bert Sproston, Danny Winter (Bolton); HALF-BACKS: Cliff Britton, George Smith, Busby, Joe Mercer; FORWARDS Billy Elliott (West Bromwich Albion), Jack Martin, Maurice Edelston, Tommy Lawton, Jack Rowley, Willie Watson (Huddersfield Town, later Sunderland, and England), Doug Hunt (a former colleague of Rowe's at Spurs), Archie Macaulay and Mullen.

They left England a day late, following the unconditional surrender of all German forces on May 7th. They travelled from London Paddington to Swindon, departing the following morning in a Vickers Warwick transport plane taking around five-and-a-half hours to get to Naples. Arriving at Pomigliano airfield, 16 km from Naples, Rowe's group, wearing tropical uniforms to cope with the heat of southern Italy, spent their first night under canvas before being ferried by Army truck from city to city. To help avoid occasional hostility from allied troops who had been risking their lives, it was thought the professional footballers should utilise the

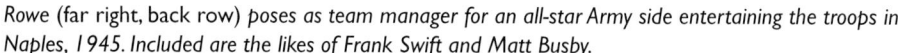

Rowe (far right, back row) poses as team manager for an all-star Army side entertaining the troops in Naples, 1945. Included are the likes of Frank Swift and Matt Busby.

Toward war's end Rowe poses (far left) with a United Services side in Belfast. Back row, left-to right: Rowe, Mullen, Busby, Edelston, Carter, Swift, Macauley, Barnes, Mortensen, Welsh (in uniform), Scott. In front: Matthews, Joy and Lawton.

same no-frills transport (trucks with little suspension). Some games would be played in front of as many as 40,000 troops.

The day after Busby and Rowe's men listened to King George VI's declaration of the end of the war in Europe, on VE Day, May 8th, they began their tour at the Vomero Stadium, Naples, where No. 3 Army District (selected from units based between Bari and Gibraltar) were beaten 6-0 on a surface scorched bare. After touring the remains of Pompeii they travelled 240 km (150 miles) to Rome, stopping en-route to visit the ruins of the 6th Century abbey at Monte Cassino. Rowe and his colleagues also witnessed displaced Italians in Valmontone resorting to cave-dwelling or living amongst the ruins. The following day in Rome, Rowe and Busby led the others for an audience with Pope Pius XII. Having just witnessed the immediate sufferings of war, some will have then felt uncomfortable at attending the opera, so a return to the soccer field (beating an 'Army in Italy' team 10-2) may have been welcome. Another long drive, of around 200 miles across mountain passes to Ancona on the Adriatic, saw a District Services team beaten 7-1. Despite heavy defeats, one can imagine how morale rose when servicemen found themselves competing against the greatest British football talent of the time.

A couple of hours further up the coast, in Rimini on May 17th, the all-star line-up faced a Naples-area XI, champions of the Central Mediterranean Forces, which included Arsenal's record signing, Bryn Jones. Here the stronger opposition only lost 2-0. Then, following what Lawton described as a '…hair-raising journey across mountain passes 3,000 feet above sea level' Rowe's group arrived in Florence. When beating a 5th Army side (including some Brazilians) 10-0 on May 20th, they received abuse from battle-worn compatriots on the terraces, the mildest of which included catcalls of 'PT Commandos' or 'D-Day dodgers'. There is no record of how Rowe felt when abused by fellow countrymen fresh from battle, but Tommy Lawton took the view that back in England footballers had been playing to entertain civilians suffering bombing raids and deprivation so, he said, why not '…do the same for the troops.'

At this point Lawton and Mercer returned to England to take their places in the England side to play France at Wembley on May 26th, Busby and Rowe taking the remaining group back south to Naples to face a Central Mediterranean Forces side. 23-year-old Tom Finney, whose career had only just begun at Preston before the outbreak of war, had by now taken his place in Rowe's side having served in the Eighth Army in Egypt as a tank driver. Before returning to England, the squad paid a short visit to Salonika, Greece, where all bar big Frank Swift were struck down with sandfly fever.

There can be little doubt Rowe's experience of working with high-quality players consolidated his ambition to pursue a post-war managerial career.

PEACE AND A RETURN HOME   Back in England Arthur informed wife Pom that he intended to give management a try for three years. Should he fail, he would pursue a career in the upholstery trade. Britain remained on rationing, but the birth of the National Health Service and the Welfare State provided a strong sense of hope and regeneration. One happy event Rowe attended in 1945, whilst still in uniform, was the wedding of younger brother Frank. As for Spurs, Peter McWilliam had left White Hart Lane for good in 1942 due to concerns over his wife's health. Despite an unexceptional managerial record, his emphasis on short-passing football had left a lasting mark at Tottenham, something Rowe would one day take to the next level.

CHELMSFORD CITY   On July 4th 1945, having been short-listed with former Spurs' colleague Willie Hall, 38-year-old Arthur became manager of Southern League Chelmsford City. As the resumed operations immediately on cessation of hostilities (unlike the Football League, which remained suspended for another year), Rowe had just six weeks to locate players, organise trials, set-up training schedules and convey his tactical approach to a hastily thrown-together group of players. The war in the Far-East continued until August 14th so many pre-War players

A portrait from the 'Essex Chronicle' suggests the photographer was subconsciously thinking of Orson Welles in the 'Third Man' when capturing this moody shot of Rowe.

remained on active service. Yet Rowe's preference to dive straight into competitive football, rather than waiting a year to manage a Football League side proved to be a successful career move. Having been stationed with the 1st Battalion 4th Essex Regiment close by, Rowe had watched wartime games at Chelmsford. Formed just two seasons before the war, City had reached the FA Cup fourth round in 1939, which now benefitted Rowe as City were thus exempted from the 1945-46 preliminary rounds. But Rowe faced many unique challenges, particularly locating and hiring players, and those pre-War players who returned to the Club had of course aged a full six years.

One who intended to return was centre-half and captain Alan Sliman, but his plane was attacked by fighter planes over Germany just two-and-a-half weeks before Rowe took over. Badly wounded, Sliman survived the flight back only to die in hospital. Such tragedies aside, one advantage Rowe temporarily shared with his fellow Southern League bosses was the part-time hiring of Football League players, with no fee required to be paid to the League club concerned. Meanwhile, during the War the nearby Marconi Company, developers of radio, television and defence systems, had rented stands in Chelmsford's New Writtle Street stadium for storage purposes, so volunteers were sought to make the stadium ready for action.

SEASON 1945-46   Ten days after his appointment a '…bronzed and fit' Arthur Rowe visited the stadium to meet those players who had reported back. He was described as '…modest, genial, and enthusiastic' and confident he would put City on the football map. For now he assisted in training the available players two evenings a week whilst setting about increasing his squad, saying 'So many men are in the Forces, and don't know exactly when they are coming out, and there are the claims of other clubs to be considered. I have a number of players in mind, but there is always an "if" about it.' New players would also require a residence and a job outside the game. Also, as this first post-War season saw the Southern League reduced from 23 clubs to just 11, the novice manager had to organise friendly matches to fill the many gaps in the schedule. Players needed to be kept match-fit and money had to flow through the turnstiles. When Rowe first addressed the club's shareholders he received a hearty reception but, aware of the complications he faced, he quietly played-down any exaggerated expectations.

On the field Rowe immediately put his theories of what would became known as 'push-and-run' into practice. Indeed one watching journalist described the new manager '…subordinating individual stars to a team pattern, giving players a collective purpose, infusing in them a spirit of team before self.' He also encouraged defenders to be constructive rather than mindlessly hammering clearances downfield. The first home fixture in six years took place against fierce local rivals Colchester United on August 25th, 1945. Colchester were able to name their side 24 hours ahead but Rowe needed every minute to locate 'guest' players. By then 500 stand seats had been cleared of Marconi's stored materials but, one day ahead of the game, Rowe still sought people to man the turnstiles. The make-up of his side ranged from 21-year-old centre-forward 'Denny' Foreman to his own former Spurs' colleagues Jimmy McCormick and goalkeeper Jack Hall, while City captain

Bill Parry remained from lifting the Southern League trophy back in 1939. Despite playing some good football, City, mostly consisting of players whom had never played together before, conceded both Colchester goals from defensive errors, the *Chelmsford Chronicle* writing: 'It was a bad start for the City. Nobody realises that more than the players themselves. Changes will have to be made. That is a matter for Manager Rowe. I hope he will be given a free hand. Mr Rowe knows a footballer when he sees one.'

A typical example of the random nature of post-war team-building occurred that very afternoon. An Oldham-born half-back, Clifford Eaton, a professional before the war, watched the game having travelled to see his sister in Chelmsford. He bumped into former colleague Jack Hall who let an interested Rowe know about his capable wing-half friend. Needing a full-time job and an engineering moulder by trade, Eaton was fortunate captain Parry himself was employed in engineering locally and a position was found. By such vagaries of fortune the new manager gradually constructed a competitive side. When Chelmsford travelled the short distance to Colchester for the return match he included four more newcomers, one of whom, Buchanan, scored the winner in a 4-3 victory. Following this another ex-playing colleague of Rowe's, Andy Duncan, arrived.

Aside from the Southern League, City also competed in the London and Mid-Essex leagues, so the intense administrative duties involved stood Rowe in good stead for the future. After defeating Cheltenham 9-1, City moved into second place having put on '…as delightful an exhibition of cohesive, determined football as any one of the 4,000 spectators could have wished to see'.

When fans began complaining about admission charges one City director explained that the gate for the first game had been £260, of which £110 went to Entertainment tax, £70 to pay the players (and other expenses), leaving only £80. On top of that were the costs for restoring the stadium and, when covering travel costs for the following away match they were left, he said, with around £20 for other contingencies. Rowe's managerial baptism of fire continued when one of his full-backs still serving in the Forces was transferred north. Rowe became frustrated with guest players, saying: 'You never know whether they are going to turn up', but a second friendly win over League side Southend led the local press to describe City as of 'Third Division status'. 19-year-old centre-half Brian 'Jake' Farley, employed at the Hoffman Bearing plant, starred, but soon began his National Service. Most of Rowe's part-timers worked a full week plus Saturday mornings foregoing their Saturday match fee if City had a far-off fixture requiring morning travel. Their fee was also subject to income tax, one player saying this left him with little more than £1, and Arthur was delighted when his club pledged to press the Southern League to increase match fees to £5. Councillor Langton echoed his manager when saying '…you get the best out of anyone only when you pay and treat them well.'

With City in second place an exuberant Rowe told the press: 'Now for the Cup!' As well as the 1st round proper of the FA Cup against League side Northampton, there was the Southern League's own cup, split into Eastern and Western sections (the winner of each to meet in a two-leg final). Having been refused, by the Minister of War Transport, to take a special train of 2,000 supporters to cheer them on at

Northampton, City crashed 5-1 and, missing three regulars, conceded five more in the return but Arthur stayed positive: 'There is no gloom here. I think we may win the Southern League. Then, of course, there is the Southern League Cup.' When a much-changed side beat Cardiff City Reserves 5-2 the interest centered on a '…strong and constructive' guest at centre-half, a locally-serving Lancastrian named Charlie Hurst, of whom more later. Meanwhile the manager was concerned with attendances. Despite the then Chelmsford population of around 60,000, City's average attendance of 4,000 hardly assisted claims for Football League status. On the plus side an 8-2 victory at Worcester City in December led to forecasts Chelmsford could be champions by season's end. In difficult times Rowe was acquiring quality (if ageing) players who excelled at Southern League level.

When Third Division Clapton Orient, managed by former playing colleague Willie Hall, arrived for a friendly, Rowe was saddened to see that his pal had lost the lower part of his right leg to thrombosis. Hall soon suffered the loss of his other leg, too. Then, in a 6-2 defeat of Bedford Town on Christmas Day, Rowe fielded another pre-War Spurs' colleague, outside-right Freddie Sargent, but simultaneously lost Clifford Eaton with a broken ankle. However it was obvious Rowe was enjoying his success. Just turned 39 he was surprisingly described as '…rather boyish-looking' despite prematurely greying hair. His '…somewhat frequent frown' was jokingly ascribed to guest players not turning-up on time!

City reached the new year unbeaten since that opening-day defeat and in second place but with games-in-hand and Rowe conjured up another quality guest, Wolves' wartime forward Alf 'Slim' Somerfield (who immediately scored against Hereford). Rowe already knew just nine further points would clinch the title. Then, as a sign of the times, a Southern League Cup contest away to Swindon Reserves was played in muddy conditions created from housing Prisoners of War in huts constructed on the playing area. Rowe then replaced a sick Foreman with trialist Len Duquemin, a Channel Islander who had arrived at Spurs only to be loaned out to Chelmsford before he had donned a Tottenham shirt. Duquemin, a significant figure in Arthur's later successes, scored the only goal in a 3-1 defeat but City did enough in the second leg to remain in the competition. A 3-2 League win over Worcester took City closer to the Championship and enabled Rowe to relax at a Supporters' Club dance that evening. Then, triumphing 4-1 at Bedford Town in the Southern League Cup, the onlooking '…silk-hatted and frock-coated' President of the Southern League, said Chelmsford's display '…did credit to the Southern League competition.'

City's final three League matches were away. At this time two pre-war Chelmsford players finally returned and one can imagine Rowe's mix of anticipation and trepidation — would they have the skills he needed? Was he not already sufficiently covered in their positions? How painful would it be to reject them? One, Jack Roberts, had served as one of Wingate's 'Chindits' in the Burma campaign and it was thought he had lost his life, but now Rowe immediately put him in the side.

A 5-1 Cup defeat of Bedford Town saw City creep closer to the 'double' and a 2-1 away League win at challengers Bath City on March 23rd all but clinched the title. With City's better goal average Hereford now had to defeat Bath by a large margin a fortnight later in order to steal the title. At around this time City trainer

Chelmsford City captain Bill Parry receives the Southern League Cup trophy, Rowe thus capturing both trophies in his first season.

Benny Welham said: 'I'd like some of the critics to know what a happy lot we are. Mr Rowe is one of the best.' A week later City overcame Guildford City 5-3 and, on Saturday April 6th, Hereford failed to prevent Rowe's men finishing champions of the Southern League East Division. That same afternoon, City were defeating Cheltenham in the Cup so the Championship victory was celebrated that evening.

Rowe could hardly have begun his managerial career in better style. Against all the odds he had constructed a 'settled' team. With City now confronting a two-leg Cup Final against Western Division winners Worcester, the Press described 'Manager Arthur Rowe's clever, judicious team building, done in spite of discouraging obstacles resulting from the war.' In the first (away) leg of the Cup Final, City took a commanding 3-1 lead before Worcester pulled it back to 3-3. In the Southern League's history only one club had previously achieved the 'double'. Could Rowe repeat it in his very first year of management? City duly took the field in front of a season's record home crowd of 8,372, all of whom were prepared to celebrate and sing the praises of Arthur Rowe, and that they duly did, City claiming the trophy 9-4 on aggregate. Rowe's victorious side was: Radcliffe; Roberts, Parry; Statham, Farley, Eaton; Sargent, Duncan, Foreman, Somerfield, Burley. By then, only four men - Farley, Parry, Foreman and Burley - remained from Rowe's initial team selection back in August.

Vice-Chairman Langton said that under Rowe the club '...had succeeded beyond our fondest hopes' and some optimistically believed Chelmsford would be voted into the Football League that very summer. To great cheers League President A. J. K. Darnell handed over the huge Championship Shield to captain Bill Parry, the *Essex Newsman* writing: 'Standing around watchfully in the background was the man who has done so very much to make the season a success—Manager Arthur Rowe. For him, Saturday must have brought a great sense of pleasure and relief. It has been a difficult season for him.' Yet Rowe had achieved the following superb statistics (incorporating all games played by Chelmsford City in 1945-46): 41 played, 31 won, 5 draws, 5 defeats with 140 goals scored and 66 against.

This would prove a tough act to follow. Having won the 'Double' results inevitably declined a little over the following two seasons as more sides, some powerful, returned to the Southern League but Rowe was to bounce right back in his fourth season. Meanwhile another 'ghost' from City's past turned up that spring of 1946 after six years' war service overseas, strongly-built full-back Leslie Pyle. In advance of being de-mobbed that summer, he made sure Rowe was aware of his availability.

'SUCCESS IN SOCCER' — NEWSPAPER ARTICLES   In 1946 Arthur wrote a series of articles for the *Chelmsford Newsman-Herald*, his first venturing to explain several recent British sporting disappointments: 'Like all other people who have had to live on British [wartime food] rations for over six years, I am sure that we are not in that first-class physical condition vital to sports classics. Especially is that true by comparison with the American athletes, who in large numbers have enjoyed a far more normal way of life than ourselves during war years. But there is more to it than that.' An unusually critical Rowe suggested British sportsmen and women failed to take sport seriously when competing internationally: 'This "happy-go-lucky" attitude, that is so characteristic of our outlook, although very pleasant, is not conducive to success,' he wrote. 'Some of the intensity of purpose, and planning, that our Russian visitors, the [Moscow] Dynamos, showed [during a 1945 exhibition tour], maybe a little more of the national fervour of the Continental, would not come amiss to what very often seems like indifference in our attitude.'

A second article emphasised that his successful City side were not individuals but 'a *team* of triers, all imbued with the idea of success as a team.' Rowe expressed a preference for the 'real trier' over the 'individualist' who can never be relied upon: 'When he does have one of his off-days, it often means an unsettling, and a disturbing, of whatever balance the team may have.' On another occasion Rowe touched upon something which would ironically cause himself grief in later managerial roles: 'The vital need is that manager and trainer should be of a single mind as to what is needed, both on and off the field. So that, in all circumstances, the players will be receiving advice and counsel that is consistent.'

Rowe's future successes were achieved with minimal expenditure — he was rarely presented with an open cheque book and generally adopted the playing staff available to him, confident enough to convert also-rans into champions.

SEASONS 1946-47, 1947-48   During the 1946 summer break it was announced that £1250 was to be collected to concrete the stadium terraces, utilising unskilled labour including German prisoners-of-war. At the meeting Vice-Chairman Langton emphasised the degree to which the club's accomplishments were down to Rowe. 'We would have won the English [FA] Cup as well, but we wanted to give others a chance!' said Langton. Rowe received a tremendous reception when he rose to speak: 'The things that I have worked and planned for have borne a rich reward' he said, pointing out that in winning both League and Cup they had overcome competitors who depended considerably on 'star' guest players. City's success, considered Rowe, was down to the club's efforts to ensure players played with a smile '…instead of a grouse.'

Rowe then had the initiative to send a dozen complimentary match tickets each week to pupils at several schools in the area, thus exposing them to Southern League soccer. Realistically expecting the new season to be tougher as more players had now returned from wartime service, the manager would only commit to a top-six finish. In October Lancastrian Charlie Hurst finally joined full-time. Surviving Dunkirk in 1940 he had remained in Chelmsford becoming a toolmaker. His 4-year-old son Geoffrey later netted a World Cup Final hat-trick. Indeed, had Rowe not persuaded Hurst senior to play for City one might ponder whether England would have won the World Cup in 1966, as young Geoff ultimately joined the closest 'big' club, West Ham United, where his game flourished under manager Ron Greenwood. Around this same time Arthur also fielded a newcomer in City's Reserves - 5ft 7in centre-forward Syd McClellan. Fast with an accurate shot, he scored twice, and would reappear in Rowe's career later.

After an embarrassing FA Cup exit to amateurs Cambridge Town, Chelmsford bounced back to beat Dartford 7-0. City playing with 'thrust and purpose' and brought '…delighted fans to their feet.' A 4-2 home win over Gloucester City saw Chelmsford go top but soon Rowe learned that even occasional setbacks could trigger harsh press treatment. A close 3-2 defeat at local rivals Colchester was criticised despite appalling conditions and City being forced to play for 75 minutes with 10 men. One fan's criticism provoked an angry outburst from the normally placid manager. The fan demanded to know why Foreman had been dropped and asked that his letter and any subsequent reply from the club be printed. The manager responded to the newspaper, perhaps too hastily, by phone: 'The club is run by the directors and myself. We run it as we think best. When I am unsuccessful, I expect to get the sack. For the moment, I have no time to waste on tripe like that.' Picking-up the phone was a rare error of judgement. Composing a letter would have given Arthur time to respond in more considered fashion. The *Chronicle* then castigated him for his uncustomary display of anger: 'Surely by this time [Mr Rowe] should know that ordinary courtesy to reporters is among the elementary qualifications of the manager of a football club. The press is much greater than Mr Rowe, and when properly addressed he should mind his manners and return an answer which even if he chooses it to be uninformative, should be at least polite.' This was clearly a rare occasion when Arthur let his guard down.

Yet despite injury setbacks City were still having a good season, at least until one of the coldest winters on record arrived creating a fixture backlog. Meanwhile Rowe wrote to other ambitious Southern League clubs proposing they combine to organise a London luncheon to which the manager and a director of each London League club would be invited, with a view to getting their sympathetic support for inclusion in the newly-proposed regional Fourth Division.

In March 1947 the Football League and Football Association met to discuss the fixture backlog resulting from the severe winter. The government did not want catch-up games played in midweek as, without floodlights, afternoon kick-offs encouraged workers to down tools and watch football at a time when it was prudent to increase productivity-levels, so the season was to be extended until June 14th. The Chelmsford boss immediately pointed out that player's annual contracts terminated on May 3rd so that even those players the club intended to off-load would have to be signed up for another whole year. His early managerial career seemed to overflow with such complications!

As for off-loading players - some of Chelmsford's squad were veterans, but he expressed his general belief that the best team '...is one which contains three "old" hands, four "middle-agers", and four "youngsters."' He added: 'What a man may lose in speed as the years go on, he more than makes up in skill and cunning.' Meanwhile, if his desire for a staff of nothing but full-time professionals was to be realised, Chelmsford's attendances needed to treble. City had been a significant stepping-stone in his career, but such frustrations now led Rowe to apply for the manager's role at Third Division Watford. However a trip to see Watford play Crystal Palace dampened his enthusiasm, although he still attended an interview. City's 1946-47 season ended with a 5-1 defeat at Exeter, City ending a mere fifth this time.

An erratic start to Rowe's third season, 1947-48, began rumours of his imminent resignation, but a substantial crowd showed up to witness City's attempt to overcome a 3-0 deficit in a Southern League Cup second-leg tie with Colchester. All Main Stand seats were occupied long before kick-off and the *Chronicle* lyrically described Rowe's evident pleasure: 'As the setting sun fell low behind the roof-tops it caught the beaming face of City Manager Arthur Rowe—delighted at the thought of the revenue. He leaned on the steps of the stand gazing across the field. It was so full he couldn't find himself a seat at his own show.' However, City again fell to their fierce local rivals, but only by the odd goal in three. Rumours now began that Rowe had applied to manage Swansea. In denying this he confessed to applying for the manager's job at no less than First Division Portsmouth. Clearly his confidence knew no bounds and, when City went down 3-1 at Worcester, he unleashed another angry outburst. This time, perhaps born of frustration, he targeted his own supporters following the unhappy departure of one of his players. In his programme notes the manager explained that Ron Gunner's departure had not been due to his police duties but to terrace barracking. 'I have no sympathy with the person who imagines that by abusing a player, or players, they will help them to do better,' adding, 'When he does things wrong, and being human, he will... will it help him at all being abused? I leave you to answer this question yourself.'

Then City exited the FA Cup at the hands of neighbours Colchester, so Rowe would have to wait a further 12 months for a chance of much-needed FA Cup income and his mood will have worsened on hearing their victors had drawn First Division opposition, going on to defeat Huddersfield Town before a substantial 16,005 crowd, before knocking out Second Division Bradford Park Avenue, leaving them with a trip to First Division Blackpool. Stanley Matthews' side would win 5-0 but United grabbed a share of the revenue from a 29,500 attendance justifying Rowe's belief that FA Cup success was essential. The income and prestige gained facilitated Colchester's election to the Football League two years' later.

At one stage in 1947-48, with no one team showing consistency, an emboldened Rowe expressed his personal satisfaction that Chelmsford were at that moment leading the Southern League, the Eastern Counties' League *and* the North Essex (colts) League, while sitting second in the London League. 'There must be some merit in the play of any club which, in these four competitions, head three and are second in another,' said Rowe. But, always conscious of the wider picture, he was then estimating a further loss of around 400 spectators per game due to the part-abolition of petrol rationing; car-owning fans now better able to take to the road on Saturdays as an alternative to watching football.

Staying on the theme of transport and with no bus service when City's Reserves defeated Bedford 5-1 on Christmas Day 1947, City player Arthur Moss was compelled to cycle from his Maldon home to New Writtle Street, a 10-mile one-way trip. By the time he got back home after the game, he said he was '…a little bit fagged!' With Sargent and Duncan pairing-up again on the right and McClellan on fire in front of goal, City were in fact showing steady signs of improvement at this point. For the first Saturday of 1948 Rowe arranged a friendly against Spurs at White Hart Lane where McClellan put Chelmsford ahead, Spurs equalised, then a frail 19-year-old called Tommy Harmer put the home side in front before half-time but City then struck no less than four times to run-out 5-2 winners, McClellan's hat-trick making a lasting impression on Spurs' officials.

As part of a national 'Service of Youth' scheme, Rowe then began giving up two evenings a week to lecture local Essex youth groups on soccer. A pessimistic newspaper article then further encouraged his quest for a Football League club post. Even the lowest-placed Third Division clubs, claimed the writer, were averaging attendances between 13 and 20 thousand, so would retain their League status as City were clearly unable to match that. Rowe had made a committed effort to raise the club to another level, informing the Press he had contacted some quality players. He was particularly seeking one senior, experienced player who might also fill the duties of assistant-manager.

Charlie Hurst then struck a goal his World Cup-winning son would have been proud of, the 'keeper barely moving as his 25-yard blast entered the net and a 2-1 win saw City finally get one over their big rival but by this stage Rowe was experimenting for the future and, despite having led the table at times during the season, City finished season 1947-48 down in ninth.

SEASON 1948-49 Rowe engaged in intensive pre-season team-building, first acquiring Plymouth Argyle inside-forward Marcus 'Spud' Murphy, a speedy player with good ball control and distribution. He topped that when approaching a full England international who was to combine playing with coaching and assisting him. This was 34-year-old wing-half Frank Soo, then of Luton but famous for a 12-year spell with Stoke City. Rowe said 'I have been looking for a chap who can take the captaincy—a man who can really lead the side. It pleased me no end to think that Frank Soo was interested.' With an English mother and Chinese father, Soo first appeared for Stoke around the same time as Stanley Matthews, later captaining the Potters and representing England in nine wartime internationals, his arrival indicating just how ambitious the Chelmsford manager could be were funds made available. City could now make a firm push for inclusion in the rumoured new Fourth Division.

Frank Soo (left) with RAF colleagues in Copenhagen, 1945, including Spurs' Ron Burgess (second left) and Ted Ditchburn (far right), as well as Ronnie Rooke and Stan Mortensen.

But the 1948 Football League meeting frustrated him. While the two clubs propping-up the Football League received 47 votes to stay, only two votes went to the strongest applicant to join the League, Colchester, while City were one of thirteen sides getting absolutely no votes at all. 'We did not expect this wholesale rejection', said Rowe and his name was immediately linked with Second Division West Bromwich Albion. Meanwhile, when a fan at a supporters' meeting raised the issue of player abuse, that rarely seen facet of his character - anger - once again raised its head: 'I cannot understand the intellect of anybody who deliberately goes out of his way to barrack a player—the silly clowns who keep shouting "Yah" at the top of their voices. They are confounded fools.' Indeed, Rowe's words were repeated all over the country. On a positive note, Arthur was now about to sign another quality player, Clancy McDermott, one of the best wing-halves in the Southern League, and, in addition, a man sought by several Football League clubs, 30-year-old Irish inside forward Liam O'Neill. The *Chronicle* then highlighted the need to encourage greater local support: 'Mr Arthur Rowe is a popular and very efficient manager. Get him out to village meetings more often. People want to see him and to hear him.'

But then, in the midst of all this optimism, tragedy struck. City winger Freddie Sargent, Rowe's former playing colleague, was taken ill with gastric problems, even apologising to him for his enforced absence before he collapsed at home and an emergency operation failed to save him. Arthur would have been devastated, but immediately set about securing the immediate financial needs of Sargent's widow, organizing a collection through the *Chronicle* and arranging a charity match between Chelmsford and Spurs.

For the third game of the season, City's attendance rose to five figures for the local derby with Colchester, who took a 1-0 half-time lead but Soo was said to play '…a real captain's game'. He kept the ball on the ground and in motion, encouraging his new teammates to do the same, and City ultimately took both points. Over the following four games Rowe's new side stepped-up to another level, dominating opponents and rattling-in goals. With reporters quoting 'inter-passing moves', 'fast, along-the-carpet' football and 'all-round team work,' it is clear he had instilled 'push-and-run' into his revitalised squad. The manager was delighted too when 7,659 attended the Fred Sargent memorial game. Despite missing Soo, City looked every bit as good as the opposing side, at least until the last 20 minutes when Spurs' winning margin rose to 5-1. At least Sargent's widow received £1,100, more than half the average house price at the time. City then reached the first round proper of the FA Cup with perhaps Rowe's strongest-ever side: Francis; Bidewell, Wager; McDermott, Pyle, Soo; Plunkett, McClellan, Butler, O'Neill, Burley.

City were expected to beat Western League side Weymouth, but trailed 2-1 in the final minute when O'Neill smashed a left-foot drive home from the edge of the area. However the referee instead awarded a free-kick against Chelmsford, saying a City player had run into an offside position. Even Weymouth players and officials agreed there was no question of offside and an unusually bitter Arthur Rowe penned a letter of protest to the Football Association. His anger was understandable: with a young family, career advancement was essential and FA Cup success will have practically guaranteed that. Then Rowe's side, the strongest he had ever put out, exited the Southern League Cup too, after a thriller with Colchester, Rowe's side still groping for consistency. The cup exits also gave rise to rumours that Soo, with a career history of jumping-ship, was already angling for a Football League return and proof seemed apparent when both player and manager avoided questions on the matter. Paying Soo a considerable salary, directors had gambled on his contribution to advance in both cup competitions.

However things picked-up in the Southern League and, playing 'copybook' football, City found themselves holding first place in the table. Then, however, Chelmsford fans were struck a hammer-blow in the first week of February 1949. 'ARTHUR ROWE MAY BE LEAVING CITY', headlined the *Newsman*. Second Division Brentford needed a replacement for their retiring manager and with City now out of both Cups, the Chelmsford boss admitted to applying. But, regardless of personal ambition, he continued City's team-building, acquiring Irish centre-forward Tommy Byrne before the Clarets rattled in no fewer than eight goals against Kidderminster.

Then in mid-March rumours surfaced that Rowe was about to be offered a position at his beloved Tottenham, presumably to assist manager Joe Hulme. The *Chronicle* quoted Rowe responding: 'So far as I am concerned there is nothing in it.' Events contradicted this but with Hulme still in place Rowe issued more denials. Following a spell of illness Hulme had returned to work at White Hart Lane on March 7th claiming he was now in good health, only for Spurs to immediately relieve him of his duties, which one doubts they would have done had someone not been set to take his place.

Despite rumours of Rowe's possible departure and with Colchester coming within a point of City, the players then stylishly beat Lovell's Athletic 5-1. Colchester lost their game-in-hand while a Gillingham win saw them pull level with City, this before Rowe's men moved ahead again, beating Hereford in a 4-2 thriller. Rowe kept pushing his men on, week-after-week, in a thrilling climax to the season. At Easter, City picked up four points from six as Colchester dropped out of the running. At this point one national newspaper announced Rowe was the man Spurs wanted, suggesting previous boss Hulme had voluntarily retired, when the Spurs' board had actually asked Hulme to resign on the grounds of ill-health. Now Rowe admitted to having applied for the post, but only, he clarified, once '…it was presumed vacant.' Yet clearly Spurs had sounded him out some months earlier.

Now Tottenham waited on reference letters from the War Office, mailed to Spurs' Chairman Fred Bearman. One was from H.M. Prince, Lieutenant-Colonel, Secretary, Army Football Association. Prince wrote that Rowe's role as manager of the Army team during the greater part of the war required '…a man of considerable tact and high technical ability to dictate policy on the field and maintain discipline both on and off the field.' He added: 'Arthur Rowe has these qualities.' He continued: '[Rowe] has a very pleasant personality, commands the respect of all the players, and has the ability of moulding eleven individuals into a successful combination.' In only one respect, wrote Prince (with tongue firmly in cheek), did Rowe fall short of requirements. This was in regard to '…the social point of view', which, however, it was felt he could successfully handle despite being '…an abstainer and non-smoker'! The letter ended: 'It would give the greatest pleasure to all those in the Army Football Association who knew Arthur Rowe during the war, if he is appointed to the managership of your club.'

Returning to Rowe's quest for the Southern League title, City dropped a home point to Merthyr, the *Chronicle* now accusing City of persisting in short-passing when they might have benefited from more 'long pots' at goal. Two days later, in poor conditions, Gravesend and Northfleet arrived and despite heavy pressure from City won 2-0, leading fans to despair as they headed for the exits. With Gillingham winning at Barry and Merthyr overcoming Worcester, they now surrendered their place at the top - a point behind Gillingham - and with both sides each having just one more game to play, City needed a win at Torquay whilst hoping rivals Colchester would overcome Gillingham. However the possibility of City now losing the Championship paled in comparison with events that followed.

On May 4th 1949 it was officially announced that Arthur Rowe was leaving to manage Tottenham Hotspur (to officially start on July 1st). Adding salt to the

In 1948 Lovell's Harry Clarke (later of Spurs) faced Rowe's Chelmsford.

On May 6th 1949 the Essex Chronicle *headlines Rowe's departure.*

wound Soo simultaneously announced his own departure. The timing could hardly have been worse, with Chelmsford's final game yet to be played. Of his imminent departure the *Chronicle* wrote: 'The City will lose… a manager whose judgement of a player is invariably better than that of his critics.' Some hoped Soo would apply for the vacant job but instead he left to coach Isthmian League St Albans.

Now, with heavy hearts, City did their utmost to claim the Championship at Torquay, Butler giving them the lead just after kick-off, but Torquay equalized. City pressed again in the second period and took the lead for the second time through Shalcross before Burley set O'Neill up to give them a two-goal advantage. Despite Torquay's late second the final score was 3-2 to City. However, Colchester had lost by the same margin to Gillingham, the Gills taking the title by just one point. Rowe would have much desired to depart having returned the Southern League Championship shield to City's trophy cabinet, but nobody could quibble about a runners-up position, nor the six other trophies Rowe had guided the club to in his tenure at New Writtle Street.

At a dinner in honour of the City players, wives and families, Alderman Langton described the outgoing manager as '…the hardest-working and finest manager any club could wish to have.' He added: 'We have also lost a friend. Right from our hearts we wish him the very best in his new job. We cannot speak too highly of him.' Rowe's initiation into football management had been a hard-earned success, the regional Press mentioning local football fans who had previously travelled to London or Southend to watch football but now stay to watch Chelmsford, adding, significantly: 'Many say the class of football seen at New Writtle Street is equal to that of [Football] League soccer.'

The excessive demands of his first managerial role had set Rowe up well. In his early days at Chelmsford he had jokingly admitted to working 26 hours a day and even when departing from the club, he continued to spend two nights a week at the ground as the club sought to appoint his successor: 'I want to see everything fixed up before I go,' he said. It appears likely that from early March until mid-July Rowe had simultaneously guided both Chelmsford and Spurs.

One City player yet to sign a new contract was Syd McClellan, whose resignation from his job at Fords suggested Rowe intended to take him to Tottenham. Young City centre-half Jake Farley was another early target of Rowe, Spurs paying what was said to be a 'substantial fee' for the young man. At the beginning of August, now ensconced behind his White Hart Lane desk, Rowe was surprised and gratified to receive a cheque to the value of £200 from the directors of Chelmsford City. When replying to thank them he added: 'It is of immense satisfaction to me to have done what I set out to do at Chelmsford – to make it a happy club and to leave it in a stronger position than when I took over.'

Meanwhile, the *Chronicle* referred to Tottenham Hotspur as '…one of the wealthiest clubs in the country,' adding 'any worries that may come [Rowe's] way will not be financial ones.' Future chapters cast doubt on that confident prediction but for now Spurs fans were about to enjoy an extraordinary treat — the first truly great, jaw-dropping Tottenham side was about to take flight and soar.

8

The Ultimate Dream

MANAGING SPURS 1949-50

'I have left a happy little club to return to a big club. I think my first efforts will be directed to seeing that the big club is as happy as the little club I left.'
ROWE ON LEAVING CHELMSFORD CITY

'I was left alone with a very great football authority.'
FUTURE WORLD CUP-WINNING MANAGER ALF RAMSEY, ARRIVING AT ROWE'S OFFICE ON HIS FIRST MORNING AT WHITE HART LANE 1949

In Arthur's absence Spurs still languished in the Second Division (the modern equivalent of the EFL Championship). The first post-War Football League season (1946-47) saw Tottenham appoint Joe Hulme as manager, this despite a lack of managerial experience and his close affiliation with Arsenal. Long-serving coach Jimmy Anderson was to assist him. Having finished sixth in that first season and eighth in 1947-48, as well as reaching an FA Cup semi-final, things seemed to be heading in the right direction. By early 1949 Spurs were in the top three in the Second Division and Hulme had little reason to suspect his job was under threat. He had mostly 'made do' with staff he had inherited and was believed to be earning less than his players so he was certainly no drain on Tottenham's resources. However Spurs directors attending Freddie Sargent's memorial game the previous September had been impressed by Chelmsford City's performance and expressed their interest in Rowe's availability when asking Arthur's wife Pom whether her husband was happy at the Essex club. Whatever her response, Rowe was quickly pencilled-in as Hulme's potential replacement should things go awry.

As with Rowe, Hulme could similarly be described as a 'nice fellow', a characteristic which suited demanding directors but events took a turn for the worse for the manager in early 1949; a cathartic 3-0 FA Cup defeat to Arsenal was followed by him falling ill. It was perhaps this which triggered an update on Rowe's availability. The Spurs boss appeared to have returned to work by February 18th but two weeks later he missed a home defeat by Cardiff which prompted headlines in the *Tottenham and Edmonton Weekly Herald* of 'PROMOTION HOPES ALMOST GONE', and 'MR HULME GIVEN NOTICE'. As there had been no official statement, Hulme's assistant Anderson was left to offer an explanation, saying that publication of the news was due to '...a leak', a *faux-pas* which suggested that the club had already lined-up a replacement.

As we have seen, negotiations for Rowe appear to have begun at least as early as the beginning of March. According to the press, other candidates in the frame included Manchester United's Matt Busby, who, it was quoted, would cost the club

£2750 in compensation. Clearly a gamble on a popular ex-player was far more palatable. Despite his continuing employment at Chelmsford, Rowe will clearly have been consulted on the playing side of things at White Hart Lane from early March. When Spurs ended their season with a 5-0 win at Plymouth, Arthur joined them in the West Country soon afterwards.

Hulme had been taking Spurs in the right direction, but too slowly to appease the board. Bitter over his treatment, he never managed again, instead becoming a successful journalist. Len Duquemin, who had of course guested for Rowe at Chelmsford, was the only significant player he brought into the club. Typically, no money had changed hands and just before Hulme's departure the *Herald* had drawn attention to the 'parsimony' of directors '…in not signing-on outside talent.'

As for Rowe, he had already achieved four of five personal ambitions: to play as a boy at White Hart Lane, to bear Spurs' cockerel crest on his chest, to captain the side and represent England. Now appointed manager, he had completed the set. *The Sunday Dispatch* considered he had probably taken on '…the greatest opportunity in soccer since the day when Herbert Chapman arrived at Highbury.' Spurs' official handbook stated '…if [Rowe] does for Spurs what he has done for the less glamorous Essex club, everybody officially connected with Tottenham, plus its scores of thousands of regular supporters, will be abundantly satisfied.' Arthur himself said: 'I have left a happy little club to return to a big club. I think my first efforts will be directed to seeing that the big club is as happy as the little club I left.'

Nevertheless he had a lot on his plate. Since relegation in 1935 Spurs had spent seven seasons (either side of hostilities) in Division Two. It was most likely a condition of Rowe's employment that long-serving Jimmy Anderson remained as second-in-command. Having served Spurs for 41 years, by 1949 Anderson had entered his last decade as a working man. Having failed to make the grade as a player, Anderson was assistant trainer before serving in World War I, then scouted in the 1920s before

Spurs' all-time greatest era begins. Rowe takes his place behind his desk.

With Jimmy Anderson in the background, Rowe talks tactics with apprentices.

THE ULTIMATE DREAM: MANAGING SPURS 1949-50

running Northfleet until World War II. Yet it is clear from players of the time I have met that for a start Anderson was far from competent and not taken seriously by the players, and also not fully supportive of the manager. Anderson may even have served as the directors' ear in Rowe's office. After all, in the ten seasons before the war he had seen no fewer than five managers come and go and knew it was safer to ingratiate himself with the board rather than with a passing, managerial stranger.

Arthur would begin with an unremarkable £1,500 a year salary, no more than about twice the average pay of a First Division player at the time. Although not joining Spurs until a year later, half-back Ralph Wetton told me how he had heard of the surge of enthusiasm experienced by the players when their new boss immediately had all the first-team placed on the maximum permissible wage. *The Sunday Dispatch* wrote how fortunate Rowe was that Spurs had decided to invest in order to get the club back to the First Division. Invest in salaries, yes. However, over time Arthur would benefit little from the club's indisputable wealth. Likewise the *Dispatch* questionably added: 'Arthur knows he has a completely free hand, a thing which previous managers never had. With the power of the wealthiest club in the country behind him, there is no reason why he should not take it to the top of the soccer world.' History tells us that ultimately it took five long years before the board enabled him to enter the market in a sufficiently big way (and that for just one player). The club was frugal, verging on tight, preferring to lean on the discovery and development of local talent. Defendants of this approach could point to the likes of Eddie Baily, Charlie Withers, Les Bennett, Les Medley, Tony Marchi and others, whilst from farther afield came Burgess (Wales) and Nicholson (Yorkshire). Yet another local, 20-year-old Peter Baker, signed amateur forms for Rowe that June and would later be acclaimed as the right-back in the great Spurs 'Double' side.

The new manager accepted that team strengthening was not easy and clubs then enjoying a post-war financial boom had no need to sell their best talent. However

Rowe on the training ground, new boy Alf Ramsey is at back, part-obscured by a rather dubious-looking Tommy Harmer in the centre-foreground.

suspicions of tight-fistedness remain. Even before his arrival the *Herald* had accused Spurs of not spending when new blood was necessary, this despite being '…one of the richest clubs in the country.' One renegade director went as far as to suggest the club '…did not want promotion.' To this the ever-loyal Anderson responded: 'No player is too dear if he is the man we want. If we find a first-rate man, money will not stop us.' This became an oft-repeated Spurs mantra. By the end of February 1949 the *Herald* had disappointedly concluded '…it's too late for Spurs to buy promotion,' adding when reporting Hulme's demise: 'It is essential that moves be made to strengthen the team by judicious buying of first-class men. Other clubs get them; why not the Spurs with all their wealth?' The writer added: 'Spurs must put their house in order. An end must be put to all the gossip, rumours and conjectures which invariably surround them. The veil of secrecy must go. Directors must learn the lesson of taking supporters into their confidence and so foster a happier spirit.' Intriguingly, the report added: 'A notice to this effect was posted in the players' dressing-room.' Who posted it? The players themselves? Or was it Hulme, realising his time was up? What was Arthur getting himself into?

Indicative of the kind of internal pressure any new manager faced, the club's own match programme notes following an April defeat at Barnsley included such pointed remarks as 'It is my unpleasant duty to chronicle another setback…', followed by 'This sort of thing happens to all clubs, but it has happened too often of late to the Spurs. Correspondents are angry about it.' These criticisms came even with directors' favourite Anderson temporarily in charge. But Rowe will have shrugged off any reservations — after all, he now managed the club he worshipped as a boy. He said his only remaining ambitions were for Spurs to win the FA Cup again and capture the Football League Championship for the first time. He would work hard to foster the team spirit which, he said, is the backbone of any team, irrespective of class or ability. His first step in that direction was to arrange for the players to lunch together every day. Rowe clearly succeeded, Eddie Baily saying: 'We all took equal praise when winning, and shared the blame if things went wrong.' Rowe enthusiastically pronounced: 'I have returned among friends who, I know, will give me every help in doing what is required.'

But …were they all friends?

Arthur had been unofficially pulling the White Hart Lane strings from his Chelmsford base since March so will have been involved in compiling the retained players' list while, more significantly, he was behind at least one of two significant acquisitions. March saw the arrival of 6ft 3in centre-half Harry Clarke from Welsh Southern League club Lovell's Athletic. If Clarke was not already known to Rowe (the player had grown-up just seven miles from White Hart Lane), he will have impressed when facing his Chelmsford City side in Southern League action. Clarke now belatedly began a Football League career at the age of 26. Of greater significance, Rowe was also behind a prolonged but determined effort to acquire the final member of his 'big five' (the other four truly essential players being 'keeper Ditchburn, driving half-backs Nicholson and Burgess, and playmaker Baily). Number five was Dagenham-born full-back Alf Ramsey.

In early March Anderson had been delegated (on behalf of Rowe who was still at his desk in Chelmsford) to complete Ramsey's signing before the March 16th transfer deadline. Indeed, at one point Anderson phoned Arthur at Chelmsford to discuss the ongoing negotiations. But by deadline day the only firm offer for Ramsey had come from Sheffield Wednesday (with whom Southampton aimed to seal a useful player-exchange deal) but the player did not relish a move north. Although Anderson had arrived to bid for Ramsey, the player himself was not informed of Tottenham's interest, the Saints favouring the exchange deal with Wednesday. So Anderson left empty-handed. At 4.30pm Ramsey was told he was needed urgently at The Dell where he was finally informed of the Tottenham bid. But by the time Saints' manager Bill Dodgin arrived in London to tell Anderson that the player was happy to sign, insufficient time remained to beat the deadline, so the player was compelled to stay in Southampton reserves. The transfer itself finally went through 11 days after Rowe had officially taken charge, Saints receiving £4,500 plus winger Ernie Jones, who was valued at £16,500.

Aside from joining a famous club, Ramsey was happy to return to life back with his parents in Dagenham, 13 miles from White Hart Lane. In early July 1949 he received a letter signed 'Arthur Rowe' requesting his presence at pre-season training. It has been claimed the name 'Rowe' meant nothing to him. However Ramsey said that '...in a very short time [Rowe] and I were to become the closest of friends and "football barmy".' Both manager and club believed they had signed a 27-year-old, not a player eight months shy of 30, although even had Ramsey's real age been known it might not necessarily have scuppered the deal (Rowe being mainly concerned with a player's abilities). As for the subterfuge over age it was not

Rowe, with trainer Cecil Poynton, chats with Spurs' first-teamers. Clearly he already has their rapt attention, particularly that of future managerial greats Bill Nicholson and Alf Ramsey (far right).

ARTHUR 'PUSH-AND-RUN' ROWE

Rowe's big five: Ditchburn, Nicholson, Burgess, Baily and Ramsey.

uncommon for players who had lost playing years to the war to falsify their age. The full-back was to be one of the foundations for Rowe's plan to alter the club's playing style, while goalkeeper Ditchburn would meanwhile become the manager's first line of attack, a unique notion at that time.

Ron Burgess recalled the new manager changing the entire outlook at Tottenham: 'His inspiration and encouragement when I was just a lad on the Tottenham books had done a lot for me, and I felt that his return to his old football "home" was a bright omen for the future.' Dismayed with the growing trend toward Chapman's defend-and-breakaway approach, Rowe was determined his Spurs would be an attacking, fast-moving, 'give-and-go' side. After the dramatic rise in goalscoring following the offside law amendment, goals-per-game had begun to drop in the years before the war, not solely due to Chapman's withdrawal of one inside-forward and the centre-half taking on a purely defensive role but also to other factors such as the growing inclination for goalkeepers to cover more ground within their penalty area, rushing from their line to intercept overhit forward passes.

The tall, slim Vic Buckingham, Rowe's former defensive playing colleague, remained on the playing staff. He had been a regular during Hulme's three seasons at the helm but now approached 34 and never featured in Rowe's first team. However, having coached on the Continent, Buckingham was happy with Arthur's offer to coach the Tottenham juniors. Absorbing his boss's general principles of how the game should be played, the adventurous Buckingham later coached the likes of Ajax and Barcelona. Meanwhile, Cecil Poynton, another ex-playing colleague, continued as trainer, Anderson taking care of the Reserves. Meanwhile, the five particularly significant representatives of Rowe on the pitch were:

TED DITCHBURN (goalkeeper) who became a first-teamer in 1946-47 and represented England in 1948. At 6ft 1in, Ditchburn was physically imposing and acrobatic. Bill Nicholson would compare Ditchburn's speed off the line and bravery to Spurs' great Irish international 'keeper of the 1960s and 1970s, Pat Jennings. Rowe turned him into Spurs' first line of attack.

BILL NICHOLSON (right-half) had joined the groundstaff in 1936. Playing for Northfleet between 1936 and 1938, he made his Spurs debut at 19. He, like Rowe, became a physical training instructor during the war, afterwards attaining the FA coaching badge. A first-team regular from 1946-47, he was always on the move, covering his team-mates when necessary.

RON BURGESS (captain and left-half) was only 11 years' younger than Rowe. As a boy he worked in the Welsh coal mines before joining Spurs in 1936. The tall Burgess had been working in a Chingford metal works when Spurs decided he wouldn't make it in the professional game. Offered the option of a return train fare to Wales or keeping his factory job, he opted to return to Wales, but before leaving went to watch the 'A' team play. When one player failed to turn-up, Burgess stepped-in and scored twice, after which manager Jack Tresadern decided to retain him after all. He was an excellent tackler and header of the ball who also possessed stamina, speed, agility and great ball control. Playing colleague Ralph Wetton told me Burgess was '…one minute leading an attack and the next clearing off the line.'

EDDIE BAILY (inside-right) was only 5ft 7in tall but capable of fearsome shots at goal and possessed excellent close control. Nicknamed 'The Cheeky Chappie', he first played in Spurs' juniors in August 1939 before army service in Europe. A communication breakdown at war's end led Spurs to think Baily was 'missing in action'. He himself, having heard nothing from White Hart Lane, signed for Chelsea, who later had to cancel his contract so, as with the case of Burgess, Spurs all but lost the player. Rowe said he had '…never seen a man play a moving ball either way with either foot as quickly and accurately as Baily.' Of all the players Rowe inherited, it was Baily who most suited his system.

ALF RAMSEY (right-back) had grown up on his father's Dagenham small-holding and represented Dagenham Schoolboys and Essex Schools. Playing for the army during the war he impressed Second Division Southampton who signed him. He originally played up-front but when Southampton needed a full-back, was switched there. He had already turned 27 when becoming a regular first-teamer and won a first England cap in 1948, but injury cost him his place at Southampton.

For Ramsey's first day of pre-season training that July Rowe, with typical concern and awareness, asked two players who lived in the same area of Essex as Alf, 'Tex' Henty and Chris Adams, to surprise the new man at Barking train station and travel up with him, which they did. They accompanied him all the way to the manager's door and introduced him, Ramsey later recalling: 'I was left alone with a very great football authority.' 'Like you,' the manager smiled, '…I'm a "new boy", and I think we should become good friends.' The new signing was immediately taken by his new manager's quiet personality and warmth. It was also clear, according to Ramsey, '…that Mr Rowe had definite and original ideas as to how the game should be played; to me they were ideas, too, which I liked.' Before Ramsey's first pre-season practice match Rowe gave his first serious tactical talk, the basis of which was: 'Play football all the time. Make it quick. Make it easy.' Ramsey recalled how players were swept up in Rowe's plans, excitedly talking in groups during training, at lunch and on their way home, discussing the manager's ideas and how they might be adapted or improved. For example, the right-side trio comprising full-back Ramsey, outside-right Walters and inside-right Bennett, discussed how best they could combine together when in possession. Rowe himself was always receptive to players' ideas, if preferring to have the last word. After the limited, direct style Ramsey experienced at Southampton, he was quickly inspired.

After Rowe added two other forwards to the staff, Billy Rees and Bobby Cook, Julian Holland lyrically described that first summer: 'The feast could now be prepared. The ingredients were ready on the green-topped table, and the new *maître de cuisine* could compose his banquet. His was no wooden spoon.' Other managers had sought success with a costly accumulation of great footballers (as with Chapman at Arsenal). Rowe, on the other hand, took Hulme's playing staff, adding only the extremely frugal additions of Ramsey, Clarke, Rees and Cook, and had them playing a style foreign to English football. His unique approach was described by Holland as something which '…tore outrageously at the foundations of all that had seemed most stable in English soccer.'

Rowe later recalled to John Motson that when arriving as manager, '…the club had a group of very good players, and by good I mean by their willingness to be… not taught, but… "advised".'

ENGLISH FOOTBALL IN 1949   By this time the Chapman style predominated in English football. As journalist Willy Meisl described it, post-War players had to model their play on '…the mechanized, the robot style, the safety-first, speedway brand of football.' Meisl felt that 'solidity, rapidity,' and 'reliability' had replaced 'originality, individuality and adventurous spirit'. 'Precise short passing' and '…clever positioning' were thought to baffle the modern British player. As Graham Morse points out in his biography of Sir Walter Winterbottom, most clubs in the early post-War era '…wanted nothing to do with new thinking.' In fact, from what transpired later, one must believe that the Tottenham directors were

Mickey Durling caricatures of Rowe's 1949-50 squad, plus the Manager himself and trainer Cecil Poynton. This appeared in the Playfair Football Annual.

quite unaware Rowe was to launch something revolutionary. Most managers then did little more than select the team, watch them play, then deal with administrative matters during the week while a trainer ensured the players did endless laps of the pitch. Rowe, on the other hand, intended to indoctrinate his new charges with a new, alternative, thrilling approach in the strong belief it would ensure success, entertainment and financial gain.

While a short-passing game demanded ball skills and a sharp brain, 'spoiling' (as Willy Meisl referred to Chapman's approach) essentially required strength and stamina, hence a style more easily adopted by less talented and/or less adventurous teams. Chapman himself had the huge advantage that Arsenal could afford the most skilled performers available to occupy the critical roles in his teams. From Rowe's description, the pre-1920s Barnsley side had gained much FA Cup success by getting the ball up-field by the most direct means (in the modern age known as the 'percentage' game — if you do it often enough, it will eventually produce dividends, often due to defensive error). This was anathema to the new Spurs boss, who cynically described it as: 'You get stuck in, whack it a long way, and gallop!'

He demonstrated his determination to achieve success when he cut the players' summer break short by a week taking them to Epping Forest rather than working at the stadium, a practice rare at the time but something he would do each pre-season. Half-back Ralph Wetton told me it was '…smashing, the kind of thing Arthur did.' He was quick to tell the players that Spurs would be promoted. Perhaps it was this positivity which later encouraged protégé Ramsey, on becoming England manager, to state that the nation would win the World Cup.

THE ROWE REVOLUTION Journalist Bernard Joy wrote an eye-witness account of the historic moment on the training ground when Rowe first demonstrated what would become known as 'push-and-run' (note: Les Medley once said Rowe called it 'push-an-run' but Rowe himself later preferred the term 'give-and-go', but 'push-and-run' is how it became commonly known).

Rowe, standing ten yards from the touchline, asked Ron Burgess to throw it to him. He then played the thrown pass first-time to winger Medley, waiting a few yards up the line (one-touch). Trainer Cecil Poynton timed this. It had taken two seconds from Burgess's hands via Rowe's foot to Medley. The Spurs manager again asked Burgess to throw the ball to him, but this time controlled it before pushing it second-touch to the waiting Medley (two-touch). 'Four seconds!' called Poynton. Finally the manager demonstrated how the throw-in would so often be dealt with during the course of an average match. First controlling the throw with his stronger foot (his right), he then tapped it forward with the left before using his more accurate right foot to deliver the ball to Medley (three-touch). 'Eight seconds!' called the assistant this time. Rowe then made the telling if obvious point that holding the ball before delivering a pass provided defenders with time to mark colleagues who moved into space expecting a pass. Also Medley, seeing he was now closely-marked, may have instinctively begun to move to a new space, the move most likely breaking down. The onlooking Ramsey was extremely impressed by how quickly his new colleagues took these theories on board.

The new Spurs manager proceeded to spend pre-season training with stopwatch in hand, practising his basic 'push-and-run' theories, telling them it was a simple game if your team kept possession and passed accurately to '...the same shirts you wear.' The more accurate the pass, the quicker and better the attack. Summing-up, Rowe told his men: 'I am certain we can do it, if we all pull together.' He told the press that pre-season would initially include walks in the mornings followed by training games such as basketball and head tennis, to ensure co-ordination of mind and muscle. In the second and succeeding weeks there was to be a concentration on ball work. Just before the season's start, dead-ball situations would be practiced. When released from physical activity Rowe's players would enthusiastically talk football. The manager's composed, quiet personality and his honest smile quickly won over any doubters. Ron Burgess recalled: 'We were all agreed there was something in it. But would it work out on the field?' Rowe believed that winning over Burgess was key to winning over the entire group.

Ramsey recalled that the new manager had '...the happy knack of making everything, no matter how trivial, seem important, and it did not take us long to see that his aim was to develop a game to suit the footballers at his disposal, not trying to fit the players into a set game which might have meant upsetting their whole approach to the game,' something Rowe later himself confirmed: 'It is wrong, to my way of thinking, to adopt a pattern and then seek the players who will fit that pattern.' Ramsey would fondly recall that whenever the manager said 'Now, I've been thinking...' the players would immediately anticipate something pleasurable, so much did they enjoy his refreshing ideas and suggestions.

Julian Holland noted that Rowe could converse with the players '...at their level.' His primary aim was to make his players accept the premise that possession of the football equated to '...being on the attack.' The side in possession of the ball is the only side capable of scoring and, in order to retain possession against opponents who would challenge strongly for the ball, accurate control and passing was essential. The added requirement was speed, hence his slogan: 'Make it Simple,

Rowe preaching his 'push-and-run' ideas. Once again, those most enjoying this appear to be future World Cup-winning manager Alf Ramsey (standing, left) and future 'Double'-winning manager Bill Nicholson (next to Ramsey). Others here are (at back) Ditchburn and Clarke, with Bennett, Burgess, Rees, Withers, Duquemin and Walters around the table.

Make it Quick.' Rowe later recalled: 'I said it so often they must have been tired of listening to me.' 'Push-and-run' came most naturally of all to Baily, of whom Rowe said: 'I've never seen a man play a moving ball either way with either foot as quickly and accurately as him.' After one early 'push-and-run' practice, Rowe asked captain Burgess his opinion. 'I can't wait to try it out in a League game', was his captain's response. Indeed, Burgess was confident the new tactic would sweep the country.

Rowe once explained to Norman Giller how he had two 'teams' of players on either flank: 'We used to operate in triangles, with Eddie Baily, Ronnie Burgess and Les Medley particularly brilliant at the concept out on the left. Over on the right Alf Ramsey, Billy Nicholson and Billy 'Sonny' Walters were equally adept at keeping possession while making progress with simple passes.' Other than making themselves more available to help their full-backs, Rowe admitted in 1960 that one reason he had his wingers Walters and Medley play deep was his recognition that neither were '…strong-running raiders', saying, 'short of buying two other wingers who were—which would have cost a lot of money—we tried to do something different with the two we possessed.'

Right-winger Walters was recalled by Bill Nicholson as '…an up-and-down grafter who excelled at stealing into positions behind defenders.' He was also blessed with a firm shot. The career of his counterpart on the left, Les Medley, had taken off on return from RAF service in Canada. He made full use of speed and close control with both feet. He was also strong-willed, once refusing to play for at least a month having been replaced pre-match when already changed and about to take the field.

As a player of many talents, captain Burgess will have harboured more concern than most that individualists who held the ball were frowned upon in Rowe's system. But Burgess himself became supremely enthusiastic, saying that the system '…depended entirely upon every man playing the team game, each section of the team dovetailing with the others, with no gaps anywhere. Each man had to cover, and be covered, if our short passes were to be effective.' Rowe believed any player could succeed in 'push-and-run', even individually skilled performers. For example, the supremely individualistic Stanley Matthews, had he been schooled in 'push-and-run', would have continually moved into space to make himself available for the ball and, as a result, he would have received the ball more often and would less frequently have had a full-back standing on his toes or coming straight through him once the ball was played to him.

Physical fitness was essential, Bill Nicholson considering 'push-and-run' impossible '…unless all ten outfield players were one-hundred-per-cent fit.' If players were to be comfortable in multiple positions on the field (according to the flow of the game) the demand on them is physical as much as technical. There was no time to switch off and 'take a breather'. In future Spurs' keeper Ron Reynolds' only prior experience, at Aldershot, training had involved a lot of running around. 'But with Arthur, it went on in the mind, it was about creating spaces, angles, having ideas of your own within the set-up of the team.' Reflecting on those early days, Nicholson wrote how vision was essential, the constant movement of eyes and head: 'The receiver has to know where his colleagues are before the ball reaches him. It

Trainer Poynton and Manager Rowe bookend the basic eleven men who would capture successive Championships.

Players are (back): Nicholson, Ramsey, Clarke, Ditchburn, Willis (who would share the left-back role with Withers) and Burgess. (Front): Walters, Bennett, Duquemin, Baily and Medley.

requires intelligence. And it calls for movement off the ball, the most important ingredient.'

Rowe could hardly wait to apply his theories in the second level of the Football League. Of course, some players had greater skills than others, but, said Rowe, '…you had to try and make all of them feel that they had a big part to play.' When training at White Hart Lane the first-team plus a few fringe players such as Ralph Wetton, Colin Brittan and Tommy Harmer, would occupy the home team (or 'Top') dressing-room. If a player's gear was in the 'Top' dressing-room, said Wetton, you '…knew you were in.'

Addressing Tottenham's Annual Meeting in the last week of July, the new manager refused to make any promises, assuring only that '…as long as I hold this position the club will be the happiest in the country.' Captain Burgess later recalled: 'There seemed to be a new air of confidence throughout the whole club, an atmosphere such as I had not known since I joined.' Season tickets sold out before Spurs held their first public trial matches, which were usually between first-team and reserves, or sometimes one side incorporating the first-team attack against a side incorporating the first-team defence. For the first public trial, Rowe's five-man first-team attack would play for the 'Reds' against his chosen first-team defence for the 'Whites'. The first-teamers selected that afternoon would comprise his first-team of choice for some time to come:

Goalkeeper: Ditchburn;
Full-backs: Ramsey and Withers [or Willis]
Half-backs: Nicholson, Clarke and Burgess
Forwards: Walters, Bennett, Duquemin, Baily, Medley.

Excitement was such that the two trial games drew record receipts (all profits going to charity).

SEASON 1949-50 The first test for 'push-and-run' took place in sweltering heat at Brentford, on August 20th 1949. On a bone-hard and dusty pitch the home side, unprepared for the new tactic, crashed 4-1, the goals coming from Bennett, Duquemin and two from Medley. One reporter immediately forecast the Second

THE ULTIMATE DREAM: MANAGING SPURS 1949-50

Division would be a walk-over for Spurs, but Burgess recalled it took several weeks '…to really get into the swing of ["push-and-run"].' Despite the result, Alf Ramsey admitted little would have made critics sit up and take notice.

On the morning of the first home game, against Plymouth Argyle, just two days later, a white-sweatered Rowe lapped the track at White Hart Lane. The Spurs' programme notes stated 'We have tarried too many years in the wilderness' and suggested this would be Tottenham's season. Spurs took most of the first-half to find their feet until Ramsey put them ahead from the spot. Baily and Medley finished the scoring in a second-half performance described as 'devastating'. The manager called the display 'not bad' afterwards, only too aware that Argyle had barely escaped relegation just three months' earlier. Rowe's reticence was not misplaced, defensive errors five days later leading to a 3-2 home defeat by Blackburn, the *Herald* chauvinistically describing Rowe's jittery players as '…a bunch of excited schoolgirls, getting in each other's way in their over-anxiety.' The 'anxiety' was more likely an excess of enthusiasm. The reporter exposed his unfamiliarity with 'push-and-run' when accusing Spurs of 'fiddling about' in front of goal. As Spurs acclimatised themselves to the new tactical approach, some errors were inevitable.

Three games later Tottenham sat in first place, on the path to netting 50 goals in a phenomenal 22-game unbeaten run, during which Ditchburn claimed no fewer than 11 blank sheets. Writing in the third decade of the 21st Century, Rowe's 1949-50 unbeaten League run still remains to be topped by any Tottenham Hotspur manager, including the likes of Nicholson, Burkinshaw, Venables, Redknapp, Pochettino and Mourinho. Not only did 'push-and-run' produce goals it prevented them at the other end. An unchanged line-up certainly helped, as did Rowe's insistence that all teams representing the club should engage in 'push-and-run', ensuring good results at all levels.

The second of two 1-0 victories which followed, at home to Sheffield Wednesday (who later became Spurs' closest challengers) saw the visitors exhausted from chasing an elusive ball shifted around with speed and accuracy. However, still unfamiliar with 'push-and-run', the *Herald* correspondent criticised Spurs' tendency '…to tip-tap with the ball in the penalty area – which is always dangerous.' The truth was that as Spurs' deftly played their way out from the back they were retaining possession, thus minimising goal chances for their opposition. Critics and fans alike wondered at how this immense improvement had been achieved despite so few changes to Hulme's line-up. The *Herald* inanely put this down to the improved spirit around the club, failing to credit the new playing style. Indeed, the newspaper had begun to snidely criticise it utilising expressions such as 'pattern-weaving' and 'tip-tap'. The retention of possession was even considered a '…waste of energy and ineffective.' One might be forgiven for thinking Spurs had *lost*, not *won* five games in a row! Persistent criticism, despite happy fans, successful results and growing attendances, was something Rowe would have to learn to contend with.

Spurs' 25-year-old central striker, the swarthy 5ft 11in Channel Islander Len 'The Duke' Duquemin (pronounced 'Dookmin'), had of course briefly played under the manager at Chelmsford. Before signing for Hulme in January, 1946 he had worked in the market garden of a monastery during Guernsey's German occupation.

He was capable of ferocious shooting and powerful heading, but perhaps more significantly he was always in motion to make himself available and held the ball up well. Rowe would have preferred him to find the net more often however, hence his perpetual search for a prolific scorer.

Leaving the pitch on September 24th after a sixth consecutive win, this time 2-1 over Leicester, an opponent exhaustedly gasped that confronting Rowe's Spurs had been '...like trying to catch pigeons.' In nine games Spurs had scored 21 and conceded just 7. In those times teams sharing the same points total were separated by dividing the goals they had scored by those they had conceded so Spurs' differential of '3' provided no clearer indication of how successful Rowe's tactics were proving to be. The only substantial doubt concerned the quality of reserve strength available to him but only a quarter of the way through Spurs' 22-game unbeaten run captain Burgess wrote '...there was no happier bunch of chaps in the country, and no more confident team, either.' Opposition sides were given little opportunity to steal the ball, although Rowe did have to tolerate the tall Bennett's occasional dwelling on it. Despite his ball skills and goalscoring Bennett did sometimes defy 'push-and-run' by shaping to pass before sharply dummying his way past opponents. Rowe may have turned a blind to this ploy as it provided an occasional alternative to rigid, rhythmic 'push-and-run'.

Strugglers Bradford Park Avenue arrived next and their uncompromising, direct football kept Rowe's side at bay until Spurs' relentless, high-tempo passing produced a final score of 5-0. As the manager put it, '...when the dam [finally] burst we were irresistible.' Possessing the best defensive record in the entire Football League, Spurs had dropped just two points from 20. Despite a further comfortable win, over Coventry, the writer of Spurs' own programme notes made it clear he had little taste for Rowe's methods. He praised a Swindon Town reserve side facing Spurs' reserves for their going '...direct for goal' while Rowe's reserves were only doing a lot of '...pattern-weaving', a pointed phrase which became one of several, repeated put-downs of Rowe's methods, suspiciously shared by both club programme and local press. Despite his success, the manager had to contend with pernicious claptrap emanating from within White Hart Lane until his final day in the Spurs' hot seat. Two Spurs players of the time independently confirmed to me that the programme notes were compiled by two club directors (of which, more later). The rare loss of a single point at Luton in October drew complaints of '...over-elaboration' which nullified speedy approach work. Yet Spurs' thrilling playing style had drawn a record 27,319 to Kenilworth Road.

A week later at White Hart Lane both Spurs and visitors Barnsley received an ovation at the climax of yet another fast, thrilling and hard-fought game won by the home side. One particular Barnsley player missed both encounters with Spurs that season, first through injury and then international duty, but he had been thrilled when reading about Spurs' exciting new style. The player concerned was Northern Irishman Danny Blanchflower who himself pined for a chance to perform such soccer. One day, thanks to Rowe, his chance would come.

Following a 1-0 win at Upton Park, the manager tried to acquire an unnamed 'Scots star' but without success, a pattern much repeated over coming years. Rowe did occasionally benefit from a quality youngster already on Spurs' books, as in the case of the 16-year-old, six-foot, Edmonton-born Tony Marchi. There was something of a trend at Spurs to play right-footed half-backs at left-half, thus the right-footed Marchi (pronounced 'Mark-Eye') followed in the steps of Ron Burgess and Spurs' 1921 FA Cup Final winning captain Arthur Grimsdell. Marchi explained Rowe's faith in this tactic: 'If you're right-footed, and you're playing in midfield, it's easier for you to work with your right foot to kick it out to your left-winger. If you are on the right-hand side, if your weaker foot was on your left, it would be harder to play it to your right-winger.' Marchi told me Rowe was, for him '…like a second father… a couple of times he took me up into the stands to sit with me, to explain things, to help me.'

The highlight of Spurs' 22-game unbeaten League run was saved for visitors Sheffield United on November 12th. With his side already five goals behind at half-time the visitor's centre-half, feeling outnumbered, asked the Spurs manager how many players he had out on the field! For once an official Tottenham publication could only react positively: 'The football [Spurs] played …was as fine a display of machine-like, accurate team football that has been seen on the ground.' Walters' hat-trick topped the scorers and, at 7-0, the *The Times* wrote: '…for decency's sake, the massacre was ended,' adding, '…the mounting of [Spurs] attacks resembled the smooth, unhindered approach of a wave gathering speed and volume.' Already named 'Team of the Year', Spurs were by then the equivalent of three wins clear at the top and it was a measure of their superiority that their opponents that afternoon ultimately finished in third place. One reporter proposed that the onlooking England manager Walter Winterbottom should select the entire Second Division Spurs' side to represent the nation! As recently as 2019 *The Guardian* recalled this very game (describing it as a 'remorseless skewering') under the banner of a regular Friday feature entitled 'PREMIER LEAGUE: 10 THINGS TO LOOK OUT FOR THIS WEEKEND'. There was Rowe's portrait sitting alongside the likes of Jurgen Klopp, Jamie Vardy and Steve Bruce.

At Blundell Park, Grimsby, Spurs lost Walters to injury and were 2-1 down at half-time. Trooping into the dressing-room, the players were met by Rowe calmly advising 'You can do it'. Ramsey recalled how he and his colleagues were inspired by this: 'Every one of the lads had the utmost confidence in [Rowe's] ability to successfully diagnose a game and to prescribe some sort of "success medicine".' Ramsey added: 'When Arthur said something in that quiet manner of his, you knew he wasn't talking for talking's sake.' The manager had said they could win, and his players then lost any doubt. With Spurs' confidence regained, Ramsey robbed the Grimsby left-winger, went on a jinking run and ended by shooting home from the six-yard line. It was a rare example of a solo effort from a Rowe coached side and even the Grimsby spectators applauded. With eight minutes left Medley scored the winner fulfilling the prediction.

Now 14 games unbeaten, a colossal 62,783 poured into White Hart Lane to see a 3-0 win over Queens Park Rangers. The *Herald* correspondent 'Arrow', watching Spurs' 3-1 win at Preston on a morass of December mud, insightfully identified that Rowe's men appeared to move faster than their opponents but only because they made the ball do the work: 'It is obvious that a player can move faster without the ball than with it, particularly on a heavy ground' this performance also confirmed the manager's opinion that 'push-and-run' could succeed in the worst of conditions. Around this time Rowe was asked what Spurs did to achieve their fitness and replied that they '…simply carry on a tradition of "…letting the players train themselves". Some need strenuous training which would leave others half-dead on match days. Spurs sensibly find out which method suits the player best. Each one's psychology is carefully studied, in order to get the most from him.' For 1949 this thinking was clearly ahead of its time.

Ramsey once described the players' basic weekly training schedule at Tottenham. On Monday they ran some laps followed by ball practice on the hard surface of the car park; on Tuesday they did eight laps before withdrawing to the gym where they used the punchball, rowing-machine and skipping-rope, and, afterwards, Rowe would try out a new tactic or hold a practice match; Wednesday's five-a-side games were loved so much by the players that the trainer struggled to bring proceedings to a close; on Thursday lapping was followed by sprinting practice and massage; on Friday just a couple of laps followed by sprints and body exercises. So, far less ball-work and far more laps than one might have imagined under Rowe's direction, although no more than practised at other clubs of that era. Before releasing the players on Friday the manager would finally gather the players to discuss the following day's game, encouraging input from the players themselves.

New bargain-buy Bobby Cook had disappointed as a stand-in for Walters so, after just three games, Jimmy Scarth came in. Cook would prove to be the first of several 'economical' purchases during Rowe's time in charge who failed to meet requirements. However Spurs had still gone 17 games undefeated, their goal average had almost doubled and home attendances were nearly 10% up over Hulme's final season. 'Push-and-run' was boosting the club's finances, yet a rare dropped point just before Christmas saw the *Herald* quick to criticise, saying Spurs had 'fiddled' and over-elaborated — these had become standard put-downs on the rare occasions when Rowe's team faltered. Spurs then took seven points from eight, moving nine points clear at the top and seven months with the new man in charge saw the club declare a record net profit of £49,000 by the turn of the year. The boss had relaxed his strict adherence to 'push-and-run' a little due to mid-winter pitch conditions, the *Herald* quickly pleading for a return to '…making the ball do the work and advancing with precise passes', even quoting from Robert Browning's *Home-Thoughts, from Abroad*: 'Spurs must aim at recapturing that first "careless rapture"'. By the dawn of the new decade Arthur Rowe's first 25 games bossing his beloved Spurs had seen no fewer than 20 wins, four draws and a solitary defeat. Now they were to travel to First Division Stoke City in the FA Cup 3rd round.

Extraordinarily, however, the *Herald* suddenly chose that moment to forget that 'first careless rapture', previously insightful columnist 'Arrow' now suggesting Spurs needed to '…cut out a lot of the useless tip-tap stuff!' So 'useless' was this 'tip-tap stuff' that Rowe's boys led the Division by ten points! Was 'Arrow' bowing to pressure from within the club itself? Expressions such as 'tip-tap' and 'pattern-weaving' were mirrored in the club's own match programme. There was by now an established, iniquitous pattern to openly undermine Rowe's successful and popular methods. A football club's local newspaper is often subjected to pressure from the club to control its critical comment. Was the *Herald* tailoring its opinions to satisfy the club? The opinions of less discerning Spurs' fans will surely have been influenced when reading programme criticisms 'reinforced' in their local paper. The pressure the manager bore from this, coming as it did from both his own club and the local newspaper, is immeasurable. Any slip, any poor result and caustic comments were ready and waiting from publications that should have been the last to criticise. This theme, sadly, is returned to later in this book.

Despite being so maligned on their own doorstep, Spurs overwhelmed First Division Stoke City with precise, high-speed soccer. Indeed Stoke had only 'keeper Dennis Herod and international centre-half Neil Franklin to thank for keeping Spurs' winning margin down to the solitary goal which clinched a fourth round place. Afterwards Rowe said: 'We'll take on anybody these days. I would sooner have my team than any other.' He pointed out his side had hit the post three times: 'That's not bad shooting—it's bad luck.' Indeed, illustrious football correspondent Ivan Sharpe believed the score should really have been 8-2 to Spurs. One wonders what the quick-to-criticise directors' suffered that afternoon? Irritation? Frustration?

Inevitably, however, just when Rowe needed a comprehensive League win to follow-up the Cup giant-killing, Spurs' hit the buffers. Over-confidence saw Spurs crash 3-0 at Leeds United, but they had at least drawn the biggest Elland Road attendance (50,400) since 1932. Leeds' 18-year-old centre-half John Charles, soon to become one of the all-time greats of world soccer, excelled against Duquemin and the defeat was hardly a disgrace — Charles' side were to finish fifth. Rowe believed it was his side which '…played the football' while Leeds '…got the goals.'

Another two points were gleaned in 2-1 win at Gigg Lane, Bury before Spurs again faced First Division opposition in the FA Cup 4th round. Sunderland were armed with prolific attackers such as Ivor Broadis (31 goals in 75 appearances for Tottenham in the Wartime League) and England international Len Shackleton. Despite the cold (the White Hart Lane pitch was described as being like an ice-rink), more than 66,000 made it through the turnstiles. In his pep-talk Rowe said to his men: 'Sunderland? Well, what about them? *We've* got four internationals in *our* defence!' Rowe's talking-down the opposing side was a psychological tactic his pal Vic Buckingham replicated years later when managing mighty Barcelona. Although Sunderland took a fortunate lead, the goal proved to be a red rag to a bull; Spurs tearing Sunderland's First Division defence apart. With both wingers having drifted into the middle, it was Walters who got to a through pass first to score the equaliser before Bennett '…screwed a header in off the post' to give the home side a 2-1 half-time lead (incidentally only one winger should have been in the middle as Rowe instructed that if one winger should drift inside, the opposite one should remain 'anchored' to the wing). Spurs proceeded to add no fewer than three further goals before the end. Second Division Spurs had heavily beaten a team on track for a third-place First Division finish, captain Burgess later recalling Spurs fans '…yelling in a wild frenzy of jubilation.' All this took place in front of Stanley Rous and members of the International Selection Committee. The result should have put paid to any remaining doubts as to Rowe's managerial and coaching talent. The downside, as always occurs following success, was the resultant increase in expectation. In addition to promotion talk the odds of carrying-off the FA Cup itself now fell to just 9-1. This despite a tough fifth round draw away to yet another First Division side, Everton, although even Rowe himself was confident of success at Goodison Park, perhaps recalling that time 12 years' earlier when captaining Spurs to Cup victory over the same opposition.

Once again Cup success presaged a rare League defeat, this time at Leicester, but Spurs remained far ahead of the rest in Division Two as they prepared again for Cup action. A win at Goodison would see Spurs in the FA Cup quarter-finals. In just four minutes, with a strong cross-wind gusting across the pitch, a bouncing ball in Spurs' penalty box grazed leggy centre-half Harry Clarke's arm. Penalty! Rowe firmly believed it was 'ball-to-arm', but Eddie Wainwright put Everton ahead. Spurs came close on four occasions and remained in command for the rest of the game but finally exited the FA Cup due to that one, questionable penalty. At least they were now free to fully concentrate on reaching the First Division.

Indeed they quickly collected two more points at Bradford Park Avenue, only for the *Herald* to cast a shadow at the most inopportune moment, reminding readers that the last occasion Spurs went up (with Rowe as captain) they had gone back down inside two years, the newspaper adding that other recently promoted sides had also struggled! Fortunately it failed to deter Rowe's men as they prepared to face fellow promotion challengers Southampton. A thumping 4-0 victory saw the manager defy his normal humility, predicting his side would finish with a points total closer to 70 than 60. The *Herald* now turned the heat upon the club's directors, suggesting that with a record profit forecast for his first year in charge, the club should not be 'sparing with their profits' when it came to strengthening the side. But, while the *Herald* was highlighting 'fabulous' fees being paid by other clubs, Spurs' scout was simultaneously scouring Scotland, Ireland and Wales — regions then viewed as bargain-basement markets.

After a rare goalless draw on a dusty, dry pitch against struggling Luton, Rowe felt obliged to hit back at the *Herald* for it's pessimism and the newspaper apologised, writing '[Rowe's] is the kind of confidence which will stand Spurs in good stead against the buffetings of fate in soccer's premier competition, and his inspiration may yet lead the club to even greater successes.' Inevitably, this affirmation of faith in the Spurs' manager presaged a rare defeat at Barnsley where Nicholson was lost to injury early-on. The setback was sufficiently catastrophic in the *Herald*'s eyes that it began calculating which sides might mathematically still overtake Rowe's men. Considering Tottenham, with two games in hand, possessed an 11 point advantage over second-placed Sheffield United, this was a pitiable exercise in futility. Should they continue to gather points at the same rate (1.61 per game) Spurs were on track to add a further 29 points for a final total of 82. For reference the average points total of the previous ten promoted Second Division runners-up had been a mere 55. The notion that promotion was at risk was patently absurd and could only have been maliciously intended. The pessimism was quickly dealt a blow as Spurs beat West Ham 4-1, leaving just two points from 16 required to guarantee promotion.

THE ULTIMATE DREAM: MANAGING SPURS 1949-50

April 1st 1950. The victory at QPR which saw Rowe capture the Second Division Championship with no less than seven games still to play. Here Duquemin is foiled by the home side's 'keeper.

So on April Fools' Day 1950 Spurs travelled to Loftus Road to secure those two points from relegation-threatened Queens Park Rangers. Indeed, goals from Medley and Baily secured Rowe promotion at his first attempt as a Football League manager. His beloved 'Lilywhites' were finally back in Division One for the first time in 15 years, and with no less than fourteen points still to play for. It had been an unprecedented, glorious and stylish achievement, gained in the face of persistent, malevolent criticism from both within and without. The *Herald* suddenly conceded Spurs had enjoyed a marvellous season yet felt obliged to add: '...the only regret was that Cup lapse.' So, at the very moment of great triumph, the *Herald* criticised Rowe's Second Division Spurs for a 1-0 away defeat to a First Division side. 'Full marks to manager Arthur Rowe for his first season's work' was their sheepish afterthought.

The club's own programme's contributors now jumped on the bandwagon too, gushing fulsomely about the achievement. Spurs' President Lord Morrison, who had served as Labour Prime Minister Ramsay MacDonald's Parliamentary Private Secretary and had played schoolboy soccer in Scotland, attempted to compensate for the club's lack of praise for Rowe in later programme notes, congratulating him for '...a fine job of work in his first year as manager.' He also praised the team '...for the kind of football that delights the heart of every lover of the game', comments far removed from those of the directors responsible for match programme notes. In an interview with George Scott, the manager modestly emphasised Spurs' good fortune in suffering so few injuries. When asked about buying players to better confront First Division football, he suggested he would keep faith in the players who had achieved promotion, justified by their strong Cup performances against First Division sides. 'If we can get what we want, we shall buy,' he responded, before adding 'but the idea of playing second fiddle is not always palatable to a player of ability,' strongly suggesting he would stick by those who achieved promotion. Scott called promotion 'The great moment of The Great Day in [Rowe's] life' and described how undemonstrative Rowe was, how he '...speaks mildly and laughs rarely.' 'My success is like one of those fantasies come true,' Rowe told him. Scott wrote of the risk the manager took when walking away from his 'pleasant and successful' job at Chelmsford to manage a club of star players whose directors and fans were frustrated by so many years in the Second Division 'wilderness'.

1950-51 Spurs staff pose with the Second Division Championship shield, Rowe at far right, seated.

Promotion had vindicated all Rowe's theories and, in Scott's words, 'Tottenham play with the selflessness of an orchestra.' The Spurs boss had guided the club back to the First Division for the first time since injury had left him a sad, helpless spectator 14 years' earlier, watching as his club tumbled back to Division Two.

With three more points required to clinch the Championship nearly 67,000 crowded into White Hart Lane to heap praise on Rowe's side before kick-off against Raich Carter's Hull City, but Carter had set his side up to play attractive soccer too, and in doing so achieved a scoreless stalemate. This was acceptable to Spurs' fans luxuriating in the knowledge they were now confirmed followers of a premier division club. The following day Preston (Tom Finney and all) visited. In celebration of the long-awaited return to the First Division the Enfield Central Band played and the players were publicly congratulated ahead of kick-off by Lord Morrison, Chairman Fred Bearman and Manager Rowe himself. Typically, following pomp and celebration, Spurs trailed in at half-time two goals behind where Rowe told his men: 'You're doing fine. Keep playing football and you'll pull it off.' Put under continuous and severe pressure the Preston defence began kicking into touch regularly. Finally Bennett pulled one back, setting White Hart Lane on fire and soon Medley, cutting inside from the left, let fly with a terrific shot to bring Spurs back to 2-2. Spurs were a goal and a point from clinching the title. Only minutes remained when Walters bravely dived to meet the ball with his head. He made contact just before cannoning into a defender. Laying unconscious and black-eyed on the pitch, he was unaware of the delirious roar inside the stadium, hats flying in the air. The Second Division Championship had gone to Tottenham at Rowe's first attempt. His first-season success at Chelmsford had been followed by immediate promotion on taking charge at his beloved White Hart Lane.

After just a day's rest, and with the job already done, Spurs then came away from the return at Boothferry Park, Hull, pointless. Indeed, they were to come away pointless from four of the final five fixtures, which became mere exhibitions for a side which already had the Championship in the bag. The 61 points total they had nevertheless garnered was still two points higher than the average Championship-winning total during those times (before two points for a win was raised to three in 1981). Indeed, those remaining games had been made more difficult by injuries to Nicholson, Withers and Baily, while Clarke had gifted Grimsby their winning goal and two of their conquerors had still been in the hunt for promotion themselves.

Yes, a little of the gloss had been rubbed off the presentation of the Second Division Championship shield by Arthur Drewry, President of the Football League but Rowe could still say it was one of the happiest days of his football life, hoping Spurs would '…deliver the goods' year after year. In his speech, Drewry said that no team had been more worthy of the honour and terminated his speech as follows:

'1900 Spurs won the Southern League Championship. In 1901 they won the Cup for the first time. In 1920 they won the Championship of the Second Division. In 1921 they again lifted the Cup. In 1950 they topped the Second Division. In 1951…'

At that point Drewry's words were drowned by a great burst of cheering, the implication of what he was about to forecast clear to all. In his own after-match speech in the recreation room, captain Burgess said he hoped for another celebration next season '…when we win the League Championship or the Cup—or both!' This brought a big smile from his manager. Burgess said it was the manager who deserved the bulk of praise, '…for it was his spirit and inspiration, reflected on the field by the wonderful fellowship of all the players I was privileged to skipper, that made us into the "team of the season", as the soccer writers described us.'

But even at this moment of extreme triumph, joy and tremendous optimism, the *Herald* were oddly compelled to emphasise Spurs' capture of only 18 points from their last 16 games: 'This does not seem the kind of form that will set the First Division on fire.' Reading this one is surprised the manager did not resign on the spot. Clearly it was deemed by the editor to be a suitable response to Rowe's Spurs having won the Second Division Championship with five games to spare, with the best defensive record in the entire Football League, and masterminded a new unbeaten Club record. What level of miracle could command positive treatment in the *Herald*? Were they in thrall of certain club directors opposed to Rowe?

Spurs still faced two very tough final away games and lacked Withers, Nicholson and Baily as they travelled to top-half side Swansea. This was followed by the truly difficult prospect of taming Sheffield Wednesday, who were fighting arch rivals Sheffield United for the other promotion places. After the dry surface at White Hart Lane of the previous week, the Vetch Field pitch was muddy, and this time the Spurs' short-passing game suffered. Swansea played their best football of the season and only splendid work by Ditchburn in goal and Ramsey, Clarke and Willis ahead of him, kept the home side to their eventual, one-goal victory. Having long-since polished off the Second Division Championship there could be few better occasions to lose four games on the trot. However, a full strength Spurs then turned-in a great performance at Hillsborough, in a game played at a furious pace, and would have won but for poor finishing. This led to an extremely fortunate goalless draw for Sheffield Wednesday, the point proving enough for them to join Spurs in the First Division.

It should be noted that ever since Arthur Rowe lifted Spurs out of the second level of English football, the Club has spent only one season outside the top flight of English football. There is absolutely no doubt that Rowe's immediate success of 1950, gained not with investment in players but a change of tactics, should be permanently recognised at the splendid new 'Tottenham Hotspur Stadium', preferably in the form of a statue, or at least in the form of a bust to partner that of his pupil, Bill Nicholson. Yet that summer of 1950 Rowe still had greater glory to achieve for the 'Lillywhites'.

Despite results faltering once promotion was assured, Spurs were still all of four victories ahead of Wednesday (today that would translate into a whopping 12-point advantage). Commentators more astute than those employed at the *Herald* were brimful of praise. Ivan Ponting emphasised that when Rowe arrived Spurs had been only a 'tolerably enterprising but unexceptional second-flight outfit.' The *Playfair Football Annual* called Rowe's Spurs '…the perfect football machine.' Maurice Smith of *The People* described Rowe's side as 'Those streamlined, supercharged Spurs whose secret lies in their ability to reduce soccer to its simplest equations—and to work them out at top-of-the-class speed and accuracy', while *The Sunday Telegraph*'s John Moynihan wrote: 'Tottenham had lain dormant and forgotten in the Second Division since the war, but the arrival of Arthur Rowe as manager changed their history.'

Leading scorers in 1949-50 had been Medley on 19 and Duquemin, Walters and Bennett on 16 each. Spurs' total of 81 League goals was 14 ahead of second-placed Sheffield Wednesday, while Rowe's 'revolution' had created club record attendances, the average of 54,405 topping the entire Football League. Nearly 7,000 more fans per game had seen Spurs than during the previous season, gross receipts at White Hart Lane were the highest in the club's history. It would not be the last occasion when Rowe and his style of football produced a sizeable increase in a football club's attendances. Meanwhile Arthur himself gave most of the credit for his side's promotion to Alf Ramsey, '…one of the best full-backs I have ever watched, a nicer fellow never walked, a grand influence on-and-off the field.' In the space of twelve months the rookie Southern League boss was now to compete face-to-face with the likes of Matt Busby of Manchester United, Stan Cullis of Wolves and Tom Whittaker of Arsenal.

Before the summer break a Spurs' touring party set off on May 6th for matches in Germany and Belgium. Almost exactly a year earlier Italian champions Torino had perished in an air disaster returning from a friendly in Lisbon. This was so fresh in everyone's mind that the Spurs' party travelled in three separate groups, insured for nearly £400,000. This was followed in the first week of June by a promotion celebration held at the Savoy Hotel where the Marquess of Londonderry praised Rowe as '…that wizard of football,' adding that the club owed their manager a debt they could never repay. Spurs' Chairman Bearman responded, calling Rowe '…the manager of the year who has managed the team of the year.'

Meanwhile there was little rest for Spurs' England trio of Baily, Ramsey and Nicholson, plus the uncapped Ditchburn, who then travelled with the rest of the England World Cup squad for the tournament starting in Brazil on June 14th. With

THE ULTIMATE DREAM: MANAGING SPURS 1949-50

Rowe opens new Spurs' Supporters' Club premises, supported (right) by captain Ron Burgess and Les Bennett.

Spurs thus providing more players than any other single club (despite being a Second Division club when the squad was selected), the *Herald* expressed the reasonable concern that they could suffer in the upcoming season due to too much summer football. The newspaper also blindly shared the commonly-held home expectation that the England side, despite qualifying only by overcoming the much smaller home nations, would go far in the competition (for the sad truth, see Chapter 13). Nicholson was a non-playing reserve, while Baily only featured in the 1-0 defeat by Spain. Alf Ramsey, on the other hand, endured all three World Cup encounters and once famously replied with rare humour to someone who asked if he had played in the USA disaster in which England lost 1-0 to a hotchpotch of part-time players representing a country without a professional league: 'Yes, and I was the only bloody one who did!' Within seven weeks the England four would run out to play First Division football against Blackpool and the great Matthews.

That summer Arthur Rowe opened the Spurs' Supporters' Club. Meanwhile a quote of his appeared in an official publication, *The Spurs of 1950*: 'There is understanding and goodwill, with everyone connected with the club that now entitles me to say that Tottenham are indeed, a happy club.'

But could it remain so?

9

Push, Run and Succeed

ROWE: HIS METHODS AND BELIEFS

'You play nineteen-twentieths of the game without the ball and that's when you do your thinking. That's when you do your real playing.'

ROWE, *ASSOCIATION FOOTBALL* 1961

With his first season as a League manager and his first championship in the bag, this is an appropriate moment to review Arthur Rowe — the man, the tactician, the man-manager and the pattern of play for which he is most associated — and the state of English football at the time.

Rowe viewed an eleven-player team as a single force, rather than a collection of individualists. As footballer-turned-journalist Eamonn Dunphy put it, the pre-Rowe period was a time '…when managers sat in their offices and the best players made it up as they went along… skilful forwards faced powerful defenders in a series of personal battles.' Visiting the UK to play exhibition games at the end of the Second World War (see Chapter 7), the Moscow Dynamos surprised witnesses with a style similar to 'push-and-run', leading football columnist and author Brian Glanville writing '…their football was …a triumph of socialism over individualism'. As with 'push-and-run' everyone works for the common good. Rowe disagreed with fellow managers who told new players to '…just play your own game, son', believing instead that a new man should adjust and conform to the team's methods.

ENGLISH FOOTBALL WHEN 'PUSH-AND-RUN' ARRIVED To fully grasp why Rowe's Spurs took English football by storm (and set the club on its current path today) it is necessary to understand the prevailing English approach at that time. The sport had graduated from individuals simply trying to dribble or force their way through until, from around the 1870s, team members began passing it to each other to achieve the same aim. Passing had previously been considered 'unmanly'. Later came the short-passing of Glasgow's Queen's Park, Newcastle United and the 'Wembley Wizards' of Scotland in the late 1920s. All, directly or indirectly, influenced Rowe.

OFFSIDE CHANGE AND CHAPMAN'S THIRD BACK By the time Rowe returned as manager at White Hart Lane in 1949 the English game remained rooted in Chapman's response to the offside rule change (see Chapter 3). Three to four attackers (two wingers, the centre-forward and occasionally one inside-forward) were outnumbered by six 'defensive' opponents (three backs plus two defensive half-backs and one deep inside-forward). Unlike Rowe, whose core belief was to win, not just draw, utilising an entertaining, crowd-pulling style, the mantra at Arsenal was 'what we have, we hold'. At the first whistle they had one point. If they retained it, their points tally increased. A second point was a bonus they achieved mostly with a reliance on breakaways. However, for less-talented sides aping Chapman's approach, their hasty, booted clearances rarely found a colleague and, on the occasions they did, that colleague would lack the mobility and control of Arsenal's Alex James and most likely turn possession over to the opposition. Therefore physique, height and/or speed became more sought-after than skill. Willy Meisl recognised that 'in two out of every three attempts [the ball from deep] would go straight to an opponent or over the touchline.' The game became more about power and running. Indeed, by the mid-1950s, Matt Busby complained that English players could be sorted into three categories:

(a) The POLICEMAN — whose main task was to prevent his opponent from utilising his skills.

(b) The GREYHOUND — who chased any ball sent ahead of him and, should he reach it, cross it in the general direction of the goal.

c) The BULLDOZER — a player simply capable of boring, blasting or blundering his way down the middle, forcing the ball through any obstacle toward the goal.

These, Busby sadly realised, were the kind of men most in demand at that time. Goal chances began to come as much through defensive error as craft and skill, while a development on what became known as 'Route One' or 'Kick-and-Rush'

Rowe braves the summer sun to get his point over in pre-season.

was, in modern parlance, to play the ball long '…into the channels'. This often led to a desperate chase by forwards who would try to catch up with the ball before a defender reached it or it ran out of play, denying the public more intelligent, sophisticated football.

At the time of writing, a change for the good is finally sweeping through the English game as the likes of Guardiola, Klopp and Arteta inspire younger coaches. Yet even at the end of the 20th Century spectators still required considerable patience if they hoped to experience Arthur Rowe's 'electric shock' (see Preface). The majority of English clubs persisted in hitting long balls from defence, most being comfortably claimed by the defending team, with the ball shepherded back to the goalkeeper who launched it back down-field. There were exceptions, of course. Brian Clough would never accept that approach from his Derby County or Nottingham Forest trophy-winning sides. One consequence of hitting long balls out of defence is that the player responsible can take a short physical and mental break. 'Push-and-run', on the other hand, requires that all eleven players are permanently alert and mentally involved in the progress of the game.

A 21st Century Premiership contest between managers Tony Pulis (then at Crystal Palace) and Sam Allardyce (West Ham), saw periods when defenders on both sides happily smashed clearances from end-to-end which had three benefits for the teams as it kept the players' limited ball skills unexposed, lifted responsibility from their shoulders and kept an ill-informed majority of each club's fans happy that danger has been averted. Meanwhile the other 20 players remained spectators. Hunter Davies quoted Spurs' defender Phil Beal advising a team-mate who was getting flak from fans for misplaced passes. He told him to momentarily forget short-passing and just bang the ball up-field, saying, 'A belted ball doesn't look as bad if it goes to one of their men, but a short pass which goes to an opponent looks diabolical.' Even today, few fans resist shouting 'Clear it!' when fearing the breakdown of a short-passing defensive move.

ATTACKING FROM THE BACK / TOTAL FOOTBALL   Prior to 1992 a goalkeeper could still collect a back-pass by hand, so many matches became a procession of fly-kicks from one penalty box to the other. Even 40 years' earlier Rowe had encouraged Ted Ditchburn to use a short, half-volleyed kick or, better, an accurate, targeted throw, to ensure the ball arrived at a colleague's feet and an attack commence. Thankfully, enlightened coaches today select goalkeepers as much for their confidence on the ball as for their agility and safe hands.

Twenty years after Rowe's side had been building from the back, little had changed in the English game when Fourth Division Mansfield striker Ray Clarke left to play for Ajax, where he suddenly found himself hitting 38 goals in one season. As Clarke has said, in the lower leagues in England the game had all been '…bang it up to the front.' At Ajax, with play starting from the back, it was technically, said Clarke, '…a different planet.' But with Clarke so successful at Ajax that he ended up in their Hall of Fame, it comes as little surprise that his career had begun under Bill Nicholson at Spurs, where he told *Back Pass* magazine, 'it was all "push-and-run" and play to feet'.

DEBUNKING LONG BALL THEORY   The Wolves team managed by Stan Cullis, at its peak between 1953 and 1960, was the most often quoted English long-ball side. Cullis appeared to have less confidence in his players hitting three (successive) passes to cover a distance of 50 yards than for one of his players to hit the target with a single long pass. As this contradicts Rowe's theory, that a series of 15-to-20 yard passes are a safer way to ensure possession is retained, one can but assume Cullis had less faith in those players at his disposal to play and control short passes than did Rowe. I would suggest Cullis rarely expected a long pass to be controlled by his player, assuming it just as likely that an opposing defender, under pressure, would miscontrol it, thereby surrendering possession to his strikers. Cullis also feared that the short-passing approach kept the ball outside the 'scoring zone' for too long. Similarly he wanted the ball in his own side's defensive zone for as short a time as possible. So the midfield was bypassed.

Cullis's lieutenant on the pitch was Bill Slater, who took basketball as an example of how a sport with little physical contact and always played in ideal conditions, became predictable. Yet what greater predictability is there than sending long balls forward in soccer? Slater actually opposed summer football on the basis that better pitches would reduce the 'natural hazards' of winter conditions! He was happy to settle for the limitations of football performed under British climatic conditions than learn from nations who took the sport forward.

CHARLES REEP AND HIS DAMAGING STATISTICS   The statistics gathered by accountant Charles Reep were the driving-force behind the approach of the likes of Cullis and would come to mislead generations of English coaches during the remainder of the 20th century.

Reep had kept statistics when watching RAF games and those of the then struggling Fourth Division side Swindon Town in 1950. At the time Swindon were scoring only half as many goals as the teams finishing in first place, so they were hardly proficient goalscorers. Reep also included goals scored by Swindon's visitors, but as the away side they will mostly have engaged in 'smash-and-grab' goals involving few passes. Put simply, as the skill level of most of the games he recorded was low, players rarely attempted multiple passes for fear of surrendering possession, so his statistics unsurprisingly established that most goals resulted from a big boot down-field, most likely due to defensive errors in dealing with them. Reep's crusade thereafter sorely delayed progress in British soccer.

Even Charles Hughes, FA Director of Coaching, expressed the belief that 'the facts are irrefutable and the evidence overwhelming' that '…direct play is far preferable to that of possession football.' Hughes had a similar eye for misleading statistics as Reep. The reduction in goals scored in nine successive World Cup Finals led Hughes to deduce that '…football is not as good as it was', which ignored the higher quality of defending at that level and instead pointed the finger at a rise in possession football. These two men had presumably been sleep-walking while Rowe's short-passing, 'push-and-run' game had accounted both for Spurs *scoring* more goals than any other side in 1949-50 and also for Spurs *conceding* the fewest goals in the division. Spurs surrendered possession far less than sides mimicking

Chapman's Arsenal. After the dreadful error of appointing former Watford boss Graham Taylor as England manager, Hughes then brazenly announced: 'The Watford controversy [regarding Taylor's preference for the long-ball approach] is going to become the England controversy, because that is the way we are going to be instructing at coaching courses from now on.' One hopes the by-then elderly Rowe never became aware of this dismal intention. Journalist Jonathan Wilson has since shown that moves involving just three passes or less, Reep's preferred method, actually produce 'fewer' goals than moves of four passes or more.

Pep Guardiola's Manchester City, when winning the Premier League in 2017-18, averaged five passes per goal yet totalled 106 goals. Furthermore, moves with multiple passes often draw fouls leading to additional goals deriving from subsequent free-kicks or penalties, a factor Reep failed to include in his statistics. Significantly, too, sides confronted with teams who keep the ball moving tire far more quickly. When his Watford side lost 7-2 on aggregate to Sparta Prague in the UEFA Cup, Graham Taylor, as if to excuse his men, said of the Czechs: 'When you gave the ball away, they didn't give it back to you.' Clearly Sparta didn't play it long. Taylor had repeated the folly of Cullis about 25 years' earlier when his Wolves faced Barcelona in the European Cup. Future England manager Ron Greenwood: 'The Spanish side swallowed the long balls and spanked Wolves hard: four goals in Spain, five at Molineux. Wolves' percentage game suddenly looked poorly.'

Unlike Cullis, Rowe would have sought perfection no matter what industry he had been involved in (no doubt he will have been the perfect upholsterer had football not interfered). He might be criticised for aiming at perfection when pitches had nothing like the snooker-table evenness common to the Premier League today, but not for him the dependence on defensive error and physicality. In 1960 Rowe referred to the long-ball approach as 'a complete absence of common sense'. Possibly as part of a tit-for-tat between Rowe and the Wolves' manager, a quote from Cullis in his autobiography can be seen as a direct attack on Rowe's more sophisticated approach: 'I cannot stress too often my belief that people who talk of short passes and on-the-ground moves as the essence of good football do not help the progress of football in Britain.' Progress?

However, it shouldn't be thought that Rowe's methods completely outlawed a long pass. For example, he was happy for Ramsey to drive long balls for centre-forward Duquemin to use his chest to 'kill' or redirect them to the feet of attacking colleagues, which, said Rowe, allowed Spurs to '…build up from an advanced position.' He also advocated chip passes, as England manager Walter Winterbottom pointed out: 'Alf Ramsey was a man for judging a chip pass just over the head of a player into the direction of an on-running forward.' But, as Danny Blanchflower said, the margin of error increases incrementally the further a pass travels. Rowe himself said that if he had possessed players '…who could have kicked the ball fifty yards with exact precision all the time, perhaps I might have used that'.

A TEAM MOVING AS ONE   According to Johan Cruyff, 'Total Football' was based on dividing a team into four banks of players (including the goalkeeper as one bank), separated by gaps of 10-15 metres, i.e. a safe distance to move the ball between the banks, echoing Rowe's conviction, as recalled by both Vic Buckingham and Roy Summersby, who played in Rowe's promoted Crystal Palace side: 'That's something Arthur taught us, the team moves up-field together, and gets back together - you don't have these big gaps.' Palace's John Jackson told me how Rowe would utilise a piece of garden trellis to help illustrate 'push-and-run' having coloured bits of the trelliswork with a Biro to represent 11 players, he used it to graphically indicate how all the players should maintain their distance from each other.

THE DISMAL PREMISE Wolves' Bill Slater believed that to secure victory in soccer it was essential to first concentrate on avoiding defeat. Slater: 'If players attacked to open up their game in order to entertain spectators and without regard to winning, then this would threaten and ultimately destroy the competitive basis of their play.' Contradicting this, Matt Busby said in 1957: 'Good Continental teams will play football right from their own goalmouth, whereas most teams in the Football League desperately strive to get the ball as far as the halfway line before worrying about a constructive move.' Controlling the game by keeping possession, on the other hand, keeps the opponent on the back foot. Aspiring to retain the ball in the opponents' half is surely the greatest form of defence.

ENGLISH FOOTBALL'S INSULARITY By the mid-1950s in England there remained a lack of awareness of advances taking place on the Continent. Yet Peter Doherty, a strong, early proponent of coaching, had written of his involvement when Manchester City toured Germany in the late 1930s and City won only one of five games. 'Throughout the tour the Germans had … kept the ball on the ground, finding their men with carefully placed passes,' he recalled. After the war, when he was then playing for Derby in Czechoslovakia, Doherty recalled County being swept off their feet by the locals' '…fast, scientific football.' The Czechs had continually '…kept the ball on the ground', running '…intelligently into the open spaces'. This led Doherty to plead for youth coaching in the UK. As John Cartwright, who appears later in this book, has expressed it, Continentals played with a '…controlled, thoughtful approach, whereas ours [has tended to be] a fierce, fighting approach.' Rowe himself said that at the time of the Hungary defeat of England in 1953 (see Chapter 13) British football had gone back a decade: 'We had stood off from development, satisfied that the deployment of a totally defensive centre-half was the answer to everything. Other countries resisted this. They were irritated by it. They tried other ways of playing and we just buried ourselves in contentment.'

So, this was the state of English football when Rowe took up the reins at White Hart Lane. England was a nation whose football community frowned upon practicing with a ball, refused to accept it no longer led the soccer world and whose aspirations were relegated to kick, rush, bully and hope. Having successfully trialled his 'push-and-run' in the Southern League with Chelmsford, Arthur Rowe immediately 'pushed-and-runned' Spurs into England's premier division. Since then Spurs have remained a fixture in England's top flight (with one single season's blip) up until today.

THE THINKING BEHIND 'PUSH-AND-RUN'   Rowe considered there were three accepted ways to get the ball from one end of the field to the other:
(a) LONG BALL: this is too-often intercepted, or simply too difficult for the receiver to control under pressure from defenders. Also, defenders in the attacking side 'switch-off' momentarily as they follow the passage of the ball from a distance.
b) DRIBBLING: this requires a degree of individual genius (perfect ball control, a low centre-of-gravity, body-swerve and other trickery) and tends to be only spasmodically successful. Also, excessive dribbling leads to team-mates momentarily 'switching-off', losing their 100% concentration.
c) PASSING: with short-passing every player remains involved, constantly seeking space whilst keeping within safe passing distance, giving their teammate in possession several options to quickly move the ball on.

Rowe considered himself a player of average ability, one who worked to develop those attributes with which he was blessed. Rowe: 'Kids always imitate the stars of their era. Look at all the boy wingers who try to play like [Stanley] Matthews or [Tom] Finney. That style may be fine for a Finney or a Matthews, but for the vast majority of young 'uns it is all wrong. They just haven't got that natural body swerve and deceptive shuffle.' He added: 'The straightforward push-and-gallop past the back would bring 'em better results,' and added, 'as a player I really had no problem. I was just not gifted. But I could do one job simply and, I think, well. From my own experience I learned that it was better to concentrate on a player's strength than bang away at his weaknesses. Some have it — some will never have it. Yet nearly everyone can do at least something well.'

As ex-Spur Ralph Wetton told me: 'With Arthur Rowe's way of playing you could be just an ordinary footballer; if you could pass the ball accurately and were fit, then you got on.' Conversely others considered that only the most technically able could play 'push-and-run' successfully. Blanchflower held the view that 'push-and-run' '…took a lot of skill to conceive and perform', and Bill Nicholson too said '…you've got to have the players who can do it.' Years later, when Rowe inherited the management of lowly Fourth Division Crystal Palace, the question

Push… Run…Push… Run…Push…! [Reproduced from an early 1950's soccer annual]

on everyone's mind was '…could he succeed with 'push-and-run' as well as he had with top-level Spurs?'

To indicate just how efficient 'push-and-run' could be, Rowe's centre-forward Len Duquemin told Deryk Brown: 'We didn't hold the ball and we didn't dribble, that would have been fatal. After a while we became so confident that we could lay the ball off without looking.' Malcolm Allison, the innovative coach of late 1960s' Manchester City, emphasised the added importance of speed. Inspired by Rowe, Allison talked of a successful First Division side playing against a struggling side. The successful team pass the ball so quickly that on occasions they probably pass it unnecessarily, as it has become a confident habit. But if they allow that speed to drop, then '…their level will often sink to that of their inferior opposition.'

THE ORIGINS OF 'PUSH-AND-RUN' AND HOW TO COACH IT   Arthur Rowe recalled how when he went walking with pals as a boy, they would kick a ball against the walls of houses while walking along the pavement. '[People] told us to clear off, but that's how it started,' he said in 1986, adding, 'You just think what a kid does when he's playing with his mates in the playground at school. If he can't get past somebody, he flicks the ball against the wall and takes the rebound. That's exactly what we did.' Rowe modestly denied having invented 'push-and-run': '"Push-and-run" is as old as the hills. I tried to teach people the mechanics of it so that they could make it happen in any part of the field.' He realised that 'push-and-run' techniques were already employed, but only in brief spurts. 'At Tottenham,' he said '…we tried to make it happen all the time.' Rowe had first introduced his Spurs men to the idea by utilising the wall in the Spurs' car park. Then he paired each of them with a playing partner and told them to repeat the process using the partner instead of the wall. Once they all agreed it was feasible, Rowe told them, 'It's just as easy on the field if you *believe* it's easy.' Spurs' inside forward Eddie Baily said: 'We used to work in triangles and squares'. The 'wall' in Rowe's approach was player B supporting player A (the man on the ball). B probably has a defender pressing him hard from behind, so A would pass it sharply to feet. B, holding off the challenge, would play the ball first-time back to A who, by then, had moved into space.

Ralph Wetton confirmed this: 'In my early days as a footballer people used to say "Never pass to a man that's marked". Well, Arthur contradicted that, saying that's exactly *when* you want to pass it to him.' The great Tommy Lawton agreed with these principles: 'How on earth can you keep possession if you are going to pass it into an open space, so risking that an opponent will get to the ball before a colleague?' Also, with defenders drawn to the ball, space is freed-up for team-mates to run into. This can be witnessed regularly in Pep Guardiola's sides, a player suddenly finding himself in acres of space so his team-mate, with a first-time pass or flick, can play him in on goal or with a chance to cross accurately, unhindered by a defender. Opponents begin to feel outnumbered, confronting eleven players always in motion and always available to receive the ball. But the passes themselves needed to be short and quick to avoid interception. They also required space.

Rowe talked of space and its importance when in debate with Blanchflower and others: 'People often ask "How do you find the open space?" But what is an open space? It simply meant it was the advantage one of your own players gave you by being in an intelligent position to receive the ball. But that, of course, is one of the sure ways of creating an open space. If you give the ball to a man who is marked, move up for the return, and the return is made, you anchor the defender, who of necessity can't move away from the man you've given the ball to in case he keeps it. So you get the desirable position you are all looking for all the time, of two men playing against one. That is the set-up pass.'

Rowe took great interest in how much of a 90 minute game any single player had possession. He sometimes stated this as five minutes, at others only three. Rowe talked of a typical player who plays 85-87 minutes without the ball. That, said Rowe, 'is when you do your thinking. That's when you do your real playing. Any clown can play with the ball when he's got it. It's the good fellows who get into position to receive.' If anything, Rowe very much over-estimated the time an individual player spends on the ball. In the early 1960s Bernard Joy, watching a game featuring the two greatest English players of the period, creator Johnny Haynes and goalscorer Jimmy Greaves, measured the time each spent on the ball. Out of the 90 minutes, goal-poacher Greaves had the ball for less than two minutes but even Haynes, a busy and dominant midfielder who was always demanding the ball, was only in possession for 2 minutes and 42 seconds. However, as Rowe calculated, the average player possesses the ball ('possession' encompassing a lot of single touches in 'push-an-run') between 30 to 40 times, which, he said, no doubt with a twinkle in his eye, 'is not so discouraging'! Also, as Johan Cruyff wrote: 'It isn't the man on the ball who decides where the ball goes, but the players without the ball.' Bernard Joy backed this up, calculating that as many as '80 per cent of bad passes are due not to the kicker, but to his team-mates.' Players supporting the man on the ball should ask themselves the question: 'Can the ball see me?' In other words the ball should always (metaphorically) have a clear view of the supporting player. Furthermore, players without the ball should move toward the man in possession, not *away* from him, as tended to be common practice in the English game.

Meanwhile Rowe believed individual running with the ball slowed attacks, giving defenders time to regroup. An essential element of 'push-and-run' was speed which kept defenders off-balance. As Ferenc Puskás once said: 'The ball must be moved about quickly, preferably on first contact.' Rowe again: 'The only way you keep your formation and keep some organisation in your team is by the ball being moved from man to man, thereby playing everybody into the game rather than playing them out of it. One of the strongest things we tried to teach at Tottenham was that this formation has got to be preserved at all times. There [mustn't be] individual running with the ball until you came, roughly speaking, to the last thirty yards of the field, when you were within your opponents' last defensive zone. Then you could run.' Ralph Wetton confirmed that Rowe, while not unhappy for wingers to dribble or outpace their full-backs, preferred them to exchange wall passes with their inside-forward. The Medley - Baily left-side duo were notably effective in this way. Famed cricket journalist John Arlott once praised Rowe's Tottenham Hotspur: '[They] dribbled the ball little; yet the patterns of their passing were perpetually absorbing,' adding, 'it was simple but effective to remember that a wing-man who tried to run round a back with the ball stood a good chance of losing it.'

When Julian Holland compared Rowe's Spurs to Chapman's Arsenal, he commented: '"Push-and-run" goals are scored at as fast a pace and with as little warning as the "smash-and-grab" goals of Arsenal. But they are much more beautiful to watch.' Holland would have enthused similarly had he witnessed the dynamic beauty of Arsène Wenger's turn-of-the-Century Arsenal side or Guardiola's Manchester City. It is impossible to watch film of either side in action without identifying a link to Rowe.

TAKING PLAYERS' OPINIONS ON BOARD There were two players whose backing Rowe most appreciated. Ron Burgess would usually agree promptly with a proposal of Rowe's, whereas Ramsey might ponder a little, then say 'Yes, I think you are probably right.' Indeed, Rowe once told the BBC that when Burgess and Ramsey gave the green light to his plans, 'It was a tremendous reassurance to myself.' On one occasion Ramsey suggested to Rowe that Spurs start the next game slowly, and then begin to speed things up as they began to feel their feet, to which his manager responded: 'How will you know when the others have found their feet? How will you know when they have warmed up?' On reflection, Ramsey agreed, so Spurs continued setting-off at top speed. Rowe always preferred to set opponents back on their heels right from the kick-off, even if it did risk errors. Eddie Baily once told Norman Giller: 'We were the thinking man's team. Players like Alf, Bill Nick and Ronnie Burgess were obsessed with tactics, and of course dear Arthur Rowe was the man who led us with clear and concise instructions. There was no mumbo-jumbo.'

THE ORIGINS OF 'TOTAL FOOTBALL'? Before joining Spurs right-back Ramsey was accustomed to playing long, diagonal passes to his left winger, which took him periodically out of the action. Rowe, with his firm belief that long passes increased the chance of lost possession, instructed Ramsey to instead make 15-20 yard passes to his own right-winger, who came deeper to receive it. This ensured greater accuracy and kept Ramsey within supporting distance of his winger. This ploy also created a problem for the opposing full-back — should he follow the Spurs winger up the field, leaving space for exploitation behind him, or should he leave the winger unattended, free to receive the pass? Rowe: '[Alf] very soon himself saw the logic and the safety of kicking within his distance accurately.' Winger Walters was also happy as he became more involved. Left-winger Les Medley once explained another Rowe ruse regarding defending deep on the right. On those occasions he would sometimes surreptitiously move across to the right and rarely would someone go with him. Ramsey would pass it to the deep-lying Walters who would then first-time it to the unmarked Medley ahead of him. Eddie Baily said this ploy paid off many times, adding: 'Les [Medley] scores most of his from inside-right.' Of course, once a team had cottoned on to the ruse of Ditchburn throwing out to Ramsey, their left-winger would harass the full-back, who was compelled to play it back again to Ditchburn, whereby the left-winger would scurry after the ball only for Ditchburn to pick it off the winger's toes and throw it out, over the onrushing winger's head, back to Ramsey who could then launch an attack unchallenged. As an alternative, Ditchburn might throw it long to centre-forward Len Duquemin who would play it off instantly, to Baily or Bennett, so that 'push-and-run' could smoothly resume.

DEAD-BALL PLOYS   Never one to rest on his laurels, Rowe and sidekick Vic Buckingham now considered how more success might be achieved from free-kicks taken in deep, wide positions. A free-kick deep on the right would see Ramsey as the taker. Assuming the opposition's defenders would line up approximately 18 yards from goal, Rowe proposed that as Ramsey was on his run-up to the ball, all the Spurs attackers (facing the kicker), should move across from left to right, dragging defenders with them. As they did so, outside-left Les Medley would remain glued to the left touchline. Ramsey simultaneously sent his kick high toward the space in the left side of the penalty box vacated by the defenders, beyond the reach of the 'keeper. Into this space Medley would sprint at top speed to meet the ball with only the 'keeper to beat. This move required a lot of sustained and repeated practice. Rowe was so precise that he would time the flight of the ball to calculate how far Medley could run. This ruse often met with success, from free-kicks on both sides of the field, with his left-back the provider if taken from the left and outside-right Walters the likely scorer.

Likewise Ramsey recalled a lunch-time discussion one day when the paucity of goals from corner-kicks was discussed, so new ideas were tried, such as the short corner zipped to the feet of an inside-forward who would lay it back first-time into the path of an advancing wing-half to shoot from the edge of the box. This illustrates the intensity (for those times) with which Rowe studied his sport, seeking means of surprise to add to the already considerable potency of 'push-and-run'. 'We got a great deal of extra fun in trying to outwit the opposition,' wrote Ramsey, adding '…everything suggested by manager Arthur Rowe was not only aimed at achieving success, but making everyone thoroughly enjoy their football.'

DEFENDING   Rowe preferred his defenders to either intercept opponent's passes or quickly tackle before the receiver had the ball under control. Should either

A successful Rowe dead-ball ploy illustrated in the London 'Evening Standard'.

approach fail, they were to jockey the attacker long enough to ensure there were at least two defenders between ball and goal. Rowe was also an early exponent of 'pressing', saying 'It is vitally necessary for the success of this "defence in depth" method that the forwards and wing-halves, when beaten for possession, should never give up. They should chase the opponent with the ball, harrying and spoiling, to allow their own defenders to retreat in formation and cover the most likely goalscorers.' He preferred man-for-man marking, something centre-half Harry Clarke felt freed him '…from the doubts that worry many defenders.' Rowe also said '…a defence that retreats in formation is less vulnerable than a defence whose defenders advance towards the opponent with the ball.' As far back as 1951 Rowe wrote in the *FA Bulletin*: 'We believe, in short, that when in possession, all players are attackers, and when not in possession, then all players are defenders.' Very advanced thinking for the time.

Brought to Crystal Palace by Rowe at the age of 17, John Holsgrove recalled the manager emphasising '…that when you have the ball you [the team] have 10 attackers and when you have not, you have 11 defenders.' Clearly this is the root of 'Total Football', yet Dutch master coach Rinus Michels and Johan Cruyff are generally heralded as its innovators (see later in this chapter). The players of Pep Guardiola, today's pre-eminent practitioner of Rowe's style, are required to remain 100% focussed for 90 minutes, all concentrating on finding the space to receive a pass, and even looking ahead to the next pass, should the ball come their way. The man on the ball thus has the luxury of various options to find a team-mate, precisely that which sets the Rowe-to-Guardiola method apart from the long-ball enthusiasts. 'Long-ball' encourages players to periodically switch-off, becoming little more than spectators. On the contrary, when all ten outfield players move from end-to-end of the pitch, they remain too close to the action to take a mental 'breather.' This can be witnessed in TV clips of the great Liverpool sides of the 70s and 80s (often considered to have utilised Rowe's basic idea) — it is rare the entire 10 outfield players do not appear somewhere on the screen simultaneously, whether they are attacking, occupying the midfield, or defending their own penalty area. They always thus appear to outnumber their opponents.

As Vic Buckingham has confirmed, in certain situations the ball *could* be passed *back*, as long as the pass was sure to reach a team-mate. Rowe even encouraged this in Spurs' own goalmouth and despite how dangerous it could appear, they were rarely-if-ever punished for it and could then build another forward move. Opposing sides found 'push-and-run' a physical *and* mental challenge to handle when so many opponents were constantly on the move, seeking space.

Not that it wasn't mentally and physically demanding to its practitioners, too. It was essential that every member of the team believed in it and that they maintained concentration and energy levels throughout 90 minutes. Rowe told players new to the system that they should imagine themselves as members of a tug-of-war team: 'A good tug-of-war team can pull more than their own weight if they pull together and believe in themselves, thereby winning over a heavier, stronger team who are not so together and not so confident.' Eddie Baily once said 'We cannot afford to lose concentration for a second — we must know exactly where the others are in case we have to find them with a pass.' So, despite his love of 'push-and-run', Baily also found it exacting, and Tony Marchi told me it was mentally tiring, but added: 'It became like second nature.' The method clearly fits Jonathan Wilson's category of an abstract approach to playing the game of football. The English game had remained rooted for too long in the notion that, as Wilson puts it, '…heart, soul, effort, desire, strength, power, speed, passion and skill' are all you need to succeed — put the best eleven players out on the field and success will naturally follow. On the contrary, 'push-and-run' was colourfully described in a *Daily Telegraph* match report as '…for all the world like a wave gathering momentum as it races to the far distant shore', The writer adding '[Push-and-run] is all worked out in triangles and squares and when the mechanism of it clicks at speed… with every pass placed to the last refined inch… there is simply no defence against it.'

Rowe once said 'push-and-run' '…does not demand a special type of player. But everyone has to sink everything into the team for the sake of efficiency.' In Rowe's eyes it followed therefore that '…a team will "make" a player more often than a player will 'make' a team". Emphasising this, Rowe pointed out how only Duquemin and Clarke of his team had not been selected for representative games (from England 'B' side to full internationals), although Clarke's turn eventually came. Some players were required to alter their playing style more than others, particularly Burgess, 32 at the time. He had always enjoyed running with the ball and on one pre-Rowe occasion had dribbled around seven opponents before scoring, something he would not attempt under Rowe, who required the player to pay a little more heed to his defensive duties (Charles Buchan considered this 'team' over 'individual' approach turned players into mere 'cogs in a machine'). But there was a further benefit from foregoing individualistic play. When Rowe coached the entire playing staff to play 'push-and-run' a reserve player could easily step up for an injured colleague, smoothly fitting straight in, rather than bringing in a player whose individualism could disrupt the entire rhythm of the side.

In 1970 full-back Arthur Willis, reminiscing with Rowe, said 'Good days weren't they, Arthur? I wasn't really a player, was I? But I could play your way.' Rowe said this was the nicest compliment he had ever had. As Rowe said, 'The right method [of play] can make a bad player good, a good player very good, and a very good player great.' He himself numbered the great performers in his Spurs side as only 'two or three' - presumably Burgess and Baily plus Ramsey. 'Ramsey', said Rowe, 'became the dominant character of the team. But he in particular didn't start that way. He gradually changed himself to fit the picture.'

In a magazine article Rowe further justified his belief that 'push-and-run' could function with just three or four outstanding players when asking readers how many players in historically famous teams could they recall by name. For example, of the first 'Busby Babes' Manchester United side, most would select Roger Byrne, Bobby Charlton, Duncan Edwards and Tommy Taylor. In Rowe's view that small core of greats would inspire the rest. Author J T Bolton summed Rowe's Spurs of 1951 up when writing: 'You may shed a tear over the idea that in this football as played by the Spurs there is no place for the player who hangs on to the ball. But if you like thrills, if you like to have your breath taken away by the speed at which the ball travels from man to man, then watch the Spurs.' Even Stanley Matthews once spoke enthusiastically of Rowe's 'push-and-run' saying it '…was a purist passing game… it was an innovative style… and it worked.'

But a year or so later, Matthews' views were not so positive in conversation with Spurs winger Les Medley. They were watching a schoolboy match in which a wing hopeful was a good dribbler but usually failed to find a partner with his passes, which Medley blamed on the influence of Matthews. Matthews' riposte was that first-time passes were 'panic' passes, they were passes of players with no confidence in their own ability, which was of course nonsense. Medley added that an entire team interpassing and changing positions as in 'push-and-run' leaves all the opposing defenders guessing, not just the one full-back whose concern was Matthews. Medley ended with the definitive put-down, saying that, in effect, at Tottenham all the team engaged in creating scoring opportunites whereas at Blackpool they depended almost entirely on Matthews to provide them.

FOOTBALL MANAGEMENT   In a 1969 interview Arthur Rowe said the secret of his success as a manager was 'applied common sense', adding '…it is not what you have got; it is how you use it that counts. A great player can be completely wasted in a team if he is not used properly.' When praised for his managerial talents, Rowe's response combined both sharp criticism with humility: '50 per cent of the people in the [managerial] game are bluffers. So a decent manager is halfway there when he starts out.'

LUCK   Like Napoleon, who once said 'Ability, experience, and integrity were important; without luck they were useless', Rowe was extremely conscious of the significance of luck in running a successful football club. When once asked what was the most vital factor for football success, he surprisingly said 'The run of the ball' or 'the luck of the game, …you've got to have it.' Endeavouring to prove his point Rowe reviewed how luck played a big part in the case of individual players, for instance the career-ending injuries of old Tottenham colleagues such as Greenfield and Hall. He talked, too, of two players of his acquaintance who had played together for the England schoolboys team, one of whom signed for a wealthy and famous club, the other joining a club less wealthy and less famous. Playing in a poor side, one had been passed over several times for International selection. The other soon established himself internationally and won a Cup medal. Financially he had received three benefit payments from his club and supplemented that by using his fame to write a press column. Rowe considered both players would have progressed equally had they enjoyed similar opportunities so it could be seen that luck was the decisive factor. Rowe's belief might be applicable to individuals, but as far as football clubs are concerned, over a league season luck can rarely be seen as of primary significance. Luck will no doubt have occasionally turned against the likes of mid-20th Century Real Madrid during their five year dominance in Europe but the quality of their players, coaches, and organisation, plus, as Rowe conceded, character and courage, would, over five seasons, have overcome occasional ill-fortune.

COMMUNICATION SKILLS   As is obvious from the many examples in this book, Rowe's articulate verbal and written communication skills were unrivalled. Ralph Wetton, in conversation with the author, perhaps expressed it best: 'He could talk all day, Arthur, and not one of us would be asleep.'

RELATIONS WITH PLAYERS   Having played so long under Rowe, 'Double'-winning Spurs' boss Bill Nicholson was left with the conviction that honesty was the primary quality of a football manager, while columnist David Miller once wrote: 'Everything with Arthur was logical and simple, and all put across with an unaggressive modesty that was possibly his ultimate undoing.'

Rowe's character was well expressed in a celebratory booklet published by Spurs in commemoration of his first season as manager in 1950: 'That strong face, topped now by iron-grey hair, immediately gives out a feeling of confidence and the thought, "I can open out with this man". His forthrightness, intolerance of inefficiency, kindliness and ability to make an instant decision are bywords at Tottenham, and unknown and star alike rest content under his care. His philosophy is simple: "I treat the player as I myself like to be treated".'

One of few things Rowe was intolerant of related to sartorial matters. Ralph Wetton, recalling how the manager periodically stood by the players' entrance at 10 am just as they arrived for training said, 'He'd call you over and say "Have a hair cut next time before you come in," "Have a shave" — all that kind of thing!' Days or weeks would pass without further inspection, then suddenly Rowe would be there again, so, added Wetton '…you had to be on your toes all the time.' Players generally addressed him as 'Arthur' or, in the case of captain Ron Burgess at least, as the even more matey 'Art'. All those I have met who worked with him unfailingly held him in the highest regard, so despite addressing him with familiarity, he still commanded their respect.

When I asked Wetton if Rowe was strict enough, he said the manager could occasionally 'come down' on people but qualified that by saying, 'To me, he was ideal. He was compassionate, he'd listen to you.' Asked if he could recall a moment when Rowe reprimanded him, Ralph recalled his relegation to the 'A' team. Disgruntled, he retired to the billiards room and told teammates his sorry tale. One told him: 'I wouldn't have that, Ralph.' So he plucked up the nerve to see Rowe. 'I knocked on the door and he said "Come in", so I went in and Arthur was sitting at his desk, writing. He said "Oh, hallo Ralph, have a seat." So I sat there, and he looked up, so I started telling him what my grievance was. But he carried on writing. I'd worked out what I was going to say before I went in there. I was going to get straight to the point.' With no response, Ralph muttered on and on. Rowe finally put his pen down and tore Ralph off a strip, beginning: 'Now *I'm* going to tell *you*…!' so Ralph quietly left Rowe's office, chastened and with nothing achieved. But such moments were outweighed, recalled Ralph, by occasions when Rowe would call a player into his office and announce he was getting a pay hike when none had been requested, because '…he thought you deserved it.'

Spurs 'keeper Ron Reynolds said of Rowe: 'He wasn't afraid of his players, there was no insecurity, no paranoia about him, that he had to show he was the boss, as so many managers do.' Nicholson recalled: 'Most of the players [during Rowe's tenure] liked a pint of beer or a lager, but weren't big drinkers' while some, typically for the time, were heavy smokers, particularly, recalled Nicholson, Bennett, Willis, Ditchburn and Walters. One imagines Rowe was applying his acute sense of humour when giving a talk about managerial discipline in 1970. He said: 'If you are in charge of players, you let them do as you like!'

One thing Rowe would never do is either criticise or praise a player in front of team-mates. Rowe told Billy Wright just after his first season as Spurs' manager that at all times you have to treat footballers as individuals. 'You've got to work on a man-to-man basis and meet the lads on their own ground. One fellow might like a joke. Another may have serious inclinations and might resent leg-pulling. A manager, I think, has to study such things and really get to know the fellows with whom he is dealing.' A prime example of Rowe's approach to handling players was related by Ralph Wetton. 'Every Tuesday night we used to play darts in one of the local clubs. Not all the team played: Ramsey never went, nor did Bill Nic. But Ron Burgess, Ted Ditchburn, Arthur Willis and Sonny Walters were among those who played. We'd have a good night and the next morning you'd see these lads training, despite all this beer they'd drunk. During a spell of poor results Arthur asked one day: "How's the darts going?" and someone said: "We've packed it in." His response was "Well, get it going again." He was like that. He used to put his finger on things.'

One thing which did test Rowe's patience was any occasional bypassing of 'push-and-run'. Tony Marchi confirmed to me that Rowe demanded all the club's sides play 'push-and-run' and recalled a 9-0 Reserves' victory over Swindon early in the manager's reign which Marchi himself had taken part in. The following morning all those who had played were summoned individually to Rowe's office at White Hart Lane. 'One-by-one he gave us such a bollocking, because we were not doing 'push-and-run'. Arthur said "I don't care about the score, the way you played was terrible – no 'push-and-run', nothing!"' 'So he could be angry, then?' I asked. 'Oh, yes!', Tony replied with conviction.

A tribute to Rowe from his players appeared in the 1950 celebratory Tottenham booklet: '[Arthur] is a man's man. Understands the game from the manager's and player's angle. His tactics have proved sound and easy to follow. His efforts have built a fine team spirit and he has earned our respect both as "Arthur" and the

"Guv'nor." He takes a licking far better than we players and has the happy knack of giving a word of sympathy or encouragement at the right time. He always seems to be able to pick out the strengths and weaknesses during the course of the game. Despite his long experience of football, he is still happy and content to learn.' However, Rowe's apparent ability to deal with defeat was almost certainly a deception, intended to take the pressure off his disappointed players. From his later health problems it might be deduced that to maintain morale he internalised the anguish he suffered when things went badly.

TEAM SPIRIT   An end-piece to a 1950 promotion booklet article had Rowe praising the '…unity of desire, a unity of purpose and method,' and the '…understanding and goodwill, with everyone connected with the club.' He continued: 'I see no real and lasting success, for any team, that is not representative of a happy club,' describing team spirit as that abstract quality which makes ordinary teams good, and good teams great. So many of his similarly sincere, deeply-held convictions might be transferred to almost every walk of life. Ron Burgess recalled that Spurs in Rowe's time was a supremely happy club and '…the man who did more than anyone to promote that happy family spirit was Arthur Rowe himself.' Alf Ramsey recalled that when he first joined Spurs he soon realised he was working for a quiet but determined manager (not unlike how Ramsey himself would become), while journalist and Pegasus player David Miller wrote that Rowe '…had a way of talking football which I can only call the Horlicks manner – he made players feel calm, relaxed, adjusted, and able to sleep better!'

TEAM SELECTION   Rowe once said: 'I always tell young managers the same thing. At the start of the season pick your best team, write it down on a piece of paper and tuck it away in a drawer. Halfway through the season, if things are going wrong, dig out the piece of paper and look at the names because the first team you pick each season is always your best team.' In other words, give it another chance. Clearly, Double-winning Spurs boss Bill Nicholson learned this lesson of Rowe's as evidenced from a conversation with Hunter Davies in 1972: 'You should always know at any time what is your best team and you should stick to it,' adding the equally important factor (ignored with today's squad system) that 'It's only through playing together that a team can get better.'

In 1946 Rowe pointed out something which has become even more critical for modern-day managers to confront: the handling, with understanding and encouragement, of those players who do not find their names on the team sheet. Rowe said '…no player likes watching', something he identified as an understandable cause for discontent. To combat this he would explain the situation to the individual concerned and not leave him forever benched to sit and watch, instead giving him occasional opportunities to play. Certainly most players enjoyed working with him and few ever wanted away.

The 21st Century English Premier Division, with its lack of regular, competitive reserve leagues and large squads of top-level performers, many left to sit matches out week-after-week, would have been a deplorable situation for the considerate

Rowe. His aims in those more innocent times, were purely and simply to '…give all players a "fair break"'.

BEYOND FOOTBALL   When he re-encountered Rowe on his return to manage Spurs in 1938, Peter McWilliam said something to him which implied that, politically speaking, he thought Rowe had '…become a red.' Yet, in the summer of 1950 Rowe reacted strongly to news that Clement Attlee's Labour Government was considering setting up a Ministry of Sport. Rowe responded: 'If the Government thinks that by the establishment of a Ministry of Sport, which would ultimately control professional as well as amateur sport in the country, they would increase efficiency and raise the standard of football overnight, they are as mistaken as they were when they nationalised some of British industries and her transport undertakings.' Yet the actual basis for the Government's plan had actually been to ensure greater national success in international sports with proposals to invest in sporting facilities and coaching.

FITNESS   In 1950 Rowe said: 'I always believed, when I played for the Spurs, that I knew better than anyone else when I was thoroughly fit. Our late trainer, George Hardy, also shared my view, and I shall always insist that a professional footballer, with his living depending upon his being in the best possible condition, will go all out to achieve this fitness without anyone chasing behind him telling him what to do, and, most annoying of all, *what not to do*.' Viewed from today's world, Rowe's liberal approach seems naive — achieving fitness to the levels required to play 'push-and-run' surely required all team members to achieve a common level of fitness. One unfit player and surely the system would flounder. However, one eye-witness to Rowe's training sessions when he later managed Crystal Palace, assured me the players had never been fitter.

CATCHPHRASES   As an ex-player himself Rowe could speak the players' vernacular, as when he criticized (albeit humorously) a fashionable coaching phrase of the time (probably Walter Winterbottom's): 'peripheral vision'. Rowe translated this for his players as: '…seeing out of your arse'. Remaining with that part of the anatomy, Ron Greenwood once described his brilliant but sometimes languid West Ham midfielder Trevor Brooking as casual and lethargic. To further convey this tendency, Greenwood quoted Rowe's expression 'He needed a squib [firecracker] up his backside'! In similar vein Rowe described the busy, scampering Johnny Byrne as a 'midfield kerfuffler' ('kerfuffle', according to the dictionary, being 'a state of noisy, confused activity'), and on another occasion as '…a fiddle-arsed midfield player.'

But Rowe became more renowned for the short, simple, memorable expressions or mottoes he used to convey his basic soccer principles to players, such as:

'Make it simple, make it accurate, make it quick' [sometimes shortened to 'Make it simple, make it quick'].

'A good player runs to the ball, a bad player runs after it.'
'He who holds the ball is lost.'
'A rolling ball gathers no moss.'
'When not in possession, get in position.'

Arthur would pin some of these instructional phrases on the walls of the White Hart Lane dressing-room and Eddie Baily recalled that they would occasionally be chanted aloud by players during practice matches. Ron Greenwood himself may have picked-up on Rowe's use of catchphrases, using such as 'Simplicity is genius' (which sounds like a Rowe hand-me-down). Rowe added several similar catchphrases in the Crystal Palace FC rule book he produced in the early 1960s (see Chapter 18), while an advertisement placed in the Crystal Palace programme for Arthur Rowe's testimonial game featured a cartoon in three stages humorously illustrating another of Rowe's pronouncements:

'If we make space... we get time... and time means space!'

Bill Nicholson believed Rowe's slogans were necessary: 'You have to keep reminding players what they should be doing, because few of them are capable of acting instinctively.' One imagines Rowe explaining this rather more tactfully. According to Steve Perryman, Bill Nicholson came up with 'Play the way you are facing,' and 'When the ball dies, you come alive.' He has also been credited with 'The man without the ball makes the play'.

Bernard Joy wrote appreciatively that Rowe's 'make it simple, make it quick,' applied to the manager's instructions as well as to the team's play on the field.

REFEREEING   While he could be critical of refereeing standards, around the time of his greatest successes Rowe said: 'To get hot and bothered in disagreement with decisions we cannot alter anyway is really a waste of time—however annoying the incidents may seem. The whistle is the law.' Ron Greenwood thought on similar lines, saying '[Referee's] decisions were matter-of-fact; like the weather or the ground conditions, they had to be accepted.' Certainly it would have been way below the dignity of Rowe to throw tantrums in front of the fourth official, behaviour often enacted by today's managers if a 50/50 throw-in near the halfway-line has gone against their side. After all he had learned to play to the whistle the hard way. Playing for Spurs one afternoon he stopped after his own full-back had appeared to foul his opposing winger. The linesman had flagged but the referee, seeing the winger recover, allowed play to continue. The cross which followed was about to be met by the opposing centre-forward's head when Arthur plucked the ball out of the

air with his hands. Only then did the referee blow his whistle… for a penalty! 'I'll never forget the look our goalkeeper gave me,' recalled Rowe.

At a London Society of Referees meeting in 1955 Rowe supported a Russian idea that only the captain of a side should be allowed to query the referee's decisions and a proposal of his own was that matches should be refereed by regular teams of officials (the referee and two linesmen), always working together, game-after-game. Other Rowe criticisms still pertain 60 years later: the lack of consistency between referees; the referee who fussily asks for the ball to be moved six inches before a free-kick can be taken, and the one who stops a free-kick from being taken quickly. Late in his managerial career, speaking to another referees' group, he told them to '… be firm but not ostentatious,' adding '…don't make players look chumps or they'll start to play like chumps and act like them.' In those days of amateur referees, he was an early proponent of full-time officials: 'How can you expect a man who has been working all the week to go out on to a field on a Saturday and keep up with men who have been training all week for that particular thing?' He said this in

Rowe addressing a referees' group.

October 1960 — it took another 41 years before referees gave up their five-day-a-week occupations to referee full-time.

POSSESSION FOOTBALL   As late as 2013 much-travelled manager Harry Redknapp complained about English football's continuing reliance on 'prehistoric' tactics: 'We desperately need coaches who believe in retaining possession.' Former England and Barcelona coach Terry Venables commented in the 1990s: '…[English] teams tended to tire in the final ten minutes, but if they kept the ball and passed it, they would conserve their energy right through to the end, while the opposition would tire having had to chase around to try to recover possession.' But it also required pace and incisiveness.

In 1990 Bryan Robson suggested an unfamiliarity with the benefits of possession football when talking about his revelation when playing for England: 'It's harder to get the ball back once you lose it.' Yet Johnny Haynes, a predecessor as captain of England, had been promoting possession football nearly 30 years earlier: '…always [at Fulham] we try to keep that ball busy, keep it moving around. Forward or backward is of less importance, provided it is moving and we keep possession.' Around the same time Rowe commented that '…the side that has the ball has got the advantage. And when one fellow has it there are ten fellows in his team who haven't, and it is up to the ten to get into the best positions they possibly can to receive it from the one who has.' He ended with the statement that the play of his Spurs side '…was based on the belief that possession of the ball is all that matters and you are better off with the ball in your own penalty box than to have the ball in the opposition's penalty-box with two players fighting for it.' A direct jibe at the prevailing long-ball approach of that era.

SUMMING-UP   Writing of the two leading English club sides at the time when Rowe arrived on the post-war coaching scene, Manchester United and Arsenal, Julian Holland explained that: 'United had played with five interchanging forwards (an 'unorthodox orthodoxy'), playing off-the-cuff rather than to a pre-set strategy; [while] Arsenal had added further pages to their authoritative chapter on defence.' Holland continued: 'But Tottenham were writing something new. And the handwriting was that of their manager, Mr Arthur Rowe. It was a new science of attack, a new conception of attacking football.' Edward Grayson wrote in the *FA News* that Rowe '…re-thought and resurrected for English football the then decaying concept of attack, without which it will forever wither and die.'

10

'Push-and-Run' Conquers England's Best

MANAGING SPURS 1950-51

'The Tottenham Hotspur team …established a new benchmark for tactical sophistication with a brand of football that brought a dash of colour to a monochrome postwar world.'

TIMES OBITUARY OF EDDIE BAILY 2010

In the summer of 1950, with the joy and anticipation of the White Hart Lane faithful knowing no bounds, neutrals questioned whether 'push-and-run' could succeed in the top flight of English football. The *Daily Mirror* confidently stated that Rowe's 'same recipe' would '…bring fresh triumph to the club and greatly increase the distinction of football throughout the First Division.' Rowe encouraged his men in pre-season, telling them: 'If you try a thing once and it's good, you try it again.' But wouldn't First Division sides tackle sharper? Wouldn't they anticipate faster? Might they not suffocate Spurs' sparkling forward motion by sheer numbers?

Yet Eddie Baily recalled the confidence of his teammates, while the manager himself was convinced his side would not be disgraced. Arthur Rowe did however come up with an astute idea to focus his players on how 'push-and-run' might be nullified by opponents. He asked them each to imagine they themselves were opposing 'push-and-run', giving them each a week to suggest how to counter the system. The resulting consensus was: 'Drop away, give [Spurs] the midfield, drop away, drop away…'. But Rowe had no desire to adjust his side's attacking style, saying '"Real" football plays a greater part in this league. In the Second Division it is more of a fight.' His confidence was boosted by how his side had dispatched First Division Sunderland and Stoke from the Cup and how only a debatable penalty had seen Spurs succumb to Everton.

Rowe then sold Billy Rees to help fund his £18,000 capture of inside-forward Peter Murphy from Second Division Coventry City. Murphy, described by Rowe as having 'no frills', was a good passer and a handy scorer. Another newcomer was 'keeper Ron Reynolds, who only arrived due to a typical Spurs' part-exchange deal, yet proved to be a quality back-up for Ditchburn. Rowe also, finally, got 17-year-old apprentice half-back Tony Marchi's signature on a professional contract. However, one other local boy got away from Rowe that summer, one who would become a very big fish indeed. The snub-nosed 15-year-old's performance in an 8-2 English Schoolboys victory over Scotland at Wembley that previous spring had caught Rowe's eye. The manager considered the boy a very good player, '…who plays

'Make it simple, make it quick' is the Spurs' recipe for success

In Epping Forest the players enjoy Rowe's lecture as they anticipate First Division football in season 1950-51.

our type of football.' He admired his quick movement and knack of finding the open spaces. The lad had even spent much time playing football in Jubilee Park, a couple of miles north of White Hart Lane. Despite his excellent dribbling skills, his 'Rowe-disciple' coach, a Mr Sanders, told the boy dribbling wasted time and energy. The boy was Johnny Haynes, who would be captaining the full England side 12 years' later when he recalled: 'Mr Sanders showed me the light' by proving '...that the ball can run faster than the man, that "send it, don't take it" was a sound football philosophy... the only real basis for quality football at all levels.' Haynes' team even occasionally practised at White Hart Lane, receiving coaching from the likes of Baily, Ditchburn and Duquemin. Despite a personal passion for Arsenal, Haynes was surely guaranteed to play a future role in Rowe's soaring Spurs. Haynes described Rowe visiting his parents one Sunday afternoon. 'He was kind and straightforward. I would go on the ground staff, train with the top players, be taught and coached by them and get every chance to develop.' Haynes' father told Rowe his son would decide, 'It is his own life.' He then took his boy to meet Arsenal manager Tom Whittaker, but a tour of Highbury backfired, the surprisingly insecure boy overwhelmed by its luxury. He later wrote: 'I could not see myself getting through to the top at Arsenal with all those star players.' So surely he would jump at Rowe's offer? No. Instead he joined unfashionable First Division strugglers Fulham, choosing the time-consuming daily commute from North to South-West London.

Johnny Haynes proved to be the first of two outstanding young English discoveries to slip through Rowe's clutches. When I asked Tony Marchi, who played alongside Haynes in the Edmonton Schools side, why he thought the boy turned down Arsenal and Spurs for Fulham, he responded: 'All I can say to you is something happened that we shouldn't be talking about. It's got to be.' Bill Nicholson was certain that Spurs themselves offered no financial inducements to parents during his own, later term as manager of Spurs and strongly believed they hadn't done so before. Over time and in common with fellow managers such as Ted Fenton at West Ham, Rowe would watch a procession of up-and-coming talent slip through his hands. Frustratingly, Haynes later wrote enthusiastically about the "short" football Fulham played, adding '…we always try to keep that ball busy, keep it moving around.' So there is little doubt Haynes could have been the ideal fulcrum around whom Rowe could have rebuilt his side in later years.

Meanwhile, perhaps recognising that few of his reserves were strong enough when needed in the first team, Rowe was encouraging the strongest candidates to improve their versatility. In this way they could fill-in for the first team to avoid, as the *Herald* bluntly put it, '…bringing in a weak reserve.' Off the field the recent ending of petrol rationing had led Spurs to extend the fans' car park to meet greater demand from motorized fans, yet, with players' pay remaining strictly controlled under the Football League's maximum wage regulations, few of Rowe's players themselves could afford private cars. On match days Eddie Baily took the bus from Clapton, conversing with fans until the traffic seized up, when he would 'leg it' the rest of the way along Tottenham High Road!

In pre-season Arthur once again took his players out to Epping Forest where, running in the countryside, players suffered far fewer blisters than running on the streets. With further concern for the welfare of his players Rowe had new showers, tiling and jet sprays installed in the White Hart Lane dressing-rooms. A newsreel of around this time shows a be-suited Rowe coaching 17-year-old winger Douglas Spivey on the White Hart Lane pitch. The commentator says: 'Long ago manager Arthur Rowe set his mind against depending on transfers to build his team: train what you can and buy what you can't, that sums up the Spurs' outlook on soccer.' Rowe was probably resigned to the reality that adequate transfer funds were unlikely to become available. Meanwhile, on August 9th, Rowe took part in a BBC TV series called *Sports Magazine*, hosted by Max Robertson, in which Spurs players were shown in pre-season training. Comedian Jimmy Jewell was included to boost the show's audience.

At the shareholders' meeting just two days before Spurs' Division One baptism, a defiant Rowe fired a 'shot across the bows' of two antagonistic directors (of whom more later) declaring his side would not change their style, '…for anybody *or* a lot

Rowe and Spurs lost local boy Johnny Haynes when he instead joined unfashionable West London club Fulham. He was instead greeted at Craven Cottage by (left to right) Archie Macaulay and brothers Eddie and Reg Lowe. Suspicion over the boy's rejection of both Arsenal and Spurs never went away, as Tony Marchi made clear to the author.

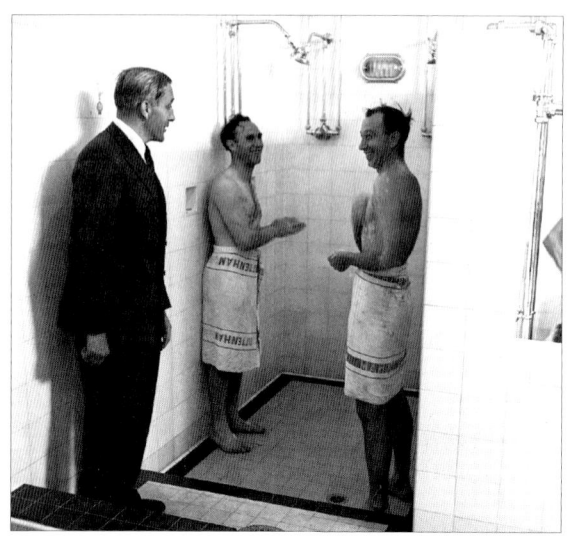

Rowe checks to see how winger Les Medley and captain Ron Burgess enjoy new showers installed in the summer of 1950. Footballers evidently (and modestly) showered in towels in those times!

of money.' Predicting a top-half finish, he continued: 'Since the old offside law changed and since the Arsenal introduced their system of play (very successfully it must be admitted) football, to my mind, has been of a negative type. Our method is better—that the team is more important than the individual.'

The big day finally arrived on Saturday, August 19th, 1950, with nearly 65,000 packed into White Hart Lane. Rowe might have hoped for easier opponents than Stanley Matthews' Blackpool to launch 'push-and-run' at the top level, the 'Tangerines' having finished just four points behind champions Portsmouth the previous May. At the first whistle the visitors slipped straight into gear, Spurs struggling for long periods. The 35-year-old Matthews was having a big say, Rowe agreeing after the game that with left-back Charlie Withers' tendency to rush in to the tackle, Ramsey should have been switched over from the right to jockey the winger more. In film-clips one Matthews' dummy sees Withers crash to the seat of his pants and in another Burgess has to double-up on the England winger. With comic exaggeration, Ralph Wetton told me of another incident: 'Matthews has gone down the wing, and Charlie's gone haring out at him from infield. He's sliding into Matthews at full speed, and Matthews has stopped. Charlie's gone past... and he's gone down the tunnel!' Baily's excellent goal was Spurs' only response to no fewer than four from the visitors. It had been a hugely deflating day but Rowe, considering the score misleading, pronounced: 'In spite of what happened the team will occupy a proud position by the end of the season.' Rowe learned that opponent's passes more often found their target in Division One football, leaving fewer scraps to feed on. Of course others were quick to say Spurs had met their match but, as skipper Burgess wrote: 'It wasn't that we played badly, but Stan Matthews had one of those days when it would have taken a Sherman tank to have stopped him.'

Rowe had to conjure up a smile that evening as he was honoured by *Sport* magazine as 'Manager of the Year'. Club President Lord Morrison will have given his manager a boost when commenting on England's embarrassing demise at the

World Cup, saying that new ideas and new methods were needed to restore the nation's football prestige and that this was where Spurs came in. After all, he said, every football writer had paid tribute to the kind of game played by Spurs. Once again, Morrison proved a far better judge of the sport (and Rowe's contribution to it) than certain Tottenham directors.

Rowe made just one change for the trip to Bolton. Mindful of shaky confidence after their opening-day defeat, he told his players: 'Just play your normal game, keep the ball moving and the goals will come', firmly adding: 'Forget last Saturday!' After torrential rain before kick-off Spurs fell behind, and things looked bad, but debutant Peter Murphy, replacing Bennett, ignored his new manager's credo, embarking on a lengthy dribble before striking home a cross-shot to tie things up. Spurs then added no less than three further goals, picking-up their first Division One points since April 1935. Spurs were thus given a timely confidence boost for the short trip to face Arsenal. After 15 years without a League encounter between the North London rivals, fans queued all night to get in.

The game naturally presented a contrast in styles; the Joe Mercer-skippered Arsenal relying on long passes down the middle or out to the wings. Although naturally right-footed, the more Ramsey-like Willis came in at left-back for Withers (who Marchi described as more of 'a terrier, a tackler'). The 'Gunners' went ahead when a wind-assisted cross-cum-shot evaded Ditchburn's outstretched fingers but then Ramsey's trademark looping free-kick dropped toward Medley, rushing-in from the left. Arsenal, aware of the ploy, had a defender follow the winger's run, only for Burgess to tell Medley 'Leave it!' before heading it home himself, off a post. In the second-half Walters flicked home Medley's deep cross and with time running-out it looked as if Rowe would emerge triumphant from his first derby as Spurs' manager. Sadly, Nicholson brought Lishman down and Walley Barnes crashed home the spot-kick to salvage a draw. But for their missed chances Rowe felt his team would have won, but it remained an excellent point for a newly-promoted club. Two days later Bolton went two-up at White Hart Lane but Spurs took the points when striking four in reply. After their opening day Blackpool calamity, Spurs

Rowe's diagonal free-kick ploy from a deep, wide position ploy worked again at Highbury. Burgess (on the ground) heads Spurs level at 1-1 in a game which ultimately finished 2-2.

Watched by Les Bennett, Len Duquemin leaps to nod home one of his two goals in a 4-2 home win over Bolton in the fourth game of Rowe's opening top division season as Spurs Manager.

had now picked up five of the subsequent six points and one fan said their football was '…just like the good old days — only faster'!

After just one point from the next four, Spurs faced Matt Busby's first powerful Manchester United side, who started strongly but Spurs eventually got on top, Walters' drive beating 'keeper Reg Allen for the only goal of the game. A clash of styles followed, this time at Championship runners-up Wolves, managed by long-ball supremo Stan Cullis. Spurs lost by the odd goal in three but the match was described as '…a classical example of first-class football played at top speed.' Rowe's only concern was the failure to take chances, which, he said '…shows up more in the First Division because of the higher standard', adding 'We get fewer opportunities now, so we can't afford to miss any.' To add punch against Sunderland Rowe replaced Bennett and Duquemin with young striker Dennis Uphill and the speedy Syd McClellan, who had followed the manager from Chelmsford. McClellan suffered a bad clash of heads after just 20 minutes, Spurs playing-out 70 minutes with ten men. But as the Sunderland defender involved in McClellan's incident was himself being treated, Uphill beat two defenders before setting-up Baily to give Spurs a 1-0 lead but they ultimately had to settle for a creditable draw.

Rowe, unable to clinch a deal for Bolton's legendary England striker Nat Lofthouse, instead signed Alex Wright from Second Division Barnsley for £12,000. Wright ultimately made just two appearances for the club. When later nominating Lofthouse as one of the best centre-forwards he had encountered, Rowe wrote: 'Everyone who loves football loves a fighter', suggesting Arthur felt his forward-line lacked aggression. Spurs now began a sequence of matches which would have a profound affect on the club's fortunes. At Aston Villa captain Burgess limped on the wing for at least three-quarters of the game, during which time Villa went ahead. Ten-man Spurs equalised through Murphy, but after Villa recaptured the lead, Spurs took both points with goals from Medley and Duquemin, the *Birmingham Mail* rating Spurs' 'textbook' football as good as any in the division. Despite then being without Ramsey and Baily (both playing for England in Belfast) and with injured Burgess replaced by tall, 23-year-old Colin Brittan, Spurs beat Burnley 1-0, reaching the dizzy heights of seventh. After a 2-0 win a week later at Chelsea, 'Lilywhite' fans now began to anticipate more than just survival.

Against Stoke Tottenham found the net three times from four attempts before both wingers added to the score, Bennett finishing off an astonishing 6-1 win. Walters scored one of the goals after running 30 yards to meet a free-kick from left-back Willis, the standard Spurs' ploy paying-off again. When asked if his side found life tough in the First Division, Rowe replied: 'The whole point is whether or not you play good football. If you do, then the higher you go, the easier it becomes.' The *Herald* now had to admit that '…for sheer football ability, Spurs are streets ahead of most clubs in the upper sphere.'

Eating away at Arsenal's slender lead at the top, Rowe's men then beat Portsmouth, League champions in the previous two seasons, 5-1. This prompted the temporarily supportive *Herald* to point out that Rowe's side barely cost as much as the sum Sunderland had expended on just one player, Trevor Ford. The *Herald* wrote: 'Soccer is a team game and that success can only be built upon teamwork.' Things were going so well that, after the Portsmouth game, centre-half Clarke complained to teammate Nicholson: 'I only touched the ball nine times. I didn't get a kick, or a header!' At Goodison Park Spurs avenged their narrow defeat in the previous season's FA Cup, beating Everton by the odd goal in three, although this time victory owed much to 'keeper Ditchburn. Not a single point had been dropped in seven matches. Could things get any better? Well… next to arrive were second-placed Newcastle United, only defeated once in nine away fixtures to date and second-only to Arsenal defensively. But this proved to be the extraordinary, landmark 7-0 victory already described in Chapter 1, a win which saw Spurs leapfrog their illustrious opponents and sit behind Arsenal at the very top.

After the game Rowe warmly reflected on elderly mentor McWilliam: 'It is good and satisfying to know that in recent years, when Peter had seen us play, he was content that we were "…playing fitba". When Peter was content with our "fitba", then I knew we had made the grade.' After all the criticism of Rowe and his methods since taking over, the *Herald* man at the match was compelled to write this time: 'In [Rowe's] short period with the club he has produced results whose effect will be felt wherever first-class football is played. He has recognised and applied a fundamental truth—that soccer is a team game and that team-work alone can bring success.' Duquemin received particular praise on this occasion, his team-mate Tony Marchi telling me that 'The Duke' was '…ideal for push-and-run… he was kind of like a wall. We used to push the ball up to him and he used to push it back.'

Graham Rowe told me how his dad arranged for him to sit pitch-side at home games and fondly recalled the Newcastle game, particularly a moment after the fourth or fifth Tottenham goal when Newcastle 'keeper Fairbrother picked the ball out of the back of the net with a wry smile on his face. Fairbrother, he recalled, '…knew that Spurs were unstoppable on that day.' The string of five games that ended with the Newcastle slaughter had seen Spurs average more than four goals a game, this against the cream of English football (indeed, Newcastle were to lift the FA Cup that season). Aside from one penalty, Spurs' goals to date had again been spread evenly among the five forwards: Walters 4, Bennett 3, Duquemin 3, Baily 5 and Medley 6. Defensively, Spurs had conceded just four in seven.

However, as so often occurs, a landmark success is quickly followed by a reverse. An unchanged side at Huddersfield went down 3-0, Spurs returning pointless for the first time in ten outings. Yet the now positive *Herald* still identified a plus: 'If a team can be as glorious in defeat as in victory, it is a team with a future.'

Writer John Moynihan then poetically described the misty afternoon when second-placed Middlesbrough visited: 'White Hart Lane was painted silver like a Whistler nocturne, and the stand roofs stood contentedly on the vapour...'. However, the scale of Newcastle's defeat now saw opponents setting themselves up to make life hard for Spurs. On this occasion England international Wilf Mannion's sublime skills outshone those of his counterpart Baily, and on a heavy pitch the score ended 3-3, which was no disgrace. Travelling to Blackpool to avenge their opening-day defeat, Spurs coped better with Arctic conditions this time and with Willis and Nicholson designated to control Matthews, an excellent late Duquemin header put Spurs back on the winning track. At a stroke, both the season's opening day disappointment and the post-Newcastle dip had been forgotten. Ramsey had played well at Bloomfield Road despite a personal matter he broke to Rowe on the train back south, asking for two or three days off to get married. While with Southampton, Ramsey had fallen in love with a married woman, waiting three years for her divorce to come through.

The first of fourth-placed Spurs' rash of Christmas games was against second-placed Arsenal, whose points tally Spurs could equal with a win, so the result carried even greater significance than usual. Excessive fears of a huge attendance for this fourth versus second place derby actually reduced the crowd to around 54,000. With a jaded-looking Arsenal relying on battering-ram methods, Spurs were faster, more methodical and possessed a sweetly-moving forward line. They cut their visitors open and should have scored far more than Baily's effort when he slammed his shot past 'keeper Swindin from the edge of the area. Of course, for many Spurs' fans, this result rather eclipsed the many other pleasures of the season. Two days later, on Christmas Day, Spurs took a point at Derby, even with Burgess

A cartoon from the cover of an official Tottenham programme depicted Rowe spending Christmas dreaming of a Spurs League and F.A. Cup double for 1950-51.

and Baily rested. The Derby County directors rated it '…the finest game that had been played on the Derby ground for many a day.'

When the same clubs took the field at White Hart Lane two days later, the Spurs' programme cover featured a caricature of Rowe contentedly sleeping in his armchair with feet planted on the mantelpiece, dreaming of his 11 players marching in high-stepping unison toward the League Championship and FA Cup trophies. The caption read: 'He also serves who only sits and waits.' One might imagine an egotistical manager of today tossing some toys out of his pram had his own club suggested he merely sat and snoozed while his team led the table. The plain truth was, of course, that had Rowe not taken charge when he did, there is no way Tottenham Hotspur would have been breathing down the necks of the League leaders that Christmas.

Returning after his injury-struck debut three months' earlier, McClellan scored twice against Derby that afternoon to leave Spurs just a point behind leaders Middlesbrough. Adding to Tottenham's joy, both Arsenal and Manchester United failed to take a single point from their Christmas games. Seeing 1950 out, Spurs' home derby with Charlton was attended by Prime Minister Clement Attlee. Despite McClellan's success against Derby, Rowe restored Duquemin and, on a treacherously frozen pitch, Spurs played in lower gear than usual, but still scored the only goal of the game, a one-touch affair; Willis's precision forward pass directed by Duquemin's head to Walters, who quickly found the corner of the net. Just 19 months after Rowe had taken over a mediocre Second Division side, Spurs finished 1950 sharing first place in Division One.

Their first competitive fixture of 1951, *Festival of Britain* year, was an FA Cup 3rd round tie at Huddersfield. Spurs sought revenge for their earlier League defeat at Leeds Road, but Burgess recalled light '…so bad we could scarcely follow the flight of the ball' and two late strikes put Spurs out of the Cup. At least they could now fully concentrate their efforts on finishing as Champions for the very first time in the club's history.

The first League encounter of the new year took place at Manchester United's Old Trafford on January 13th. At 1-1, Clarke's misjudgment shortly after half-time allowed Jack Rowley to score and, although Spurs continued making chances as they threw caution to the wind, it finished 2-1. The *Herald* summed things up positively: 'The thing now is to refuse to lose grip, and to continue playing football of Saturday's standard'. With Middlesbrough losing at Arsenal, Spurs hung on to first place, but Wolves, a side better suited to mid-winter conditions, were next up at White Hart Lane. Two months' of bad weather saw mud affect Spurs' swift-passing game. However one day, during a practice session at a soggy White Hart Lane, Rowe spotted that instead of passes being, as Alf Ramsey expressed it, '…grabbed by some unseen hand', the ball travelled fast and true, and the manager wondered why. Rowe then realised that no sand had recently been applied to the pitch, so thereafter he instructed it should never be applied and home performances improved as result. The Wolves encounter was played at full stretch, Murphy's tireless performance compensating for Baily's tired one. It was Murphy who crossed accurately from the goal-line to Walters, whose sliced effort rolled on for McClellan

to flick the ball past England international Bert Williams. Ten minutes into the second half Walters headed just inside the post before Wolves pulled one back, but Spurs took the points, 2-1. Rowe would later regard this win and that gained at Blackpool as the greatest achievements of the season (more so than the annihilation of Newcastle) because when Spurs met them, both Blackpool and Wolves had been potential champions.

The Spurs manager customarily studied forthcoming fixtures and now declared: 'I find our programme most favourable.' It seems unlikely Rowe would tempt fate, especially as when he said this Spurs were only ahead on goal average, although the fact was, no less than 11 of their remaining 15 fixtures were against sides in the lower half of the table and Spurs were also free of cup distractions. Indeed, on 4th round day, Rowe organised a friendly against Cardiff to keep the players match-fit. During the game two opposing players collided and neither could continue. 14 years before substitutions were first permitted, two reserves took the place of the injured men. When asked afterwards if substitutions like those should be allowed in competitive matches, Rowe was surprisingly opposed: 'In friendlies, I thoroughly agree, but in a sustained league struggle over a long period, injuries are usually cancelled out.' 'Our lack of injuries,' he continued, '…apart from that to McClellan [in the 1-1 home draw with Sunderland] when we still took a point, is due to our fast, skilful football which does not rely on the strong tackle.' As his Spurs managerial career progressed, however, Rowe might have reconsidered this particular theory.

Entering February a scoreless draw at Roker Park saw the towering Clarke keep Sunderland's £30,000 centre-forward Trevor Ford well under control. With Middlesbrough losing 1-0 at Manchester United and Arsenal and Newcastle taking a point off each other, Spurs crept clear at the top. After four weeks without a home game, Aston Villa arrived to play on what Burgess described as 'treacle pudding'. Baily capped a fine performance, hitting a glorious goal from 25 yards and Medley put Spurs two-up, but, with lowly Villa fighting back to 2-2, it took a Ramsey penalty to take Spurs' points total to 41. Middlesbrough were on 40, Newcastle 36, Manchester United 34 and Blackpool 32.

At Turf Moor they faced a Burnley side with the division's best defensive record. The home side went ahead before an awkward bounce struck Clarke's hand, the referee judging it intentional, the converted penalty sealing a rare Spurs' defeat, but they recovered with a 2-1 home win against struggling Chelsea. Around this

'PUSH-AND-RUN' CONQUERS ENGLAND'S BEST: MANAGING SPURS 1950-51

Opposite: *Syd McClellan (9) flicks home against Wolves after Walters' (also in the picture) had miskicked his attempt.*

Rowe restored Duquemin to the attack at home to West Brom on March 17th 1951, and it paid off, the Channel Islander finding the net three times (including this one and that shown at the foot of the page) in a 5-0 home win.

time Assistant Manager Jimmy Anderson fell sick and Rowe, with considerable relief no doubt, asked the infinitely more capable Vic Buckingham to fill-in. Then, however, Rowe himself fell sick, missing the trip to Stoke City, whose programme notes described Rowe's Spurs as '…one of the great sides of this generation'. If only Spurs' own programme contributors had been so appreciative. But, on the day, Spurs failed to take their chances, the game petering-out to end goal-less.

Restored to full health, Rowe selected both Bennett and Duquemin against West Bromwich Albion, hoping to resolve the dip in firepower. It took only ten minutes for fans' hero Duquemin to hammer home Nicholson's perfect through pass, and only 'keeper Jim Sanders kept Spurs out until the break. But, in the second-half the floodgates opened, Duquemin completing a hat-trick before Bennett, from Duquemin's assist, struck a shot so hard it entered the net and cannoned off the stanchion back into play. This was powerful stuff. Murphy then ran from his own half, fending off a series of challenges until reaching the goal-line where he pushed it back for Baily to net for a final score of 5-0. This performance took Rowe's side a comfortable five points ahead of the rest and inspired the onlooking former West Brom and England centre-forward W. G. 'Billy' Richardson to proclaim 'Arthur Rowe has changed the face of football with this stuff.' On occasions Spurs' build-up play was so thrilling that goals were mere icing on the cake – akin to so many well-crafted Manchester City goals under Pep Guardiola's command.

Two wins and a draw over Easter then led Rowe to make a rare, bold forecast: 'Notwithstanding Manchester United's strong challenge, I believe we have an

outstanding chance of bringing the League shield to London for *Festival of Britain* year.' He pointed out that his side had remained on top despite what he called 'Britain's wettest winter'. But, as well as Manchester United, Blackpool were also on a run of 10 wins from 11. Nevertheless the season still looked to be Spurs's best since Rowe had captained them to third place in 1934.

The first of the final six fixtures was at home to struggling Everton, who only lacked a goal from their surprisingly strong first-half performance. Home fans were becoming restless and only a disallowed effort by visiting centre-forward Harry Catterick finally inspired Spurs into action. Bennett slipped a perfect pass into the stride of Walters who hammered home an unstoppable shot. Ditchburn still had to prevent an equaliser before the well-rehearsed Ramsey free-kick routine increased Spurs' lead, Medley's replacement Murphy making that late dash from the touchline to meet the kick with his head. Bennett then completed the scoring for a fifth 'double' of the season. Could Rowe really capture the Championship? Meanwhile United, Blackpool and Arsenal also won while fading Middlesbrough collapsed 6-0 at Derby and Spurs' next opponents, Newcastle, took only a point.

Although Newcastle would clearly have liked to avenge their earlier 7-0 loss at Tottenham, they also had more than half-an-eye on the upcoming FA Cup Final. Walters put Spurs ahead after only seven minutes, yet again from the now established free-kick move ('The old gag once more' as the *Herald* put it). Spurs played out the rest of the first-half with copybook football and in the second-half, with Clarke keeping a tight grip on England's Jackie Milburn, Spurs held out until the final whistle. Further joy arrived with news of Manchester United's defeat at Stoke, putting Spurs a full six points ahead. The maximum points total United could now muster was 57 so to win the Championship they needed four successive Spurs' defeats in the remaining games, three of which were at home. When told the Championship was all over bar the shouting, the manager said nothing …but his grin spoke volumes!

Not only was the first of those home games against bogey side Huddersfield, but Ramsey was absent on England duty. Spurs came close four times before Glazzard put Huddersfield ahead. With Spurs trying to pull that goal back early in the second half, Huddersfield instead found the net again. 55,000 had expected to witness their 'Lillywhites' clinch the title, but the visitors achieved the only double over Spurs all season. Meanwhile United had cut the gap to four points.

By now Middlesbrough had dropped out of contention but remained tough opponents for Spurs' final away trip. Fortunately for Spurs, Boro's talisman Wilf Mannion had picked up an injury with England and midway through the first-half Murphy curled a 30-yarder over 'keeper Ugolini's head to put Spurs ahead. However, Spuhler tied things up and, in the second period Tottenham had to settle for a hard-earned point. Watching on was none other than Peter McWilliam, Rowe no doubt disappointed his side hadn't put on a regal show in front of his mentor. At least Blackpool had also now dropped out of contention, but Manchester United predictably defeated Wembley-fixated Newcastle, so the gap between Rowe's Spurs and Busby's United had shrunk to a mere three points with two games remaining. Rowe's men were not quite yet there.

Meanwhile the Vic Buckingham-coached Pegasus (consisting of Oxford University and Cambridge University students) had amazingly captured the FA Amateur Cup, beating Bishop Auckland in front of a reported 100,000 spectators. Pegasus captain Ken Shearwood made it clear that the biggest influence on Pegasus derived from Rowe's White Hart Lane (see Chapter 16) '[Buckingham] wanted us to play it simply and quick, push and run stuff, give and go, our wingers coming right back and collecting the ball from defence, everyone playing a part and taking responsibility'. Indeed, reporting on the game at Wembley, Bernard Joy wrote: '… during their inspired spell in the second-half, Pegasus produced soccer worthy of the Spurs themselves.'

Returning to the title race, the advantage still lay with Rowe's men, as no matter what United achieved they had to rely on Spurs slipping. Going into the penultimate weekend a win for Spurs at home to relegation-threatened Sheffield Wednesday would give them 58 points, United now only able to achieve a maximum of 57. However in their fight for salvation the Owls had won their previous three games. Just before that all-so-important encounter, a long-arranged friendly with Scottish champions Hibernian took place, and afterwords one Scottish writer described Rowe's side as 'entrancing' to watch, adding: 'You get the impression that everything [Spurs] do is planned by a shrewd soccer tactician.'

During that same week the Spurs' Season Ticket Holders' Association presented each player and official with a cigarette lighter. The lighters were optimistically inscribed 'T.H.F.C. League Division 1 champions 1950/51'. The non-smokers, (few existed in those times) included the hirsute pair Ramsey and Duquemin, grateful perhaps to receive hair brushes instead. At the presentation dinner Rowe unreservedly exhibited his optimism when addressing the guests: 'At the beginning of the season I thought we should certainly finish in the top half, probably in the top six and had hopes of finishing in the first three. Now I can say with some justification that the First Division Championship will come to the club for the first time in its long and honourable history.' Guest of honour on the night was that idol of the schoolboy Rowe, Arthur Grimsdell, who the Spurs manager addressed directly, saying 'You were the finest sportsman of them all, and a man to whom our present captain, Ronnie Burgess, is very much akin.'

One can imagine that following both the happy trip to Edinburgh and the fans' dinner that Spurs' spirits were high when Sheffield Wednesday arrived on April

Rowe's Spurs' hero from childhood, Arthur Grimsdell (centre) was a guest as Tottenham celebrated the Club's first-ever League Championship, which Rowe won at his first attempt. Captain Burgess is on the right.

28th 1951. Manchester United had hardly made it easy on Spurs, powering to a 6-0 victory over the self-same Huddersfield who had won at White Hart Lane. The Spurs groundsman had meanwhile lightly watered the pitch, no doubt at Rowe's request, to better suit the home side's swift give-and-go style, and once the game got under way, Spurs dominated. Driven forward by Nicholson and Burgess and playing some beautiful football, chances were, however, frittered away. As Burgess later pointed out: 'To say the game was tense would be putting it too mildly.' Ditchburn was hardly a spectator either, twice called upon to make full-length saves. The attendance had been reduced this time to a mere 46,645 due to BBC Television screening the second-half of the FA Cup Final live but those who did attend roared louder-and-louder as Spurs came ever closer to scoring. The *Herald* report takes up the story with only seconds left before half-time: 'Burgess sent Baily away. With eel-like speed he wriggled past three defenders while Medley switched places with Duquemin. In a flash the ball was transferred to Medley and sent on to Duquemin, who, with both full backs bearing on him and [Dave] McIntosh leaping at his feet, crashed home…'.

Despite the diminished attendance Burgess later recalled: 'I have heard the Hampden roar and the Ninian Park roar, but they were mere whispers to the Tottenham roar that greeted that goal.' Hearing during the interval that rivals Manchester United had gone two goals better in their game, Spurs stepped up the pace, Wednesday relying on rash, booted clearances or the brilliance of McIntosh in goal to prevent additions to Duquemin's goal, but they still sought an equaliser and scrambles took place in both goalmouths. Tension rose again around the stadium, but another goal could not be conjured up, that dramatic Duquemin strike had proved to be the gold-plated Championship-clincher. The *Herald* reporter wrote: 'Hats off to the Lilywhites. Hats off to 'The Duke'. Hats off everyone.' He continued: 'Fans wildly cheered as Lilywhite hugged Lilywhite, while defeated Wednesday players sportingly congratulated their victors. Directors stood with delight in their box and policemen smiled.' Burgess recalled: 'I have never heard such a racket, and never experienced such excitement. The crowd went crazy. I don't think any of us, players and spectators alike, will ever forget it.'

Despite Manchester United's superb run from January onwards, Spurs' fans could celebrate their club's first-ever Championship after 69 years of existence, Rowe succeeding where the previous nine Spurs managers had failed. Not only had

At last Spurs finish at the top of the English football pile. Rowe's players celebrating here, from left-to right, are Nicholson, Medley, Walters, Willis, Duquemin, Burgess, Ditchburn (almost hidden), Murphy and Baily.

he guided them out of the Second Division at his first attempt, he had followed that by winning the League Championship, also at his first attempt.

Unlike the more historically-acclaimed Herbert Chapman, who after joining Arsenal in 1925 spent five years (and a lot of Arsenal's wealth) to achieve some success (the winning of the FA Cup), Rowe had now overseen two championships from two attempts. Furthermore, for neutral spectators there was absolutely no question that Rowe's side was far greater value for money. Yet Rowe would speak non-judgementally of Chapman's contrary approach: 'Chapman decided that he wanted a certain player for inside, or wing half back, and went out for him. In that way he bought whom he thought would do that particular job and said to the man: "You needn't do anything different from what you have been doing—go and play your own game." He got the players to do what he had in mind and left it at that. In other words, you can't get a carpenter to do a bricklayer's job.' Significantly however, Rowe, unlike Chapman, had hardly disturbed his club's bank account, taking the Second Division 'tools' he was presented with before turning Spurs into by far the finest side in the country. Rowe had become only the third manager to win Second and First Division Championships in successive seasons. The equivalent today would be topping today's 'EFL Championship' then capturing the Premiership 12 months' later, a feat yet to be achieved.

Meanwhile, champagne flowed liberally in the home dressing room, one bottle delivered to the dressing-room of relegated Sheffield Wednesday. The *Herald* described proceedings and summed-up: 'Supporters and well-wishers surrounded Arthur Rowe, Spurs' manager, when he slipped into the dressing room. For some members of the cheering fraternity the past weeks have given them many anxious moments. Those Championship points were hard to get, but always there has been football, glorious football. Spurs have set a new soccer standard. For sheer artistry their fast, open style has no equal. And, above everything, it has all come from teamwork. Home fans have been lucky to see the "team of the century" almost every other week….' [yet a team so often criticised by the self-same newspaper].

Rowe himself said 'Our success …vindicates good football.' His was a perfect riposte to Chapman, who famously told his Arsenal players: 'Pretty football does not pay.' Rowe had taken what had been a mediocre Second Division side to the pinnacle of English football within just two seasons. For the record, the Spurs' side for this Championship-winning game of 1950-51 was: Ditchburn; Ramsey, Willis; Nicholson, Clarke, Burgess; Walters, Murphy, Duquemin, Baily, Medley.

A week later Liverpool arrived for the final game of the season and Spurs put on a suitable show for their celebrating fans. But the visitors also contributed to a game played at terrific speed and in one 15-minute spell the ball went from end-to-end without it ever once leaving the field of play for an interrupting goal-kick, corner or throw-in. The champions finally went ahead in the 57th minute with a classic Rowe-designed goal, Willis accurately finding Baily near the halfway-line, a flick across to Burgess, who drew two opponents to him then found Nicholson in space, a swift, accurate pass and Walters rushed in to find the net. Murphy, a good, economical Rowe purchase, scored six times in the final nine games, the last proving to be Spurs' final goal of an extraordinary season, resulting from a

ARTHUR 'PUSH-AND-RUN' ROWE

This group photo commemorating Spurs' capture of the equivalent of today's Premiership has Rowe confined to back left, while the Chairman claims prime position behind the trophy. Furthermore, Rowe's persistent critic, director Dewhurst-Hornsby, stands centre-stage between Ditchburn and Clarke. The players featured are (back) Ramsey, Withers, McClellan and Uphill.
2nd line down: Brittan, Duquemin, Ditchburn, Clarke and Bennett.
Seated: Nicholson and Burgess.
Front: Medley, Willis, Baily and Walters.

four-man move involving Medley, Walters and Duquemin, which left Murphy to strike home a superb drive. It had been 20 years (13 seasons allowing for the War) since the Championship had been won with as many as 60 points which saw Matt Busby's Manchester United pipped by four points. On the final whistle thousands of fans invaded the pitch before Burgess received the Championship trophy.

On presenting it, the President of the Football League, Arthur Drewry, said: 'All clubs in the Football League are proud of Tottenham. They are proud of the Spurs not only for winning the Championship, but for the way they have done it.' Drewry added that he had received reports from people all over the country about the fine and sporting football Spurs had played, and referred to Rowe as '... the man who planned your successes,' a statement interrupted by the players with shouts of 'Good old Arthur!' When Drewry asked what Spurs would achieve in 1952, there was a chorus of 'LIFT THE FA CUP!' On receiving the trophy, captain Burgess first thanked the fans, then Rowe. Fans chanted 'WE WANT ARTHUR, WE WANT ARTHUR!' until Rowe appeared to cheers. In his impromptu speech the Spurs manager revisited what he had said at the season's outset: 'It's a great truth that you try things once and if you like them you try them again. That is what we are hoping to do in the future.'

Writing at the time, Rowe reflected on this joyous moment:

'Practically the whole of my football life has been associated with Tottenham—the four years I spent with Chelmsford City from 1945 until 1949, plus the war years, are the only periods I have

been away from the club. And now, as manager of the club I have the privilege and pleasure of being closely connected with as grand a bunch of good players, who are also good fellows, as I have ever known. I am a very proud man to be thus associated with these players. I sincerely congratulate them, and thank them for their good football, good fellowship, and honest endeavours. Their efforts have allowed me a pleasure and honour that I never knew as a player, and I humbly share with them the joy of the 1951 Championship, one of our club's greatest triumphs, and one that will live through the years.'

Captain Burgess would write that if ever a man deserved a full share of the glory, 'that man was Arthur Rowe, our manager—and good friend', adding, 'It was his philosophy that we followed.' A philosophy which, of course, depended on every man adhering to pass-and-move, from defence through to attack, yet, ironically, that very summer, the *FA Year Book* chose to include an article which contained the statement 'Anyone who has tried to coach will know how impossible it is to mould a group of players to a fixed pattern of style.' One presumes the *FA Year Book* had gone to press before Rowe had so gloriously disproved that statement.

Charles Buchan wrote: 'Spurs were the most attractive team I had seen since the war. Their simple 'push-and-run' methods were carried out with great speed and accuracy.' John Arlott wrote: 'Tottenham Hotspur's forward moves were the most exciting football we have seen for years.' Ivan Sharpe said it was no surprise Spurs had continued their success at the higher level, as '…theirs was football of top class', and he admitted with embarrassment that at the commencement of Spurs' first season in England's premier Division he had pleaded for a concession to be made in Spurs' case, that they be excused from possible relegation by season's end on the noble grounds that '…they were setting such a fine example up and down the country by their essentially constructive, cool-and-collected style'! A 2010 *Times* obituary for Eddie Baily stated that Rowe's side had: '…brought a dash of colour to a monochrome postwar world.'

Ten years on Rowe himself wrote: 'In the Second Division in our promotion year at Tottenham we thought we were three years ahead of our time. When we got to Division One I knew we were five years ahead. Yet all we had really was the truth of this matter of football; the truth cleared of any conditional thinking.'

Spurs' future 'Double'-winning captain Danny Blanchflower said anyone who saw Rowe's 'push-and-run' Spurs would never forget it. 'As much as they were efficient, they were unpredictable. They were thrilling to watch, players were encouraged to improvise, the ball moved along the ground at remarkable speed and with devastating accuracy.' Eamonn Dunphy has written that before Rowe, English football was essentially based upon personal, on-field battles between naturally gifted players, skilful forwards and powerful defenders: 'English football had never been, in any formal sense, a contest between two units.'

In seeking to challenge accepted practice and improve the sport, managers such as Rowe exposed themselves to more pressure from their club directors than most, laying their livelihoods on the line. Similar (though lesser) courage had been shown by Chapman at Arsenal with his third-back approach following the 1925 offside-law change, but, unlike Rowe, Chapman's success had been significantly underpinned by considerable financial support. Rowe, on the other hand, took a group of largely

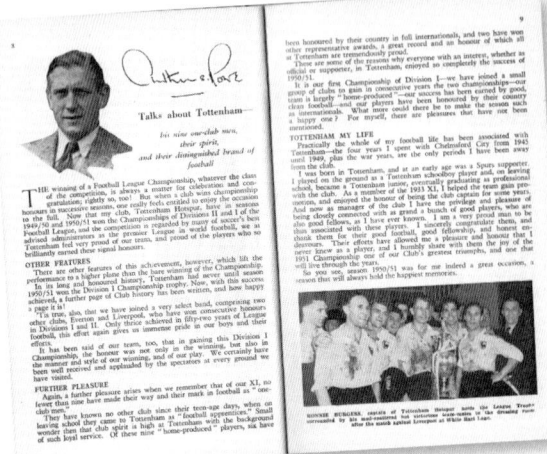

In that summer's *Playfair Annual* Rowe rejoiced in his achievement of capturing Spurs' first-ever League Championship. Of his players he wrote: 'Their efforts have allowed me a pleasure and honour that I never knew as a player, and I humbly share with them the joy of the 1951 Championship, one of our Club's greatest triumphs, and one that will live through the years'. Sadly however, the memory of it has long occupied a distant second-place to that of Bill Nicholson's expensively-assembled 1961 Championship-winners.

average footballers and inspired them to believe in his daring, alternative approach, ultimately winning the biggest prize in English football.

Spurs had totalled 82 goals, the highest in the entire Football League that season. Once again, goals were spread across the front line: Walters had 15 (top scorer), Bennett and Murphy (sharing the inside-right spot) scored 15 between them, Duquemin 14, Baily 12 and Medley 11. Even more remarkably for a side which, unlike Chapman's, did not place a priority on defending, Spurs had conceded fewer goals (44) than all but two other First Division sides in '50-51. This defensive record would not be bettered by Spurs for twenty years (33 in 1970-71, but that was a season when total goals scored was 23% down on 1950-51). Even Nicholson's much-lauded 'Double'-winning side of 1961 conceded 11 more than Rowe's (bettered since by Mauricio Pochettino's Spurs, but in four games fewer than in either season). Ralph Wetton explained this defensive advantage of Rowe's 'push-and-run': 'We didn't lose many games, we really steamrollered everybody, we were scoring four, five, six goals at a time. As a result we didn't have to defend very much and apart from that, in defensive terms we had blokes who could play.'

Within 48 hours of that final League game, the then leading Austrian club side, F.C. Austria, arrived for a friendly. It was the first of two games forming part of the *Festival of Britain* celebrations. A weary Spurs lost 1-0, for once rather dominated by a side playing a similar game to that which Rowe himself preached. It was a further warning for those in English football who rigidly clung to the conviction that 'British' was 'Best', and at the same time highlighted the fact that, in the UK, Rowe was alone in trying to compete with nations whose aspirations for the sport were higher. Jimmy Anderson then took charge of a Spurs team that travelled to play Racing Club de Paris, the local Press describing a Tottenham side defeating the home side 4-2 as '...the best eleven ever seen in France'. There followed a week's tour of Denmark, too, the Tottenham board always seeking to utilize the off-season for money-making tours. So the weary champions could not rest yet.

Spurs' Championship-winning celebration was held on June 2nd 1951 at the Savoy, the entertainment including popular singing trio The Beverley Sisters. The

Marquess of Londonderry proposed an excellent toast which may have innocently ruffled the feathers of certain directors. He said his greatest pleasure was to see Spurs' brand of football, to see movements started from goalkeeper and backs, and to know that if all clubs tried to emulate Spurs there would be less criticism of football throughout the country. He concluded that Spurs were a '…really great side' moulded by '…sportsman and architect' Arthur Rowe. Rowe himself spoke, 'Keeping,' said the *Herald*, '…his stock high by proving to be an equally great orator.' The triumphant manager thanked everyone, from Spurs' international players down to the groundsmen, the painters and everyone else in-between, for their cooperation. 'We have a grand bunch of boys at Tottenham who believe in the club and the method of football they are trying to play. Team-work, fellowship and friendship prevailed at White Hart Lane,' he said, '…and there was all-round happiness in the club.'

On Sunday, June 10th, success gained Rowe a guest spot on national radio alongside popular comedian Ted Ray. Discussing Rowe's life and career he was asked what had been his proudest moment. 'I have it every week when Tottenham take the field,' he replied. As to hopes for the future, he said: 'To see Spurs play as during the last two seasons—not for winning, but for the way they play.' No doubt an uncontrolled spasm of distaste crossed the faces of his ambitious directors following those words. For them winning *was* the priority and some gave every impression of wanting to bring Rowe and his methods crashing down.

By mid-June and preparing for season 1951-52, Rowe denied offers had been made for Bolton centre-forward Nat Lofthouse and/or Chelsea centre-forward Roy Bentley. He continued: 'Perhaps someone wants to buy us a centre-forward, but even if they sent him "carriage paid" he would have to compete with four others for the position.' His reference to 'someone' wanting to buy a centre-forward appeared to be a subtle hint regarding miserliness in the boardroom. He would have another crack at the League Championship with what remained, basically, Joe Hulme's squad.

Sadly Vic Buckingham left Spurs that summer for his first step on the managerial ladder at Third Division North Bradford Park Avenue. Having begun coaching under Rowe at Spurs and working with Pegasus, the Bradford job was the next step in an illustrious managerial career with the likes of Ajax and Barcelona later to be added to his CV. On leaving Buckingham was asked if he would create Bradford in the guise of the streamlined Spurs: 'There is only one Spurs. They are a really great side, with a great skipper and fine manager. Only Arthur Rowe has the secret of their success, but *I have learned a lot from him.*'

Rowe had put two trophies in the White Hart Lane cabinet in just two years. Any 'push-and-run' sceptics had been put to shame, if not, sadly, those in the White Hart Lane boardroom. No matter how much he embellished the club's reputation and no matter how much he boosted its finances, there remained, just a corridor away at White Hart Lane, those who continued to snipe. Could he shrug them off and repeat his success in 1951-52?

11

Pleasure and Pressure

MANAGING SPURS 1951-52

'When it was all going right, when it was flowing, I'd sit there transfixed at some of the stuff they played. I was jealous for that team. I was anxious for them to do justice to themselves. That was the only pressure. All the rest was sheer pleasure.'

ROWE TALKING OF HIS SPURS'S SIDE IN *FOOTBALL DIGEST MONTHLY* 1974

Before season 1951-52 got underway, Arthur Rowe lifted the burden of expectation from his players' shoulders and forecast a top-six finish, which rather conflicted with the triumphal tone of the club programme: 'May 1951-52 write another memorable chapter in the club's history.' The *Herald* also believed Spurs could take the Championship for the second year running, but on the dubious premise that Rowe's side was 'young enough', yet of the four outstanding outfielders only Baily remained under 30. Driving-force Burgess was 34, Nicholson 32 and Ramsey 31. For the future, Rowe had at least now taken on promising young Welsh full-back Mel Hopkins as an apprentice.

Any review of Rowe's time as Spurs' manager prompts the question: Why did the club purchase so few top-level players to prolong the team's success on the field? Despite Spurs' wealth there was continual, minimal investment in both players and managerial staff. After all, McWilliam had left the club to seek far better rewards elsewhere, and Hulme was said to be paid less than those who called him 'Boss'. Little dispelled the notion that Rowe's hands were tied in the transfer market, although Rowe's frequent defence of older, experienced players hardly assisted him. Indeed, he believed that the fear was not so much that a player might be too old—but too young, once saying: 'I've seen and played with some very young thirty-fives, and also some very old, and tired twenty-fives.' He also believed that a dip in energy could be compensated by the positional sense that experience provided. As Rowe's pal Matt Busby once put it: 'The trouble with football is, that just as you learn, and realise the easiest way to play, you find it's time… to pack up!'

When Rowe visited Tottenham's Rowland Hill School that summer to present medals to children who had excelled in local sports, he received one of the awards himself, a badge he should have collected 30 years earlier as a 14-year-old! Meanwhile, Spurs again spent pre-season walking and running in Epping Forest, but an injury suffered by Sonny Walters in practice kept him out of the opening games. It was the first in a catalogue of injury setbacks. In a public trial match centre-half Clarke incurred both ankle and knee injuries. So, beginning the defence of their Championship Spurs already lacked two regulars to face the tough prospect of Middlesbrough away. Debutant 'Jake' Farley, who, like McClellan, had followed Rowe from Chelmsford, replaced Clarke. Bennett had already put Spurs ahead but within eight minutes young Farley slipped under pressure and in trying to recover diverted Mochan's shot past Ditchburn for a debut own-goal. Both Farley and Ramsey were then blamed for Middlesbrough's second, but eventually only poor shooting saw the champions fail to equalise. 'We shall be all right and I think we shall be able to hold our place,' said Rowe.

In Spurs' first home game, against Fulham, 21-year-old Derek King replaced Farley, but Rowe lost Baily to injury this time, yet despite this the home side won, 1-0. Three days' later Spurs defeated West Brom 3-1 in their second home game but unbelievably lost a third centre-half to injury, King. This left a patched-up side to travel for the return at Craven Cottage. McClellan, selected to replace Duquemin, scored in a 2-1 win and Rowe's injury-struck side had somehow collected six points from eight but a heavy defeat followed when Rowe's makeshift side ran out at Cup-winners Newcastle. After a fourth minute Ditchburn error Newcastle had scored three more by the 35th minute only for Jimmy Scarth (in for the injured Walters) and Bennett (with an acrobatic overhead kick) to make it 4-2. But Newcastle, perhaps eager to avenge last season's 7-0 humiliation, added another three, Chilean striker George Robledo grabbing a hat-trick. It was Spurs' heaviest defeat for 36 years.

In a five-year period when Newcastle won the FA Cup three times, only the margin of Spurs' defeat was a surprise and a philosophical Rowe saw the positives: 'It was a great game between two sporting teams. Play almost reached classic heights.' Girding himself for criticism, Rowe pointed out that for two years he had fielded an unchanged team almost every week, but this time he had lost three centre-halves alone. However, some criticisms were extraordinarily harsh, one fan castigating the Spurs boss personally: 'Why all this ballyhoo about the maestro manager, Mr Arthur Rowe? The public are getting just a little fed up with it. After all, when he took over he did not have to build up a team—it was already cut and dried for him.' A team, the correspondent neglected to point out, which had been rooted in Division Two until Rowe arrived. Even now, despite the injuries, the reigning champions had still won three out of five. What could have provoked such a vitriolic reaction?

Despite Murphy joining the injury list, Spurs took a deserved point at Burnley, which set the stage for a significant moment in Spurs' post-War history, Rowe granting a debut against Bolton to the painfully slim, baggy-shorted Tommy Harmer. At 23, Harmer stood just 5ft 6in tall and weighed a mere 8st 12lb, his seemingly over-sized head perched on a frail body. Brian Glanville recalled how on that day 'Harmer's cockney impertinence and extraordinary ball control won him a place in [the crowd's] favour'. With Spurs one-up early on, Bennett eventually headed the second in a 2-1 win following a quick-passing combination featuring Harmer, Ramsey, Walters and McClellan. In the following home draw with Burnley, Spurs' fans barracked certain players, possibly encouraged by criticisms appearing in both the *Herald* and the official club programme. However, one fan leapt to Rowe's defence, attacking fickle supporters '…who demand goals and care little for good football. Personally, I am happy when merely seeing good football.' Despite the injury list Spurs were, after all, only two points behind the leaders. At Stoke, they were three goals to the good by half-time and, instead of easing-off, piled on the pressure, adding three more for their highest away score in 19 years. Rowe, ever the realist, pointed out that Stoke were, in truth, a poor side but the recovery following the heavy Newcastle defeat had been superb.

Before Manchester United visited a week later, with 70,882 fans arriving to witness the Championship holders take on the current League leaders, Rowe bristled with rare anger when a reporter stated 'he had heard' Duquemin had asked for a transfer. Rowe: 'If you visit all the pubs and cafés in Tottenham and surrounding districts you can "hear" many strange tales, but take it from me that neither Duquemin nor any other player has walked into this office to ask for his transfer.' The game witnessed the return of the dependable Clarke, whose particular strength was on his left side, providing an efficient barrier to right-footed centre-forwards who would, as Rowe pointed out, '…run into Harry's stronger side.' A convincing performance against Busby's side saw Spurs' opening goal, a low, angled shot from Medley, arrive during that sweetest of periods, just 20 seconds before half-time. With Clarke keeping 14-goal Jack Rowley quiet, Walters added a second, to send Spurs into fourth place.

Two days' later the Charity Shield match between League champions Spurs and FA Cup holders Newcastle saw Rowe collect his third trophy since arriving back as manager. It was an early opportunity for Spurs to respond to the seven goals conceded at St. James' Park and shots rained-in on the Newcastle goal in the first quarter, only for Milburn to evade Withers and shoot past Ditchburn. Murphy soon equalised before Bennett leapt high to score the winner for Spurs' first Charity Shield success in 30 years. Yet fans soon focussed on the next fixture; Arsenal at Highbury. In just six minutes the ball zipped from Nicholson to Ramsey to Murphy, who, spinning on the edge of the area, beat Swindin with a low shot into the far corner. Many of Arsenal's passes went astray while those of Rowe's side rarely did. Harmer's shot came back off a post, Spurs' lead kept to just 1-0. Then, 15 minutes into the second period, the tall, powerful Cliff Holton equalised with a bullet-like header, Spurs at least satisfied that their point took them to third place.

In a September 1951 draw at Highbury, Arsenal's Alex Forbes slides in to halt a burst into the penalty area by Spurs' captain Burgess.

Two days later Rowe's great mentor Peter McWilliam passed away. The Spurs manager paid this tribute — 'Our present team, with its "push-and-run" slogan is simply following his teaching, for our application is to push the pass and run into position.' Clearly this confirmed McWilliam's influence on the manager, although Rowe also recalled McWilliam's side mixing triangular passing with longer passes, particularly cross-field to the wingers. That same day Rowe contacted Tony Marchi's army camp commandant in Basingstoke, requesting the player's release from National Service duties to play for the Reserves at Southampton that evening. Southampton were one of the first clubs to install floodlighting, having experienced play under lights when touring South America. This run-of-the-mill reserve fixture thus became the very first-ever competitive football match played in England under lights. Rowe later recalled: 'I remember picking [Marchi] up from his Army unit by car for this game. The crowd of 13,000 was at least three times as large as for the ordinary reserve matches played in daylight.' Short of a centre-forward, Rowe wanted Marchi to fulfill the role and not only did he play well but he scored the opening goal in a 2-0 victory, years later telling me how proud he was, having scored the first-ever goal in a competitive game under floodlights in England!

At this point, Rowe jettisoned Harmer to reinstate his fit-again, first-choice pairing of Bennett and Baily. Despite Rowe's appreciation for the Harmer's skills and character, the youngster's inclination to delay a pass or set-off on an occasional dribble reduced the efficiency of 'push-and-run'. Harmer himself admitted his talents did not fit. Rowe's usual first-choice eleven made each other appear better than perhaps they were due to their strength in combining continuously at speed, anticipating what each other was likely to do next. Harmer, on the other hand, was reluctant to release it straight away. Like Rowe, future England captain Johnny Haynes believed '…in a quicker use of the ball', and that dribbling was only positive if defenders rushed into the tackle. If instead they jockeyed the dribbler, there was, said Haynes, '…no profit in it', adding, 'the man who holds the ball and dribbles incessantly throws great strain and responsibility on all the other players.' I asked Ralph Wetton if Rowe had a good relationship with Harmer. 'Oh yeah,' he replied with conviction, '[Tommy] didn't get played very often but he was a favourite of Arthur's. And of course, Tommy,' added Ralph, '…couldn't get up-and-down the field. I used to play behind him a lot, and I liked him, but he made me do extra work.' However, it could not be denied that Harmer's first eight appearances produced six wins, one draw and just the one loss.

Wearing black armbands in memory of McWilliam, Spurs then lost 2-1 to strugglers Manchester City, dropping three places and the *Herald* headline 'SPURS' CHANGED TACTICS WORRY FANS' suggested Rowe had moved to a long-ball approach. Certainly, with the speedy McClellan up front, players will have been tempted to play the ball into space. 'With a down-the-middle attitude against modern defences there is neither goals nor the best of football' said the report, which might have been composed by Rowe himself. The irony of a newspaper so often aping the anti-'push-and-run' opinions of Spurs' own match programme now criticising Rowe for abandoning the tactic, was not lost. Yet, after another defeat, this time at struggling Derby, the Spurs programme returned to criticising

November 3rd 1951. Despite the proximity of two Wolves defenders, Duquemin, on the ground with arm raised, has headed Spurs' fourth goal in a thrilling victory. Walters and Bennett celebrate.

a '…tendency to overdo the passing to one another'. 'Push-and-run' would only be tolerated in the boardroom when producing trophies (which, ironically, it had plainly and efficiently achieved) but any setback was to be pounced upon. Rowe himself will have been disappointed enough to find that all four Spurs' sides in action that day had lost, as he took responsibility for all levels of the club, even forecasting all results in advance, on this occasion saying 'We drew four blanks where I frankly expected we would register four wins.' Then, following the gain of just one point from six, Rowe lost four players to international call-ups yet Spurs still overcame Aston Villa 2-0 at home. Villa half-back Danny Blanchflower, facing Spurs for the first time, was hugely impressed.

So far 1951-52 had been quite unlike Rowe's first two seasons in charge, losing players to injury and international calls. Against Villa the tall, 24-year-old half-back Ralph Wetton came in for his debut. Although born in County Durham, Wetton had grown up in the Tottenham area, watching Spurs play before the War. It was only October yet Wetton was already the 20th player to appear in the first-team before Rowe then lost Willis, suffering a hernia, and Burgess, who pulled a thigh muscle during a 'backs-to-the-wall' 1-0 win at Sunderland.

Entering November, tenth-placed Wolves arrived and went two up despite Spurs' beautiful football, but Bennett and Walters tied the game just before half-time. Then Duquemin was sandwiched between two defender, leaving Ramsey to beat England colleague Bert Williams from the spot. With three minutes remaining and Wolves fighting for a point, Duquemin headed the best goal of the game, clinching a thrilling two points for the champions. Ralph Wetton told me a story of team-mate Medley during this game. Doubts about Ramsey's continued selection as England right-back had arisen so it was proposed that England captain and half-back Billy Wright might be switched to full-back at Ramsey's expense. As a gesture to the England selectors, Wolves trialled Wright in the full-back role at Spurs. Medley, something of a non-conformist, said to Ralph as Spurs took the field, 'Just give me the ball, anytime you like, I'm going to make a mug of this bloke.' Medley turned

Wright every way you could think and he never played right-back again. Medley himself, Ralph added, was nobody's friend, '…a bit of a loner, off the field' and he was soon to clash with Rowe.

The Spurs boss then watched a transfer target, Arsenal's Cliff Holton, score a hat-trick for an FA XI against an Army XI but, as always seemed the case, the manager drew a blank. For whatever reason Holton joined the growing list of strikers Rowe failed to bring to White Hart Lane. Neither McClellan nor Duquemin fully suited his needs, particularly in goalscoring terms. Meanwhile, Spurs still shared second place behind Arsenal as they struggled to a draw at second-from-bottom Huddersfield (who even lost their goalkeeper to injury). Rowe predicted Spurs' finishing would improve, adding '…some team is likely to be hit with an avalanche when this happens in the near future.'

Against struggling Chelsea the waterlogged White Hart Lane pitch saw 'push-and-run' bogged-down, and there were frequent bursts of hilarity from the terraces as players tried vainly to keep their feet. At 2-2, Duquemin dexterously beat Harris on the turn before sidestepping the 'keeper to hit the winner, proving Spurs had the stamina to overcome a heavy surface. Wetton confirmed to me Rowe's belief that 'push-and-run' could be played in any conditions, adding 'that if you could play it on the White Hart Lane pitch then you could play it anywhere!' With December approaching, Spurs were still favoured to retain the Championship but first confronted League leaders Portsmouth, whose Fratton Park ground faced a strong gale from the Solent. Pompey took a first minute lead against the wind, adding a second and final goal in the second-half. Again Spurs finished with passengers, Nicholson with an old groin injury and Medley a pulled muscle. Rowe unusually admonished his players: 'I told the lads I did not mind them ever being beaten by a more skilful side, but regretted their going down to a more determined one.'

Moving into December, Spurs missed Nicholson at home to Liverpool, meanwhile Ramsey's nemesis, Scottish winger Billy Liddell, had scored twice by the 17th minute before Bennett and Walters pulled it back to 2-2. Ramsey was, as usual, kept at full stretch by Liddell and, with twenty minutes left, he appeared to cleanly whip the ball away from his foe in the area but a spot-kick was awarded, Liddell completing his hat-trick. Unlike most wingers of the time, Liddell enjoyed facing Ramsey, explaining: 'When Alf won the ball he always tried to use it effectively, rather than clear it quickly. That gave you the chance to chase and try and win it back.' Team-mate Wetton defended his teammate: 'Alf was the best positional player I've ever seen. They said he lacked pace and all the rest of it — he wasn't really quick, old Alf, but his brain was lightning. He could see an opening before the opening was there, while his covering in defence was immaculate.'

Two successive defeats illustrated just how quickly things could turn against a Tottenham manager. One fan felt things were going wrong while another reasoned that Spurs merited a poor patch after two seasons of continuous success. Neither correspondent, however, mentioned the string of injuries. The *Herald* believed that 'push-and-run' was faltering: 'There is a tendency to receive the ball first and think where to put it afterwards.' At Blackpool's waterlogged Bloomfield Road the home side was missing both Mortensen and Matthews, yet took the lead. As Spurs pressed hard for an equaliser the injury bug struck again, Wetton limping to the wing and Spurs trailed south after a third successive defeat. The change in fortunes coincided with excessive rainfall plus, of course, the rash of injuries. Rowe also pointed at fewer chances being created: 'The difference between this year and last is that last year we missed as many opportunities and still won, but this year we cannot afford to miss.' The defeat led the local newspaper to dampen fans' hopes with phrases such as 'Spurs' chances of a third Championship in successive years faded considerably.' Yet Rowe's side were still in the running for the title. Rowe's three trophies in three years seemed quickly forgotten whenever a result or two went against Spurs.

They began the second half of the League programme at home to struggling Middlesbrough, Rowe moving Bennett to centre-forward, accompanied on either side by Murphy and Baily. Murphy scored after fifteen minutes from another of Rowe's pre-planned short corners and Murphy (again) and Bennett then scored either side of half-time, making it 3-0. Using the tall Bennett as a target man, a ruse to help overcome the soggy conditions had been a great success, Spurs eventually winning 3-1. Prior to the game Rowe had called the team together for what he called '…an extension of the normal weekly chats.' At this time the prickly Medley took exception to something Rowe said, the manager pointing out that no matter Medley's feelings, he, unlike others, had not been dropped in nearly three years. But Rowe was confident the tide had turned.

Rowe travelled to watch FA Cup 3rd round opponents Scunthorpe and Lindsey United for his customary brief on opponents before every game. Ralph Wetton confirmed Rowe '…would go through every player, right from back to front and tell you how to play them.' With the Championship shield now in the trophy cabinet, the club wanted the FA Cup trophy to join it (the Final in those pre-Premiership, pre-Champions League times was the big annual spectacular of English football). Some already believed it was Spurs only real chance of 1951-52 silverware. In the face of such defeatism, it was that very week that Rowe, for the second year in succession, was presented with the 'Manager of the Year' trophy. The presentation was made by former light-heavyweight boxing champion of the world, Freddie Mills. Rowe humbly pointed out that the award '…was all due to a fine bunch of players who honoured the white jerseys with a cockerel badge.' As Mills made the presentation, Rowe said he had heard about the boxer's '…upper-cuts so was glad Freddie had something in each hand!'

Inevitably following such an occasion, Spurs lost 3-1 at West Brom, this despite opening the game with some of their finest football. This may have been one of the occasions when 'push-and-run' opportunities went begging. The constant tip-tap passing from defence to frontline can become so rhythmical that by the time the ball arrives inside the penalty area, several options still present themselves: 'Shall I shoot?' 'Shall I slip it to the colleague to my right, or the one to my left?' One saw this frequently when watching Wenger's turn-of-the-millennium Arsenal at their best. By the time a player is one-on-one with the 'keeper he has to switch-off the repetitive desire to find a colleague. If not, the opportunity goes begging. Conversely, in the traditional 'up-and-under' game, the only option is often to strike the ball goalwards. Rowe took the view that provided his side kept splitting the

Rowe proudly clutches his 'Manager of the Year' award, received from boxer Freddie Mills (far left). Spurs players supporting their manager are (l-r) Nicholson, Burgess, Ramsey and Duquemin.

opposition asunder, enough goals should result and missed chances shrugged-off. However, on the back of four defeats from five, the Tottenham match programme chose to quote a *Birmingham Argus* report on the Hawthorns game which included this barbed criticism: 'One felt that Spurs had lacked enthusiasm, they were there it seemed to play football and if they could not succeed by scientific methods they were not going to resort to energy and enthusiasm. It seemed a surprising policy in the circumstances.' That Spurs' own directors should happily quote this snide, contemptuous indictment of their own side was stooping to a new low.

One can well imagine journalist Willy Meisl had Rowe's directors in mind when he wrote: 'In the opinion of the average director the crowd did not pay to see good football, but a fierce fight for a ball, tough tackling, speed and strength, in short, action. Where it led to was far less important than that something was happening every minute.'

Away at Charlton on Christmas Day, Rowe brought back the popular Harmer but his real surprise was to field Finchley amateur outside-left George Robb, this allowing Medley to switch to the right in place of the rested Walters. Robb could hardly be said to have followed the traditional path into the Football League. Having joined Spurs as a schoolboy he had resisted other clubs' offers of professional terms, desiring to pursue a teaching career at Finchley's Christ's College whilst turning out for Athenian League Finchley. On the heavy Valley pitch Robb was to be the star, creating Spurs' first and third goals, and capping it all by claiming the second himself. Watching his England Amateur wing partner Robb from the stands was Tony Pawson of Pegasus, who had been enticed to see the game by Charlton Athletic, who were similarly trying to persuade him to turn out for them, but Pawson too had a career outside football. Spurs' handsome 3-0 victory restored some self-belief prior to hosting the reverse fixture just 24 hours later. Charlton included the amateur Pawson this time, but Spurs were on fire from the first whistle, Murphy and Walters soon making it 2-0. As for Pawson, the only pre-match instruction from his captain was to strike corner-kicks to the far post. Four minutes' short of half-time, after so much Spurs' pressure, the slight Pawson went to take his first corner and duly swung his right boot as hard as he could at the heavy leather ball. However, as he did, his standing foot slipped from under him, so the ball not only remained earthbound, but travelled diagonally back, hugging the pitch. By pure chance it travelled into the path of Kiernan who smacked it home for 2-1. Kiernan then headed another from a Pawson cross with 60 seconds remaining in the half, and Spurs had surrendered their lead. In the second-half Charlton were saved only by 'keeper Bartram but Pawson then collected a goal-line clearance from Ramsey and, eyes tightly shut, struck a rising drive wide of Ditchburn, thus completing his extraordinary Charlton debut and snatching both points from Spurs' grasp.

Tottenham had three days to recover before hosting Newcastle United's big guns in the final fixture of 1951. Despite his five goals in 13 appearances, Murphy was dropped, never to play for Spurs again. Harmer, yet to feature in a losing side, returned. The watching Field Marshall Montgomery of Alamein may have mistaken the quagmire of a pitch for a commando course. Baily had already struck the bar by the seventh minute, which is when Duquemin's determination took him past centre-half Frank Brennan before he passed through for Walters to score. Desperate to avenge their crushing defeat back in September, Spurs proved again that 'push-and-run' could still work despite the surface. Early in the second period another brilliantly contrived move involving Harmer, Baily and Walters ended with a Duquemin flick for Medley to double Spurs' tally. Ten minutes from time George Robledo (admired by Rowe) netted a superb reply, but Spurs held on for victory.

Nicholson's return and the win over Newcastle persuaded the *Herald* to begrudgingly concede that Spurs were, after all, still in the chase for the Championship and, despite more heavy mud, the first game of 1952 at Bolton would be referred to as a 'near-classic'. After 25 minutes Bolton took the lead but, once again, 'Harmer the Charmer' mesmerized the opposition, netting his first goal in League football. Nicholson, Baily and Duquemin each struck the crossbar and Clarke kept England's Lofthouse quiet, Spurs moving into fifth place. After removing Scunthorpe from the Cup, Spurs were then pulled out of the hat to face… Newcastle United, a fourth meeting of the two clubs inside five months. A home League win over Stoke followed lifting Spurs to fourth place behind Portsmouth, Manchester United and Arsenal.

At Old Trafford Busby's United sought revenge for their defeat at White Hart Lane and, on a frozen pitch, only Ditchburn kept them out until after the break when Johnny Berry's cross deflected in off Ramsey. But Spurs were still in it until United added another four minutes from time. Although United had no more than equalled the score by which they had lost to Spurs just months' earlier, the *Herald* chose the moment to write off hopes of a second Spurs' Championship. Yet Rowe's side were well-placed in sixth with 26 points to play for. One imagines Rowe's dismay that a newspaper read by so many fans was so eager to prophesy doom. 'What', he must have feared, '…will they throw at us if we are knocked out of the Cup next Saturday?'

On the day around 70,000 were present for the fourth round clash. Injuries hardly favoured Spurs, and Bennett even pulled a muscle preparing for the game. As for the notorious pitch, that morning Rowe had inspected the frozen surface and found it '…just to our liking,' adding 'It was soft on top, yielding to football stud depth, and solid underneath.' But a dramatic thaw due to pre-kick-off sunshine suddenly left the pitch resembling a bog. The delicacy of 'push-and-run' was difficult to maintain and the Magpies went ahead when Nicholson gifted the ball to Billy Foulkes whose first-timed, diagonal pass found Robledo near the penalty spot. Ditchburn plunged head-first at the striker's feet but too late to prevent the goal. Spurs came closest when Duquemin's looping header dropped onto the bar but, by half-time, Spurs had fallen two behind, before Robledo's left-footer as Spurs chased the game finished things off. At least Spurs had fallen to the eventual Cup winners. 'Lady Luck was against [Spurs],' stated an unusually empathetic *Herald* report, before more typically adding, '…it is impossible for the light-weight Lilywhites to play feather-bed football on the White Hart Lane pitch.' 'Feather-bed football' might be added to the lexicon of cynical 'push-and-run' criticism. Commenting on the Cup exit, the Tottenham match programme stated: 'Last Saturday, much to the regret of all—Directors, Management, Players and Supporters, the Spurs had to say farewell to the FA Cup for another season.' Of course, the directors are placed first in the order of those suffering the Cup exit.

A week later, as the nation mourned the passing of King George VI, Arsenal arrived at White Hart Lane with the pitch little improved. As the sides lined up before kick-off and after the crowd removed their headwear, a brass band played *Abide with Me* before a minute's silence was observed. In the fifth minute a corner caused confusion between Nicholson and Ramsey, Don Roper scoring. A Walters' header tied things up but a third of the way through the second-half Clarke's clearance struck the referee and diverted to Arsenal's Alex Forbes who hammered the ball home from distance, putting his side back in front. Despite a great fightback, the score remained a fortunate 2-1 to Arsenal. Spurs had conjured-up plenty of 'might-have-been's so the game could in no way be perceived as a disaster.

Unless, that is, you happened to be 'Fanfare' in the *Herald*. Headlined 'ARTHUR ROWE ANSWERS HIS CRITICS', 'Fanfare' boldly forecast: 'Now nothing short of a miracle will enable [Spurs] to overtake the leaders,' pointing out, laboriously, that to retain the Championship shield Spurs would need to win each of their 12 remaining matches, the current leaders would need to lose four of theirs and hope that the White Hart Lane pitch would change from a mud heap to a firm playing surface. 'Fanfare' continued: 'The first is unlikely, the second possible, and the third extremely remote.' A casual reader might have assumed Spurs' three consecutive defeats had been inflicted by run-of-the-mill sides, not the three most powerful clubs of the era: Manchester United, Newcastle and Arsenal. As for his first two points, history shows leaders United would indeed drop seven points by season's end, just one short of the eight points suggested as 'unlikely'. As for Rowe's 'written-off' Spurs, would Fanfare's pessimism inspire Spurs to prove him wrong?

The *Herald* also raised the hoary proposal to switch to long-ball tactics, to which Rowe boldly responded: 'Any attempt to alter [our style] would upset more fans than would be pleased.' With a rare burst of anger he also struck back at a national newspaper quoting him as saying that if Spurs' fans did not like his team (and by inference, his management), then they should go elsewhere. Rowe, said the *Herald*, was well aware of the importance of spectators in professional football, and of the loyalty they felt toward the club. To the suggestion that his 'push-and-run' style should be changed when grounds were heavy, Rowe replied: 'There is nothing wrong with the style, whatever the state of the pitch. In each of our two games with Newcastle and Arsenal, we had as much of the play as our opponents…'. He felt that 'push-and-run' could not be turned on-and-off like a tap, adding that the problem was not the tactic but the application of it which was to blame. 'Fanfare' had to concede that in recent home defeats, Tottenham's '…skilful and scientific' performances had been good and the games thrilling to watch.

A week later Spurs encountered a better pitch at Manchester City, though they still had to contend with fog. Bennett came back in for Duquemin while Baily was replaced by Uphill, who was harder to knock off the ball. Perhaps it had dawned on Rowe that having two vertically-challenged, ball-playing inside-forwards in the side (Harmer and Baily) was one too many for a side whose title successes had depended on an alliance of two taller attackers (Bennett and Duquemin) to complement Baily. In the ensuing 1-1 draw Ditchburn's misjudgement (due to the fog) accounted for City's goal. Walters saved the point when beating City's former prisoner-of-war 'keeper, Bert Trautmann. The on-form Medley broke a toe late in the game, missing no fewer than six run-in fixtures. But, in breaking their run of defeats, Spurs rose to sixth. By now Manchester United, eight points (four wins) ahead of Spurs, had moved into first place, followed by Arsenal and Portsmouth.

Yet despite the rise up the table, the *Herald* now suggested that Spurs had 'NO INTEREST LEFT' in either League or Cup competition and should therefore overhaul their 'football machine'. This implied ditching "push-and-run", the newspaper appeared to pander to those Spurs' directors who wanted an end to it, successive Championship successes or not. Rowe's side were just seven points behind with 24 points left to contest and in no way could be written-off. What was the newspaper's motivation for it's continued pessimism?

For the visit of Preston North End Rowe pulled off a masterstroke, surprisingly replacing injured outside-left Medley with half-back Burgess, the reliable Wetton slotting into the captain's half-back role. Burgess recalled Rowe calling the players together a few days before the game. 'Ron,' he said, 'you always like to get up among the forwards and have a go, so what about "having a go" on the left wing?' Despite Rowe's unfamiliar forward line-up of Walters, Uphill, Bennett, Harmer and Burgess, Spurs dominated the opening quarter-hour, a Burgess shot being blocked on the goal-line. Thereafter play was end-to-end, before Harmer's long, looping shot was fumbled into the net by the Preston 'keeper. On this occasion Spurs were criticised for playing too many long balls down the middle, some thinking Rowe, conscious of the uneven White Hart Lane surface, had put 'push-and-run' to one side, perhaps waiting for the weather conditions to change. The restoration of Bennett and inclusion of Uphill suggested a desire to cash-in on their aerial strengths and, on this occasion, the justification was a 1-0 victory, catapulting Spurs to fourth and the gap with United (who didn't play) closed to a mere six points.

Spurs next faced strugglers Derby County on a much-improved pitch so Rowe restored his iconic forward line-up aside from the injured Medley who was replaced by Chris Adams who had a hand in both opening goals. In the 22nd minute he played a perfect ball for Baily to unleash a shot on the run which bounced from the 'keeper's chest for Walters to hook home. Ten minutes later Adams himself scored with a measured lob from outside the area and by half-time Duquemin made it 3-0. A Bennett drive and an own goal produced a final score of 5-0, the victory facilitated by a playable pitch. With leaders Manchester United dropping a point at home to Aston Villa, the gap with Spurs closed to one point. What were the doom-sayers now thinking at the *Herald*? Indeed, Spurs continued at their peak, dazzling home side Aston Villa with even Spurs' own programme scribe swallowing a bitter pill, pronouncing: 'What a treat it was to see our lads moving with the old polish and rhythm'. After Villa's many lucky escapes in the first-half, a spasm of quick-fire passing nine minutes after the break involving Ramsey, Nicholson, Walters, Bennett and Walters (again) ended with Duquemin firing home. Four minutes later Adams hit a strong cross from the left to Walters who touched it directly into Duquemin's path, the swarthy centre-forward volleying home for his second, before Walters tapped home for a final score of 3-0. A stylish, dynamic, comprehensive victory. So where were the doubters now?

The *Herald* now conceded Spurs were at least challenging Arsenal for second place even if trailing five points behind United. Yet correspondent 'Fanfare' still brushed aside the four-game unbeaten run, writing: 'Spurs' bid for League honours appears to have come too late.' Of course, a delighted Rowe contradicted this pessimism: 'The machinery has never run so smoothly, the forwards have never used the ball to better purpose, and individual players have not reacted better all season.' Even a Villa fan wrote: 'May I thank you for the grand exhibition put on by your team at Villa Park. Yours is the football we like to see, win or lose.' Again, what a contrast to the poisonous opinions held in Spurs' own boardroom.

When Sunderland visited in mid-March, Duquemin, Bennett and Baily prevented the Sunderland half-backs from supporting their forwards, who included Welsh international Trevor Ford and England's Len Shackleton. After twenty minutes Duquemin struck his fourth goal in three games but, defied by 'keeper Mapson, Spurs could not complete their victory until Bennett sharply despatched a deflected Burgess shot into the roof of the net. Spurs were in the midst of their best run of form of the season but Busby's United also picked up maximum points with a 2-0 home win over Wolves - Spurs remaining third with seven games left. A fifth successive victory would have been a tall order as Spurs travelled to face the self-same Wolves at Molineux, and Ramsey missed out with a blistered foot. Both sides immediately tore at each other but the wind made control difficult and Wolves went ahead only for Baily to equalise 60 seconds later, and that is how it remained, Spurs maintaining their unbeaten run. However Portsmouth leap-frogged them into third place. Compensation came with news of United's surprise defeat at bottom side Huddersfield, Spurs creeping one point closer to the leaders.

The following Tuesday Spurs left the Championship chase behind them, playing a showcase friendly in Brussels against Austrian champions FC Austria. The entertaining 2-2 draw impressed a Belgian newspaper: 'Never has such precise, purposeful and progressive football been played by any two teams.' Others claimed it was the finest game ever played in Belgium. Certainly for Rowe personally it was a game which would always remain of enormous significance (see Chapter 22).

Returning to League football on April 2nd, Spurs entertained the surprise conquerors of United, relegation-threatened Huddersfield Town. A snowfall followed by a thaw had turned the pitch to glue and the encounter would only be recalled for a glaring refereeing error. At 0-0 after 90 minutes, stoppage time was being played. Baily, who had incidentally just incurred the referee's displeasure, prepared to take a corner-kick on Spurs' left. His kick struck the referee full in the back, poleaxing the official face-first to the ground. The ball rebounded to Baily, who quickly placed the referee's 'return pass' onto Duquemin's head for the winning goal. Rightly Huddersfield pointed out that the goal was illegal, a dead-ball kicker is not allowed to play the ball twice before another player has made contact with it. But, having regained his footing, the referee went across to confer with his linesman, who had missed the infringement, so the goal stood, two points going to Rowe's men. Relegation-threatened Huddersfield's bitter complaints fell on deaf ears and the loss of the point was liable to send them down. Some wondered why the referee took up such a strange position for a corner in the first place. Fortunately for the FA and the referee, the two points Huddersfield lost at White Hart Lane did not determine their eventual relegation. Meanwhile the *Herald* was finally confessing their earlier, negative forecasting had been misplaced.

As the FA Cup semi-final between Arsenal and Chelsea, to be played at neutral White Hart Lane, had been twice rescheduled due to the weather, Spurs' own games had also been rescheduled. Meanwhile Busby's men stumbled again, losing 1-0 at Portsmouth. Over Easter Spurs would face just two opponents, Portsmouth at home and Preston away. The two sides ahead of them, United and Arsenal, were both faltering. Could Spurs still retain the Championship? Would the much-maligned Rowe achieve an extraordinary THIRD first place position from three seasons as Spurs' boss? Tottenham's magnificent comeback this time, if maintained, could even be viewed a greater accomplishment than their first Championship. Not playing on Good Friday, Rowe's men were delighted to hear that both United and Arsenal had only taken one point that day, but the next afternoon United restated their intent, conquering Liverpool 4-0.

That same day Spurs had home advantage against challengers Portsmouth. For once the pitch was hard and dry, the groundsman watering it a little prior to kick-off. Both Ramsey and Medley were now fit and for the first time in 21 outings Rowe fielded his classic forward line: Walters, Bennett, Duquemin, Baily and Medley. Spurs tore into Pompey right from the start but, against the run of play, the visitors went ahead. However with Spurs' forwards combining at speed, it was not long before Duquemin received from Ramsey, evaded Jack Froggatt, rounded the onrushing 'keeper at pace and shot left-footed into the net. On the half-hour the ball passed from Withers to Medley to Duquemin to Baily who, outwitting his marker, slammed a shot high into the net. This prompted the *Herald* to write that Spurs were now '…dispelling any doubts about their being titled the "Team of the Century".' Just before half-time Baily made it 3-1 with no further goals added in the second-half. Yet such had been their mastery, Spurs could have run up nine or ten.

In 1974 Rowe recalled of this period: 'I've never had greater pleasure from football than that [early 50s] team gave me. When it was all going right, when it was flowing, I'd sit there transfixed at some of the stuff they played. I was jealous for that team. I was anxious for them to do justice to themselves. That was the only pressure. All the rest was sheer pleasure.' Clearly, had it not been for the disruptive injuries suffered in the first-half of the season and poor mid-season playing surfaces, Spurs' supreme confidence, spilling-over from their Championship success, would have seen them conclusively reclaim their title. The only other thing they lacked were back-up players of top-notch quality when first-teamers were sidelined. Yet they still remained a point short of second place and, on Easter Monday, Manchester United demonstrated their firm intent to hold off Rowe's Spurs, thrashing Burnley 6-1. While Spurs were dropping a point at Preston, Arsenal claimed a rare win which meant that to retain the Championship Rowe's men now needed to win all three remaining fixtures whilst relying on United and Arsenal to slip-up. With United now on 52 points, Arsenal on 50 (with a game in hand on both United and Spurs), Rowe's men followed on 48.

On the penultimate Saturday Spurs arrived at Anfield, a ground where they had failed to taste success in thirty years, and things behind the scenes at White Hart Lane were suddenly unsettled. Medley had been omitted from Spurs' 18-strong end-of-season tour party to Canada due to fears that he might choose not to return to the UK, his Canadian wife having failed to settle in England. Had he stayed in Canada without the club's blessing he would have forfeited benefit money and other sums from the footballers' provident scheme which were due to him.

McClellan came in for Medley and Spurs edged Liverpool in the first-half, Rowe's ploy being to send the speedy McClellan through on goal at every opportunity. After half-an-hour Ramsey, once again struggling against Liddell, came up-field to take a free-kick on the edge of the area. He chose to let fly himself, the 'keeper choosing to fist it back to him, and this time Ramsey passed for Duquemin to shoot home through a crowd of players. After half-time Spurs stayed on top, hitting the

Rowe once said of watching his Spurs' side: "I'd sit there transfixed at some of the stuff they played."

Here he looks similarly satisfied merely watching a practice game alongside director Fred Wale.

post in the very first minute, but, with eight minutes left Liddell again escaped Ramsey and his bouncing effort found the net. So Spurs again came away with just a point, falling four points behind both United and Arsenal, and, sadly the single point United took at Blackpool now put them out of Spurs' reach. They could still match United's points total but were too far behind on goal average. So, after a great challenge for the title, Rowe's boys now competed with Arsenal for the runners-up spot. Both Arsenal and United played their penultimate games on Monday April 21st. United took both points when beating Chelsea, moving to 55 points, while the maximum points Spurs could now hope for was 53. But Arsenal lost 3-1 to West Brom, leaving their final points total a maximum of 55 too, and Arsenal's final League fixture was away at United. Even if Arsenal were to lose at Old Trafford, Spurs would still have to win both their final two games in order to claim the runners-up spot from the 'Gunners' on goal average,

Blackpool arrived for the first of Spurs' final two contests, Medley returning following resolution of the Canadian tour issue. It was another close, fast and skilful game, again blighted by injuries, Blackpool losing centre-half Hayward and Ramsey falling heavily, bruising a shoulder. Both men continued as wide attackers. At one point trainer Cecil Poynton was signalling for Ramsey to receive treatment when Medley sent over one of many crosses and Ramsey, injured arm close to his side, managed to score when 'keeper George Farm failed to hold the ball. Blackpool went down to ten men in the second-half, Hayward not returning, and Baily hit his fourth goal in six games, for a final score of 2-0 to Tottenham. Spurs were now two points short of Arsenal, who capitulated in their final game by no less than 6-1 at a Championship-celebrating Old Trafford. The Gunners now depended on Spurs failing to win at Stamford Bridge if they were to finish as runners-up. Busby's

Alf Ramsey, later criticised for his dourness when managing England, joins Rowe and Edward 'Ned' Liddell (manager of various clubs) in finding something trainer Cecil Poynton has said amusing.

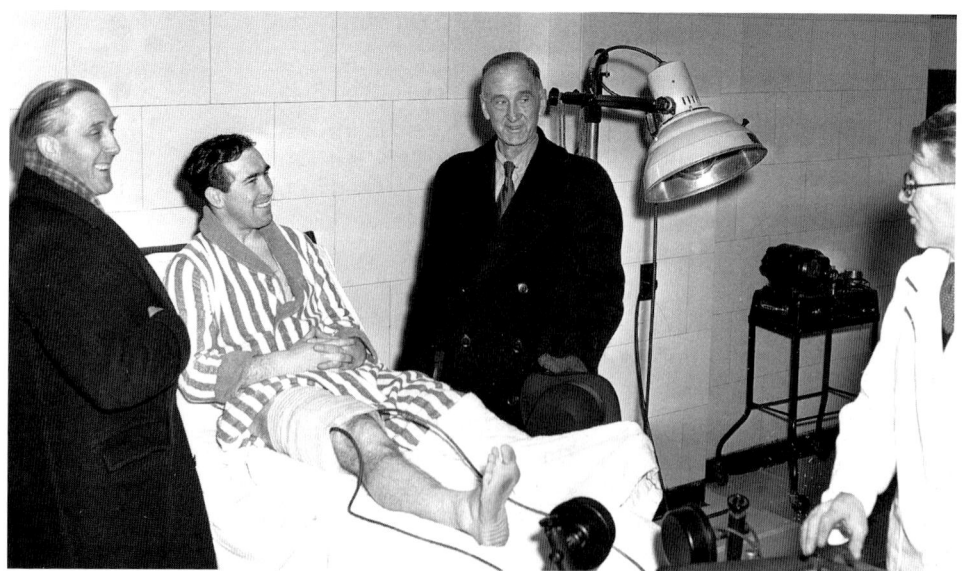

United had meanwhile deservedly finished in first place, having been runners-up in no less than four of the previous five post-war seasons. They fended off challengers in great style, winning their final four home games with an aggregate score of 19 goals to two.

Back at White Hart Lane the club began replacing the turf which had proven a stumbling-block to Rowe's ambitions for a third successive Championship success. Before then Spurs travelled to Stamford Bridge and picked-up the two final points needed for their final runners-up place, pipping the 'Gunners', their fierce rivals, for second-place. They had fallen short of a repeat Championship by a mere four points, picking up no silverware despite their injury-impeded efforts. Rowe's resistance to criticism and persistence with 'push-and-run' had all but paid off.

The sniping Tottenham directors responsible for programme notes had to confront the reality of another successful season. Even without silverware, second spot in the First Division was a rare achievement in the history of the club. Second (or higher) has only been achieved four times since, the latest in 2017 under Mauricio Pochettino. Typing his season summary, the Tottenham director responsible was perhaps biting his lip as he did so: 'Looking back over the season we have much to pride ourselves on, for the team has put up a grand fight, and provided us with many stirring games.' Arthur Rowe had achieved no less than two Championships and one runners-up place in three seasons. Finishing a close second this time, Rowe had proved conclusively that the previous two seasons had been no fluke. Had it not been for the catalogue of injuries, who knows?

For all the talk of Rowe's potent attacking force, Spurs had achieved the best defensive record in the First Division (51) and Rowe could pride himself too on his reserves topping the Football Combination, the London Mid-Week team finishing runners-up, and the 'B' team winning the Metropolitan League Cup. 'Push-and-run' ruled!

Years later Danny Blanchflower reflected that Rowe's first-team failed to win silverware that year simply because, by season's end, Burgess was 35, Bennett 34, Nicholson 33, Ramsey 32 and Medley 31. The Irishman added that '…while "push-and-run" called for clear heads and clever footballers, it also required stamina and good general fitness, such was the tempo at which it was played.' As renowned philosopher and Spurs' fan A. J. Ayer wrote, 'push-and-run' was '…a style which is very beautiful to watch when it is successful but one which makes very heavy demands upon the players' energy.' However, Ralph Wetton felt this an exaggeration. 'You weren't doing an awful lot of tackling for one thing, and secondly, it's not as though you were carrying the ball.' Yet no less a figure than Bill Nicholson sided with Blanchflower, saying 'push-and-run' was impossible '…unless all 10 outfield players were 100 per cent fit.'

Three days after clinching the runners-up slot, Spurs were defeating Racing Club de Paris in a floodlit friendly. That same day Newcastle United beat Arsenal at Wembley to win the FA Cup. Had Rowe's men not fallen to the Magpies in the fourth round and subsequently enjoyed the 'Magpies' Cup draw fortune (two of their three ties against Second Division sides) then clearly Spurs' chances of Cup success would have rated just as high. Without today's Champions' League

ARTHUR 'PUSH-AND-RUN' ROWE

Summer 1952. The Spurs' party photographed en-route to Canada. Standing at the left are directors Dewhurst-Hornsby and Heryet, followed by Bennett, Burgess, Uphill, Wetton, McClellan, Ditchburn, Medley, Clarke, Harmer, Duquemin and Rowe. Crouching in front are Willis, Walters, Gibbins, Withers and back-up goalkeeper Ronald Ward.

qualification, second-place in the League, despite the enormity of the achievement, was then a poor substitute for Wembley success and of course the White Hart Lane boardroom demanded silverware.

The day before setting sail for the Canadian tour, Rowe conceded that the season had ended far better than at one time seemed likely, the surge up the table in the final 12 games sufficient, said Rowe, to '…win any Championship in any season.' The *Herald* columnist described the manager's demeanour as having become sunnier. And so it should have done — after all, he had more than proved the *Herald*'s doomsayers wrong. But Rowe faced reality when addressing the likelihood of 'cracks' appearing in the team, saying the club would utilise their 'junior talent' or '…be prepared to buy players'. As few fans believed money would be made available for players, talk of utilising 'junior talent' will not have appeased the critics amongst them. One new face was 20-year-old inside-forward Gilbert 'Dickie' Dowsett, who had watched Rowe's Chelmsford City as a boy. Rowe also signed apprentice full-back Mel Hopkins on a professional contract and attempted to sign forward Tommy Orr from Morton but the Scot was clearly seen as another bargain-buy, unlikely to supply the quality required to ensure Spurs' continued success. With all the travelling due that summer, could Rowe suitably rejuvenate the side before it was plunged into another demanding League season?

On May 13th 1952 the Spurs party sailed for Quebec, initially without Ramsey, Nicholson and Baily who were on England duty. The two directors accompanying the Spurs' party were W. J. ('Bill') Heryet and E. ('Eddie') Dewhurst-Hornsby. Heryet would report on the tour in the official club handbook for season 1952-53.

PLEASURE AND PRESSURE: MANAGING SPURS 1951-52

Ahead lay a demanding, five-week, coast-to-coast tour of Canada, finishing with two games against recently-crowned champions Manchester United. Reviewing the high scores they were to achieve against limited Canadian opposition, one can but deduce that the tour was unnecessarily long just when a break from football was needed. Spurs' players ran out onto seven soccer fields in Ontario, Saskatchewan, British Columbia (3 games), Alberta and Manitoba, travelling by rail approximately 3000 miles across the entire North American continent — and back again. With combined scores totalling 73 to Spurs and 5 to their local opposition, it would seem an exercise in futility. McClellan netted 9 in one game alone, while Ralph Wetton recalled the score in a game with a Saskatchewan team reaching about 14-0 at half-time, at which point Rowe told his players: 'If I see any of you blokes take the mickey out of these lads, I'll have you off. If you get through, stick the ball in the back of the net. Don't belittle them.' Rowe's only concession was to agree with the Saskatchewan coach that Ted Ditchburn could change places with the local 'keeper. By the end, the score was contained to a mere 18-1!

At least most games took place before capacity crowds so perhaps the tour paid for itself. But surely Rowe worried about his players' powers of recovery for the upcoming League season, by which time the knives would be re-sharpened, ready for any sign of failure. For now, maintaining the myth of British/English soccer dominance, it was deemed better for Spurs directors to purr with pride as the goals flowed in. The players will have gained little, Ditchburn, for one, gaining a tan and little else. Six weeks after the end of a demanding season, Spurs' ageing stars were still running around football pitches under hot and humid conditions. The final game would take place on June 15th before setting sail back to Liverpool. The vital trio of Baily, Nicholson and Ramsey had stayed in action even longer, having first taken part in England's post-season tour.

The *Herald* joined the Spurs' directors in celebrating the trans-Atlantic tour as if the results were of significance: 'Spurs fans will go on talking about it for months, and if there are disappointments to come in the future, the past few weeks will afford some consolation.' But would Spurs' demanding directors (and the niggling *Herald* reporters) be consoled by the results of these one-sided contests should League results disappoint come August? The most significant aspect of the tour came at the very end, League runners-up Spurs routing champions Manchester United first in Toronto, then again the very next day, in 90 degree New York heat. Around 25,000 spectators watched each game. All five Spurs forwards scored in the 5-1 victory over the champions in Toronto where the Canadian fans firmly supported the 'Lilywhites', while Duquemin hit four of Spurs' seven in the New York match. But, significantly, Bill Nicholson suffered a bad injury during the Toronto game and returned urgently to England for treatment to an injury which proved extremely costly once the League campaign began.

Despite United fielding their strongest side, the Toronto-based *Globe and Mail* wrote: 'Tottenham's marked superiority was there for everybody to see. The Spurs were more alert, better conditioned, and played at high-speed, oblivious to the strength-sapping potential of a burning sun and an 85 degree temperature.' The game at New York's Yankee Stadium was covered by a local newsreel team and

Spurs line up with Manchester United in New York's Yankee Stadium, summer 1952. Players, from left to right, are Ditchburn, Withers, Clarke, Medley, Ramsey, Brittan, Wetton, Duquemin and Bennett.

provides a rare chance to see snippets of just how slick Rowe's side could be at their best. Referring to the sides mostly as the 'Manchester Uniteds' and the 'Tottenham Hotspurs', the local commentator says 'The Manchester booters, in the white pants, aren't in the same league at all here in the Yankee Stadium,' adding, 'The Hotspurs are giving their old rivals a lesson in how soccer should be played.' In one edited version of the newsreel a slick Tottenham 'push-and-run' move, mostly first-time passes, can be admired. Another nice sequence shows Burgess in possession just outside the centre-circle in his own half, with United's number 10 challenging. Burgess sells him a neat dummy and drives forward into the centre-circle toward Bennett, who, with a United player almost standing on his heels, seems to be in Burgess's path. But Bennett, with his marker crashing into him, plays the ball off Burgess's feet, short to [possibly] Wetton, who likewise sends it forward, first-time, to Burgess, who has continued his run in true, triangular, 'push-and-run' style. He turns and sends a ground pass into the path of a colleague, at which point the reel of film unfortunately ends. But it was a brief cameo of typically sharp 'push-and-run'. The *New York Herald Tribune* wrote that Tottenham had '...controlled the play throughout despite the fact that Manchester led in corners.' Clearly United (who, unlike Spurs, had included in their tour some testing confrontations with Mexican, Swedish and Turkish sides) had tired in the second-half. Incidentally, during the entire five weeks away, Rowe never failed to write daily to wife Pom.

Back home, at the Football League Annual meeting, Tottenham suggested increasing the number of promoted and relegated clubs to four, in order to stimulate more interest and increase competition right up until the end of the season. Customarily, those running the League were resistant to change, the motion failing. It took another 35 years before the four sides finishing immediately below the top two automatically promoted sides would compete in a stadium-packed end-of-season mini-tournament to decide the third side for promotion. That there are six places for teams to compete for until the end of the regular League season has resulted in exactly the effect Spurs (or was it Rowe?) campaigned for way back in the 1950s.

Also that summer Spurs installed a new pitch drainage system following the weather-induced setbacks suffered in the winter of 1951-52. But of greater significance in the long term, Rowe succeeded in acquiring a training ground at Cheshunt. This was a significant legacy of his managerial reign at White Hart Lane. With space for three pitches, Cheshunt would be used by the club until the 1980s when it was sold for £4 million. Naturally it also saved wear-and-tear of the White Hart Lane pitch. Tony Marchi explained to me just how limited facilities were before Cheshunt: 'There was no training pitch, you had to do your five-a-sides under the stands, or in the car park. We used to dodge between the bloody girders as we were doing five-a-sides underneath the stand. At White Hart Lane the car park used to be an "L" shape, so one goal used to be here and the other goal used to be there [pointing to the other end of the "L"]!' In 1960, Rowe, having long since left Spurs, was free to castigate the club for it's attitude to the Cheshunt purchase, saying there was '…opposition from some quarters — we were wasting a lot of money that wasn't going to be used and one thing and another, that was the cry. It was all right to spend money renting a ground on a Saturday afternoon, but it was all wrong to invest in a scheme that would show profits in the future. That's the sort of muddle-headed thinking you can get at times in football.' A clear indication that the soft-spoken Rowe could be driven to clash with directors over financial tightness, which may go some way to explaining their criticism of his tactical approach, a possible case of 'tit-for-tat'.

Cheshunt was further commended by the *Herald* as an answer to finding young players for the future and thus avoiding the indulgence in '…costly and speculative deals in the transfer market.' Were these comments based on statements Rowe had made, or, as would seem more likely, the board? They will surely have enjoyed the prospect of the Cheshunt investment preventing income being spent on ready-made, quality footballers.

Ralph Wetton recalled that Rowe himself was so excited at the time of the Cheshunt purchase that he couldn't wait to break the news to the players in Vancouver, announcing:

'I've got some good news for you. We've just bought a training ground in Cheshunt.' 'He was over the moon', said Ralph. But would this progress arrive a little late to benefit Rowe himself? The weary joints of his great side's principal performers were beginning to creak. Could Rowe squeeze another season of success out of them?

12

Dreams of Wembley

MANAGING SPURS 1952-53

'We have been on the floodtide of success.'
RARE POSITIVITY EXPRESSED IN SPURS' MATCH PROGRAMME 1952-53

'He could talk all day, Arthur, and not one of us would be asleep.'
SPURS' RALPH WETTON IN CONVERSATION WITH THE AUTHOR

Despite having come so close to a third consecutive Championship, Rowe's playing staff was ageing, while 'push-and-run' was beginning to be successfully countered by opponents. That summer of 1952 three key men were undergoing surgery: Ditchburn, Nicholson and Walters. On the plus side, the quality of Rowe's football had produced record gross profits of £73,725 for season 1951-52 and gross receipts were up by no less than 20%. But despite investment in the pitch and training ground, the Second Division playing squad he had inherited was yet to be reinforced with players of First Division experience, although at least Rowe's achievements were recognised by the club in its official report: 'These three past seasons form a memorable period in the club's history in which our manager, Mr Arthur Rowe, and his players, may take justifiable pride.'

Even the club's programme notes said of the same period: 'Our players have added much to the high reputation the club has gained wherever football is played throughout the world. We have been on the floodtide of success'. On August 2nd, the Spurs manager will have been delighted, too, to hear that Hungary had won the Olympic Soccer Gold in Helsinki, although he said it came as no surprise to him. Of course it was Rowe himself who had originally been selected to coach the Hungarians when the Helsinki Games were originally scheduled for 1940.

A week later British Pathé screened a fashion documentary for cinema audiences entitled *Men About Town*, filmed at the Victoria and Albert Museum. Instead of professional male models the producers selected leading male personalities to pose stiffly in frilly shirts, top hat and tails, 'plus twos' and tweed suits. They included comedian Richard 'Stinker' Murdoch, television and radio presenter Eamonn Andrews and actor Derek Bond. Sports figures also featured in the shape of England wicketkeeper Godfrey Evans, renowned cricket commentator and journalist John Arlott, golfer Arthur Lacey, athlete Roger Bannister, rugby international Wilfred Wooller, cricketer and footballer Dennis Compton and… Arthur Rowe. In one excerpt the camera pans from Bannister to Lacey before the commentator says 'Angora has won the toss for Tottenham Hotspur manager Arthur Rowe and tweeds for rugby international Wilfred Wooller.' Wooller stands alongside Rowe, peering at the magazine Arthur is clutching, but neither blink. The participants have been instructed to act as tailors' dummies, and the only acting Rowe engages in occurs when a young lady appears among all the waxwork-like males. In common with all the others, Rowe turns his head sharply as the commentator intones in his rich, early-BBC tones, 'They needed that feminine touch to prove they were anything but dummies.' It seems odd that the normally unassuming Rowe agreed to take part, although his fee will have handily supplemented his Spurs' income.

As for Spurs' pre-season preparations, for the second-half of the Public Trial match Rowe selected 20-year-old Peter Baker, who played at right-back for the Blues (reserves). This moment could be viewed as the very beginning of Spurs' great 'double' side and Rowe would even one day recommend Baker as successor to Ramsey in the England international side. In the trial, the Blues embarrassed the first team, 3-2. Meanwhile Vic Groves, a 19-year-old forward then playing for amateurs Leytonstone tried-out in pre-season and was signed on amateur terms.

West Brom visited to open season 1952-53, yet with both Spurs' wingers indisposed, Scot Alan Grubb and Les Dicker (who had been with Rowe at Chelmsford) came in. Despite his recent surgery Nicholson took the field, only for his damaged knee to survive mere minutes, so he now missed the following six matches. Only ten fit men now faced a side which ultimately challenged for the title. Ramsey and Withers were too often caught up-field leaving the lanky Clarke to cover, this despite already having a deep-lying centre-forward to worry about (converted winger Ronnie Allen). The ten men still went ahead, but the final score was 4-3 to the Albion. Nevertheless Rowe's depleted side had contributed to a thrilling encounter and the manager, conscious of West Brom's qualities, said 'I am confident... that we shall still do well this season.'

However, Rowe's looming problem is best summed-up by the fact that only four of the Reserves' side losing at Cardiff that day ultimately made any real impression in the first team (Hopkins, Marchi, McClellan and Reynolds). For the first away fixture at Manchester City, Wetton stood-in for Nicholson and amateur George

Cricketer and rugby union international Wilfred Wooller and Arthur Rowe model fashions at the Victoria and Albert Museum during the summer of 1952.

Robb finally made his second appearance. Despite Walters and Medley being sorely missed, a Duquemin goal saw Spurs hang on for a well-deserved victory. Medley returned for the tough trip to Newcastle, but took Grubb's place on the right, McClellan coming in on the left to replace Robb, who instead lined-up for Athenian Leaguers Finchley, this the equivalent of a Premiership side of today allowing a player to turn out for an amateur club on Saturdays. The rapidly growing catalogue of team changes was hardly conducive to consistent performance and Spurs began relying heavily on Ditchburn. At St James's Park Ditchburn turned creator, throwing long and accurately to McClellan out on the left, who raced off, evaded two challengers and shot past the advancing Ronnie Simpson. Although Spurs soon conceded an equaliser it was a well-earned point.

On September 1st, Spurs had an opportunity for their first double of the season but Manchester City wingers Roy Clarke and Jimmy Meadows gave Ramsey and Withers the run-around. City went 3-0 ahead before Robb led a late Spurs' revival. Baily's quickly-taken free-kick was nodded in by McClellan then Robb added Spurs' second. With seconds to spare a City defender handled in the area. In almost complete silence 'keeper Trautmann set himself as Ramsey placed the ball on the spot for the last kick of the match. He ran forward, hammering the ball goalwards, but it struck the crossbar and spun up… up… up… into the air before gravity brought it spinning back to earth, Trautmann failing to grasp the ball which spun into the net. This incident induced one spectator to leap with joy, leaving him with a broken ankle!

At home to promoted Cardiff the pacy McClellan ignored 'push-and-run', bypassing three defenders, drawing the 'keeper and shooting left-footed into the corner of the net. The lead lasted just two minutes but Spurs' winner came when the ball sped from Willis to Bennett, then Duquemin, who scored from a tight angle. Spurs then suffered two close defeats, first at undefeated Liverpool, then at Sheffield Wednesday, with injuries incurred this time by Bennett, Burgess and McClellan. Nicholson's absence was now being keenly felt and, when he did finally return for the home game with Liverpool, it was his midfield partner Burgess who had to drop out. Here Rowe granted a League debut to 19-year-old Billingsgate eel-skinner Vic Groves, making him the eighteenth different player Rowe had selected that season and it was still only mid-September. With Spurs a goal behind at the break, Groves' debut goal triggered a wonderful exhibition of football, especially from Baily and Harmer. Groves grabbed a second before Harmer completed the 3-1 victory, the *Herald* describing the '…delightful, artistic manner in which [Spurs] wore down, and then crushed, their opponents,' notably adding '…do not let us cast aside the brand of soccer with which Spurs have brought honour to Tottenham in recent years.'

Despite Groves' goals, Rowe restored Medley to face Arsenal and, in front of 69,220 White Hart Lane spectators, Spurs should already have been two-up before Ditchburn's throw to Willis was quickly robbed by Jimmy Logie whose cross was diverted home by Peter Goring's knee. Early in the second period Milton made it two after Robb lost possession and, with Spurs trying to salvage something, a breakaway saw Logie shoot past Ditchburn, Harmer grabbed a consolation but the mood of the Spurs faithful was summed up by Willis ending the game limping on the wing having broken a bone in his foot. Criticism mounted again, much of it aimed at Ditchburn's attempts to play out from the back. Yet the game had been full of good football although Rowe's men occasionally appeared slower than their opponents, and 'Push-and-run', without the required speed of application, was unlikely to achieve another Championship. After three consecutive seasons of success, Spurs now sat in the lower half of the table and the *Herald* even described some fans as '...full of bitterness' against '...club personnel.' Some Spurs' men were considered insufficiently aggressive. Other fans wanted hefty kicking. Others felt defenders were too adventurous. Rowe was continuously critiqued by those who preferred to live in the past.

The injured Willis and Burgess missed the arrival of defensively-strong Burnley, but the Championship-winning forward five of Walters, Bennett, Duquemin, Baily and Medley finally teamed-up again while Robb was excused Spurs duty so he could turn out for Finchley again. He appeared to enjoy the best of all worlds: maintaining his teaching career, maintaining good relations with amateurs Finchley and enjoying occasional spells in the First Division limelight. The Burnley game became a scrappy affair, a result of strong winds combined with the visitor's negative approach. The encounter was illuminated four minutes after the break, however, when Ramsey sent a free-kick to the far side where Withers played it forward to Medley. Withers received it back on the overlap, crossed for Duquemin who headed high into the net. Ramsey gifted Burnley an equaliser, but in the final minute a desperate Medley cross from the left was caught by the wind and sent dipping and swerving into the net. It was two points gained, albeit due to meteorological good fortune. However the Spurs manager, aware of his team's shortcomings and seeking a prolific striker, turned to Newcastle's Chilean international George Robledo, scorer of 39 goals the previous season, but the Magpies were reluctant to part with the 27-year-old and asked for a sizeable fee. A consolation that week was Rowe's acquisition of Peter Baker's signature on professional forms, the player later to capture four major medals with the club.

Spurs travelled to Deepdale without Ramsey and Baily (both on England duty) but Burgess and Medley had returned. Preston, who would lose the title that season by the narrowest margin in English football history, did more of the attacking and Angus Morrison's cross-shot proved to be the winner. In 11 games Rowe had fielded an unchanged side only the once and, at Derby, one full-back (Ramsey) returned just as the injured Withers was replaced by 17-year-old debutant Mel Hopkins. Rowe, knowing his squad urgently required strengthening, skipped the resulting goalless draw to go scouting. Disturbingly, however, the Tottenham director responsible for negative match programme notes enjoyed the hospitality of the Derby boardroom after the match and proceeded to print criticisms of Spurs' play he had heard there (with Rowe absent, critical comment will have flowed more freely than usual). Despite then being the most successful Spurs' manager of all time, Rowe had considerable cause to watch his back.

Next opponents Blackpool had achieved eight wins from 10, but the great Matthews was missing, injured, and, on the half-hour Blackpool's stand-in goalkeeper Harry Sharratt failed to collect a corner and Duquemin put Spurs ahead. Baily, back to his best, made it 2-0, and even the referee assisted, awarding a successfully converted penalty (put away by Ramsey) after a Blackpool defender kicked the ball against a colleague's hand. A second from Baily completed a 4-0 win and Spurs climbed to 10th. Then, at the 14th attempt, Rowe finally fielded his classic (if creaking) Championship-winning side at Stamford Bridge and will have appreciated the Chelsea match programme notes which highlighted how often Spurs had missed star players through injury: '[Spurs] hope soon to recapture in full the machine-like touch that carried them to success—smooth, high-speed push-and-run football.' Sadly, the Chelsea encounter itself was scrappy, Willis putting through his own goal and, at the other end, a Ramsey spot-kick being saved. However, Ramsey did convert a second spot-kick before the end but, by then, Chelsea had scored again, through McNichol, Spurs returning home pointless.

With 'push-and-run' again under the microscope, Ralph Wetton recalled one morning when the Spurs manager addressed the players, saying: 'No training this morning.' 'He used to do this every so often,' Wetton recalled, 'and he used to talk. He could talk all day, Arthur, and not one of us would be asleep. He said: "I don't see any smiling faces anymore. What's wrong?" So one or two piped up. He said "Well, if you're not happy with the system, I'll change it. We'll work out something else. How do you feel about that?" The players said "No, we want to stick with it." So he said "Right. Well I'll tell you where you are going wrong." So he started. He said to Les Medley: "You're not coming back like you were. You're staying too far up-field and we can't get hold of you." And he turned to three or four of the blokes who weren't doing their jobs. He ironed it all out and we went from there, and that

After 'keeper Sharratt's error, striker Duquemin slams home in the 4-0 victory over Blackpool, with Walters (near left) and Bennett in support.

was it.' Although, with further tough opposition coming up, things would fail to improve immediately.

As with Rowe's Spurs, their next opponents, Busby's United, were also struggling, the common denominator being that both sides had experienced a lengthy summer tour. For Spurs, Uphill replaced the unfit Bennett and in six minutes it was his cross (an overhead kick) which Walters headed home before a deflected shot beat Ditchburn. For twenty minutes of the second-half Spurs were back in control, but, with 15 minutes left, Berry robbed Ramsey then ran from halfway for the winner. With more defeats than wins in the first third of the season, 'Fanfare' described '… long faces and grumbles from many quarters.' Ralph Wetton for one didn't agree that the summer tour was a factor in the poor start in 1952-53, considering it more of a relaxing 'holiday' but one article published at the time did suggest the North American tour was at least partly responsible for the drop in form.

More gloom was on the horizon for Spurs fans; a third successive loss at Fratton Park, Portsmouth on November 8th was compounded by the transfer-listing of 32-year-old Les Medley which emerged after their next fixture. Pointing out it would take a high price to replace the winger, the *Herald* stated that '…it should not stop Spurs from buying, for their bank account is healthy.' This was perhaps designed to put the Spurs' board on the spot. Although the club was now fifth from bottom, if viewing their situation as a 'cup half full' Spurs were also a mere nine points off first place with 52 points still to play for. Medley was missing for Spurs but they sped out of the traps when Bolton arrived at White Hart Lane. However, after 13 minutes Ramsey imprudently supported an attack which already incorporated Nicholson and Burgess and, when Spurs lost possession, Trotters' inside-left Harold Hassall raced 40 yards with Ramsey and Nicholson trailing in his wake. He then sent the ball out to his winger, pulling defenders out of position and leaving the great Nat Lofthouse unattended to stab home the resulting cross. But Bennett equalised and that is how it ended.

The reason for Medley's absence then became clear. Having decided to emigrate at season's end as his Canadian wife had been unwell, he had asked for assurance that Spurs would still pay the £600 benefit due should he have stayed. Having received no assurance, he was further angered to find a note from the manager stating he had been transfer-listed. Not delivering such information in person seemed unlike Rowe. Had the board told him that a replacement for Medley would not be acquired unless he first received a fee for the winger? Rowe conveyed the distressing news to Medley in writing having departed early that day to take a Football Combination representative side to Brussels. With Medley's future earmarked for Canada it was unlikely he would have found another club to provide income for his five remaining months in England. He was also losing a benefit that was all but due. Once back from Brussels Rowe received the board's assurance that Medley would, after all, get all the dues owed him and this guaranteed Medley's services until season's end. For Rowe this episode will have added to the stress of increasing criticism from press, fans and 'spoiled-for-success' directors.

This time the *Herald* took Rowe's side, blaming the poor season to date on the players: 'It is reasonable to expect the players to carry out dressing-room plans, and a stern warning should be given to forwards who persist in individual moves and to defencemen who sacrifice their role of stopping the opposition [when going] up-field in efforts to score goals.' This reference to 'gung-ho' defending exposed the correspondent's lack of understanding of Rowe's system, depending as it did on a more fluid approach to players' roles. If, for example, Ramsey 'pushed,' he would also have to 'run', expecting Nicholson to cover for him. More to the point, if it wasn't for his club's resistance to spend, why had Rowe been unable to attract a determined striker (the likes of a Lofthouse, Holton or Robledo) to the club? Surely, had the money been in his hands, Rowe would not have denied himself (and the fans) the pleasure of including a prolific sharpshooter in his side?

Conversely, should Rowe have stood by his ageing stars? Matt Busby, having finally won the League Championship in 1952, wasted no time in telling his board that the team needed remodelling. 'Something must be done and I am going to do it. I must be drastic and make big changes,' said the Scot whose nature was perhaps steelier than Rowe's. Thus were born the famed 'Busby Babes', their success only halted by the horror of the Munich air crash following further Championship successes in 1956 and 1957. However, in view of Rowe's demanding directors it must be clarified that it took Busby's transitional United side all of FOUR YEARS to return to the top. Would the Tottenham board have been so patient?

Another concern for Rowe was heavy terrace barracking of Eddie Baily, whose form was hardly helped when Medley increasingly ignored the basic tenet of 'push-and-run' and kept possession. Baily was declared 'unwell' for the trip to Aston Villa, who were on a good run, but Harmer, his replacement, demanded so much attention from the Villa defence, particularly Blanchflower, that his fellow forwards and half-backs were gifted time and space. Spurs took control right from the start, Bennett hooking home a Walters' cross and, just beyond the hour, Ditchburn threw long to Dicker at outside-left, who found Harmer whose cross to Walters was played square to Duquemin, who struck it home — another fine example of Ditchburn as the first line of attack. Dicker made it 3-0, thus ending a run of five winless games and Villa fans considered Spurs' attacking play the best they had seen that season.

Harmer's performance again raised the question: why was he not a regular in Rowe's side? The player himself claimed he could '…last ninety minutes with the best of them,' as proven by his Villa performance, but he lacked speed and tended to take a few touches after collecting a pass, thus defying the successful application of 'push-and-run'. This was one soccer essential Rowe shared with long-ball adherent Stan Cullis; they both admired skilled individuals but demanded their talents be devoted to the benefit of the team. Harmer himself held no personal grudge against Rowe, believing his limited opportunities were due to Baily's form. Bill Nicholson felt that size and weight were the more significant issues, saying that Harmer was '…a player opponents thought they could intimidate.'

With confidence returned after the Villa success, Spurs now met both table-topping sides: Sunderland and Wolves. By half-time Sunderland's costly Trevor Ford had put the Rokerites two-up but, when Spurs quickly forced a corner in the second-half, the referee introduced a white ball and this immediately landed in the back of the Sunderland net via little Harmer's head. Spurs then drew level through

1952-53 saw full-back Peter Baker (left), sign for Rowe as a professional, eventually becoming Ramsey's successor. Meanwhile Les Medley (centre) was in his final season with Spurs before emigrating to Canada. When acquiring young Ron Henry (right), Rowe had completed Nicholson's future 'Double' side's full-back pairing (Baker and Henry would thus earn four major medals each).

Duquemin and pressed hard for a winner but the visitors' 'keeper barred the way. But three points from four, achieved on heavy pitches, restored Spurs' spirit and Rowe's men were now just four victories behind leaders Wolves, with December yet to arrive. The *Herald* stated: 'Should Spurs fight to victory [at Wolves] there will be many fans and critics ready to change their minds about the Lilywhites' chances of winning the Championship in [this] Coronation Year.'

The Spurs party were delayed by fog on the way to Molineux, the players changing into their playing strip on the train. As the pitch was icy in places, slushy in others and covered in sawdust, for once the manager instructed his men to utilise the long ball, but from habit they still engaged in constructive football despite struggling to stay on their feet. Even with an injured Burgess finishing the game on the wing, Spurs took a point from the League leaders and remained undefeated for a fourth successive match. During the week that followed Rowe finally brought a player in, but only by resorting to a seemingly desperate swap deal, Chris Adams being exchanged for Third Division South Norwich City's centre-forward Roy 'Stick' Hollis, a sunken-cheeked, slim six-footer. Hollis had scored more than a goal every other game but only at the bottom end of the Football League. With so much money in the bank, why was Rowe having to resort to exchange deals for players ill-attuned to top-level football? Inevitably, Hollis, already 27, would not prove a success.

After beating high-flying Charlton, Rowe again admitted 'push-and-run' had been put to one side, telling the *Herald*: 'The old formula has not been discredited or discarded, and in due course every effort will be made to swing back into the quick, fluid style.' Indeed, the *Herald*, ironically commented that '…games have become less entertaining.' But points were being picked up and further uplifting news for Rowe arrived through the mail: a licence to install floodlighting (although lights were not as yet sanctioned for Football League games) at White Hart Lane.

Moving into the second-half of the season Spurs' short-passing game returned at West Brom (now managed by Vic Buckingham), forcing the home side to defend desperately for the first 30 minutes. Dicker put Spurs ahead and the lead was nearly increased, but before half-time Reg Ryan and Ronnie Allen replied for Albion, and that is how the score stayed. Although Spurs' unbeaten run had ended, it had occurred against a side soon to press hard for the Championship itself and Rowe believed that signs of a return to Championship-winning form had became apparent. In the spirit of Christmas, the *Herald* was expressing exaggerated optimism regarding Spurs' back-up players, but, if truth be told, even Wetton and Brittan were hardly the equal of Nicholson or Burgess. Hopkins had played well in his solitary appearance, and amateur Groves starred on his debut against Liverpool but too much time had passed with insufficient player investment.

Indeed, aside from the unfit Burgess, Rowe reverted to the Championship-winning line-up for Middlesbrough's arrival on Christmas Day. Les Bennett, wanting to spend a rare Christmas Day at home, told his manager he was sick, but a suspicious Rowe talked the player into turning out. Although Bennett proceeded to put Spurs ahead, he was soon hobbling on the wing. His colleagues were slogging through the mud as, despite a new drainage system, the home pitch still held water (Tottenham were perhaps as frugal with drainage as with team-building). At half-time there was little sign of the extraordinary 45 minutes that followed. Appreciating that an injured Bennett would not make best use of the rare grassy patch out on the right, Rowe smartly restored Walters to the wing so that Bennett could utilise his heading ability at centre-forward. Ten minutes into the half Duquemin's free-kick rebounded to the limping Bennett, who still beat 'keeper Ugolini. Three minutes later, having apparently run-off his injury, Bennett passed to Baily and Spurs were 3-1 ahead. Then Baily added a fourth. As Middlesbrough tried to get back into the game, an unmarked Duquemin headed the fifth, before a rare misplaced pass from England star Wilf Mannion was collected by Medley whose 30-yarder was parried by Ugolini for Bennett to complete his hat-trick. A minute later the unnerved Ugolini fumbled Baily's effort and the 'crippled' Bennett snapped-up an astonishing, personal fourth. In a 7-1 victory, almost every Spurs' attempt had found the target.

Afterwards Rowe said to a sheepish Bennett: 'When you feel better, Les, I'll expect FIVE goals', and 48 hours later Bennett was indeed fit enough to start on a pitch where snow had replaced mud. Rowe will have instructed his players to pepper the by-now nervous Ugolini with shots on target and, in the 25th minute, the 'keeper could only push a shot out for Duquemin to knock in. Then Walters gave Spurs a two-goal half-time cushion. Just four minutes into the second-half Duquemin's cross was deflected in for an own-goal and with twenty left, Baily set Bennett up to fire his fifth goal past Ugolini inside three days. Spurs moved up to tenth and were just two wins shy of where they stood 12 months' previously when they finished as runners-up. Despite their earlier pessimism, the *Herald* now talked of an 'outside chance' Spurs could win the League and also made them a good bet for the FA Cup.

Newcastle were the first visitors in Coronation Year, 1953, Burgess surprisingly taking the number seven shirt in place of an injured Walters, Rowe's preference to field a player less than 100% fit and out of position confirmed his limited faith in the reserves available to him. After Ditchburn had brilliantly saved from Milburn, Medley rounded his full-back before sending over a swinging centre, Burgess ran in from his unfamiliar wide right position to head past Simpson, putting Spurs ahead. Just two minutes later Baily crossed low and Burgess fired home his second. However, within minutes Newcastle pulled it back to 2-2 through Milburn and Davies but with eight minutes remaining Spurs sealed the points; the ball sped from Medley to Bennett to Baily to Burgess, who threaded it through for Duquemin to finish off a classic 'push-and-run' move to snatch the victory. With one defeat in nine, Spurs now sat just six points behind new leaders Sunderland. Despite their poor start to the season, Spurs had both out-scored the League leaders and conceded fewer goals.

Rowe made his Cup aims clear when he fielded his Championship-winning XI in the third round at little Tranmere Rovers. After three Spurs' 'goals' were called offside in the fog, the minnows took the lead which they held until the hour mark when Bennett equalised and the First Division giants were relieved to take the train south having secured a replay 48 hours later. This time no fewer than nine Spurs' efforts would find the net, Sid McLellan bagging a hat-trick to defeat tired Tranmere 9-1. After a goalless draw at newly-promoted Cardiff, Harmer, his 25th birthday approaching, finally requested a transfer. He bore Rowe no ill-will and the manager himself said he would gladly have the player back should things not work out. Before returning to the Cup trail, Spurs extended their run to seven League and Cup games without defeat, struggling to a 2-1 home win over Sheffield Wednesday.

The fourth round draw sent Spurs on their travels yet again, this time to Deepdale, Preston. This was a good omen — on the two previous occasions when the name 'Tottenham Hotspur' was engraved on the FA Cup, the Lancashire club had been one of the victims en-route to the final. On this occasion Preston had beaten Wolves 5-2 in the tie of the third round and had won eight consecutive home games. North End's main threat was their great right-winger Tom Finney. Rowe doubled-up at left-back, Withers sporting the number 11 shirt at Medley's expense. It was Withers who made an entirely unexpected contribution in the third minute, his in-swinging corner-kick travelling directly into the Preston net. Despite the doubling-up of Willis and Withers on Finney, it still took the England winger just ten minutes to earn a penalty when he was tripped. Twice the wind blew the ball off the spot, and when Finney's foot finally made contact Ditchburn got a finger to his shot, but the ball still rolled over the line for the equaliser. Then, despite much Spurs defending, Withers, of all people, shot his second past 'keeper Thompson just before the break. Another Preston equaliser took it to a replay at White Hart Lane but, clearly, Rowe's defensive ploy to counter Finney had been a masterstroke, keeping the club in the competition. In a total of 164 competitive games for Spurs, Withers' two goals were the only two he ever achieved!

The day before the replay Ralph Wetton went to the billiards room where he encountered a 21-year-old clutching his £10 signing-on fee (equivalent to approximately £300 today). This was Johnny Brooks, Spurs having beaten Arsenal, Manchester United, Liverpool and Chelsea to his signature. Brooks was a teenage fan of Rowe's Championship-winning sides and Spurs paid Reading just £3,000 in cash plus two reserve players in part exchange. Brooks, later referred to as 'Mr Adonis', spent all his signing-on fee on clothes when he went to collect his club blazer from the tailors in Bruce Grove. He possessed a powerful shot and Terry Venables, who later played with him at Chelsea, described him as 'brilliantly gifted' and 'oozing class'. After three years as manager, Brooks was Rowe's first significant signing, although he was unproven at First Division level.

55,600 cup-crazy Spurs fans then turned-up for the Preston replay on February 4th with the prospect of Third Division Halifax in the next round. Within eight minutes Duquemin back-heeled into the net from Baily's assist and despite Preston pressure thereafter, Spurs held on to win 1-0. Young Spurs' fans who were already looking forward happily to the following morning's end to sweet rationing could now go to bed dreaming of Cup success too.

72 hours later, Spurs faced local rivals Arsenal at Highbury, knowing a win would bring the sides level in the table. For 23 minutes Arsenal resisted Spurs' attractive passing patterns, Duquemin striking the home crossbar, but confusion between Bennett and Willis saw Arthur Milton cross and Cliff Holton smash a left-footer past Ditchburn. This spurred the *Herald* reporter to take another gratuitous swipe at 'push-and-run'. He hypothesised that Spurs had '…paid no heed to this [Arsenal] lesson on how to score goals in the minimum number of moves.' Early in the second-half Spurs defenders took a breather, mistakenly thinking the ball had crossed the goal-line, only for 'cannonball' Holton to strike a shot in-off Ramsey guarding the line. Seven minutes later Ramsey hesitated, expecting a handball decision, and Lishman tapped-in a third, before Jimmy Logie beat Ramsey to a cross for a final, devastating derby scoreline of 4-0. The *Herald*, covering the adventures of both Spurs *and* Arsenal, saw things this time only through rose-tinted glasses. It had been only a second defeat in 15 outings yet a pointed attack was launched on everything Rowe's Spurs stood for. Exhaustion from the Cup replay was overlooked, and the writer poured scorn on Rowe's methods. Arsenal, he suggested, had given Spurs '…a decisive four-goals answer to [my capitals] THIS TYPE OF FOOTBALL,' adding: 'Spurs lost because the forwards decided to be "modern" in the belief that their pretty football would mesmerise the Highbury players.' This bitter criticism of Rowe's successful methods will have encouraged less-savvy Spurs' fans (and directors) to up the pressure on Rowe. Yet a match report by the knowledgeable and erudite former Arsenal star Bernard Joy, impressed by Spurs' many chances, saw it far more realistically, headlining: 'ARSENAL FLATTERED BY 4-0 WIN.'

On Valentine's Day 1953 Spurs travelled north for their first-ever meeting with Third Division North side Halifax Town, who had already dispatched two First Division sides, Cardiff and Stoke. Rowe had sent scouts to watch Halifax while the Cardiff manager, Rowe's former playing colleague Cyril Spiers, had provided him with some tips. Despite 4-6 inches of snow on the pitch at Halifax's ramshackle Shay ground, nearly 37,000 attended, a Halifax record that still stands today. As the game progressed, conditions became similar to those encountered at White Hart Lane. Rowe had told his men to treat Halifax as League champions and Spurs eventually dominated but it took nearly an hour before Bennett shot left-footed into the roof of the net. Two more goals were added and, after two successive championships and a runners-up position, Rowe had now taken Spurs to the FA Cup quarter-finals... but would they finally get a home draw? No! This time they had to travel to Second Division Birmingham City.

By now Rowe's focus was on Cup success, yet a Duquemin hat-trick saw Spurs draw 4-4 at home to Championship-challenging Preston seeking revenge for their Cup exit. Spurs now seemed marooned in-or-around tenth place in Division One, slipping to the equivalent of four wins behind the leaders. Rowe now organised a special practice match designed to combat Second Division Birmingham's strengths and take advantage of their weaknesses. For this the first-team wore their standard white shirts while Rowe wanted his reserves to resemble Birmingham, to which end he borrowed royal blue shirts from his friend Ted Drake at Chelsea. Spurs already had a second strip utilising blue shirts but they were NAVY blue and Rowe insisted that to properly represent Birmingham they must be Chelsea's ROYAL blue!

So, on Saturday February 28th 1953, Spurs took the field at St. Andrews. City hit Spurs with quick, no-nonsense tackling and before long five of Rowe's men were nursing injuries and self-preservation became as important as the need to win. Birmingham went one-up after 24 minutes and held the lead up to the break. Before sending them back out in search of an equaliser, Rowe encouraged his men to stay composed in the face of provocation. It still took Spurs 30 minutes before Bennett equalised with a firm header to take the contest back to White Hart Lane. An unusually bitter Rowe called for a change of referee for the replay, saying Birmingham's performance was the worst exhibition of 'so-called' football he could remember, adding: 'I was never a carpet-slipper player myself, but some of the incidents were just too bad to believe.' The semi-final draw was announced before the replay so Spurs knew their reward for overcoming Birmingham would be a semi-final contest with Stanley Matthews' Blackpool.

Despite missing the injured Nicholson and Clarke, a fine Duquemin goal put Spurs ahead by half-time. Birmingham pulled level before Bennett added an excellent second for Spurs, but once again, with just seven minutes left, the never-say-die visitors sent the game into extra-time during which no goals were added. The two clubs' chairmen then tossed for regional advantage on a neutral ground. In keeping with Spurs' terrible luck with Cup draws, the Spurs' chairman lost the toss and, instead of a London venue, Spurs would have to travel to Wolverhampton.

This second replay meant Spurs' had to play three games within nine days, Rowe rested no fewer than five players for the League game at potential semi-final opponents Blackpool. Tragedy struck, too, when the three-week-old son of Sonny Walters died on the day of the match. In came six non-regulars. With so many stars missing, Ditchburn kept the score down to 2-0 and thoughts could now be entirely focussed on the Cup. With three defeats from their last four League games, the second Cup replay now took-on greater significance if Rowe's critics were to be kept at bay.

Two days later Spurs, with their six stars returned to the line-up, took the field to face Birmingham at Molineux. Once again Spurs were forced to work hard but, with just 12 of the 90 minutes remaining, Burgess threw in to Walters near the right corner-flag. A give-and-go with Burgess left Walters to manoeuvre his way along the by-line before shooting the winning goal from a tight angle between Gil Merrick and his near post. With Walters' devastating personal loss in mind, there could have been no better candidate to score the decider. Rowe was finally 90 minutes away from fulfilling his dream of leading Spurs out at Wembley. The *Herald* now piled on the expectations: 'All are convinced that Spurs will be one of the Wembley finalists in this Coronation year.' Most neutrals, however, desired to see semi-final opponents Blackpool win so that veteran Stanley Matthews could finally receive a winner's medal at the third attempt. Again Rowe rested first-teamers for the home League game with Derby County. With a mere 48 hour gap before the next League game (against relegation-threatened Chelsea), fewer than 14,000 spectators were rewarded as Rowe's makeshift side hammered County 5-2. Ramsey, Nicholson, Clarke and Medley then continued 'resting' for the London derby with last-placed Chelsea. Duquemin was made captain in recognition of it being his wedding day, but this failed to bring good fortune. He lost the toss and Spurs lost the game. With excitement mounting for the semi-final, another outstanding Spurs' full-back of the future was then signing amateur forms for Rowe. Shoreditch-born Ron Henry had been spotted at Woolwich during his National Service with the Royal Artillery. In two years he was to turn professional and make his Spurs' debut, and, like Peter Baker, would capture medals for both League and Cup in 1961.

In preparation to face Blackpool at Villa Park, Rowe decided there was no definitive strategy for dealing with Matthews, simply choosing the tougher-tackling Withers over Willis and, despite a lack of match practice, he restored Nicholson and Clarke. Most believed Blackpool were the stronger attacking side so it was critical that Spurs' forward line should click. The 90 minutes to come would be chock-full of drama and incident, with Spurs determined not to repeat their late collapse against the same side and at the same stage five years' earlier under Joe Hulme. For the six survivors from that day, Ditchburn, Nicholson, Burgess, Baily, Duquemin and Bennett, this was their chance to turn the tables. All now was set.

Spurs attacked from the first whistle but, in only their second foray forward, Blackpool won a corner. Taking the kick Matthews saw main target Stan Mortensen heavily marked, so instead drove his kick to the near post where Bill Perry had come across from the far left. Ditchburn came to collect but Perry got there first, looping his header over Ditchburn's hands and in off the crossbar. Thereafter Spurs controlled more than 80% of the play, Blackpool relying much on Farm in goal and breakaways featuring Matthews. As *The Guardian* reported: 'One glorious [Spurs] move went the length of the field with the ball on the ground and not a Blackpool player touching it.' At one stage Baily headed against the bar while McClellan broke clear and looked set to equalise only to be stopped by a last-ditch tackle. Spurs' frontline picked up the pace at half-time following words from Rowe and, within five minutes, a sweeping attacking move, ended with Bennett crossing low from the right to Walters who, with his back to goal and near the edge of the six-yard box, motioned to bring the ball under control but instead allowed it to run to Duquemin, who opened his body before guiding his shot with the inside of his left-foot into the left side of goal. 1-1!

But Bennett then received an accidental blow when leaping for a high ball, his right eye almost closing completely. Clearly dazed, he remained a passenger on the left wing for the final half-hour. With time running out, Spurs kept pressing in search of the winner. McClellan twice broke clear to beat the 'keeper, each attempt agonisingly coming back off the post. A free-kick slammed against the bar and there were two penalty shouts. A winning goal for Spurs had to come. Indeed, if not for the woodwork Spurs should already have been on their way to Wembley but as the one-and-a-half minutes of time added for the treatment administered to Bennett drew to an end, the referee put his whistle to his lips. As the better team on the day, Spurs remained confident they would win through in extra-time. However, the final whistle still hadn't been blown when referee Arthur Ellis awarded a free-kick for handball by Baily, who indicated the muddy mark made by the ball on his shirt in vain. Stanley Matthews later recalled Ellis checking his watch again at this point. From the free-kick, Blackpool hoofed the ball forward to winger Perry, who slipped it to Ernie Taylor, who in turn tried to return it to Perry. But the ball instead looped over Ramsey's shoulder as he ran toward his own goal, Perry hard on his heels. Ramsey waited for it to bounce and it did, but surprisingly high, so with Perry breathing down his neck, he waited to play it again, which he chose to do with his chest, but with insufficient force. The ball ran from him, toward his own goal. He stretched out a leg but could only push the ball gently into the path of an unmarked Mudie, who had smartly moved to cover the space between Ramsey and Ditchburn. Mudie spun-and-hit a left-foot shot just as Ditchburn flung himself at his feet, the ball rolling into the unguarded net. Clarke, who should have been tight on Mudie, threw his head back in despair as Ditchburn remained on his knees, head down. There was barely time to kick-off when the final whistle sounded and the Spurs men dragged themselves from the field.

Baily recalled it as the first time he had seen Rowe's team with their heads down. Ramsey suffered a quiet despair, weighed down by the gravity of his oh-so-late error (ironically, eleven months' earlier he was quoted as saying: 'Mistakes by full-backs can turn victory into defeat. Safety-first must be the slogan'). In the stands Rowe must have felt quite wretched. He later recalled the post-match dressing-room scene to Ken Shearwood: 'I never saw a sadder-looking bunch sitting in a dressing-room. I felt so sorry for them, because most of that side would never get another chance to play at Wembley, they were too old'. Shearwood recalls Rowe describing how a director had pounced on him after the Blackpool game: 'To make matters worse one of the directors railed on-and-on at me about Ramsey. In the end I told him to shut his mouth'.

Some commentators of the time considered this the best Cup semi-final of all time. Nobody could foresee that it proved to be the prelude to 'The Matthews' Final', without doubt still the most talked-of FA Cup Final in the tournament's history, but it should really have been 'The Rowe Final', or 'The "Push-and-Run" Final'. Performing on the perfect Wembley surface Spurs would surely have illuminated the big occasion with their inspiring, crisp, pass-and-move style and the odds against Bolton would have been stacked high. The injured Medley's telepathic link-up with Baily had been missed, while Bennett had of course been left groggy

just as Spurs were taking command. Although Ramsey did not absolve himself of any blame for the winning goal, he also pointed to his best pal's contribution to it — had Baily not disputed the free-kick rather than quickly taking-up a covering position, then the kick may not have been taken so quickly. But Rowe would neither have chaired a post-mortem nor pointed a finger of blame.

The *Herald* ruefully reflected on the joy of Spurs fans earlier that day, tossing coins to children as their coaches passed through villages. The return trip will have been long and testing. Spurs had dominated yet lost the Wembley dream when it was there for the taking. The realisation slowly sank-in, too, that for the second successive season no further silverware was to be added to Rowe's collection. That the most memorable final of all time would materialise from Spurs' misery was an added, cruel twist. Most neutrals would soon forget the equally-stirring semi-final.

One can imagine Rowe absorbing the accumulated pain of his players. He said: 'There shall be no criticism of any player or of any deed. The whole team played well and according to plan, but hitting the upright and crossbar, having an injured player for nearly half the game, and going out as we did in the dying seconds after clearly being on top, is just sheer misfortune.' It was a 'misfortune' that prevented Rowe from adding FA Cup success to his fledgling yet outstanding CV, success that may have kept his carping directors at bay. Villa Park had probably been the last chance for Rowe's ageing side to seriously challenge for the Cup.

Four days later the dejected squad travelled to Old Trafford to resume a League programme now offering little incentive. It was a pivotal moment for both teams. Busby's new 'Babes' were beginning to be pieced together just as Rowe's 'push-and-runners' were beginning to creak. Clarke went straight out of the team again, surely confirming he had not been 100% fit for the semi-final, while Bennett's knock was serious enough to keep him out of the next four games. Spurs only lost by the odd goal in five, but it was their fifth League defeat in seven. Even struggling Portsmouth came away with a point from the Lane and, at one point during the game Ramsey found himself in a similar position as during those closing moments

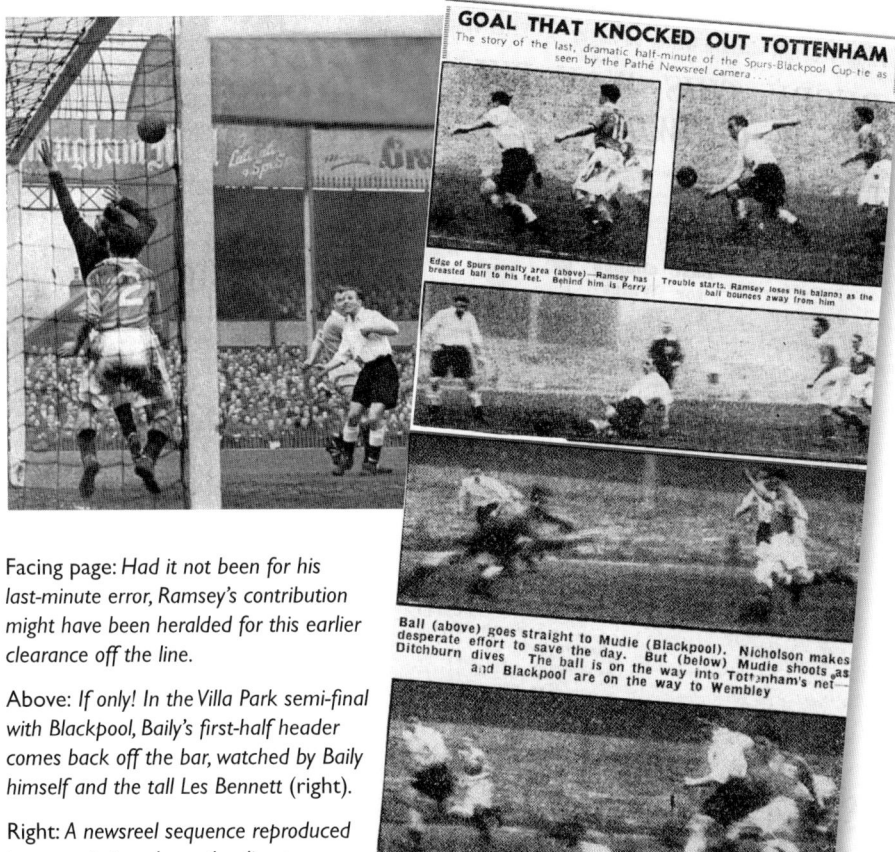

Facing page: *Had it not been for his last-minute error, Ramsey's contribution might have been heralded for this earlier clearance off the line.*

Above: *If only! In the Villa Park semi-final with Blackpool, Baily's first-half header comes back off the bar, watched by Baily himself and the tall Les Bennett (right).*

Right: *A newsreel sequence reproduced in a newspaper shows the disastrous last-minute Blackpool winner following Ramsey's error.*

against Blackpool, facing his own goal with the ball at his feet. Just before passing back to Ditchburn, someone in the crowd shouted 'Don't give away another!' which surprisingly drew a curt smile from the usually surly Ramsey.

With three clubs leading on 43 points (Preston, Charlton and Wolves), Spurs, in no danger of relegation, sat in 12th place on 33 points. Aside from the exciting, if finally tragic, Cup run, Rowe's reserves topped the Football Combination and led in the Combination Cup. But even a 1-0 Easter home win over relegation-threatened Stoke provoked criticism, Spurs failing to take full advantage of an injury suffered by Stoke's 'keeper for 75 minutes of the game, leading the Tottenham programme to lambast the club's own players, particularly Baily and Bennett. Meanwhile, with his future away from Spurs, Medley had begun defying instructions, holding the ball and taking on defenders, thus slowing the pace of the game. Inevitably, left-side partner Baily, very self-critical by nature, suffered. Rowe once said how much he appreciated the compassion Matt Busby showed United players who were suffering poor form, saying: 'The reason why a boy can't produce this or that on a particular day may be something he doesn't understand himself. The manager's job is to try and discover why this is and, if possible, correct it.' Baily's barracking from

Left: *Johnny Brooks, a debutant over Easter 1953.*

Right: *George Robb, coaching schoolboys. More of an individualist, he was hardly the ideal replacement for the departing Medley, for whom 'push-and-run' had come naturally.*

the terraces persuaded Rowe to leave him out of the firing line for several of the remaining games.

Twenty-four hours after Stoke Spurs travelled to Burnden Park, Bolton to face the team they would have faced at Wembley. Young striker Alf Stokes was given a trial run and Spurs won 3-2. For the final Easter game, the return at Stoke, Rowe reinstated Baily, nearly 160 miles from any critical, baying home fans and 21-year-old Johnny Brooks was the debutant this time. In four days over Easter Rowe had utilised six players with an average age of 22, the others being Brittan, 25; Harmer, 25; King, 23; Marchi, 20 and Stokes, 20. However, on this occasion the home side struck two second-half goals without reply to ease their relegation concerns. Rowe was looking to the future again when making no fewer than NINE changes against Aston Villa, for whom Blanchflower scored with a rare header. Spurs equalised with a fine move, McClellan finishing from Duquemin's perfect through ball. The draw sent Spurs' points total crawling up to 38. That same afternoon Pegasus were at Wembley for their second Amateur Cup Final, this time beating Harwich and Parkeston, 6-0. That Pegasus still utilised Rowe's methods was in no doubt, judging from this report: '...hardly a pass was wasted; in the scoring of two of their goals, eight Pegasus players criss-crossed in perfect unison without an opponent touching the ball.' Another report stated that Pegasus appeared to have 22 players on the field, '... tantalising opponents who were a yard behind the pass for most of the afternoon.'

Meanwhile, right-back Peter Baker had impressed Rowe so much during an A-side draw with an experienced West Ham side that, with Ramsey on England duty, he was selected for the visit to Sunderland. Baker was the last of no less than ten players introduced in '52-53, so Rowe could hardly be accused of failing to identify a need for change. However most, aside from Brooks, had came through the ranks or did not demand transfer fees. Despite the increase in wealth emanating from Rowe's success, it stayed locked away in the White Hart Lane vault.

Spurs' penultimate game of 1952-53 saw title-chasing Wolves visit Tottenham and it being Medley's final game prior to emigrating, Rowe named him as captain. Despite Wolves having so much to play for, Rowe's mid-table Spurs lorded it over the visitors, winning 3-2. Marchi had impressed in Nicholson's role while Medley finally bowed-out after 46 goals from 164 League appearances.

Spurs ended in ninth place after a 3-2 loss in torrential rain at Charlton, finishing thirteen points behind eventual champions Arsenal. Spurs had lost no fewer than 12 games by just the odd goal and drawn 11. Spurs had continued making many chances and just one more goal in each of those 23 games would have put them on 64 points, ten more than Arsenal. Of course, for a long period in season 1952-53, the League programme had taken second place to Rowe's Cup ambitions. Ageing players also picked-up injuries they might well have avoided when they were younger and they were slower to recover, so team changes could no longer be regarded as misfortune. The knock-on effects of that punishing summer tour (eight points dropped in the first seven games alone, those which Nicholson missed due to his tour injury) had contributed to a loss of around 6,500 spectators per home game, biting into those gleefully-banked tour profits.

For an end-of-season tournament in Scotland, Spurs stayed in the coastal town of Largs before facing Hibernian at Ibrox Park. While there Spurs broke local by-laws, one local resident contacting the police to report a '…bunch of young men' playing football on an '…unfenced grassy plot' near the sea front. No charges were preferred and Rowe said everyone had been 'charming' about it. Is this an amusing tale or yet more evidence that the club were unwilling to rent proper training facilities?

Despite releasing seven players Rowe's only close-season targets appeared to be amateurs Groves and Robb. On departing, Medley thanked players, fans and well-wishers but showed no gratitude to the Tottenham Club or management. He would play in Canada until 1957, later playing and coaching in South Africa. Robb finally signed professional forms that summer, at the advanced age of 27, so he would no longer be a midweek-only, back-up player. Yet Rowe still permitted him to continue teaching at Christ's College, believing it would not interfere with his football and believing it could even aid his fitness. Tony Marchi told me Robb was '…a true amateur who could dribble and was very hard to knock off the ball' but as with Harmer, dribbling was not ideal for 'push-an-run'. Yet Rowe considered the capture of Robb as the most important signing he had made, although, aside from Ramsey, and perhaps Murphy, what other significant signings had there been?

Rowe also signed newly promoted Sheffield United's right-winger George Hutchinson, 23, that summer, as back-up to Walters. But again, time would show that Hutchinson did not make his mark and one wonders why a side just promoted to Division One was happy to sell a player to a rival. Presumably putting a brave face on restricted circumstances, Rowe said: 'We are well satisfied with the fine bunch of players we now have and only someone really outstanding would tempt us into the market again.' But it is clear he still craved a prolific striker. After failing to get Lofthouse and Robledo, his target now, aiming considerably lower, was the Scot, John Dick. So Bill Nicholson accompanied Rowe to Glasgow, the two calling on Dick's mother's house to offer the player a professional contract. Dick himself would recall that 'the Spurs people' were none too happy, following such a long journey, to hear he had just signed for West Ham's Ted Fenton. Dick later said 'I didn't fancy Spurs', offering no further explanation. Had the Second Division 'Hammers' offered a superior financial deal than Rowe could offer at First Division Spurs?

Just how could Rowe entice players of ability and experience to White Hart Lane? When could he seriously plan for another Championship bid, or that trip to Wembley for which he so yearned?

13

The Hungarian Revolution

…AND ENGLISH DECLINE

'The myth of England's invincibility was shattered with a brand of football that England had already seen from Spurs …and, for some reason, ignored.'
RALPH L. FINN ON ENGLAND'S CRUSHING DEFEAT BY HUNGARY NOVEMBER 1953

'…the passing of Puskás, Hidegkuti and the rest was all Rowe.'
DAVID LACEY OF *THE GUARDIAN*, ON THE GREAT HUNGARIANS

While Arthur Rowe had brought a breath of fresh air to English football, few of his compatriots realised just how far behind the best of the soccer-playing world English football had fallen. At international level the degree of descent would be farcically exposed in 1950 and 1953. Sadly, aside from the case of, for example, Spurs, Liverpool and Brian Clough's Nottingham Forest, little further improvement occurred before the birth of the Premier League. In both 1953 and 1954 the country which had invented the game was humiliated by the nation some considered to have based its style on Rowe's own 'push-and-run': Hungary. This chapter sets out to review how and why English soccer had fallen behind.

BRITISH RESISTANCE TO COACHING An article in *The FA Year Book 1951-52* refers to criticism that young players were being over-coached and, as a result, not developing their individual style of play. Those critics exemplified the prevalent belief that skills could not be taught, which left the stage open only for (a) those naturally endowed with skill or (b) those who showed willing regardless of whether they possessed minimal talent. Presumably the famous 'wing-wizard', Stanley Matthews himself, never considered he would so easily have skipped around so many full-backs had those self-same full-backs been specialist-coached (in, for example, jockeying, tackling and intercepting). Jimmy Greaves, another natural endowed with almost unnatural skills and speed, believed that coaches stifled '…the natural instincts of players and turn them into robots.' In England ignorance ruled — Arsenal and England star David Jack, for example, told England manager Walter Winterbottom that there was only ONE way to pass the ball: with the inside of the foot. On being told there were Continental players using the outside of the foot for passing, or a knee for bringing the ball under control, Jack replied: 'That's rubbish.'

When Rowe was captain of Spurs in the 1930s, English football administrator C. E. Sutcliffe bullishly proclaimed: 'All the training and coaching in the world will not make a player the least bit better.' Sutcliffe will never have contemplated cushioning the ball and passing in one move, or redirecting the ball with the chest, or (like Jack) kicking with the outside of the foot. This 'head-in-the-sand' distrust of coaching persisted for decades to come. A 1951 article promoted the notion that 'most' managers know the average British lad is a better "natural" footballer than a boy of similar age from any other corner of the world.' Clearly, if that were so, coaching could only set these boys back!

In 1949 the Director of PE at the University of Birmingham acted as liaison and interpreter between the manager of a well-known English football club and a visiting German sports writer. When the visiting journalist enquired about soccer training methods in England, the University Director acting as translator was appalled to learn how basic they were, and almost too embarrassed to put them into German. Bernard Joy believed that the English were naturally conservative, averse to change, something Arthur Rowe expressed as '…our slightly stodgy temperament.' Joy continued: 'We [preferred] brawn to brain, the bludgeon to the rapier. Continentals point to the long passes and heavy tackling we made, the hefty boots and padded shin guards we wore, and the emphasis on stamina in training.'

Rowe again: 'The Continentals fundamentally are far more artistic; it pleases them better to exploit the art and craft of football rather than brute force and strength.'

LACK OF YOUTH COACHING IN BRITAIN The childhood football training memories of Spurs' Tony Marchi, born in the 1930s, differ little from football correspondent Mick Dennis's description of the situation 80 years later. Marchi: 'Schoolmasters used to do the coaching and all they knew was to show you how to tackle with two feet, collect the ball and "hit it up the field"! And dribble, take people on, get it across goal.' An American baseball coach Rowe met in wartime simply could not believe it when Rowe told him that hardly any British schools employed a specialist coach for the national sport.

LACK OF TECHNICAL SKILLS TAUGHT AT AN EARLY AGE Even thirty years after England met Hungary at Wembley in 1953 Charles Hughes at the FA was preaching that games were best won by launching the ball into what he called the 'POMO' ('Positions of Maximum Opportunity') when he should instead have been concentrating on the development of basic ball skills, particularly in

Comparitive footwear for the England versus Argentina international at Wembley in 1951. England's on the left, Argentina's slipper-like, lightweight boots on the right. Which style aided close ball control?

school and youth football. This negligence horrified the likes of Ron Greenwood and John Cartwright (later Technical Director at both the Professional Footballers' Association and the National School of Excellence). Working at Lilleshall between 1989 and 1991, Cartwright was shocked that his so-called 'elite' fourteen year-olds lacked basic skills which should have been acquired much earlier, from the age of seven. Most of them were one-footed and had played 11-a-side only (hence insufficient touches on the ball), believing the game was essentially, as Cartwright put it, about '…knocking the ball forward and scrapping for it in midfield.'

WHO NEEDS A BALL?   During Rowe's soccer lifetime, training was almost entirely about physical strength and endurance. Even well into the second-half of the twentieth century training at English clubs was full of running with barely a football in sight - unsurprisingly this led to poor ball control. Bill Nicholson recalled being a groundstaff boy at pre-War Spurs: 'When we had a spare moment we would kick about under the stands using a bundle of old cloth tied up into a ball.' Rowe's playing contemporary Ted Fenton recalled having '…a session with the ball only once a week,' unless, he added, '…we managed to steal one'! In pre-season training during the summer of 1950 Rowe actually gave *each* of his Spurs players a ball, albeit a small one, for the players to use at their own discretion. Tony Marchi described the ball as rubber and a bit larger than a tennis ball. Rowe's idea was that they could use the balls in the many corridors at White Hart Lane, kicking them against the walls and hitting them on the rebound. 'We don't want a team of jugglers,' he said, 'but the practice will be useful in increasing the quickness of kicking a ball springing from all angles.'

Arriving at Fulham at 17, in 1950, future England manager Bobby Robson found most of the training sessions took place without a ball, while Danny Blanchflower satirically summed-up training at Barnsley as '…running, followed by running, then some running, with a little bit of running to finish off the day.' A hero of Blanchflower's, Peter Doherty, described a standard training session in 1947: 'Players lope aimlessly around the track in small groups, talking to relieve their boredom, and wondering whether they can "drop out" inconspicuously.' Why not give the players a ball to control while they ran, thought Doherty, convinced it would increase concentration and erase some of the drudgery. Arsenal manager Bertie Mee, a qualified physiotherapist, would point out that constant running around the track actually caused metatarsal injuries. Of course, while this was going on in England, the great Hungarian Ferenc Puskás did all his training with a ball at his feet, including road-running. Combining running with ball control was inconceivable in England.

Back at Barnsley Blanchflower asked manager Angus Seed if he could have a football and Seed's famous reply was that if he was given a ball the '…others would want it.' Unsurprisingly Danny left Barnsley for Aston Villa in the hope of better things. During the transfer negotiations Blanchflower said he was happy with the terms but wanted to clear one thing up before putting pen-to-paper. The club officials girded themselves, assuming he was about to request an under-the-counter payment but all Blanchflower demanded was to train with a ball in the afternoons! He later sardonically suggested that the lack of a ball in training was due to something in-bred in the English character, something derived from English public school custom, that whatever an Englishmen sets out to achieve, it must include suffering! The result, according to Blanchflower, was that '...we neglected to match the advancing degrees of skill and speed with the ball with the advancing degree of our physical fitness.'

When the Swedish FA employed British coach George Raynor they asked him to '...make our players hungry for the ball like the English — you will keep it from them'. But the enlightened Raynor ignored this instruction and most of the Swedes' training was indeed done with a ball. He took Sweden, hitherto football minnows, first to Olympic glory in 1948 when they won the gold medal at Wembley. He also coached them (as host nation) at the 1958 tournament.

Rowe's former playing colleague and later club trainer, Cecil Poynton, confirmed that under Rowe Spurs trained a lot with a ball. When taking over as manager of Sheffield Wednesday another former colleague, Vic Buckingham, switched the training concentration from fitness to ball work at all times. Decades later Johan Cruyff's response to trainers who demanded a lot of running was: 'I say don't run so much. Football is a game you play with your brains. You have to be in the right place at the right moment, not too early, not too late.'

BASIC BALL CONTROL As late as 1960 Rowe defended Walter Winterbottom's FA coaching scheme, saying: 'If anything, it is too progressive, as we tried to coach assuming a standard of ball control that did not always exist.' He added: 'The Continentals were more sensible, and went on teaching the basic skills, such as trapping, kicking, dribbling and heading, and generally making the player the master of the ball. Because we are British, we assume we can do all these things, and we try to go one jump ahead and concentrate on team play and tactics.' By 1963 FA Secretary Dennis Follows seemed genuinely surprised when reporting that, '...in the basic skills and ball control, the foreign players have developed much faster than the home product.' England's Jackie Milburn, impressed after facing Argentina in 1951, could only put the South Americans' superior ball control down to their use of modern, lightweight, flexible boots!

Even thirty-four years after England's defeat to Hungary at Wembley Terry Venables, on returning from coaching Barcelona to manage Spurs, said: 'Having worked with the supremely talented and highly technical footballers of Spain, it came as a shock to realise just how far below that standard were the skills of the players I was now coaching.' Meanwhile, children and youth players in England continued to play 'kick-and-rush', often on full-size adult pitches where they inevitably did a great deal of running, but little of it with a ball at their feet.

LONG BALL — BEST FOR BRITAIN? When John Moynihan described a 1947 contest between Great Britain and a Europe XI at Hampden Park he said the GB side, who won 6-1, used the long ball to '...counteract the close passing of the European side', sarcastically adding: 'Loud was the crowing. British football was seemingly invincible.' Of course, we can now reflect that it was actually a really bad day for British football, helping prolong the myth that British was best.

BLIND TO CONTINENTAL ADVANCES   Until the 1950s the England national side had played just a third of their games against nations outside of the British Isles, but even many of these had been against small nations with half or less of England's population (approximately 56 million today). From Romania (approximately 19 million today) down to Norway or Finland (approximately 5.5 million today). Excuses had been plentiful for an eventual 4-3 defeat to Spain in 1929: a hard pitch, the heat and the 'threatening' spectators. The other 30 games were against the home nations (Scotland's population is approximately 10% that of England's, the Republic of Ireland's 9%, Wales 5.8% and Northern Ireland 3.4%). Ignoring these telling facts, as late as 1951 the author of an article in the Football Association's own journal about the Home International tournament wrote: 'A few [people] even maintain that the four international sides which make up the competition cannot be said to be equally matched.' Only crass ignorance could have led him to contest that claim. This was written a year following England's disastrous first entry into the World Cup Finals for which they had only qualified by overpowering those self-same (relatively tiny) home nations.

Even Spain's 1931 7-1 defeat by England was blamed by Willy Meisl on a goalkeeper unfamiliar with the physicality of England forwards. In 1932, when England won 4-3 at home against the close-passing Austrian 'Wunderteam' (see Chapter 4), an unbiased *Observer* reporter pointed out that Austria had run England close even with two players not fully fit. Indeed, the Austrians '…always knew where each man was in position and positional play is 60% of the art of football.' Unlike this reporter, the English football authorities learned nothing from it, but the *Observer* spelt it out: 'Ball practice is quite a minor part of a footballer's training in England and team-work is supposed to grow as naturally as wild flowers. What fallacies are these!'

Until the 1950s the England national side had played just a third of their games against nations outside of the British Isles, but even many of these had been against

A typical forthright article by Rowe appeared in World Soccer *magazine in 1960. He wrote of those in British football who were* 'turning a blind eye' *to* 'the rising supremacy of European and Latin countries'.

small nations with half or less of England's population such as Romania, Norway and Finland. At schoolboy level, it was as late as 1956 before the England national side faced a nation from outside the British Isles. Defeating a nation of similar size, West Germany for example, the *FA Book For Boys* crowed: 'England's schoolboys have little to fear from Continental opposition at present.' The statement 'have little to fear' says it all. The FA saw no improvement was necessary in the coaching of English boys.

Bernard Joy was mystified by home opposition to the development and improvement of players: 'Our coaches, like Jimmy Hogan in Austria and Arthur Rowe in Hungary, gave them the correct fundamentals and naturally are mortified today to see them flourishing abroad while they have been neglected at home.' In 1960 Rowe referred in *World Soccer* magazine to the 'supremacy' of European football. Fresh in his mind at that time were Real Madrid's majestic 1960 conquests of first Eintracht Frankfurt by 7-3 in the European Cup Final and then Peñarol of Uruguay 5-1 in the Intercontinental Cup. Rowe said those (rare, televised) performances should have finally convinced anyone who had forgotten the lessons of Hungary at Wembley in 1953 '…that British football was not so good.'

ENGLAND ISOLATIONISM — WHAT WORLD CUP? A dispute with FIFA over 'broken time' payments being allowed for 'amateur' players competing in the Olympics in 1928 led to the home nations leaving FIFA and therefore excluding themselves from the first three World Cups. After Italy won the 1934 World Cup they came to play England at Highbury where they lost 3-2 in a violent confrontation, some claiming England were therefore the best side in the world. When England finally made an appearance in the World Cup Finals of 1950 they fell to none other than the USA, whose side comprised a group of part-timers who had practised for just one day before setting out for Brazil! England's preparation had hardly been better, training for a few days at non-League Dulwich Hamlet's ground in South London where they were not even permitted to use the full-size pitch. Following their loss England had to beat Spain to stay in the tournament but lost 1-0. Eliminated so early, the FA party then displayed no interest in seeing the final tournament games and packed their bags and went home. Meanwhile Olympic champions Sweden (with one-fifth of the population of England) finished in third place.

Meanwhile Willy Meisl stayed to report on the climax to the tournament while all bar one of the British journalists took the first plane home. Journalists from other eliminated nations such as Italy, Germany and France all stayed, to learn what it takes to win a World Cup. Eight years later, at the Swedish World Cup of 1958, English correspondents once again quickly fled the country after England's early elimination, thus few could describe at first-hand Brazil's superb football as they won the trophy for the first time. Back in 1950 Meisl pointedly explained the absence of British journalists: 'Britons …will not realize what has happened to their soccer until they have experienced a string of humiliating defeats, and home defeats at that! …only seeing for themselves is, to [the British], believing, and they must see it not once but repeatedly.' He was critical, too, of the British press, who kept up the illusion that English football was strong, keeping their readers happy enough to keep buying their newspapers. However just as Willy predicted, a humiliating home defeat was just round the corner.

Following the 1950 tournament four FA meetings were held to review the failure. Opinions were invited from managers, former international players and football club directors. Inevitably, Arthur Rowe was enthusiastic enough to contribute. Meanwhile England captain Billy Wright put the greater skills of the Brazilians down to their being coached every single day, the coaching including ball work. Nor did he see any problems with the Brazilians' fitness levels: 'They are athletes as well, they can do 100 yards in 10 or 11 seconds, each and every one of them.' With classic, unintended irony, this filmed interview was interlaced with footage of Wright's Wolves team-mates training on the terraces at Molineux. What were they doing? They were throwing a medicine ball at one another! No wonder jokes at England's expense proliferated, such as: 'What do you call an English player's second touch?' Answer: 'A sliding tackle'. Or the typical English centre-half of the period who, as striker Alan Birchenall once put it, '...could trap it as far as I could kick it.' The fact was that English football had barely progressed since Rowe's recollection of an early twentieth century Barnsley side that, in his words, '...got stuck in, whacked it a long way... and galloped.'

ENGLISH FOOTBALL COACHING IN 1953 Despite being a former Arsenal player himself, Bernard Joy acknowledged the truth when writing '...the wholesale and third-rate imitation of the tactics which swept Arsenal to triumph-after-triumph in the 1930s ushered in the era of negative football which toppled England from world leadership in the game.' In 1946 Tommy Lawton witnessed 'mass coaching' in Switzerland, fearing that '...within five years we in Britain would be playing second fiddle to the Continentals.' Lawton added: 'I was only two years wrong.' When coaching in Holland in 1954 Lawton noticed how much training equipment was available, forecasting that within ten years Holland would be a force in football. Indeed, from 1968 to 1973 Dutch clubs reached every European Cup Final, winning four out of five and the national side also reached successive World Cup Finals soon after. Lawton was spot-on again.

As far back as the dawn of the twentieth century, Swedish international Karl Gustafsson had travelled to study the English approach and was disappointed. When revisiting England in the 1950s he found little had changed. 'Many seem not to know that the ball can also be kicked along the grass,' he wrote. He also found that the English (Rowe excepted) didn't appreciate the importance of playing when not in possession of the ball. This raises the question as to why Rowe's tactical revolution was not as quickly imitated by other clubs as that of Chapman, nor adopted by Walter Winterbottom, the man responsible for the performance of England internationally.

In 1953 Bernard Joy noted that coaching had still not really caught on in England whereas in most other countries it played an important part. Joy had come to realise that without a coach to drive and encourage the players they slackened, became slipshod, or gave up altogether. 'Under pressure from a coach, on the other hand,' said Joy, '...they are forced to continue to do their best, just as they are, of course, under match conditions.' He had seen South Americans, such as the Uruguayans, moving vigorously in training for over 90 minutes, with no time for chatting or tomfoolery, forced to keep going '…at their specialized ball practices.' Meanwhile, in Britain, soccer balls tucked safely away until Saturday, players all over the land were lapping, tossing medicine balls, then …off to the pub.

HERE COME THE HUNGARIANS   Fourteen years after Rowe's work in Budapest, the England side was still unbeaten at home against nations outside the British Isles and, on the morning of November 25th 1953, English prejudice suggested the visiting Hungarians would be sent packing later that day. However the visitors arrived at their peak and it is important to tell their story here as their style of football was an exemplar of Rowe's 'push-and-run' and the forthcoming match would rupture English football like no other event before or since.

Without doubt some of the Hungarian side running out onto the Wembley turf will have come under instruction from coaches who attended Rowe's 1939 Budapest sessions. Ferenc Puskás once said his own father's training sessions were to involve a lot of one- or two-touch five-a-side games and also included the practice of set-piece moves, a speciality of Rowe's. As we have seen, their national coach in 1953, Gusztáv Sebes, had been present at Rowe's pre-war sessions, but many of the budding Hungarian players and coaches with whom Rowe worked will have seen their football careers put on hold due to the outbreak of war and only by the early 1950s will some of them have been reaching their peak.

The previously mentioned Jimmy Hogan has regularly been credited for contributing to Sebes' 1950s' success but Hogan's final work in Hungary dated back a quarter of a century. So who most influenced that 1953 side, Rowe or Hogan? Esteemed author and journalist Jonathan Wilson has written that at the time Rowe travelled to Hungary he '…was so inculcated in the [short-passing] style from McWilliam, that he went to Budapest to lecture on it…'. But there is also no doubt from reviewing Hungarian articles describing Rowe's activities in 1939 that part of Rowe's remit was to follow FA guidelines of the time. Concentration, for example, on physicality, such as the use of the shoulder and the slide tackle. He also encouraged long, crossfield passes and he even preached Chapman's third-back game. However, unmonitored by the FA, Arthur no doubt took advantage of his time with the Hungarians to spread his own, preferred, 'push-and-run' gospel, and with far greater enthusiasm.

In a later conversation with Ted Drake, Rowe said of the Hungarians: 'They have never as a whole taken very kindly to the stopper centre-half'. Willy Meisl later clarified this commenting, 'Hungarian soccer… has successfully proved that one can combine the so-called third-back game with classical soccer, one can even play it with all the emphasis on attack and goal-scoring.' Meisl's statement breathes life into the notion that Rowe, a faithful believer in the attacking centre-half, had almost certainly applied a far more positive slant to Chapman's 'stopper' approach when in Hungary.

A month before Hungary's arrival at Wembley, a match was organised between England and a 'Rest of the World' side (this so named despite the glaring absence

Hungary's Puskás about to receive the team gold at the Helsinki Olympics of 1952. Rowe had of course been offered the chance to coach Hungary for these very Olympics before war intervened.

of players from any continent other than Europe). England's lack of technical finesse was still exposed, however, even without opposition players from the other six continents. Benefitting from a gift goal they still trailed 4-3 with time running out when they were awarded a dubious penalty which Alf Ramsey hammered into the roof of the net.

This poor performance led to press suggestions that English clubs should organise morning *and* afternoon training to increase fitness. Rowe responded that he had no intention of recalling his Spurs' players in the afternoons, pointing out: 'If all the players of both teams [England and Hungary] were lined up and told to sprint the length of the field the majority would undoubtedly finish in a nothing-between-them bunch. It was not better speed or stamina, but the application of the short-passing game which gave the 'Rest of the World' team the edge over England. The visitors moved the ball quickly from 'A' to 'B' and then ran into open-space 'C', just as Spurs did in their most successful season.'

England's opponents that afternoon included players of six different European nations who had played together for only around 50 minutes before running out at Wembley. Yet, as Meisl pointed out, this scratch side '...clicked together' and '...passed with incomparably greater precision' than the English. Were it not for Ramsey's late penalty, a defeat might well have caused the FA to sit-up and encourage change before Hungary arrived.

HUNGARY'S SOCCER REVOLUTION Hungary cemented their place as one of the greatest-ever soccer teams on four occasions: at the 1952 Helsinki Olympics, against England at Wembley in November 1953, against the same opponents in Budapest in May 1954, and at the World Cup in Switzerland which followed that year. Arthur Rowe had originally been lined-up to coach the Hungarians at the 1940 Helsinki Olympics before war intervened (see chapter 6). Instead, the Hungary team at the rescheduled Helsinki Games in 1952 was coached by Sebes who had led them on an unbeaten run of 32 consecutive matches. While the Hungarians trained together regularly, England's players would meet up just a day-or-two ahead of their fixtures, the team having been selected a week ahead of a game.

Sebes watched England play the 'Rest of the World' before testing the Wembley turf himself, even measuring the pitch and asking Stanley Rous if he could have some English match balls so his players could practice with them (which they did once Sebes had found a similarly-sized pitch to Wembley's)! Incidentally, Sebes commented that when kicking an English ball, it was like kicking solid wood!

PRELUDE TO ENGLAND v HUNGARY (November 25 1953) Having lost star winger Tom Finney in the week before the game, England called Spurs' George Robb up for his debut. *Times* journalist and Rowe admirer Geoffrey Green forecast a Hungarian victory, saying that in the light of England's struggle against the 'ROTW' side, '…they shall one day soon wake up and find six goals in the back of the net.' On the contrary Charles Buchan wrote with typically misplaced confidence: 'We have the men to beat the brilliant Hungarians.' All that was needed, added Buchan, was 'close-marking', adding: '…do not expect a goal flood.'

Prior to the game Buchan joined a strong contingent of former and current English players watching the Hungarians training. They included Bernard Joy, Tom Finney, Ron Greenwood, Johnny Haynes, Dave Sexton and Malcolm Allison. Joy recalled a Hungarian coach throwing high balls at the centre-half who was being harassed by a colleague mimicking the typical, burly English centre-forward. Up the other end of the pitch another coach was feeding a supply of balls for leading scorer Puskás to strike first-time at goal, which he did, no matter the height or speed the ball came to him. The full backs struck low, zippy and accurate one-touch passes to each other while a triangle of players worked their way along the touchline, interpassing as they went, very much in the Arthur Rowe style. Buchan was particularly impressed how the 'Magyars' trained with the same degree of application and effort as if it

England versus the 'Rest of the World'? A SMALL world indeed (but then the Trade Descriptions Act was not to come into force for another 16 years)!

were a game. Haynes was impressed that Hungary hardly did any lapping and spent most of the session with the ball. 'Imagine,' Haynes must have been thinking, '...training with a *ball*!" Incidentally, Haynes himself agreed with Peter Doherty's notion that running in training could just as well be undertaken WITH a ball just as well as WITHOUT. As Walter Winterbottom once said, ever-so-slightly ironically, 'A billiards player does not train by walking round the table!'

The Hungarians ended their session with an eight-a-side game played in half the field, with the ball constantly moving and players repeatedly finding space to make themselves available for a pass. With 16 players in only half the normal pitch size, thinking-time is reduced to a minimum. As with 'push-and-run', each player had to foresee where he would play it before it arrived, shaping his body so as to lay it off first-time. Such skills were not acquired in England, time instead devoted to lapping or tossing medicine-balls. Willy Meisl, by now utilising 'we', 'us' and 'our' when discussing English football, commented: 'What had retarded our soccer development was just this barbaric trend of being bent on destruction, on spoiling the other fellow's and team's ideas, not to allow them to develop a plan, in short ...on stopping them. Never mind that we ourselves could not produce anything worthwhile either...'.

In the build-up to the Hungary encounter, extraordinarily over-optimistic English newspaper headlines proliferated, such as:

'HUNGARY'S FANCY STUFF WON'T BEAT ENGLAND'
'MAKE 'EM RUN ENGLAND!' and the truly inspiring:
'RELENTLESS TACKLING WILL SHAKE THE HUNGARIANS'

However, as the *Observer*'s Tony Pawson recalled, 'Finney, and those of us who watched [Hungary] kicking in before the game, were less certain. For the Hungarians not only juggled the ball on thigh, boot or head with a subtlety not seen at Wembley before, but their practice shooting was fierce and true as the shots seared past [goalkeeper] Grosics.'

It had twice recently taken late Alf Ramsey penalties to rescue England's home record (in the 70th minute against Austria and 90th against the Rest of the World), which led Max Marquis to point out that Ramsey's penalties '...had artificially prolonged the undefeated home record'.

CONSTRAINTS ON WINTERBOTTOM   Team selection was out of manager Winterbottom's control so he adopted an attitude of quiet resignation. In addition to managing footballers whose individual skill levels were way behind the Hungarians, he depended on player combinations selected by FA councillors. So it was colossally ironic that in the summer of 1951, the FA's own *FA Year Book* spoke of the 'overriding problem — that of building an assured, CONSISTENT [my caps] team...'. England's performances were therefore unsurprisingly described as 'somewhat erratic'!

The England team (particularly in the 1930s and 1940s) remained competitive with other European sides only due to the quality of the individuals available for selection, individuals whose skills had developed naturally from playing street football, often against multiple opponents, and in confined space. But by World War II other nations had caught up on skills, and developed tactics. When Winterbottom took charge he was very conscious that the supply-line of naturally-talented ball-players was already drying-up, so a formal programme for developing players was necessary. It wasn't until 1957 that Winterbottom succeeded in persuading the FA that his team had to be selected with balance and cohesion in mind. For example, the choice of one defensively-inclined half-back and one attack-minded half-back [or midfielder]. One more physically-imposing man in the middle of the attack, accompanied by a sharper, slighter, poaching companion, etc.

25th NOVEMBER 1953   On the morning of the big game Chelsea's Ron Greenwood arrived for training at Stamford Bridge where the session included '…obligatory laps around the pitch'. After a bath he learned that transport had been organised for players who wanted to see the international match. Over at White Hart Lane Arthur Rowe, no doubt licking his lips in anticipation and perhaps looking forward to meeting some old Hungarian acquaintances, had likewise organised tickets for his players. Ralph Wetton recalled how he and the other players prepared to board the coach to Wembley when 'Arthur asked "Well, what do you reckon then?" and everybody said "Ah, we'll slaughter them" and Arthur was the only one who thought otherwise.'

West Ham's Dave Sexton, Malcolm Allison and Jimmy Andrews watched the Hungarians warming-up on a patch of grass near the Wembley stadium greyhound track. Andrews, later a coach and manager, was unembarrassed to admit years later that he had pointed Puskás out to Malcolm Allison, saying 'Look at that fat little chap there… we'll murder this lot.' Allison himself would later point out that great English players such as Matthews, Finney, Haynes and Charlton had reached their stature '*despite* our system not *because* of it', adding 'We have many diamonds in English football, but how many of them are properly polished?' This was an occasion when Allison spoke as eloquently and concisely as Rowe himself.

Ron Greenwood recalled the portly captain Puskás waiting in the centre-circle for the coin toss, flicking the ball up a few times, catching it on his knee before killing it dead on his toe. At that time this kind of skill was seldom evident in the British Isles. To prove he was not the only astonishing conjuror in a Hungary shirt, Puskás finished his circus act by nonchalantly flicking the ball with his heel to Zoltán Czibor who, without pause, carried on where Puskás had left off. In film footage of that moment the England players are out of shot so we are spared the likely sight of them engaged in booting the ball vaguely in each other's direction, between little bouts of jogging and hand-warming. As Terry Venables bluntly put it, the home nation's footballers at that time were: '…terrible plodders.'

As the teams took the field West Ham manager Ted Fenton correlated their respective playing kits to the quality of football about to be unveiled. 'We [England] looked old-fashioned as we went out on to the field—long shorts, flapping shirts, shin guards that would not have been out of place on a wicketkeeper.' On the other hand, said Fenton, Hungary appeared 'smart' and 'super-fit', delightfully adding, 'chromium-finished.'

THE HUNGARIAN REVOLUTION ...AND ENGLISH DECLINE

This cutting depicts the moment a header from Kocsis struck the post (following a delightful chipped cross from Puskas). But the ball was not cleared and Bozsik hammered a right-footer into the other side of goal for Hungary's fifth at Wembley.

Winterbottom had done his homework, telling his defenders to hold off tackling until the right moment and to keep an eye on those supporting the man on the ball and seeking space. Yet Hungary went ahead in 42 seconds! Hidegkuti had feinted to shoot (throwing Billy Wright off balance), before arrowing a right-footer into the top left corner. Sebes had instructed Hidegkuti and the rest to continually switch positions knowing England's defenders would follow their individual opponents around the pitch leaving gaping holes for Bozsik, in particular, to fill.

England equalised but Merrick's weak fly-kick eventually led to Hidegkuti striking his second into the left-hand corner of the net from about eight yards, 2-1. From England's re-start Ernie Taylor immediately lost possession in the centre-circle and, after an exchange of passes, Budai shot hard and low but two yards wide of the far post drawing a collective 'OOOHHH!' of relief from the home crowd. It was soon 3-1 anyway, and the third proved to be one of the most famous goals in soccer history. Puskás began the move in his own half, the ball moving smartly between four players before Czibor, from the wide right-hand corner, passed diagonally back toward the near corner of the six-yard box where Puskás brought the ball smartly under control. Wright desperately slid in to block the expected shot just as Puskás put his left foot on the ball, dragging it back all in one movement, leaving the England captain sliding embarrassingly out of play. Puskás then half-turned before slamming a left-footed shot inside the near post past Merrick's despairing left hand. The Hungarians then strolled calmly toward Puskás, almost as though this was a common occurrence rather than one of the greatest goals ever scored! A fortunate deflected fourth for Hungary followed before Mortensen pulled one back before half-time. England were 4-2 down.

In the second-half Ernie Taylor carelessly lost possession for Bozsik to advance quickly, his shot deflecting into the far left corner for Hungary's fifth. A high ball from the right touchline was then back-headed on to Puskás, just outside the left side of the area. He gently brought it under control with his left foot and, under no pressure, lobbed it gently to the far right of the area where Hidegkuti raced in unchallenged to volley home at the far post. England 2 Hungary 6. At that point the cameraman captured England defender Jimmy Dickinson trudging slowly back to take up his position for yet another restart, scratching his head in mystified Stan Laurel fashion. Hungary could then afford to gift England a penalty which Ramsey converted for a final score of: England 3 Hungary 6.

England had got off extremely lightly, having had five shots on target to Hungary's twenty-one. At the final whistle the exultant Hungarians engaged in a group hug, as (according to one poetic correspondent) '…a mist came down to enshroud the wreckage of English football.' The home players returned forlornly to their dressing-room, 'speechless, silent, no discussion', as Stanley Matthews recalled. Significantly Ralph L Finn wrote: 'The myth of England's invincibility was shattered with a brand of football that England had already seen from Spurs …and, for some reason, ignored.'

Twenty-one years had passed since Austria had embarrassed England with their vastly superior technique, yet few, aside from Rowe, had apparently learned anything from it. Others felt the defeat might be part explained by the highly politicised Sebes associating football matches with the struggle between socialism and capitalism. Rowe himself touched on this in *World Soccer* magazine in the early 1960s: 'In the post-war years, under the auspices of their communist government, anxious for international successes [the Hungarians] adopted a methodical and purposeful system of training that gave a greater effect to their natural ball play. Whilst the circumstances [under Communism] could have been happier for the Hungarian people as a whole, there can be no doubt that their football benefitted enormously.'

Afterwards John Thompson perceptively commented: 'When Hungarian players passed the ball they seemed to know instinctively where to put it. The English in contrast were doubtful of their colleagues' whereabouts and wasted precious seconds looking around them.' In addition, added Thompson: 'The English made two moves to bring the ball under control to every one made by their opponents.' Had the England team combined the best of Rowe's Spurs (Ditchburn, Ramsey, Nicholson, Baily etc.) with the addition of (say) Matthews, Wright, Mortensen and Finney, and been coached for a week in advance by Rowe, they may still have lost, but without disgrace and, more significantly, the national side will have been on the right path for the future.

REACTION Desmond Hackett of the *Daily Express*, who had been so confident of triumph before the game, wrote that England had 'moved stiffly' in comparison to the Hungarians. The Liverpool *Daily Post* reporter wrote 'I confess to never having enjoyed football so much – and yet so little! – at one time.' On a lighter note, Stuart Hylton in his book *From Rationing to Rock: The 1950s Revisited*, aptly described the England collapse at Wembley by borrowing Churchill's turn of phrase: 'Within less than half-an-hour of the kick-off [England] were 4-1 down. They were beaten in the air, on the ground and in terms of tactics.' Hylton's punchline followed: 'At half-time the Hungarians were even better at sucking oranges'. Geoffrey Green wrote: 'English football …must awake to a new future.'

'The Wembley crowd had seen the future of football, and it lived abroad,' added Hylton, while Jonathan Wilson has since pointed out that defeat by Hungary '…was not the moment at which English decline began but it was the moment at which it was recognised.' Rowe will have agreed. Sadly, however, a new future for England would have to wait. Greenwood recalled his Chelsea manager Ted

Drake attending the 'emergency' conference of English managers which Walter Winterbottom called to find ways of restoring English soccer pride. At the very next Chelsea training session Drake, having voiced how impressed he had been by what had come out of the meeting, called all his players together, and, referring to the Hungary game, talked enthusiastically of '...how new the future [of soccer] was going to be...'.

Then ordered his men to do twenty laps around the pitch!

Sándor Barcs, President of the Hungarian Football Association, summed-up the reality of that 1953 game, 'What [England] played was industry and what we played was art.'

YET MORE PUNISHMENT Six months later England had the opportunity to restore national pride, this time at Budapest's Népstadion. Prior to this, England had beaten Scotland 4-2 (yet the corner count was 15-2 in Scotland's favour), before losing 1-0 to Yugoslavia in Belgrade. Despite these warning signs the English Press was again bursting with misplaced optimism: 'SPEED WILL CONQUER PUSKAS & CO' read one, while another claimed: 'OUR TOP BOYS WILL WHIP HUNGARY'.

However watching reserve Johnny Haynes recalled a period of twenty minutes in the second half when Hungary '...played football of a quality beyond my wildest dreams, paralysing us in midfield and simply pouring on goals galore in an exhibition of concentrated majesty...'. Arthur Rowe, reflecting later on his own time in Hungary, wrote that even back then it was a nation producing fine footballing individuals: '...to my mind the great Hungarian side of 1953-54 was in no way superior, individually, than some of their predecessors. Certainly, György Sárosi and Zsengellér would live comfortably in the company of Puskás and Kocsis.' This repeat 'fiasco' led Charles Buchan to declare: 'We are many years behind Hungary, and other Continental teams, in all the essential points; speed, ball control, distribution and team-work.' Fitness, too, according to Hungarian sources.

Puskás exchanges pennants and flowers with England captain Billy Wright before the calamitous 7-1 Budapest defeat in May, 1954.

Unlike most others, Geoffrey Green accepted reality: 'As a team [England] were outpaced, out-manoeuvred, and out-thought. Defence, as one has seen before, was drawn into the most grotesque shapes by the fiendishly clever decoy work of a superbly swift Hungarian team.' The home side themselves were amazed England had failed to change their tactics despite the Wembley disaster.

'It was the only way [the English] knew how to play,' Puskás said afterwards.

Stuart Hylton again came up with an antidote to these depressing commentaries on English football: '…England went to Hungary to teach those upstarts a lesson. In front of a delirious home crowd of 92,000, England taught them how to be gracious in defeat, losing 7-1.'

Most English clubs seemed unable to recognise the need for skills improvement, or tactical change. As Terry Venables wrote: 'Even …when the Hungarians made us look like dinosaurs in football terms during the 1950s, we had been slow to react to new ideas.' Willy Meisl said that part of the reason for writing his book *Soccer Revolution* in the mid-1950s was to help '…save British soccer drowning in an ocean of mediocrity.' Of the 7-1 embarrassment, Meisl rightly summed the English up as '…pupils apparently unwilling to learn any lessons.'

1954 WORLD CUP FINALS   Hungary, despite being by far the best side in the tournament, only finished runners-up in the 1954 World Cup. Puskás suffered an injury in an 8-3 qualifying victory over West Germany and returned, not fully fit, to play in the final against the same opponents. In Brian Glanville's opinion Puskás had been kicked out of the qualifier by the German centre-half. In the Final the Germans led 3-2 with just two minutes' remaining when a superb effort from Puskás found the net but the goal was disallowed for offside, although many were convinced he was onside when the ball was played to him. Indeed, the watching Matt Busby called it '…a travesty of justice'. Allegations also circulated that the German side had been dosed at half-time with an amphetamine-based drug '…developed by Nazi scientists to make soldiers fight longer and harder.' World champions or not, Sebes could still claim four years of almost continuous success, an amazing thirty games undefeated before that unfortunate World Cup Final.

ENGLISH FOOTBALL AFTER 1954   The Football League held a meeting shortly after England's crushing defeat in Budapest but the poor quality of the nation's football was not touched upon. Instead the continuing drop in attendances was discussed, yet nobody seemed to draw the parallel between the low quality of play and disappearing spectators. The FA did however set up a conference of English managers to improve the preparation of the England side and those attending included Bill Ridding, Jimmy Seed, Ted Drake, Andy Beattie, Matt Busby, Rowe (of course!) and Vic Buckingham.

Another meeting, this time chaired by Arthur Drewry, President of the Football League, included Rowe, Busby and Buckingham, and, among others, Stan Cullis and Ted Fenton. Fenton was delighted such a meeting was taking place but recalled that patriotism was much to the fore. Drewry ended the meeting by saying 'We must have more [meetings]' yet six years' later Fenton and the others were still waiting

THE HUNGARIAN REVOLUTION ...AND ENGLISH DECLINE

Rowe, pictured between pals Matt Busby and Vic Buckingham (just one eye in shot, on the right), attends a meeting of prominent English club managers chaired by Sir Stanley Rous (at head of table). They discussed the outcome of the Hungarian defeat of England in 1953, a game which exposed just how far behind the English game had fallen in World terms...

Aside, that is, from Rowe's own, thrilling Spurs!

by their phones. However, the FA did belatedly hold regional meetings in 1962 and as a result Alf Ramsey was appointed as the first man to devote all his attention to the management of the national team. There were also meetings to plan England's hosting of the 1966 World Cup.

COMPETITION AGAINST OTHER CONTINENTAL SIDES   Rowe very much favoured English clubs competing with European sides. When Chelsea won the League in 1954-55 they were one of 18 Continental sides invited to take part in the first European Cup competition. However Alan Hardaker, Secretary of the Football League, refused permission on the grounds there were too many fixtures already. Throughout his tenure as Spurs manager, Rowe arranged friendlies against strong European competition. Ralph Wetton recalled: 'We played FC Austria, they were the best in Europe, and we had a two-week tour of Germany. We played Racing Club de Paris every year, home and away. We played a team from Austria in Brussels, we played Hamburg, Frankfurt, Stuttgart'. Preceding the European Cup, these matches were treated as contests of national pride.

LACK OF PRACTICE FACILITIES IN ENGLAND   Even by 1963, and in common with so many English club sides, Fulham did not have a practice ground, so when the weather was inclement they simply couldn't use a ball in training, as their Craven Cottage pitch had to be protected. Johnny Haynes recognised that two of the few English sides who *did* enjoy their own practice fields (thus regularly training with the ball), Spurs and Burnley, also happened to be two of the most successful of that era.

CHAMPIONING THE LONG-BALL APPROACH   As mentioned in Chapter 9, Stan Cullis's Wolves were the club most renowned for success with the long-ball. Bernard Joy wrote at the time: 'Wolves' backs and goalkeeper are intent on clearing their lines and the short pass is rarely used… the style is admirably suited to heavy grounds which prevent far-flung passes from running out of control and [simultaneously] bog down close passing.' Notably, however, when Wolves' Championship-winning side were confronted at Molineux by the Rowe-inspired (but Nicholson-led) Spurs in October 1959, they were pounded 4-0. They fared poorly too when qualifying for the European Cup. Although they reached the quarter-finals, Cullis' Wolves were crushed by Barcelona 9-2 on aggregate, as they only rarely kept possession of the ball. What Wolves *did* have, as Bernard Joy recognised, was a good sprinkling of '…the English virtues of vigour and determination'. However, as against Spurs, that proved inadequate when confronted by superior skills, speed and better ball retention. Returning to Spain, Barcelona coach Helenio Herrera stated what was obvious to those beyond British shores, that English clubs still played without method or technique, and still employed a physical style Continentals had abandoned years before.

Perhaps the most famous example of Wolves' approach to the game was their 3-2 challenge match victory over Hungarian champions Honvéd in December 1954. Before that game Cullis had told his apprentices to water the pitch and 'roll the moisture in' (this on top of four days of incessant rain). So, while the Honvéd side included seven of the Hungarians who had torn England apart on the impeccable Wembley turf the previous year, their defeat by Wolves owed most to a playing surface described by Geoffrey Green as 'thick glue' - the Hungarians had certainly not lost to a team of greater talents. Before the muddy surface took its toll Honvéd had raced into a breathtaking 2-0 lead, but their tiring legs in the quagmire saw them eventually go down 3-2. Cullis was far from alone in this, Ted Drake actually suggesting England games be switched from the pristine, flat playing surface at Wembley to over-used, muddy club pitches. 'Why not let them challenge us under our natural wintry conditions?' Drake asked. But conditions such as those were far removed from those English teams would face when it really mattered, in international tournaments in South America or Southern Europe, where they encountered players who could 'kill' long balls stone dead. However, back home, a Wolves' air ball, if aimed accurately, would 'die' on Molineux's soggy surface, their forwards collecting it to make ground or else take a shot. Who needed ball control?

PLAYERS LACKING DESIRE TO IMPROVE THEIR SKILLS   Arthur Rowe compared an average British player with an average Continental in his usual concise manner, describing typical Hispanic footballers in training: 'If Rodríguez can do it ten times with his left foot and fourteen times with his right, it's a challenge to José. And José accepts it and tries to do something about it. In our [British] stolid, phlegmatic way we say: "Look at that fellow showing off", and it passes with no more thought.' In a discussion about the need for English players to extend their daily training period, Rowe said: 'If you're aiming at improving your skills, adding to your repertoire, then the only way you will acquire this higher grade is by coming back and doing something about it, and this is the very thing I've always found the average professional footballer very reluctant to do.'

ROWE OR HOGAN?   Bill Nicholson's opinion was that although the great 1950s Hungarians probably learned more from Rowe than he from them, Hogan's influence may have been greater still. The most telling point in Hogan's favour came in the aftermath of Hungary's humbling of England at Wembley, when President of the Hungarian FA, Sándor Barcs, stated: 'Jimmy Hogan taught us everything we know about football', although that could simply be a personal opinion from a man (Barcs) who had been young and impressionable when Hogan first worked in Hungary. But Hungarian team manager Gustáv Sebes also credited Hogan: 'When our football history is told, [Hogan's] name should be written in gold letters' but Sebes will have been impressed by Hogan as he played under the Englishman. It could be the case that Rowe's brief but telling work with Hungarian coaches, interrupted by the war, was ultimately overlooked. The essential factor in any argument over whose influence was the greater would be that Rowe's work occurred far closer in time to the 'Magical Magyars' of the 1950s. His work had been carried out specifically at the request of the Hungarian authorities to improve the general level of coaching just before the war, which might suggest that whatever Hogan had achieved was by then in need of upgrading or updating.

One of the greatest thinkers on the game, future England manager Ron Greenwood, linked Sebes' Hungary and Rowe's Spurs together when saying that Hungary's display at Wembley had '…proved to me beyond all doubt that football can be a game of beauty and intelligence, a lovely art as well as a muscular science,' adding, 'I had seen generous hints of it in the Spurs' push-and-run side when they won the Championship in 1951 under Arthur Rowe.'

In *Soccer Revolution* Willy Meisl wrote: 'The Hungarians feted Jimmy Hogan as the man who laid the foundations for their two victories over England. Of course, that happened forty years ago. In a previous chapter you have read that Arthur Rowe is considered the man who helped the Hungarians modernize their tactics.' In 1954 John Graydon of the *Sunday Graphic* traced the roots of Hungary's success. writing: 'It is not by accident …that Arthur Rowe, the Tottenham manager, was at one time a coach in Hungary.' Another leading light of Fleet Street, Ken Jones, wrote that arriving in Hungary Rowe '…planted the seeds which were to bloom with such stunning colour at Wembley in 1953.'

Conclusively, the normally modest-in-the-extreme Rowe told Norman Giller that the 'push-and-run' he introduced to his Spurs players was 'very similar to the style I introduced while coaching in Hungary before the war.' Giller, recalling another chat with Rowe in the 1970s, told me '[Rowe] was not the boastful type to claim credit for what the Hungarians achieved, but he made no secret of the fact that his time in Hungary had set new standards of football.' Summing-up, Giller told me 'The Hungarians at Wembley in 1953 and in the massacre in Budapest the following year had "Arthur Rowe" written all over them'. Of the Budapest game Geoffrey Green added: 'These Hungarians have probably achieved at this point of time as great a mastery over a football as any team in history.' David Miller, writing about the invitation for Hungary to play at Wembley in 1953, said 'Hungarian football had been steadily developing for fifteen years' (which again coincided with Rowe's spell in Budapest). The Hungarians, he added, had long since recognised the importance of coaching, '…and had 900 qualified coaches training their young players.' Just how many of those coaches had attended Rowe's sessions in 1939?

Rowe believed the drastic social and political change which Hungarians underwent between pre-war times and the post-war Communist state had changed their approach to the sport drastically. In 1960 Rowe added, 'I must say that the Hungarians were just as great a team of "pure" footballers when I went there coaching as they were when they beat us at Wembley [in 1953]. I was staggered by their ability. But there was one vital difference between those two eras, and this is not something that happens very often. The pre-war Hungarian as a person, was a pleasure-loving individual, keen on song, wine and what have you. To him life was a bowl of cherries; hard work went very much against the grain. Football was one of their pastimes, an art to be enjoyed but for the post-war Hungarian, to be a great footballer was a passport to a good living in a country that was behind the Iron Curtain, where life wasn't very pleasant, and if somebody said "gallop a bit faster", you galloped a bit faster if you wanted to eat, and you worked a bit harder. Therefore their football became much more pungent, much more incisive, much more determined, much more ultimate in its performance.'

He referred to this post-war change on another occasion: 'If their way of life was [still] as free, comfortable and happy, I don't think we should have seen the pungent Hungarian side of 1953.' Rowe's work in Hungary then, shortened by the oncoming war, was a contributory factor in the advancement of the game there. The coaches he had impressed in the spring and summer of 1939 will have passed on his enthusiastic teachings to players and coaches who followed. Rowe, impressed when attending a Sebes lecture at Lilleshall in 1960, said: 'I would say [Sebes] is a great man: simple, sincere, without pose or affectation,' who '…understands the game almost intuitively, and more important, he is able to put his thoughts in simple terms, and convey them to others.' Rowe might have been describing himself.

'NONE SO BLIND…' In 1960 Rowe wrote in *World Soccer* that British football '…needed to absorb the lessons offered by the first-class Continental sides.' Rowe wanted no obstacles put in the way of English players, coaches or spectators should they wish to view football from other countries. However, he was realistic enough to add the following proviso: 'Yet there is an old and certain saying "There are none so blind as those who do not wish to see" …but there are those who *do* wish to see, and this is a privilege that should not be discouraged.' To be certain, Rowe, as one of those who *did* wish to see, will have been thinking of such as Malcolm Allison, Ron Greenwood, Dave Sexton and others, those more open-minded, younger coaches of his times, those flushed with the enthusiasm to counteract the prevailing and dated British approach to the 'Beautiful Game'.

14

Toil and Torment

MANAGING SPURS 1953-54

'They were right tight skinflints, you know, the board of directors.'
1950'S SPURS' PLAYER TONY MARCHI, IN CONVERSATION WITH THE AUTHOR

'...niggardly people [had] broken [Arthur] down at Tottenham.'
ARTHUR WAIT, CRYSTAL PALACE CHAIRMAN AND CLOSE CONFIDANT OF ROWE'S 1961

Spurs '...ALL SET FOR RECORD-BREAKING SEASON' headlined an article which ignored concern over the average age of Rowe's side (soon to reach 32) and the lack of talented new blood. Even two years earlier, Alf Ramsey had written of players starting on 'the downhill journey'. He notably added: 'I am not even prepared to state that the Spurs can keep on top for any considerable length of time.' The concentration on Cup success during 1952-53 had left Rowe with his poorest League points total as Spurs' manager, although he had come close to four continuous years of trophies (including the League runners-up spot in 1951-52). Publicly the Spurs boss optimistically declared: 'I believe we have the right material.' Yet aside from the promise of Third Division novice Johnny Brooks, too little had been invested in players. Robb was clearly no Medley while George Hutchinson was rated by Tony Marchi as no match for Walters.

When the Championship-winning side (less the departed Medley) took on the Reserves behind closed doors in pre-season, Nicholson and Burgess were replaced at half-time by Marchi and Wetton. The enduring influence of Nicholson and Burgess could be seen in the 4-0 half-time lead which was cut back to 4-1 by the finish. In August Rowe showed interest in Hibernian's Scottish international striker Lawrie Reilly but needless to say, no deal transpired and Reilly proceeded to net a phenomenal 185 goals in 253 appearances for Hibs, his average of 1.5 goals every two games would surely have made some impression at Tottenham, too.

The annual public trial match between the 'Whites' (basically the men who started under Rowe four years' earlier) and the reserves saw the 'Whites' scrape a 5-4 win. Rowe may have seen this as confirmation he had sufficient quality in reserve or, from another perspective, that his 'old guard' had faded too far. A leg strain meant Nicholson would again miss a season's opening game. Clearly little had been done to improve on the previous season, yet Spurs opened the season with promise, taking eight points from ten.

After a 2-1 defeat at Sheffield Wednesday, Spurs hosted Charlton and Robb scored twice in a 3-1 victory. Another home fixture saw Walters and Bennett score in a classic 'push-and-run' performance. A late 'push-and-run' move begun by Ditchburn ended with Robb making it 3-0 before visitors Middlesbrough pulled one back, only for Duquemin to hit a fourth seconds from the final whistle. It had been a classic Rowe performance, Spurs climbing to third place. This led the *Herald* to boldly forecast 'Spurs are a good Championship bet this season', but Rowe himself was aware that Middlesbrough were not the strongest opposition (indeed they would be relegated by season's end). Spurs next faced three away games, the first at Charlton where Vic Groves, the amateur who had refused Rowe's offer to turn professional, came in for Duquemin and netted the only goal.

However, an injured Bennett was missed for two games, the first at Rowe protégé Vic Buckingham's high-flying West Brom where Spurs were hit first by a Ronnie Allen goal and, after half-time, by a header from Johnny Nicholls who also ended the scoring when pressuring Ramsey into an own goal. Buckingham had added accurate 40-yard passes to feet to the 'push-and-run' mix, prompting Bernard Joy to write: 'Whereas Spurs wafted across the field in delightful waves, West Bromwich were more staccato, using one or two violent thrusts forward to vary the rhythm.' Forty-eight hours later Spurs faced Burnley at Turf Moor, with Brooks replaced by Harmer and the tall, muscular Marchi running-out at centre-forward following goal-scoring success in the Reserves. Frustrated in the transfer market, Rowe now sought an alternative to Duquemin from within but on this occasion, Spurs again returned pointless.

In a 'thrill-a-minute' encounter at home to struggling Liverpool, full of clever, fast soccer, a goalkeeping error saw Ramsey's 40 yard lob put Spurs ahead. Then Walters thumped home first-time from a tight angle before Liverpool pulled one back for a final score of 2-1 to the 'Lillywhites'. Rowe was absent that afternoon, sizing-up Chelsea's 20-year-old centre-forward Bobby Smith in action against his own reserves. Ruminating on the paucity of goals, Rowe said his forwards '…lose their virility in the last thirty yards' a problem throughout the club, not just the first team. Rowe then faced criticism at the Annual Shareholders' Meeting, responding 'We are doing all right. We have some points and we will do better as the season goes on.' One imagines he failed to aid his cause when explaining that Spurs were (after all) competing with 21 other clubs, and could '…only hope for a share of success.'

Rowe's successive championships, achieved whilst barely disturbing the club's bank balance, were now held against him, as though his earlier miracles could be repeated regardless of his ageing playing staff. When Rowe then offered the directors and shareholders 'continued good football', it will likewise have gone down like a lead balloon, the board clearly having little desire for quality, just results. Rowe pointed out that Arsenal had lost six from eight, the latest was by no fewer than 7-1 at Sunderland. Rowe then laid it on the line, saying all managers had one big fear, that their team would collapse from old age. 'A good manager tries to plan his team for the future.' This was surely an indirect plea for transfer funds. When all those present adjourned (to watch the first-ever floodlit practice match at the stadium before inspecting the new visitors' dressing room) one could imagine a tangible release of tension.

TOIL AND TORMENT: MANAGING SPURS 1953-54

In an unusually off-guard moment, Rowe here could be contemplating how to rejuvenate his side despite lacking the funding to bring in younger players suiting 'push-and-run' requirements.

After a third defeat in five Spurs travelled to confront arch-rivals Newcastle United where, on arrival in the North East, Ramsey heard his mother had been taken seriously ill. So, with both Burgess and Nicholson on the treatment table, Ramsey became a further absentee, returning on the midday train. Twelfth man Derek King filled-in for Ramsey and despite missing three key players, Spurs went ahead and Ditchburn made a double penalty save. It took Newcastle over an hour to equalise before, with ten minutes left, Robb put Spurs ahead again and in the last minute Baily completed an exceptional 3-1 victory.

Two days later the annual friendly with Hibernian proved costly, McClellan breaking a bone in his ankle. Such friendly encounters brought in extra income for clubs in the days before the League Cup or European club competitions existed. Indeed, Rowe proposed that the club's planned installation of floodlights could enable an annual mini-tournament between leading English and Scottish club sides and he put it to the Tottenham board. He suggested that England be represented by Arsenal and Tottenham, and Scotland by Glasgow Rangers and Hibernian (who had won the Scottish League title four times between 1948 and 1952). Each club would play six matches, the four clubs meeting each other home and away. 'These games would in my opinion have given us all the extra games that are practicable in addition to the present arduous League season,' said Rowe. But the Spurs directors told him they did not think the scheme worth proceeding with. 'A mistake, I thought', said Rowe. 'A cup competition between Hibernian, Rangers, Arsenal and Tottenham had all the makings of a first-class tournament that had real crowd appeal.' Rowe's mistake may have been to suggest that income from the tournament go toward strengthening his playing staff.

Ramsey returned from compassionate leave to face Manchester United, and George Hutchinson made his debut in place of the injured Walters. Both Nicholson and Burgess returned yet, considering their success at Newcastle, one wonders why stand-ins Brittan and Wetton had not been retained. United led at half-time but Spurs pressed for most of the second-half until the 88th minute arrived. With

Clarke off the pitch having a cheek wound stitched, Bennett had dropped deep, and from there he swung a pass across the field to Ramsey, who quickly lobbed the ball down the middle where United full-back Bill Foulkes lost his footing, leaving Duquemin to ensure Spurs added a point to their total. But during the week that followed, Rowe discussed Spurs' growing reliance on their defence, which, he said, '…is bound to concede goals as long as the forwards fail to keep the ball moving in their opponents' half for long periods. Attacks break down, chances are missed, and the defenders are called in to cover-up or to stem the tide far too often.'

On September 29th Rowe put Harmer in for Baily for the first floodlit game ever played at White Hart Lane, a friendly against Racing Club de Paris, who, one-up at half-time, were 5-1 behind by the middle of the second-half, only to score twice more for a final score of 5-3. Fans of Harmer who demanded his selection for the first team accused Rowe of using him as a 'performing seal' in friendly games such as this. Perhaps in response to this criticism Harmer stayed in for the trip to Bolton where Spurs held out until Burgess, defending a cross, accidentally knocked the ball from Ditchburn's grasp for Lofthouse to net. Attempts to tie the game led instead to an error gifting Hassall the second. Sinking to ninth this was hardly the time to host Arsenal, yet still nearly 70,000 attended. The visitors had recently signed Rowe's old playing opponent, Tommy Lawton, and were gaining ground on Spurs. From kick-off the usual pattern quickly developed, Spurs applying lots of pressure only for an unmarked Jimmy Logie to score. Then Milton made it 2-0 and with Spurs pressing high up the pitch, Nicholson's desperate tackle resulted in a penalty which Forbes converted. A Ditchburn error made it 4-0 by the end of a half in which Spurs had 80% possession. Robb pulled one back in the second-half but, in typical fashion, Arsenal had taken the points by defending in depth and breaking fast.

A good result against Arsenal would have restored Rowe's status with directors, shareholders and fans alike. The *Herald*'s 'Fanfare' believed that players were staying put and asking for the ball to be returned to them instead of passing-and-moving.

Les Bennett leaps to head for goal against Manchester United in a 1-1 draw at White Hart Lane at the end of September 1953. The stocky Duquemin (who scored Spurs' late, late equaliser) and grimacing Baily look on.

Furthermore, Robb was venturing on solo runs and Walters was starved of passes. Columnist 'Fanfare' had the last word on it: '"Push-and-run" must be re-introduced, with immediate replacement of any player who fails to attempt to carry out the blackboard instructions'. So the *Herald* was overlooking its criticisms of old.

At Cardiff Baily turned-in a great performance, but a penalty awarded for another ball-to-hand incident saw Spurs return pointless. The plain truth was that Spurs had already lost as many games as in their entire Championship-winning season. Rowe had used Brittan, Marchi and Wetton whenever Nicholson or Burgess were indisposed at half-back. He had used King or Gibbins if Clarke was missing at centre-back. He had used Baker and Hopkins when Ramsey, Withers or Willis were unavailable at full-back. Up front he had used Brooks for Bennett, McClellan for Duquemin, Harmer for Baily, and Groves for Walters. Yet time-after-time the old faces returned. But with teams packing their defence to counter 'push-and-run', it was necessary to both increase Spurs' tempo and maintain it for 90 minutes, and this was extremely testing for players in their early to mid-thirties. Danny Blanchflower, when recalling Rowe's great Spurs' side, said: 'Eventually they reached a peak... some players must naturally decline but do so gradually and when-and-how to replace them is a difficult task, others naturally ease up when they reach their destination.' The famed Hungarian coach Béla Guttman, best known for successive European Cup wins with Benfica in the early 1960s, believed that no football team could maintain success for more than three years without major changes to it (he actually called a manager's third year with a club the 'fatal' year). So why did a club as rich as Tottenham invest so little in players during Rowe's tenure?

But it should also be pointed out that, as Ron Reynolds recognised, the act of dropping men he admired and respected '...played on [Rowe]'s nerves.' As, too did letting the club and fans down when results were disappointing. It is almost certainly the case that the impression of some Spurs' stars that Rowe could, as one put it '... take a licking far better than we players' was false. In reality his nature was surely to suppress and disguise his worries and concerns. He would have felt obliged to sustain the spirit of his men with a facade of calm and confidence. But, as Guttman believed, there is also a time limit for the perpetuation of the coach's influence over a given group of players. Familiarity eventually breeds contempt, especially when results begin to fail. Coaches move on to other clubs, strike early gold again before eventually the process repeats itself. Malcolm Allison, shortly after his greatest coaching achievement (his first spell with Manchester City) wrote: 'Inevitably a coach loses his edge with a certain set of players. In the last period at Manchester City I sensed that we had all become too familiar, a kind of complacency had taken hold of both myself and the players. It is at times like that a man should either move on—or radically change the emphasis of his work' but Rowe's devotion to Spurs will have ruled out a search for new pastures. He was clearly imbued with the tantalising notion that, with some fresh talent added or not, his side might just still have a trophy or two within its grasp.

When Spurs beat lowly Manchester City, Duquemin scored early but the highlight, shortly before half-time, was a picture-book, five-man move ending with Robb heading past Bert Trautmann. The final 3-0 result was a first win in five.

Rowe then took his side to face the expensively-constructed Sunderland side who had beaten Arsenal 7-1. Goals from Robb, Walters and Duquemin failed to prevent a defeat by the odd goal in seven. With the arrival of November, two more points were picked-up at Chelsea before Spurs fell victim to food poisoning before taking the field at Blackpool. Not ideal conditions for coping with the likes of Ernie Taylor and Stanley Matthews, and it was that very pair who conjured up the only goal of the game. With Spurs dominating the last twenty minutes, a local paper headlined: 'FINAL WHISTLE WAS SWEET MUSIC TO BLACKPOOL', while *The Times* meanwhile wrote that the match '...revived one's faith in the British game.'

Spurs gained a further two points when third-placed Huddersfield Town arrived at the lane, yet after Duquemin had scored early the visitors controlled much of the game. Hopefully Rowe will not have read his own club's programme notes before the game. They referred to the Chelsea game of a fortnight earlier: 'Either Chelsea are a lot better side than their League position would indicate, or we have sadly deteriorated... .' Even the *Herald* censured the programme writer on this occasion: 'Spurs may not be the team they were—the attack needs more punch—but overall they are as good as most.' Of all the criticism from his own club Rowe had to endure, it was notable that the one thing the club programme did not blame Rowe for was the failure to enter the transfer market!

Three days after England's humiliation against Hungary, Spurs faced struggling Sheffield United. Robb and Ramsey had suffered at Wembley and there was no let-up for them at Bramall Lane. The Blades dominated despite Spurs going ahead. One United winger, Alf Ringstead, grabbed a hat-trick, while Derek Hawksworth was too fast for Ramsey on the opposite wing. It ended 5-2, Tottenham's biggest defeat in over two years and they tumbled to thirteenth. Not a great moment then to confront a Wolves side undefeated since August, yet Spurs dominated the first-half, ahead due to Bennett's picture-book header, his 100th League goal. But within eight minutes of the restart Wolves were 2-1 up in a superbly entertaining game. Duquemin equalised just before the hour only for Johnny Hancocks to win it with 12 minutes remaining. Blame was again placed on Ramsey's shoulders for his occasional bursts up-field, from which he now struggled to recover — his immediate opponent, Mullen, had provided the crosses for all three Wolves' goals. It was also very much past-due for Rowe to purchase two ready-made, technically-adept and hard-running wing-halves to replace Nicholson and Burgess.

A week later Spurs won 2-1 at Villa Park but it was something of a 'smash-and-grab' victory, the visitors surviving heavy early Villa pressure in both halves, headers from Baily and Walters finally put Spurs ahead before Danny Blanchflower's 25-yard drive beat Ditchburn late on. Despite Spurs' move up to twelfth, their own match programme praised Villa's 'open game', a further sly, public dig at 'push-and-run'. Ironically Blanchflower, a man of intelligence and wisdom, was at that very time desperate to escape playing that self-same 'open' style which the poison-penned Tottenham programme contributor was then promoting. Ramsey was replaced by 22-year-old Peter Baker to face Sheffield Wednesday at White Hart Lane, while Burgess returned for Brittan. Perhaps this was the moment Rowe should have given someone else a consistent run in Burgess' position, but on this occasion Spurs gained a fortunate victory after going behind, their three goals including an own goal and Baker's lengthy clearance being picked up by the wind and sailing over the 'keeper's head.

A few days later the entire staff of Tottenham Hotspur Football Club sat down to Christmas dinner, the meal taking place not at the Dorchester, but under the stands at White Hart Lane. Spurs' Vice Chairman Greville Wagstaffe Simmons (who passed away just a month later) said it was a gathering of one happy family, only to choose this festive occasion to address recent poor form on the pitch: 'I am not going to hide the fact that some of us (the directors) had a certain amount of anxiety as to what was going to happen, but you have done much indeed to relieve our anxiety.' As the *Herald* put it, when Wagstaffe Simmons finished his speech '…the bleak shadow of the Second Division seemed to pass, and the comic hats worn by the gay gathering were again tilted to a jaunty angle.' To be fair, the 87-year-old Vice Chairman had greater credentials than most directors when it came to running a football club. He had played amateur football, had joined the FA Council in 1901, and had refereed cup-ties and internationals. He was also said to have '…a very charming disposition' confirming similar opinions expressed to me by ex-players. Perhaps he had felt pressured to voice the concerns of his malevolent co-directors (of whom, more later) but he continued to go over Rowe's head, publicly reprimanding the players, suggesting they should, '…by determination, skill and science, dictate the play in future matches to bring more honour and more glory to this famous club.' So, in front of his men and attired in his paper hat, Rowe had thus received a public slap on the wrist.

Directors Heryet, Dewhurst-Hornsby, Taylor and Wale rose after the speech to drink to the health, happiness and success of the players, while Rowe (presumably through gritted teeth) thanked the directors for attending. Considering the nature of the Vice Chairman's speech, Rowe was probably compelled to add this rallying cry at the dinner: 'No player and no team can command success, but every player should apply his abilities in such a way as to deserve it.' Burgess replied for the players, putting their poor form down to not having had the best of luck, a sentiment which will have stuck in certain directors' throats. With that, Burgess and Les Bennett broke the unseasonal turn of events to lead a vocal rendition of 'MacNamara's Band'.

Clearly a Victorian attitude still prevailed during Rowe's time in charge at White Hart Lane, but, as Brian Scovell wrote, by the time Nicholson had later assumed Rowe's role it was finally recognised by the directors themselves that '…they had little expertise about football and left it to the expert.' As the *Topical Times* had jested as far back as 1935: 'When is a football manager a real manager? Answer: When he's allowed to manage.'

After two draws with Portsmouth over Christmas, Spurs would have needed to win all 17 remaining games for any chance of winning the title, so the FA Cup once again became the priority. On the first day of 1954 Rowe travelled to watch struggling Third Division North side York City triumph 3-1 at nearby Darlington. Said to again be searching for a centre-forward, rumours abounded that his directors had denied him the necessary funds and there had been fruitless tours of

Scotland in search of an affordable prospect. At Darlington he witnessed two goals from York's 19-year-old Dave Dunmore, who had been recommended by Rowe's former playing colleague Jimmy McCormick, then York's manager. Dunmore finally joined on February 11th for the sum of £10,500 but despite his promising skills a considerable drawback would prove to be both his deferred National Service and the completion of his trade apprenticeship.

Despite the optimism derived from a new arrival, a trip to Middlesbrough proved a gruelling experience. The four team members not part of the Championship-winning side (Hopkins, Marchi, Wetton and Brooks) performed reasonably well but Spurs succumbed 3-0. Now in the bottom half, Spurs at least had a nine point cushion over bottom side Liverpool but the *Herald* resorted to an unsubtle cartoon referring to the fading Spurs' 'Old Brigade' of players, depicted wearing long beards and glasses, propping themselves up with walking sticks. Was this aimed at Rowe… or the Tottenham Hotspur board?

For the FA Cup third round Spurs were drawn away for the fifth successive draw, this time at Second Division Leeds, who had just hammered Second Division leaders Leicester 7-1. Despite the beards-and-glasses cartoon, the *Herald* now asked Rowe to select his 'old team' to ensure a good result and indeed, in came Willis, Nicholson, Burgess and Baily for Hopkins, Marchi, Wetton and Brooks. In 35 seconds Walters scored from Baily's assist but in pressing forward to increase their advantage Spurs conceded twice, the second headed home by the powerful 22-year-old future Juventus legend John Charles. As Rowe later noted, Leeds had countered his deep-lying wingers, their backs moving up-field to stay tight on them (Rowe resolved that issue over time by getting Duquemin to exploit space left by the opponents' advanced full-backs). Bennett equalised but before half-time Ramsey deflected a shot into his own goal. With the minutes ticking by one can imagine the ordeal Rowe, now sitting in the 'last-chance saloon', was going through, but Bennett then came up with a second equaliser. Final score 3-3.

The Elland Road game proved to be the last Rowe would attend that season. He had suffered a severe nervous breakdown. When later describing the character of Alf Ramsey as England manager, author Max Marquis expressed the belief that Ramsey and Rowe possessed a common trait. They both '…appeared calm and equable on the surface, but [Rowe's] illness revealed that there was only a thin crust over the internal volcano of emotion and pressure.'

As the club made a concerted effort (with the collaboration of the local press) to keep the reasons for Rowe's absence from the public, the precise dates of his sick leave are not easy to determine. One report (long after the event) had his illness striking in December but clearly he was still actively running the team at Leeds on January 9th and he had in any case spoken at the club's Christmas party. The actual first reporting of his illness, by which time he was hospitalized, occurred around January 16th, following the Leeds replay.

Meanwhile Assistant Manager Jimmy Anderson took over the day-to-day running of the first team and presided over that rematch. No changes were made and Spurs ran out onto a White Hart Lane pitch which combined lake with muddy foreshore. Ron Burgess described it as '…one of the worst surfaces I have had to play on,' yet Spurs still dominated the first-half, grabbing a goal lead through Bennett. Apparently Anderson and trainer Cecil Poynton thought champagne would assist Spurs, as this is what the players were reportedly dosed with at half-time. Leeds fought hard to stay in the competition but Spurs ultimately scraped through to the fourth round. The inspirational performance of captain Burgess confirmed both his desire for belated personal success in the Cup and, no doubt, his desire to win for Rowe, his ailing boss to whom he owed so much.

WHAT CAUSED ROWE'S BREAKDOWN? As Brian Glanville has reported and as independently confirmed to me by two of Rowe's players, a couple of particularly distasteful Tottenham directors '…constantly sniped at Rowe's tactics, saying how pleased they were whenever they saw the ball played high and long.' Tyrannical club directors seemed an integral part of the English game in those times, wealthy men believing they could dictate on football matters regardless of their singular lack of experience in the sport. Their stern Victorian upbringing

Summer, 1953. Rowe and Spurs directors review the 1953-54 FA Year Book. From left-to-right are: Rowe, Fred Wale, Fred Bearman (Chairman), Bill Heryet and 'Eddie' Dewhurst Hornsby. Persistent sniping from Heryet and Dewhurst Hornsby would make Rowe's job virtually untenable.

forbade any capacity for respect, sympathy or empathy with staff, including the manager they themselves had appointed. I suggested to Brian Wait, who knew Rowe well, that despite the malodorous treatment he received from those board members, Rowe himself would never have denigrated or bad-mouthed them. 'No,' said Brian, '…absolutely not. He was a gentleman.'

When meeting Ralph Wetton (this before I came upon Glanville's disclosures) he, too, specifically pointed the finger at the self-same pair of directors Brian Glanville has since publicly identified: F. 'Eddie' Dewhurst-Hornsby (the 'forbidding figure in his broad-rimmed hat') and W. J. 'Bill' Heryet. In a 2004 *Times* article, Glanville categorically stated that it was these two who '…drove Arthur Rowe into an nervous breakdown in the 1950s.' 'For them,' wrote Glanville, '…push-and-run was a heresy', adding that they even went as far as '…eulogising long-ball tactics in the match programme.' Ralph Wetton referred to them as two 'bastards', adding '…sneaky blokes, and it got Arthur down.' It speaks volumes when viewing the 1950-51 Championship-winning team group photo that the sole director proudly taking his place plumb-centre amongst Rowe's players (all 'push-and-runners') is a very tall, white-haired man, the very same 'F. Dewhurst-Hornsby', happy to soak up the glory Rowe had brought to his club with the very tactic he, Dewhurst-Hornsby, despised.

When raising Rowe's breakdown with Tony Marchi, asking if he knew what may have been the cause, he could only say 'Oh, I could tell you a story about [Arthur's illness], but I don't think you should print it. Because…' Tony hesitated, before thinking out loud then trailing off: '…well, probably *all the people who did it to him are dead…*'.

Those last few words remained in my thoughts as I drove away from Tony's house.

Rowe's dedication to his job and to the football club he loved will have afforded him limited capacity to absorb persistent, nagging criticism on top of the everyday stress that came with the job. His spirit had finally been broken by two unscrupulous individuals. When I sought Marchi's confirmation that it truly was pressure from directors which most contributed to Rowe's breakdown, he responded: 'Well, that's what it was all about.' Author Max Marquis believed that in view of Rowe's character, his honesty and popularity, '…it would take a particularly unpleasant man to do [Rowe] a dirty trick.'

The closest we can get to knowing Rowe's own opinions on his mental stress while at Tottenham can be gleaned from a speech given in 1961 by a later employer of his, Crystal Palace Chairman Arthur Wait (see Chapter 17). Having become a very close friend of Rowe's, there can be little doubt Wait's comments were based on private disclosures. Ever-concerned for Rowe's health, Wait proposed that it must never happen that, at Crystal Palace, worry and lack of support would affect: '…the health of the man who took Spurs to successive championships, and was then shown such a lack of consideration by club and supporters alike…'. Wait, a much-admired and respected club chairman who held Rowe in the highest esteem, then pointedly added that, '…niggardly people [had] broken [Arthur] down at Tottenham.'

TOIL AND TORMENT: MANAGING SPURS 1953-54

At the time of the final game ever played at White Hart Lane, Brian Glanville wrote of how, for him personally, Rowe inspired more memories of the old stadium than anyone else, and in doing so repeated that the major cause of the manager's stress-related illness at Tottenham was the behaviour of 'two *sinister* directors.'

In the twenty-first century, it is hard to comprehend the ignorance and lack of understanding for stress-related mental illness or instability which prevailed in the middle of the twentieth century. When relating this tragic and sad moment in Rowe's career I chose to credit the club's board for at least keeping the nature of their manager's illness within the walls of White Hart Lane (although it is of course feasible that, in those very different times, neither Rowe nor the club wished to be publicly tainted with the stigma then attached to any mental illness).

So, in January 1954, the resilience of the kindly, sensitive and dedicated manager, with Spurs' blue and white running through his veins, had finally wilted. Less than three years had passed since his superb 'push-and-run' Championship success and he had since kept his side comfortably in the top flight, a side recalled to this day for their thrilling, entertaining soccer. Ironically it was his extraordinary early success which contributed to exaggerated expectations in the boardroom. The surprise and suddenness of his collapse only emphasised how self-controlled he had been.

Ralph Wetton recalled one particular incident: '[Arthur] hadn't been well for some time. He'd been a little bit… distant. He broke down one morning in the dressing-room, as he was talking to us.' This possibly refers to the very event following the Leeds Cup-tie. Graham Rowe was unaware of his father's torment prior to his breakdown, explaining to author Martin Cloake that '…he was essentially a quiet man and if he voiced any problems it was to my mother, not me.'

STRESS AND THE 1950s CLUB MANAGER As a 1950s football manager Rowe was hardly alone in succumbing to pressure. Several contemporary managers were similarly brought to their knees during that era. The first managerial experience of genial future England boss Joe Mercer was with Sheffield United in 1955, where he discovered there were no fewer than fifteen directors! Mercer immediately realised it would be tough to keep all fifteen happy. Mercer was also very aware that much of the success of clubs such as Wolves and Manchester United was due to the strong, individual will of managers Stan Cullis and Matt Busby. Mercer ultimately exchanged the 'frying-pan' of Sheffield United for the 'fire' of Aston Villa and, like Rowe, he quickly experienced success but, when results faltered, he too became the object of criticism, eventually collapsing from what was referred to as 'nervous exhaustion'. In those less enlightened and more insensitive times the *Daily Sketch* headlined this as '*MERCER CRACKS UP*'.

A further example was the death of Arsenal's 58-year-old manager Tom Whittaker four days after managing his side to victory over Spurs in October 1956. Found to be suffering from 'nervous exhaustion' he was instructed to take a six-month break from the game. Even the aforementioned granite-tough, strong-willed and independent Stan Cullis at Wolves suffered strains on his health. After season 1955-56 he received medical advice to take a month's rest. On one occasion a new director arrived at Molineux who, according to Cullis biographer Jim Holden, addressed the esteemed Wolves boss as a common lackey: 'Just you remember in future that you're not dealing with your schoolboy players when you deal with me, Mr Cullis.' Sure enough, when his side was in the midst of a series of defeats which had taken them to the foot of the First Division table, Cullis fainted at his desk. Doctors again ordered him to rest but the Wolves' directors saw fit to sack a manager who had won the Midlands club six major trophies in just over a decade just three weeks into his recuperation (Rowe being one of those who quickly sent Cullis a letter of sympathy and understanding). The director-manager relationship seemed to be a case of businessmen keeping their working-class managerial employees in their place, whilst happily sharing the acclaim whenever success was achieved (as with Dewhurst-Hornsby).

A graphic example of the power which directors of Rowe's era commonly exerted over the manager can be witnessed in a scene from an early 1960s documentary about West Brom, called *The Saturday Men*. When first viewed it I had to reverse the film to be sure I had heard correctly. In a Victorian-style boardroom the Chairman gives manager Archie Macauley the chance to describe the previous Saturday's game to those directors who, said the Chairman, '…hadn't been present.' Macauley sombrely describes the team's victory before 'recommending' that 'we' play the same side for their next League match. The only conclusion one can draw from his use of 'recommending' is that the board seriously believed they could overrule (on football matters) the man they paid to manage.

Following his collapse, Rowe was treated at a sanatorium in Kent and underwent electroconvulsive therapy (ECT), a treatment for severe depressive illnesses first developed in Italy in the late 1930s. Two electrodes are attached to the scalp before an electric current is passed through them, causing convulsions which are thought to 'reset' the brain, returning the patient to the person they were before their illness.

On January 16th 1954, with the public told Rowe was recovering from influenza and bronchitis, Jimmy Anderson prepared the side to face Vic Buckingham's second-placed West Brom. Once the game was underway Spurs, as so commonly the case, made more chances than their visitors but, ten minutes from the break Ronnie Allen put Albion ahead and Spurs failed to find an equaliser. Although Anderson had announced he would only select what he called 'whole-hearted triers', he initially persevered with similar line-ups to Rowe's.

At bottom-placed Liverpool Spurs came away with a point, their defending said to have been less 'polished' than usual, suggesting Anderson was instructing defenders to hack the ball away whenever danger threatened. The resulting surrender of possession might explain Spurs' failure to beat a side propping-up the table. When describing Spurs under Anderson, Julian Holland wrote: 'At times their play was no more than a shambles.'

Returning to the FA Cup, Spurs' reward for beating Leeds was, unbelievably, a *tenth* away tie from the last twelve draws, this time at Maine Road to face in-form Manchester City. Finding the pitch frozen on arrival, Anderson and trainer Cecil Poynton took the initiative to visit a Manchester shoe shop where all except Ditchburn and Ramsey chose soft, rubber boots to aid their stability. Ditchburn kept Spurs in the game until the rubber-booted Bennett scored what proved to

Jimmy Anderson, a long-standing Tottenham employee, favoured by the Board, proved an inadequate assistant for Rowe, who one suspects would have benefitted tremendously had the likes of the talented Vic Buckingham filled Anderson's role instead.

be the winner. One headline read: 'MANCHESTER TONIC FOR MR ROWE'. Indeed Rowe was well enough to pen the players a letter from his sick bed: 'Thanks lads for a great result on Saturday. Keep fighting. Best wishes to you all.'

For the fifth round Spurs were drawn away for the twelfth time in fourteen draws, their opponents to be Second Division Blackburn or Hull. Avoiding First Division sides will have boosted Rowe's men, who were determined to reach the sixth round as a tonic for their beloved manager.

At home to a feisty Newcastle in February, an hour passed before a goal arrived, Ramsey's long ball enabling Robb to score from 22 yards. Robb (again) and Walters completed a 3-0 win. Baily was now jumping into 50/50 clashes he would previously have pulled out of. Rowe's philosophy was: 'Some like a tackle, others don't, so you have to assess the player's value on the other things he does. I am well aware that the ball player who also likes to 'get [stuck] in' is the perfect footballer, but there are not many of them about.' This aligns with Rowe's theory to create a team of many talents and make them function as a unit, combining each of the players' strengths for the benefit of the team. He knew that the odds of uncovering a single individual encompassing all the most desirable talents were slim.

With Spurs back in the top half of the table Rowe will have been further boosted when Anderson completed the signing of Dave Dunmore on his behalf. Spurs next visited Old Trafford where the developing 'Busby Babes' won 2-0. Spurs then travelled to Hull for their FA Cup fifth round tie but even though their opponents lost a man injured in just the third minute it still took an hour before Bennett finally put Spurs ahead and even then the home side equalised, the visitors only crawling into the sixth round after a replay. Then the quarter-final draw not only teamed Spurs with the most powerful opponents left in the draw, West Bromwich Albion, but it was also yet another *away* tie, now making it eight from eight! Rowe might have been forgiven for feeling the odds were stacked against him. His spell as manager would ultimately witness the unlikely odds of Spurs being drawn away in the FA Cup no fewer than fourteen times in seventeen draws.

Anderson took Spurs to Highbury next, where Spurs had not won for twenty years. Dunmore replaced Duquemin for his debut and, after twenty minutes, he combined with Marchi before Baily delivered a through ball which Robb despatched to put the visitors ahead. Dunmore and Marchi were also involved when Robb scored his second, shooting on the turn from Walters' corner. Just five minutes into the second period Walters headed a third and that is how it finished. For once Spurs had taken their chances. It's unlikely Rowe had been well enough to attend, yet he was not forgotten by the *Herald*, a caricature of his beaming face appearing in their weekly cartoon, the caption reading '…everyone in Tottenham was delighted. Mr Rowe too!'

After heavy snow at home to Bolton the game was level at 2-2 when Dunmore leapt high to nod home the winner yet, for some reason, Spurs' momentum stalled, and the Anderson-led Spurs suffered five consecutive defeats. One was against Cup quarter-final opponents West Brom, a side on fire at that time and leading the First Division table so, for the third season running Spurs had been knocked out by the eventual winners. This was likely to have been the game at the Hawthorns which Ralph Wetton recalled when describing Anderson's limitations:

'[Anderson] said,"Right lads, let's open the game up a little bit, let's make some longer passes."

'So Alf [Ramsey] said: "Well, what do you mean, longer passes?"

'Anderson replied: "About twenty yards."

'"TWENTY YARDS!" said Alf, incredulously, and everybody laughed.

'Anderson was absolutely clueless. The blokes just took no notice of him.' Sadly, this is a commonly-held view of Anderson among players of the time, Ernie Walley (later Assistant Manager at Chelsea) bluntly used the word 'useless' to describe Rowe's assistant.

Burgess, his Cup dreams over, would now return only for a 'final hurrah' in the penultimate home game. As for Baily's struggles, return passes to him were infrequent now that the individualistic Robb had replaced Medley. When asked if Baily found life harder partnering Robb, Ralph Wetton said: 'Robb was an amateur, and played like an amateur. He just got his head down and ran'. On the contrary Wetton referred to Medley as 'an artist.' No doubt Rowe, with insufficient financial support, was perfectly aware that in Robb he had been forced to settle for second-best.

Now change was really in the air, the combined age of the eleven Spurs men who took the field at Maine Road to face Manchester City dropping by an astonishing 39 years (the absence of Burgess and Bennett alone accounting for much of that). But both Brooks and Dunmore failed to impress in a heavy defeat. Meanwhile that week, in mid-March 1954, Bill Nicholson was named chief coach, a significant landmark in the club's history, although for now he also continued playing. A club director made the announcement, not Anderson, and presumably Rowe gave his blessing. Nicholson, concerned about his niggling knee injury, had volunteered for the coaching role. Ramsey was another candidate but unlike Nicholson, lacked an FA coaching badge.

The Spurs' match programme for the home game with Sunderland expressed extraordinary negativity: 'We have a very stiff lot of fixtures for the remainder of the season and are not likely to pick up many [points] in our away games.' Was this written by directors to lessen pressure on Anderson? Goalkeeper Ron Reynolds finally made his debut, aged 25, having waited four years for Ditchburn to step down but multiple team changes saw Spurs struggle at the back and they were short of ideas up front. Errors by Ramsey played a part in all three Sunderland goals and as for Johnny Brooks, it seemed he sometimes needed something extra in his half-time tea, reports again describing how he faded in the second period.

Two days later, on Monday March 22nd, Arthur Rowe walked back through the doors of White Hart Lane for the first time in ten weeks. It was only a visit and its purpose went unrecorded, although he did have a meeting with Vic Buckingham later in the day. Had Rowe been summoned from his sick-bed to help stall a run of disastrous results? Was he merely demonstrating his fitness to resume his role? Was he meeting Buckingham to discuss the possibility of his old pal taking over his job? Whatever the reason for Rowe's presence at White Hart Lane that day, Anderson remained in charge until season's end, this despite four successive defeats and the creeping fear of relegation. Demands rose again for investment in experienced players. To this Anderson voiced the club's standard and tired response, that the club would invest only '…providing the player is up to standard, but he must be a lot better than those we have on the books.' The *Herald* now regretted Rowe's absence, appealing for 'push-and-run' to be reinstated at Chelsea. That afternoon, mostly due to 'keeper Ron Reynolds, who even saved a penalty, Spurs kept Chelsea at bay, at least until Johnny McNichol finally netted a winner. Anderson's side had now managed just one goal in five successive defeats, and five of the six remaining matches were against sides higher in the table.

Against Blackpool the restored Dunmore showed great skill when beating three defenders to set Baily up to put Spurs ahead and although the final score was a 2-2 draw it at least represented Anderson's first point from ten. Harmer was reintroduced at Huddersfield and took no time in making his point. At the kick-off he received from Dunmore before setting off on a 25-yard run before setting-up Brooks to put Spurs in front. Three more goals were added before, as the *Herald* put it, 'Harmer crowned a wonderful performance by nonchalantly lobbing the ball over the goalkeeper's head' but this 5-2 away win was soon forgotten when Spurs fell 2-1 at Preston. Then Ron Burgess returned for his final game in the Lillywhites' shirt, at home to Sheffield United, the 2-1 win confirming Spurs' safety for another year. It was a fine moment for Burgess to bow-out after 324 first-team appearances but, without him for Spurs' final home game on Easter Monday, a Preston side lacking Tom Finney tore Anderson's side asunder, winning 6-2. The *Herald* slammed Spurs for lacking '…modern ideas', a clear put-down of Anderson's Neanderthal approach. Tottenham's heaviest defeat had taken place in the final home game in front of loyal fans hoping to see their side finish with a bang. Many will have hoped to see a restoration of 'push-and-run'.

Instead Spurs signed-off on a sad, disappointing season against new champions Wolves at a celebrating Molineux. Despite going down 2-0, Spurs had not disgraced themselves against their strong opponents. However, the defeat saw them finish the season just four teams clear of relegated Middlesbrough and Liverpool.

In their review of the season, the *Herald* made it clear that Anderson's error was to turn his back on Rowe's 'push-and-run': 'Let's face it, this long ball punt, this hit-and-hope-for-the-best, will satisfy no one, not even if it wins a match or two.' Thus only by his glaring absence was Rowe's contribution to Tottenham appreciated. The *Herald* also noted: 'Marksmanship can be secondary. The Championship side also missed chances—they could afford to, for they made more of them.'

Instead of being at the hub of Rowe's sharp inter-passing, poor Dunmore had been ploughing a lonely furrow. Capable of bringing the ball down no matter how it was delivered to him, and occasionally nutmegging his opponent, Dunmore usually found himself with nobody in sufficient space to pass to. Meanwhile Anderson reported that Spurs had scouts busily hunting talent in 'England, Scotland, Ireland and Wales.' One or two players were under consideration but, he said (and this caused not a modicum of surprise) 'for one reason or another' no deals had been clinched!

Since promotion in 1950, Spurs had finished 1st, 2nd, 10th and now 16th, although there's little doubt that had the manager not fallen ill in January he would have attained more points than Anderson. The players, lacking faith in the stand-in manager, missed Rowe's benevolent, sympathetic encouragement, his tactical know-how and man-management skills. More than anything, they will have missed the exhilaration of performing 'push-and-run'. Meanwhile, behind the scenes and despite being retained, Willis and McClellan found their pay had been cut, dispiriting news which was leaked to the Sunday papers, who were of course obliged to point out that Tottenham Hotspur was 'one of the richest clubs in the country.' The never-complaining Willis, playing well whenever called upon, had served the club for 17 years, and fans wrote to express their disgust.

A post-season tour to Austria and Germany led by Anderson, garnered three defeats and a draw, results bearing little comparison with those gained when Rowe had led Spurs on foreign soil.

Finally, on Monday, May 17th 1954, Rowe walked back into White Hart Lane. Described as 'looking incredibly fit', he had been absent for nearly five months. Immediately going into conference with Anderson and new player/coach Nicholson, discussions ranged from the weaknesses of the previous season's side to a review of future prospects. The inevitable conclusion was to go into the market, particularly for what the *Herald* referred to as 'quick, hard-shooting inside men.' But, as so often in the past, no player of that description turned-up, either before or during the season which followed. When Rowe, Anderson and Nicholson came to review season '53-54s statistics, it was noted that wingers Walters and Robb had been responsible for nearly half Spurs' 65 goals from 42 League matches. As for defending, Ramsey had increasingly struggled to stay with his winger. The most damning statistic was that the same eleven players had taken the field for consecutive matches on only six occasions. Rowe made it clear that the approach on the field was now to return to normal: 'We have our problems, but we also have our plan,' adding pointedly, 'stylish football will never be abandoned at Tottenham.'

However, the fixtures for season '54-55 included some tough early engagements, which immediately prompted concern in the *Herald* for the returning manager's health: 'Mr Rowe will need the support of the critics and fans, especially in these early games.' But, by late June, Rowe's return had regenerated optimism at White Hart Lane, columnist 'Fanfare' writing: 'This column has never ceased to plug the 'push-and-run' formula, although I'll admit I have had many long discussions, and even arguments, with Mr Rowe when I believed there were flaws in the set-up. In these discussions, however, Mr Rowe has always come out on top. He has a theory which he is prepared to discuss down to the last detail. He has a plan which has been devised to minimise errors, and which, if followed through thick and thin, must pay dividends in providing first-class entertainment, and should bring individual and team honours in the years to come.'

The 1954 World Cup Finals were televised in the UK for the first time and *Herald* columnist 'Fanfare' identified a clear similarity to Rowe's 'push-and-run' in the play of the Hungarians as they beat West Germany 8-3 and South Korea 9-0 in the qualifiers. A Spurs supporter also picked up on this: 'Spurs fans are realising that the Hungarians have set the whole world talking with a style which, in essence, was the one which set Britain talking only a few seasons ago. And what is good for Budapest would certainly be good once again for White Hart Lane.'

But, as season 1954-55 approached, Rowe needed more than pure 'push-and-run'. He needed cash. In the course of the approaching season Bennett was to turn 37, Nicholson 36, Ramsey and Willis 35, Ditchburn 33, Clarke and Withers 32, and Duquemin and Walters 30. A continued persistence with the 'old guard' would see a team taking the field with an average age of 33. When I suggested to Tony Marchi that he was one of the young players who Rowe could and should have promoted earlier, he replied '[Arthur] was so loyal, he didn't want to hurt anybody'. Yet although the likes of Wetton and Brittan had done well as temporary replacements at half-back, their predecessors' boots were simply too big to fill from within, while Brooks and Dunmore had yet to prove themselves as adequate replacements for Bennett and Duquemin.

Rowe needed to acquire exceptional, experienced talent, preferably aged 22 to 26, with the technical ability and enthusiasm to master 'push-and-run'. Without a change in approach from the boardroom, could Rowe balance the demands of restoring success while at the same time protecting his own health?

15

Ignorance and Violence Around Him

MANAGING SPURS 1954-55

*'This proved to be a fleeting glimpse of what
English football might have become.'*
'*THE EDUCATED LEFT FOOT*' WEBSITE ON ROWE'S 'PUSH-AND-RUN' SPURS, FEBRUARY 2017

As Arthur Rowe holidayed on the Isle of Wight that summer of 1954 the *Herald* was pronouncing: 'Never have Spurs faced a new season with such uncertainty.' Beginning pre-season training ahead of other clubs Rowe said no player had a right to be in the team: 'We shall play the fittest and the men in form in our endeavour to fight back to the top. All players are expected to be 100 per cent fit and to carry out the club slogan of "make it simple, accurate and quick."' The Spurs match programme spoke of the '…many promising young players on our books' who '…will be called upon' in the coming season. Composed by directors, it surely translated as 'no player investment can be expected'. This had been the board's mantra twenty years earlier when success was achieved largely with home-grown players (under Percy Smith) and led to a failure to invest in the experience and quality to prevent Spurs' swift return to Division Two.

In training Rowe had his men playing in positions other than those they usually filled, for example left-back Hopkins at inside-left, centre-half Clarke at centre-forward and inside-right Bennett at right-back. This, said Rowe, was 'to help the regulars get the feel of what their colleagues expect from them when everyone is in the proper position.' A significant loss that summer was Ron Burgess, who left Spurs to combine playing with coaching at Second Division Swansea Town. Having lost several playing years to the war, 'push-and-run' had provided Burgess with belated success. One wonders if Rowe had retained him back in the spring purely so his captain would qualify for his five-year, £750 benefit (more than a third the price of an average house).

When Tottenham did (finally) grant Rowe a transfer fund later that season, it required all of it to capture just one player to compensate for the departure of Burgess. For now, Rowe would yet again depend heavily on those remaining from his 1951 Championship-winning side. Fans desperate for team rebuilding flooded the *Herald* with comments and suggestions. With so little of Rowe's 'push-and-run' side captured on film, the comments of these supporters contribute to one's perception of individual players. At left-back Willis was said to have 'more class' than Withers. One correspondent felt Marchi and Wetton should be the half-backs as they were both capable of powerful shooting. Marchi was further considered to be 'thoughtful, confident' and 'sure-footed'; Wetton 'a grand distributor, hard to beat' and possessing 'speed and determination'; Walters was '…the only Spur who goes straight for goal'; Duquemin should retain his place at centre-forward as he was '…the most constructive centre-forward in soccer; perfect distribution', while Baily, one reader wrote, should be '…left alone by the crowd'.

These were times long before rash, ignorant and abusive opinions could be irresponsibly espoused on social media. Fans back then handwrote and posted constructive, considered opinions and Ramsey, for one, believed spectators could identify things a manager or coach had missed. One correspondent perceived that the team had often looked jaded in the second half of games prompting my question to Tony Marchi whether fitness levels under Rowe had dropped over time. He denied this but added that later, under Bill Nicholson's management, training methods were devised to increase endurance.

Spurs' performance in a pre-season friendly against Lille Olympic in Boulogne worried Rowe sufficiently for him to recall players for additional, afternoon training before the League season opener at Aston Villa. Marchi would eventually become the regular replacement for Burgess but at that time he was doing National Service, so Brittan played at Villa Park, while Rowe surprisingly chose 23-year-old debutant Dickie Dowsett to stand-in for Walters. Some fans were disappointed with the selection of Ramsey over the promising Baker, but Rowe had chosen Ramsey to assume the captaincy from Burgess. So the full team was: Ditchburn; Ramsey, Withers; Wetton, Clarke, Brittan; Dowsett, Bennett, Dunmore, Baily, Robb. Fans attending a reserve contest with neighbours Arsenal heard 15-minute tannoy updates from Villa Park where, before kick-off, captain Ramsey placed a pre-kick-off arm around Dowsett's shoulders, assuring him 'If you're in trouble, I'm 45 degrees inside of you and I'm always there.' Spurs fans were soon able to celebrate Rowe's return to the helm, Bennett and Baily putting their side two-up, before Villa half-back Danny Blanchflower pulled one back from the spot. Such was Spurs' domination that Villa fans broke into a first-day slow hand-clap and two late goals, including one from debutant Dowsett, gave Spurs a 4-2 opening day win. The return of 'push-and-run' had produced far more goal chances than under Anderson's leadership and when Rowe commented afterwards on the '…return of the fine team spirit among the lads', it firmly illustrated the degree to which morale had plunged under Anderson. Those fans at White Hart Lane cheering news from Birmingham were simultaneously celebrating the four goals which polished-off Arsenal Reserves, a good day all round for Rowe. As for Dowsett, he had to return to National Service duty, history showing he was never selected again, although he did claim an impressive total of 101 strikes from 191 League games during spells with Bournemouth and Crystal Palace.

Dunmore then struck a hat-trick in a 3-2 home victory over champions Wolves, before Sunderland arrived and took the lead at White Hart Lane. A great strike by Dunmore was then disallowed, knocking the spirit out of Rowe's side. With a packed defence, Sunderland eventually departed with both points and a customary problem persisted: the breakdown of Robb's link-up play with Baily. For a Spurs side averaging thirty, the return with Wolves then arrived too soon. Despite Robb and Walters putting Spurs ahead, a slow, jittery defence conceded four times in just twelve minutes after the break, and that is how it stayed. Clearly the defence needed tightening before the trip to Highbury, although Spurs started brightly against an Arsenal side including 35-year-old Tommy Lawton. After Withers was injured, Jimmy Logie and Doug Lishman scored the Gunners' winning goals. When Busby's 'Babes' then arrived, Rowe's surprise choice to replace Wetton was 17-year-old debutant Alan Woods, but the former's defensive capabilities were missed in a fourth successive defeat. Pressure was mounting again.

Three more changes were required at Sheffield Wednesday, including King for Clarke. Spurs dominated but only went ahead after half-time when McClellan lobbed Harmer's pass over the 'keeper. Young Hopkins then failed to prevent winger Alan Finney crossing for Jack Shaw to equalise. But keeper/creator Ditchburn found Baily, who played a one-two with McClellan before shooting home in-off the 'keeper. With two minutes left and two points on the cards, Duquemin pressured his opposing centre-half into a booming, do-or-die clearance which happened to find the feet of England international Jackie Sewell who beat Ditchburn after rounding both King and Woods, Wednesday thus snatching a point at the death. Despite this late blow, the losing streak was at least over and Rowe could not be accused of failing to experiment, the side now incorporating six changes from that which started the season. Yet with pressure growing Rowe was obliged to clarify that the accent now was on re-building. 'We would naturally like to finish near the top, but I am not driving the youngsters, who must get experience', he said. Then, without explanation, the *Herald* wrote 'Spurs are willing to buy' adding, ominously: 'There's confidence in Mr Rowe in the chair.'

Rowe persisted with the side that so nearly won at Hillsborough for the return at Old Trafford, but within twenty minutes United were 2-1 ahead, and that is how it finished. Five of Spurs' nine opponents to date were to finish in the top six. The last of those was Portsmouth, against whom McClellan put Spurs ahead, but after Reid equalised it took a late Ditchburn penalty save to preserve a point. The *Herald* reacted strongly to this Spurs performance, stating that '…everyone, including the manager, players, spectators and directors are well aware such exhibitions must be stopped', this despite Rowe making it clear that he regarded the season as one for rebuilding and the newspaper knew the manager could only work with what was available to him. The *Herald* finally clarified responsibility, writing that the *directors* '…must be prepared to sanction buying the right players whatever the cost'.

Tensions at White Hart Lane will have soared when Spurs produced their worst performance since leaving Division Two. Away at bottom side Blackpool and one-up at half-time, they conceded no fewer than five without reply in the second period. Les Bennett had been restored for this game but it sadly proved to be his final appearance. Later describing Rowe as 'a tactical genius', Bennett had totalled 117 goals from 294 games. Recoiling from pressure applied at a shareholders' meeting the previous week, the magnitude of the Blackpool defeat was a double blow for Rowe who had told the shareholders: 'We have had the misfortune of losing our greatest players, Nicholson, Burgess and others at the same time, and must hope the younger players, bolstered-up by the more experienced, will do the job.' Rowe's plaintive use of 'must hope' is clearly significant. He was without other options. Yet Chairman Fred Bearman still claimed that a cheque would be signed '...for any player Mr Rowe wants and thinks he can get'. However, a further five months would pass before that cheque was signed. Keeping a tight grip on the club's purse strings, directors were presumably too easily impressed by the Reserves' success.

Rowe was now forced to put coach Nicholson in the side to face Charlton. He also restored the competitive Marchi while Brooks replaced Bennett. For twenty-five minutes Spurs looked set to end their eight-match winless streak. At that point Ramsey sliced a low shot from John Hewie over his shoulder and past Ditchburn. A tragicomic moment which disheartened Rowe's men and Stuart Leary headed a second before things worsened. Hopkins had played a few nervy back-passes but, in the 57th minute, his luck ran out, Bobby Ayre scoring from another to make it 3-0. Brooks pulled one back before Dunmore surrendered possession and Ayre completed the scoring at 4-1. According to the *Herald* reporter however, home fans surprisingly remained supportive: 'When a small band of young fans started a feeble slow hand-clap on Saturday, I shut my eyes and thought "this is it". I awaited the dread sound to be increased, but instead I heard angry voices—of protest against such clap-trap. The hands were silenced, and within minutes came the more welcome sound of a miniature Tottenham roar.'

Some Spurs' men were now bristling at new captain Ramsey's abrasive criticisms, his tongue sharper than that of the more genial Burgess. On occasion Nicholson and Ramsey bitterly clashed. Rowe had begun planning for the unqualified Ramsey to fill a coaching role, which left the fully-qualified Nicholson fearing that his planned post-playing career was under threat. Rowe was meanwhile expressing how appreciative he and his men were with fans who demonstrated 'loyalty and good sense', and said he was keeping an active eye on the transfer market. What Rowe knew he needed more than anything however, aside from that seemingly unaffordable target, a snapper-up of chances, was an inspiring and powerful leader-of-men. A costly commodity.

Meanwhile amateur Vic Groves left to finally turn professional at Third Division (South) Leyton Orient. His success there eventually earned him a transfer to Arsenal, where he was captain for three years. But although Groves thus appeared to have been 'one who got away', Orient manager Alec Stock later wrote of the young Groves' dislike of training, and an occasional lack of enthusiasm to play the game at all, flaws which Rowe will have identified for himself.

Now in penultimate place, Spurs welcomed League leaders West Brom on October 9th. Rowe's decision to keep faith with his forward line of McClellan, Baily, Dunmore, Brooks and Robb paid off even before he had taken his seat in the stands, Robb sending in a shot which bounced off 'keeper Jim Sanders for McClellan to score. By the 24th minute it was 3-0, McClellan with his second and Ramsey converting from the spot. West Brom would manage just a lone reply in Spurs' finest performance so far. At that point Rowe finally made a purchase, although the fee hardly rivalled the £34,500 Sheffield Wednesday had forked out for Jackie Sewell or the £30,000 Sunderland paid for Trevor Ford. Rowe paid £10,000 for stocky, speedy Irish winger Johnny Gavin, who arrived not from Arsenal, nor Manchester United, but Third Division (South) Norwich City. It was yet another bargain-basement buy, not that Gavin was Rowe's major target that autumn. No, his prime target would indeed create a dent in Spurs' bank balance. This was an international, an experienced First Division leader of men. A thoroughbred, someone potentially as influential as the departed Burgess. More than anything, he was a huge admirer of 'push-and-run'. But for now, Gavin would have to do. He was introduced at outside-right at Newcastle, where Spurs were quickly 3-0 down before the home side lost their 'keeper and the visitors recovered to earn a point in a 4-4 draw.

After a floodlit friendly defeat to Austrian club Sportklub Wacker, Spurs then faced a Preston side gunning for the Championship. Rowe bravely restored Hopkins to counter none other than Tom Finney but it was Ditchburn's brilliance which saw the first-half end goalless. Soon after the break 'The Preston Plumber' headed home before his side lost full-back Willie Cunningham to injury. Gavin then produced a corner from which Dunmore equalised and was also involved when McClellan scored his eighth goal in eight games. With two minutes left Ramsey completed the 3-1 victory from the spot. Gavin had been involved in all three goals, while Hopkins was congratulated on his performance by the great Finney himself. Spurs had now taken five points from six.

Two days later, on October 25th 1954, a 14-year-old Essex schoolboy made the first of what would ultimately be hundreds of appearances at White Hart Lane. Representing London Schoolboys against Manchester, he struck a post with a superb cross-shot before running the entire length of the adult-sized pitch only to run out of energy when attempting to shoot. He finally found the net in the second-half. Rowe anticipated signing the boy, named Jimmy Greaves, as an apprentice. Indeed the player himself later spoke of his 'destiny' to join Spurs from school. Rowe spoke to Jimmy's tube-driver father of the great opportunities awaiting him at Tottenham, the Spurs boss painting as bright a picture as he could. Jimmy's father was particularly impressed with Rowe's personal concern for the welfare of young players and admired, too, the fact that he had not stooped to offer illegal financial incentives to obtain his son's signature. Furthermore, Jimmy's dad admired the football played under Rowe. It was agreed that as soon as Jimmy Greaves left school a few months' later he was to join Spurs.

Meanwhile Rowe's principal transfer target was soon revealed. The leader-of-men for whom he had been promised funding was also a target of Arsenal's. He was the 28-year-old Aston Villa and Northern Ireland midfielder Danny Blanchflower. Why was he in such demand? Well, he was a natural, inspirational leader of men, once described by Terry Venables as 'aristocratic' in bearing. Quick-thinking, not over-physical, Blanchflower relied on awareness and anticipation defensively, while going forward he was graceful, skilled and an accurate passer.

Spurs then travelled in good heart to face Sheffield United. Yet by the time Dunmore found the net with eight minutes left, his side were four goals behind (with one more to come) and a disappointed Rowe believed the Blades should have been beaten. No doubt with a sizeable intake of breath, he added 'Things will turn our way', yet still more bad news followed as it emerged that Blanchflower had suffered knee ligament damage on international duty putting his transfer on hold. The only positive that week was Rowe's selection of a Spurs' star of the future in a side to play Cambridge University. This was Terry Dyson, 19-year-old son of a jockey, who had been spotted playing for the Royal Artillery during his National Service. Rowe signed the 5ft 3 in winger in a café opposite the Woolwich barracks in December, and Dyson would become an integral part of Spurs' 'Double' side.

A week later, on November 6th, McClellan broke an arm at home to Cardiff and Spurs conceded two second-half goals, tumbling back into penultimate place. Having totalled eight goals from ten games, McClellan was a big loss. 'By thunder, there'll have to be a considerable all-round improvement if the club are to avoid relegation,' the *Herald* now proclaimed, simultaneously offering Rowe their support: 'Perhaps, when [Spurs] find their rhythm, we shall be glad they always tried to play true football, even when their future looked so black.' Before crossing London to face mid-table Chelsea, goalkeeper Ditchburn asked Rowe to leave him out and Ron Reynolds played in the remaining 29 League and Cup games. Sadly Reynolds had already conceded twice by the eighth minute at Stamford Bridge. Aside from Gavin's goal in reply, Spurs also twice hit the woodwork while Dunmore missed an open goal, but 2-1 is how it stayed. This meant victory over struggling Leicester City had become essential and Dunmore was the provider for three first-half goals, two by Robb and one from Gavin. In the 65th minute Dunmore was again the provider, his long cross struck home by Baily. Leicester pulled one back before Gavin collected his second for a final score of 5-1, a result which took Spurs above Arsenal in the table. Rowe then signed defender Ron Henry on professional terms after a successful trial. With Baker, Dyson and Henry on board, plus his targeting of Blanchflower, Rowe was already setting the stage for Spurs' sixties 'second-coming'. Of course, he had the boy Greaves lined-up to join, too.

A successive victory followed, at Burnley, taking Spurs up to eighteenth, giving Rowe some respite from the incessant pressure. That week he again tried to sign Robledo, cabling the player in his native Chile in an attempt to lure him back to England. As an excellent passer and superb finisher, Robledo would have given Spurs a refreshing boost. But, of course, Rowe's attempt came to nothing. Earlier in the season Rowe had planned to blend three or four new players into the side, and would have felt satisfied if achieving a midway finish in the table. To date, Reynolds, Hopkins, Marchi, Gavin, Dunmore and Brooks were keeping more established players out of the side. But would these economical changes to his Championship-winning XI capture further silverware?

Mid-table Everton's arrival on December 4th was sadly littered with defensive errors, firstly two by Reynolds, then young Hopkins, under no pressure, put into his own goal. Baily only reduced the deficit two minutes from the end. This performance prompted the *Herald* to demand that 'guilty offenders' be 'severely reprimanded.' Robb was one target of criticism. Still training at Finchley during the evenings and teaching during the day, he was clearly out of the loop for team-talks, team planning and daily camaraderie with his team-mates. Rowe should perhaps have given Robb an ultimatum to end this state of affairs, particularly as the player still defied 'push-and-run'. This was confirmed by Johnny Haynes, who played alongside Robb for the England 'B' side: 'You could never hit a ball instinctively to the wing and know [Robb] would be there. And when you came up square with him for a return pass he would just take off with the ball.' However, the only man standing down for the upcoming game at Manchester City was Nicholson, who finally quit for good. Soon he coached the England Under 23 side to a 5-1 defeat of Italy and continued playing in the reserves or the 'A' side, offering on-the-spot guidance and encouragement to developing players.

ARSENAL AND SPURS COMPETE FOR BLANCHFLOWER   Returning to the race to sign 28-year-old Danny Blanchflower. It began in earnest in October 1954 when Arsenal manager Tom Whittaker travelled to the Aston Villa chairman's home to meet the player and complete a deal. Blanchflower was both excited to (a) escape Villa and (b) taste London life. As a regular contributor to the *Birmingham Evening Mail* he hoped to pursue a journalistic career and what better than to be close to Fleet Street? Whittaker was shocked by the fee requested (rumoured to be £40,000) but promised his club would outbid any other. The following morning he was informed that his dear friend Arthur Rowe had since been given permission to meet the player. Despite being happy to pledge himself to Arsenal, Blanchflower was happy to meet the Spurs boss (after all, he had once described Spurs' style of play as 'soccer delights') but he had inevitably heard of the club's miserliness. As if to confirm this, the *Herald*'s usual topical cartoon that week included a depiction of the Tottenham Hotspur office safe alongside a caricature of Blanchflower. A label affixed to the safe pronounced 'NOT TO BE PARTED WITH'. The cartoon was a powerful challenge to the board that they finally share Rowe's ambitions.

Aware of Rowe's uncertain health Blanchflower did wonder if, were he to choose Spurs, he might soon find himself working under a different manager, one with whom he would have far less in common. Unlike Whittaker, who met the player at the Chairman's residence, Rowe instead met Blanchflower in the Villa Park billiards

With this cartoon the Tottenham Weekly Herald confirmed common knowledge that funds were unlikely to be made available for Rowe to maintain Spurs' success. Perhaps this cartoon helped open the safe door at last?

room, which Blanchflower, believing Rowe to be 'a sincere and unpretentious man', actually preferred. The Irishman immediately …warmed to Rowe, finding the Spurs boss direct, honest and lacking pomposity. 'Well, my boy, how about it?' asked Rowe. Blanchflower pointed out how Arsenal would outbid any other club, but Rowe said his club were not '…out of it yet.' Perhaps testing Blanchflower out, the Spurs boss made it clear that his club would not offer any improper inducement to encourage him to sign for them but the player himself said he would not want to come by money dishonestly. However he did seize the moment to express his conviction that, considering the size of fee discussed, he, as the talent for sale, was clearly worth a commensurately high salary. This impressed Rowe, who said he wanted players who would fight for themselves and what they believed in. Rowe said he hoped the Irishman would come to Spurs '…because we could do big things together.' He saw Blanchflower as someone to inspire his young players, intimating that Danny would captain the side. He left the player in no doubt that he would be the fulcrum of his second great Spurs side.

Blanchflower said 'Rowe knew I would like …the atmosphere of good football for the sake of good football.' For his part, Rowe was aware of Blanchflower's belief in football as an intellectual entertainment and as a sport not intended to be played in the air, that 'real' football should be played 'on the carpet'. Blanchflower was impressed by Rowe: 'A player can only judge a club by its manager and as I sat talking to Arthur Rowe that day in the [Villa] billiard-room I realized that no club could have a better manager'. However this did not prevent the forthright Irishman from asking awkward questions, particularly on what life at Tottenham might be like were Rowe to cease managing the club. He also mentioned the club's reputation for penny-pinching — would the Tottenham board support the manager financially, or might he prove to be the limit of their investment? Rowe replied that he understood rumours about how the club functioned and could only tell the player that he and the board were trying to 'deal with them'. As for his own job security, he said he wouldn't like to promise anything on that account. 'A manager,' he added, 'could never be certain of how strong he was.' Rowe's final word on this matter was acutely diplomatic; that if Blanchflower were to join Spurs then his [Rowe's] own position would be strengthened, on the simple grounds that '…a manager is as strong as his team.' A few years earlier Rowe had already left a powerful impression on Blanchflower during a brief, unplanned encounter (described later), which contributed to giving the manager the upper hand over Whittaker.

By the end of the interview the player's enthusiasm for Arsenal had taken quite a knock. Both Whittaker and Rowe had bid £28,500, entering into an unusual agreement whereby neither club's offer would exceed £30,000, the ultimate decision to be left to the player. With extremely unfortunate timing, this was the moment when Blanchflower suffered his knee ligament damage, so the chasing clubs put their bidding on hold until his recovery could be assured. But Blanchflower was meanwhile telling colleagues that his move to Tottenham was in progress, subject to a fitness test once the treatment to his knee was completed. For Blanchflower, Tottenham's clear intent to pay a big fee for his services encouraged him to believe they might invest further in new blood. But the sand in Rowe's hourglass was meanwhile seeping away; he will have cursed the timing of the Irishman's injury — another cruel blow.

A few weeks later the still unfit Blanchflower and the Northern Ireland team attended a lunch at London's Euston Hotel. At one point Villa manager Eric Houghton telephoned to let the player know he was going to Tottenham. There followed a phone call from Rowe asking Blanchflower to be ready to jump into a taxi outside the hotel, to avoid the Press. The player duly hovered in the hotel entrance, feeling like a secret service agent as he rushed into the back of an arriving cab where Rowe confirmed Spurs had agreed to buy him, subject to an examination of his knee. 'As I drove around in a taxi with Arthur Rowe my feeling of wanting to become a Spur was complete,' wrote Blanchflower later, adding, 'I was ready to go to the Moon with [Rowe] and with Tottenham Hotspur.' Arsenal had stuck on their offer of £28,500, Spurs had called their bluff when agreeing to pay the top limit, £30,000. For once credit was due to Spurs' directors. It was, after all, a record fee for the club, but the *Herald* believed Blanchflower's capture should only be seen as a first step to pull Spurs clear of the relegation zone.

The unlikely location for Blanchflower to actually sign on the dotted line was the premises of West End boot and shoe manufacturers Headlam & Sims, producers of both the 'Arthur Rowe' and 'Danny Blanchflower' trademarked football boots. Snatching Blanchflower from right under Arsenal's nose, Rowe had laid the second of the two main foundations for Tottenham Hotspur's greatest-ever period of success (to this day). The first of the two foundations was also Rowe's, of course, 'push-and-run', which would be continued by his eventual successor, Nicholson.

Blanchflower was a regular in the Northern Ireland side and became captain. His sardonic humour was legendary. When talking on BBC radio in the early 1960s, Blanchflower's Irish side had just created an upset by defeating England 2-1 at Wembley. He said: "All our success has been built on failures really, we are the greatest moral victors in the world. When we get defeated it is a moral victory for us. This was one of the black spots where we defeated ourselves by winning."

Blanchflower said that in Rowe's Spurs he had finally found a club where players actually tried to pass the ball to one another! That previously mentioned first encounter with Rowe had taken place in March 1952, after Blanchflower had been playing for Northern Ireland against Wales at Swansea. Leaving the stadium the player had spotted Rowe and assumed the manager was there to watch his captain Ron Burgess play for Wales, but, as Blanchflower passed him, Rowe said: 'Well played, lad,' this despite the two not having met before. He recalled: '[Rowe] had come humbly and quietly to the back-door just to give a young player a word or two of encouragement.' Rowe would recall the Irishman's 'big, sparkling eyes' as the two men sized each other up. Blanchflower would subsequently play 382 first-team games for Spurs, picking up no less than four major trophies in one three-year-period and remains a strong contender as the greatest player ever to wear the 'Lillywhite' shirt. His arrival at the club is all down to Arthur Rowe whose humour and warm regard for Blanchflower shone through a description he later applied to the Irishman: 'He's fairly respectful most of the time; then every so often he gives somebody a kick in the crutch, and I think "Good old Danny".'

By the time Blanchflower had been signed, his new manager was already contemplating a tweak to 'push-and-run', conceding that tactical systems get 'found out'. 'The time for a change comes when everyone has become grooved into a style to which all the answers are well known', the manager explained. He realised, for example, that opponents had begun to sit back against his side: 'There might be some man-marking. The team had to be renewed, but so did the style we played.' Blanchflower was the perfect catalyst for a re-shaped 'push-and-run' approach. Author Phil Soar quoted Rowe talking of his plans when signing Blanchflower: 'The team I had in mind was Blanchflower at right-half with little Tommy Harmer at inside-left as the axis of another, somewhat different side. Those two had the combined skills to carry us forward.'

Taking part in his first Spurs five-a-side practice, Blanchflower was firmly struck by how differently his new club approached the game and of how they had a 'more definite rhythm' to their play, '...as if the players were more related to one another' and collectively trying to '...control the game and direct the course of play.' At Villa he felt the team were not controlling the game but dashing after it '...in the hope of keeping up with it and perhaps finishing in front!' During those five-a-sides Danny was impressed by '...the great degree of combined play that stood out for the unaccustomed eye to see, and the speed and skill with which it was accomplished in that small area of play.' These commentaries, coming as they do from an already established international, demonstrate just how unique a football practitioner Rowe was.

With the signing of Blanchflower, Rowe was finally and substantially transforming his team, illustrated when comparing the League Championship winning side of 1951 with (his potential, Blanchflower-led side of December 1954:

Ditchburn	GOALKEEPER	Reynolds
Ramsey	RIGHT-BACK	Ramsey
Withers/Willis	LEFT-BACK	Hopkins
Nicholson	RIGHT-HALF	Blanchflower
Clarke	CENTRE-HALF	Clarke
Burgess	LEFT-HALF	Marchi
Walters	OUTSIDE-RIGHT	Gavin
Bennett	INSIDE-RIGHT	Harmer
Duquemin	CENTRE-FORWARD	Dunmore
Baily	INSIDE-LEFT	Baily
Medley	OUTSIDE-LEFT	Robb

THE BLANCHFLOWER ERA BEGINS Rowe's evolving line-up took the field for Blanchflower's debut at a muddy Maine Road on December 11th 1954. The Irishman was soon feeding passes through to his forwards and Spurs were twice denied by the linesman, the first when Blanchflower's free-kick resulted in Dunmore beating Bert Trautmann with a superb shot. However, the game petered out into a

Even before the purchase of Blanchflower, Rowe had been trying to refresh his side. Eleven days before Blanchflower signed, only four of the manager's ageing Championship-winning side turned out for the win at Burnley (Baily, Clarke, Nicholson and Ramsey). But it had been a low-budget transformation. Posing at Turf Moor are (back) Gavin, Nicholson, Clarke, Reynolds, Ramsey, Marchi and Hopkins, while Dunmore, Baily, Brooks and Robb are seated.

goalless draw, but it was the first clean sheet of the season. Afterwards Blanchflower said: 'Spurs are a grand bunch of fellows, they are all for playing good, methodical football, and that suits me fine', while Rowe said it was the first time in weeks he had been able to sit back with confidence and enjoy a match.

Having yet to move house, for his home debut Blanchflower travelled down with the opposition, his former Villa teammates. Within three minutes a glorious move saw the ball pass swiftly from Baily to Blanchflower, back to Baily, back through to Blanchflower and on to Gavin. Both Gavin and Robb attempted to finish off the move before a wild clearance found Hopkins, who shot wide. But the first goal of the Blanchflower era was soon to arrive, a 25-yard Baily effort, deflected off a defender. However Villa equalised before both sides then missed from the spot so, ultimately, just one point was earned. Despite gleaning only two points from Blanchflower's first two appearances, they nevertheless took Spurs above Arsenal. It was then that 37-year-old Les Bennett was sold to West Ham United, while Ditchburn joined Wetton, Harmer and Withers on the transfer list.

There followed away and home fixtures with Bolton over Christmas, Brooks putting Spurs ahead at muddy Burnden Park and Dunmore making it 2-0 ten minutes into the second period. The home side pulled one back but Reynolds' outstanding performance ensured Blanchflower's first victory, and newspaper reports now focussed on the Irishman's contribution, much to Baily's irritation, as recalled by Tony Marchi: 'Although Eddie and Danny were friends, they always had arguments.' Baily no doubt sympathised with old pal Ramsey, whose influence on the team was clearly threatened with Blanchflower's arrival. The home return with Bolton, just two days' later, again saw chances missed until ten minutes into the second-half when Ramsey's free-kick saw the ball travel quickly between Blanchflower, Gavin, and finally Baily, who snapped-up a simple chance. Out of the blue Brooks' shot was then fumbled over the line for the conclusive goal.

Blanchflower's arrival had produced a run of four games without defeat, with just two goals conceded. He was always demanding the ball and inspired fellow half-back Marchi to play some of his best football yet. Only goalscoring remained an elusive task for Rowe's new side, the manager telling the press: 'Many goal chances are being missed, and if we take them we will again be on level terms, and perhaps in front of, the best. That doesn't mean I'm content, but it certainly means I'm hopeful, with good reasons for being so… .'

On New Year's Day 1955 the Rowe/Blanchflower combination faced a trip to League-leaders Sunderland. For the first twenty-five minutes Spurs dominated only for the home side to take the lead before, a minute into the second-half, Dunmore's flying header tied the game. Thereafter Reynolds and his fellow defenders, emboldened by Blanchflower's confidence, held out for an outstanding away point. On signing Blanchflower, the Spurs boss could hardly have hoped for a better return than five successive games unbeaten. Tottenham quickly returned to the North East to face Third Division North Gateshead in the FA Cup third round (incidentally a ninth successive away draw). Brooks scored twice, either side of the break, this proving sufficient to take Spurs through to face Division Two Port Vale in the fourth round where, bewilderingly, at the tenth attempt, Spurs had been drawn at home. Was it Blanchflower and the luck of the Irish?

Meanwhile, having been demobbed, Ron Henry signed professional forms in January 1955, three days after a home derby with Arsenal in which Spurs sought to avenge Arsenal's 2-0 victory four months earlier. However Rowe's forwards remained bedevilled by frailty in front of goal. On a weekend of snow and fog the groundstaff cut through four inches of snow to paint the lines blue. The relatively few who braved the weather witnessed a great spectacle, Blanchflower again starring for Spurs. After Holton had struck a 25-yard free-kick against Reynolds' post, Spurs mounted several right-sided moves involving Baily and Blanchflower, all setting up shots for Gavin but on the hour mark the legendary Tommy Lawton swivelled to shoot home after a Clarke error. The *Herald* summed-up the remainder of the contest as '…nearly all Spurs, pretty to watch, but so tantalising in front of goal.' Robb, Dunmore and Brooks had again fallen short, only Gavin, unafraid to shoot, was a threat. The unbeaten run had ended in appalling conditions.

Duquemin returned for Dunmore at home to bottom side Sheffield Wednesday and after just forty seconds Ramsey calmly headed a clearance to the feet of Blanchflower who broke with 'push-and-run' to strike a long, raking pass to Gavin. Duquemin, running to the right, received Gavin's pass, played it to Baily who passed back to Duquemin, who played it first-time through to Brooks, who set up Gavin to crash it home. 16 minutes' later Jackie Sewell equalised before another accurate Blanchflower delivery set Robb up to put Spurs ahead again. Then Gavin received from Reynolds, moving it on to Brooks, who set off on a mazy run before pulling it back for Baily to score. Just before half-time Gavin headed home Blanchflower's free-kick for 4-1. This was a return to the best of times and soon after the re-start another 'push-and-run' move executed by Ramsey, Blanchflower, Gavin and Baily left Brooks clear through on goal for number five. Four minutes later Gavin's cross saw the popular Duquemin score his first goal in over a year, generating huge cheers. Finally, good work between Blanchflower and Baily led to Brooks netting his fifth from the last five matches, this time from Gavin's cross. With Spurs easing-up, Wednesday pulled another back for a final score of 7-2. Gavin had been involved in six of the seven goals. For once a lower division purchase had shown he could contribute at the top level.

The *Herald* correspondent confessed how 'grand' it was to shake Rowe's hand afterwards. One Spurs' fan excitedly told Rowe 'We'll wallop Port Vale next week,' receiving a typically calm, collected reply: 'I think we shall be alright.' The manager knew the risk of over-confidence and was aware that Wednesday were the weakest side in the division but surely he will have let out a whoop of joy when arriving home to Pom that evening. This one result may have exorcised the dour months of struggle, toil and criticism. As the *Herald* reported: 'Confidently [Mr Rowe] has said: "Keep on playing good football, the push-and-run, short, accurate and quick kind, and we'll once again take the club and English football to the top."'

The luxury of a home FA Cup tie followed, against Second Division Port Vale. With Spurs' fans expecting another goal-fest, Rowe's men this time stumbled through, 4-2. Inevitably an away draw came out of the hat next, this time a long trip to confront Third Division North York City, who had previously knocked out First Division Blackpool. It was not a tie to relish and Rowe would have preferred a home tie against a fellow First Division side. Before then, Spurs faced a trip to fourth-placed Portsmouth. By now Blanchflower was not adhering religiously to 'push-and-run', preferring, like Harmer, to occasionally hold the ball before making the perfect pass. Spurs went in at half-time content to have kept the powerful home side from scoring. Then, with 25 minutes remaining, Gavin headed home a perfect chip from Baily and within five minutes it was 2-0, again the Baily-Gavin combination. Gavin was then the supplier as Duquemin completed a convincing 3-0 victory over a side destined to finish as First Division runners-up. Spurs were now in Championship-winning form, one Spurs' player saying 'We've never seen the boss so happy.' Rowe had turned the corner, his re-modelled side having slipped into top gear and his health hopefully restored.

After Blanchflower's arrival only one defeat was suffered by the time of his 11th appearance, a February victory over Blackpool.

Here the man many consider the greatest 'Spur' ever watches as Tony Marchi clears a Blackpool attack.

A week later Blackpool arrived and despite White Hart Lane's blanket of snow, Spurs continued where they left off at Portsmouth. With 22-year-old Marchi outshining Blanchflower, and Hopkins giving Matthews little chance to impress, Robb scored two and Baily the other as Spurs won 3-2. Meanwhile Rowe's first combination of Peter Baker and Ron Henry as the full-back pairing for the Reserves would prove of considerable future significance, their partnership later contributing to Spurs winning the Championship, FA Cup twice and the European Cup Winners' Cup.

Following Blanchflower's arrival Rowe had begun experimenting with the idea of an attacking centre-half. This provides an interesting insight into Rowe's innovative thinking. Aware that it might not work, his idea was for his wing-halves to cover the opposing wingers (instead of pulling his wingers back as before) enabling his full-backs to play further infield and free-up his centre-half to be more adventurous (much in the style of his own playing days). But he needed a centre-half with the technical ability to play out from defence and Clarke was purely suited to the defensive role. He had one man in mind: the tall, leggy, 20-year-old full-back Maurice Norman of Norwich City. But, whoever it was, according to Rowe, needed to be '…a player of tremendous energy, ability, and an artist: a really good player'. Sadly, Norman's transfer to Spurs only finally went through after Rowe had left the club but he had identified in Norman a man who would ultimately represent England alongside Bobby Moore in a World Cup. One can but assume Rowe's experiment, utilising Norman, failed to materialise due to directors who had yet again 'mislaid' the key to the safe.

Danny Blanchflower recalled Rowe enjoying the pair's tactical chats: 'We used to get ideas at Tottenham, and Arthur and I used to chew over them. Conceiving them is one thing, but putting them into practice is quite another. We believed that anything worthwhile needed time for development. And it takes time to show results. Now, this is the point. Are the directors of clubs going to be prepared to wait for that? Are they going to be patient? They sit up in the box week after week and what they want are results, good results, wins. They don't necessarily want anything new-fangled and perhaps even competent. They want success, there and then. And if it is not successful on the day, it's not successful as far as they are concerned.' At Blanchflower's side when making these comments, Rowe made obvious his ingrained bitterness with directors: 'Another trouble, of course, is that if directors don't understand some new scheme that has been explained, then it is *you* who are the fool.' This was no doubt a bitter rebuke to certain directors and their view of 'push-and-run'.

Returning to the 'Blanchflower Revolution', it was widely thought Spurs would go far in the Cup. Due to face little York City on February 19th, the *Herald* wrote of three more matches '…then Wembley,' adding '…it's with high spirits [the players] journey to York.' With only one narrow defeat in the last eleven games and 25 goals scored, confidence this time was understandable, but the home side had likewise lost just one in eleven, and they, too, brimmed with confidence. Staying overnight at Harrogate before the game, Rowe's plans were hit when Gavin received news of his father's death, and he immediately set-off for home. Blanchflower later called this 'the first blow'. At short notice Walters, who had missed all 25 previous matches, travelled up to stand-in for Gavin. Inevitably, news of their team-mate's loss was dispiriting and that day the weather conditions were horrendous, travelling Spurs' fans passing countless abandoned cars and lorries on the icy roads. Awaiting Rowe's men at York was a frozen, bumpy pitch, part-coated with slush.

Inevitably York paid little heed to their glamorous opponents and, despite being hit by Robb's early goal, threw caution to the wind. In one sixty-second spell alone, the ball nestled in Spurs' net twice. After the break Duquemin's header brought a great save from York's 'keeper and a Walters' effort was headed off the line. With ten minutes left Spurs were still desperately trying to salvage the tie when a York breakaway made it 3-1. At the final whistle Rowe's rampant, super-confident 'new' Spurs trailed away with the raucous cheers of home fans ringing in their ears. The defeat, as Blanchflower put it, had '...soured the fresh new taste' adding '...the air was thick with remorse on the long train-ride back to London.' A *Yorkshire Evening Post* report suggests City had played a similar 'stylish' soccer to Spurs, but with greater urgency and spirit. Rowe's greatest desire had been to capture the Cup (if only to shake those sniping directors from his back). Endlessly being drawn out of the FA Cup hat second, the competition had been repeatedly cruel... and now this.

Questions were immediately asked. How could decisive winners at powerful Portsmouth lose to 'little' York? The *Herald* returned to 'push-and-run' bashing, claiming Spurs were simply not an 'all-weather side', that they were a ball-playing team, and 'the ball-player' is rarely 'aggressive'. They further described Rowe's side as 'lethargic', forgiving only Reynolds, Duquemin and Robb. In the rush to criticise, little heed was paid to York's having earlier travelled to knock Blackpool out, who had enjoyed home advantage. Tony Marchi, one of the losing side at York, told me, 'That game was ridiculous really, when you look at the players we had out. But this happens all the time, doesn't it? You see League One teams beating Premiership teams now.' (In more recent times Bradford City of League One, the equivalent to York's 1955 status, defeated José Mourinho's Premiership champions Chelsea 4-2 at Stamford Bridge) but such ruminations could not comfort Rowe in February 1955. 1954-55 would prove to be York City's greatest season ever — they even took Newcastle to a semi-final replay. The greatest irony of all was that four of the York side had been acquired only due to the fee Rowe paid for Dunmore.

Ditchburn is stranded and Ramsey is desperately trying to close York scorer Billy Fenton down, but to no avail. The goal cancelled out Robb's early opener.

Following York, Rowe was reported to have been sent home from White Hart Lane having experienced a relapse of his 'nervous breakdown'. However, just days later, he was guest speaker at a London referees' gathering. Far from appearing stressed or under the weather, FA referee Arthur Blythe described the Spurs' manager as '…in great form, being clear, constructive and witty' adding that he had given '…an excellent talk.' Was the mention of a breakdown an invention, or had Rowe unearthed enough willpower to attend the meeting, perhaps as a blessed relief from hectoring club directors? The most likely scenario is that a temporarily demoralised Rowe, overwhelmed with self-reproach and facing public, press and boardroom flak, had been advised to take a short break.

Four days after York, Spurs, no doubt keen for a quick rebound victory at Charlton, were prevented when more adverse weather saw the game postponed. A quick rebound victory after their Cup exit would have been just what the doctor ordered. Then the Saturday trip to West Brom was also postponed, so the grim, post-York atmosphere festered for a full fourteen days. Now, in the season's final two months Spurs had little to play for but pride. On the Monday after the second postponement Rowe, clearly recovered, phoned Arsenal manager Tom Whittaker to set up a floodlit friendly between the clubs at White Hart Lane to maintain match fitness. Rowe was also reported to have returned unimpressed from a talent-hunting trip to watch Southern League Guildford City. Assuming the referees meeting, the arrangements with Whittaker for a friendly match and the Guildford scouting trip did actually take place, then, contrary to reports, Rowe was clearly well enough to continue with his duties.

The remarkable Spurs' revival engineered by Rowe had started at Manchester City just twelve games earlier. After the shock Cup exit, another revival was called for and City were again the opponents. Rowe conducted one of his longest team talks of the season as Manchester City, inspired by Don Revie, remained in the running for both League and Cup. Indeed, City had yet to lose in 1955 and had recently beaten Manchester United 5-0, so this was a tall order for a Spurs' side with flagging spirits. But Rowe could not have asked for a better start. It took 20 seconds for Duquemin to score from Brooks' pass. City equalised but Duquemin's fierce left-footer put Spurs back in front by half-time, only for City to capture a point when equalising again halfway through the second period, both sides finishing with a point. The *Herald* described it as '…one of the most intelligent matches at White Hart Lane this season…', so Spurs appeared to have recovered well from York. A major theme of Rowe's tactical talk prior to the game had been how to deal with Revie in his unorthodox, deep-lying centre-forward role. Blanchflower shadowed him, and did it well, although in the process Spurs lost the benefit of the Irishman's usual, more expansive game.

So, despite York, Spurs had maintained their League form and now sat 11 points behind leaders Wolves and 8 clear of the relegation places. They were a First Division team in transition, yet very much holding their own. A 6-0 floodlit friendly victory over Racing Club de Paris followed before a visit to Preston on March 12th. An injured Baily, consistently brilliant since linking-up with Blanchflower, was replaced by Harmer, while Tom Finney was kept in check by young Hopkins. However,

Blanchflower's performance was, for once, indifferent and Spurs ultimately fell to their first League defeat in five, by a single goal.

Meanwhile, Rowe was about to lose Dave Dunmore. Having completed his trade apprenticeship he now had to deal with National Service, another setback for the manager, who then failed to appear at the match with Sheffield United on March 19th. His absence was put down to 'flu, a subterfuge previously utilised when he suffered his first breakdown 13 months earlier. Had he suffered barbs from directors unhappy with both the Preston defeat and the further unavailability of Dunmore, who, of course, Rowe had persuaded them to spend a little money on? Around this time Rowe's younger son Graham had turned 17. With a journalistic career in mind and thanks to his father's connections, he had been working at Reg Hayter's sports agency but he was tempted to join a school friend who had headed for Canada in search of adventure. Not that adventure was the sole purpose, however, as staying in the UK would soon mean two years of compulsory National Service. For them, working on Southern Ontario farms was a more enticing prospect. Rowe was required to sign a document granting his permission for Graham's adventure and, sadly, by that stage he was again under treatment in a sanatorium. Graham recalls: 'To get Dad's signature Mum and I went to the sanatorium. Dad was sitting on a bench, and we explained the situation to him and he signed the document. To this day I do not know whether he fully understood.' Although Pom had encouraged Graham to go, she was already missing the support and company of her husband and now contemplated the departure of her youngest son. Two years later Graham's elder brother Derek, tempted by the irresistible reports and photos his brother had sent home, would join him and later settle in Canada.

Meanwhile, since Blanchflower's arrival, Spurs had conceded an average of just one goal per game compared to 2.3 in the 20 games prior to that. Ramsey, ever-present aside from injury or international calls since 1949, was now replaced by the 23-year-old Baker. Ramsey's demotion strongly suggests Anderson was fully in charge that day as he had previously been offended by Ramsey's disrespect. Anderson believed too that both Ramsey and Blanchflower concentrated on creativity at the expense of defence (this despite statistics proving otherwise). Ralph Wetton confirmed that when standing-in for Rowe, Anderson introduced his own way of doing things, Wetton recalling one occasion when the Assistant Manager

Arthur and Pom photographed in the mid-1950s with sons Derek (left) and Graham (right).

shouted the instruction to 'whack' the ball up the field, bringing the retort from Blanchflower, 'You get on here and whack it yourself, then!'. Perhaps in Rowe's absence Anderson was being pressured to heed the long-ball preferences of Dewhurst-Hornsby and Heryet.

By then Ramsey had unhappily ceded his tactical influence to Blanchflower, who, for example, would now hug the touch-line to receive the throw-outs from Reynolds before Ramsey could react. As Tony Marchi told me, 'Alf would start to go out there and Danny had taken his place. They used to …have words!' Another significant change for the Sheffield United game was the debut of 20-year-old soon-to-turn professional Terry Dyson at outside-left in place of the injured Robb. Adapting to Anderson's tactical changes Spurs' first-half performance was dismal, yet improved dramatically after the break. Gavin scored an 18-minute hat-trick, Brooks netted the fourth, and Gavin added his own fourth three minutes from time. Anderson phoned his match summary to Rowe immediately after the game. One suspects Spurs' players had resolved at half-time to 'win it for Arthur', resorting to 'push-and-run'. Proof exists in a magazine interview with Baily that spring in which he talks of his debt to Rowe, reiterating the need to stick to 'push-and-run': 'Not for us the chancy, long ball driven up-field in the hope of opponents making mistakes', adding, 'The rest of the team are solidly behind [Arthur] in sticking to the style and methods which have paid dividends in the past.'

At struggling Cardiff Duquemin put Spurs ahead following combination play between wingers Gavin and Robb. Yet it was soon 1-1, before an improving Spurs saw Robb net a second-half solo winner, the cue again for twenty minutes of pure, exhibition football. The team had suffered just two defeats from 13 since Blanchflower's arrival yet fears of relegation had returned. 1954-55 had been a strange First Division season, few points separated top from bottom and a smattering of poor results was liable to change almost any club's situation abruptly.

Rowe was back in harness for the arrival of table-toppers Chelsea. With the home side outclassing them, the visitors resorted to physicality. When not assaulting Tottenham players they repeatedly cleared the ball up onto the terraces. Spurs took the lead through sharp interplay between Gavin, Baily and Robb, setting Duquemin up to volley home. Six minutes later Johnny McNichol made things even at half-time. More good build-up play involving Blanchflower, Baily and Robb, ended with a flicked header for Duquemin's second but Chelsea scored twice more to go 3-2 ahead. When Peter Baker handled, Chelsea's Peter Sillett converted from the spot for a final score of 4-2. A frosty Rowe said afterwards he would hate to be quoted on what he thought of the eventual champions' performance, adding that the number of their infringements could only harm the prestige of British football.

Seven months had passed since the promising meeting between Rowe, the young Jimmy Greaves and the boy's father. Now, however, the enthusiasm of Mr Greaves had been dampened by rumours of Rowe's retirement which coincided with an approach from Chelsea. The Greaves family had of course been impressed by Rowe's personal assurances that he would look after their boy, but rumours had by then arisen that due to Rowe's health issues Anderson might take over as manager, and the Assistant Manager had suggested his priority would be with the first team. History thus shows that Rowe lost Greaves to Chelsea, becoming one of many talented young Essex or East London-born lads (including Terry Venables, Les Allen, Ron Harris and others) whose parents were improbably keen for their sons to commute across London instead of training more locally at West Ham or Tottenham. Bill Nicholson explained that Tottenham failed to sign many good young players through the years '...because they never paid inducements to the parents of schoolboys' adding 'they never did when I was manager; I am certain they didn't before I took over; and I'm sure they don't now.' The loss of Greaves will have further lowered Rowe's flagging spirits.

Greaves himself confirmed that Chelsea scout Jimmy Thompson (going by a cover name of 'Mr Pope') was the 'lovely rascal' who 'sweet-talked' his father into accepting the move to Chelsea. When I asked Ralph Wetton if the likes of Haynes and Greaves would have signed for Rowe had 'back-handers' been involved, he thought they would have, but pointed out: 'I'm not sure if Arthur agreed with that sort of thing. I think Arthur relied on players "wanting" to go to Tottenham for the football experience.' Fellow Dagenham-ite Terry Venables, another Spurs' target, wrote that as a boy he 'adored to watch' Spurs' style of football and in his autobiography confirms that Rowe '...the great man of "push-and-run"' had invited him to join Spurs. As for the young Greaves, he proceeded to net a phenomenal 124 goals in just 157 League games for Chelsea. As England's greatest-ever striker, a man who regularly 'stroked' the ball into the net ('...like someone closing the door of a Rolls Royce' as wrote Geoffrey Green), he would have been the perfect addition to a 'push-and-run' side. Furthermore, Greaves later reflected that his England partnership with Johnny Haynes, the other 'maestro' who slipped through Rowe's hands, was his greatest. How close had they come to forming a devastating partnership under Rowe at White Hart Lane?

Meanwhile, uncertainty over Rowe's future and the looming possibility of the inadequate Anderson assuming the manager's chair lowered spirits in the home dressing-room. Ralph Wetton confirmed Anderson had been thrust upon Rowe

England's two greatest young stars to emerge in the mid-late 1950s, Jimmy Greaves (in the dark shirt of Chelsea) and Johnny Haynes (in Fulham's white) battle for the ball.

If only Rowe had been able to bring both these great talents to **NORTH** *instead of* **WEST** *London! He had identified the enormous talent of both players at an early age.*

as his assistant before shockingly adding, with conviction, that Anderson '…didn't really want to help Arthur.' There can be no doubt Rowe would have benefitted far more from the support of someone not in the pocket of directors and with similar ideology — a Buckingham, a Ramsey or a Nicholson.

Easter began with a 1-0 defeat at title-challengers Everton, only Reynolds saving them from a bigger defeat. Two days later relegation-threatened Huddersfield arrived at the Lane; Blanchflower failing from the spot and Hopkins slicing into his own net. With just 17 minutes left Brooks netted via the far post, but Huddersfield still left with a point. In the return two days' later 20-year-old Ron Henry was tried-out at centre-half after Harry Clarke had injured his knee in an 'argument' with a train door. The day before, Rowe had settled Henry's nerves, saying: 'Don't worry about it, there won't be many people there.' Perhaps Rowe should have been concentrating more on his own nerves, as at this point his condition was on a knife edge, and it is unclear whether he travelled. Robb was a 'passenger' following a first-minute knock and Huddersfield went ahead. The under-manned Spurs failed to equalize and they had now lost three from four, finding themselves just four points clear of the relegation places. With Rowe mainly sidelined, the remarkable, Blanchflower-led revival had begun to evaporate. At least only one relegation place now remained, as Sheffield Wednesday were already down, leaving Spurs with five matches to ensure they did not accompany them.

The first was at home to Burnley, Rowe restoring Ramsey in place of young Baker, who later confessed to trying too hard to match Ramsey's contribution to the side. Almost any points added to the 34 collected to date should have made Spurs safe but, despite a bright start, Spurs faded and the reinstated Woods was blamed for the misplaced pass which led to Burnley scoring in the 27th minute. By half-time it was 2-0 and ten minutes after the break the Clarets struck for a third and final time. Suddenly only Cardiff, Leicester and the already relegated Sheffield Wednesday remained below Spurs. With just eight points left to play for Spurs could be grateful to hear Wednesday had defeated fellow strugglers Leicester, whose next opponents were …Spurs. A Tottenham victory would transfer the pressure onto Leicester.

However, the loss to Burnley was more than Rowe could take; it appears he broke down again on returning to his office on Monday, April 18th 1955, and was again hospitalised. As earlier mentioned, it is not easy to pinpoint specific dates for Rowe's episodes of stress-induced illness. As we have seen, following his first collapse during the previous season he had apparently suffered a second episode during the aftermath of the York Cup fiasco, but had been battling to withstand further pressure since, emanating primarily, one suspects, from directors. Blanchflower said the manager's '…nerves had been worn down'. Tony Marchi's recollection of one incident may well coincide with the manager's post-Burnley collapse. He recalled Rowe addressing the players in preparation for a close-season tour. As the Burnley game took place just three weeks before season's end, with preparations for the close-season tour of Austria, Hungary and France in full swing, it seems likely that Tony was indeed recalling the Monday following the Burnley defeat:

'Arthur wanted to push the club forward and he had these blazers made, but he came down just before the tour to tell us who was going and who was not going.

Then he said he'd spoken to the directors and only those people who were going on tour plus a couple of others who had played for the first-team would get blazers. He said "I'm sorry, but none of the other players will get blazers", and began to weep. He had tried so hard to get the board to give everybody a blazer and they had said "No, no!" They were right tight skinflints, you know, the board of directors, and that's what happened. The trainer took Arthur away to his little room.' For Rowe, a man endowed with concern for others, this denial of blazers for all except thirteen of his men was symptomatic of years of boardroom tight-fistedness. Danny Blanchflower, still commuting from Birmingham, was not present when Rowe was taken ill, and later wrote: 'The news of his break-up greatly surprised me,' adding '…and I wondered what inner conflict had sapped his strength.' When I discussed this with Ralph Wetton he paused, lost in his recollections for a few seconds before quietly and sadly uttering, '…dear old Arthur.'

Behind the scenes there had been rumours of constant bickering, of Rowe being under constant attack from Dewhurst-Hornsby and Heryet. Graham Rowe has confirmed his father was suffering pressure from a boardroom spoilt by success. Exiting the FA Cup had confirmed the directors' fears that a fourth consecutive season would produce no silverware. As Blanchflower put it, the directors had failed to be patient during a 'famine' following the 'feast'. He added that erratic results, to be expected during team rebuilding, led them to doubt Rowe's ability, despite his amazing achievements for the club. Ron Reynolds wrote of '…plenty of people around the club who were only too happy to see [Arthur] start to fail.'

In his 1985 article for *The Observer* headlined, 'The Director's Obsession with Success', Blanchflower no doubt had those directors who had so badly treated Arthur Rowe in mind: 'They simply covet the social prestige and the personal satisfaction of being celebrated men of sport. The more successful their team is, the more celebrated they will be, so their obsession is not for sport, but success — continual, permanent, enduring success.' Blanchflower added that successful managers like Rowe were the object of directors' envy: 'The directors may not like [the managers] getting the "lion's share" of the glory.' Hunter Davies starkly illustrated this concept in his superb fly-on-the-wall account *The Glory Game*. He wrote of a Spurs' home victory over Liverpool in the early 1970s: 'Up in the Oak Room, the directors were having their hands shaken by friends. Each was being warmly congratulated, as if they personally had beaten Liverpool.'

During the era of Rowe's management, depressive or stress-related illness suffered by a male was viewed as a weakness and too embarrassing to even discuss. It is surely the prime reason why no Rowe biography was published during his lifetime. When the Mental Health Foundation celebrated their 70th anniversary in 2019 they reviewed previous decades and described the situation in 1950s' Great Britain as follows: 'Ignorance about mental health meant that there was extreme stigma and fear surrounding it. People with mental health problems were considered "lunatics" and "defective" and were sent off to asylums.' In today's far more enlightened times there is almost total understanding and sympathy but in 1955 Rowe suffered alone, trying to mask his inner torment. Perhaps Rowe should have adopted Bela Guttmann's approach to club management. When Guttmann's judgement was questioned by his club officials he took the view that it was he who had all the responsibility so 'why then should I have let others control me?' Maybe it was that mind-set that ensured the great Benfica coach retained his mental health.

A STRESSFUL JOB   In the 1950s the basic responsibilities of a manager like Rowe in no way compared to today, when specialists are hired to handle individual responsibilities which managers and club secretaries used to routinely share between them. A survey back in 2016 showed Spurs employed 380 staff (including players, coaches, and those in charge of administration, media, commercial/retail and so on). This paled by comparison, however, with Manchester United's average total of 869 and Chelsea's 681.

But in 1955 Arthur Rowe's duties alone will have included:
- Scouting and acquiring new players
- Selecting teams
- Devising tactics
- Motivating his team to achieve results
- Spying on future opponents
- Ensuring the maintenance, morale and fitness of (at the very least) 60 footballers playing at three or four different levels (First Team, Reserves, Eastern Counties' League, Mid-week League, etc.)
- Monitoring the success (or otherwise) of all those sides
- Deciding which players (and training/coaching staff) to retain and which to move out of the club
- Keeping the local and national press well informed (and responding to letters from the public)
- Attending to players' individual issues, including transfer requests, etc.

As Rowe himself said in 1958: 'To run a football club is a much more complicated job than many people imagine.' In 1961 writer Tony Stratton Smith criticised the system: 'It is vital today that managers spend all their time with their players; [managers] just cannot, efficiently, cope with administration as well.'

Rowe was not as fortunate as the legendary Herbert Chapman whose directors stated he '...had authority over all football matters.' Rowe's directors, on the contrary, attacked their own manager's 'push-and-run' methods with their poisonous pens and many less-informed fans will have been influenced by this 'criticism from within'. He was obliged to constantly steel himself against it but in Rowe those little men came up against someone too proud and wise to be told how to do his own job. One suspects that when employing him the directors anticipated that, being of personable nature, he would be malleable, adjusting his management approach and tactics to suit their own particular preferences. Rowe's determination, for six years, to stick to his guns whilst maintaining civil relations with these people came at great cost to his health.

Brian Wait, who knew and admired Rowe, described him to me, enlighteningly, as a man who 'spoke quietly, but with presence' but, added Brian, 'he wasn't an argumentative man' this despite the strength of his opinions. It is interesting that when reading accounts of previous Spurs managers only McWilliam and (perhaps)

Percy Smith come across as men with strong, independent personalities. The descriptions of most might equally apply to Rowe. They tended to be amiable, undemonstrative characters, perhaps the very traits Tottenham directors most valued, assuming they would take orders and tow the line, men who might, for example, shrug their shoulders philosophically when denied money to strengthen their team, or agree to change their tactics. From what we know of them, this might well apply to Minter, Tresadern, Hulme and Anderson. However Rowe, with difficulty, stuck to his tactical beliefs, and for that alone does not himself belong to the 'undemonstrative' category.

In conversation with Geoffrey Green and Danny Blanchflower in 1960, Rowe exposed the depth of his despair with club directors. Green had suggested 'The moment is ripe for English football to produce something different,' to which Rowe responded: 'Why don't you think it happens, Geoffrey? What stops it?'

The conversation then ran as follows:

GREEN: 'Well, the fear of the consequences of defeat.'

ROWE: 'From whom and for whom?'

GREEN: 'All right. We know, surely. You have to fear for the directors.'

ROWE: 'Who's 'you'?'

GREEN: 'The manager.'

ROWE: 'Ah! Right! That's a very good reason for the manager, who is an ordinary fellow with a job to keep and a family to support, not to get out of step.'

He had no stauncher ally on this topic than Blanchflower who imagined the typical, resigned response of cowed managers: 'We won't do anything, so we won't be wrong.' Blanchflower exhibited just how great an ally of Rowe's he was. Addressing his former manager directly, he added: 'It was just like you and me at Tottenham. We had many ideas, but for the reasons stated we couldn't fully try them out.' The Irishman added the bitter punchline (echoing Arthur Hopcraft): 'Here is a professional game controlled by amateurs... .'

When later managing Crystal Palace, Rowe would be left to get on with the job for which he had been appointed. Also, he would be given (within a Third and

Rowe, far right, engages in intense debate on the state of English football in 1960.

The others, left to right, are Howard Fabian (an amateur who played for Derby County), Chelsea manager Ted Drake, journalist Geoffrey Green and Rowe admirer Danny Blanchflower.

Fourth Division economy) significant sums to reinforce his team when necessary. This is how Rowe spoke of life at Selhurst Park under the benign chairmanship of Arthur Wait: '[The Chairman] is a colossal enthusiast. In many ways it is like having a very close assistant manager [something Rowe lacked at Tottenham]. [Wait] is in constant touch and he often contacts the other directors by 'phone. All of them are very busy men. The idea of delegating responsibility stems down from the board. I doubt if we hold more than four or five board meetings in a year. Everyone knows exactly what is going on though. People react to responsibility if you only give it to them.' One wonders if when Rowe specifically said the Crystal Palace directors were 'busy men' he was subliminally suggesting those at Tottenham had time on their hands to interfere with his role as manager.

Author Dave Bowler quoted Blanchflower's reflections on Rowe's collapse: 'When his [Spurs'] team faltered and the whole unreasonable reaction set in, he was appalled at the ignorance and violence around him. It drove him back to the depths of a quiet desperation.' Note the use of the term 'violence'.

For day-to-day support, Rowe had only the unqualified Anderson, who had been foisted upon him by the board and was little respected by senior players. A man whose technical football vocabulary peaked at 'getting stuck-in' or 'no messing about at the back'. Anderson had no faith in 'push-and-run'. If only the ambitious, able and popular Vic Buckingham had become Rowe's assistant, Spurs may have been assured of smooth continuity in the event of his eventual departure. Ralph Wetton concurred with this, adding that unlike Anderson, Vic was well respected by the players (and of course went on to coach no less than Ajax and Barcelona). If not for Anderson's apparent popularity with the directors, Rowe would surely have selected Ramsey or Nicholson as his assistant. Time would show that Buckingham, Ramsey and Nicholson would all find a place (alongside Rowe) in the pantheon of great British football managers. To illustrate just how diametrically-opposed Anderson and Rowe were, Ralph Wetton told me of a standard pre-match Anderson instruction to his defenders: '"If you're in trouble, lads, you know where I'll sit", by which he meant "up in the stand". You know — kick the ball up in the stand.' As an aside, Ralph damningly added: 'We used to take no notice of Jimmy.'

Arthur Rowe had no further involvement with Tottenham Hotspur after April 18th 1955. Some sources quote that date as Rowe's final day as manager of the club, but his official departure was in June. Unlike the earlier occasions when Anderson temporarily took charge of the team, now he was to have the support of newly-appointed coach Nicholson. Ron Reynolds made it clear that by then Spurs had put to one side pure 'push-and-run', resorting to getting the ball quickly to the forwards. Reynolds, despite being a huge fan of Rowe and his methods, accepted the practicality of this change at a time when confidence was low. 'When you play a one-touch, quick-moving, passing kind of game, you rely on confidence, and that comes from experience and from results.'

As for Rowe himself, the *Herald* reported that he was 'resting' in a nursing home and explained his illness on worries 'attendant' to a team fighting 'desperately against relegation.' In the remaining three weeks of the season Spurs, fighting for First Division survival with Anderson at the helm, would meet Leicester City, West

Bromwich Albion, Newcastle and Charlton. At Filbert Street Spurs went down 2-0 and had now scored just once in five matches, yet prior to the York City turning-point, they had been the country's form team having rattled-in 17 goals in four matches. Now they plunged into danger with six points left to play for. Anderson told the press that the players were very conscious of their precarious League position, '…so conscious, in fact, that it's causing worry-itis.' His solution to the 'worry-itis' was somewhat basic: 'There's nothing like a little bit of close marking to make you forget that things are not going right.' Reading such Anderson quotes reinforces Wetton's tale of how little faith the players had in him. Alf Ramsey had less than most, and other such unsophisticated Anderson mantras may have led to a confrontation between the pair, as the classy full-back was dumped for the game at The Hawthorns. The man who Rowe called 'a perfectionist' and without whom his 'push-and-run' side would fail, had played his last game for the club, leaving Spurs behind for a two-month coaching assignment in Rhodesia.

Meanwhile Buckingham's West Brom had surprisingly become another candidate for that second relegation spot and were not helped when Anderson's side came away with a vital 2-1 victory. Spurs' penultimate fixture was at home to none other than Newcastle, who, fortunately for Spurs, had one eye on the FA Cup Final to follow a week later. Spurs took a fortunate lead through Gavin, and their second goal was even luckier, United centre-half Bob Stokoe finding his own net with a 20-yard backpass. Yet despite then being reduced to ten men for the entire second-half, the Magpies pulled a goal back but couldn't find a second, thus ensuring Spurs' safety before their final day victory at Charlton's Valley.

The *Herald* then insensitively, if not maliciously, chose to refer to Rowe as '…the boss who broke down when the club looked in dire straits', but the use of 'broke down' is the first indication that by then the nature of Rowe's illness was commonly known. As for Anderson, he now began expressing his strong ideas for avoiding a similar relegation battle in season '55-56, as reported by the *Herald*: 'When Mr Anderson talks about his football he does a little miming—like rolling up his sleeves, gritting his teeth and touching his left chest, where he expects every footballer to have a tough heart.' Oh my. Summing-up the season; a poor start had been followed by nothing less than a superb Blanchflower/Rowe-inspired mid-season recovery. Emphasising how closely fought the 1954-55 season had been, had Spurs not dropped eleven points in the single month of April, they would have finished second behind champions Chelsea. Despite Rowe's remodelling of his side, Spurs had equalled the 14th-placed side on points, scored more than in the previous season and suffered three fewer defeats. Two days after the Charlton game an Anderson-led Spurs left to tour Austria, Hungary and France. Things started poorly with a 6-2 loss to Austria FC Wien and it is hard to imagine a Rowe-led side engaging in all-out 'push-and-run' capitulating to the degree Spurs did during that trip, losing all three games by an aggregate score of 14-5.

A *Herald* columnist described how much he would miss the 'pleasant Monday morning interviews' in Rowe's office. 'No matter how busy…work would stop while we chatted over a cup of tea with Mr Rowe going through the tactical successes (or blunders) of the first-team's week-end game…'. Spurs' Supporters' Club published a tribute to Rowe in their *Lilywhite* journal, which Rowe had always given up time to support. Indeed, he had always arranged for copies of it to be placed in the dressing-room, encouraging his players to take interest in supporters' activities and views. The *Lilywhite* now wished the outgoing manager a prompt return to good health, adding that '...none of us believe that the game can do without a man who produced a team which became the finest exponents of cultured, artistic football since the war.'

After his departure only Ditchburn, Withers, Clarke, Walters, Duquemin and Baily of the classic 1951 Championship side remained on the playing staff. Tony Marchi made the number 6 shirt his own (until a big-money move to Italy) and would total an impressive 260 Spurs' first-team appearances. Extensive team changes allied to the continuing lack of investment in new players (Blanchflower excepted), could explain why silverware could never have been anticipated in 1954-55 but one thing Rowe should certainly be credited with is the laying of firm foundations for the club's huge success of the early 1960s. In retrospect, the York defeat struck just when Rowe's new Blanchflower-inspired side had collected 13 points from 18, scoring 19 and conceding 8 (less than a goal per game). The internal repercussions at White Hart Lane resulting from that 'blip' on York's appalling pitch struck just as he was on the cusp of establishing his second great Spurs' side which had recovered well in the four games following York, before that physical battering by champions-elect Chelsea. However only a single point was scraped from the following four games and this, allied to incessant boardroom criticism, finally tipped Rowe over the edge.

So why had Rowe been unable to maintain his extraordinary early success? The following may all have been contributory:

LOYALTY AND CONCERN FOR HIS PLAYERS Despite a great admiration for his manager, Ron Reynolds believed that the likes of Henry, Baker and Harmer should have been promoted from the reserves sooner. Rowe's reluctance for change was exemplified when Bill Nicholson suggested that he himself should be replaced toward the end of the 1953-54 season. Nicholson put Rowe's reluctance to drop players down to his being a '...compassionate, decent man.' Something Rowe said in 1970 throws light on this; Alf Ramsey had been criticised for including Nobby Stiles in his 1970 England World Cup squad even though the player had long since lost his place in the side. Yet Rowe's opinion was 'What a wonderful thing! It was saying "I haven't forgotten what you did for me in 1966."'

SELF DOUBT In 1969 Rowe admitted that he felt like 'a round peg in a square hole' as a manager. He perhaps needed the bullish self-confidence of (say) a Ferguson, Mourinho or Guardiola. Before the outset of his managerial career he said he had felt he wasn't 'big' or 'clever' enough to manage. Did this kind of self-doubt haunt him when things turned against him?

CONSIDERATION FOR OTHERS The plain speaking Bert Head much appreciated Rowe's back-up and support when managing Crystal Palace to the promised land of the First Division in 1969 but spoke of Rowe's one 'bad trait'. This, said Head, was Rowe's '…very nature of being kind to people,' adding 'hurting people …is something Arthur does badly.' Arthur Hopcraft wrote that successful soccer management required '…the capacity to dominate, the need for "steeliness" in a man's make-up'. Admirer David Miller conceded that: '[Rowe] was too gentle, too sensitive to withstand the rigours and pressures from public and directors at the top.' As Rowe absorbed the problems and worries of those for whom he felt a sense of responsibility, his own personal pain stayed hidden.

HAD 'PUSH-AND-RUN' BEEN 'FOUND OUT'? For all the innovative, exciting soccer he had introduced at White Hart Lane, producing two Championship trophies, a runners-up season and an FA Cup near-miss, Rowe's reign ended in relative failure. At the time he bowed out at Spurs he was adjusting his entire thinking about the game to counter the tactics managers now used to nullify 'push and run'. Future England manager Ron Greenwood said of 'push-and-run': 'It was marvellous to watch and proved very successful. But opponents learnt to counter it. [When] they ran with the man and not after the ball: push-and-run's number was up.' By 1956 Rowe himself had recognized a need to return to the blackboard. The outstanding Hungarian coach Béla Guttmann never stayed longer than three years in a career that spanned twenty-five club management appointments, saying that 'In a second season, nothing will be new and it is difficult, often impossible, for a trainer to maintain their new-found impetus'.

PERSISTING WITH 'PUSH-AND-RUN' FOR TOO LONG? Despite admiring both 'push-and-run' and its creator, Bernard Joy personally believed passes could be short or long, provided the intended receiver was unmarked and the passer was confident he could find his target accurately. However he missed a significant point: the short-passing game better ensures the constant, intense involvement of all outfield players. The long pass risks breaking the 'rhythm'. Clearly few sides in the English League adopted 'push-and-run' yet many mimicked Chapman's third-back game. I would suggest those who did not adopt 'push-and-run' either doubted that their players could practise it or adopted a 'British-is-best' mentality having no time for anything regarded as 'Continental football'. The 'bulldog' British approach was essentially about physicality, aggression, 'kick-and-rush' and stopping the opponent. Some saw short-passing as 'fancy Dan' stuff, while Bill Nicholson believed few sides utilised 'push-and-run' because they believed it difficult to accomplish. Perhaps a philosophic comment by Blanchflower says it all: 'The rise and decline of "push-and run", the lesson that good things come to an end, was part of my education of football at the time' — a philosophy also applied by Johan Cruyff when considering the downfall of the Dutch 'Total Football' side of 1974: 'By definition, after a high point, things can only go downhill.' In 2008 striker Peter Burridge, who worked with Arthur Rowe later in the manager's career, told me: 'Arthur Rowe was a purist, a bit like [Arsène] Wenger now. I mean, the way Arsenal play now is wonderful [but] eventually other teams suss-you-out.' Following Rowe's departure, the *Herald* asked Tottenham fans for their opinions. Most favoured the retention of 'push-and-run', leading the newspaper to entitle their article 'A Push-and-Run Team Gives the Most Pleasure', something from which Rowe, once back to good health, will have taken great heart.

INSUFFICIENT HOMEWORK ON THE OPPOSITION?   Although Alf Ramsey once said Rowe's tactical talks didn't involve a review of the strengths and weaknesses of the opposition, colleagues of his have contradicted this, asserting that Rowe spied on upcoming opponents. Yet there seems little doubt his philosophy was to let opponents worry about his side, which chimes with the view of two-time European Cup-winning manager Brian Clough, who preferred to concentrate on his own side (90%) rather than concern himself with the opposition (10%). However as opposing sides developed ways to counter 'push-and-run', a more concerted effort to concentrate on the weaknesses and strengths of adversaries might have hauled-in a few more points for Spurs.

UNSUPPORTIVE DIRECTORS   Many of the contributory factors to Rowe's failure to maintain his Spurs success were peculiar to the club itself. With Rowe convalescing and Anderson in temporary charge the *Herald* asked its readers to suggest how Spurs' fortunes could be improved. Their responses showed how aware fans were of the limitations Rowe worked under, particularly the financial stranglehold. On Rowe's departure, one reader insisted that his replacement should have absolute authority in managing the team, adding 'I have the impression Mr Rowe and his predecessors were not so fortunate.' A second wrote '…to have a successful team, the manager must have a free hand…', while a third imagined himself in the role of manager: 'I would want …full co-operation from the directors'. A further correspondent summed it up concisely; that for years Spurs' directors had only viewed the manager as a 'necessary evil'.

FINANCIAL IMPEDIMENTS   Despite Alan Hoby of the *Sunday Express* calling Spurs 'Britain's Bank of England club', a common belief was that 'no club would sell a player to Tottenham at Tottenham's price.' As a result Rowe made do with players approaching, or beyond, their sell-by-date. There could be no comparison whatsoever between the degree of investment in Rowe's side to that of Chapman's Arsenal before the war which had been constructed for what in the 1930s was the huge total of £85,640 (the sum paid for 11 players over a ten-year period), worth approximately £225,000 in 1955. For comparison, the English transfer record in the mid-1950s was £34,500, so clearly, had Spurs blessed Rowe with similar financial backing he could have invested not only in Blanchflower but in at least five other top-of-the-range players to reanimate and rejuvenate his ageing side.

During his spell as manager fans were accustomed to the club's miserliness, one fan writing: 'For over 30 years we have heard of players having wage cuts or leaving, and it's not all rumours.' Another commented: 'Contentment breeds success, and I do not blame the players for the slide of Spurs—how can players be happy when they have their wages reduced?' In an era when players mingled freely with fans, some travelling by bus to-and-from games, their gripes about pay will have easily leaked out. The club's frugality during that era dogged Rowe and, in some respects, continued at least until the 1970s. Published examples of top players affected by the practise abound, affecting the likes of Dave Mackay, Jimmy Greaves, Martin Peters, Ralph Coates and even the dependents of the tragically-killed John White. Ron Burgess once travelled as twelfth man only to find he would not get the £8 bonus which those who played received.

In 1947 Spurs' programme notes had attempted to justify paying poor wages for players yet, later that very same year, the club could not resist bragging about their exceedingly healthy bank balance: 'We may be wrong, but we do not think that any club has previously had so large a surplus.' It was actually over £102,000 at a time when the biggest sum ever paid for a player was £15,500. Many a good player could have been bought for much less had the money been made available to Joe Hulme. An example would be the 1950 case of Charlie Wayman, who, after 77 goals in 107 games, moved from Southampton to Preston for just £10,000 (plus a player in exchange). Wayman proceeded to score 105 times in just 157 League appearances for Spurs' title rivals yet the Lancashire club's average attendances during Rowe's time as manager amounted to half those at White Hart Lane.

Spurs chairman Fred Bearman was the latest of only three men to hold that post by the time Rowe returned to manage the club in 1949. As Julian Holland wrote in the mid-1950s, the three chairmen had built the club up to be '...the richest side in the land today.' Did Berman personally deny Rowe funds? Following poor results the Chairman's co-directors would criticise his methods, believing it was cheaper to change tactics (or manager) than buy a prolifically-scoring centre-forward. Neil Carter, in his PhD thesis *A Social History of the Football Manager 1889-1966*, wrote of football management during Rowe's time in charge of Spurs: 'The directors were still the bosses who traditionally disliked delegating, did not like spending money and therefore, were reluctant to cede power to managers.' It's tempting to think Carter was using Bearman's Spurs as his example.

At the time of Joe Hulme's dismissal the *Herald* stated that Rowe's predecessor had not had '...complete authority in the matter of buying players,' so it can be taken for granted that Rowe suffered similar restraints. His directors were happy, for example, to part with a modest amount for the cut-price purchase of Roy Hollis from Third Division South Norwich City but demurred over the purchase of a top class striker. When explaining their lack of activity in the transfer market, the club once stated: 'We could not persuade clubs to part with the players whose signatures we sought to obtain.' If they were offering considerably less than the seller's valuation, then one can safely assume the player was likewise unimpressed by the club's pay offer.

As for the solitary occasion when Rowe spent a suitably high sum (for Blanchflower), Tony Marchi postulated that '[the directors] will have said "This is once, Arthur, you're not getting any more!"' (Tony furthermore volunteered that '...the Tottenham directors in them days... were tight with their money'). This is corroborated, too, in Julian Holland's tale of Dunmore's signing: 'For seasons Arthur Rowe had been denied the money to buy the fast-moving, fast-thinking centre-forward that he needed.' The fee for Dunmore, a promising but inexperienced Third Division striker, £10,500, hardly compared with the £34,500 Sheffield Wednesday had paid for Jackie Sewell three years *earlier*. As in the case of Wayman, Sewell's 97 goals in just 178 appearances repaid his fee many times over. Meanwhile, Rowe resorted to fruitless tours of Scotland seeking bargains when all five of the strikers he had tried and failed to acquire for Tottenham: John Dick, Cliff Holton, Nat Lofthouse, Lawrie Reilly, and George Robledo averaged a goal every two games during their careers.

Rowe will have been particularly frustrated if he had read Matt Busby's 1957 account of his asking the Manchester United board to finance the purchase of Tommy Taylor from Barnsley: 'The unanimous decision was "If you think Taylor is worth that money, that's good enough for us. Go out and get him, Matt."' Needless to say, Taylor struck 112 goals in just 166 League appearances. Rowe, without access to anything approaching the £29,999 United spent on Taylor (until belatedly and surprisingly granted the £30,000 for Blanchflower), continued shopping around the lower divisions. Of Rowe's 14 additions to the playing staff as manager, five came from the Second Division, five from the then basement level (the Third Division) and three from non-league football. Only Blanchflower had First Division experience. Aside from McClellan (29 goals from 78 League appearances), the three who fetched the largest fees, Ramsey, Murphy and Blanchflower, proved the most successful.

As for Dunmore and Brooks, their price suited Spurs' budget, but neither had played First Division football. Dunmore scored an acceptable nine from 33 appearances under Rowe but was inconsistent and frequently replaced (Tony Marchi considered Dunmore a 'Gentle Giant' who failed to make the most of his physique). Brooks was Rowe's biggest disappointment as he undeniably possessed creativity, speed and a powerful shot, allied to a love for the game so significant that he could not pass a park on the way home without joining in with local lads. However as Dickie Dowsett told me, Brooks did not relish '…the ugly part of the game.' Likewise Peter Burridge, who later played alongside Brooks at Crystal Palace, told me of an occasion when Palace warmed-up prior to a match. Burridge noticed Brooks nervously eyeing-up the opponents then saying 'Jeez! Look at the size of those guys!' To calm his colleague's nerves Burridge replied 'They're only footballers — just like us!' However Tony Marchi defended Brooks: 'He got hit a lot, because people couldn't stop him otherwise, because he was fast.' But, significantly Blanchflower lacked confidence in Brooks (as did the player himself, once recalling Rowe's efforts to boost his self-confidence) yet Terry Venables, who later played with him at Chelsea, included the player as one of 28 he most admired during his 40-plus years in the game, a list that included Pelé, Beckenbauer, Best, Cruyff and Maradona. Considering his youth when Rowe signed him, and, again, that limited transfer budget, Brooks had clearly been well worth a punt.

BUNGS   Arthur Rowe fully supported Spurs' aversion to the practice of clubs offering financial inducements (bungs) to parents of promising youngsters but Eamonn Dunphy has pointed out that contemporaries, even the otherwise principled Matt Busby, eventually succumbed to these under-the-counter payments so as not to miss out on young talent. Ralph Wetton told me of another 1950s' practice, that of 'finding' supplementary jobs to entice players, jobs which didn't really exist. Geordie Ralph told me that Trevor Ford (who Sunderland had paid Aston Villa £30,000 for in 1950) once told him that Sunderland had given him a "job" as a car salesman, yet the player said he never sold a car but got some money from it. When we went up there to play Sunderland, Ford asked Ron Burgess, who every club wanted, 'Do you fancy coming up here?' — tapping him up — and Ron said 'No, no, I'm alright where I am.' Ford said: 'Come on, come up here, get yourself a good job, you don't do anything, you just turn up for training every morning but at the end of the week there's a few bob in it.' The incorruptible Burgess said he was quite happy without 'that sort of thing', remaining loyal to Spurs until age finally took its toll. Clearly, such underhand activities compounded the uneven playing field for anyone who managed Tottenham Hotspur during that time.

It was not until the last week of June 1955 that the *Herald* front page confirmed Rowe's departure from Tottenham Hotspur Football Club: 'Mr Arthur Rowe, the man who took Spurs into the First Division, the man who 'invented' push-and-run, the man who guided the Lilywhites to their one and only Premier Championship and into the semi-final of the FA Cup, has relinquished his post of manager of the only club he really loved. Two bouts of illness have taken Mr Rowe away from his duties in the last two years, and now, while still convalescing, his resignation has been tendered and accepted by the Tottenham club. Spurs' Directors have appointed Mr Jimmy Anderson acting manager, while continuing to pay Mr Rowe his full salary until the expiration of his contract at the end of this year.' Having been unable to fulfill his duties since April 18th it could be deduced Rowe would therefore receive the equivalent of roughly eight-and-a-half months' salary. Considering he would require five months of treatment and recuperation, it was not over-generous.

As for the board's selection of Anderson as manager, Brian Glanville reported: 'Only a grim desire to save money could have led to Anderson's appointment in the first place, for he was hopelessly out of his depth.' Glanville had become aware from a trustworthy internal source at White Hart Lane that Anderson was being paid all of £20 a week, information which Glanville duly incorporated in a story he wrote for weekly magazine *Sport Express*. On becoming aware of this director Dewhurst-Hornsby threatened the publisher with legal proceedings. With Glanville obliged to protect his source (a Spurs' employee), *Sport Express* had to withdraw the story. One can imagine Dewhurst-Hornsby's self-satisfaction.

As for Rowe's pay-off, he himself, ever-loyal to the club, publicly stated the club had treated him 'fairly and kindly'. However, Danny Blanchflower was inevitably angered by this treatment of a sick man. Of course, the Irishman's own future was now questionable — aside from the benefit of being based in London and advancing his journalistic ambitions, the main reason for his joining Spurs had been Rowe himself and his style of football. The Irishman may even have regretted leaving Villa, especially on hearing Anderson had been awarded Rowe's job.

IGNORANCE AND VIOLENCE AROUND HIM: MANAGING SPURS 1954-55

The Herald now belatedly compensated for their past criticisms of Rowe's methods, concerned that his knowledge of the game might be lost and commending him for his voluntary work with junior sports clubs, adding: 'He was always a good sportsman, win or lose.' The writer wished Rowe a 'quick and permanent recovery', before commendably tailing-off with the statement: 'It is my view that Mr Rowe's temporary ill-health has robbed England of one of her best chances to put football back on the map.' One fan interestingly suggested the club create an 'Advisory Management Board' which Rowe should sit on in return for a '…substantial cheque', adding, 'I would also invite Arthur Rowe and Willie Hall to sit on the [Tottenham] board.' This sounded laudable, but one doubts Rowe would have been comfortable going shoulder-to-shoulder with those who had perpetually stabbed him in the back.

RECOVERY Clearly Rowe's breakdown had been severe. With so many advances in treatment, drugs and psychiatric care, his confinement today would be nowhere near as long as it was then. During that summer of 1955 he spent several months in hospital, followed by recuperation in Bournemouth from around mid-September. Alan Hoby saw him three weeks after his release from hospital, writing of Rowe's 'star' being only in 'partial' eclipse. Of talk that Rowe wouldn't be able to return to the game, Hoby, in sync with the universal respect with which journalists regarded him, concluded: 'Finished. Don't make me laugh!' In an article headlined: 'It wasn't the game that hurt me' the journalist mentioned rumours that not only was 49-year-old Rowe finished in soccer but that he was a '…sick and embittered man who is fed-up with managing, fed-up with Spurs and fed-up with football.' But on his recovery Rowe denied this, saying he was not bitter and had no reason to be. As Hoby continued: 'No backbiter, Rowe steadfastly refuses to drag into the

After suffering the breakdown leading to his 1955 departure from Spurs, Rowe spoke with Alan Hoby of the Sunday Express.

Right: *Pom and Arthur at home.*

open those behind-the-scenes policy differences at Tottenham which caused him so much wear and worry' and he believed that Rowe was starting the '...biggest come-back fight of his life—the fight to regain his confidence', adding: 'Only the other day Rowe—the thinker who brought back old-fashioned, attacking football after Herbert Chapman had destroyed it with the Arsenal game—watched his first League match since his illness.'

When asked if her husband would return to the game, Arthur's wife Pom replied: 'We must all wait and see. Somehow I can't see him settling down as a tobacconist or publican. He wouldn't be happy. His heart, you see, is in football.'

Back at White Hart Lane, Alf Ramsey had shown interest in taking on Rowe's job, but now, with Anderson (of all people) running things, he instead dipped his toe in management with Third Division Ipswich Town. In Suffolk he was to experience meteoric, Rowe-like success. However, seeing his Third Division players struggling with one- or two-touch play in practice, Ramsey, his own man, chose to concentrate instead on getting the ball from defence to attack in no more than three passes. As for Blanchflower, he now found himself playing under an uninspiring and tactically-inept novice manager. How painful was the frustration of working with Rowe for mere months instead of years. Tony Marchi confirmed that Anderson and Blanchflower were a poor match. When I mentioned Blanchflower had not rated either of his pre-Spurs managers in English football, Tony replied: '...and he didn't rate Jimmy, and of course, they had arguments.'

FROM ROWE TO THE 'DOUBLE' The following season under Anderson (with Nicholson coaching) Spurs suffered 11 defeats in their first 14 games and, in the final five, conceded an average of three goals a game. What, one imagines, were Dewhurst-Hornsby and Heryet thinking now? History suggests the board's answer was to avoid personal ridicule by freeing-up team-rebuilding cash previously denied to Rowe. First they bought Norwich full-back Maurice Norman, for whom Rowe had begun negotiations earlier that year. Rowe had of course identified Norman as a centre-half in-the-making, but it took Anderson two whole seasons before he switched him there from right-back. It was at centre-half that Norman would perform outstandingly in the early-60s' 'Double' side and play 23 times for England. So Rowe had correctly identified his best position all along. A month later £18,000 was magicked-up for the bustling, 22-year-old Chelsea goalscorer Bobby Smith, another player the former Spurs boss had been monitoring. This sudden flow of cash appears to confirm that funds for Rowe's intended purchases had been held back for as long as he remained in charge. At the end of Anderson's first season in charge he lavished a further £18,000 on Welsh international winger Terry Medwin and, in a mere seven months, Anderson's spending exceeded that which Rowe spent over his entire *six years* in charge.

Another cruel advantage Anderson somehow had over Rowe was good fortune in the 1955-56 FA Cup. Firstly, Spurs avoided drawing a First Division side all the way to the semi-finals. Secondly, only *one* of those four ties was away. Spurs finally bowed out 1-0 to Manchester City in the semis, when to the chagrin of both Nicholson and Blanchflower, Anderson incorporated no fewer than three established centre-forwards: Dunmore, Duquemin and Smith, while leaving the creative Harmer out. In the previous round Spurs had trailed West Ham 3-2 when captain Blanchflower instructed the tall Norman to move up into the forward line in a last-ditch effort to keep Spurs in the Cup. It was then Norman who managed to feed the ball to Robb on the wing and Duquemin was set up to equalise. To Anderson's irritation, Blanchflower was then acclaimed a 'genius' by the press. Blanchflower then repeated the process in the semi-final with Manchester City when they were a goal behind, again sending Norman forward. With time running out Blanchflower risked further Anderson wrath when sending Brooks forward too, but this time the gamble didn't pay off. A furious Anderson told his captain that he had made him look a fool in the eyes of the directors but it is clear from comments by ex-captain Ron Burgess that Rowe himself would have fully supported Blanchflower's onfield changes. Rowe expected his captain to be the 'boss' on the field.

Then, with Spurs fighting relegation and losing against Huddersfield, Blanchflower sent Marchi up front to try to snatch an equaliser. Again, nothing came of it, so an angry Anderson dropped the Irishman for the penultimate game at Cardiff. Blanchflower would later make it clear that his conflict was not so much with Anderson as with the board, believing the new Spurs boss had been promoted above his station, as he told Norman Giller, 'The Hungarians and Brazilians had recently shown we were light years behind with our methods, and it was so obvious that Jimmy Anderson was still living in the ark.' Anderson repeatedly asked his players to hit 'long balls', which prompted the facetious query from Blanchflower: 'What exactly do you mean by a long ball? How does a long ball roll?' Anderson's first season saw Spurs finish in the club's lowest position since Rowe had arrived as manager (18th). The following five seasons would ultimately see Rowe's pupil Nicholson replace Anderson, reintroduce 'push-and-run' and take Spurs stylishly back to the top, but not, it should again be emphasised, without the kind of enormous player investment Rowe had been starved of.

By season 1956-57 Anderson was himself sadly exhibiting signs of what Norman Giller described as '…the sort of nervous illness that had ended Arthur Rowe's reign.' Despite this, 1956-57 saw the ever-present Tommy Harmer inspire Spurs to challenge eventual champions Manchester United for the First Division title (of course, were it not for his illness, Rowe himself had planned for Harmer to play a significant role in his regenerated side). With Nicholson now running on-field affairs Spurs finished in second place, Blanchflower considering the playing style under Nicholson as essentially 'push-and-run'. With Anderson taking a back seat, the Spurs 'Double' side now began to take shape.

During the summer of 1957 Tony Marchi escaped Anderson to join Italian club Juventus for double his weekly Tottenham wage of £10, plus the-then considerable sum of £7,000 as a signing-on fee (*and* big bonuses). The highlight of Marchi's eventual post-Anderson return to Spurs would occur in 1963 when Spurs hammered Atlético Madrid to become Britain's first winners of a major European trophy. After injury ended his career Marchi managed Northampton Town, and during season 1967-68 Rowe travelled on a scouting mission to watch Marchi's side. Following the game Marchi insisted on driving Rowe to the station. Rowe had just been having a drink with the Northampton directors following the game and had picked up on something which was said. In the car he leant forward and whispered 'watch your back!' in Tony's ear. Marchi's spell in charge duly lasted a mere eight months, the club's board then being in an on-going process of hiring-and-firing no fewer than eight managers in ten years!

Returning to Spurs, during 1957-58 Anderson paid £16,000 to buy Jim Iley as replacement for Marchi, and then paid a further £35,000 for winger Cliff Jones from Swansea. Spurs managed third place in Division 1, all of 13 points behind long-ball specialists Wolves. Blanchflower was however voted 'Footballer of the Year'. Season 1958-59 started poorly, Spurs taking just nine points from the first 11 games and, on the morning of an October home fixture with Everton, Vice-Chairman Frederick Wale offered Anderson's job to Nicholson, the position confirmed before a game which saw Tottenham famously beat Everton 10-4. However, the four goals conceded was a sharp warning that the defence seriously needed shoring-up and a further eleven goals entered Spurs' net in the following three matches! Indeed, had Nicholson's disastrous run of eight losses from 12 games occurred in today's Premier League, his managerial career may well have ended almost before it began. Yet, unlike during Rowe's reign, the board granted Nicholson further substantial sums of money, including £32,000 to bring Dave Mackay in from Hearts. Yet Spurs still finished in their lowest position (18th) since Anderson's first season, conceding 95 goals, more than twice the total conceded by Rowe's 'push-and-run' side in their Championship season (indeed, even Rowe's worst-ever season had seen only 76 conceded).

Clearly the relationship between the board and manager had changed since Rowe's time in charge. 'The directors are quite happy to leave the running of the club to us two [i.e. the Manager and the Secretary]. I certainly couldn't complain one little bit about my directors,' said Nicholson. His first full season in charge (1959-60) was particularly memorable for a 'push-and-run' goal at Old Trafford involving around 20 passes from one penalty area to the other. That season saw yet more cash flow through the fortunate Nicholson's hands. Goalkeeper Bill Brown came in for £17,500 and the creative John White for £22,000. In five years since Rowe's departure, the Spurs' board paid-out approximately £175,000 to bring in ten players, with fees twice topping the then huge sum Rowe had paid for Blanchflower. Unsurprisingly Spurs finished just two points behind champions Burnley that season but a year later they finally clinched the First Division Championship for the first time since Rowe's success ten years' earlier. Blanchflower was again 'Footballer of the Year' and Spurs' 115 goals had been spread across the five forwards: Jones 19, White 13, Smith 33, Allen 27, Dyson 17. Ron Reynolds confirmed that Nicholson had '...soon returned to the methods that Arthur Rowe had used.' Likewise, Terry Dyson said the style was derived from '...the Arthur Rowe days.' If only Rowe had been able to spend as freely as Anderson and Nicholson.

Indeed, without his spending power Nicholson's Spurs may have faded at the same rate as Rowe's. Nicholson continued to spend during the rest of his lengthy reign and yet Rowe's win ratio was all but identical to Nicholson's: 48.5% compared to 49%. Even Jimmy Greaves, the boy Rowe had expected to capture for free, finally arrived at White Hart Lane, but now for just £1 short of £100,000. Nicholson's reign as manager was a world far removed from the tight-fisted White Hart Lane Rowe worked under.

So, who really was Spurs' greatest manager?

Was it Rowe, who masterminded Spurs' first-ever Championship and came so close to winning five trophies in his first four seasons (despite little financial investment)? Or Nicholson, who took Rowe's 'push-and-run', modified it a little and spent an average of £7,000 per player more than Rowe paid for Blanchflower on each of five players, in addition to utilising five players Jimmy Anderson had spent an average of £25,000 on (including Norman, Smith and Jones)?

Norman Giller, for one, believes a statue should be erected for Arthur Rowe at White Hart Lane '…in memory of the man who pumped the pride and passion back into Tottenham.' In 1969 the following statement appeared in *Charles Buchan's Football Monthly*: 'Spurs' era of success under the management of Arthur Rowe was one of the major contributions to the good name of football during the present century.' Since his period in charge until the present day, Spurs' fans have expected thrilling, quality football, so all his successors have been left with the responsibility to keep that particular flag flying. Those who have best lived up to that responsibility include Bill Nicholson (of course), Keith Burkinshaw, David Pleat, Terry Venables, Ossie Ardiles, Harry Redknapp and Mauricio Pochettino. David Lacey of *The Guardian* believed Rowe was the 1950s' equivalent of Arsène Wenger, the man who first brought the 'beautiful game' to the Premier League.

Nobody can decry Nicholson's achievement in winning the 'Double' but author Ken Ferris tells of a game against Aston Villa during the 'Double'-winning season when Blanchflower had a half-time dispute with colleagues who said they were not passing it to him because he was marked. 'That's what Villa want!' said Blanchflower. 'You're doing their job for them. The solution is 'push-and-run' isn't it? We're supposed to be good at that, aren't we?'

Reviewing the playing staff of the 'Double' side, Baker, Dyson, Henry, Hopkins and Marchi all began or developed under Rowe. Maurice Norman signed for Jimmy Anderson in November 1955 but only after Rowe had initiated negotiations for him and, finally, of course he also signed the man who would captain Spurs to all their triumphs of the early 1960s, Blanchflower.

In 1964 David Prole addressed the imbalance of praise for Rowe and Nicholson, 'The [Spurs] team of recent years has been assembled at astronomical cost,' adding 'Remember, too, that Tottenham have had TWO great teams in the post-war era, and only Alf Ramsey of the first of them [Rowe's] cost a fee.' During Mauricio Pochettino's early days managing Tottenham Hotspur, Norman Giller wrote of Spurs' tradition since Rowe of playing 'Give-it-and-Go' and added 'Pocchetino's men were remembering the "give" it bit…but forgetting to "go"!' Four years' later Pochettino's men *did* remember to 'give' *and* 'go' as Spurs' reached their first Champions' League Final.

One Nicholson advantage over Rowe was greater firmness when dealing with players, exemplified by his occasional blunt criticisms even when players were engaged in celebrating victories. On the other hand, as Terry Dyson once said, 'Bill wanted to entertain people. For him, victory was not enough. It had to be victory with a flourish.' This will have warmed the cockles of his old boss's heart. In his later years Rowe poignantly admitted he would have liked to manage Spurs to FA Cup success. He almost certainly would have were it not for his side being so regularly drawn away. But no matter the preponderance of away draws, nothing could cap Ramsey's late error in the Blackpool semi-final when Spurs would almost certainly have proceeded to win the Cup.

When reviewing his Spurs' managerial career, he reflected that his endeavours had never been fully financially supported by the Club: 'If things had gone my way I could have built the best team in soccer', interestingly adding, 'I wanted the Big Four to run Spurs: myself, Alf Ramsey, Bill Nicholson and Eddie Baily. But things just didn't work out that way.' But Rowe *had* undoubtedly contributed the foundation for what remains the greatest-ever achievements of any Spurs' side, challenged only by reaching that Champions' League Final.

Another quote from Blanchflower finally sums-up Rowe's Tottenham demise: 'A modest, sincere, democratic man like Arthur, a man of such fine and sympathetic feeling must of necessity be a sensitive man. Perhaps the doubts around him undermined his desire.' Blanchflower felt the lack of appreciation for Rowe's early, outstanding success might have caused Rowe enough distress to think that those who ran the club were simply not worth it. He concluded that Rowe was '…the victim of too much care and anxiety for the troubles of his team.'

Tony Pawson calculated the average life expectancy of an English League club manager in the 28 years following World War II as a mere three years. Despite the lack of support from his employers, Rowe had lasted nearly double that at White Hart Lane, lifting Spurs straight out of Division Two, winning their first-ever Championship, then laying the foundations for the Nicholson years. Only malicious club directors, a lack of funding and the ill-health he subsequently suffered prevented him repeating the trophy captures of his early years. At the time of writing, in the sixty-plus years since, only Nicholson and Burkinshaw have outlasted him in the manager's chair at Spurs.

Back in 1951, when rapidly hitting the heights as Spurs' manager, Rowe had written: 'One of the commonest, most repeated comments passed on the job of "Football Manager"— especially by those who have some inside knowledge of the complexities, worries and frustrations the position so often brings, is "I wouldn't have it at any price".' He poignantly continued:

'There are many managers too, who often wonder if they might not have chosen a vocation a little less precarious, and trying!'

16

A Break from the Hotseat

GOODBYE LANE, HELLO SELHURST 1955-60

'With Crystal Palace, Arthur Rowe returned from the wilderness to grace further the game he has adorned for 40 years.'

EDWARD GRAYSON, *FA NEWS*

Around the turn of the 1950s Rowe sent his full Spurs side to play Pegasus, the team comprising Oxford and Cambridge University students (see Chapter 10). Coached by Vic Buckingham, Pegasus went on to reach two Amateur Cup Finals at Wembley and, as underdogs against Hendon in the semi-finals of the 1951 competition, the players received a telegram of encouragement from Rowe, reading: 'Make it Simple - STOP - Make it Quick - STOP'. Overcoming Hendon, Pegasus then beat Bishop Auckland in the Wembley final. The *Observer*'s Tony Pawson confirmed the play of Pegasus was '…based on the Tottenham Hotspur principle of doing the simple thing quickly, and make the ball do the work.' Two years' later Pegasus were back, defeating Harwich by no less than 6-0.

In September 1955 a recuperating Arthur Rowe received a call from Pegasus founder Dr. Harold 'Tommy' Thompson, the Vice-President of St John's College, Oxford, who as well as teaching Margaret Thatcher would later, as FA Chairman, sack England manager Alf Ramsey. Thompson wanted Rowe to teach 'push-and-run' to his new recruits, seeing it as a gentle reintroduction to the sport after the trials of Arthur's last months with Spurs. Pegasus captain Ken Shearwood remembers

In 1955 Rowe was invited by Dr. Harold Thompson (above) to help amateurs Pegasus. On the right Rowe chats with Tony Pawson of Pegasus (and Sonny Walters), while Bill Nicholson speaks with Denis Saunders of Pegasus.

that on arrival Rowe was "...still vulnerable and far from fit" but recalled him telling many stories of his time managing Spurs.

Another future Fleet Street correspondent, David Miller, replaced Tony Pawson in the side, and Miller's rapid progress down the wing in a game against a British Police side at Huddersfield led a jolly Rowe to exclaim: 'David will be over that stand and into the next county before he knows where he is!' Miller later described Rowe as: '...one of the most patient and gentlemanly of men you could meet.' Another football correspondent, Alan Hoby, believed the Pegasus work was '...nudging' Rowe back to full fitness '...quicker than any medicine'. Thompson's 1955 offer had provided the opportunity of a gradual rehabilitation following Rowe's time of crisis, so can only be viewed in a positive light. Arthur clearly took great pleasure from his Pegasus involvement, on one occasion watching the ageing Shearwood take place in a defeat by eight clear goals and at the end putting his hand on Shearwood's shoulders, saying 'You're not only over the hill, you're bloody well half-way down Porlock Hill, mate!' Aside from the eight goals that day, Shearwood's only regret was 'failing' Rowe when not winning the Amateur Cup that season.

Also around this time Rowe kept himself in pocket as a goodwill ambassador for the manufacturers of his trademark boots, 'Headlam & Sims'. He travelled to promote the Arthur Rowe brand 'Slimline' and 'Streamline' boots which proved to be a further spiritual restorative, especially when Rowe encountered admirers delighted to make his acquaintance. Rowe's son Graham, possessor of a mint pair of Slimline's at his Los Angeles home, told me: 'It was one of the first low-cut boots'. An earlier version had been adopted by Buckingham's Cup-winning West Brom in 1954. Rowe, kitted-out in a dark overcoat and a black homburg hat, would present Ken Shearwood with a pair, saying, with tongue in cheek, 'See if they'll improve your game a bit!'

Then, on becoming manager of West Bromwich Albion in August 1957, Vic Buckingham hired Rowe as his Chief Scout. The only record of Rowe's 14 months in that role is a trip he made to watch Crystal Palace's 20-year-old goalkeeper Vic Rouse in action. No subsequent bid appears to have been made for the future international 'keeper but Rowe may well have been distracted by Rouse's 18-year-old forward teammate, Johnny Byrne. Rowe saw enough to recommend the then

'Arthur Rowe' branded boots manufactured by Headlam & Sims.

A BREAK FROM THE HOTSEAT: GOODBYE LANE, HELLO SELHURST 1955-60

Scouting for West Brom, Rowe travelled to run his eye over Crystal Palace's future Welsh international 'keeper Vic Rouse (left). He was distracted however by the precocious skills of Palace's 18-year-old Johnny Byrne (right). Although West Brom failed to capture Byrne, who would later play for England with distinction, Rowe and Byrne were destined to form a great partnership of mutual admiration.

diminutive teenager to the Albion. 'I was immediately taken by Byrne's ability with the ball,' Rowe later recalled. 'He was not applying it quite right, but at least he had got it. Some never have it.' Rowe identified Byrne as a potential long-term successor to Albion's deep-lying centre-forward, Ronnie Allen. Although nothing came of this, Rowe and Byrne would later team-up.

After nine months of scouting, during which time Arthur appeared as a guest on an episode of *This is Your Life* about Matt Busby in January 1958. That May Rowe was approached by, of all clubs, Arsenal, who had just sacked manager Jack Crayston - the position eventually going to former Gunners 'keeper George Swindin. Why Rowe didn't become Arsenal boss is a matter of pure conjecture. It may be that he was following doctor's orders to avoid such a high-profile position so soon but, for a man with Spurs running through his veins, working for their arch-rivals was perhaps out of the question. Considering the dour, if successful, Arsenal side of the late 1960s, one might imagine Rowe setting Highbury crowds alight with stimulating play so similar to that introduced later by Arsène Wenger.

During that same summer period Rowe was also the choice of Fourth Division Crystal Palace's chairman Arthur Wait to replace Cyril Spiers, coincidentally the 'keeper during Rowe's first season as a Spurs' player back in 1931. Spiers had failed to win Palace a place in the new national Third Division, so they were instead condemned to the newly-formed Fourth (basement) Division. On leaving, Spiers said: '[Crystal Palace] is the finest club I have ever been with,' so could well have recommended his pal Rowe as his successor. As for Palace Chairman Wait, he was that rare combination: ambitious and successful in business, yet kindly and sympathetic. As for his club, it was described at that time by journalist Bob Pennington as follows: 'For years we have talked of the Palace potential; the size and scope of the vast, natural bowl that is Selhurst Park; the carriage trade that was only waiting for a winning team to attract them from the opulent dormitory of Surrey.' Wait believed that Rowe would regain his touch away from the harsh spotlight of the First Division. Arthur thought Wait's offer over long and hard but Wait's son Brian stressed to me that Rowe had been 'very reluctant', not wanting '…to run a club again.' He instead recommended wartime colleague George Smith, who had just had success with Sutton United, and Smith enthusiastically grasped the opportunity. Blunt and outspoken, Smith proceeded to set himself the target to take the club then nicknamed the 'Glaziers' straight back up into the new Third

Division. However, over the coming months, Rowe would remain firmly in the chairman's thoughts.

Until Smith's arrival Division Two had been the peak of Palace's achievements. Smith was a man who deserved to succeed, but some players recoiled from the intensity of his training sessions, which Roy Summersby, who joined Palace later that season, told me were '…really brutal.' Colleague Terry Long told Don Madgwick (in Madgwick's excellent *Palace Heroes and Legends*) that Smith occasionally lost his temper, some players regarding him as 'some kind of nutter' but he at least encouraged his side to play from the back. The only two real 'stars' Smith inherited were captain Johnny McNichol, a title winner with Chelsea in 1955, and the boy Rowe had enthusiastically recommended to West Brom, the precocious, highly-talented Johnny Byrne.

Smith's reign began superbly with a 6-2 home victory over Crewe, before the Glaziers went six games without another victory, Smith publicly angered by his side's inconsistency. This and Smith's occasionally abusive treatment of players will have concerned Chairman Wait. Indeed, in October, Wait was back in touch with Rowe. Smith himself had already confessed he needed help and Rowe finally joined the club as combination assistant manager and chief scout. Wait later believed this role gave Rowe his confidence back. As for Smith, he said: 'I am honoured to think that the most successful manager since Herbert Chapman should come and act as a subordinate to me.' Beginning what would become his longest stay with any club on November 1st 1958, Rowe admitted: 'I am not a magic man who is going to pull Crystal Palace out of trouble just like that'.

Within two days Rowe oversaw the signing of winger Ray Colfar from Smith's former club, Sutton, and three further players were to arrive before season's end. One strongly suspects Wait harboured a plan to slide Rowe into the hot-seat should the abrasive Smith fail to improve on the average results achieved to date, while in the meantime the Chairman could assess his health. Rowe's return to football administration was met with pleasure across the entire spectrum of English football, Sports barrister and journalist Edward Grayson writing: 'With Crystal Palace, Arthur Rowe returned from the wilderness to grace further the game he has

In November 1958 Rowe became Assistant to wartime colleague George Smith, Manager of Fourth Division Crystal Palace. Smith is at the far left, while Arthur Wait, the Chairman, is third from the left.

A BREAK FROM THE HOTSEAT: GOODBYE LANE, HELLO SELHURST 1955-60

adorned for 40 years,' adding that fans of Tottenham Hotspur '…will never cease to have more than just a sneaking regard for his adopted club [Crystal Palace] which has so generously preserved his talents.' As for the Palace playing staff, Terry Long told me how uplifted and excited he and his colleagues were when hearing that the distinguished, Championship-winning manager was joining their little club.

Being of the same generation, Chairman Wait would form a close bond with Rowe. Aside from their Edwardian childhoods, both Arthurs also had a lifelong obsession with their local football club but as far as boardrooms go, Rowe now found himself in enormously better company than he experienced at White Hart Lane. Wait, despite having grown up a fifteen-minute stroll from Selhurst Park in a road cheerfully referred to as 'Death and Poverty Street', now owned his own successful building company. The hardships of his early life had been alleviated by watching Palace in action and he now had a burning ambition to take the club to the top flight. Johnny Byrne said of him: 'The chairman is a matey man. I could talk to him straight without any of this toffee-nosed stuff you get from some directors of other clubs.'

However if Wait had intended Rowe to be a calming influence on Smith, it had not taken effect two weeks later when Smith took his side to amateurs Ashford for a 1-0 FA Cup 1st round victory. According to Terry Long, at the final whistle a far from satisfied Smith witnessed his players tucking into a plate of sandwiches and cakes which the amateur club had kindly prepared. Furiously accusing the players of a lack of effort, Smith yanked open the dressing room door and threw the entire spread of food down the corridor. If Rowe was present he will surely have been mortified, but he was probably away scouting, as soon to arrive were winger Gerry Priestley and inside-forward Roy Summersby. The stocky 23-year-old Summersby was a creative, goal-scoring wing-half or inside-forward who had once played alongside Johnny Haynes for London Schoolboys. As early as 1953 Bernard Joy had said of the then 17-year-old: 'He …excels at distribution' and '…keeps passes on the ground for his forwards', so Summersby fitted Rowe's preferences to a tee. Making his debut in a 2-0 win at Walsall before Christmas, he was identified as the brains behind Palace's attack and scored a debut goal, the first of many collaborations between the reserved and quiet Summersby and 'life-and-soul-of-the-party' Byrne.

After Christmas, with Palace now moving up the League, one national newspaper suggested Rowe was wasting his talent with a Fourth Division club, Smith responding: 'Arthur has only just got here and we are certainly not losing him yet!' A setback at Bradford Park Avenue then saw one newspaper refuse to print Smith's angry reaction. Roy Summersby recalled how the spiky Smith, following defeats, '…nearly had fights with players', adding 'George used to tear players to shreds sometimes, until they nearly cried.' This facet of Smith's character was presumably absent during his wartime association with Rowe.

Nevertheless six victories from nine followed, the Smith-Rowe combination galvanising the side into promotion form. A 4-0 win at Workington saw two visiting players visit Palace's dressing-room to thank the visitors for the '…football lesson they had been given'. Considering the long-ball style Smith employed later in his

In the summer of 1959, content to be once again involved in the game he loved, Rowe took time out to bodysurf in Newquay.

career one might assume Rowe was by then exercising some influence over the playing style. Two days' later Rowe was sporting a different 'hat', managing a British Army side against the Belgian Army at Stamford Bridge.

With ten games left Palace had struck 73 League goals yet, when losing 2-0 at home to Carlisle they had played it long and high. Then five Easter points out of six revived faint hopes of promotion, but Palace's League form withered at the final hurdle. Despite Smith's copious team changes, Palace finished three places adrift. Smith had failed with this first attempt at promotion but he and Rowe had at least upped Palace's scoring rate by nearly 30%, and their points total, too, was up 20%. In the final of the Southern Floodlit Cup, Palace played superbly against a strong Arsenal side in front of over 30,000 spectators, eventually losing by just the odd goal. That night Palace had worn white shirts with a triple hoop of claret and blue across the chest for the first time. Hooped shirts were uncommon and, in view of Rowe's pre-War experiences, brought to mind the Hungarian national shirt and that of Honvéd. With Smith denying the shirt design was his, it remains to this day identified with Rowe.

Player unrest arose at the end of Smith's first season with one player returning to his Lincolnshire home with no intention of returning, only Smith's forgiveness bringing him back. Smith then acquired Dave Sexton, 29, scorer of more than a goal every other game for Brighton. Sexton had been a confirmed fan of Rowe's Spurs. With Byrne about to report for two years' National Service, Sexton was quality cover. Another arrival was Johnny Gavin, now 31, who had of course been with Rowe at Spurs.

Smith and Rowe's forward line for the 1959-60 season now looked promising; Gavin and Sexton were on the right, the lanky 27-goal Mike Deakin in the centre and Byrne at inside-left. At Rowe's imaginative suggestion, Smith introduced five-minute, across-the-pitch, six-a-side contests before kick-off, this to replace the standard, casual kick-about. It was designed for the players to '...play themselves into the groove *before* the whistle instead of *after*,' as Smith put it. However, one point from Palace's first two games drew the comment: 'Pretty football alone isn't enough', Palace said to look '...more like boy scouts hunting butterflies than soccer commandos.' Yet the Glaziers then won five of the next seven. On Wednesday, September 23rd, a Ron Burgess-managed Watford side arrived containing a twin strike-force of Rowe's former transfer-target at Spurs, Cliff Holton, and former Spurs' forward Dennis Uphill. Yet Palace astonishingly scored four in each half, winning 8-1. Three days later Palace crashed to a 3-4 home defeat against lowly Chester prompting the volatile Smith to tell the press 'If we don't win promotion this season, I quit'. He later denied this was intended for publication but said he would stick by his words. After 8-1 victims Watford then beat Palace 4-2 in the return at Vicarage Road it was Rowe who spoke on behalf of the manager, saying: 'The team are not playing the quality football we think they can', a statement suggesting he was now no longer confined to administrative or scouting duties.

Four away losses then provoked the inevitable question: 'Has any side ever won 8-1 followed by four successive defeats?' but Palace had played excellent football in spasms, and, to his credit, Smith kept the same line-up to face Barrow at Selhurst Park. Fewer than 10,000 looked on as Palace went four goals up by half-time. By the 89th minute Byrne was sending a shot skimming across the grass for his second goal, the final one of the night. In between a further four goals had hit the Barrow net, the final score 9-0! Although Sexton and Byrne were praised for their probing and accurate passing, the real star was Summersby, some suggesting his play was of international quality, while his four goals made him the first post-war Palace player to score more than three in a match.

Yet the ambitious Byrne remained concerned about the preceding four defeats on the trot and Smith reluctantly put him on the transfer list. However, six wins from nine followed, before Deakin departed for Northampton and the prolific 28-year-old Alan Woan arrived in exchange. An improved financial proposition then convinced teenage father Byrne to remain at Selhurst Park after all, perhaps due to his relationship with Rowe, whose kindly support and advice was more palatable than Smith's authoritarian approach. An unpaid collaboration of Byrne and Rowe, both supporting an Epsom-area five-a-side youth football competition, organised by a young man named Chris Hassell who reappears later in Rowe's story, demonstrated the growing, fruitful relationship between Byrne and Rowe. Also around this time Rowe was chosen as one of three leading figures in a forum to discuss the state of the game with Geoffrey Green of *The Times*, with a contribution to a four-volume, encyclopaedic treatise on soccer. Extracts from this forum are included where appropriate in this book. The only other panel member who was Rowe's eloquent equal that day was none other than Danny Blanchflower, who was on the brink of enjoying his greatest playing success at Spurs.

When eighth-placed Palace won 2-0 at Northampton, a serious knee injury suffered by Sexton cast a deep shadow over the rest of the season. Carried from the field after colliding with the 'keeper, Sexton's injury presaged a lengthy and painful attempt to regain fitness. With Sexton in the side Palace had averaged nearly 2.5 goals per game but one goal per game without him, so this was a tremendous blow to Smith's hopes of promotion at his second attempt. When Gillingham arrived for the last game of 1959 their philosophy was clearly 'stop the main man and you stop the team', Byrne thus given a rough passage.

Setting Smith and Rowe's promotion quest to one side for a moment, January 1960 saw calls for a hike in footballers' pay, which had fallen back since it had exceeded the average non-footballer's pay in the late 1930s. Now the set maximum wage for players over 20 years of age was just £20 during the season and £17 in the summer. To give this some perspective, the average gross household income at the time was around £19 per week and the average non-player expected to earn that for around 45 years until retirement, while the average career lifespan of a footballer (according to the PFA, even today) is only eight years. So the Professional Footballers' Association began discussing strike action to increase salaries, but more significantly, to remove the salary cap.

In a lively discussion with Chelsea boss Ted Drake, Rowe favoured extracting more from fans' pockets. He estimated the cost of a fan's trip to the cinema with wife and children, buying them 'some nuts or ices or something' to be around 'seven or eight bob' [a 'bob' equating to 5 new pence, so 35 or 40 new pence]. The minimum cost to watch the LIVE entertainment of football then was around the equivalent of 10 to 12.5 new pence. 'What about this "poor old fan"?' continued Rowe, blaming Football League clubs for not increasing the price of admission after the war at a time of growing prosperity and enthusiasm. Surely it would have been wiser to remember that booms don't last for ever. And had they raised the price then, it would have been accepted.' In this conversation with Drake, Rowe betrayed his approval of gambling, perhaps rooted in his earlier, greyhound-owning days 'I don't hate betting. I don't hate the pools. I love a few bob on. It makes life interesting. You can back your opinion and you can lose or win, depending on how big a mug you are.' One can be sure his attitude would have changed had he lived to witness the human ravages caused by today's compulsive, online gambling.

Returning to Palace, a disastrous start to the new year saw them plunge 7-1 at Notts County, a club who admittedly finished top scorers in the entire Football League that season, but when Smith blamed a lack of fitness for the result, trainer Jack Blackman angrily walked out. A 2-1 home defeat to Walsall saw Palace criticised for 'tap-tap football', yet attendances at Selhurst Park had increased by nearly 20% since the Smith/Rowe partnership came into being, bucking a national trend of diminishing crowds. Sexton's recovery to appear in the next six games inspired a revival, but after promotion-challenging Torquay were held 1-1 at Selhurst Park, an explosive Smith accused his men of being spineless. Only miracles, he said, would now see Palace promoted and they proceeded to take just eight points from the following 16. After nearly two years as manager, Smith had become increasingly frustrated. When Palace lost 4-0 at Rochdale in March six changes were made for Workington's arrival, including an apparent 'slap on the wrist' for Byrne when moved to outside-left, his least favourite role. The 1-0 defeat resulting from Smith's gamble all but extinguished Palace's promotion hopes.

Following a first victory in six games, at Doncaster, Crystal Palace were managerless the following week. It was first thought Smith had honoured his pledge to quit but the truth was that he had been sacked by Chairman Wait. Following an away win and with successive home games to follow, something had clearly forced the issue. In a significant incident later in his chairmanship, Wait would take a star player's word against that of his manager. The chairman had a tendency to form close relationships with players and he particularly hated to see young Byrne unhappy, but Smith will have regarded players questioning his decisions as insubordination. Yet Byrne was not alone, the *Advertiser* disclosing that Smith had '…set up a storm by his criticism of the players', adding, 'through spokesman and skipper Johnny McNichol, the players hit back.' The temptation for Wait to remove the conflictive manager had now become too strong. It was Rowe himself who issued a statement to the press. It later transpired that Smith had been asked to resign on the Monday, and to produce a letter of resignation, but he had dragged his feet over producing the letter. Wait will have preferred the press and public to believe Smith had honourably kept his word and resigned.

So, five years since managing a side Arthur Rowe now took temporary control of Crystal Palace for the three Easter games. With morale low, Wait, with a remote chance of promotion remaining, may have felt a belated roll of the dice might still (just) lift the club out of the bottom division. At Easter the chairman told the press that no applicant was being sought, strongly suggesting it was Rowe's job. Meanwhile Smith, perhaps learning from the errors of his ways, later spent nine years in charge of Portsmouth and Wait later credited Smith with Palace's drive to attain First Division status. Rowe backed this up: 'George had got the club out of a rut. He fired the club and got it moving the right way' but Smith himself, asked in 1969 how he viewed his Palace career, replied: 'I worked like a slave and got no bloody thanks for it.'

So, Rowe temporarily moved into Smith's chair on April 15th 1960. The temptation to benefit from the experience of a man much admired and liked by the players, will have been irresistible. As far as the quality of football under Smith was concerned, Roy Summersby told me that Smith '…didn't really play the way Arthur wanted to play.' Proving the manager had not been comfortable with the short-passing game, or 'push-and-run', Summersby later played under Smith at Portsmouth, where, said Roy, it was '…all up-and-unders — the ball would always pass over my head!'

With Byrne re-energised by the managerial change, Rowe began Easter with a 1-0 victory over Exeter City, the *Advertiser* reporting that Palace had '…responded with more spirit, more determination, more skill than recently.' The following day Palace dominated Northampton without taking their chances and, in the last minute Smith reject Mike Deakin scored a winner, so Palace's faint remaining hopes of promotion were all but erased. At Exeter on Easter Monday Rowe made a number of further changes and, with little now to play for, Palace trailed in 2-0 down at half-time yet Gavin, now rejuvenated under Rowe, struck twice to salvage a draw. While Rowe and the team were down in the West Country that Monday afternoon, the other three Palace directors were in deep discussion with Chairman Wait over the vacant manager's position. A new man coming in would likely result in Arthur Rowe's exit from Selhurst Park.

17

It's Arthur!

A PALACE OF DREAMS 1960-61

'I am living through the most exciting adventure of my life. Crystal Palace are top of the Fourth Division. I have never known a happier club in football.'

ARTHUR ROWE 1960

There had still been no word about the vacant manager's position when Palace lost by the odd goal in three at promoted Torquay United on April 23rd 1960 but two days later Chairman Wait called another board meeting and, on departing, simply said...

'It's Arthur!'

Five years on and away from the intense spotlight of Division One, 53-year-old Rowe could gently dip his toe back in managerial waters. His Crystal Palace now joined Nicholson's Spurs as practitioners of a rare, enlightened form of the game. Rowe knew the players well enough to be confident he could take Palace up. He would boost spirits which had flagged under Smith. For Terry Long, the appointment was a major turning point '...for the club and for me personally', continuing '[Arthur] promoted a way of playing that finally saw the club really moving in the right direction... and with style.' For Johnny Byrne, Rowe was a match made in heaven: two intelligent men, one young, the other a father-figure, but sharing similar footballing beliefs. That summer the *News of the World*'s Bob Pennington spelt-out the significance of a superb boardroom/manager/player

At Crystal Palace there developed much mutual admiration between the two Arthurs, Chairman Wait and Rowe. At last Rowe was spared unsupportive directors.

triumvirate: 'Byrne was the major hope of Arthur Rowe in proving that football, pure football, will take you to Division One. Yet I would say [Rowe's] alliance with Chairman Wait was every bit as vital.' Rowe was of course compelled to rebut doubts regarding his health, telling the press that he wouldn't have taken the job had he been concerned.

His first two official games in charge were the last two of season '59-60, beginning at home to Bradford Park Avenue. Rowe was unaware that both 'keeper Vic Rouse and defender Terry Long had long been ever-present so his decision to trial a reserve 'keeper ended Rouse's unbroken run of 78 appearances. Similarly Rowe wished to review a young reserve full-back, only for the *Advertiser* to point out Long's amazing record of 193 League and Cup games. So Rowe dropped another player instead, switching Long to right-half so that young Roy Lunnis could be assessed at right-back. Summersby's fifteenth goal of the season then gave Rowe a golden start as the official manager of Crystal Palace. Then, before their final League game, Palace arranged a money-spinning friendly with Spurs. Despite Byrne's absence on Army duty, Palace drew 2-2 against a Spurs' side that included four men from Rowe's time: Blanchflower, Henry, Harmer, and Dyson. Those four, plus Nicholson, will have been greatly heartened to see Arthur back doing what he did best.

Palace's key summer purchase was to have an enduring impact on the club. Half-back George Petchey, 28, was an accurate passer with a forceful style. Starting out at West Ham (alongside the likes of Malcolm Allison and Dave Sexton) he then made 255 League appearances for Queen's Park Rangers. Attending the final QPR home game, Rowe located Petchey afterwards, saying 'Well done, son' and telling him he had been the best player on the field. What followed might be called "tapping-up" today, but, as Petchey put it, he and Rowe then 'bumped into each other' at White City underground on the way home, Rowe telling the player that he was exactly the wing-half he needed. The player had previously encountered Rowe when shopping for a pair of his trademark boots and the former Spurs boss made sure he would not have to pay for them.

Petchey would later say: 'Arthur was the best manager I ever worked with. When he told you how he wanted you to play, it was easy to understand. He encouraged you to pass the ball. That was all I ever wanted to do, and all I ever wanted to teach.' At Fourth Division level Petchey's contribution matched Blanchflower's at First Division Spurs. Rowe told Petchey he aimed for three promotions inside ten years to elevate Palace to the First Division for the first time in the club's history. Petchey said he would still be there when that took place (and it did — and he was)! Arriving at Selhurst Park, Petchey said he found '…the best club in London', adding, 'going to Crystal Palace under Arthur Rowe was such a pleasure, finding such a nice, happy atmosphere — a brilliant environment to play football.'

A national newspaper then reported that Palace were seeking 'an old-fashioned outside-left', a description which tickled Rowe: 'I visualised a player in long trousers and a flowing moustache.' The man in question was QPR's Pat Kerrins but more significantly Rowe also captured 30-year-old Ron Heckman, a goalscoring inside-forward or winger who had originally been with Rowe as an amateur at Spurs, and who had since accumulated 59 goals in 177 appearances with Orient and

Millwall. Rowe also attempted to buy Orient striker Peter Burridge but, having purchased Petchey, hesitated, Burridge instead joining Millwall. Although Rowe would eventually get his man.

That spring Real Madrid beat Eintracht Frankfurt 7-3 in the European Cup Final at Hampden Park in one of the finest games ever played. Rowe was so impressed that he purchased a copy of the film from the BBC to show and inspire his Fourth Division payers. Meanwhile a full-scale trial game at Selhurst Park more than satisfied him. 'The whole movement was smooth, balanced and progressive,' he reported. Roy Summersby told me how Rowe would emphasise the importance of timing runs — 'when to go'. He would get the players to take their field positions before getting them to pass the ball between themselves until he called for a through ball into the path of the inside forward. If the timing was wrong he called them back and they had to do it again. 'Once he got the timing right, the inside-forward was through on goal.' Summersby enthusiastically adding: 'I'm convinced Rowe's way of playing can't be beat.' The chairman's son, Brian Wait, attended some training sessions and believed Palace's fitness levels had increased under the new manager but something Rowe now abandoned was the pre-kick-off, warm-up game, explaining: 'I like the idea physically and practicably but psychologically it

Having been appointed as full-time manager following the sacking of Smith, Rowe meets new additions to his playing staff in pre-season 1960-61. From left-to-right they are: Ken Jones, George Petchey, Peter Vine, Pat Kerrins, Roy Lunnis, Jim Mason, Brian Lewis and 'keeper Ray O'Dell.

never worked out. To work properly it had to be taken seriously to gear the players up to match pace [and] unfortunately, some of the remarks passed by spectators seemed to affect some of the players.'

A week before season 1960-61 was to begin, John Matthews of the *Advertiser* reported: 'Sitting easily in the managerial chair is a man who has sat in more illustrious seats in the past — Mr Arthur Rowe.' 'Arthur's "come-back" to League management,' added another journalist, Peter Morris, '…is not before time'. Palace's pre-season public trial match, Whites (first-team) v Colours (reserves), saw the Whites (Rowe's first-team choice) lining-up as follows: Rouse; Long, Noakes; Petchey, Evans, McNichol; Gavin, Woan, Byrne, Summersby, Heckman.

Petchey's arrival allowed Summersby to move back up front to cash-in on his goalscoring ability with Byrne playing down the middle. Goalkeeper Rouse had begun mounting attacks Ditchburn-style with accurate throw-outs, primarily to his full-backs, ensuring possession was retained. Rowe explained why the 5ft 8in Byrne would be the focus of the attack: 'I said to him one day, "Why don't you play up the front?" He said, "I'm not big enough."' Rowe replied that all the players he had trouble with as a centre-half were little guys. Byrne tried it, liked it, and would eventually run rings around distinguished centre-halves such as World Cup-winner Jack Charlton. 'Byrne [said Rowe] had what Eddie Baily had — the ability to play the ball quickly and move as soon as he had played it.' Ambitious for his new protégé, Rowe could imagine Byrne walking into the full England side.

So, on Saturday August 20th 1960, Rowe's side took the field at Selhurst Park to face newly-relegated Accrington Stanley. As soon as the whistle sounded the question arose: 'What are a side producing this brand of soccer doing in the Fourth Division?' It took Byrne only a minute to open his 1960-61 account and although Accrington equalised three minutes later Woan scored two in quick succession, George Petchey telling me he had not touched the ball before realising his new side were 3-1 up! Heckman made it 4-1 from Byrne's through ball and just after the half-hour Byrne, for once defying 'push-and-run', tricked his way past three defenders to add his second. Accrington pulled one back and walked off 5-2 down at half-time then Woan completed his hat-trick on the hour. Byrne topped that with two more of his own and when Heckman completed his own double Palace had begun with an extraordinary 9-2 win. The hat-tricks of Byrne and Woan remained the only first-day trebles by a Palace player until Dougie Freedman repeated it 43 years later. Having experienced little success at West Ham and QPR, Petchey felt inspired: 'It was the first time I'd won by such a big margin, and the first time I'd seen so many people so happy.'

Roy Summersby, too, animatedly recalled this game: 'From the kick-off Johnny [Byrne], myself and Alan Woan passed the ball between us and ended with a shot on goal! Straight the way through! I couldn't believe it. It was *so* exhilarating. To me, that's the way to play football. I had never experienced that before — at Millwall it was all "up-and-under".' Terry Long recalled: 'We were so slick at times that the opposition couldn't get near us. Sooner or later one of us would get clattered up in the air because they would become so frustrated, but most of the time they couldn't tackle you because you didn't have the ball long enough.'

The architect of this destruction of Accrington played it down, Rowe admitting that while there was a lot of good football from his side, '…some was not so good — but it would be foolish to say that I was not satisfied.' Clearly he was confident 'push-and-run' was achievable by the players at his disposal. Meanwhile, any early reservations Petchey harboured about Byrne evaporated rapidly. 'I used to say to him: "If you start to run away, I only see your backside and I'm not going to give it to you. I'll turn and give it wide or somewhere else." And, to his credit, I never said that to him again.' Petchey admired Summersby too, 'The great thing from playing behind the pair of them was they didn't react and run away from you. If you were to give it to Roy and go, he would give it back to you.'

Inevitably the attendance for the second home game rose by almost 40% and Darlington unsurprisingly arrived with a defensive mindset, Palace scraping home 3-2 this time. A big setback was the loss through injury of both Rowe's centre-halves, Evans and Choules, so the 5ft 10in Long would fill-in for the following five games. In the next game Palace were 4-0 up on a wet afternoon at Doncaster and the referee seemed likely to abandon the game at half-time, so the Palace players went back out onto the soggy turf early at half-time to start kicking the ball about and convince the official to carry on. It was a ruse which worked, Palace winning 5-1 and one Rovers reporter declaring Rowe's side the '…best seen here for many years.' For some reason this brings to mind the game Chairman Wait recalled years later: 'We arrived at the ground, the dressing room was to say the least appalling,

Two Jim Mercer cartoons from the Croydon Advertiser *anticipating* (left) *Rowe's 'Season of Hope and Expectation' and* (right) *celebrating his astounding opening 9-2 victory over Accrington Stanley.*

IT'S ARTHUR! A PALACE OF DREAMS 1960-61

After four successive winless games in Rowe's otherwise outstandingly successful first season as Palace manager, a stray cat ran onto the Selhurst Park pitch during a 5-0 victory. Thereafter the cat remained at the club, serving as a mascot.

an open stove in the middle of the room with the flue pipe up through the roof, the toilet door swinging on its hinges, etc. The complaints were growing when a gentleman stepped in with a fire bucket and said "I've brought your bath, boys." This, of course, was Rowe, who then said "If you don't want to play here any more, go out there and beat the living daylights out of them."' Wait added: 'This sums up Arthur, full of humour and yet firm.' Such conditions only furthered Rowe's ambition to take Palace up in the world.

With Palace averaging five goals-a-game the blood was coursing through Rowe's veins again and a fourth straight win, in the return at Darlington, was described as '...90 minutes of scintillating football'. It was perhaps no coincidence that the only other team in the Football League with maximum points was Blanchflower-led Spurs. Palace then dropped their first point to in-form Hartlepool, Rowe recognising that their opponents had smartly countered 'push-and-run' by stopping the runner (the man moving for the return pass).

Glowing reports of Palace's next visitors, Peterborough, new to the Football League, led Wait to forecast a 30,000 gate — which proved an underestimate! On a night when only 7,000 watched Second Division football ten miles away at Charlton, 36,478 turned up at Selhurst Park! Clearly, Arthur Rowe's brand of football pulled in the punters but 'Posh' defended solidly against Palace's well-crafted onslaught, eventually earning a 2-0 victory. As the game went away from Palace there were typical terrace demands of 'BOOT IT' or 'BELT IT!', but reporter Bob Pennington wrote: 'Palace scored one victory last night. They stuck to their faith in football... they did right by Arthur Rowe.' The manager's own response was 'The kick-and-rush style might take you up but you will soon be back.' Despite his seven goals from six to date Woan was then omitted at promotion-chasing Wrexham where Byrne won the points by dragging the ball back with the sole of his boot, Puskás-style, before striking the winner home via the 'keeper's fingertips and a post. Yet despite sitting in joint first place Palace began to be criticised for trying to walk the ball into the net. A two-day gap proved too short before facing Peterborough again at London Road, the home side going three-up in no time and, despite stand-in Long's best efforts, Posh centre-forward Terry Bly grabbed a hat-trick in a 4-1 home win. By season's end, that scoreline would actually look quite respectable as

Peterborough, who had arrived like a bolt from the blue, would notch five or more on no fewer than eight occasions that season.

The three successive draws that followed were testament to the lack of a tried-and-tested centre-half, while Byrne had been stretched by a lot of Army fixtures (on one occasion playing a total of five games in eight days)! When Southport arrived Palace badly needed a win and the return of Choules freed Long to move back to right-half. Byrne scored early on before adding two more, first drawing the 'keeper to chip over his head (his second), then controlling with his chest before dramatically volleying home, a goal described by David Prole as: '…a flash of pure genius'. After full-back Alf Noakes scored from a typical Rowe short corner ploy, Byrne collected Summersby's fine pass up the middle before striking it left-footed into the roof of the net for his fourth. Afterwards the striker nobly drew attention to Summersby's excellent set-ups. During the game a stray black cat had interrupted play and was thereafter kept by the club as a mascot, Rowe later photographed playing with it in his office. With Arsenal boss George Swindin witnessing Byrne's four goals, Rowe was obliged to say: 'Johnny is going to play soccer in a higher division… with us.' Some felt Rowe's attention to Byrne created jealousy among his colleagues, indeed the manager would later admiringly reflect on Palace's shining star: 'He had a spark that could light fires! He had this tremendous skill. This ability to take people on. John was pigeon-toed, and it gave him four ways of dealing with a ball; the inside and outside of both feet. No ball ever gave him a problem. He was great at playing it away first-time and moving off to a new position. He was so quick, defenders couldn't get near him. I would put him in the top four centre-forwards I ever came across.' In Byrne, Arthur Rowe was finally working with a striker comparable to his old pal George Hunt.

After injury struck both Choules and Byrne, Palace unsurprisingly sank to a 5-2 defeat at Edgeley Park, Stockport but either side of that game Palace enjoyed two four-goal triumphs of their own; one included a hat-trick from Summersby, while a recalled Woan had now struck eleven from ten appearances. With Byrne injured Rowe did a quick deal with Ron Burgess to sign Watford's bustling Dennis Uphill. Eleven years had passed since Uphill had signed for Rowe at White Hart Lane and in the previous season he had scored 30 as Watford climbed out of the Fourth Division. He immediately scored twice on his Palace debut, a 4-2 defeat of Barrow. Woan then lost his place to Uphill when he was injured during a victory at Gillingham, but Palace now led the table for the first time, Rowe succeeding where Smith had failed — taking Crystal Palace to the top of the Division.

Before a home game with Bradford Park Avenue Rowe inspired his players by pointing out how nearly 15,000 souls had braved appalling weather to attend, saying 'Let's make it worth their while.' Palace were indeed 3-1 up by the 89th minute and just one further goal would see Palace chalk-up 50 for the season, with 29 games left to play. Cue Johnny Byrne who set-off on a storming run from the centre of the field, taking the ball out to the wing before cutting back in, outfoxing two defenders then rounding the goalkeeper not just once but twice, before driving his shot past a defender on the line. As for the game in general, the *Sunday Dispatch* eulogised: 'If this is Fourth Division football then let's have four Fourth Divisions.'

Byrne's fifteenth of the season made him joint leading scorer in the entire Football League and, on his return to management, Rowe was again creating the best of headlines and drawing the biggest crowds.

The struggle was meanwhile continuing between the PFA and the Football League over ending the maximum wage and freedom of contract for players. In opposing a strike Rowe was strangely at odds with a public shocked to find how little players were earning. Palace captain McNichol was also concerned about the contractual constraints on players — those not in the first-team could be prevented from playing as they could not move to another club without the agreement of their present club. McNichol was duty-bound to promptly clarify that at Palace '…we are treated right and are happy.' Malcolm Allison also saw the issue differently to Rowe recalling that players then '…were naively happy to be earning their living in a way that pleased them. They didn't think in terms of exploitation and serfdom, of a system which enabled a club to hire 60 professionals because wages were so low.' The *Observer* newspaper printed the opinions of leading soccer men of the time, including Danny Blanchflower and Jimmy Hill. Rowe also contributed, this time in more positive vein:

'For many years we called the Continentals "ballet dancers" and decried their style of play. Lately it has been forcibly driven home to us that there is much to be said for the Continental style and some of our teams have adopted it. So why not, as you [the *Observer*] suggest, take a close look at the way [Continentals] administer the game? We might have *more* to learn.' This included looking at pay levels; poor pay had degraded the standard of British football and Rowe himself had been a victim of this. In order to ensure no interruption in earnings once retired from football (in his case, his option to move straight into a paid job in the furniture trade) he had lost several early playing years completing his upholstery apprenticeship. His career-ending injury meant his career earnings were further reduced. If earnings failed to cover years devoted to the game plus an allowance to invest in the future once a playing career was over, then many gifted young players would turn their backs on the game. An overwhelming majority of players were in favour of striking and even Palace chairman Wait supported the players. After all, how could he keep Byrne without paying him more than his less gifted teammates? But Wait was also concerned that strike action would lead to a subsequent loss in revenue and, worse still, damage Palace's promotion chances.

Meanwhile, despite Palace's tremendous progress, Wait remained concerned for Rowe's health and was negotiating with a First Division club to acquire the services of their trainer (an unnamed man but, according to the *Advertiser*, familiar to Palace fans). Wait had noted that after distant away fixtures the manager sometimes returned on the sleeper train in order to keep up with office duties. 'That's not good enough, because we don't want Arthur to go ill again,' said Wait. Rowe himself conceded he needed some support. On October 26th Rowe had a break when taking all his players to Wembley to watch England impressively defeat Spain 4-2. It seemed to inspire Palace three days later when they travelled to promotion rivals Northampton. Byrne scored in just 30 seconds, before a Northampton shot deflected in off McNichol's leg but with 20 minutes left Gavin reached a through ball from Summersby just before the 'keeper, crossing for Uphill to slot the winner. A 'four-pointer' indeed.

The man with Palace connections appointed as Rowe's assistant was the 6ft 2in stocky, crew-cutted Dick Graham, 38, a post-war 'keeper for Leicester City and Palace. His hiring was to prove extremely significant, both for the club and Rowe himself. Forced to retire due to injury in 1951, Graham took an FA coaching course then spent six years as trainer under Vic Buckingham at West Bromwich Albion. Whether Rowe had come into contact with Graham during his scouting engagement at West Brom is hard to establish. In an interview years later Dick Graham suggested the invitation to return had come from Rowe himself, yet Arthur Wait had been on the board when Graham had been the club's goalkeeper. Considering the marked disparity between Graham and Rowe in both character and beliefs, the origins of Graham's appointment become significant when reviewing future, traumatic events.

Despite merely being a trainer at West Brom, Graham was suddenly elevated to the status of 'Assistant Manager'. Taking up his post within a fortnight, Graham said he regarded Crystal Palace as his '…old club'. Not only was his wife from Croydon but he had also once run a pub in the town. Furthermore, he had once authored a strident weekly column covering Palace affairs in the *Croydon Advertiser*, indeed, it was so strident that in season 1952-53 he was banned by the club for blaming the staff's low spirits on the directors, one of whom was Wait. Graham was now brim full of ideas, some of which were regarded as oddball. A harsh disciplinarian, his training approach would test the players to their limits — the 'Smith' approach had returned. Arthur Wait's son Brian, fitter and stronger than most, told me Graham had challenged him to train with Palace '…and see if you can do it better.' Brian accepted the challenge and told me that Graham did indeed '…drill them very, very hard.' Palace's long-retired all-time top goalscorer Peter Simpson, who still lived nearby, was soon criticising what he referred to as 'commando-style' training. Had Simpson heard rumours circulating of players unhappy with Graham's methods?

Roy Summersby scores one of his 'double' in a 4-2 home win over Workington, the last game before the arrival of Assistant Manager Dick Graham (with whom Summersby would have little in common).

He added: 'Psychology is the way to bring the best out of players. You might be able to yell at one footballer, but it just won't wash with another.'

When Rowe spoke at the club's annual meeting, his comments might be seen as an oblique criticism of his Tottenham experience: 'This is a happy club. You can smell that when you come in. Everybody trusts each other. Too many managers have to look over their shoulder all the time, but here you get one hundred per cent support.' That same week Rowe, introduced in a newspaper column as '...the silver-haired soccer genius', said: 'I am living through the most exciting adventure of my life. Crystal Palace are top of the Fourth Division. I have never known a happier club in football. Things are right at the top, by which I mean in the boardroom, and for the Palace the future is unlimited. In terms of population, ground potential, enthusiasm, everything you can think of that any club might need, Crystal Palace can one day become one of the biggest clubs in England.'

He typically broadened his subject to that of the football business itself, suggesting it should be reviewed in the light of the growing number of competing attractions. At the time these included the cinema (500 million admissions a year in 1960], theatre, television (15 thousand licences in 1945 had grown to 5 million a year in 1960], theatre, television (15 thousand licences in 1945 had grown to 5 million by 1956), coffee bars (the first espresso machine had arrived in the UK in 1952), speedway and stock-car racing. Then 'DIY' arrived and car ownership was on a steep upward curve, with many owners restricted to driving at weekends. Rowe knew that the quality of football had to be improved if the sport were to compete, particularly as most of the other activities were enjoyed whilst sheltered from extremes of weather. He added: 'Our grounds must be modernized. That takes money, and I see no reason why some central fund, like the League's [football] pools money, should not be made available for this purpose.'

He then moved on to more familiar territory, saying '...the team with the most strength of character and personality will win' and expressing his belief in developing the psychological aspect of playing. 'A player is in possession of the ball for about three minutes in each match,' adding, 'we must learn to condition his thinking about what he is doing, and the positions he is taking up, for the other 87 minutes.' What Rowe said next could equally apply to today's 'Total Football': 'I do not want *centre-halves* and *outside-rights*, and so on, in my team. I want *footballers*. The game has suffered from too much specialization in play.'

Returning to Palace's promotion bid, five successive victories were followed by a narrow loss to Oldham but they clung to first place and were about to lose just one of their next 16 games. In the first, against Workington at Selhurst Park played on a muddy surface, Byrne's confidence on the ball brought accusations from opponents of 'big-headedness', echoed by some Palace fans in the crowd whenever he slowed 'push-and-run' down to play 'keep-ball' but still three games short of the halfway mark in season 1960-61, Palace had already notched 59 goals. It was hardly a coincidence that only Nicholson's Spurs had scored more.

It was at this juncture that Dick Graham arrived to take up his duties. Before leaving West Brom, club captain and future England manager Bobby Robson made a presentation to trainer Graham on behalf of the players, saying: 'If you have sometimes felt we were kicking against your ideas, we hope you appreciate that we now know you were doing it for our good.' On Graham's first morning back at Selhurst Park genial goalkeeper Vic Rouse recognised the new Assistant Manager as he walked from his car. However, Vic took offence when Graham blanked him after he had proferred a friendly 'Good morning'. Graham's spiky manner chimed little with Rowe's and it remains a real conundrum as to why such disparate characters ever worked together. After all, Rowe had once expressed just how important it was for a 'manager and trainer to be of a single mind.' Yet this essential ingredient, absent from his partnership with Anderson at Spurs, seemed highly unlikely to be established with Graham.

An extraordinary 33,699 turned up for a rainy FA Cup second round tie with Watford at Selhurst Park. From the way Ron Burgess's side passed their way out of defence, Rowe's influence in a game described as 'scintillating' was visible in the play of both sides. A replay was required and Woan was due to replace Gavin. However Woan then suffered a pre-match injury the like of which is unlikely to befall Harry Kane today... he suffered a concussion after cracking his head on the coal bunker at home, but Rowe risked him. The replay was goalless until injury time which saw none other than Tommy Harmer's indirect free-kick take a touch off someone's head and enter the net, a further unfortunate FA Cup exit for Rowe, who then faced the accusation of Spurs-bias for selecting Uphill over Woan, but he responded jocularly: 'I am said to have a Tottenham bias. Well, have we done so badly if I have? If Danny Blanchflower became available at some time I would not mind having him!'

Returning to the removal of the maximum wage, when Rowe addressed a meeting in December 1960 he argued against it by citing Spain, where most clubs had become mere cannon fodder for the only two clubs (Real Madrid and Barcelona) capable of paying sizeable signing-on fees and salaries. 'If that kind of situation ever happened in England,' said Rowe, '...I think it would kill football.' Had he lived to witness the success of the Premier League Rowe may have reconsidered, although by the third decade of the twenty-first Century, four rich sides continually finish in the top six, with Arsenal and Tottenham thereabouts. So at the dawn of each season the basic aspiration of the remaining 14 clubs is to preserve their Premiership existence and earnings. Rowe will have seen this as justifying his 1960 statement. But Rowe was concerned that football needed to counter more comfortable attractions: 'If we don't offer football in a more enticing way, I think we are going to fall by the wayside.' Meanwhile, club chairmen rejected further PFA proposals so the threat of strike action in 1961 grew.

As for Palace's promotion push, in a five-game spell they succeeded in achieving three successive away wins book-ended by two rare goalless home draws. At York one could imagine Rowe shuddering as he entered the Bootham Crescent ground for the first time since Spurs' shock Cup exit five-and-a-half years earlier. But the short corner ploy Rowe had introduced led to Petchey's long lob deceiving the 'keeper and entering the net before Heckman clinched Palace's win. News came through that Peterborough had lost, leaving Palace three points clear. On the last weekend before Christmas, in front of just 3,341 spectators at Accrington Stanley,

IT'S ARTHUR! A PALACE OF DREAMS 1960-61

Palace scorched into a three-goal lead and despite Stanley fighting back to draw, a local reporter said Palace produced '…a brand of football that has not been matched at Peel Park this season.' Rowe could not have been happier at this halfway point of the season. Incidentally, Palace's playing staff had presented Rowe with a highly original Christmas card. With 'push-and-run' in mind, it showed a bell-push on one side while pinned on the other was …a well-known laxative.

Meanwhile the PFA had given clubs one month's notice of a strike to begin on January 21st, 1961. The *Advertiser* then set Palace captain Johnny McNichol up against his manager in print, each man presenting his conflicting opinions. Rowe felt the players should have accepted the Football League's offer before waiting a couple of years to see how things worked out (Jimmy Hill quoted Rowe as saying around this time: 'Strike? They must be barmy!'). Rowe sided with the clubs' stance which said they could only pay in accordance with what they were taking at the turnstiles. From this distance in time, Rowe's belief that clubs could not increase players' pay comes across as naive: 'You can't economise on footballs or football boots. You can't travel on the railway any cheaper, you can't cut down on your coke and coal bill', he said, finishing with, 'that leaves only one thing.'

That 'one thing' presumably being laying-off players. As has been seen, playing staffs were overlarge but only because low pay made it affordable. The clubs were now prepared to field amateur players or juniors to ensure the fixture list was fulfilled, ensuring their deal with the football pools companies would not be interrupted. Chairman Wait became concerned that fielding juniors would cost the club the promotion that he and Rowe had so yearned for. But if clubs did play through a strike without their stars, how many fans would turn up? Would admission prices be reduced? How many hired amateurs would be happy to be branded as blacklegs? Meanwhile, public sympathy still remained almost entirely with the players.

On a lighter note Rowe's fear of losing Byrne to a big club may have been lessened when he learned that the player's wife, Margaret, had just knitted a white sweater with claret and blue hoops (Palace's shirt design) for son Kevin! Meanwhile the family of a 17-year-old goalkeeper selected for the FA Youth side shared the same home-delivery baker in Brighton with Palace captain John McNichol, who then became the conduit for a trial at Selhurst Park. Appropriately the young 'keeper's surname was Glazier. Impressed following the trial, Rowe gave Glazier a Glazier's [!] contract and, when later sold, he would become the most expensive goalkeeper in Football League history.

Successive scoreless home games now led to demands for Woan's reinstatement and Byrne's restoration to centre-forward. Ironically, fans had initially derided Rowe's moving of Byrne to the middle. 'I was told I was barmy, that it was a waste of talent, that Byrne was too small,' was the manager's comment. As for the Woan/Uphill debate, Rowe pointed out the nine wins, three draws and two defeats since Uphill had arrived, saying 'Whether you think [Uphill] is a good player or not, that's not a bad record,' adding 'he scraps his hardest when things are toughest.'

Palace's average Fourth Division attendance under Rowe now extraordinarily exceeded that of several second-level clubs competing for promotion to Division One. Then, on a day when Peterborough pounded Carlisle 5-0, Palace reached half-time goalless against Doncaster, the crowd growing restless. Rowe switched Uphill and Byrne and within a minute Petchey's incisive through pass saw Byrne (now back as central striker) put Palace ahead and, by the finish, it was 5-1 to Palace, who entered the New Year in that coveted first place. After a surprise loss away to Chester, they would then win seven of the following eight games.

Finally, on January 9th 1961 clubs accepted the end of the maximum wage, richer clubs having realised its removal gave them the chance to tempt the best players away from financially-weaker clubs. However, the 'retain-and-transfer' clause remained in their contracts, meaning they were still unable to take their services wherever they chose, as in any other profession. So the players rejected the offer until it also assured freedom of contract. Rowe once again suggested they accept the offer, again as a basis for further discussions but, with just three days left before the strike was to begin, the League caved in. The strike was off and a player could now be paid the market value for his talents *and* was free to leave his employer to work for another as-and-when he chose.

Meanwhile Palace's seven victories began with a ninth away win, at Hartlepool, a feat then equalled only by… Nicholson's Spurs. Byrne, now suffering fan abuse due to his Palace pay hike, responded by putting his side ahead at home to Wrexham, but the visitors struck twice in a minute before he curled a free-kick over the wall for Woan to volley an equaliser. With three minutes' left, Byrne raced through the mud, jinked past two defenders and powerfully steered his shot home for the winner, maintaining Palace's five-point lead. Wait now talked excitedly of constructing a new cantilever stand to hold 20,000 and the happy atmosphere improved further with news that Sexton was close to a return.

Struggling Chester visited for the last match of January 1961 and perhaps the last thing they needed was a referee mistakenly starting the game a few minutes early. With fans still queueing to get into Selhurst Park, Summersby's superb ball through the middle was brilliantly steered home by Byrne. Those who were inside the stadium had still not settled down when Byrne hammered his second, in-off the crossbar. Only then did the clock strike three! Chester gamely pulled one back before Summersby restored Palace's advantage. Before the game Rowe had heard of Byrne's short-listing for the England Under-23s so had encouraged the player, saying 'This could be vital'! Fifteen minutes into the second-half Byrne's cross saw Summersby score with ease and, before the end, Petchey's ball up the middle found Byrne who beat the 'keeper with precision for his hat-trick and a final score of 5-1. With Peterborough still engaged in the FA Cup, Palace had opened a seven-point lead. A witness to the game was Chelsea's Stan Crowther, who said: '[Palace] are the best footballing side I've seen this season. It must be a wonderful side to play in: you can see the method that is instilled in them.' With 16 games still to play, Palace had already equalled their goals total of the previous season (84).

Byrne and Rowe were reunited the following day. Chris Hassell had again organised a five-a-side youth tournament which both attended, Byrne taking son Kevin along, wearing that home-knitted Palace top. Following the previous tournament Byrne had refused Hassell's offer to pay his expenses while Rowe replied: 'Thanks for your letter old son, and I'm glad I was able to help', adding

Rowe and Byrne (with son Kevin sporting a sweater knitted in Palace colours by his mother) happily gave up their time to support a local 5-a-side youth tournament. Inset: The young Chris Hassell, whose organisation of the tournament so impressed Rowe that he would eventually become Club Secretary at Crystal Palace.

that he had received, '…a black look from the wife for being out on Sunday!' When Hassell later sought an administrative job in the game, Rowe put in a good word when he applied to Chelsea, telling him: 'Have phoned Mr Battersby [Chelsea's Club Secretary] re. the post and given you a real 'build up' — But I believe it's true! Best wishes lad.' The young man was not offered the role but within months, on Rowe's recommendation, Hassell became Assistant Secretary at Selhurst Park and soon graduated to Club Secretary. He later held similar roles at Everton and Preston, before ending an illustrious career as Chief Executive of Yorkshire Cricket Club. Meanwhile, Byrne added England duties to his already crowded schedule when becoming the first-ever Fourth Division player selected for the England Under-23s to face Wales on February 8th 1961. Of Byrne's selection, Rowe said: 'I couldn't be happier if it was my own son.'

With Rowe then contracting 'flu, Dick Graham took charge for a 2-0 defeat at Carlisle and openly admitted afterwards that Rowe's influence had been missed. It was a defeat Palace could ill-afford as Peterborough had beaten Stockport 6-0. Another 'keeper discovery of Rowe's had meanwhile made his debut for Palace's reserves. This was 18-year-old John 'Jacko' Jackson, whose hero as a boy, ironically, had been Ted Ditchburn. As for Byrne, after training with the full England squad he had made his England Under-23 debut against Wales. Also making his first appearance was 'keeper Gordon Banks, future star of two World Cup Finals, while the second of England's two goals came from future World Cup-winning captain Bobby Moore. It was the first of hundreds of occasions when Moore and Byrne would take the field together.

Despite his excellent return of 23 goals from 46 appearances, Woan was then sold to Aldershot, much to the annoyance of fans. However, Rowe had identified the greater benefit Byrne gleaned when accompanied by the more physical Uphill. Rowe then returned for a 4-1 win over Rochdale, but Palace's score was topped by Peterborough, this time beating Exeter 7-1. At Mansfield, Byrne crossed for Petchey to rocket home a header before Summersby clinched Palace's fourth 'double' of the season. It goes without saying that Peterborough also won that day but, a week later, they faced promotion rivals Northampton, presenting an opportunity for the Glaziers to move further ahead should they win at Barrow, which they did, 3-0, despite a muddy pitch. Four days later Byrne did, after all, play against Scotland Under-23s (who won 1-0) and Rowe could hardly wait to write to Chris Hassell: 'So very nice, young John's success! So well deserved too for he's a great lad, I'm tickled pink.'

On March 4th Noakes rattled the Gillingham crossbar with his spot-kick, Palace stumbling on for another 38 minutes before Byrne mis-hit a shot only to see the bounce escape the grasp of 'keeper John Simpson. Hardly a goal to impress the Barcelona scout recording Byrne's every move on his tape-recorder. Byrne also had an assist, his chipped free-kick met by Gavin's head, Simpson getting a desperate hand to the ball only for Summersby, in his 100th successive League appearance, to cement the victory. With just eleven games remaining the only big story should have been Rowe's outstanding return to management, but Peterborough stole the attention again with a 7-1 victory over Aldershot. The Palace boss was now working on strengthening his team in the likely event of promotion and was said to be in the hunt for a First Division inside-forward. He could do this in the confidence that, unlike at Spurs, money would be available. Then, however, with the worst possible timing, Palace suffered four successive defeats, starting at Bradford Park Avenue, and an ankle injury forced the dependable Terry Long out after 214 consecutive appearances.

Then, in his fifth game in eight days (including Army fixtures), Byrne will have left Rowe glowing with pride and satisfaction. Playing for England Under-23s against

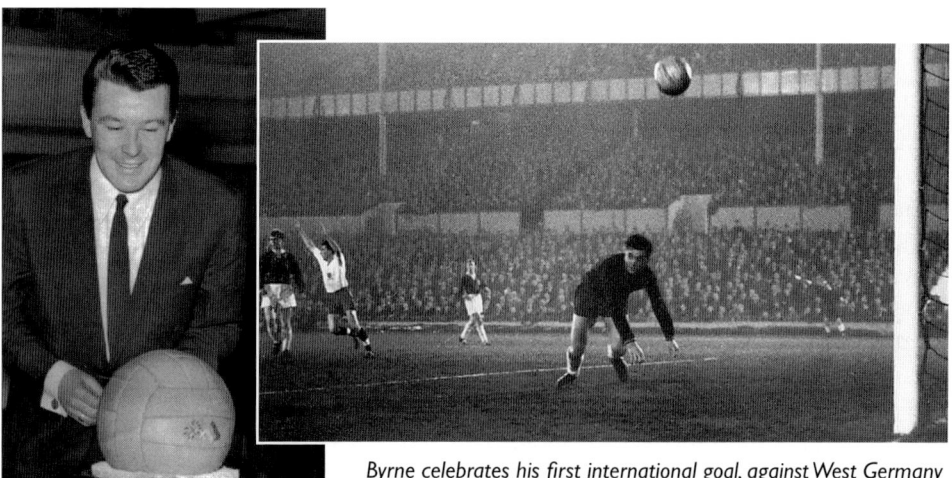

Byrne celebrates his first international goal, against West Germany Under-23s at, of all places, White Hart Lane.

Left: *He examines the post-game reception cake.*

West Germany at White Hart Lane, he not only scored his first international goal as England comprehensively won 4-1, but was the star of the evening. Talk began of Byrne's selection for the following year's World Cup finals and future England manager Ron Greenwood, then coaching the Under-23s, promised that if ever he became a club manager he would try to sign the Palace man. Although the boy Rowe (as West Brom scout) had spotted in 1956 already brimmed with natural skills, he only fully blossomed with Rowe as his manager and mentor. He had honed Byrne's awareness of team-mates, the need to constantly find space, his instant control and his first-time passing. It was a fine coincidence that England manager Walter Winterbottom had selected this match for an intense statistical study, involving no fewer than 70 onlooking coaches. Each had to record specific skills performed by all 20 outfield players on the pitch. The *FA Year Book* published the final statistics, player-by-player. The accompanying article, written in that publication's sterile style, drew particular attention to the (unnamed) 'England centre-forward,' who '…made no less than 106 contacts with the ball.'

Byrne, for of course it was he, had also made had no fewer than 12 attempts on goal and 62 'runs off the ball'. Despite being a Fourth Division player his points total of 240 led his nearest rival's total by 65. Some considered that Byrne's transfer value had doubled that night, even Stanley Matthews, the only man still playing from Rowe's own playing days, pressed for Byrne's inclusion in the full international against Scotland: 'Here we have a young man with superb ball control, speed and shooting power—the hallmarks of the great centre-forward.'

As if that wasn't enough, Johnny then scored six for his Army side the following day! Unfortunately he finally ran out of steam when promotion rivals Northampton arrived at Selhurst Park. Summersby gave Palace an early lead but Northampton quickly replied twice, finally winning 3-2. The result was good news for Peterborough, whose own win that day pushed Palace out of first place after five months. Armchair critics in South London were quick to direct their ire at Uphill, who had now netted in just one of his previous 12 outings. Not pretty to watch, Uphill needed goals if the less-informed fan was to be satisfied, and the prolific Woan, his departure lamented by many, was about to torment Palace.

At least one erudite and insightful Palace fan came to Rowe's defence that week: 'Palace, thanks to Arthur Rowe, have shown the Press and the public the best football and produced the happiest results since the war.' However the correspondent added, ominously: 'If Aldershot win, and our old friend Alan Woan scored two or three, Arthur Rowe's name would be mud.' Aldershot did indeed make things difficult, netting twice, the second, inevitably, from Woan. Petchey was then pushed up-field and scored from Summersby's through ball but, for a third consecutive game, Palace finished pointless, prompting a nasty jibe at 'push-and-run' from Dick Graham's friend John Matthews of the *Advertiser*: '[Aldershot] have a rugged spirit—guts if you like—that carries them through against more artistic sides like Palace, who cut pretty patterns but cut no ice.' So Palace, according to Matthews, had presumably 'cut no ice' when scoring an average of nearly three goals a game in the 37 games up until Aldershot. What (or who) in a magnificent Crystal Palace season could have so warped Matthews' normally reliable perception? Peterborough, with games in hand, now moved away from Palace, prompting the *Advertiser* headline 'HOPE OF TITLE RECEDING FAST'.

The Easter weekend included two meetings with fierce local rivals Millwall. Reviewing his team's form Rowe felt recent bone-hard pitches had favoured '... defensive, big-kicking sides,' emphasising how even Nicholson's Spurs had faltered of late. The home Millwall derby on Good Friday saw thousands of fans from London's Docklands contribute to what would prove to be the highest Fourth Division attendance of all time, 37,774. Millwall forced the pace and won corner-after-corner then took the lead. Before Palace could hit back, a long, driven goal kick evaded Choules for Peter Burridge to beat Rouse to the chase, striking the ball low into the net to make it 2-0. Palace thereafter struggled to a fourth consecutive defeat and Rowe conceded: 'The football we were playing has disappeared. It is up to the players and myself to try to get the rhythm back.' Being Good Friday, they had only 24 hours to achieve that.

Taking to the Selhurst Park turf again, they faced mid-table Oldham. Tall, direct winger Tom Barnett came in for Gavin and Rowe restored the much maligned Uphill to the centre. Multiple changes were unlike Rowe but games were running-out. *Sports Special* TV cameras were there and six minutes of highlights demonstrate Rowe's instructions were to quickly close Oldham down:

> Right from kick-off Byrne and Uphill press Oldham defenders into a hasty forward pass and wing-halves Long and Petchey soon take possession. Byrne nearly creates the first goal, exchanging passes with Summersby, feinting to skip past a defender, playing the ball into left-winger Colfar's path, before Summersby's downward header from the resulting cross is parried away by the 'keeper for a corner. Petchey, facing his own goal, collects a wild Oldham clearance, turns on a sixpence, switches the ball onto his left foot and strikes a sweet through ball bisecting the defenders straight into Summersby's path as he enters the right-side of the penalty area. With just the 'keeper to beat, Summersby tries to find the far corner of the goal with a calculated, side-footed shot but it just skims the far post. Although he should have scored, it had been a classy attempt.
>
> With tension mounting and Palace so badly in need of something after four consecutive losses, things worsen when Oldham take the lead. As Palace go to the centre-circle for the re-start, Byrne and Summersby take up positions either side of Uphill, and Byrne claps his hands together, rallying the flagging troops. As commentator Alan Weeks points out, 'Crystal Palace have been attacking almost constantly'. Then relief arrives as Colfar finds his way past the right-back and crosses to the edge of the left-hand side of the area with his back to goal Uphill directs his pass first time into the approaching path of Byrne on the edge of the area, and his left-foot volley is only pushed by the 'keeper onto the post and in.
>
> Uphill is then shown bringing the ball in from wide left before passing short inside to Colfar who chips a ball up to the far post. An Oldham defender's headed clearance only reaches Byrne who, retreating, has his eye firmly set on the dropping ball before trapping it and moving forward. Nobody challenges him and from the edge of the area he shoots left-footed into the left-hand corner. The

ensuing celebrations include several small boys running onto the pitch and Byrne, mobbed by colleagues, takes time out to shake one young fan's hand before the game restarts - 2-1 to Palace, ten minutes into the second half. There is a late scare with nine minutes remaining when Oldham are awarded a penalty and Selhurst Park is paralyzed into silence. Branagan strides up and shoots right-footed along the ground, aiming at the left hand corner, Rouse scuttles across, but guesses correctly, staying on his feet and watching the ball roll past the post. Captain McNichol thrusts both arms in the air. Then the final whistle sounds.

Palace had taken two points for the first time in seven matches but Peterborough retained their two-point advantage so Rowe's Championship hopes were sliding. Travelling the seven-and-a-half mile return trip to Millwall's Cold Blow Lane ground just 48 hours' later, Palace needed to avenge their Good Friday defeat. After 30 minutes Heckman smashed home a rising drive just inside the post. Within minutes it was 2-0, the same player preventing a ball going out of play then moving in on goal and firing an angled shot against the far post, Barnett tapping in the rebound and Palace claimed the two points. Uphill had again demonstrated his effectiveness, one fan saying how much he admired Rowe for '…allowing his knowledge of football to override the screams of those who fail to realise that with Uphill alongside him, Byrne is a different player.' So Palace ended Easter 1961 with a satisfactory collection of four points from six. Later to join Palace, Millwall's Peter Burridge recalled a post-match visit by a smartly-dressed Byrne to the Millwall dressing-room and summed up Byrne's performance in two words: 'Seriously good.'

Rowe now believed just two of the remaining ten points would guarantee promotion, even if Peterborough were inexorably closing-in on the Championship. Owing to their FA Cup exploits, Peterborough still had 16 points to play for against Palace's 10. But one Palace fan stated happily: 'I say to all those critics of Crystal Palace that we have had the best football this town has had for many years. And to those who want to tell Mr Rowe who to pick and how to play, I say don't be foolish, because Mr Rowe is the finest manager we could have.'

Byrne, playing against the French Army in Algeria, missed the trip to Workington which followed, while Colfar and Summersby played despite having been suffering 'flu. A penalty conceded by McNichol proved to be the only goal of the game. Rowe's headaches grew when Petchey then suffered a pulled muscle and Byrne picked-up an injury in Algeria. Peterborough then beat York to move four points clear. Second place was probably now as good as it could get for Rowe but at least promotion was all but certain (the only other club with a remote chance of promotion, York, needed to win all five remaining games). So a week still promising much for Rowe began on Monday, April 17th, when his great love, Tottenham Hotspur, managed by his apprentice Nicholson, defeated Sheffield Wednesday 2-1 to claim the First Division Championship for the first time since his own Spurs side had beaten the same side in claiming the title exactly ten years' earlier. On this occasion the man who Rowe brought to Spurs, Danny Blanchflower, had been the driving force, the shining example, the biggest contributor to the triumph. Showing their appreciation, Spurs' fans had rushed onto the White Hart Lane pitch at the final whistle, chanting 'WE WANT DANNY!' recalling similar chants ten years earlier, of 'WE WANT ARTHUR!'

Two days later, both points at home to Aldershot would take Palace into the Third Division. Meanwhile York, still retaining faint hopes of promotion, travelled to Accrington Stanley. Palace first held a board meeting, Chairman Wait announcing the club had 'agreed on the players we were looking for' for the now all-but inevitable Third Division season of 1961-62. Ominously, Aldershot arrived armed with former Palace strikers Alan Woan *and* Mike Deakin (who had moved from Northampton). After 15 minutes Woan steered a pass into the path of winger Taylor, who chipped the ball over the onrushing Rouse. The ball was entering the net anyway when Deakin gave it a final nudge, stifling the home crowd's celebratory mood. Wishing so much to reward their much-admired manager and their fans, the Palace side grew anxious but, eventually, the visitor's offside trap failed and Byrne stroked a high pass through for Summersby to run onto before shooting low past 'keeper Millard. Rouse pulled-off a miraculous save from a close-range Woan volley as time ran out before, with just three minutes' remaining, Petchey's cross was nodded forward by Uphill. Goalkeeper Millard hesitated and Barnett, getting his own head to the ball, found the net for the winner. As Barnett leapt high in celebration, Rowe and his directors slumped with relief and, after Palace almost

19th April, 1961. Promotion to the Third Division at Rowe's first attempt is celebrated in the home dressing-room. The players, left to right, are captain Johnny McNichol, Ron Heckman (who had been a Spurs' apprentice under Rowe's management), goalkeeper Vic Rouse and full-back Alf Noakes. Despite the occasional reverse, this success put Palace on the path to becoming the 'Eagles' of today.

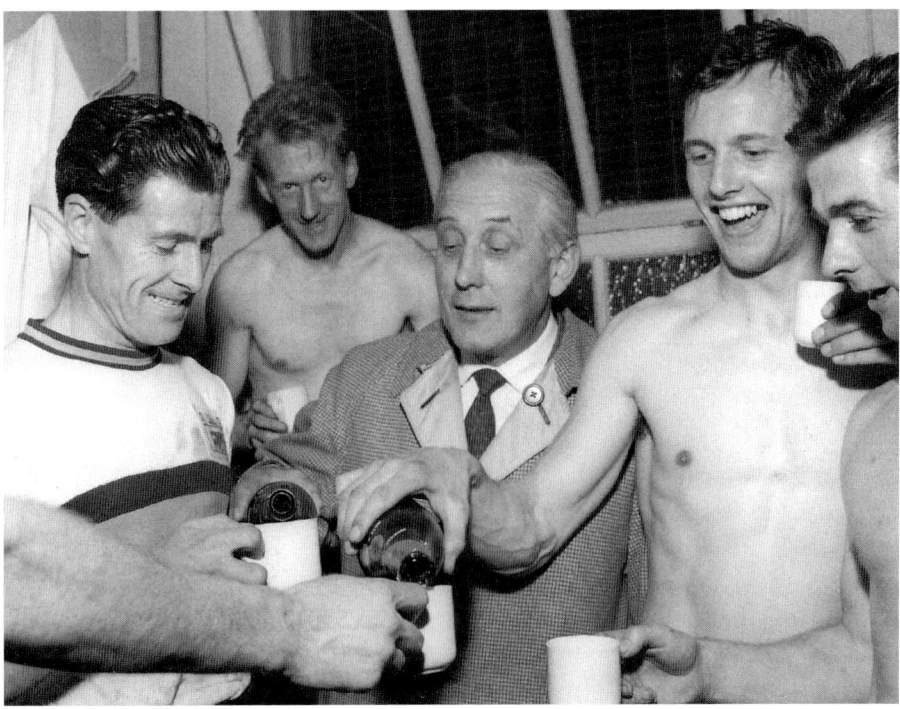

made it 3-1, the final whistle sounded. During the match Tiddles the cat, now the Club's official mascot, had repeated his trick of wandering on to the field of play, timing his re-appearance perfectly.

For an extraordinary third time in three managerial roles Rowe had tasted success at his first attempt. First Chelmsford, then Tottenham, now Crystal Palace. Had it not been for the fairy-tale first Football League season enjoyed by Peterborough and Byrne's excessive international and Army commitments, the Championship would surely have been Rowe's. Chairman Arthur Wait was delighted that following eleven long-suffering years as a Crystal Palace director, he had finally enjoyed a promotion. After the game Rowe poured champagne, surrounded by his victorious players. He said 'I am as happy as I was when Spurs earned promotion into the First Division 11 years ago. And that's saying a lot'. Following the bitter end to his White Hart Lane days he so richly deserved to enjoy such success again.

On April 24th Desmond Hackett of the *Daily Express* wrote: 'Arthur Rowe, creator of England's finest football, will most certainly put on that familiar wrinkled brow and quizzical air when he reads today that I have named him Football Manager of the Year.' Hackett also drew attention to the success of Rowe's pupil Nicholson and his 'Double'-winning side, and also to that other pupil of Rowe's, Alf Ramsey, whose Ipswich Town side had simultaneously gained promotion to the First Division. Hackett ended his tribute by naming Rowe 'Mr Crystal Palace' and, although Rowe would never lose his deep-set love for Spurs, there is little doubt that he had taken his latest club very much to heart, too. After all, it was the club which had given him another chance. In view of later developments, it should be noted that Assistant Manager Dick Graham commented: 'I regard it as an honour to work with Arthur Rowe. I am convinced he is the greatest man English soccer has known.'

Meanwhile Johnny Byrne, feted on all sides, was named in the full England squad to tour Portugal, Italy and Austria. This, he said, made him feel he was walking on air, and he was also soon to be demobbed from the Army. In celebration he said: 'Mr Rowe is a great chap who has helped me a great deal.' In that evening's match programme Rowe returned Byrne's tribute: 'One of the great pleasures and rewards that a manager can enjoy is to watch the progress of a young lad from his teenage days of immaturity to the day when one can lean back and say "Well, he's made it." The nicest thing about the lad's progress is to know that his progress as a person has matched his football advance.' As skipper Johnny McNichol put it, only under Rowe's management had the immensely promising Byrne truly 'arrived'.

Palace took full points from their final three outings. At Crewe, despite missing both Byrne and Long through injury, Palace were said to look '…champions all the way' and the gap with Peterborough was reduced to three points. On the tenth anniversary of his Spurs Championship success this result meant Rowe had steered Palace to their all-time away win record, 13 of 23 games and, with two games remaining, a record points total of 60. The night before Palace's penultimate fixture against Stockport, Peterborough travelled to Southport knowing that were they to lose their remaining two games, Palace could still claim the Championship. Southport raised Palace's hopes when finding the Peterborough net no less than

On April 26th 1961 Byrne cheated his Army 5-a-side colleagues so that he could arrive at Selhurst Park just in time to help Palace gain two crucial promotion points against Stockport!

three times, but the prolific visitors inevitably scored three too, which confirmed them as Champions.

Palace needed a win against Stockport to at least protect their runners-up spot from Northampton and Bradford Park Avenue, and Byrne nearly didn't make kick-off, arriving from his Army camp with just minutes to spare. Here lies a story, the like of which will never be repeated: committed to playing in a five-a-side Army tournament that same day, Byrne planned to leave for London by car as soon as his side were knocked out but his team kept advancing further than he had anticipated, and the minutes were ticking by. At this point he offered to go in goal. This done, he 'arranged' for an opposition goal or two to enter his net, enough to ensure elimination from the tournament. Then, he beat a hasty retreat leaving Warwick just after 3pm and with no M40 in those days, he arrived at Selhurst Park with just five minutes' to spare for the 7.30 kick-off! Poor Johnny Gavin was stripped and psyched-up to take Byrne's place. Rowe gave Byrne quick instructions and out he went into rain, thunder and lightning. Despite the appalling weather, a solid 15,822 had turned-up. It remained scoreless at half-time and Stockport, defending desperately, looked like holding out. Then, just past the hour mark, Palace earned a corner-kick, Byrne knocking it short. Receiving it back, he weaved his way along the by-line, avoiding four challenges, and the crowd's anticipation rose. Byrne shot, the 'keeper could only palm it away and Summersby picked-up his 23rd goal of the season, a strike which also broke Palace's highest scoring total for a single season. Then Byrne again drifted past several defenders before hitting a low pass through the middle into Summersby's stride, and the chunky inside-forward shot under the diving 'keeper for his second. Stockport pulled one back but Palace gained their two points. Byrne's disloyalty to his Army unit had not been in vain!

Going into the last game Northampton were required to beat Mansfield by a 3-0 margin and depend on a York win over Palace in order to capture the runners-up spot. Meanwhile the Palace players were playing for a share of a £220 bonus for finishing second and, five minutes into the second-half, with the score 0-0, Byrne pressured centre-half Jackson into an error, Summersby following-up to tap in the only goal of the game. The 17,885 fans at Selhurst Park returned home happily clutching souvenir promotion brochures.

Palace's points total was the club's highest-ever, 64, yet another record under Rowe's watch. Summersby had taken his personal goal total to 25, just five short of Byrne, while the York victory was Palace's 29th in all (one more than Peterborough) and another all-time record for the Division. Finishing just two points' short of Peterborough, Palace's 64 points and 110 goals would normally have seen them crowned champions but at least Rowe had now put Crystal Palace truly on the map. Without doubt it was this promotion which provided the initial impetus for Palace's swift rise right through the Divisions over the following eight years. When Rowe had been appointed, one supporter mocked Wait's comment that keeping the club running would require 20,000 gates at Selhurst Park. Yet under Rowe's leadership that had all but been achieved: a final average gate of 19,092, which exceeded that of two First Division sides. Rowe had proved once more that attractive, buccaneering, front-foot, passing football went hand-in-hand with financial gain, income through the turnstiles having increased by 27% under his management. Wait claimed it had been the club's 'best post-war season', not only due to promotion but because '… there was some grand football to watch.'

Bob Pennington quoted Wait on Rowe: 'He does what he likes, how he likes, when he likes. But above all — he *knows*. Then there is the rich humour of the man that has saved us in many a crisis.' Terry Long said: 'Arthur Rowe was the best manager. Just his way and the way he wanted to play. Simple, straightforward. Push-and-run, give and go. Everybody loved it, because you were always involved. It was a lovely, relaxed way to play football.' 'Relaxed' is an interesting description. Perhaps it felt relaxed because it involved perpetual motion and involvement, with little time to dwell on what might be about to happen.

Rowe looks on as prizes for the Crystal Palace Advertiser's 'Player of the Year' awards are presented. The main award went jointly to Terry Long (second-left), and Johnny Byrne, who is represented by his wife Margaret, Byrne himself away on England duty. The other players are captain McNichol (left) and Vic Rouse.

When the *Crystal Palace Advertiser* polled its readers for 'Palace Player of the Year' (the result a tie between ever-dependable Terry Long and the intoxicating Byrne), Rowe typically praised the newspaper's invitation to the resulting prize-giving event for having included Palace's back-room staff. At the club's own celebratory banquet, special guests included Rowe's mutual admiration team of Ron Burgess and Alf Ramsey. After Wait had paid tribute to the players and staff he then (as also mentioned in Chapter 14) gave an assurance that, at Palace, Rowe would not be shown the 'lack of consideration' which contributed to his ill-health at Tottenham, adding a plea to all connected with the football club: 'Let us be behind him and don't let us see him broken down again.' One can only assume Rowe was unembarrassed by these references to his Tottenham setbacks. Presenting Rowe with a marble clock, Wait confirmed he had indeed been first choice as manager before the appointment of Smith '…but after his serious illness he lacked confidence in himself. Not now, though. He's done us proud. He is a First Division manager and I hope he will be one with us.'

Rowe himself introduced some levity when referring to the club's swear box, which in a turbulent year under Smith had tallied £16 and 15 shillings (approximate value £375 in 2022). In the season just finished, however, the total was only £11 and 5 shillings. 'Up to Easter, I believe there was [only] about 30 shillings [£1 and 10 shillings]' the manager laughed, 'then came adverse results!' With the assembled gathering chuckling, Rowe paused for comic effect, before adding: 'I put in £10!'.

The manager was then overwhelmed with emotion when paying tribute to the one person to whom he attributed so much of his success — his wife Pom.

Simultaneously that spring, Nicholson's Spurs, with their roots firmly set in Rowe's 'push-and-run', became the first side in the twentieth century to simultaneously win both League Championship and FA Cup in the same season. In a 1960s article on how most English clubs still only paid lip-service to coaching, Sir Stanley Rous, Secretary of the FA, wrote: 'It is no accident, I believe, that the Spurs have for long been a club that views coaching seriously, that really believes in it and takes steps so that it can be carried out in all weathers. If many clubs, especially at the middle and lower levels, ceased merely to pay lip service to coaching, the standards of the whole game could be raised dramatically.'

Wait announced an increase in admission prices for Third Division football, but, unlike many administrators in the game today, he saw the common sense in not increasing admission for children — after all, children were the fans of the future. Also, after the lack of financial backing he had suffered at Spurs, Rowe was delighted to work with a board which understood the requirement of team building. He was confident about the Third Division challenge. 'All the teams who have come out of the Fourth Division have finished in the top half of the Third,' he said. It will then have been a painful duty for him to release seven players, but one who was kept on the payroll was Dave Sexton, despite his prolonged absence and the ongoing treatment on his knee injury.

The first man Rowe bought that May was none other than former England international centre-forward Ronnie Allen, 32, who had been unhappy at West Brom since Vic Buckingham's departure, and had announced his intention to move into club management. For that reason he claimed to relish the opportunity to work under Rowe. Rumours had it that Palace had trebled Allen's pay to £60-per-week. According to Allen himself, Rowe intended him to 'general' the forward line, aside from passing-on his experience to younger players. Although slight in stature, only 5ft 8 in and 11 stone, Allen had an eye for goal and was strong with either foot. Starting out as a winger, he eventually became a deep-lying centre-forward and made his England debut in the first international following the landmark 6-3 home defeat to Hungary in 1953.

Identifying that centre-half was a position to be strengthened, Rowe also snapped-up West Brom's promising 20-year-old centre-half Brian Wood who, by the end of his first season, would be voted Palace's 'Player of the Year'. Needing a left-back, Rowe acquired the experienced Roy Little, veteran of two FA Cup Finals for Manchester City, and speedy Charlton winger Eddie Werge, scorer of 19 goals in 44 League appearances. Another arrival was ball-playing inside-forward John Cartwright from West Ham, capped by England at Youth level and, like Bobby Moore, inspired by the progressive coaching ideas of team-mate Malcolm Allison. Ron Greenwood's dismissive assessment of Cartwright was that the player himself knew too well how talented he was, thus assuming success would come easily, but the Palace boss felt he was worth a gamble.

Meanwhile, Johnny Byrne left for Lisbon with England, anticipating a debut full cap before the tour was over, but, despite commentators rating him above both Bobby Smith and Gerry Hitchens, he remained on the bench. While he was away Italian side Fiorentina enquired after his availability, Rowe telling the press 'They are wasting their time' but Rowe and Wait were agonising over just how big a pay hike their star player would command now that rich Italian clubs were sniffing around. So when Byrne returned, Rowe asked how much he would want to sign a new Crystal Palace contract. Byrne replied, 'I don't know. You tell me,' and Rowe, with fingers no doubt crossed behind his back, offered double what the other players were on. With no hesitation Johnny accepted, putting his faith in his manager and mentor masterminding Palace all the way to the top. 'In effect we got [Byrne] cheap,' Rowe admitted later.

At the end of July Rowe moved house, finally settling south of the Thames, in Mitcham. By then he was also on the verge of signing another First Division player, another off the West Ham conveyor belt, the 20-year-old inside-forward Andy Smillie, a good friend of Bobby Moore. Rowe believed that Smillie '…could become nearly in young Johnny Byrne's class.' Good with both feet, he had won England Youth caps. With several inside-forwards coming in, and Byrne unlikely to play centre-forward with Allen's arrival, it increasingly appeared that 25-goal Summersby would move to half-back, risking the break-up of his excellent partnership with Byrne. Nevertheless the *Advertiser*, impressed with Rowe's acquisitions, boldly announced: 'That dream of a swift, elevator-like rise into the Second Division becomes more of a reality', adding…

'Palace obviously mean business.'

18

A Bold Start, then…

MANAGING CRYSTAL PALACE 1961-63

'…it was the triple blending of chairman Arthur Wait, manager Arthur Rowe and player Johnny Byrne that made Crystal Palace the most exciting club outside the First Division.'

BOB PENNINGTON, *NEWS OF THE WORLD*, ON CRYSTAL PALACE FOOTBALL CLUB 1960-61

Having bolstered his playing staff to confront Third Division football, Rowe holidayed in Spain while Arthur Wait was encountering 'football mad' locals in Bermuda. This persuaded him that Palace should tour there the following summer in belated recognition of promotion. The chairman also planned a showpiece friendly to inaugurate Selhurst Park's new floodlights.

In pre-season Byrne listed five reasons for remaining with Crystal Palace, including how the directors '…treat professional footballers as human beings', how he also had '…the best and wisest manager in football', that he enjoyed the '…civilised atmosphere,' and finally, that he had 'never once heard [Rowe] bawling out or praising an individual in the presence of others'. Byrne was also content with Palace's new bonus system: for attendances over 16,000 players would receive an extra £1 per thousand. As the average home attendance in 1960-61 had been over 19,000 and larger gates were now inevitable, the incentive was considerable at a time when the average house cost £2,500. At 30, George Petchey was also happy with Rowe's suggestion to combine playing with coaching the apprentices.

However, a lot of the optimism was deflated when Palace crashed 7-2 to fellow Third Division side Reading in pre-season. Despite the game's friendly status, Rowe admitted '…seven goals against you is serious …you can't say it does not mean anything.' Meanwhile Byrne featured alongside the likes of Johnny Haynes and Bobby Charlton in a Football Association XI facing Spurs in the annual Charity Shield match at White Hart Lane. In Palace's Public Trial match, first-team versus reserves, Rowe immediately dispelled the notion that the experienced Allen would perform his deep-lying centre-forward role, fielding him instead at outside-left, Byrne taking the central role. This proved to be a very contentious decision.

With new men Allen, Little, Smillie and Werge all starting at Torquay in August, Palace's scintillating football almost saw them four-up in the opening half, but although Allen created an early goal for Byrne, only Summersby's effort was added, for a final score of 2-1. Next, Notts County arrived at a Selhurst Park buzzing with anticipation and, with Palace's front men repeatedly switching positions,

County struggled. Werge put Palace ahead before his cross was nodded home by Summersby. Late on, Smillie added two for a final score of 4-1, the close-to 30,000 spectators earning each man a £12 bonus. With two win bonuses of £4 each, the season's first week saw up to £20 extra enter the pockets of the players (the equivalent of £450 at the time of writing).

However, Rowe suffered a blow when captain McNichol broke his arm at home to Swindon, but the visitors too, lost a man before Allen opened his Palace account from the spot. Four minutes into the second-half Smillie nodded into the path of Byrne, who half-volleyed home. Swindon then struck back before Allen's second penalty completed the scoring. Three wins from three put Rowe's promoted side ahead of the pack and the manager might have been forgiven if recalling his 1949-50 Spurs' side which had similarly climbed a division without a dip in results. However, realist Byrne bluntly stated in his new *Advertiser* column: 'Don't let us kid ourselves that the team are playing well. Far from it; we're just not clicking at all.' He admitted that against Swindon he himself had held the ball more than normal '...in an effort to slow the game down while we collected our thoughts, but even that went wrong.'

Two away draws followed before Palace were overwhelmed by powerful visitors Northampton, who that morning had spent £7,000 on Rowe's former target at Spurs, powerful Cliff Holton. Werge became Palace's second long-term injury victim before centre-half Len Choules was outfoxed by striker Pat Terry who was left free to chip Rouse. Under pressure from Holton, Rouse then punched into his own net and the score reached 3-0 when Holton's spot-kick almost took the net with it. Palace pulled one back before Holton shot against the onrushing Rouse, the ball rising conveniently for the same player to nod into an unguarded net. Uncharacteristically bitter about the refereeing, the Palace boss claimed fouls on both Choules and Rouse and considered the penalty offence was minor. Down to ten men against a prolific scoring side, the defeat nevertheless failed to prevent criticism of 'push-and-run' resurfacing. An extremely poison-penned John Matthews wrote:

Supported by Roy Summersby (right), Byrne scores at home to Swindon in August 1961. The 3-1 result gave Rowe his third win from three following promotion from Division 4.

Croydon Advertiser *chief Palace correspondent John Matthews (left) appeared to mimic the same 'language' as both Assistant Manager Dick Graham (right, with Rowe) and ex-England forward Ronnie Allen. His anti- 'push-and-run' comments became increasingly biting, although the time came when he would look back upon Rowe's methods with nostalgia.*

'[Palace] pushed and ran, flicked and twisted intricately, and carried about as much bite as a toothless dog'.

Considering the loss of two men to injury, the adjustment to a higher level of play and the bedding-in of four new signings, results had not been disastrous. Byrne meanwhile denied a rift between himself and Allen. Rowe restored Uphill to add physicality against Queen's Park Rangers, but this meant Summersby stepping down after 125 consecutive league and Cup games. Smillie soon put Palace ahead and some quick-fire 'push-and-run' between Byrne, Uphill and Smillie set Allen up to score from a tight angle but Rangers replied twice, Palace settling for a point. As at White Hart Lane, criticism of 'push-and-run' only arose when results faltered. That evening BBC radio presenter Jacob de Vries unwisely asked Rowe 'Does [push-and-run] work in the Third Division or is it only for the big brothers of the First and Second Divisions?' Rowe responded: 'When [my men] do it, yes [it works], but we are not doing it well at the moment. At Tottenham, we had Eddie Baily, a natural; we have not got a natural, but when it does work in a lower division it can be even more pungent than in the First Division.' When Rowe said he did not possess a 'natural', was he highlighting Byrne's growing tendency to retain possession for too long? When De Vries dared suggest Palace might benefit with greater use of the long-ball, Rowe bluntly responded: 'I think we have had more long-balls, to my annoyance, this season than last. That is what I call "hope football". You cannot live on that. You must have purpose and pattern.' This rare display of irritation may have been provoked by two of the recent additions to the staff whose clear preference was for long-ball football (of which, more later).

When Byrne's performances were blamed on close-marking, Rowe countered: 'Every first-class player must expect tight-marking' he said. To the suggestion Byrne would do better playing in a higher division, Rowe batted straight back: 'I met some people who saw the [First Division] Fulham-Bolton game last week and then came and saw the last half-hour of ours. They said our football was much the better.' He even had a snappy response when asked about improving the stadium: 'People will watch good football from bad surroundings, but they will not watch bad football from good surroundings.'

Palace met QPR again in the first round of the League Cup, this time suffering a heavy defeat. After conceding four goals in the first five games, eleven followed in the following three, by which time eight players were being treated for injuries and

Byrne had yet to catch fire. Rowe was not fooled by a 3-0 win at blustery Barnsley, bluntly saying 'Barnsley are not a terribly good side', and Palace proceeded to take just one point from the next 10. Meanwhile, Rouse became the victim of anti-'push-and-run' venom, the loudest voices wanting him to hack the ball down-field, but one lone voice pointed out that '…nine-out-of-ten big kicks by goalkeepers are headed straight back by a towering centre-half,' adding '…especially with a forward line as small as Palace's.' For Rowe, Palace and Byrne (now left out of the 'shadow' World Cup squad), the introductory Third Division season had proved underwhelming. Gifted with the type of freedom to strengthen his side which had been unavailable at Spurs, perhaps Rowe had introduced too many new faces too soon. He then demonstrated his muscle, leaving Allen out for the visit of Portsmouth, now managed by George Smith. An early physical assault on Byrne by 36-year-old wing-half Jimmy Dickinson (a veteran of England's 1953 and 1954 defeats by Hungary) symbolised Smith's intention to interrupt 'push-and-run'. Heckman still put Palace ahead but Portsmouth equalised and then hit a late winner. Smith's grin as he strode into the Palace boardroom afterwards evinced his bitterness when sacked 17 months' earlier and he made it clear to all present that 'justice had been done'.

Aside from their West Brom connection, neither Ronnie Allen nor Dick Graham were believers in 'push-and-run', particularly if practised outside of the top level. Graham later became renowned for his belief in winning 'ugly'. In omitting the much-heralded Allen, Rowe seemed compelled to show the ex-England star who was boss. With five defeats from 13 games, albeit in a higher division, Chairman Wait was forced to deny his club was in crisis. The *Advertiser*'s Matthews then broke the story that Allen did not relish playing out wide and had requested he be played at centre-forward. Matthews then stated: 'He will have to do it via the reserves.' The impression given is that a famous former England international had confided his woes to a 'star-struck' provincial journalist. Rowe himself would surely have kept such disagreements private. Now Rowe was compelled to issue a strong public rebuke, stating that the ex-England man would play a few matches in the reserves until '…he adapted his style to Palace's needs.' Clearly such public discord between star player, Assistant and Manager will have encouraged the very stress levels Wait had resolved to protect Rowe from. It had never been likely to be an easy season as Palace faced higher-quality sides and many raised their game at Selhurst Park in front of attendances up to three times greater than they were accustomed to.

Then Rowe took what for him was the unprecedented step of publicly criticising a player of his by name, bluntly telling the press: 'If Johnny Byrne had been able to show us his best form straight away, our problems would never have begun.' The manager also chastised Byrne for retaliating on the pitch when provoked, Chairman Wait crediting him for the resulting improvement in the star player's self-control. Yet Byrne almost immediately worsened matters when publicly rebuking young team-mate Brian Lewis for himself retaliating when fouled.

Following a home draw with Southend, Matthews' match report now mercilessly criticised 'push-and-run' with cynical, cutting phrases, including: '…Palace footled their way to what looked like another reverse…' engaging in '…round-the-houses stuff that took so long to build up.' He also cynically threw in for good measure Palace's '…zig-zag patterns'. Odd that Matthews, an otherwise splendid reporter, should be so unsupportive of the self-same tactic which had brought extraordinary success and pleasure to spectators just four months' earlier (indeed, history shows that Matthews would later reflect on Rowe's era with dewy-eyed nostalgia). The journalist had clearly been swayed by his long-standing friendship with Allen's close friend Dick Graham. When I asked another *Advertiser* reporter of the time, David McClelland, about the relationship between Graham and Matthews, he replied that they were not merely close but '*very*' close.

For Rowe this was beginning to uncomfortably echo the *Tottenham Herald*'s support of 'push-and-run' criticisms made by Spurs' directors. Encouraged by Matthews' comments, letters from fans critical of Rowe's methods began appearing in print, this a mere 13 matches since Palace's promotion. One specifically referred to the manager's disinclination toward using the long ball, adding: '…but Northampton, Lincoln, QPR and others have exploited it…'. Refusing to alienate fans, Rowe tactfully responded: 'When people stop writing about football, they are losing interest in the game.'

That Allen was filling his preferred centre-forward role, but in the reserves, suggests Rowe had resigned himself to using the well-paid Allen only as back-up for Byrne. After the last of five poor results, an otherwise respectable 3-2 defeat at Watford, Rowe knew he had to tighten his injury-hit defence. At least back-up centre-half Evans had now recovered and Rowe's defensive changes saw an instant turn-around in fortune. Yet the real surprise was up front: Byrne moving to inside-forward to accommodate Allen, finally granted his wish to play down the middle. At Shrewsbury, Evans kept prolific striker Arthur Rowley at bay and the forwards benefited from Summersby's support. However, on the day luck played quite a role in a 5-1 victory. Uphill's weak shot had crept inside the post before Rowley equalised, then Allen put Palace ahead again. Thereafter no fewer than three Shrewsbury defensive errors ended the scoring although Allen took much of the credit. However, Rowe will have been happier that his new-look defence had kept the home side to just the one in reply. This result triggered Palace's best spell, winning nine of 14 League games and reaching the FA Cup third round. When third-placed Peterborough arrived the attendance was down on the club's Fourth Division meeting, but a crowd of 28,886 was still phenomenal. In the 28th minute Allen scored from a 'push-and-run' move and more superb football saw Byrne (twice) and Uphill take the score to 4-1. With a minute left, Hudson made it 4-2, but there was still time for Allen to turn and slam his shot into the roof of the net for a princely finale to a first home win in seven. A draw at Northampton left Palace just six points short of the leaders, so a successive promotion was still on.

The *Advertiser* then finally admitted Allen's performances had been disappointing, but added that Allen's difficulty had been to fit into a side concentrating on the '…short ball.' One wonders why Matthews failed therefore to question Allen's decision to join a 'push-and-run' club? Had Allen seriously not expected to play 'push-and-run'? Or had he harboured alternative reasons for joining the club? Rowe admitted: 'I am in an invidious position. I was instrumental in getting Allen; I am instrumental

George Petchey (left) admires Roy Summersby's superb volleyed goal from Johnny Byrne's cross in a 2-0 win over Newport County.

in dropping him. Ronnie has got friends in the game who are friends of mine [Vic Buckingham, for one] and I like the bloke. This situation is as embarrassing for him as for me. But I just cannot pick the team from players I like.' Presumably, as an international Allen would never have imagined being left out of a Third Division side but Arthur Rowe sought perfection and, as with Tommy Harmer, some players did not fit. A second goal at home to Newport County made one wonder why Allen was needed at all, especially for those witnessing Byrne's exquisite lob from the left met by Summersby's unstoppable volley. In this game Summersby was heralded for his '…cultured football and unflurried but accurate distribution.'

Then, following the feisty nature of the home League defeat to George Smith's Portsmouth, a phenomenal 30,464 turned-up for the Cup meeting with the same club. When Rowe stated: '…our lads have *every* incentive to win', it suggested revenge for Smith's crowing over his side's League victory. As Dickinson had snuffed Byrne out of the League encounter, Rowe instructed Uphill to in-turn to harass Dickinson this time. Seven minutes after half-time Byrne put Palace ahead and, within minutes Uphill's low shot was fumbled by the 'keeper and Heckman scored from close-in. Buoyed by the two quick goals Palace played continuous, fast 'push-and-run' and, in the 81st minute Rowe was vindicated for his choice of Uphill over Allen when the ex-Spur set-up the third and final goal, Heckman's second. Rowe was quick to point out that his decision to select Uphill against Portsmouth did not make him any cleverer than he had been the day before. 'I had to make a decision and not be afraid of what people thought. If you are going to live in this game, you have got to back your own judgement. I did not want Jimmy Dickinson to control this game as he did in the League match in September.'

Three days later Rowe told shareholders: 'I would not say that we are playing our best team, but it is our best team of the moment'. This perhaps inferred that his 'best team' depended on Allen's will to fit the system. Vice-chairman John Dunster supported Rowe over Allen and objected to the local press advising the Palace manager who he should select. Dennis Uphill also spoke on the subject of Allen that week: 'Even if you have no faith in my ability, then I think you should have plenty in Mr Rowe — even if he picks me ahead of Ronnie'. Meanwhile Rowe had discovered a young defender named Alan Stephenson playing for London Schoolboys. The tall, slim Stephenson's destiny was to captain Crystal Palace and later partner the great Bobby Moore, but at that time he was reluctant to pursue a football career following his earlier rejection by Leyton Orient. To help Stephenson simultaneously pursue another career option, Rowe helped find him a 9-to-5 role at the *The Times* newspaper, the boy training two nights a week and playing for Palace juniors on Saturdays.

The first of two League games before returning to the Cup trail saw Rowe's men play some delightful soccer against Grimsby. Smillie scored twice from brilliant through balls, the first supplied by Allen, the second Petchey. Grimsby replied but Heckman made it 3-1 before Smillie completed his hat-trick. Afterwards Byrne publicly apologised for having twice kicked the ball away in anger: 'I realise how pathetic I was. Strolling around as though the park was my own and, to top it all, have the referee book me for a show of arrogance.' When Palace then overcame Coventry at Highfield Road Long was unusually tormented by his winger, Stewart Imlach, whose name went into Rowe's notebook. Allen's penalty and Uphill's winner raised Palace to fifth, Rowe declaring: 'Promotion is definitely on.' The improvement, he said, was down to a tightening of the defence, not, he pointedly added, due to 'the "Byrne-and-Allen" show.' Meanwhile, Rowe was then further personally buoyed by a Croydon-area soccer-lover's observation: 'I see quite a fair amount of local football, and I have been quite impressed by the genuine attempts on the part of local teams to play football. Personally, I think this can, in part, be attributed to the example set by Mr Rowe since he has been manager of Crystal Palace. No doubt most of these players have seen the Palace and benefitted accordingly.'

Byrne then became only the third Third Division player to be selected for England — he would make his debut against Northern Ireland on November 22nd 1961[*]. Byrne quickly acknowledged Rowe's help: 'Arthur has done a lot for me. I am certain his way is the proper way to play soccer'. When Byrne took the field at Wembley Rowe, Wait and Byrne's Palace colleagues watched from the stands. The player said he didn't feel nervous, this despite teammates including Bobby Robson, Johnny Haynes and Bobby Charlton but it had perhaps been unwise of manager Winterbottom to field two debutant strikers in one game (Ray Crawford from Ramsey's Ipswich Town partnered Byrne). Although failing to score Byrne did get all three of his chances on target, as well as setting Crawford up for a chance which was struck against the crossbar in the 1-1 draw. He had done enough to attend a pre-World Cup 1962 England get-together where players watched film shows and learned of problems they might encounter in South America. Inevitably, this raised Byrne's hopes of making the trip.

A fourth successive League win, 1-0 at promotion-chasing Port Vale on December 2nd, saw Palace climb to fourth which left Palace with a fighting chance of successive promotions but Bristol City then left Selhurst Park with both points, Palace's second defeat in 11 games. Torquay's visit then proved to be a memorable 600th

---

[*] *There have been five overall as of January 2023 - Tommy Lawton (1947-48), Reg Matthews (1956-57), Byrne, Peter Taylor (1976) and Steve Bull (1989).*

career appearance for Allen. Being the penultimate Saturday before Christmas, the attendance fell to 13,834, but after just six minutes Allen crossed for Heckman to head Palace in front. Uphill added two more before Torquay replied. Then, five minutes after the restart, Byrne made it 4-1. A second for Heckman and another reply from Torquay took it to 5-2 before Allen's cross provoked an own goal, for 6-2. Up until then Allen had been involved with five of the goals. Then Byrne was held in the area and Allen took the penalty. However, changing his mind when running-up, Allen slammed it over the bar. Time still remained for a seventh Palace goal via Smillie's head. Who provided the cross? Allen, of course, in what some considered his finest performance for Palace. But Rowe was unimpressed with his side, blaming '…too many below-par individual performances.' He will have been concerned too that his defence had conceded five times in two outings, a statistic that was about to worsen.

Rowe granted 21-year-old centre-half Brian Wood his debut at Swindon. On a semi-frozen surface, a crude home side frequently hammered the ball skywards or into the stands but 'keeper Rouse was unusually uncertain on crosses, Wood suffered a tough baptism and Swindon's 19-year-old winger Mike Summerbee was too hot to handle for veteran McNichol. 0-0 at half-time, Swindon struck five times after the break - a 7-2 victory one week and a 5-0 annihilation the next! A trip to Hull's frost-bound Boothferry Park followed and, despite Uphill's return, Palace soon conceded twice. However, thanks to some superb football it was 2-2 by half-time and Palace began thrilling spectators with soccer which would have been admired even in perfect conditions. Just a minute into the second-half a superb passing spell ended with Byrne smashing a left-footer home to put Palace ahead for the first time before Petchey's 25-yarder completed a 4-2 victory. A local freelance reporter, free of the *Advertiser*'s anti-'push-and-run' bias, wrote: 'Palace served up some brilliant soccer, showing far the better ball control, keener tackling, smarter anticipation and, above all, passing that was so accurate it mocked the conditions.' Palace had already scored 59 times, a similar rate to the promotion season.

Palace were drawn away to First Division Aston Villa in the FA Cup 3rd Round on January 6th 1962 but in the build-up to the game the sad news was received that

Left: *Aside from the great Tommy Lawton, Byrne became the first outfield player from the Third Division to represent the full-England side when appearing against Northern Ireland at Wembley in November 1961.*

Right: *Three weeks later he was back in Third Division action for Palace, looking on as Uphill's effort beats the Torquay goalkeeper for one of Palace's seven goals.*

Dave Sexton, after 12 goals from 28 appearances, had finally been forced to retire. There can be little doubt however that his future management and coaching career owed more than a little to Rowe's influence. Meanwhile Allen was approached by both Chester and Accrington Stanley to be their manager. He turned them down, he said, because he could learn more from '… watching someone like Arthur Rowe at work.' Like Graham, however, his wife was from South London. What if a similar opportunity were to open-up at Selhurst Park?

Arriving at Villa Park Rowe, trying to banish painful recollections of Spurs' semi-final defeat of 1953, joked on entering the away dressing-room: 'Hello, it must be an important game today, Byrne is stripped already' (the player being renowned for still wearing his jacket even as his colleagues prepared to run out onto the pitch). Rowe had set a tactical plan. Aware that a common Villa ploy was for lanky striker Derek Dougan to flick-on long punts from deep, Rowe played twin centre-halves, Petchey supporting Wood in the middle. This left Summersby teamed with Allen in the middle in a 4-2-4. Rowe also asked Allen to double-up with full-back McNichol to help snuff-out international winger Peter McParland. This is a rarely known example of Rowe utilising special tactics to counter opponents.

Palace fell behind when the referee diverted Allen's pass to Vic Crowe, who slipped it quickly to Harry Burrows, whose low cross-shot beat Rouse. But, on an ideal surface for 'push-and-run' (wet but firm), Palace had been playing superior soccer to the First Division side long before Byrne ghosted past two defenders and hammered a 20-yarder into the top corner. With the 2,000-or-so Palace fans still celebrating, Cartwright sent a pass cutting through the Villa defence, goalkeeper Sims dived but failed to retain the ball and Uphill poked home. By half-time Villa were level via McParland's header, yet Rowe's men still left the field at the break with applause ringing in their ears, having played their way out from the back instead of utilising the more customary 'big boot'. Early in the second-half Heckman's firm cross from the left was met by Byrne's head and the roof of the net bulged, only for Dougan to promptly scramble another equaliser. Palace were giving their all in a

The side Rowe put out to face First Division Aston Villa at Villa Park in January 1962. Third Division Palace were twice ahead but eventually fell 4-3 to a freak goal in the dying seconds of injury time. Back: *Long, Summersby, Petchey, Rouse, Wood, McNichol.* Front: *Allen, Byrne, Uphill, Cartwright and Heckman.*

magnificent match until, two minutes from time, Rouse made another of great save, this time from Alan Deakin, and Palace fans anticipated a money-spinning replay. A questionable amount of injury time took the clock to 4.55pm, with some in the Press Box putting their notebooks away.

Deakin then pushed a pass out to Burrows, 35 yards from goal, with Dougan and McParland waiting in the middle, frantically waving for a cross. Burrows fired it over, through the mist. Distracted by the two attackers Rouse allowed the ball to pass over his outstretched hands, leaving defenders behind him desperately trying to keep it out, but the ball nestled in the net. Palace were out of the Cup in the cruellest fashion and Rouse's earlier great saves were now forgotten. At the final whistle Allen, determined for a good result on his return to the Midlands, picked the ball up and kicked it furiously into the stand. For Rowe it was another last-minute Villa Park knockout, but he will have appreciated this comment from a Villa fan: 'If this is Third Division football, let us have more at Villa Park' and even more, from another: '[Palace are] *the best team to play at Villa Park since Spurs last season.*' Villa reached the quarter finals where they lost to eventual winners Spurs, so Palace had done well to push them so close.

Arthur Rowe meanwhile had initiated an informal group of London club managers for periodic meetings. 'It will help us to get to know each other better and help us to understand several tricky problems,' he said. Then Chairman Wait invited top Czech side Slovan Bratislava as opponents for the official opening of the new Selhurst Park floodlights but he continued to aim higher, holding two meetings with the directorship of five times European Cup winners Real Madrid. An excited Rowe said that for top Continentals, '…the game is a craft and an art, with the main thought always that the possession of the ball is the one thing to go for and keep' but could Rowe and Wait seriously expect the likes of Ferenc Puskás and Alfredo Di Stéfano to face little Palace? Admission prices would require a big hike to cover Real's fee.

Following the Cup exit at Villa Park, Rowe dropped Rouse in favour of 18-year-old Bill Glazier, explaining that '…in the long run it could be the best for Vic.' Rouse's dry sense of humour would suggest he greeted Byrne's bogus news report about him that week with a chuckle: 'Vic Rouse has a bad back. Rumour has it that he has been bending down to pick the ball out of the net too often lately.' At home to Halifax, Palace hit the net four times but the visitors themselves struck three, for a final score of 4-3. Having now conceded a worrying three goals per game in their last six fixtures it was a bad time to visit prolific-scoring QPR, but a win would take Rowe's side into third place. However on a muddy pitch few passes reached their target. In one single action Byrne failed with three attempts before Rangers netted the only goal of the game. As Rangers were to top-score in the entire Football League that season Rowe at least saw the positives in how Wood and Glazier had stiffened-up his defence, some even considering Wood the better buy from West Brom than Allen.

But a 3-1 home defeat by Barnsley triggered a mass exit of home fans. Palace's mid-season run of seven wins from nine games was now a fading memory, Rowe saying the Villa defeat '…had taken the stuffing out of some of the players.' While

Byrne was simultaneously exposing disagreements between his colleagues over man-for-man marking, the unease between Rowe and Allen persisted and Byrne said he would be glad to get away to join the England party for training.

Despite heading the Third Division scoring table, the last thing Palace now needed was a trip to Portsmouth, who were unbeaten at home. Byrne put Palace ahead but the defence capitulated and Palace returned pointless. At Roots Hall, Palace rescued a point against Southend even after losing Wood following a clash of heads, but five winless games saw a second promotion fade from view. So the two Arthurs met with Johnny Byrne. For a newly promoted side, Palace had accumulated a healthy 34 points from 32 games, not bad when just two points were awarded for a win, and were they to earn all 28 points still to play for they would total 62, which in some years was enough for promotion. But it was clearly the right time for Rowe and Wait to cash in on their star asset and they announced his availability, the chairman admitting: 'Byrne would be 26 or 27 before we could hope to win a First Division place.' Arsenal and Chelsea enquired first, while Rowe contacted West Ham's Ron Greenwood, who had of course once said he would buy Byrne should he become a club manager. In his autobiography, Greenwood would refer to Byrne as no less than the '…Di Stéfano of British football' but the player himself had some regrets: 'Palace are a second home for me… to leave is a wrench.' As for Rowe, he at least had some positive news, having just captured Alan Stephenson's signature on a professional contract. If Palace fans had only known then just how outstanding Stephenson would become, their sorrow over Byrne's loss would have been tempered.

The friendly with Slovan Bratislava went ahead, Byrne marked by Jan Popluhár, who a year later would be the losing captain in the World Cup Final. A brilliant Byrne-inspired Palace overturned the top Czech side 3-2. Poor weather and Byrne's impending departure then saw the lowest crowd so far witness a 2-1 defeat of Shrewsbury. Before turning his attention to the trip to high-scoring Peterborough, the manager and his players attended a Croydon Chamber of Commerce lunch where the manager confessed his passion for Crystal Palace Football Club, saying: 'I hope I shall live to see the day when there will be a great big stadium that will be the best in the country.'

At Peterborough, Rowe re-established the Byrne-Summersby combination. Despite his high regard for Rowe, Summersby never understood why the manager had undone his goalscoring partnership with Byrne, preferring to move him back to the 'engine-room'. After all, Rowe always had outstanding half-backs in his sides: Nicholson, Burgess and Blanchflower, for example, and he had similar faith in Summersby. A Glazier error saw Peterborough go two ahead, Bly adding to Hudson's earlier goal. Although Byrne pulled one back, the 'Posh' eventually added two more. Palace's erratic afternoon climaxed in a mad chase to reach Peterborough Station by 5.16. Their fleet of hired taxis became becalmed in traffic and Byrne and Smillie took to running with a mile to go. Two cycling autograph hunters leant Byrne and Smillie their bicycles and, as Byrne put it, he and Smillie finally '…rode in triumph into the station'. In such a manner did Byrne's outstanding contribution to Crystal Palace Football Club (and his close partnership with Rowe), end.

Byrne's move to Upton Park proved timely for West Ham manager Greenwood, as his side had just crashed 6-0 at Burnley. Palace fans, still awaiting news, ominously noted their idol's absence from the side to play at Bradford Park Avenue. On a surface of ice and mud, Palace performed so badly in a 2-0 defeat that locals considered Palace the worst side to have visited all season. Byrne's departure was a firm signal to both fans and playing colleagues that promotion would have to wait. The *Advertiser* reported events in the style of a state funeral: 'It was at 1.10pm that Palace's blackest moment of the season came' — the moment the 22-year-old who many even today consider the single greatest player in the history of Crystal Palace FC signed the contract taking him to West Ham United for a fee of £65,000 including an allowance for the return to Palace of 24-year-old forward Ronnie Brett. At that time £65,000 was the highest fee to have passed between two English League clubs and would have purchased around twenty average family homes.

Brett had not even been Rowe's primary target for part-exchange. That had been a young half-back who until then had made little impact. The player's father had played under Rowe for Chelmsford and advised his son that dropping two divisions might enable him to become an established first-teamer. Rowe, who held great stock in friendships and character, will have been keen to sign the young man. His name was Geoffrey Hurst. A player who, ironically, would later credit his partnership with Byrne for his development as a striker and thus for scoring the only-ever hat-trick in a World Cup Final. Greenwood, despite then describing Hurst merely as a '…strong, honest wing-half', had a notion the player might succeed as an attacker, so had politely turned Rowe down, Brett arriving instead.

Wait glumly said of Byrne's departure that it was '…the worst day's work we have ever done,' adding '…the boy is worth far more than money to us.' He continued: 'I feel especially sorry for our manager, Arthur Rowe, who will have to reshuffle the plans he had built around Johnny for this season and next.' Rather than using part of Byrne's fee to pay-off the club's overdraft, Wait would much preferred to have

Byrne signs for Ron Greenwood of First Division West Ham. Byrne had maintained loyalty to Rowe and the Club despite risking his personal progress. Below: Compensation for Rowe came when his highly promising find, centre-half Alan Stephenson, signed a professional contract.

seen Byrne leading Palace's attack to attract bumper Second Division attendances. Byrne's international career, cut short by injury, would see him net eight times in a mere eleven England appearances while at Upton Park he became the catalyst for West Ham's best-ever side, forming part of a talented quartet with Hurst, Moore and Peters. When describing the success of Rowe's 1960-61 Palace side, correspondent Bob Pennington had described the '…blending of chairman Arthur Wait, manager Arthur Rowe and player Johnny Byrne that made Crystal Palace the most exciting club outside the First Division.' Now Arthur Rowe had to restore belief that his side could still advance without their greatest talent.

Before Real Madrid arrived Palace faced seven League games beginning with Reading at home. The injured Werge, Allen, Uphill plus of course, Byrne were missing and Palace lost even though the visitors suffered a broken leg victim. Only 12,507 passed through the turnstiles and Palace spirits plunged further. As with all managers Rowe had a chairman hovering over his shoulder but, instead of contemplating his dismissal, Wait was instead concerned only for his manager's health. At least Rowe now had the distraction of coaching his Third Division side against the greatest club side in the world, before a spirit-reviving trip to sunny Bermuda. Byrne, choked to miss Bermuda, would at least turn out as a guest player against the Spanish aristocrats.

A 2-1 defeat at already relegated Newport was hardly surprising considering the loss through injury this time of Petchey and Smillie, but Rowe was still worryingly reported to have gone down with what was reported as 'flu. In front of the smallest home crowd since October 1957 (7,041) and with Graham in temporary command Palace struggled to find a way through against 2-1 winners Hull, and Allen's display was so poor that even John Matthews wrote of the ex-England man's contribution: 'For a man of his great ability and experience [Allen's] performance was not very creditable.' When Graham and director John Dunster called by Rowe's home later with a report on the game, they told him that the 'majority' of the side had fought hard. It is unlikely Rowe expected the 'majority' to include Allen, who then failed to appear in any of the remaining eight games or the showpiece friendly with Real Madrid. Rowe put the run of poor results down to a loss of the '…pattern of play' ['push-and-run'] and that as a result '…we merely became the same as every other team.' He added: 'We must try to find it again.' Was Allen banished as being the major cause of the lost 'pattern of play'?

Season '61-62 had witnessed the expected step-up in quality of opposition but nobody could have anticipated the disruption caused by Allen's arrival. Perhaps Rowe, too, had contributed to Palace's disappointing season, perhaps introducing too much new blood but there was also the glut of injuries. When one fan referred to the '…stubborn insistence on a method which, although labelled "push-and-run", has mostly been nothing of the sort', his criticism inadvertently reinforced Rowe's own assessment: 'push-and-run' had not been consistently adhered to. Another, more positive correspondent happily recalled occasional 'scintillating displays of classic football'.

But at least one game, at Bradford Park Avenue, offered a pointer to future success. Wood shared central defence duties with slim 17-year-old debutant Alan

Stephenson which also freed-up Summersby to return to the front line. Four missed chances saw Palace settle for a 0-0 draw but a clean sheet, something not achieved in the previous 16 outings, meant a celebration of sorts was in order. Some fans still feared a massacre against Real Madrid, but Rowe himself was greatly looking forward to it, saying: 'When we invited Madrid it was not to a challenge game but as an exhibition. At our best we could not hope to live with them and neither could about 80 or so of the clubs in the Football League.'

Meanwhile, to end the season, Palace faced four sides fighting for promotion (one of them twice). As delighted as Rowe had been with Stephenson's performance, he did not want to risk the young man at Grimsby, explaining: 'I am a great believer in letting a boy get his feet wet and letting them dry again after he has had his baptism'. In the event, Palace came close to taking both points but there was no shame in the resulting goalless draw against a side promoted at season's end.

The last home fixture before Puskás and Di Stéfano planted their illustrious feet on the Selhurst Park turf was against Coventry City and Brett found the net, but crew-cutted Scot Stewart Imlach, his name already jotted down in Rowe's notepad, set up Roy Dwight's equaliser. Nine minutes into the second-half Smillie conjured the ball over his shoulder before scoring with a dipping volley off the far post. Imlach then set up Dwight's second equaliser, the final goal of the match but at least Palace had now gone undefeated for three games. But, at Brentford, Palace's last fixture before the red carpet was rolled out, the Palace men trod carefully in fear of injury and duly crashed 4-2, ex-Spur Johnny Brooks netting twice for Brentford. Not quite the result Chairman Wait required to sell those expensive Madrid tickets and with Palace having gone nine games without a win, the word 'relegation' was beginning to be heard.

Rowe's men had to put their League form behind them to face some of the greatest players in the history of football. Real Madrid had qualified yet again for the European Cup Final and leading their glittering array of talent was Alfredo Di Stéfano, twice-winner of the European Footballer of the Year title and the imperious Hungarian torturer of England back in 1953 and 1954, Ferenc Puskás. Included too were Spanish internationals Francisco Gento at outside-left, Luís del Sol at inside-right and, at the back, international centre-half José Santamaría. Aside from raising Palace's profile and attracting new long-term support from South London, the official purpose of the encounter was to open the new floodlights. A lavish Park Lane Hotel reception was also held, at which Wait said 'I feel it a great honour that the greatest club in Europe came to play a poor little Third Division club.' As per the custom of the times, Wait raised a toast to Her Majesty the Queen. However, having done so, he was compelled to likewise toast the then Franco-led, fascist Spanish State.

As the game approached, a relaxed and healthy-looking Rowe gave several on-pitch TV interviews. In one, standing before the main stand and bathed in sunshine, he fielded questions from the BBC's John Timpson. With the players training just behind him, he was asked about the high ticket prices, responding with a smile: 'Well, the best is worth more than the ordinary, isn't it? I mean, Real Madrid are the best, everyone must want to see them. I want to see them myself, never mind

Three all-time soccer greats chat at the Park Lane Hotel reception which Crystal Palace held for the visit of the great Real Madrid: Ferenc Puskás, Arthur Rowe and Alfredo di Stéfano.

anything else!' He added: 'If it stays like this [Rowe looks to the sky to a backing spring chorus of birdsong], I think everything will be alright.' Timpson suggested the game might prove no more than a '...procession', but Rowe took no offence. Indeed, he pointed out that in the European Cup Final against Eintracht Frankfurt, '...there were a lot of goals there, the majority of them for Madrid and naturally, we can expect something like that, but who knows?' Still in the midst of a testing season Rowe was clearly enjoying a return to the national limelight.

However, in common with Palace's oscillating fortunes that season, the sunshine turned to heavy rain on the day, curtailing the number of last-minute spectators drawn by pre-match publicity. Having not insured against abandonment, Wait anxiously followed weather reports. Palace needed at least 25,000 to turn up if only to meet their financial obligation with Real Madrid. As it was, 24,740 eventually braved the elements, which proved just enough. The side Rowe sent out to compete with the greatest club side in world football was:

Rouse (Glazier, second-half); McNichol, Little; Long, Wood, Petchey; Brett, Summersby, Byrne (guest), Smillie, Heckman (Lewis, second-half).

Real wore their hallowed all-white strip, Palace switched to their change kit of pale blue shirt with narrow claret stripes, and claret shorts. By kick-off time fog was added to the raw, damp conditions and Wait's worries grew. He recalled standing with Rowe, looking out at torrential rain and fog, having just presented Real Madrid with a cheque for £10,000. 'It looked at one time as if we and the Spanish Ambassador would be the only ones there', he later recalled.

Of 20-plus press photographers attending, only two extreme optimists crouched alongside the Madrid goal. Those at the other end were soon snapping away, the European champions going two-up in eight minutes. First Puskás' put Tejada clear, his cross easily nodded home by the fast-arriving Di Stéfano. Within 60 seconds Palace defended a free-kick but Tejada found captain Gento and his volley flew past Rouse. Rowe's heart must have sunk — for all his realistic expectations, he will not have wanted his side trailing so early. The fear of a double-figure Madrid total rose in the minds of even the most optimistic Palace fans, while Rowe himself will have been hoping a good performance might help erase the disappointments

A BOLD START, THEN... MANAGING CRYSTAL PALACE 1961-63

of the League season. However Byrne, whose temporary return had engendered conflicting emotions in the home crowd, then had the Madrid defence at full stretch before passing inside for Summersby to strike a shot which 'keeper Araquistain hung onto. By the 29th minute Palace were performing what the *Daily Mirror* described as '…delightful push-and-run stuff' and when Brett put Byrne through on the right, the resultant cross led to a brilliant headed goal from Heckman. This stung 'Los Blancos' into action and a Puskás free-kick swerved past Rouse, making it 3-1 (but what did the score matter when the Selhurst Park score-sheet already listed Gento, Di Stéfano and Puskás)! Six minutes from half-time, the visitors really rubbed-in their superiority with a walking-pace move which still undid the Palace defence, Sánchez finding the net.

Rowe then granted Glazier a pre-arranged run-out for the second-half, and the youthful 'keeper soon walked tall having made two superb saves from Puskás. Palace fans then cheered another Palace goal, Byrne wriggling through before crossing for Smillie to make it 4-2. But by far the greatest moment for home fans came in the 70th minute, when the longest-serving Palace player on the field, right-footed defender Terry Long, used his left foot to strike home a cross-shot which travelled 30 yards without rising more than six inches off the ground until it stretched the far netting. Palace suddenly trailed by just one goal. Of this memorable moment Desmond Hackett wrote: 'The thousands who came to applaud the fine arts of Real Madrid suddenly found themselves roaring with cup final ferocity. For the unbelievable

Rowe clearly enjoyed the limelight when interviewed in the build-up to the friendly with Real Madrid.

Left: Press build-up for what was only a friendly encounter was huge. How would a mere Third Division side fare against the five-times winners of the European Cup?

Below: Di Stéfano heads Real Madrid ahead, leaping in front of Palace captain John McNichol.

Johnny Byrne, guesting from West Ham United, looks on as a Real Madrid defender desperately clears a threatening Palace attack.

happened in the second-half when Palace became as menacing as their masters.' Puskás then struck the post but Madrid's other attempts were dealt with by Glazier and a final score of 4-3 had a nice ring to it — Real had maintained their reputation and Rowe's Palace had surprised not only their magnificent conquerors, but their fans and the onlooking press. As for Byrne, Real Madrid's Santamaría said Byrne '…was one of the most difficult players to stop I have ever played against', while Di Stéfano described Byrne as 'world class'. Puskás, in Muhammad Ali fashion, said Byrne '…would not be in the wrong place with Real Madrid, but he talks more than I do!' This is how Real Madrid lined-up: Araquistain [Vicente, second-half]; Casado, Miera; Sánchez [Ruíz, second half], Santamaría [Marquitos, second half], Pachin; Tejada, Del Sol [Pepillo, second half], Di Stéfano, Puskás, Gento.

Just two days later attention returned to dour Third Division football. At promotion-chasing Bournemouth on Good Friday Palace dominated the second period only for a defensive mix-up to let in 'Dickie' Dowsett (Rowe's Spurs discovery, now Bournemouth's top-scorer) to snatch the only goal. The following day Port Vale were the first side to tread the Selhurst Park turf since Real Madrid. Glazier finally achieved a shut-out after 13 attempts but Palace only collected one point. The two remaining games produced another goalless draw and a 2-2 draw at fifth-placed Bristol City. This proved a nightmare for Wood who suffered cartilage damage, costing him his trip to Bermuda. Also, had it not been for going down to ten men, Palace may have achieved that elusive win on the final day.

The Palace boss could at least take comfort from four clean sheets out of the last seven outings, saying 'There were many matches drawn when our football deserved a victory' before adding 'there are no points for deserving — only doing!' Summing-up, he said the season '…had us on edge, waiting for things to go, always promising to go, and never really clicking into top gear' but Arthur Rowe could take credit for the advances of youngsters, particularly Glazier and Stephenson, while his junior side had won an Amsterdam tournament. Smillie, more than justifying Rowe's faith in him, ended with an excellent 19 goals from 39 League and Cup appearances but the manager still had to confess that 1961-62 had been one of the most frustrating and disappointing seasons he had ever experienced. Injury or sickness repeatedly prevented him from fielding his first choice line-up, while Byrne had often disappointed. 'When he did perform,' continued Rowe, '...as against Aston Villa, Bratislava, Real Madrid and Hull City away, then we were lifted. I reckon he was only at 50 per cent of his form in other games. Right until the time he left we were still waiting for him to play at the level we know he can play.' Aside from Byrne the only other individual to single-out for criticism was Ronnie Allen who clearly lacked the will to adjust to 'push-and-run'. So much had been expected from these two outstanding talents; Byrne would initially continue in the same vein at Upton Park, managing just a single goal from 11 West Ham appearances and missing-out on the 1962 World Cup squad.

There had been an overall drop of approximately 60,000 fans through Palace's turnstiles compared with the previous Fourth Division season. Palace finished 15th of 24 teams, although 11 of the 18 defeats were only by the odd goal, and Palace scored just four fewer than champions Portsmouth. Other plusses had been Rowe's successful introduction of Wood and Glazier, while Stephenson had shown he had a tremendous future ahead of him. Indeed, Rowe now selected the 17-year-old to replace Wood on the plane to Bermuda. As for the tour itself, big scores indicate games were hardly competitive but an enthusiastic Rowe still said it had been the best tour he had ever been on.

That summer Rowe produced a snappy Crystal Palace FC rule book for presentation to each member of the club's staff. 'The best results on the field can only be achieved', he wrote in the book, '...when there is all-round co-operation

A happy group of Palace players and officials in Bermuda during the summer of 1962. This was their belated reward for the 1961 promotion. Rowe stands alongside Assistant Manager Dick Graham and trainer Ted Brolly. Ron Brett, in white shorts, who had joined in part-exchange for Byrne, stands at the bottom of the staircase between Roy Little and John McNichol.

and teamwork, and a happy atmosphere.' With season 1961-62 in mind, he will have been compelled to emphasise that. In standard Rowe fashion, each page included a catchphrase (see also Chapter 9), the first proclaiming: 'Remember! A happy club is a sure foundation for a successful club', followed by: 'No player can command success, but every player can deserve it.' One essential, added Rowe, '…is whole-hearted effort and determination. This is well put in such sayings as:

"A winner never quits and a quitter never wins."

"It's not the size of the man in the fight but the size of the fight in the man."'

Rowe continued: 'And still on the subject of courage what about this one? – "All men are equal 'tis said but it's what they are equal TO that matters."'

Some were Rowe originals, but he admitted collecting others and modifying them to make them relevant to football. For example, he utilised the old saying 'A fool and his money are soon parted' but added '…likewise a fool and the ball'. Instead of 'Look before you leap', Rowe has 'Think before you pass'. Instead of 'A bird in the hand is worth two in the bush', Rowe has 'A pass on the ground is worth two in the air'. His catchphrases gave 'colour' to his rule book, giving the players, as he said, '…a good reason for taking their books out from time to time and reading them.'

He rounded it off with: 'In a great team, all minds must think alike.' But on that score, sadly, he continued to work in the company of two influential men who did not appear to share his own footballing beliefs.

SEASON 1962-63   Rowe had to rebuild his post-Byrne side, strengthening weaknesses. At the end of June he finally captured Millwall striker and captain Peter Burridge, who had notched 56 goals in just two seasons at The Den. Rejecting Millwall's insignificant reward for his success Burridge was happy to accept Rowe's £35-per-week offer. The 5ft 9in, well-toned striker possessed a lethal left-foot and, in time, played a huge role in Crystal Palace's ascent. He had been a fan of Rowe's Spurs, his idol Ted Ditchburn. He had then joined the RAF voluntarily instead of two years' compulsory National Service, which lost him three years of his football career. So he was already 24 when starting out with Leyton Orient and 28 by the time Rowe came calling. Burridge recalled sitting in the manager's office when his potential new boss noticed he was born in 1933. 'I was thinking he was not going to sign me after all but in the end he said "OK" and that was that!' Rowe had probably assumed him to be around 25 at most. It was of course an echo of Alf Ramsey's transfer to Spurs.

Another capture was Coventry winger Stewart Imlach, who had so impressed when facing Palace. The diminutive Scottish international, an FA Cup winner with Nottingham Forest, had partnered Eddie Baily at Forest (coincidentally Burridge had also partnered Baily at Leyton Orient). Imlach's career is described in his broadcaster son Gary's award-winning book, *My Father and Other Working-Class Heroes*. Of his dad's remaining in Division Three when joining Rowe, Gary wrote that he would at least be playing '…stylish football for a sympathetic boss.' Rowe also acquired experienced Charlton left-back Don Townsend (described as 'a classy passer' and father of Andy) while his final capture was the understudy to Blanchflower at Spurs, Bill Dodge. Of course, even four newcomers combined

Left: *Rowe's four summer signings in pre-season training, 1962, winger Stewart Imlach, left-back Don Townsend, midfielder Bill Dodge and striker Peter Burridge.* Below: *Burridge finally scores his first of many for Palace (against Shrewsbury, Allen watching).*

could not adequately replace one Byrne and the burden of replacing the England man's goal quota fell on Burridge. Palace's public trial was then bedevilled by injuries, particularly Petchey's twisted ankle, but Burridge achieved a fourth strike in four pre-season outings. Rowe's final whistle verdict: 'A good match… and they can all play football, can't they?'

Palace, notably without Allen, began the season at home to a Halifax side kicking everything in sight. Imlach's entire career was thrown into jeopardy when one wild, early tackle left him limping throughout the rest of the game. By Monday, fluid had formed on his knee. A bitter Rowe criticised the referee, who he felt should have sent two Halifax players from the field. Meanwhile Burridge nearly got off the mark, evading two defenders before 'keeper Downsborough parried his shot and the eventual goalless draw failed to lay Byrne's ghost to rest. Then both Imlach and Petchey were missing at Shrewsbury and Palace fell two behind early on. Rowe's half-time talk produced an improved display but the game finished 3-1. Cartwright had performed well but he was never to fulfill his promise and later, as a successful youth coach, he openly admitted to promising youngsters that as a player he had been a 'coward' on the pitch, thus encouraging his 'pupils' never to pull out of a tackle.

Palace's winless run now extended to 15 games across two seasons and Rowe bluntly admitted his side had '…played as badly [at Shrewsbury] as I have known.' At Eastville, Palace's build-up play was easy on the eye, but, in the final quarter, Bristol Rovers struck twice, while for the return with Shrewsbury Rowe reinstated Allen in his preferred role at centre-forward. Allen's performance was far more committed, yet Palace still fell two behind before Burridge rounded the 'keeper to open his Palace account. Five minutes after the restart Allen tied things up at 2-2 and it was cruel on Rowe to then witness five Palace near-misses involving the

The tragic Ron Brett's short-lived return to Crystal Palace saw him play just seven League games plus his penultimate appearance, against Real Madrid, starring in the same forward line as the man whose place he had taken in the Palace side, the guesting Johnny Byrne (right). Roy Summersby is the man in the middle.

woodwork or goal-line clearances. By the following morning, August 30th 1962, with only two points captured, Rowe may have wondered how far his chairman's patience could stretch.

But he was about to be struck by news putting any sporting torment in the shade. Having sat alongside Cartwright watching the Shrewsbury game, Ronnie Brett spent the rest of the evening in London with West Ham's reserve 'keeper Brian Rhodes. In the early hours their car collided with an articulated lorry, Rhodes suffering mere cuts and bruises but with seat-belts then not compulsory, poor Brett died at the scene. On hearing the shocking news Rowe said 'It is a terrible tragedy—a terrible shock.' He may have harboured a degree of guilt, having presented Brett with few opportunities since his return to the club. Now, in a cheerless, sad and shocked atmosphere, Rowe prepared a side to face Brighton. With Wood being Rowe's third loss to injury in just four matches, Stephenson made his second first-team appearance. In Brett's memory black armbands were worn and a minute's silence observed. After 21 minutes young Stephenson's rare error gifted Brighton the lead. Stephenson then suffered a hefty boot to the face, returning to the field only as nuisance-value on the right-wing. These setbacks sapped belief from Palace, but with just twenty minutes' left Petchey equalised. Then, five minutes' later, Stephenson shook off both his error and his injury to meet Allen's corner-kick firmly with his head, finding the net and leaping high in celebration. Sadly, however, a last-minute Brighton equaliser further prolonged the wait for a victory.

By this stage, Arthur Rowe had experienced a prolonged period of adversity: the disappointing season 61-62 (especially the failure of Allen and Byrne to combine their tremendous talents and live up to expectations), the departure of Byrne without first achieving Second Division football and, perhaps, a feeling that with so many injuries and Brett's tragic loss, luck was against him. Moreover, he was working with at least one colleague who was unsupportive and lacked sympathy with his fundamental footballing beliefs. It was just 16 months on since Rowe proclaimed: 'This is a happy club,' adding, 'everybody trusts each other.' But, as at Tottenham, Rowe now had cause to look over his shoulder. From this distance in time it seems extremely odd that Chairman Wait had granted Dick Graham the title of 'Assistant Manager', rather than 'Coach' or 'Trainer'. He was 'Trainer' at West Brom. As 'Coach' he might justifiably have applied for the manager's role in the event of Rowe's departure. But, as 'Assistant Manager' he would be in prime position to apply for the manager's role in the event Rowe faltered. Meanwhile, Graham's long-time colleague Allen, too, was publicly seeking a post-playing career as a coach or manager. A struggling Third Division side provided both men with a chance to get on the managerial ladder. Brian Wait told me that without doubt 'internal factions' were active behind Rowe's back around this time, while Rowe himself will no doubt have been punishing himself for Palace's mediocre results since he had thrillingly elevated the club from Division Four. Rowe was enduring pressure similar to that he had encountered in his final season at White Hart Lane.

Forty-eight hours after the Brighton draw both centre-halves were unavailable to face high-scoring QPR. Dodge made his debut and Rowe rested Burridge after scoring just one goal in five appearances. The game followed a familiar pattern, QPR fans applauding Palace's sharp inter-passing while at the other end Rangers struck four times. Despite Palace often missing four or more men through injury, John Matthews returned to the use of snide expressions such as 'genteel attackers' and 'cross-the-park football'. In so doing he critically ignored the negative effects of Byrne's departure and Allen's arrival. Rowe had lost one supreme footballer (the 'jewel in his crown') who fully backed his methods, gaining instead a fading star who had signed-up to play 'push-and-run' yet had little or no appetite for it. A fixture away to Carlisle, propping-up the table, was a 'must-win' affair. Wood returned and after just three outings in his preferred central role, Allen moved back to the wing to accommodate Uphill. Palace soon trailed but recovered to lead 2-1, at last on track for that face-saving victory, even toying with their opponents. But, with seven minutes remaining, a long range shot deflected past Glazier. If Rowe had felt stress at Tottenham, managing a Third Division side who had now gone twenty games without a win will have been a tougher pill to swallow.

Ronnie Allen sits alongside Dick Graham in a team group photograph when both men were employed by West Bromwich Albion.

From last-placed Carlisle, Palace next entertained first-placed QPR. To counter the League's highest scorers, the experienced Rouse returned in goal and Rowe went with a back four. In the 24th minute Allen directed a firmly struck, airborne corner-kick back toward Summersby, 20 yards from goal, who found the net with a thunderous volley. With supreme reserves of effort and determination, Palace then kept Rangers from scoring for the remaining hour. The winless run was over at last, Palace fans surging onto the pitch to celebrate. Palace then failed to build on those two points when Bert Head's negative Swindon arrived in mid-September, but a 0-0 final score at least meant Palace had gone three games undefeated, Rowe putting this down to fielding '…something like our best team'. At Hull, Petchey, prominent in repelling early attacks, suffered a first-half ankle injury but continued. With no substitutes permitted Palace's approach became more pragmatic yet worse followed when Imlach suffered a re-occurrence of his early-season knee injury and was to be out for 14 long months. With just nine-and-a-half fit men Palace still earned a further goalless draw yet Rowe may have preferred a defeat than suffer the critical loss of both Petchey (sidelined for four more games) and Imlach, out for the foreseeable future.

At least, with the future in mind, consolation for Rowe came with the expected capture of outstanding 16-year-old inside-forward David Sadler from Maidstone United. 'If Sadler decides later to join a professional club I don't think we will be second', he said. However Rowe was pipped for Sadler, but only by old pal Matt Busby at wealthy Manchester United. Sadler thus joined Haynes and Greaves in the list of outstanding young talent slipping through Rowe's grasp, going on to collect four England caps, two League Championship medals and a European Cup winners medal.

Whenever first-choice players had returned from injury there had been an upturn in results but Townsend was next to join Imlach and Petchey on the treatment table. However Evans did then return to keep Peterborough's prolific George Hudson from scoring in yet another goalless draw. Summersby was next on the injured list before Palace set off for a League Cup tie at Second Division Leeds United, a club poorly supported but on the brink of becoming one of the strongest sides in the country. Rowe failed with his suggestion that to guarantee a much higher attendance the tie be switched to Selhurst Park. Leeds fielded not only the likes of Gary Sprake, Jack Charlton and Norman Hunter, but also the great Welsh international John Charles and were challenging for promotion under Don Revie. However a depleted Palace side still dominated, Long putting them ahead from 25 yards. But late in the game Jack Charlton headed an equaliser before a winner from Storrie arrived too late to re-start the game. The attendance was a mere 7,274, prompting Rowe's bitter reminder: 'If Leeds had come to Selhurst, with John Charles, for a replay, we would have had 25,000 here'. So having been knocked-out of the League Cup by the last kick of the game and denied bumper box-office replay takings, Rowe's most challenging spell at Palace continued.

Only two injury victims returned for the home game against Barnsley, who arrived with an offside trap. Rowe didn't watch the entire game as he took in an amateur international at nearby Dulwich, maintaining his interest in David Sadler.

So Dick Graham was in charge for the afternoon, which might explain Rowe's comments on the segment of the Barnsley game he did witness: 'There was no constructiveness about it. We are simply not geared to the long ball game'. Palace dominated but two defensive errors saw them go behind before Allen pulled one back. It was a first defeat in six and another inquest was called-for. Meanwhile Peter Burridge was still struggling to transition to 'push-and-run'. As George Petchey told me: '[Peter] liked to run on to things and whack them with his old left stick', Burridge himself confirmed this: 'We were playing nice passing in midfield but I just wanted it up-front and I was just not getting a good supply of the ball to have a few pots at goal.' A constant change of personnel around him will not have helped and history shows Burridge eventually became a Palace goalscoring legend.

Away to hotshots Northampton; Summersby returned for Allen, and fatefully, as things transpired, took over the captaincy for the first time. The home side went two goals up, but the *Advertiser* report, presumably submitted by a Northampton-based reporter, stated: 'Northampton's own fans, brought up on a diet of sheer thrust, had to admire Palace's clean moves. Especially in the second-half, as Northampton were knocked out of their complacency by quickly built-up attacks.' Indeed, Summersby twice found the net only to be given offside. Holton then made it 3-1 before Palace pulled one back through Lewis. Considering Northampton were to finish as champions, Rowe's men had put up a good show but the odds facing him rose further when Lewis then twisted a knee before the end.

As with Imlach, Holton's performance against Palace cemented his name on Rowe's wishlist. Confronted by growing fan unrest, the Palace boss was typically honest: 'They are justified in moaning. So am I. It has been most disappointing.' He went on to bemoan his team resorting to the occasional long-ball, although Palace had returned to short-passing at Northampton but Rowe then made allowances for his squad, saying that players had been bought '…to blend with young John [Byrne], and when he left, the pattern did not work out. We have not been able to play the forward-line we wanted …I envisaged an attack consisting of Lewis, Summersby, Burridge, Smillie and Imlach, with cover from players like Werge, Cartwright, Uphill, [Stan] Forster and Heckman.' Injuries meant his first-choice forward line had been unavailable for 11 of the 13 League games to date.

It is hugely significant that Rowe was omitting Allen from both his first-choice *and* second-choice forward lines, surely confirming the player's disinclination to adapt to 'push-and-run'. His talent, after all, was undeniable. Yet, as was the case with Anderson at Tottenham, Assistant Manager Dick Graham was unsupportive of Rowe's ideology, and, furthermore, he had a relationship with Allen going back to their West Brom days together. Moreover, Graham and Allen's wives both came from South London and both men were ambitious to get on the managerial ladder. Peter Burridge told me that when chatting together players would occasionally say 'For God's sake, don't tell Ron', believing Allen was Graham's 'spy in the camp', something independently backed-up, unprompted, by another player of the time.

Yet when he had left Albion, Allen had publicly stated: 'Arthur Rowe and I think along the same lines when it comes to soccer'. But mentions of Palace resorting to long-ball football when Allen participated increased suspicions that Rowe was being undermined. As an England international Allen knew he could rely on fan support, one of whom wrote demanding a club statement '…on the subject of the treatment being served out to this still fine player' while another called for a fans' boycott until Allen was restored to the side.

Defending poor results, Rowe referred to the absence through injury of the likes of Smillie, Summersby, Imlach and Petchey, asking: 'What would Spurs be like without Greaves, White, Jones and Mackay?' His continual loss of defenders in particular had prevented his establishment of a settled defensive unit. At Southend Rowe resorted to desperate moves, bringing-in reserve full-back Bert Howe (so that the 37-year-old former forward McNichol could play up front) and putting tall full-back Lunnis at centre-forward. However, the injury hoodoo struck again, Summersby succumbing early and Lunnis himself picking up a visible bump on his leg. Still, Palace took the lead when a rare 'up-and-under' down the middle was headed on-the-bounce by Smillie, over the onrushing 'keeper. Then, in the first minute of the second-half, Southend scrambled an equaliser and Werge found his own net. Smillie made it 2-2 but Southend still snatched a winner. Although it was only October, Palace already looked out of the running for promotion.

A short yet disturbing *Advertiser* report, for some reason set in bold type, then covered a Reserves' defeat at Shrewsbury. It failed to name which Palace official was in charge, but whoever it was, he wasn't happy. A club statement read: 'On Saturday at Shrewsbury, with probably the strongest second-eleven forward line fielded this season, the team gave one of their poorest displays. Following this poor display, the forwards have been told, in no uncertain manner, that they are paid to play AWAY as well as at HOME.' The forward line concerned comprised Stan Forster (a Rowe acquisition from Southern League football), Cartwright, Uphill, Burridge and Allen. Whilst it is difficult to imagine either Rowe or Wait being comfortable with players being so publicly shamed, it is equally hard to imagine all five men performing in a uniformly lacklustre fashion. Confusingly, despite the public dressing-down, one of the three, Uphill, was immediately promoted to first team duty. Things at Selhurst Park were clearly growing more and more sour.

In this bitter atmosphere Palace again confronted Northampton Town. Winger Ron Newman, signed that morning from Leyton Orient, was rushed into the line-up at outside-right, McNichol remained upfront and Rowe was boosted by Petchey's return. Yet it still took Northampton only three minutes to go ahead and by the break it was 0-2. Fan displeasure began to make itself felt, but, just after the hour Smillie made it 2-1 only for the injury jinx to then claim not just Long, but Townsend too. Palace fought on with just nine fit men yet kept the final score down to 2-1 to a side which eventually finished as high-scoring champions. The *Advertiser* now suggested the home dressing room be renamed 'Out-Patients Department'.

With a third of the season gone Palace had just nine points, relegation form, and the worst seasonal pitch conditions were yet to arrive. Fan disquiet now focussed on Wait, who told the Press he and Rowe were racking their brains to sign a quality centre-forward who could hold the ball up and score regularly. 'But where are they? Do you know one?' Wait asked plaintively. Rowe believed Burridge would benefit from dovetailing with another quality strike partner.

Rowe enjoyed a rare respite from his Palace tribulations when Alf Ramsey sought his opinion before accepting the FA's offer to become England manager. Rowe's advice suggests he was basing his opinion on his own experience as Tottenham boss, that the national side would be easier to manage as Ramsey would be working with the nation's best players as opposed to competing as Ipswich boss against clubs possessing far greater spending power. Ironically, the FA also sought Rowe's advice before committing to Ramsey, Rowe telling the FA: 'If you looked the whole world over, you couldn't have found a better man.' As for Ramsey's later pronouncement that England would win the 1966 World Cup, Rowe believed this was '…an expression of [Ramsey's] fierce desire and a subsequent conviction that it could be done. It was no cheap, throwaway phrase; it was studied.' Even as a World Cup winner the now 'Sir Alf' still sought his former manager's advice.

Despite Palace being five short of Rowe's first-choice side at Layer Road facing fourth-placed Colchester, they suddenly looked like promotion challengers again - two goals from Smillie capturing Palace's second win in sixteen. Even Rowe sceptic Matthews wrote that Palace's team work and pattern of play '…positively flowed at times and when they were ahead, Palace moved in close, intricate patterns, defying Colchester to take the ball.' For Rowe this 90 minutes was just what the doctor ordered. Would Palace's fortunes now turn?

One fan of 'push-and-run' suggested that the manager should start reporting poor refereeing decisions to the FA and that if asked for justification, he should simply supply them with his injury list… were there a piece of paper large enough to write it on! There can be no doubt that 'push-and-run' was undermined by intimidating challenges then accepted as legal by referees. As another fan added, Byrne had left Palace '…while he still had two legs.' Talking of whom, Rowe had accumulated the names of fifteen prospective replacements and looked beyond their skills, for example categorizing some as not '…of the desired off-field character', while fees for others were prohibitive. On the plus side it was around then that Rowe first spotted a local Thornton Heath-born boy playing for his Catford school. This was David Payne, who ultimately made 318 Palace appearances, many at the top level, as well as representing England Under-23s.

At home to Notts County, a less than 100% fit Summersby replaced the now sick Werge, before Rowe lost McNichol with a broken jaw in just the second minute. So for 88 of the subsequent 90 minutes it was 10 v 11, and even the 10 included Little despite his having a dislocated shoulder had to be re-located on the pitch. Palace's strong half-back line led a fighting display thereafter, only centre-forward Jeff Astle, later of West Brom and England, causing them problems. Burridge's lob veered just wide of a post, before Smillie put the ten men ahead. Thereafter Palace tried to keep possession, this only failing when Rouse was impeded on the ground as a cross-cum-shot dropped into the unguarded net. The incensed 'keeper uncharacteristically chased the referee to the halfway-line, to no avail. But Palace had now achieved three points from four against the third- and fourth-placed clubs. Poor McNichol, however, had made his last appearance. Rowe then paid a very heavy price for keeping a promise. Fielding his first-team for charity at Corinthian Casuals, Petchey's ankle problems returned and he missed a further four games.

Petchey, Smillie and Allen (right) watch as Dennis Uphill gets in a header against Notts County. Palace took a point despite playing most of the game with only nine-and-a-half fit men.

The *Advertiser* then asked why the club hadn't paid out one large sum for a single player of considerable ability to replace Byrne, instead of smaller amounts for 'lesser players'. Rowe's response was that he believed the sums paid for Burridge, Imlach, Smillie and Allen were not inconsiderable, adding pointedly: 'If we bought a class centre-forward tomorrow, it would not put all the injured players back on the field.' A fan's comment was heartening: 'I hope that the club continue their attractive style of play; fluent team play is the answer to brawn.'

Bournemouth centre-forward Dickie Dowsett had become Rowe's prime transfer target and forunately a stomach complaint prevented him from posing a threat when Palace then visited Dean Court. Rowe restored Summersby to the front line and Burridge nearly volleyed Palace into an early lead before a Rouse error saw a header bounce into his net. Before half-time Jimmy Singer added two more. After Rowe's half-time talk Palace at least conceded no further goals in the second period and, at one point, Bournemouth fans showed appreciation for Palace's short, sharp passing in midfield, leaving John Matthews to snidely suggested their applause was only in gratitude for Palace's failure to cause their side any problems. Matthews' waspish pen ignored Rowe's loss of five first-choice players through injury.

Allen then returned from the wilderness for an FA Cup first round victory over Southern League Hereford, while Rouse's Bournemouth error saw Glazier return. This time the popular Rouse played his 257th and final game for the Glaziers and he considerately informed the young 'Jacko' Jackson of his intentions to leave, as he was aware Jackson himself had been considering giving up the game knowing that two strong 'keepers were ahead of him in the queue. Then both Lewis and Imlach, Rowe's injured first-choice wingers, broke down in a comeback trial, the latter soon facing surgery.

With Matthews encouraging yet more fan complaints about Allen's 'treatment', Rowe responded: 'I try to pick the team that I think will, at the moment, do the best for the club. At present that is not easy because of injuries, but, although I make mistakes, it is an honest selection.' He appeared uneasy to admit the real reason for omitting Allen public. One fan, thinking it a 'folly' to persist with 'push-and-run' now that Byrne had gone, wrote: 'Time after time we have seen attacks break down because of an obsession with short passing, which is so easy for a defence to break up before any danger threatens.' Another writer called for the end of five-a-sides in practice, '...because the close-passing, small-pitch techniques that [five-a-sides require] gets players into bad habits when it comes to the real game of football.' Yet of course the reality is that small-pitch, five-a-side drills get players into the very *best* of habits!

Palace's quality of play was again praised at Bradford Park Avenue, only for the home side to snatch the lead. It even went to 2-0 before Allen reduced the deficit but defeat left Palace in penultimate place. Relegation to the League's basement was now a justifiable fear but, as at White Hart Lane, Rowe remained determined to prove doubters wrong.

At a board meeting a £67,000 profit was glumly announced as it primarily comprised Byrne's transfer fee. In his own address the manager mentioned pre-season optimism due to the arrivals of Imlach and Burridge, but the Scot had missed more than half the games through injury while, 'force of circumstance has not given Burridge the chances to play in the [line-up] as I envisaged he would be.' Rowe also mentioned the many other injuries which '...have carried on'. Before drawing the meeting to a close, Wait uttered words now deemed fatal by managers: 'There is no loss of confidence on the part of the board in our management and no loss of spirit in the dressing-room.' Three days later confidence did perhaps start to wane when the attendance for third-placed Watford's visit plunged to just 10,716. Glazier risked life and limb diving around his area but was unable to prevent George Harris's winner. Palace had now arrived in last place, with no fewer than four sides slated to go down.

With an FA Cup second round tie at home to Fourth Division Mansfield approaching, Chairman Wait answered the injury crisis by promising one new signing with more to follow. 'Three good wins' the chairman added, would probably see Palace clear of danger. Typically, Petchey broke down in training again, and even Mansfield were unlikely to provide respite, sitting as they were in second place with nearly 50 goals scored at the halfway point in the season. They will have been confident to defeat a last-placed side now only able to field four first-choice outfielders.

As with any side struggling to get results, criticism of the man in charge mounted, two fans writing with opinions anticipating those that Dick Graham would later express. With his friendly links to Sports Editor Matthews, one might almost imagine Graham penning these himself, using pseudonyms. One of the correspondents (coincidentally named 'J. H. Matthews') listed three specific changes he believed to be required if Palace were to avoid tumbling back into the Fourth Division:

(a) Allen to play every remaining game.
(b) Style of play must be changed (Palace build-ups too slow).
(c) A proven goalscorer should be acquired.

Rowe had of course already acquired a 'proven' goalscorer (Burridge) and the transfer of a second (Bournemouth's Dickie Dowsett) was then in progress. As for

Allen playing regularly and the playing style changing, then Rowe would clearly have to go. The correspondent added: 'It would be unfortunate if the club were to be relegated through blind adherence to a plan which has proved to be a failure,' an extraordinary opinion blindly ignoring the momentous 'push-and-run' success of 1960-61. To support his view further, Matthews wrote of '…the number of leading players and managers' who had recently been almost '…unanimously agreed that the only answer to the current retreating defence is "rapid strike" combined with frequent and hard shooting.' The second letter, from a 'W. R. Froom', promoted similar opinions, that 'push-and-run' required world class players, and added: 'One only has to note the position of Peterborough for proof of what forceful, long-ball tactics can achieve.' As for Graham, 'forceful, long-ball tactics' were to become his trademark. Reading these opinions Rowe must have despaired, especially as they came 24 hours before super-confident Mansfield arrived, having just scored a towering average of four-goals-a-game in their previous 12 outings.

Perhaps to boost morale, Wait reported that the arrival of the 'goal-snatching' forward Rowe had lined-up, would take place immediately following the Cup tie, and promised further additions to replace some of the injured. Just one of Rowe's injury victims, Long, was fit to face Mansfield. As for Imlach, following a cartilage operation, his injury-scarred season was already over by November and to cap it all centre-half Wood now fell sick… Nevertheless, Palace had more of the early exchanges against Mansfield but striker Ken Wagstaff put the Stags ahead. Burridge equalised 12 minutes later but, seconds after the break, a weak clearance provided Wagstaff's second. Then injury struck again, top-scorer Smillie limping out to the wing and, with just 15 seconds remaining Palace were on their way out of the Cup. At that moment Burridge, driving into the penalty area, crashed to earth. The referee pointed to the spot, simultaneously blowing the final whistle: the penalty would be the last kick. Allen stepped-up to take it knowing he had to find the net directly — any rebound off the 'keeper would signal the end of the game. Mansfield tried to unsettle the player as he struggled to locate a muddy penalty spot. Then he ran up… and the net shook! Palace's team of 10-and-a-half men, already missing six regulars, had achieved a replay, which took place just two days later. Smillie had recovered but Wood remained unwell, making it six of Rowe's first choice side missing. The manager gambled heavily, moving the attacking Werge back to left-half so that Summersby could add firepower up-front, yet Mansfield raced into a two-goal lead, Uphill nearly made it 2-1 before Long inadvertently diverted Hall's shot past Glazier, 3-0. After the break Roy Chapman struck two more, although a Mansfield own-goal inspired a fightback with Summersby scoring but, by the final whistle, the score had risen to a horrendous 7-2.

Burridge recalled his colleagues sitting dejectedly in the dressing-room. In retrospect, had Allen fluffed that last-minute penalty in the first game, a 2-1 home defeat would not have been remotely as punitive. For Rowe, the combination of this Mansfield debacle, the endless stream of injuries, the tenuous relationship with Allen, the loss of Byrne and the struggle to turn results around, triggered a further breakdown. According to the late Dick Graham's son, Mark, when his father arrived for work at Selhurst Park the morning after, he found a dishevelled Rowe slumped over the wheel of his car at Selhurst Park, where he had possibly spent the night. Graham took care of him and drove him home.

The Palace chairman's son, Brian Wait, came to know Rowe well and feels certain the manager suffered occasional, extreme depressions, only, as Brian says, '...it wasn't called that in those days', a time when mental health was stigmatised and professional help hard to find. In the post-war, macho world of soccer his condition will have been viewed as a sign of weakness. Rowe will have felt compelled to conceal and fight the duress he was under, alone. On reflection one suspects the Tottenham directors, having lived through two World Wars, viewed their manager's condition as unacceptable and one doubts they would have offered a shoulder to lean on.

The official Crystal Palace club statement (no doubt composed by Chairman Wait) read: 'The many injuries and misfortunes that have befallen the club this season have had a very adverse affect on Mr Rowe's health. The directors have therefore sent him away to recuperate until he is fit to resume office. Indeed, he is now well on his way to putting many thousands of miles between himself and club worries. We are sure that the gentlemen of the press who were given evasive answers to their questions yesterday will forgive us and appreciate that it was only done to protect one of the greatest gentlemen in football.'

The stress had been clearly visible to some. The *Advertiser*'s John Matthews, whose niggling, negative commentaries influenced fans and surely contributed to Rowe's condition, now wrote that it had '...been obvious that the strain' had been '...telling on him.' Meanwhile Peter Burridge first heard of Rowe's having been 'rested' on the TV, '...and I thought, well, that's the end of it.' Vic Rouse could only recall brief moments when Rowe appeared sad or morose, so the gravity and suddenness of his collapse came as a surprise. When I asked someone of Rowe's close acquaintance if relations with Graham may have contributed to his illness, the answer was a very firm and concise 'yes'. He then added: 'There was aggravation between Graham and Rowe' which sent '...poor old Arthur up the wall.' Terry Long, too, suspected Rowe and Graham didn't see eye-to-eye and said Graham was interfering with the tactical approach on the field. I should point out that I phoned Dick Graham himself to try to set up an interview, but he was unwell at the time and it never took place before he passed away. He was keen to speak to me and of course I would have appreciated his own account, particularly regarding this unfortunate period.

In his 1969 history of the club, the late Roy Peskett, 21 years the *Daily Mail*'s top football correspondent, wrote of Dick Graham taking over the team from the '...quietly spoken' Rowe '...at a most difficult time', before immediately adding: 'Whether or not it was the upsets behind the scenes, but [Palace] were almost immediately hurled out of the Cup, 7-2, by Mansfield.' I have not uncovered any other mention of specific unrest at that time and perhaps Peskett's wording invites misinterpretation. What history does spell out is that Rowe's modern, Continental-style Palace were about to temporarily fall into the hands of a man who became renowned for promoting the very unenterprising, physical, long-ball style which Rowe rightly claimed hindered British footballing progress.

Brian Wait told me that in his opinion Rowe was not an argumentative man, that despite his strong opinions, '...he was never going to stand up for a fight' instead bottling his feelings. When he needed full support Dick Graham, possessing a totally incompatible football philosophy, was hardly the man to provide it. When accepting the post as assistant to a man renowned as 'Mr Push-and-Run', there can be no doubt Graham was fully aware of the style of football Rowe expected him to help put into practice. Had this evident conflict begun to diffuse the players' focus? Had some of them lost faith in their manager's strongly-held beliefs?

A week later stand-in boss Graham was blessed with the kind of fortune Rowe had been short of as he oversaw a 2-1 home victory over Reading, of which more later. During the week following that game Wait was interviewed on the Selhurst Park pitch by TV reporter, and spoke of the '...thousands of miles' that Rowe had put between himself and his football worries (when in truth, he was recuperating just five miles away in Mitcham). When asked if there was news of a Rowe return, Wait said: 'Well, I had a nice letter from [Arthur] this morning saying how he was enjoying himself, how the weather was good, the sun was shining, but he won't be back for some time,' adding, not entirely with conviction, 'he's in Canada with his two sons'. The interviewer asked for Wait's forecast for the rest of the season. 'Certainly they'll pull up,' he replied, 'only twice this season have we fielded the team we expected to field, through injuries. We've had a minimum of six up 'till last Saturday' [the Reading victory].' Asked if he still had confidence, Wait responded 'every confidence', managing a slight, curt smile, clearly relieved the interview was at an end, a man unfamiliar with being anything but totally honest. The chairman's intention had clearly been to prevent members of the press contacting the Rowe family home. Wait said that he hoped Rowe would stay away for at least a month, '...but you know how Arthur loves his football. I am scared we will see him back before then.' The chairman himself will have been burdened with guilt, having encouraged Rowe's return to club management but he should have reflected instead on Rowe's declaration during his first season as Palace manager that he was '...living through the greatest adventure of his life'. For Rowe, that immediate success at Palace had reassured him just how talented a coach and manager he was.

A week or so after the Mansfield Cup replay Chairman Wait uncomfortably fields questions about Rowe's absence from Selhurst Park. He was determined to avoid the Press interrupting his manager's recuperation.

As for John Matthews, he now sheepishly wrote, 'Whatever the views of the public on whether Mr Rowe's policies were to their way of thinking or not, I am sure everyone will wish for him a speedy recovery.' A long-standing and literate *Advertiser* reader, despite being a critic of 'push-and-run', compensated for Matthews' obsequious statement when writing 'We all wish Arthur Rowe, certainly a "fine gentleman of football", a speedy recovery to health and strength. He has, we all know, tried to bring "class and culture" to the Third Division.'

Although the 7-2 demolition by Mansfield is regularly quoted as the event which brought Rowe down, his breakdown had been on the cards for some time and only a drastic upsurge in the team's fortunes may have prevented it. This latest FA Cup calamity summed-up his extraordinary ill-fortune when it came to the competition: the uncanny way Rowe's Spurs were almost always drawn away; the Ramsey slip-up in the 1953 semi-final; the Rouse error at Villa Park; and now a last-minute penalty-kick, without which he would at least have been spared the harrowing replay. A further irony is that had Rowe's health survived Mansfield, he would almost certainly have experienced a change of fortune, for when Graham stood-in to take temporary charge of the Reading game five days' later both the influential Petchey and first-choice centre-half Wood were fit to return. Also, Rowe's desperate search for a striker had finally materialised with the arrival of Dickie Dowsett on the very first day of training after Rowe's collapse. Dickie, looking forward to a reunion with Rowe, was surprised when arriving at Selhurst Park to find Graham greeting him; four days of training later and keen to impress, Dowsett took his place in an already considerably strengthened line-up from that which Rowe was reduced to utilising at Mansfield.

In common with his initial reign at White Hart Lane, Rowe had experienced phenomenal early success at Palace before falling victim to a stress-induced depression. Unlike at Tottenham, however, once returned to full health, Palace Chairman Arthur Wait would ensure Rowe had a job for life. Indeed Rowe would spend far longer at Crystal Palace than he had spent managing Spurs. After approximately two months of recuperation he returned to do some scouting, and it was noticeable that Wait was in no hurry to confirm the novice Graham as manager until he was totally convinced Rowe could not return to the hot-seat.

Reflecting on Rowe's time as Palace manager there should be no diminishing his achievement. Despite the club's lowly status when he arrived, he converted the playing staff to 'push-and-run', thus ensuring promotion was immediately achieved. In that first season there were goals galore and fans flocked through the Selhurst Park turnstiles. Decades later the quality of the football is still warmly recalled by Palace fans and players of that period. Over time his impact diminished but this story has already identified several pointers as to why this occurred.

Firstly there was the departure of his one unique, supremely talented and inspirational player. Johnny Byrne's ability to conjure up something special when the going was tough had been lost, lowering team morale into the bargain. Then, as at Spurs, there was the growing familiarity of opposing clubs with 'push-and-run', although at the lower level this tended to take the form of increased physicality.

'Opponents,' said Terry Long, tried to '…stop us dictating the pace.' In those times referees regularly turned a blind eye to tackling of a nature outlawed today and there was a wider acceptance of 'playing the ball with the man'. Not, as Terry Long admitted, that all fouls on Palace men were deliberate. With 'push-and-run', said Terry, 'You'd already passed [the ball] on to a teammate by the time [the opponent was] able to put in a challenge.' On the other hand, George Petchey recalled once hammering on the referee's door at half-time, demanding to know when the referee planned to start blowing his whistle or do something to stop the fouling. Unprotected by officials, some Palace players will have occasionally hid or ducked-out of challenges.

Also, as with his great Spurs' side, Rowe had several players over the age of 30. Even if older players' legs withstood 90 minutes of 'push-and-run', their recovery from injury was slower. Not that Rowe had failed to introduce young blood, for example Glazier, Lewis and Stephenson. However the saddest parallel with his White Hart Lane experiences was that at Selhurst Park Rowe was not backed by certain staff members who lacked belief in his football ideas. With players spending more time in Graham's presence than in Rowe's, could this have reduced some players' faith in the manager's theories? Peter Burridge has an alternative opinion: 'At the Palace I don't think we had the players of the quality required for "push-and-run",' adding, 'we played a lot of stuff in the middle of the park but if you don't score…?' Peter is the only person I have interviewed who felt player quality was a factor, yet Rowe's side had initially succeeded superbly before the injury glut and the growing influence of staff members holding contrasting tactical ideas.

Arthur Rowe himself later said of his Palace side of 1962-63 that they were '…as fine a squad as the club have had for a very long time,' a squad he thought could win the Third Division title that year, adding poignantly: 'Then I was sick just before Christmas.' But on this occasion he failed to include mention of the preponderance of injuries his side had suffered — it is hard to credit but in the twenty League games before falling sick, Rowe had only been able to field his strongest promotion-challenging eleven *twice*. Furthermore, Rowe was later keen to emphasise that the side which won promotion the following season was mostly his, although the tactics were Graham's. To reinforce Rowe's belief in that 1962-63 side, by the time of his ill-health Palace could have been in second place on points had they found the net just once more in drawn games or those lost by just a single goal. Free of injury and sickness, there is little doubt his first choice eleven would have made all the difference.

David Prole summed-up Rowe's Palace revolution in his book *Football in London* (written in 1963): 'What glamour there is in the lower divisions attaches itself to clubs like Palace and has done for some seasons, with the production of one player of genius, Johnny Byrne, several others of excellent standards, and, for a spell, a manager like the great Arthur Rowe. In recent years at least Palace have played football of a calibre worthy of a far higher grade.

19

'Push-and-Run' to 'Kick, Bollock and Bite'

CRYSTAL PALACE 1963-66

'Arthur Rowe may think in terms too advanced for us and the technique of some of his staff, but a club with Crystal Palace's crowd-potential must plan boldly.'

A FAN'S COMMENT AFTER ROWE'S SUCCESSOR DICK GRAHAM HAD
ABANDONED 'PUSH-AND-RUN' MARCH 1963

Arthur Rowe remained at Crystal Palace Football Club until retirement age but, initially, as he recuperated, Dick Graham ran the first team and the football retreated into the past. Rarely has any group of footballers been subjected to such an abrupt change. Exit Rowe, ruling sympathetically and insisting on enterprising, exciting, short-passing football. Enter Graham waving a big stick and insisting on intimidatory 'percentage' tactics.

Goalkeeper John Jackson told me Graham was '...very, very hard', while George Petchey went further, calling Graham "...an angry man', adding '...a lot of players resented him, as a coach'. A more positive slant comes from Peter Burridge who says that under Graham '...we jumped higher and ran harder and we were a good defensive side', adding that he '...made us very aware that it was a hard, tough old game'. Meanwhile Jackson would always remain grateful for Graham's specialist goalkeeper training and Petchey admitted he had some good ideas before

Trainer Dick Graham, Rowe's controversial successor as Manager of Crystal Palace, puts Alan Stephenson, John Sewell and John Holsgrove through their paces at Selhurst Park in around 1965.

commenting '...but the football ideas, that he needed, he didn't have'. Graham accepted that Petchey talked the game better and, in time, invited him to coach the side. Nevertheless the pair had an explosive relationship, George telling me: 'I didn't take prisoners when I was telling him my views and... I thought he was a prat.' In old age, Dick Graham claimed he had been reluctant to take over from Rowe as he had been happy coaching. He did not see his methods as a 'brutal philosophy' but only as a response to the club's perilous League position. However, Graham would stick with those methods even after safety was achieved.

Graham quickly banished Rowe's breathtaking give-and-go style in favour of the long-ball-dominated, physically-intimidating approach which had left English football trailing the world. His unsophisticated football, bending of the rules and inclination to be content to grab an early lead and then look to defend it, quickly saw a Palace side who had been universally admired in the lower division under Arthur Rowe, become disliked wherever they played under his successor. An episode which perfectly sums-up 'the good, the bad and the ugly' of English football in the second-half of the twentieth century.

On December 1st 1962 Reading were the visitors for the first game after Rowe was taken ill and they expected to combat 'push-and-run', but instead were confronted with the 'percentage game'. Palace still conceded early on but 25 minutes from time debutant Dowsett set Allen up to score and, before the end, Heckman added a second. As already hypothesized, if Rowe had benefitted from fielding such a strong line-up against Mansfield just a week earlier, there would almost certainly have been no Cup replay and Rowe's health may have remained intact. Instead it was Graham who benefitted, not only from the return to fitness of Petchey and Long but also the debut of Rowe's latest addition to Palace's attacking strength, Dowsett (so popular at Bournemouth that an abstract likeness of him appears on AFC Bournemouth's club crest to this day). Naturally Ronnie Allen, with his former West Brom colleague in temporary command, would now be ever-present until season's end.

Graham's crude ditching of 'push-and-run' immediately came under fire from one Rowe admirer, who wrote: 'Long ball adherents must spend much of their time chasing loose balls, relying on opponents' errors for success,' adding an extremely pertinent, Rowe-like observation: 'Many writers to the *Advertiser* advocate the long ball game because it is used by the division leaders [Northampton]. May I point out that it is used far more extensively by most of the stragglers as well.' The writer closed with a tribute: 'I do not know Mr Rowe personally, but I do know that he has fully earned the respect he is accorded in football circles. There are many obvious reasons for the Palace decline; it is not necessary to make a very fine man the scapegoat.'

Despite Andy Smillie being described as '...one of the best forwards afield' and creating Allen's goal in a 4-1 defeat at Port Vale, Graham never selected him again. The same applied to fine servants Heckman and Summersby. When first arriving at Selhurst Park, Allen had stated 'I don't think I have ever come across a club with more team spirit and general friendliness than there is in the dressing-room at Selhurst.' Yet Graham would now lay that to waste. Publicly Rowe kept his opinion of Graham and his methods to himself, but there is evidence that Arthur's wife

Pom harboured considerable bitterness toward her husband's assistant. After all she, more than anyone, will have witnessed the duress her husband had suffered.

The Port Vale defeat triggered a player revolt, almost certainly due to post-match criticisms from Graham. The quiet, reserved Roy Summersby, who made no bones about his admiration for Rowe, had of course only recently (and reluctantly) agreed to step in as captain in McNichol's absence. 'I got stuck with the [captaincy] for a while,' Roy told me, and it thus fell upon him to collect thirteen players' signatures on a letter to Chairman Wait expressing their reservations about Graham and his methods. However the board felt compelled to reject the letter — after all, the last thing they needed was further upheaval when the League position remained perilous.

One player of the time said he and his colleagues began going around the club in fear. Furthermore, there was concern that Allen (described by one colleague as 'aloof' and by another as 'snide') was Graham's 'spy-in-the-camp'. The excellent professional Summersby was told by Graham he would never play for Palace again and this alone suggests Rowe's return as manager was now unlikely. Two players formerly with Rowe at Spurs, Heckman and Uphill, along with Long, were then ordered by Graham to change for training in the narrow referee's dressing-room. Yet Long, despite Graham's punitive action, remained in the first-team, perhaps due to the mutual respect Long enjoyed with Chairman Wait. A highly-regarded and popular man with a pristine playing record, Long had no idea how he had offended Graham. Perhaps a facial expression of his had been misconstrued. How things had changed in the two years since Rowe said he had never known a happier club in football!

With 'push-and-run' now on the scrapheap, a full team of players never appeared again: Rouse, Lunnis, McNichol, Dodge, Evans, Summersby, Newman, Cartwright, Uphill, Smillie and Heckman, while Imlach was shunned by Graham for a long time, even once recovered from injury. Uphill bitterly recalled: 'Palace was a good club. It was enjoyable, and we were all like a family together,' adding: 'It all broke up when Dick Graham came along.' Even Burridge, who considered Graham had a beneficial affect on his own career, admits to having once had an explosive face-to-face confrontation with him. The irony is that around ten years earlier, the self-same Graham had criticised the Palace board of directors and management in his regular *Advertiser* column, writing: 'Professional footballers are very sensitive human beings, not just machines; they must be treated like men, not a lot of children.' Seeing as how a seemingly spiteful Graham was forcing experienced players to change in a tiny room which young Palace apprentices then gleefully referred to as 'the naughty boys room', I pointed Graham's article out to Alan Stephenson, whose bitter bust-up with Graham would later make the national press, and he, too, saw the irony in this, saying it was a shame Graham didn't practice what he had earlier preached.

Yet some players thrived under Dick Graham. Burridge was one, and Stephenson would always respect Graham for his defensive coaching: 'We were a very well-organised, well-drilled team. A lot of training sessions were spent on ...man-marking, tackling and closing down, that sort of thing.' Yes, Graham had a lot to offer the game and he worked hard despite the pain of his career-ending back injury. He was passionate about everything he tackled, whether as a goalkeeper, columnist, running a supporters' club, coaching or managing. Soon after assuming control of the team he developed what then was an original strategy: keeping a 'special training squad' of fifteen from which the first eleven would be selected. This was in the days when only a twelfth man stood by on match days in case of last-minute injury or sickness. In such fashion Graham confronted the threat of relegation head-on.

In mid-December 1962 Graham circulated all League clubs with a list of players surplus to his needs, which further suggested the long-term future of the club had slipped from Rowe's hands. From then on the quality of soccer plummeted in equal measure to the steady collection of points. A 2-2 draw at Halifax, during which Petchey was dismissed, was described as 'robust', an unsurprising adjective considering future first-teamer David Payne's recollection that Graham's rallying call, replacing Rowe's 'Make it simple, make it quick' was… 'Kick, Bollock and Bite'. By then Rowe was resting in Broadstairs, the club saying he would be away until the end of January at least. 'He has definitely *not*, at the moment, stated he is giving up [football] or going to live in Canada,' reported the press. A player Rowe had initiated transfer negotiations for, 33-year-old ex-Arsenal striker Cliff Holton, weighing-in at 13st 8lbs and 6ft 1in tall, then joined from Northampton Town. One reason for Holton's delayed arrival involved the player's unwillingness to train full-time due to his role as general manager of an engineering firm, but the player's other condition confirmed Rowe had made the initial approach. Holton later said Palace '…were playing entertaining football but getting poor results. I wasn't very keen to be part of this kind of set-up,' continuing 'I told them straight, "If that's the way you want to play, there's no point in my joining." I have always believed in the philosophy that if you can't play well and win, the next best thing is to play badly and win' - this suited Graham perfectly. Holton depended much on strength and aggression but he was also a pretty good passer, and, in 1952-53 he had totalled an extraordinary 19 goals from just 21 appearances as Arsenal won the title, explaining Rowe's desire to bring him to Spurs as a more prolific replacement for Len Duquemin. Holton made his Palace debut in the Boxing Day derby with Millwall and the core line-up that day would remain until the end of season 1962-63 and for much of 1963-64, too: Glazier; Howe, Townsend; Long, Wood, Petchey; Werge, Holton, Dowsett, Burridge, Allen.

The trio of strikers, all signed or sought-after by Rowe, had totalled 79 League goals between them in the previous season and the Millwall defenders' fear of Holton freed-up space for his colleagues, a possibility Rowe had identified. Burridge put Palace ahead while Dowsett rounded the 'keeper for his first Palace goal in a 3-0 win. So often a critic of 'push-and-run', John Matthews now ruefully confessed that now Palace no longer passed the ball out of defence, it '…tended to lessen the quality of their football'. Yet even George Petchey confessed a grudging respect for Graham: 'I met a lot of people afterwards who would have loved to have had Graham's aggression, the way he wanted the team to play. Graham said to me once, when we had cut out all the fancy stuff and bought Cliff Holton, that he wanted me to "Hit Cliff, all the time." I said: "But he won't fight for it." "Yes he will," said Dick,

"I'll make him fight for it!" So that's what we did. We whacked it to Holton and he flicked it on for Burridge or Dowsett or whoever.' Classy stuff.

Behind the scenes a group of Rowe's players still suffered the indignity of changing apart from their colleagues, at various times this group included Evans, Heckman, Imlach, Long, Rouse, Summersby and Uphill. Graham damned them publicly: 'Fair criticism is always welcome, but whatever is finally agreed at team meetings must be done out there on the field and kept going. If team discipline is slack, you are in trouble.' The common denominator among the exiled men was their high regard for Arthur Rowe who must have been horrified by it all. Even John Matthews failed to hide his disgust: 'It was a pity that such an action should have taken place when good spirit and teamwork is an essential.' Author and broadcaster Gary Imlach, whilst appreciating Graham's own recollections for inclusion in his biography of his father, remained inclined to use the adjective 'tyrant' when describing the 'stand-in' manager. In the New Year, Palace hero Summersby was placed on the transfer list; at 27, he needed to get his career back on track. Then, in the second week of January, Wait told the press the 'atmosphere' at the club had been cleared while Graham had set a target of a point a game from the final 22 fixtures.

That English winter of 1962-63 remains the coldest since the seventeenth century so postponements quickly decimated the fixture list. The first playable fixture of the year fell on 12th January, one of only eight League fixtures played that day and it only went ahead thanks to Brighton's considerable investment in tar-melting machinery, sand and peat. Palace won 2-1 at the Goldstone Ground with goals from Holton and Burridge, the latter now feeling more at home, recalling his high-scoring Fourth Division experiences when running onto hoofed passes from deep or headed flick-ons.

In the last week of January 1963, Rowe volunteered to do some scouting and Chairman Wait even talked of easing him '…back into the manager's job', adding that Dick Graham would continue to '…help take the load off Mr Rowe's shoulders. What happens when Mr Rowe is fully fit is not so certain, but the two-men-in-control arrangement could continue.' One imagines Wait's words were designed to avoid further distressing the man (and friend) he so admired. By now Graham had changed the entire focus, style and tactics of the side, and with just one loss in five games, a return to 'push-and-run' looked ill-advised until relegation could be ruled out.

Palace played just once between 12th January and 9th March and during that time the club stated Rowe would return to take up 'light duties', but then added that '…by mutual agreement the responsibilities for the playing staff, team selection, training and all matters concerned with players will remain in the hands of Mr Graham.' One imagines Rowe's wife Pom persuading her husband to put any idea of a management return firmly behind him.

Meanwhile full-back Bert Howe was becoming the embodiment of Graham's approach, his often mistimed tackling becoming what he would be most renowned for. When Palace returned pointless from their only game in February, at Swindon, Graham for the first of many future occasions faced criticism for the physicality epitomised by Howe, responding 'I have told our lads to play it hard, to try to win the ball by hard but fair tackles.'

In the third week of February the club was contacted by the Professional Footballers' Association on behalf of Evans, Rouse, Summersby and Uphill, who had not been selected for reserve games nor even practice matches. Three clubs were interested in Rouse but had been unable to see him in action. Graham's inconsiderate response was that aside from the fact few games had been played due to the weather, his priority was with first-teamers and 'possible' first-teamers. As a former 'keeper himself one might have expected greater empathy with Rouse, yet over time Graham also engaged in confrontations with Rouse's successors between the sticks, Bill Glazier and John Jackson. Ultimately the Professional Footballers' Association forced Graham to include Rouse and the other 'rebels' for the next scheduled reserve fixture.

Then, during the first week of March 1963, Wait officially announced Graham as manager with Rowe taking the title 'General Manager'. However the chairman still hedged his bets, saying that things would be reviewed again at season's end. One might imagine Wait's nightly prayers for Rowe to return to full health as he had already developed concerns over Graham's confrontational tendencies. For now Rowe would watch future opponents, help Graham's tactical planning and assist scout Charlie Revell. As Rowe later recalled he also worked with the schoolboy and youth sides '…to try to pep them up a bit.'

The 'big freeze' ended in Britain on 6th March (remarkably the first frost free morning of the year) and football resumed with a huge backlog of fixtures to complete. Palace began well, garnering 9 points from 14 and Graham publicly drew the line between his ideas and those of Rowe's. He said that unlike Rowe and 'push-and-run' he didn't '…restrict the players to any set pattern of play,' adding '…it is a nonsense to say we are foregoing the short stuff exclusively in favour of the long ball.' Yet fans who had waited almost three months to see their side run out at Selhurst Park were none too impressed when, in mid-March, Palace shut-up shop against Bournemouth once Allen had put them ahead. Graham, addressing the press, then exposed his lack of respect for Rowe's methods: 'The sudden determination I introduced into the side probably came as a surprise to clubs who thought they were on an *easy touch*.' So there it was. 'Easy touch'. Which concisely confirms Graham's dismissive attitude to his former boss's tactics.

A turning point in public reaction to the abandonment of the 'beautiful game' occurred at Coventry where, according to a now discomforted John Matthews, Graham's side engaged in '…late tackles, trips and obstructive methods'. Matthews named this a 'Black Day', adding: 'Palace have been respected on many grounds for their football skills and general ability to keep their game on a higher plane than most. I am afraid their reputation took something of a knock at Highfield Road.' Coventry boss Jimmy Hill could only splutter: 'I'm speechless.' Graham blamed the referee and 'the "whipped-up" crowd', while his cultured description for the afternoon's display was that it '…was a bit meaty', a term unsurprisingly not to be found in Rowe's technical soccer dictionary. Next, at home to Colchester, Palace hurried, scurried, and sent streams of long balls forward. It required someone to steady the ship, for just a smidgeon of football to be played. They fell behind in the 72nd minute yet, as one commentator wrote: 'Still Palace unmethodically pushed away; passing badly, shooting badly and making little or no impression on the veteran ['keeper] Ames.' The Selhurst Park attendance was 25% down on the previous home match and Palace now, in addition to playing ugly, were leaking points.

In defending growing accusations of deliberate rough play, Graham finally and publicly exposed his deep-set opposition to Rowe's 'push-and-run': 'We believe in playing soccer strongly', he began, adding, 'this is a man's game and it will not be won easily or by *tip-tap methods*.'

There it was. It had slipped out.

Tip-tap methods.

So it appears that, all along, Graham had held a dismissive view of his illustrious superior's glorious 'push-and-run'. A critical attitude which had likely spread to Graham's former press colleague Matthews, thus exposing Rowe to negative coverage from the leading local newspaper. Graham had purported to support his boss for 20 long months but only now was his clear contempt for Rowe's methods publicly exposed. Graham had accepted the post as Rowe's assistant in full knowledge his boss was renowned for 'push-and-run', so it is hard to accept the defamatory expression 'tip-tap' had only now, suddenly, entered Graham's vocabulary. Had he not previously used it derogatively, maybe in front of Rowe's players in training, and almost certainly in the company of Allen? Rowe's stress-related relapse had proven extremely convenient for a trainer granted a job title which practically made him a 'shoe-in' for the manager's chair.

A reader's riposte to Graham then appeared in the *Advertiser*, defending his predecessor. It was such a considered and eloquent piece that one is tempted to believe Rowe himself may have composed it: 'The clamour [from fans] for retaliatory power-play has been successful, with doubtful results. Push-and-Run provided sufficient chances, the weakness was in the finishing. Holton would have had more opportunities [under "push-and-run"] if he had been used as a "remedy" instead of a "disruption".' The writer added: 'Arthur Rowe may think in terms too advanced for us and the technique of some of his staff, but a club with Crystal Palace's crowd-potential must plan boldly. One injury-plagued, unsuccessful season [1961-62] should not have been allowed to disturb the longer-term objectives.'

The correspondent continued: 'The British public is beginning to realise the gulf between our own standards and those of the rest of Europe. Clubs equipped to meet the changes that must follow will quickly prosper.'

As for the writer's notion of 'clubs equipped to meet the changes prospering', one needs look only at the 1970s' Liverpool side (often mentioned in the same breath as Rowe and 'push-and-run') which conquered the best of Europe, winning the European Cup no less than four times in the 70s and 80s.

Graham, however, was intent on taking soccer in a reverse direction, which is clear from Palace's attendance for the next home game, which had dropped to just four figures for the arrival of strugglers Bradford. Fortunately Palace played more football than of late and Bradford crashed 6-0. After then gaining a further point at Millwall, Graham targeted 10 points from the remaining 24 to guarantee safety.

Were it that Rowe had remained in good health, the addition of Dowsett alone would have created more openings for Burridge, and with a fit Petchey the manager would have been able to move Long to right-back and Summersby to right-half — always his strongest combination. In that event the season could conceivably have been turned around and Graham's ugly, negative methods would not have damaged the club's reputation.

A further flurry of goals saw Palace win all three Easter fixtures, but multiple goals in a game would thereafter become a rarity. Now all but safe, Palace's Friday night win over struggling Reading was comically described as a: '…series of missed traps, missed headers and a string of wildly-booted clearances.' The following Wednesday second-placed Peterborough arrived, embarrassing Graham's side with their own neat passing style as they took both points. Arthur Wait bullishly said the players still aimed for a top-six finish, but Graham himself preferred to glance over his shoulder at the other end of the table. Three days later Palace went 2-0 up against promotion-seeking Port Vale, before protecting what they had but a defensive error by Wood left Palace barely snatching the two points Graham felt necessary to ensure safety. Whatever the 'means', however, the 'ends' could be celebrated.

There is no denying that Palace's continuing Third Division existence had looked precarious following the Mansfield Cup defeat, but at that time there remained a whopping 52 points still to contest. With Dowsett, Long and Petchey available to him, it was not improbable that a recovered Rowe could have engineered salvation himself. Petchey, who Graham had been using despite his carrying an injury, finally dropped out for a 1-1 home draw with Hull. The fact that Graham had been fielding Petchey half-fit demonstrates just how significant the player's loss had been for most of Rowe's final ten League games in charge, as well as the Mansfield Cup encounters. However there were now just 16 days to play out Palace's remaining five games.

When drawing at Bristol City, an unimpressed reporter described the game as '…a competition to see which team could kick the ball highest and furthest.' Burridge's bicycle-kick equaliser proved to be the only touch of class. With five points from the final eight Palace finished seven points clear of the drop. After Rowe stepped down Palace earned 35 points from a possible 52, all credit to Graham. Terry Long accepted this, but was compelled to add '…it was a horrible way to play.'

With season 1962-63 over and Graham off on holiday, it was Rowe who was left with the unfortunate task of fielding transfer enquiries for players loyal to him such as Lewis, Summersby and Smillie, men who, had it not been for his illness, would have remained firmly in his plans. One understandable free transfer was that of ageing, yet super-versatile, ex-skipper McNichol. John Cartwright, another free, would soon turn to youth coaching and it will have been music to Arthur Rowe's ears when Cartwright eventually became no less than the Technical Director of the FA National School of Excellence.

Returning to comparisons between the idealistic Rowe and his no-nonsense successor, Graham had begun to copy the great Peter Doherty in having his men wear numbered shirts foreign to their historically-established positions on the field. In those pre-squad-numbering days, shirt numbers told spectators and opponents which role a player was filling. The single central defender, for example, was number '5', his direct opponent, the central striker, number '9'. Reporting on Graham's random numbering policy against Bristol City, the *Advertiser* was unimpressed, reporting that '…only Bristol City seemed reasonably untroubled by it all.' Unlike the breathtaking magic of 'push-and-run', the ploy contributed little to 'the Beautiful Game'. Another Graham tactic was to hinder the opposition's tactical planning by announcing his team at the last moment. He would delay handing stand tickets to the four of his 15-man squad who would not take part until the very last moment. Players will have been getting into their playing strip when Graham would surprise them with a stand ticket. 'Jacko' Jackson recounted the occasion when something went amiss with the plan and it was only realised at the last moment that only ten players were changed, ready to play. 'Who's missing?' a panicking Graham asked, before realising who it was: 'Go and get him!' he shouted. The player concerned was by then sitting sadly in his stand seat muttering 'I'm never going to play for this club again!'

These petty practices suggest limitations causing Graham to grasp anything that might give his side a smidgeon of advantage. George Petchey, who would become the first British coach to collect all UEFA coaching badges, considered Graham was no master of the arts of soccer. Esteemed future broadcaster Jimmy Hill, then Coventry City manager, later recalled how during Palace's visit that March 'We had been kicked to pieces by Dick Graham's Crystal Palace team…'. Thereafter Hill rarely hid his contempt for Rowe's successor.

Graham's soccer philosophy symbolised the very thinking Rowe had set out to quash with 'push-and-run'. Indeed, had Willy Meisl not written his excellent *Soccer Revolution* as early as 1956, he could have been accurately describing Graham's football philosophy in 1963. Like Rowe, Meisl considered a concentration on PREVENTING rather than CREATING goals: '…morally and mentally makes all the difference in the world. The first is a negative attitude: I am out to spoil; I am destructive. As long as I can stop the other chap from winning, I am a success. I have accomplished my main task. In the second case I am inspired by a positive outlook [as with "push-and-run"]; I want to create something; I am constructive.' Meisl significantly added: 'SPOILING can be more easily and quickly taught; it can almost be drilled like square-bashing; it needs far less technical skill, if any. Fighting spirit can make up for many glaring soccer deficiencies, so can robustness.' Playing negative soccer, wrote Meisl (and here he truly damns the likes of Graham), is 'easier', and his description of 'scrounging points' would prove particularly true of Graham's following season (1963-64), when 13 of 23 victories would be achieved with a single-goal margin, and a further 10 points scraped together with 0-0 or 1-1 draws (this despite the quality of players available to him). The average goals per game under Graham progressively declined from nearly 2-per-game during that 1962-63 relegation-avoiding spell to a mere 1.21 by the time of his departure in

1966. Under Rowe, goals-per-game had been little short of 2.5. As goals are what spectators most appreciate, attendances under Graham inevitably fell away.

Returning to that spring of 1963, Rowe will have enjoyed watching Bill Nicholson's Spurs score five as they won the European Cup Winners' Cup live on TV. The alternative activity for Rowe that same evening would have been to watch Graham's men fight-out a goalless draw with Coventry. Meanwhile, in May, Roy Summersby, a tremendous servant of Rowe's, finally escaped 'jailor' Graham to be reunited at Portsmouth with, of all people …George Smith!

Unlike Rowe's board at Tottenham, Palace Chairman Wait appreciated that if the club were to buy players, the preferred policy was to pay more rather than less. Buying players of £6,000 or so, only to find they were inadequate, often left the club obliged to give them away, so was counter-productive, which of course echoed Rowe's experience at Tottenham. At Palace lessons had been learned from the relatively costly signings of the experienced Dowsett and Holton — 'Their value has been proved,' Wait said. Graham then contradicted the policy, purchasing West Brom's Billy Birch, a striker who, having never made the Albion side, would never find the net for Palace.

Away from Palace duties, in 1963 Rowe became first Chairman of a newly-formed London Football Coaches Association, still existing at the time of writing. Founder members included Walter Winterbottom, Bertie Mee (later Arsenal's 'Double'-winning manager), Ron Greenwood, Jimmy Hill and Tommy Harmer. Meanwhile Byrne, selected by Ramsey for his a second England cap, scored twice as England hammered Switzerland 8-1. Rowe will have purred at the news.

SEASON 1963-64   Back at Selhurst Park in August, a beaming Rowe posed for the staff group photo. He appeared reassuringly healthy, content now to enjoy his back-room role. Working at a club he had grown to love, he would spend 13 years serving the 'Glaziers', more than double his time as Spurs' manager. The erudite Peter Burridge best summed-up the Rowe-to-Graham transition: 'Thinking back to Dick's way of playing, we were getting a lot of stick from the press but we didn't lose many games …Dick said "Stop them scoring goals for a start and then get stuck in! And train hard."' Peter then stated that which could only previously have been assumed - 'Of course, Arthur hated him.'

As General Manager Rowe retained as much dignity as possible, and there is a clear distinction between Rowe's treatment when having to step down from his managerial role at White Hart Lane and losing his role through similar circumstances at Selhurst Park. This time, appreciated for his experience, grace and humour (as well as bringing some much-needed good press to Selhurst Park), Rowe still had a job and Chairman Wait valued his knowledge, friendship and advice. After Graham's early face-off with the players, Wait will have feared that things could blow up again at any moment. What better than to have Rowe waiting in the wings, ready to stand-in if needed?

1963-64 proved an extremely significant season for Crystal Palace FC and although Rowe worked mainly in the background, it was mostly his players who wore the Palace colours. Moreover, in a pre-season interview on the pitch Dick

Crystal Palace, summer 1963. Players only, back: Howe, Holton, Townsend, Wood, Glazier, Jackson, Stephenson, Petchey, Long, Little. Middle: Imlach, Griffiths, Allen, Burridge, Dowsett, Fuller, Forster, Werge, Birch. Front: Dick Graham (third from left), Rowe (third from right), then the first-ever female Club Secretary Margaret Montague who would be succeeded by young assistant Chris Hassell (far right).

Graham graciously credited Rowe for putting together a good squad of under-17 apprentices and explained how this had enabled him to cut the professional squad to just 18. That autumn Rowe invited lanky half-back John Holsgrove, 17, for a two-month trial, the boy signing amateur forms and soon Holsgrove was captaining the England Youth side. Graham meanwhile paid Southend £4,000 for 20-year-old Bobby Kellard, a tigerish, diminutive midfielder who had played for England Youth alongside the likes of Terry Venables and Martin Peters. His talents, being a native of Edmonton, may have been known to Rowe.

Something Peter Burridge said confirmed Graham's limited ambition to engage in skilful soccer. When concerns were raised regarding the use of the well-worn Selhurst Park pitch for training, Dick Graham would say: 'It's no use having a bad team and a good pitch (or a bad pitch and a good team)! Get some water on it to make it difficult to play on.' Conversely, whenever Rowe chose to apply a little water to the pitch his intention had been to assist the passage of a zipped, accurate, ground pass. For away fixtures Graham sometimes utilised a defensive set-up from the first whistle to frustrate the home fans, whose jeering would cause their side's confidence to wane. However, if the home side *did* snatch an early goal, Palace could be dead in the water, forced to open up, exposing themselves to counter attacks. When Graham then changed the basis of the players' bonus system to league position rather than attendance, his players were incentivised to defend a one goal lead rather than add to it.

Meanwhile, Rowe had heard that the late Ron Brett's life insurance had expired before his fatal car accident, so proceeds from a pre-season friendly against neighbouring Charlton went to his mother, Rowe saying the club hadn't been '…as generous to his mother as we would have liked, so we decided to help out this way.' Another pre-season friendly, against Spurs, was played 'behind closed doors' at White Hart Lane and produced an extraordinary 6-2 Palace victory, news of which found its way into the national press the following morning. Peter Burridge (who scored four) proudly recalled he had given '…Danny Blanchflower a real chasing'. When meeting Jimmy Greaves at a dinner some time later and mentioning that 6-2 defeat, Greaves replied: 'Oh no! Don't talk about that. Billy Nick gave us so much stick afterwards!'

Yet Palace's League season began with a thumping 5-1 defeat at Jimmy Hill's Coventry, despite Burridge giving Palace a half-time lead, and the *Advertiser* described Palace's lack of '…pure soccer ideas'. Second-best to a quicker and cleverer home side, Palace were castigated for their rugged play. Before kick-off Graham had engaged in his 'delaying the team sheet' scheme, reporters resorting to asking non-playing Palace squad members: 'Who is number 7, who is number 4,' etc. Perhaps Graham was satisfied this procedure had restrictedt Coventry's total to five instead of six.

When he was criticised following three out of four games ending 1-1, Graham, despite previous denials, made it clear he *had* disposed of the short-passing style, insisting, 'In the top divisions you are allowed more room to play cultured football but in this division the marking is much tighter and quicker.' Graham had spent over two years as assistant to a man who had achieved success with 'push-and-run' in the Fourth Division, yet was now claiming it was too sophisticated to perform outside the top two levels. This interview also made it clear that Ronnie Allen had never intended to do as Rowe required. Graham said, 'What is the point in buying people like Allen who have always played [an open game] if you are going to alter their style?' No wonder Rowe had felt compelled to utilise Allen so rarely. Graham, as Rowe's assistant, had stood by as his boss purchased an ex-colleague of his who had little or no intention to engage in 'push-and-run'. Presumably Graham was personally content to get a 'fellow-traveller' on board, someone whose beliefs matched his own, even if they contradicted those of his boss. Indeed Allen, freed from what he will have considered the 'shackles' of 'push-and-run', now played with '…fire and enthusiasm,' an unused description whenever Rowe had placed faith in him. He led them out onto the field, too.

Yet statistics showed that Dick Graham had tightened Palace defensively; by mid-October only 8 goals were conceded in twelve League outings. However despite winning all three home games, attendances were down on the previous season by around 25%. After a 1-1 draw at Meadow Lane, Notts County manager Eddie Lowe said all Palace had done was pack their goal to pick up the point, Graham presumably unaware that prior to meeting Palace, County had picked up just six of twenty points. As things were, Palace relied heavily on Rowe's superb goalkeeping discovery, Bill Glazier. Meanwhile, around this time Rowe penned the first of several handwritten letters to the parents of 16-year-old David Payne, who would later shine for Palace against the likes of Jimmy Greaves and Bobby Charlton.

Dick Graham's promotion plan was to win home games and steal a point away, which took a big hit with successive 3-1 away defeats, at Watford and then at Oldham. Having drawn level at Boundary Park, Palace tried to defend the point only to lose both. Graham's limited ambitions clearly led to a clash with Rowe devotees Long, Werge and Petchey, as all three were then discarded. It took seven matches before Graham restored Petchey, but Long remained 'grounded' for no fewer than 20 games. Graham said both Long and Petchey were suffering 'slight injuries', yet, in missing 20 matches, Long's injury was clearly *seriously* slight. Petchey, as Roy Summersby recalled, was not a man to put up with '…anyone talking back to him' and, by the beginning of November, the trio were on the transfer list, joining Imlach and Little. In a forty-eight-hour panic-buy Graham 'one-stop-shopped' at nearby Charlton, snapping-up half-back Fred Lucas (30) and full-back John Sewell (26), as direct replacements for Long and Petchey. Lucas would only feature in sixteen League games but Sewell ultimately proved to be perhaps the best thing Graham contributed to the football club, eventually captaining Palace (under Bert Head's management) into the First Division.

One reporter described the home encounter with Crewe as a 'Miserable Third Division clash', adding '…any genuine soccer lover must have writhed in agony.' Furthermore, spectators were amused by '…a series of miskicks, blooped clearances and indiscriminate passes…'. Reading this, one hopes Rowe was by then avoiding exposure to first team performances. Graham then signed 28-year-old Brian Whitehouse, another ex-West Brom colleague, who wasted no time in bashing 'push-and-run': 'There is certainly no room [in Division Three] for the "frilly" sort of soccer you get in the First Division and among the top eight or nine teams in the Second.' Unsurprisingly Whitehouse was later suspected of being a second pair of Graham's 'ears' in the dressing-room. When strengthening the squad Graham seemed unable to cast his net wider than his old club and it must be said that the careers of most of his former West Brom men ultimately went nowhere. By contrast at around this same time Arthur Rowe spotted and signed 14-year-old Steve Kember, who would go on to make 291 appearances for Palace and played an essential role in two promotions, gained international recognition from Alf Ramsey, and earned the club a substantial fee when sold on. That same week Rowe's half-back discoveries, Payne and Holsgrove, teamed-up as Palace knocked Chelsea out of the FA Youth Cup.

Graham then experienced a Cup disaster to equal (or out-do) Rowe's at Mansfield, Palace sinking 3-1 at Southern League Yeovil. A headline even read 'PALACE OUTPLAYED' and while Glazier was unusually responsible for two goals, the London *Evening News* stated blisteringly: 'No attempt was made [by Palace] to play Yeovil at their own game — football.' Next, facing Coventry, the club who proved to be Palace's closest rivals for promotion, Graham wisely included the 19-year-old Stephenson in a dual centre-half role alongside Wood. This turned into the big breakthrough game for Rowe's discovery and 'Stevo' was destined to be a regular in the side for the next three-and-a-half seasons until tempted away, like Steve Kember later, by a big-money move. With Rowe's driving, inspirational purchase Petchey reinstated in the middle of the park, Palace suddenly looked a much stronger outfit, Stephenson's goal holding the 'Sky Blues' to 1-1. At one point City manager Jimmy Hill, so infuriated by Graham's tactics, had left his stand seat to go face-to-face with Graham, who said afterwards: 'How often do we hear that a player who honestly plays hard is dirty? I never tell one of my players to go out and maim the opposition. I do tell them to play hard.' Stephenson, despite his own later differences with the manager, supports Graham in this particular respect: '[Graham] never had to tell me when to tackle or how to tackle. The side was not dirty but competitive, and worked hard for each other as real teams do.'

When Petchey's brilliant 30-yard volley won a point at Mansfield, putting Palace in joint second, a report referred to a '…rugged clash of spoiling tactics, certainly not for the faint-hearted', while another spoke of '…too much aimless and unimaginative football.' One might imagine Rowe's wearily shaken head. Meanwhile, at Christmas 1963, 21-year-old Chris Hassell became the youngest Club Secretary in the Football League. Five years had passed since he had impressed Rowe when organising those five-a-side tournaments. Such were Hassell's achievements in the post, the club would owe Rowe a considerable debt as the years passed (Hassell would finally end a distinguished career as Chief Executive of Yorkshire Cricket Club).

In January 1964 Arthur Rowe was interviewed about his search for young players, a role he clearly enjoyed. Way back in 1950 he wrote about the essential qualities he looked for in a young prospect, which I abbreviate here as:

- Sufficient all-round general football ability to have earned schoolboy representative honours.
- A good physique, or potential physique; a good 'big un' is better than a good 'little un'. Here he added: 'I overheard this remark, made of myself, as a scrawny, undersized schoolboy player, with a hurt that I still remember. I was glad when I filled out.'
- A love of the game. He added 'If eagerness and keenness can take this boy to the top then he is certain of success because the days ahead will test his keenness.
- Courage. 'Not necessarily physical, but the moral courage that makes for character. The courage which gives his game its purpose and power.'

Rowe added that a club developing its own young apprentices is building a player '…who is a club man, with a sense of loyalty—a priceless asset', and, '…for the successful lad, who satisfies the manager that he really has progressed satisfactorily, will come his first real success— a professional engagement. It is a great day too, for the manager—one of his great joys of this football life. He has, indeed, put into the game a little of what he has taken out, and thus— THE GREAT GAME GOES ON.'

Indeed, that very month David Payne signed apprentice professional forms at 16, showcasing how Rowe could persuade parents to put their trust in Crystal Palace. A typically charming handwritten letter to Payne's parents stated: 'I feel as confident as one can be that David will make the grade; his own personality and character will help him tremendously, for he is a nice lad. Some attendance at night school — learning anything — languages if he has the notion, will be wise, for his spare time will be intelligently spent and that's important. We usually find this out too late! I hope David does well; I believe he will.' When Rowe visited the Payne residence, David's father was in such awe of the great man that he did little but nervously talk down his own son! 'He's too casual', 'Too laid back', 'Doesn't get stuck in', 'Not aggressive enough', were some of dad's unhelpful comments, Rowe jokingly replying that those were just the qualities he liked about the boy!

Bobby Kellard, a talented, do-or-die, grafting midfielder, promised the temporarily-in-charge Rowe a goal before facing Bristol City and indeed came up with the only goal of the game. Here Cliff Holton forlornly chases Jack Connor's back pass, Kellard just visible under Holton's right arm.

By this point in the season home attendances were hovering around the 15-16,000 mark, a drop since Rowe's Fourth Division season (19,092) due, said the *Advertiser* to '...less artistic soccer.' But many fans were sad to witness their club's reputation being dragged through the mire. Goals, too, remained at a premium. The only thing to relish was the accumulation of points.

With Graham hospitalised Rowe briefly returned to the hotseat at the end of January. Coincidentally the now 32-year-old Johnny Brooks joined Palace from Brentford that week, Rowe presiding over his signature for the second time. Brooks said he was very happy to be with 'Arthur' again, adding 'He's a great fellow', but ultimately Brooks would total a mere seven Palace appearances before leaving to play in Canada. His debut came in the 1-0 Rowe-directed home victory over promotion outsiders Bristol City. Was it coincidental that John Matthews described this game as one of the more distinguished home games of the season? '[Palace's] brand of soccer shows increasing signs of quality,' Matthews pointedly added. Incidentally, the Edmonton-born Kellard promised Rowe before the game that he would get him a goal and he kept his word, his first for the club, and it proved to be the winner. Rowe made light of a critical match report which suggested Graham's methods had not entirely been banished in this game, saying: 'I can only conclude the paper who said "jeers" made a printer's error and meant "cheers"!' Two days before Palace travelled to Port Vale, Graham summoned not just Rowe to his hospital bed, but also an ally, Cliff Holton, which might confirm Rowe had indeed tinkered with the tactics against Bristol City.

Was Holton present to ensure Graham's instructions, not Rowe's, would be carried out this time? Surely Rowe will have found it extremely difficult to remain mute as Palace defenders wellied the ball clear, surrendering possession. As it was, Holton clearly had the upper hand over Rowe, with one report describing 'brawny Palace' adopting '...a ruthless policy.' Two Palace men were booked and Peter Burridge confirmed that during this match a colleague of his deliberately stamped on the 33-year-old Scottish international Jackie Mudie's ankle as he lay on the ground, leaving the home side with just ten fit players. 'Ruthless' indeed. Two late Holton strikes gave Palace the points, Rowe credited for switching wingers Imlach and Kellard during the game, crosses from Imlach 'tipping the scales'. Rowe cautiously summed-up afterwards: 'Our lads gave a sound and courageous display, even if the match was not brilliant.' 'Sound and courageous' was probably the best he could muster.

The final of Rowe's three wins standing-in for Graham saw strugglers Notts County beaten 2-0 at Selhurst Park. The game was drifting to a ninth single-goal victory before Burridge added a last-minute second, but the win was followed by typically caustic criticism, such as: 'Some wild kicking indeed by Palace defenders' and 'Palace ended up like a side fighting relegation.' This drew a surprising riposte from Chairman Wait, illustrating how desperate he was to take Palace to the top: 'I do not care if we see that sort of match from now until the end of the season as long as we can get out of this division. Then we can start playing football. I reckon I have about 19½ hours of agony to go.' As Graham left hospital with his methods rubber-stamped by the chairman, Rowe returned to the shadows.

Allen returned at Bristol Rovers, where Palace trailed 1-0 at half-time. For good reason Peter Burridge well remembered what occurred next. 'At half-time Dick was giving everyone a bollocking and then said to Ronnie Allen, sitting next to me, "Now, Ronnie, I want you to do this… [continuing to explain a tactical change]" and Ronnie turned to me saying: "What do *you* think of this?" and I replied "Well, I don't care," meaning "I don't mind", and Dick angrily shouted "You *should* care!" and I jumped to my feet and we ended face-to-face and he said "Don't you fuck with me!" and the other players were pulling me away from him.' Burridge rarely lost his composure on the pitch and his disciplinary record was pristine. Hackles

Arthur Rowe admires Peter Burridge's trusty left foot. Even the mild-mannered Burridge would on one occasion be drawn into serious conflict with Dick Graham (at half-time during a match at Bristol Rovers).

raised, he went out for the second-half to score twice, with Kellard grabbing the third, putting Palace level on points with Coventry. George Petchey could not abide Graham indulging in his 'door banging and tea cup throwing nonsense' and removed himself from the dressing-room when it occurred, telling me that Rowe himself would later act as a buffer between himself and the volatile manager.

By mid-March Palace were two victories clear of the field but Wait expressed dismay at attendances 20% below those enjoyed during Rowe's promotion season. Goals-per-game, too, had dropped from 2.4 to 1.6 and Wait made it clear rival attractions could not be blamed — a shot across the bows for Graham.

Then, with seven games left, a narrow victory over Bournemouth on Easter Saturday proved to be Palace's last that season. With five of the remaining seven games away, allied to Graham's limited ambitions when Palace travelled, there was an inevitability about this. Meanwhile, Coventry were strongly on the rebound. In the second of two Easter games, Palace went 2-0 up at Walsall before Graham pulled all 11 men back and Walsall's second and equalizing goal inevitably arrived in the final minute of time added-on. Then, in the first of Palace's two remaining home games, Palace lost to relegation-threatened Barnsley, a first home defeat, blamed in one match report on Palace's reliance on '…the big punt up the middle.' Palace's next trip was to Colchester where, despite the home side's nine games without a win, Graham fielded a defensive line-up. At 1-1 with an hour left, Palace left two up front, hanging on for a point. Reporter Mike Langley wrote: 'Palace trampled to the top of the Third Division last night,' adding that Colchester were a match for Palace at '…the brawny business of big kicking, shoving, and waist-high tackling.' As for the numbers game, Langley wrote: 'A gimmick was no substitute for skill with the bouncy ball.'

Entering the final week Palace had 59 points, Coventry 58 and Watford 57. On the last Wednesday, Palace only needed to overcome already-relegated Wrexham. Coventry had lost their penultimate fixture and Watford had dropped a point at home to Brentford. In front of just 3,384 spectators Whitehouse put Palace ahead (after the home goalkeeper had cleared the ball directly to him) and the final score was 2-2, one report stating: 'For most of the game one had great difficulty picking which team was going into the Second Division and which was going to the Fourth.' Had Palace played to win at Colchester, the extra point would ultimately have ensured them the Third Division Championship. As things were, a 2-0 Palace defeat to Oldham and a Watford win by at least 4-0 at Luton on the final day, with Coventry (at home) also winning, would see all three clubs tied on points. Palace's poor goal average, however, would have consigned them to another year in Division Three. Palace had won by just a single goal in ten of their 17 home victories and final day visitors Oldham were strong opponents. However, just a draw would see Palace captain Holton lift the Third Division trophy.

Palace had 60 points, Coventry and Watford both 58. With their superior goal average, a Coventry win would see them promoted over Watford. A Coventry win and a Palace defeat would see Jimmy Hill's men crowned Champions. In the event, Watford returned from Luton with no points, which at least confirmed that Palace and Coventry were up.

Coventry took an early lead against Colchester while Palace, playing even more poorly than of late, stumbled ahead due to a first-half Holton penalty. Yet within just nine minutes of the second-half Oldham had raced into a 3-1 lead! Had Graham instructed his men to defend their single-goal lead? Palace were unable to stage a comeback and Coventry hung on for a 1-0 win, so Palace lost not just the game but the Championship trophy and medals, too. Graham's extreme cautiousness had all but marooned them in the Third Division.

Nevertheless, Palace were at least now half-way to Rowe's ten-year forecast to reach the pinnacle of the Football League, although as one reporter pointed out '… seven successive games without a victory is hardly a primrose path to promotion.' No fewer than five sides finishing in the lower half of the table had out-scored Palace, one fan commenting: 'It must have been driven home to all 27,000 spectators that Palace, when playing a footballing side such as Oldham, have either lost the knowledge gained from Arthur Rowe of how to match skilful football with an equal brand, or, alternatively, are playing to instructions.'

On May 1st 1964, at the annual dinner of the 'Glaziers Club', Arthur Wait ensured Rowe was recognised for his big contribution to Second Division status: 'It was five years ago that we fell into the Fourth Division—a place we should never have been. But, under the guidance of Arthur Rowe, we were promoted back to the Third Division. Then, the person around whom he had moulded his team [Byrne] went, and, last season, dogged by injuries, things went wrong.'

Speaking of Byrne, he had by now truly found his feet in the First Division, totalling 33 goals in League and Cup as West Ham finished ninth in the top flight (Byrne was only bettered by the phenomenal Greaves, who had netted 35 in that season's League competition alone). Byrne also picked-up an FA Cup winners' medal and received the "Hammer of the Year" award (ahead of future World Cup heroes Moore, Hurst and Peters). Rowe will have been delighted and proud his 'lad' now enjoyed such success after his years of dedication to Crystal Palace. As a further assessment of Byrne's popularity at Upton Park, fan mail was sorted into three piles, one for Moore, one for Byrne and the third pile for all the other players.

When Ron Greenwood talked of Byrne's short-striding style (he seemed perpetually on his toes) it echoed advice Geoff Hurst had received from his dad, Charlie, who, of course, had played under Rowe at Chelmsford. Short strides make it easier to adjust body shape when receiving a pass. Graham Rowe tells me his dad had indeed coached him to shorten his strides when playing football, so he could 'be more nimble on the pitch', proof if required that it was indeed Arthur Rowe who introduced Charlie Hurst to this practice, and later similarly coached the young Byrne at Selhurst Park. Byrne returned to Wembley that month, sharply snapping up both goals alongside Jimmy Greaves and Bobby Charlton as England defeated Uruguay 2-1. Eleven days later Byrne went one better, scoring a hat-trick as England beat Portugal (Eusébio, Coluna, Torres and all) 4-3, in Lisbon.

SEASON 1964-65 Dick Graham utilised no fewer than nineteen players as Palace lost their first three Second Division games. The first, a home defeat by Derby County, ultimately led to goalkeeper Bill Glazier's departure, Graham striding on to the pitch at the end to publicly criticise his 'keeper. Glazier's angry response saw him dropped from the second game and he soon left when Coventry's Jimmy Hill came in with a record offer for a goalkeeper. Were it not for breaking a leg in the following 1965-66 season, Rowe's discovery had been shaping-up to be number two to Gordon Banks at the 1966 World Cup. His departure soon led to Rowe's second goalkeeping discovery, John 'Jacko' Jackson, becoming almost ever-present for the next eight seasons, a major contributor to what was then the greatest period in the club's history.

When Graham finally fixed on a settled side, Palace enjoyed five successive victories, one of which drew this bitter commentary from the manager of opponents Plymouth Argyle, Malcolm Allison: 'If Palace want to play defensive football on their own ground then their supporters will have to suffer. It reduces soccer to a farce. The crowd don't come to see eight players standing along the 18-yard box for most of the game.' A 'tit-for-tat' response in Palace's next programme notes was almost certainly Graham's, criticising Allison's tactics with the use of the term 'Continental', a dismissive adjective used by exponents of long-ball football (indeed, a style that under Graham had seen 19 of the previous season's 46 League games ending either 0-0, 1-0 or 1-1). Ronnie Allen then returned to hit a hat-trick against Charlton, but after just six further appearances departed to coach Wolves.

Meanwhile Graham recognised young David Payne's potential, signing him as a full professional. As with other Rowe discoveries such as Glazier and Stephenson,

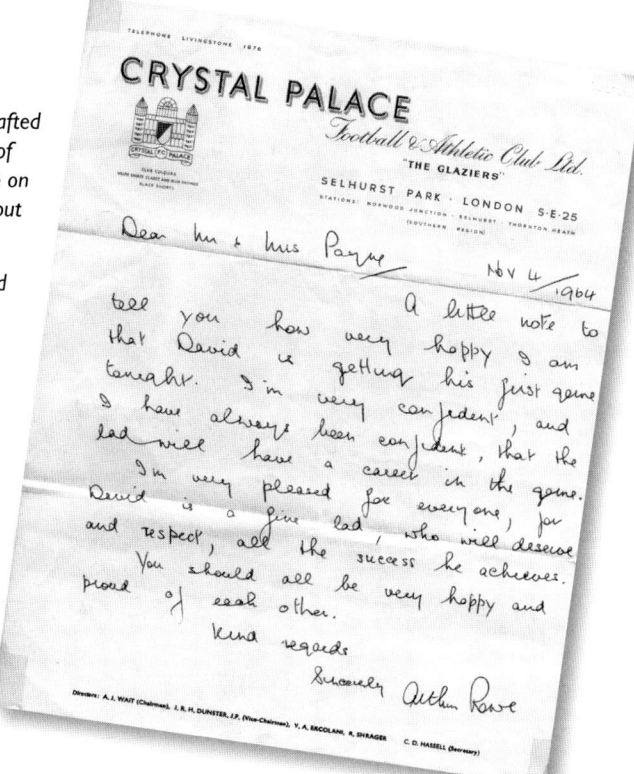

A typical, simple but sublimely crafted letter from Rowe to the parents of promising youngster David Payne on the occasion of his first-team debut for Crystal Palace:

'You should all be very happy and proud of each other'.

Payne would later be capped at England Under-23 level, but it took Graham's departure before Payne's prowess as a box-to-box midfielder was recognised. Payne made his first-team debut in a League Cup draw away at First Division Leicester City prompting Rowe to again write to the young man's family: 'David is a fine lad, who will deserve and respect all the success he achieves. You should all be very happy and proud of each other.'

Peter Burridge had clearly fitted-in at the higher level, and with goals under Graham's management hard to come by, he still picked-up 11 from just 20 appearances. However he had now turned 31 and with the arrival of a younger challenger, Keith Smith (another acquisition from West Brom), became the man who most often stood-down. In the 2-1 League Cup replay defeat against Leicester, Burridge had leapt to head Holton's cross down and past Gordon Banks, something Pelé tried and failed to replicate in the 1970 World Cup! He ultimately averaged a goal every two-and-a-half games compared to Smith's one in four. On December 24th 1964, Smith made the *Guinness Book of Records* when scoring at Derby after just six seconds, but it was Burridge who scored twice that day, one a stunning left-foot volley from 30 yards, this after first setting the ball up with his right foot. He had certainly repaid Rowe's shrewdness when acquiring him.

That Christmas Graham brought in three more forwards, including the pacy Charlie Woods from Bournemouth, and the seventh and eighth former West Brom players to join the Palace staff, David Burnside and Roy Horobin, further evidence that the manager struggled to cast his net wider. Meanwhile attendances remained 12% down on Rowe's Fourth Division season and this in the second tier! By the time Palace had progressed to the FA Cup fifth round, Graham had written Burridge off as a striker, selecting him in left midfield for a fifth round tie with First Division Nottingham Forest. Yet the supreme highlight of what resulted in an atypical, stirring victory was the goal putting Palace back in front. It was described

Peter Burridge, who Rowe had brought to Crystal Palace, was the hero of the Club's 3-1 victory over First Division Nottingham Forest in February 1965 with this left-footed volley to the top-right corner, putting Palace 2-1 ahead. On the right he celebrates with Cliff Holton and 41,000 fans.

as '…the goal that will be talked about so long as football is played at Selhurst Park.' With the score at 1-1 Holton moved out wide on the left toward the corner flag. Graham shouted from the touchline for Burridge to get forward in support. Holton's lofted pass perfectly coincided with the speedy arrival of Burridge on the edge of the area, and a crisp, clean left-footed volley saw the ball slam into the top-right corner, fragments of white toilet rolls flying up from the netting, in unison with thousands of arms all around the stadium. Holton wrapped things up with a late third and Palace were in the FA Cup quarter-finals for the very first time. It was Graham's finest achievement. Nevertheless more than half the players conquering Forest remained from Rowe's time as manager or had been spotted by him. Of these, Jackson, Burridge and Stephenson had been particularly impressive on this occasion.

Unfortunately the quarter-final draw saw Palace paired with Don Revie's highflying Leeds United and it proved to be the beginning of a protracted end for Rowe's successor. Leeds had quickly earned a reputation as masters of the dark arts of the game, the like of which Graham himself had been keen to fine-tune at Selhurst Park. Prior to the performance against Forest in the earlier round, a *Daily Mail* article had criticised Graham's team resorting to 'strong-arm tactics', adding that Palace '…prefer slide-tackles to slide-rule passes.' Palace's subsequent change of style against Forest suggests Graham had indeed been influenced by this article, but against Leeds he left out Cup hero Burridge and opted to take on Leeds at their own game. At that time the reputations of Palace and Revie's Leeds were deteriorating at a similar pace, not that either manager seemed remotely concerned. To Rowe's lasting and utter dismay, Leeds were developing a reputation for foul play and gamesmanship like nothing ever seen before, and it prompted the question: had Revie and Graham developed a mutual 'two-fingers to the world' attitude when they were playing colleagues at Leicester City?

On the night, 45,384 spectators packed Selhurst Park and Palace kept it scoreless for an hour before eventually caving-in 3-0 in a contest uglier than the worst prediction. Press acclaim from Palace's sensational Forest victory was erased at a stroke, Desmond Hackett of the *Express* writing: 'If this is the best of Crystal Palace then there were no regrets from me to see this Second Division team go down to Leeds United,' adding '…the only aspect of the game in which Palace were ahead was the discreditable total of 27 fouls against 12 by Leeds.' The *Daily Herald*'s Peter Lorenzo wrote: '… the ratio [of fouls] tells very clearly who were the principal offenders,' adding: 'I unhesitatingly indict Crystal Palace for much of the over-strong football.' Those Palace players that night who I have since met are rather ashamed by what should have been an occasion to remember. It broke the hearts of those who had cherished the Rowe's crisp-passing, high-scoring, Fourth Division promotion side. The tie also witnessed Petchey's final appearance as a player. When recalling Petchey's purchase in 1960, Arthur Rowe said: 'It is quite a job to decide who was the best bargain, Blanchflower for £30,000 or George Petchey for about £2,800. Both are first-class blokes.'

A 2-0 League defeat at home to Southampton then ended faint hopes of a second successive promotion. More fans stayed away and the attendance for the final home game plummeted to 12,175 — in the Fourth Division under Rowe, only a December fixture with Crewe fell below that figure. Meanwhile Johnny Byrne suffered a significant setback when restored for England's Wembley showpiece fixture with Scotland. He unusually featured in midfield on a day when Ramsey first fielded the England defensive line-up that would feature in the following year's World Cup: Banks, Cohen, Wilson, Charlton and Moore, with Stiles covering in front of them. With Byrne prompting alongside Bobby Charlton in midfield, England took a two-goal lead by the 35th minute. Scotland pulled it back to 2-1 before left-back Ray Wilson suffered a rib injury and it was Byrne who became a makeshift replacement. In performing this role he then suffered a career-threatening knee injury, and the game ended 2-2. Even with his thicker waistline Byrne would surely have added some extra gloss to Ramsey's 1966 World Cup success. After all, in the 15 England games up to and including the Scotland fixture Byrne had scored eight in nine of them.

When Palace drew 1-1 with already promoted Newcastle on Easter Saturday, 17-year-old Rowe discovery David Payne was described as '…playing with the aplomb of a more adult performer, always attempting to use the ball and never wilting when the men from the North-East tried some power play.' By season's end, Graham's Palace had achieved a commendable seventh place but a fierce indictment of Graham's approach appeared that summer in the *FA Year Book* as part of an article entitled 'Soccer and Sophistication': 'Last season [1964-65]… a side was able to command a position in the top seven of the Second Division having scored fewer than fifty goals up to the last week of the season [actually with four games left to play]. This is a terrible and frightening commentary on our football.' Although the author did not name the club involved, it was clearly Graham's Palace (to meet the press date, the article had been penned before Easter, by which time Palace had totalled just 49). In Dick Graham's defence, George Petchey told me he had learned a lot from him, before adding, 'A lot of people couldn't abide him. When I became coach, I was the bridge.' But during the upcoming 1965-66 season, Petchey's own relationship with Graham was again put to the test. Indeed, Graham's Palace 'project' was to last only a further seven months.

SEASON 1965-66 Graham's summer shopping left much to be desired. Two forwards, Ian Lawson and Ernie Yard made little or no impression. One new man who did prove his worth was defender Jack Bannister, but Graham's headline purchase was that of 30-year-old Derek 'The Tank' Kevan, who became the tenth former West Brom player to arrive since Graham began assisting Rowe in 1960. Kevan had just scored a creditable 56 Second Division goals over two seasons at Manchester City, but arrived at Selhurst Park patently unfit, weighing 13st 13lb. Nevertheless Graham told the assembled pressmen 'I believe I am one of the few men who know how to bring the best out of Derek.' Yet Kevan soon confessed he found Graham's training programme too tough, telling the same pressmen 'Whereas the players here are up to, say, 33 repetitions of a certain exercise, I am done at 20.' He soon pulled a muscle and his signing proved to be a disaster. In an opening day defeat at Birmingham, he was satirically described as 'economical of movement' and Palace took just four points from the first 10.

That autumn Arthur Rowe will have shared 21-year-old Stephenson's pride when he was invited by Ramsey to join the full England party for training, nine months ahead of the 1966 World Cup Finals. Although too inexperienced to be a candidate for selection, his inclusion boosted his confidence. Then, in a 2-0 Palace defeat at Preston ('...a game where brawn pushed brain into a background of mediocrity'), 18-year-old Payne was booked and five minutes' later, a second foul saw him ordered off. So with just 14 first-team games under his belt Payne asked for a personal hearing, both he and his manager believing the Preston player had play-acted. To his great credit, Graham even went to young Payne's home to explain the situation to the player's parents. But for all the manager's protestations of innocence, referees were now pre-conditioned to expect overzealous tackling from Graham's side. After a 3-1 defeat to Manchester City and losing a two-goal lead at home to Rotherham, discord brewed in the boardroom. Two days before travelling to Wolves on October 30th, criticisms of Graham's stewardship by director John Dunster upset Chairman Wait, who even offered his own resignation, only for Dunster to go instead. The grace and conviviality of Rowe's time in charge had long gone; the football was poor, popular players replaced by inadequate buys, and few had anything positive to say about Crystal Palace. Most worrying for Dunster will have been the drop in attendances since the 19,000-plus average in Rowe's Fourth Division days. Despite playing two divisions higher, the average had now sunk to just 17,592.

At Molineux a truly dire 1-0 defeat was unfortunately captured by the *Match of the Day* cameras. Filmed highlights make for tough viewing, the only Palace player to excel being hard-pressed 23-year-old 'keeper Jackson, a performance confirming the potential Rowe had recognized. Graham's men engaged in little more than hoofing and chasing. Afterwards the Palace boss was persuaded to take a months' leave, his wife simultaneously undergoing surgery at this time. So Rowe took temporary command of team administration, with Petchey controlling on-field matters. At home to Norwich the two big strikers Kevan and Lawson were unsurprisingly discarded in favour of the more mobile duo of Smith and Burridge. Rowe's discovery, Steve Kember, 17, was made substitute. The *Advertiser* duly reported increased '...mobility up front for Palace' although the game ended goalless. For the trip to Bury which followed Kevan was surprisingly restored at Burridge's expense. Had Graham demanded it? The big man shot wide of an empty net in the first minute before Palace went 2-0 behind but, with Rowe and Petchey at the helm, Palace were beginning to play some football, Yard pulling one back. Burnside's equaliser followed some swift and accurate passing and as a result it was recognised in one report that Palace '...had the resource, *if so minded*, to play effective, attacking football.' Palace returned with a well-earned point.

Was Wait testing the waters by putting Petchey and Rowe in charge for a few games? A narrow 1-0 victory over powerful Southampton followed, a report telling how Palace's attack had moved '...much more freely and incisively than of late.' The scrambled winner came from Kevan. Wait still talked of the club's 'terrific' confidence in Graham but two months later it became clear there had then been '...a minor revolution in the club administration.' On November 25th the hugely popular Kellard and Burridge were sold (Burridge having finally justified Rowe's faith with an excellent 49 goals from 124 appearances). This took place on the day of a vociferous Annual General Meeting, a spin-off from Dunster's departure. Wait reported gates were down, the club thus not paying its way. One shareholder said he didn't like the policy of scoring a single goal and then falling back on defence. He wanted to see goals and felt this was the reason that gates were down. Graham, present, rather condescendingly responded that he would love to see his team go four or five goals up, but '...the other side don't just sit back and let you do it.' He said the players become anxious about losing a lead, and '...our wingers come back to help and that is the way we play best.' Hearing this can have been of little comfort to the goal-shy Kevan who had publicly expressed his need for wingers if he were to find his goalscoring form.

Time was now running out for Rowe's successor.

A scathingly erudite fan's letter to Chairman Wait was then published. 'Some time ago, when critics were getting at manager Dick Graham, you said to the press; "If they do not like it (meaning the football and the methods) let them stay away." I suggest, sir, that the decline in gates at recent matches proves they are doing just that.' The fan added 'I do not mind paying more for my football, providing it is attractive, fast, open football; I do not mind the home team losing, if they go down to a side playing a better type of football.' He continued: 'We expect to be entertained and enjoy a good, clean game and, if possible, see the home team win.' Viewing the events which followed, this considered criticism almost certainly left an indelible mark on Wait but publicly he stated: 'Our confidence in Dick Graham is terrific and never been greater.' Then Palace were immediately thumped 4-0 at Derby. After the following goalless home draw with Cardiff (now just one win from eight), the situation grew a whole lot worse.

On Friday December 10th, 1965, Graham let slip the pressure he was now under. The team was to travel to Euston station en-route to play Carlisle the following day.

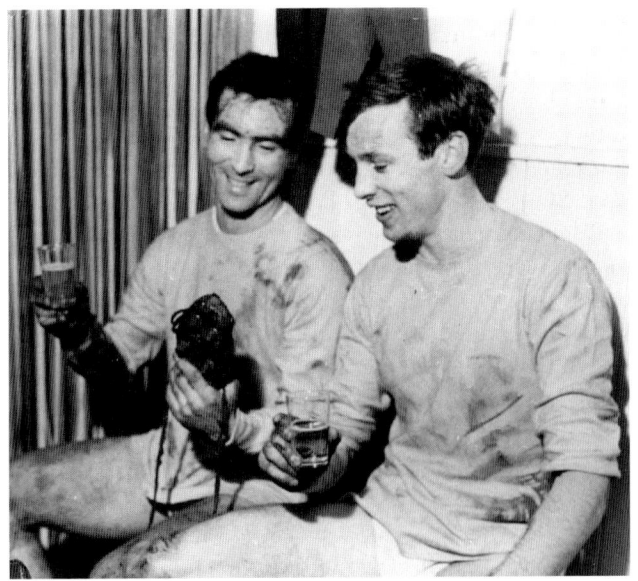

When Alan Stephenson had sat in the Palace changing room to admire Peter Burridge's trusty left boot after the 3-1 FA Cup victory over Nottingham Forest, he himself had left the field that afternoon with praise ringing in his ears after dominating England striker Frank Wignall throughout the game.

Little will Stephenson have imagined then what would take place between himself and his manager just 10 months' later at Euston Station.

Before leaving Graham asked for the players' opinions on the run of poor results. The experienced John Sewell, assuming the manager preferred honest opinions, said the wingers were playing too deep. Graham then turned to young centre-half Alan Stephenson, who had of course recently trained with the full England side and was the target of First Division clubs. Stephenson agreed with Sewell, as did several other players. Graham listened to Stephenson without comment, but, when stepping off the coach at Euston, Graham blocked the young man's path, asking: 'Where do you think you're going?' Presumably the manager had ruminated on Stephenson's contribution to the debate and now accused him of allowing transfer publicity to go to his head. Requesting the return of Stephenson's train ticket, he then told his star defender 'You can go home now.' A distressed Stephenson, proud to play for a club Rowe had enticed him to join, felt belittled in front of his teammates and headed back to the home he shared with his parents. As a consequence Stephenson's father phoned Wait, who had not travelled with the team and the chairman was shocked to find an essential player left behind. Contacted by the press on Saturday, Wait was asked if Stephenson would leave the club. 'No. He is a smashing kid and we want to keep him,' replied Wait, who now girded himself to confront his manager.

Inevitably Palace lost the game, John Jackson recalling Graham '…going mad at us', and saying Stephenson had become 'too big for his boots'. With the story hitting the Sunday papers Graham found himself in a face-off with a chairman whose strength when running his own successful business included mixing with the 'workers'. Wait's son Brian told me his dad was '…not an aloof man, he was a man's man.' After the meeting Graham told the press that what he had done had hurt him as much as Stephenson. Wait said he expected the matter would be resolved by Wednesday, the day of the regular monthly board meeting. Stephenson attended the meeting and immediately requested a transfer. The club had accepted Graham's story. With the manager at his side, the chairman chastised two journalists: 'Why don't you write a story about directors being faithful to their managers for a change?' However, for many fans frustrated with poor quality football since Rowe's time in charge, the damaged reputation of the club and the recent departure of the popular Burridge, Kellard and Holton, the story of Graham's altercation with their young, star centre-half was the last straw.

With only one victory from nine, the pressure on Graham was now intense and, unfortunately, Joe Mercer and Malcolm Allison's promotion favourites Manchester City were next up. Coach Petchey, despite his forthright nature, generally did as Graham requested but, friendly with the chief scout at City, George knew that Allison would try to defeat Graham's man-marking by starting with two men up front then suddenly dropping them back to midfield, changing places with two colleagues. 'Dick always wanted everybody to have a man to mark. He never wanted players to use their brains', said Petchey, whose own view was that the two Palace central defenders should zonal-mark, to avoid City's trap and be pulled out of position. Graham responded angrily to Petchey's zonal marking suggestion and immediately sent his coach packing, saying 'I don't want you around.' So instead of sitting on the bench for the City game, Petchey was sent to spy on Palace's next opponents, Ipswich. Inevitably Malcolm Allison did just as Petchey had foreseen, midfielder Mike Doyle performing one of the 'switch' roles and scoring both goals in a 2-0 victory. On Monday morning Petchey walked in and, referring to the City defeat, asked Graham: 'What happened?' Graham responded, 'You're fired, bugger off, go home!' George believed he had been sacked, so, in the interim he accepted the youth trainer's job at QPR and began some long-deferred decorating at home. Ten days later, however, Graham phoned him, asking him to return to duty but during those ten days he had not told the chairman about Petchey's removal from duty, probably fearing Wait's reaction, knowing full well how much Wait admired the coach.

Two days after Christmas, Ipswich Town arrived and were defeated 3-1. Stephenson surprisingly appeared at centre-forward, but with the none-too-tall Bill Baxter in the middle of Ipswich's defence, there was method in Graham's 'madness'. Height was also the consideration with the other tactical change. Speedy Ipswich centre-forward Gerry Baker was only 5ft 7in tall, a difficult challenge for tall, slim Stephenson to handle, so the smaller, nippier Charlie Woods took up position in the centre of Palace's defence. To Graham's credit, both surprise moves proved a success, Baker was kept quiet and Stephenson scored twice, one a right-footer, the other a thumping header. Of course, however, the surprise tactics may have been Petchey's, as it was he who had spied on Ipswich.

By the turn of the year Palace had scored a measly 28 goals from 23 games, with 33 conceded. Against a general upward trend in English football attendances that year, Palace's had dropped 21% from the previous season. It only now came to Wait's attention that Graham had kept Petchey's banishment from him. By the time Graham took his side to Bristol City on New Year's Day 1966 the decision had been reached to sack him. Dick Graham was to be informed on Monday January 3rd, 19 days since Wait's full backing over the Stephenson affair.

For Graham's last game in charge, at Ashton Gate, he showed foresight when awarding a debut to 17-year-old Steve Kember, and also bit the bullet by dropping the two bulky, awkward strikers he had invested so much faith in, Kevan and Lawson. Kember lined up at outside-right and Terry Long was reinstated. It was Kember who won the ball and released Yard, whose square pass saw Long score, saving Palace a point. Graham's final selection also included two other teenagers, David Payne (18) and forward Paul Cutler (19) plus, of course, John 'Jacko' Jackson (23) in goal and 21-year-old Alan Stephenson. All young men who would not have been at the club had it not been for Arthur Rowe. With supreme irony, Graham's final team selection saw Palace receive a far better press than usual. But it was too little, too late. On Monday morning at 10 a.m., the chairman waited for Dick Graham to arrive at Selhurst Park. His position with the club was terminated with immediate effect, Wait telling the Press: 'Mr Arthur Rowe has been appointed acting general manager and George Petchey as assistant to him.' Petchey was described in *The Sun* as '...a disciple of more attractive football,' having strong views on the game and how it is played, whilst possessing great loyalty to Rowe, who he so admired.

I should point out that in writing Rowe's biography I never set out to target Dick Graham for criticism and indeed he was gracious to take my phone call when attempting to arrange an interview that he was then too ill to attend. However, my personal experience of seeing Arthur Rowe's side strike seven goals in a thrilling game, only to return three years later to witness the Dick Graham-orchestrated 'street-brawl' with Leeds United encourages an emphasis on how the former's beliefs and coaching ran contrary to those of the latter. First and foremost this book's aim is to relate Arthur Rowe's lifetime dedication to the sport of soccer but along the way he had the misfortune to work with people whose inclination was more 'Chapmanesque'. This had an insidious effect on his career, almost certainly robbing him of further achievements. Fortunately it is Rowe's style of play which captivates *Match of the Day* audiences today, not that of Anderson ('If you're in trouble, lads, you know where I'll sit') or Graham ('Kick, Bollock and Bite').

Dick Graham's written statement on departing Selhurst Park ended 'This morning was a sad moment in my life' and he received a sympathetic letter written by Brian Whitehouse and signed by 21 of the Palace playing staff. Despite signing, John Sewell would later state that under Graham '…there was great disharmony in the club.' Another signature was that of the young Stephenson, who truly held no grudges, crediting Graham with making him '…the defender I became.' 'Jacko' Jackson was grateful too, for Graham's specialist goalkeeping coaching, while Keith Smith believed Graham's ideas were ahead of his time: 'It was all a bit revolutionary, and he didn't get the accolades he deserved'. Bobby Kellard once said he owed his career to Graham, benefitting from discipline he needed at the time.

Pictured the following day kissing her husband on the cheek as he poignantly clutched the players' letter, Graham's wife Anne said: 'There were people at the club who did not want him to succeed. When he was appointed they said he would not make a success of the job, and they were not going to change their minds and admit that he had been a success.' Aside from the directors, particularly perhaps, Dunster, and the man who had appointed him, Arthur Wait, the only senior figures still at the club were Long, Petchey and Rowe himself. One can well imagine Rowe suggesting to Wait that Graham's abrasive character and limited tactical ambition would make him unsuitable to manage on a full-time basis, but there is no evidence to support that.

Publicly justifying the decision to dispense with Graham's services, Wait said, 'The simple reason is that we are not paying our way at the moment.' A bonus system which paid on results yet could only be paid from good income at the turnstiles (which Graham was failing to maintain) was unsupportable. *The Sun* included more forthright Wait comments: 'And what about our public image over the last two years? It hasn't been very good has it?' When, just seven days earlier, Wait stated in the December 27th match programme that '1965 has been one of the greatest years in the history of this fine club.…', he had been unaware of the Petchey incident and was still honour-bound to support his manager. But he had now been pushed too far by a man who, as *The Sun* put it, '…seemed to thrive on controversy.'

So very unlike his predecessor.

ROWE RETURNS At the very beginning of a year that would be remembered for the England World Cup victory masterminded by his 'pupil', Alf Ramsey, the now 59-year-old Rowe was back behind the manager's desk at Selhurst Park. Yet

Rowe photographed on the day of his return to the manager's chair at Selhurst Park in January 1966.

George Petchey joins him in the office. The two men enjoyed much mutual respect.

for now he was merely 'acting' manager, mainly looking after the administrative aspects of the job, with George Petchey responsible for the first-team and tactics. *The Sun* immediately concluded (or perhaps, 'wished') that the duo would reinstate 'push-and-run'.

Dick Graham's future forays into management would include just one-and-a-half seasons at Orient, two months at Walsall and a season at Wimbledon. His longest and most successful spell turned out to be four seasons with Colchester United, for which he is most recognised and praised, although he never took them higher than sixth place in the Fourth Division. His big achievement was the club's 1971 3-2 FA Cup victory over Don Revie's by then even mightier Leeds United. Yet just days after that his Colchester side, engaged in a League encounter, were described in the *Times* as playing 'factory floor football'. As a determined man with strong self-belief, it was perhaps only to be expected that Graham's managerial career after Palace would run little smoother and, toward the end of his career, he must have regretted falling foul of the best and most amenable boss that he could ever have hoped to work for — Arthur Wait.

Nevertheless, Arthur Rowe was back at the Palace helm, this time to support Petchey and allow Wait time to ensure he uncovered the man of experience he felt the club needed to complete the forecast of Division One football by the turn of the decade.

But… what if Rowe and Petchey were to rack-up a few handsome victories?

20

Rowe's Ten-Year Pledge Achieved in Nine

PALACE REACH THE PROMISED LAND 1966-69

'It's funny, but I honestly feel after all these years in football as if I am starting all over again.'

ARTHUR ROWE INTERVIEWED BY PATRICK ROBINSON JANUARY 1966

Upon Graham's departure, Arthur Rowe sat down to chat individually with all the players. Remaining from his previous time in charge were Howe, Long, Stephenson and Wood, while he could now work for the first time with his own discoveries: Jackson, Payne and Kember. 'Push-and-run' fans hoped the club's damaged reputation could quickly be restored should the Rowe-Petchey duo be confirmed as a full-time partnership. However Wait, concerned for Rowe's health, made it clear that, in time, he would appoint from outside.

The new interim boss confessed he had only seen the first-team twice that season, the second time being that December 27th victory over Ipswich Town. Watching Graham's side twice will have been twice too often for a purist such as Arthur Rowe and he now repeated his managerial mantra: 'I have always regarded the object of football is for a team to win and provide entertainment at the same time.' In Petchey, he finally had a partner who he admired and trusted. Although he said he would only tide the team over during an awkward spell, one suspects he was keeping a promise to wife Pom whilst covertly hoping he and Petchey achieved the results which might lead to a full-time arrangement. He asked Norman Giller to report his and Petchey's appointment as a '...quiet takeover,' adding 'I don't want to see sensational headlines about this.' Knowing they would have to win every remaining game if promotion were to become a possibility, their more realistic aim was to return to a more crowd-pleasing playing style, to boost attendances (and thus income) before a new manager came in to ensure Rowe's 'promise' of Division One football by 1970 was met.

The first Rowe/Petchey side took the field at home to Bury on January 8th, 1966, in an adventurous formation of 3-2-1-4, the more creative Burnside came in for Yard, to feed a front four that included 'Stevie' Kember, who moved inside to accommodate the pacy Woods, and Palace got off to a great start. In just six minutes Kember chested-down a Smith pass, then shifted the ball quickly from right to left foot before beating the advancing 'keeper for his first League goal. Palace played a more open game but lacked a marksman. As a result Bury, including future England star Colin Bell, came back into it, but Palace took the two points. At Millmoor Kevan was surprisingly given an opportunity and in snowy conditions Burnside and Kember caused Rotherham problems, but the home side fortuitously went ahead. Palace then claimed an equaliser but the ball was adjudged not to have crossed the line, before United scored a quality second. As Palace tried to salvage something, a third was conceded. Derek Kevan never played for the Palace again.

Before a third round FA Cup tie at Carlisle, Arthur Rowe was interviewed by future novelist Patrick Robinson, then of the *Daily Express*: 'A gentle, silver-haired grandpa named Arthur Rowe accompanies [the Palace team] to Carlisle. And the strict drilling and instructions of the recently-sacked Graham are replaced by kindly words and encouragement "…to play football the natural way."' Typically principled, Rowe told Robinson: 'I don't want anyone to think I am glad Mr Graham has gone. I am not. I am employed by this club and I simply want to do the best I can for it.' As with his persecutors in Spurs' boardroom, Rowe would never publicly air his grievances, even saying 'I respect Dick's ideas. You started off with a draw with him—and you still had a draw at the end of it if you didn't let anyone in to score against you. That is sound logic. But I have the instinct to go out and try to win every match with natural, responsive football.' He did expose one gripe about the outgoing manager however, saying: 'I have been a player and I do not tend to get cross about a match. I do not believe people do things badly on purpose. I believe they fail because they cannot help it.' Rowe then let slip a desire for his return to become permanent: 'It's funny, but I honestly feel after all these years in football as if I am starting all over again.'

However, a strong Carlisle side including the likes of Chris Balderstone, Stan Harland and Willie Carlin saw Palace exit the Cup. Only Howe, Long, Stephenson and Wood had played 'push-and-run' before, so Rowe and Petchey were essentially starting from scratch. Palace's second post-Graham home match saw another 1-0 success, this time against Birmingham. The bustling Whitehouse, moved to centre-forward for the first time, snatched the only goal. Birmingham's intimidatory tackling suggested they expected a physical Graham-like performance from Palace but, as one report clarified: 'There has been a Palace revolution. They just don't play that way anymore.' As for young Payne; with Graham gone, Petchey said to the 18-year-old 'I'm going to teach you how to play!' Petchey and Rowe identified him as a creative, driving midfielder and worked on his movement, when to hold the ball, when to release it, how to take up angles plus, that 'push-and-run' essential, finding space to support the man in possession. With Petchey's coaching, the player said his game improved in '…leaps and bounds.' He and Kember would light up Selhurst Park in the post-Graham era.

At struggling Leyton Orient, Palace went two-up in just six minutes. On a muddy Brisbane Road surface and with an awkward wind behind them in the first-half, Palace played the ball in the air more often and it paid off, whilst in the second period they kept possession, ensuring victory. Again Whitehouse was on the scoresheet and Palace now had six points from eight. The following Friday at Portman Road captain Whitehouse again led by example, pulling Palace level after Ipswich had gone ahead in the first minute. 'Palace [then] settled down to play a brand of soccer that delighted the purists and gave Ipswich all the trouble they could handle' wrote former sceptic Matthews. A second from Whitehouse saw Palace on-track for another two points but Ipswich's saviour was ex-Palace favourite Bobby Kellard. Then, on Valentine's Day 1966, Stewart Imlach was signed for a second time, from Rowe's former club, Chelmsford. He was expected to contribute on the field and assist with coaching and went straight into a Palace side which should have beaten Middlesbrough comfortably although it was Imlach's through ball which set Keith Smith up to score Palace's solitary goal, the game ending 1-1. At Huddersfield Whitehouse hit his fifth goal from seven games only for the home side to grab a fortunate equaliser.

But Whitehouse was then poached by Dick Graham, now assisting Bob Stokoe at Charlton. Rowe met Chairman Wait for an hour before suggesting it unwise to keep the player and '…make him disgruntled.' Whilst regretting the loss, he equally damned the player with faint praise: 'I have a high regard for his honest endeavour.' By contrast when new captain Stephenson became a West Ham target, Rowe, his sights sill firmly set on First Division football, stated he wasn't for sale at any price.

Rowe then signed 19-year-old full-back Michael 'Chick' Maynard who had arrived from British Guiana in 1955 to become one of only a handful of black players with Football League clubs in the 1960s (the famed 'Three Degrees', Regis, Batson and Cunningham, would not break through with West Brom until the following decade). Sadly Maynard never achieved a place in Palace's first team but did later play League football with Peterborough.

The improved quality of football had seen Palace attendances rebound, although Rowe part-exonerated the quality of Graham's football when making the point that fewer fans were by then working on Saturday mornings and their day was full of attractive alternatives. Rowe was conscious, too, of the growing success of Tommy Docherty's youthful, 'mod' Chelsea side, drawing football lovers from Palace's catchment area for the chance to see the likes of Cooke, Osgood and Tambling.

When a Rowe/Petchey side then handsomely beat First Division Nottingham Forest 4-1 in a friendly, they showcased an elaborate five-man free-kick plan with one-touch passes, the leaping Smith finally heading home. To convey the quality of Palace's play that night the *Croydon Times* dusted-down an adjective rarely used during Graham's time: 'scintillating'. Back in League action, promotion-seeking Coventry overcame mid-table Palace, missing the injured Stephenson (1-0) and from then on Petchey was left in sole charge on match days, his mentor turning his attention to uncovering a goalscorer.

After renewed transfer enquiries for Stephenson, Rowe told the press: 'I am sure he would dearly love to play his First Division soccer with us.' There followed a 1-1 draw with Preston and a short trip to Charlton where Palace succumbed 1-0 to a side now including Burridge, Holton and Whitehouse. Young Kember now joined the three other Rowe discoveries as first-team regulars. With Palace still lacking punch up-front, another close away defeat followed at Norwich, but over Easter Palace took four points from six.

However, any lingering hope that the managerial duo harboured of leading Palace into season 1966-67 ended when Wait then appointed experienced ex-

Swindon boss Bert Head as manager. He was a spectator for the first match of his reign, only taking charge for the final three games. Head was an old-school manager, be-suited and office-based, which, of course, was conducive to Petchey (now appointed Coach), while Rowe became Assistant Manager. Head was a blunt man, unsophisticated tactically, his character best symbolised by a response he once gave to the *Observer*'s Barry Norman who asked if Head was looking to buy a 'striker' (then a trendy new term for 'goalscorer'). Head replied: 'Call him what you like. Some bugger who puts the goals in.' Following the interview, Norman reported on a Palace defeat to Norwich and was unable to resist typing the obvious: 'Norwich were quite well equipped with buggers like that.'

So Arthur Rowe would now be happily engaged in scouting and watching over the club's youth sides, whilst supporting Head and Petchey as an elder statesman. The Head-Petchey-Rowe triumvirate would bring about great success and eradicated the bitter taste of the Dick Graham era. However there can be little doubt that many Palace fans had yearned for Arthur to get another chance. The Rowe/Petchey combination had only achieved five victories and four draws from their fifteen League games in charge, but in so doing they converted the playing style whilst suffering the lack of firepower Graham had bequeathed them (over the entire season, his attacking purchases Lawson, Kevan, Smith, Burnside and Yard had amassed a pitiful 20 goals between them). On the other hand, defensively, Petchey and Rowe's passing game, ensuring greater possession, saw Palace concede an average of just one goal per game as against Graham's (nearly) 1.5 goals per game. The rate Palace conceded under Rowe and Petchey, goals spread over a full season, would have matched that of Second Division champions Manchester City. Had the partnership been given funds to buy-in one or two strikers of their own

Bert Head lines up at back left, next to George Petchey, then Rowe and Club Secretary Chris Hassell. Seated are Director Ralph Shrager, Chairman Arthur Wait and Director Victor Ercolani.

choice, there is little doubt Rowe would have added further achievements to his impressive CV.

Incidentally, that famous World Cup summer saw a new TV show, '*Quizball*', piloted by the BBC, a general knowledge quiz contested by players of football clubs. Stewart Imlach represented Crystal Palace and his son Gary recalled that the method to score a 'goal' was to choose either four *simple* questions or just one *hard* one, called 'Route One'. As Gary explained, 'When the Palace players complained to me [in the early 21st Century] about Dick Graham's tactics, they were using a term, 'Route One' that hadn't existed when [the manager] first screamed at them from the dugout to stop fannying about and get the ball up-field.' As with route one in the actual sport of soccer, a goal in *Quizball* might result from a hefty kick in the general direction of the opponents' goal — the 'kick' in that case often being a lucky guess to a tough question but to score via 'Route Four' the players succeeded when confidently answering four simple questions, the equivalent of four short, accurate passes. One wonders if Rowe had invented *Quizball*!

Arthur Rowe accompanied the new manager that summer, acquiring the tall, leggy Bobby Woodruff from First Division Wolves and Tommy White, an old-style, battering-ram type centre-forward from Aberdeen. The pair had watched White in the spring, possibly at Bill Nicholson's recommendation (White's brother being the late John White, of Spurs' 'double'-winners). Woodruff proved the more prolific but White was an excellent foil. A make-weight in the deal for White was wiry, red-headed centre-half John McCormick who ultimately became a rock at the centre of a defence which later faced the cream of top level attackers.

Meanwhile that summer Johnny Byrne trained in Ramsey's provisional squad of 28 for the home World Cup Finals, but his increased weight and unsound right knee ultimately saw him one of six sent home. The England manager admitted that leaving Byrne out had been one of his most difficult decisions, while a perceptive profile on the *Football England* website states: 'Had a follower of English football been told in 1964, or even 1965, that England would win the 1966 World Cup and the goals would be supplied by a West Ham player there would have been no great surprise… the fan would simply have assumed that the player in question was Byrne, not Hurst.'

Arthur Rowe, with links to both players, would have, too.

SEASON 1966-67 That summer Rowe took 16 Palace youth players to take part in a tournament in North-Western France where his side won all three League games but lost the final 2-1, with Kember adjudged the best forward in the tournament. Four of Kember's companions, nurtured by Rowe, would later break into the first-team. Meanwhile, further distancing the club from Graham's time in charge, claret and blue returned to replace the all-white strip and as if in celebration, Palace lost just three of their first 17 games, Woodruff netting in nine of the first 11. Enterprising football under Head and Petchey saw attendances rise to just under 20,000 by the sixth home game. In October Rowe enjoyed Stephenson's debut for the England Under-23s, and a month later equally relished Kember's first appearance for England Youth, playing alongside the likes of Peter Shilton and Trevor Brooking. When Palace won 2-1 at Coventry, Dick Graham's nemesis, Jimmy Hill, enthusiastically stated: '…there was no doubt that the better team won' and, by the New Year Palace were just three points behind the leaders.

Returning to Byrne, around this time Leeds' Norman Hunter described how 'Budgie' had 'destroyed' his defensive team-mate Jack Charlton as Revie's side lost 7-0 at West Ham in the League Cup. Despite his knee problem and liking for a drink, Johnny's Upton Park career looked set to continue for some time yet, but things soon took a surprising turn. By the time West Ham eventually exited the League Cup, Byrne was described as '…looking decidedly heavy.' Hammers boss Ron Greenwood needed to sell someone in order to strengthen his side and fans would not have tolerated the sale of Moore, Hurst or Peters. Only Byrne could attract a sizeable fee and, on February 15th 1967, those Palace fans who had so enjoyed Rowe's 'push-and-run' side read the headline: 'BYRNE BACK AT THE PALACE'. He had scored 108 goals in 206 games (including a phenomenal 28 in 34 Cup-ties) for the Hammers during the finest period in their history.

After Wait handed over £45,000, Byrne said it was great to be back '…among all my old friends' (primarily Rowe, Petchey, Long, Stephenson and 'Jacko' Jackson), while Wait commented 'We hope this heavy expenditure will bring Division One soccer to Palace', continuing 'Byrne is the sort of player who can make his colleagues raise their game' Wait was obliged to add, however, 'It's a gamble, I admit.' At 27 Byrne was now at only 75% of his potential. Certainly manager Bert Head had needed persuading before agreeing to Byrne's return. The only man still in the side from Budgie's last League game for Palace five years earlier was Terry Long. As for David Payne, he would now line-up alongside his schoolboy idol, telling me years later that in a 'give-and-go' set-up Byrne was '…terrific to link up with. The next time you'd play it up to him he'd turn and go at the defenders. So if you were marking him it was very hard to know what he was going to do.'

That spring Rowe experienced further success, leading his Under-17 side to the South-East Counties' League title. Meanwhile, after Byrne had initially helped Palace take five out of six points, the side suffered a painful, pointless Easter. Woodruff's goalscoring burst dried-up and much of the enthusiasm generated by Byrne's return had waned. However, in the final two games another Rowe discovery took centre-stage; the diminutive 18-year-old, floppy-haired Danny Light scoring twice in a 4-1 win over Hull City, following that up with the opener as Ronnie Allen's title-chasing Wolves lost in the final match to an identical score. This team performance was so impressive that fans invaded the pitch at the end and expectations soared for a promotion push in 1967-68.

SEASON 1967-68   Palace now had an extremely strong side; John Jackson was practically unbeatable in goal, a solid defence with Stephenson at its heart, tenacious and skilled midfielders Payne and Kember, and forwards such as Byrne, Woodruff, White and winger Cliff Jackson, all promised goals. Woodruff began with another flurry of nine from the first 11 League games. Byrne also started well and a 5-0 midweek win over Plymouth on September 6th 1967 was a superb display of 'push-and-run', largely inspired by Byrne, a memorable encounter and not just for the scoreline. Yet another complex free-kick ploy, with Kember posing to take the kick before jumping over it this time and also involving Sewell and Woodruff, ended with Byrne flicking the ball to Kember who only had to pass it home, a foretaste of the kind of sublime team goal Wenger's Arsenal would produce decades later. The press described a '…show of power, poise and pace', 'magnificent' and 'stupendous', while Payne recalls it as his all-time favourite game, saying '…we played the way Arthur Rowe would have wanted.' It was immediately followed by a similarly dominant and exciting 3-0 win over a strong Charlton side and then a 1-0 victory over QPR, Terry Long scoring the winner in a game witnessed by a new club record League attendance of 38,006, topped that day only by the games at Anfield and the Manchester derby at Maine Road. Palace sat at the top of Division Two for the first time in the club's history.

Said to be '…enjoying Palace's success', Arthur Rowe was interviewed by Peter Gillman of the *Times* who described him as '…relaxed now and distinguished'. Rowe spoke of his personal pride that six of his players were holding down first-team places and, reflecting on his time at Selhurst Park he could as easily have been referring to his spell at White Hart Lane: 'Looking back it's mixed. There's the sweet and sour — if you want to taste one you have to accept the other.' Of the current side he said, 'there's only one way to play football, pass the ball accurately then move, and that's what the Palace are doing.' Of his work with youth players he joked: 'Gardeners get more praise for growing cabbages than men get for grooming football teams', but added, 'this is a growing and expanding club and I am helping to build something tangible. It's rewarding.'

By the time Byrne scored from the spot at home to Blackburn on October 23rd, his 100th career goal for Palace, he had begun to criticise Head's management. It was ominous. Palace's vibrant start to the season evaporated as they won just six of the remaining 31 fixtures. After Byrne's previous experience under the management of Rowe, followed by Greenwood (both men more advanced thinkers than Head) mistrust grew between player and manager. Head unfortunately forecast at the time that it might take Palace five years to get to the top which jarred with Byrne's aspirations, Wait's hopes and Rowe's forecast. Despite offers to coach at Coventry and Arsenal, Petchey said: 'When I came in 1960, and Arthur said he wanted the First Division in ten years, I said I would still be at the club when it happened.'

Rowe will have greatly enjoyed one October evening in 1967 when a Palace Under-19 XI (featuring Payne, Kember, Light and other Rowe discoveries) defeated the full England Youth side 2-1. This was followed by Payne's call-up by the now 'Sir' Alf Ramsey as substitute for the England Under-23s against Wales. Payne told me that when nervously arriving at the Swansea hotel, Sir Alf approached to introduce himself as 'Alf', calling Payne 'David,' and making the young man feel welcome. Ramsey's courtesy resulted from his own first selection for England when he had likewise reported to a hotel only to be ignored, not only by playing greats such as Wright, Lawton and Swift, but by the England management. He had sat alone, feeling humiliated, before being obliged to introduce himself. Meanwhile Payne found himself changing alongside stars such as Ray Clemence, Emlyn Hughes and Peter Osgood, having some cause to feel nervous, but he was soon to be mentioned in the £70,000 bracket himself. Byrne even talked of forming as great an understanding with Payne as he had experienced with Geoff Hurst.

Most positivity around Selhurst Park at this stage still stemmed from Rowe's office. In the early rounds of that season's FA Youth Cup another Rowe find, centre-half Phil Hoadley, made the headlines. In December, with the first team reasonably placed in seventh Byrne was persuaded to improve his fitness. As Petchey recalled he was '…quite fat then but he used to train hard, I'll give him his due. He used to put black bean bags on to sweat, with a towel around his neck.' What concerned Petchey more was an entourage of friends who joined him at the bar immediately after games, John Sewell confirming that by the time he and the others had left the showers to go for a drink, '…Johnny had already had quite enough.' By then, according to Petchey, Byrne had also become inconsistent, '…one day he would do that job up-front, and the next he hadn't got the energy or the enthusiasm.' But Petchey's regard for Byrne was such that what he did in his own time didn't bother him, the upside being that '…he was teaching the others to play. He played the game right and I was ready to back him.'

However by the end of January 1968, Palace were again falling out of promotion contention, so Wait decided Stephenson's progress could no longer be deferred. It was almost an exact replay of Byrne's situation five years' earlier. Stephenson, an England Under-23 regular, was clearly of First Division quality, while bargain-buy McCormick's fine performances as stand-in had impressed. Meanwhile, a clearly unhappy Byrne publicly admitted Orient were thinking of appointing him as player-manager (to replace none other than Dick Graham). On March 11th, both Stephenson and the popular White left, bringing £100,000 into the Palace coffers. Stephenson joined relegation-threatened West Ham, the transfer fee a record for both sellers and buyers. The move boosted his chance of a World Cup place and it says much for Stephenson that of the 13 West Ham games he featured in before the end of that season, only two were defeats and the average goals conceded halved compared to the 29 games prior to his arrival.

Then, after a 2-1 defeat at Blackburn and with only seven hours left before the transfer window closed, Palace travelled south on the same train as First Division Fulham. During the journey Cottagers' manager Bobby Robson expressed his interest in Byrne to Head and the move went through just before the deadline. Assuring me that he had personally wanted Byrne to stay, Petchey said: 'I think Bert Head couldn't get on with him because Budge was an extrovert who had returned expecting to be "King Dick".' But even Rowe will have been saddened by the degree to which Byrne had deteriorated. In total, for Palace and the 'Hammers', Byrne accumulated 209 goals from 464 first-team appearances, few of them of the scruffy variety. His subsequent successful coaching career in South Africa (before the end of Apartheid) would demonstrate his enlightened views on the inclusion of South African blacks in the game and he authored at least one article promoting multi-racial participation. Dying suddenly at just 60, he at least lived to see the freeing of Nelson Mandela and the first few years of post-apartheid South Africa.

Returning to 1968 Wait, saddened by the failure of his Byrne gamble, the loss of Stephenson and the failure to achieve promotion, now talked of relinquishing the chairmanship. Meanwhile on the pitch Woodruff again ended with a scoring spree. He scored in two Easter defeats before Danny Light was reinstated for a home game with Norwich the following day. Earlier in the season, before the arrival of Mark Lazarus, the Rowe discovery had played in nine consecutive games producing seven wins and one draw. Now he helped Palace put six into the Norwich net. At Bolton, another Rowe find, defender Phil Hoadley, became Palace's youngest-ever player at 16 and 113 days, while Rowe's youth side reached the semi-finals of the FA Youth Cup, beating Chelsea and West Ham on the way. Illustrating the breadth of Rowe's involvement, at the time of the Youth Cup semi-final he was away scouting in Scotland. In Holland, Steve Kember starred as Rowe's boys beat Ajax in a youth tournament which Tottenham Hotspur had attempted and failed to win seven times — yet another feather in Rowe's cap.

SEASON 1968-69 With financial support from three new directors, work began on Wait's new grandstand. Meanwhile Arthur Rowe announced 'The kids [in Palace's youth scheme] are coming along fine'. In June Palace signed little-known Mel Blyth, 22, from Scunthorpe. Word had gone around the Scunthorpe dressing-room that Rowe was interested in experienced centre-half Frank Burrows but Rowe was instead checking on Blyth, who had come late to the game and had only 27 Third Division appearances behind him. Blyth would later tell me how much he owed to Rowe, who, as a former centre-half himself, would work one-on-one with him in training, and later the player came very close to England selection and won an FA Cup-winners' medal with Southampton.

Bert Head tried and failed to capture Birmingham's England striker Barry Bridges before the season-opener at Cardiff, and Woodruff had fallen sick, so Cliff Jackson, who since joining the club had struggled to shine playing wide on the left, filled-in at short notice. From the first whistle Cliff Jackson sparkled; too sharp for Cardiff he scored twice and created the other two in Palace's 4-0 victory. George Petchey told me he had selected Jackson as he could '…pass the thing, drop off, lay it off, play it to feet, and be able to play a bit of football.' Rowe was meanwhile casting a further eye over Bridges, but, by the end of that first week of the new season, Cliff Jackson had taken Palace to the top, creating four and scoring four of Palace's nine goals as they won all three opening games. The hunt for a pricey, established striker was happily postponed.

In early season one commentator described Palace producing '…flashes of pure soccer poetry that hinted of great things to come.' Incorporating 'push-and-run', their play was adventurous, with wafer-thin Jackson the fulcrum of the attack. Although busy with his scouting and youth activities, Rowe will have enjoyed hearing this. A 3-3 draw at Fratton Park in late September saw Terry Long replace injured captain Sewell to make his 480th and final first-team appearance. It was also the first time Kember, at just 19, captained the side. Reaching the fourth round of the League Cup Palace met a Leeds' side on their way to winning the League Championship yet Palace triumphed superbly, 2-1. The contest bore little relation to the game four years' earlier when Graham's side had capitulated in ugly fashion. This time Palace played the ball up to Cliff Jackson never more than chest-high, his fine control and sharp movement leaving England's Jack Charlton '…trailing around, totally outclassed.' As for Leeds, Brian Scovell wrote 'No bigger giant has ever been killed… or more gloriously'. Rowe will have particularly enjoyed the night, his criticism of Revie's methods undiminished.

However, despite this success Palace gradually switched their own emphasis to stopping the opposition. Kember, for example, was designated to mark Blackpool schemer Tony Green out of one game only for Palace to lose 3-0. For a League Cup fifth round tie at Burnley, striker Woodruff was dropped in favour of a defender and Palace lost 2-0. Sometimes only Cliff Jackson was left up front. The benefit of keeping the opposition occupied in *their* half of the field had apparently given way to a Dick Graham-like pragmatism. As the season progressed, with Cliff Jackson, Payne and Woodruff sidelined with injuries at various times and the likes of physical, ex-Spurs centre-half Roger Hoy filling-in in midfield, style began to take second place to the accumulation of points. At least McCormick had developed an excellent partnership with Blyth in central defence which would last for several seasons. At the end of October, Celtic winger Tony Taylor arrived, the perfect example of Rowe's 'total footballer': a speedy winger, tigerish midfielder and, later in his Palace career, an excellent left-back, Taylor told me how fondly he recalled Rowe for his advice and his readiness to help when needed. When Palace defeated Bolton 2-1 on November 2nd, the move for the winner stemmed from 'keeper Jackson who collected the ball before hurling it straight to the feet of the unmarked Kember. A quick pass to full-back Loughlan, who back-heeled to Kember, then a pass to Woodruff, who flicked on for Payne to flash a 25-yard drive past 'keeper Hopkinson. It was a goal that owed everything to Arthur Rowe's methods. Rowe and Head meanwhile scouted Scottish strikers, including a Rangers' centre-forward by the name of Alex Ferguson (the future 'Sir Alex' of Manchester United) and Kilmarnock's Gerry Queen, who impressed enough to arrive the following season. Seemingly lacking faith in the slick contribution of Cliff Jackson, Head seemed set on acquiring one of those 'buggers' who could score goals.

By January 25th 1969 Brian Clough's Derby looked certain for one of the two promotion places. When Palace lost at home to Blackpool, Head forecast the club could afford to lose another three of their final 16 games yet still gain promotion but, as things turned out, Blackpool proved to be his side's final defeat. In a similar way to Graham in 1962-63, Head used Palace's fixture backlog to psychological advantage. Their biggest task would be a trip to face Derby at the beginning of March, followed three days' later with a visit to Birmingham City. 18 home games undefeated, Derby included the likes of Roy McFarland, Kevin Hector and ex-Spur Dave Mackay, yet on the night Palace deserved more than the 1-0 victory that took them to fifth. Prospects increased further three days later when Palace achieved another 1-0 away win, this time at Birmingham City. By the end of March Palace were ahead of Head's promotion target.

After a 3-0 win over Portsmouth at Easter only one promotion spot remained to fight for, Derby having already clinched promotion. Unlike paupers Palace, Clough had spent a then huge £200,000 to support his ambitions. However, in their determination to snatch points Palace again chose sweat-and-toil over finesse,

ROWE'S TEN-YEAR PLEDGE ACHIEVED IN NINE

The post-Fulham victory celebrations saw Rowe's hatless wife Pom (light-haired, behind the player bending forward) and, alongside her, young Claire Hassell (wife of Chris), enjoying the historic promotion. The absent Rowe was also represented by his 1961 promotion captain John McNichol (right-hand image, seen behind the gentleman with the white hair). Pom will have experienced great pride, her husband's inspired football having set Palace on their upward trajectory eight years' earlier.

ARTHUR ROWE
ROWE'S WORDS COME TRUE
The words of Arthur Rowe, the former Spurs manager who took over the Palace to lead them into the Third Division eight years ago, have come true. Rowe openly stated then that Palace would be in the First Division during the sixties. When ill-health forced him to step down as club manager, he gradually took over the youth policy of the club with the title of assistant manager and his endeavours have produced such youngsters as Alan Stephenson, sold to gain the money that has paved the way for much of the present success, Steve Kember, David Payne and several youngsters who are almost ready to take their place in the first team squad.

returning from Huddersfield with an uncompromising point. The ghost of Graham had again returned, the *Daily Express* even describing Palace's tactics as '…rough, tough'. Head came clean, admitting Palace were not out to '…make friends by playing good football at this stage of the season.' Instead they now scrambled toward the finishing line. To achieve Rowe's commitment to reach the First Division (and with a year to spare), Palace needed one point, either at home to Byrne's Fulham or away to Blackburn in the final game. Neither Head nor Rowe were present to receive the accolades should promotion be achieved against Fulham. Instead Head was assessing players at Rangers v Morton and Rowe ran the rule over Celtic v Airdrie. Back at Selhurst Park 36,126 were in attendance, along with Fleet Street's finest, including Danny Blanchflower. They had come to see Palace finally reach the 'Promised Land' but by half-time Palace trailed 0-2 before Petchey's tactical changes prompted a thrilling comeback, the 'Glaziers' scoring three in the second-half to take both points. Crystal Palace had finally become a First Division club, fulfilling Rowe's ambitions with a year to spare.

As wild celebrations took place, the now very stocky Byrne left the field he had so greatly illuminated on many occasions, ignored by his former fans. But it was fitting that after Palace had salvaged the two-goal deficit, it was Cliff Jackson who topped his best-ever season in League football with the winner, his raised-arm salute adding a final gloss to the day, while Chairman Wait would harken back to the day Rowe took-up the reins at Selhurst Park. If only Arthur himself had been there to enjoy it.

As Palace's players lined the balcony of the directors' box, throwing their shirts and socks to celebrating fans below, Pom Rowe, standing alongside Secretary Chris Hassell's wife Claire, smiled broadly in the row behind. Despite many ups-and-downs along the way, Arthur's prophesy had become fact. Of course, his playing style had periodically gone amiss, but results had mostly kept on track. Six men remained on the staff to see the former manager's forecast become reality: Rowe himself, Arthur Wait, George Petchey, trainer Jess Willard, Terry Long and Rowe's former captain John McNichol (then employed on the commercial side and also seated in the Director's Box). Meanwhile Alan Stephenson was left with very mixed feelings. That afternoon he had accompanied Messrs Moore, Peters and Hurst in a 1-0 West Ham defeat at White Hart Lane, but he had nonetheless helped West Ham finish in their highest place in Division One since 1962. Yet to this day he harbours regret that he left Palace a year too soon.

On the following Monday the London *Evening News*, under a banner headline 'PRIDE O' LONDON — THAT'S PALACE', displayed a celebratory, informal team group which included Rowe himself, standing alongside Bert Head's daughter (the manager's secretary) who clutches 'Tiddles' the cat who presaged the beginning of Palace's rise to the top nine years' earlier. Palace captain John Sewell, reaching Division One at the age of 32, emphasised the significance of experienced players such as himself: 'The longer I go on playing I realise it's what's in your head that really counts.' How Rowe will have agreed.

Between Fulham and the final game at Blackburn, Palace experienced further success, winning the London Five-a-Side Tournament. Freed from the pressure of a promotion campaign, the players displayed their polished 'push-and-run' skills. The side featured both Jacksons, Payne, Kember and Sewell (three out of the five,

In April 1969 the London Evening News included a front-page group photo of those most responsible for achieving Rowe's target, including (far-left) Bert Head, Rowe and Head's secretary and daughter, who clutches lucky black cat 'Tiddles'.

At the end of May 1969 Rowe happily perches on his suitcase en-route to Rotterdam with his Palace youth party. On the far right are trainer Terry Long and George Petchey.

Rowe men). Head was meanwhile quietly confident that Palace would survive their first year in the First Division, but his reservations about the second season are interesting when considering Rowe's 'push-and-run' Spurs side's storming to the Championship back in 1951. Head believed the second season would be the real test, '…because the element of surprise has gone and in my opinion, this is the critical year.'

After 64 years Palace had at long last reached the promised land, but Rowe and Head were still hard at work, travelling to Manchester on April 22nd 1969 to run a trial for 33 young players who had been recommended by northern-based scouts. Then, on May 29th, Rowe (accompanied by Petchey) took the Palace youth side back to the Netherlands in the hope of retaining the Cup they had won the year previously.

Despite eventually serving in the background, Rowe could savour Crystal Palace's very first arrival at the summit of English football. That 1969 promotion owed so much to Palace's first, stylish step up English football's ladder, engineered by Rowe eight years earlier.

21

Every Match an Adventure

ROWE ENJOYS PALACE'S RISE 1969-71

'Now, when the game languishes, when the First Division can boast of no more than two or three genuinely inventive teams and when the overall standard lags appallingly, there is no place for Rowe.'

MALCOLM ALLISON IN HIS AUTOBIOGRAPHY *COLOURS OF MY LIFE* 1975

Arthur Wait was too emotional to deliver his speech at the Glaziers' Club dinner that celebratory spring of 1969. It was instead read by a co-director. He stated that he was '…perhaps the proudest man in Croydon, or maybe the world. I, like a lot of you, have seen my team come from being an ordinary football team to a great one.' Certainly the team had been decidedly 'ordinary' when he had arrived 11 years' earlier and, after praising coach Petchey, Wait's speech continued: 'We now come to the Man of Football, the Great Gentleman of Soccer: Arthur Rowe. What more can anybody say except that we thank him for all he has done for us and hope that he'll be with us until he retires.'

That summer Rowe spoke of players who had risen through Palace's youth system, firstly those who had moved on to other clubs for big fees, such as Glazier, Holsgrove, Stephenson and Byrne, then those about to become mainstays of a First Division Palace side: Jackson, Payne and Kember (the last two from the immediate Crystal Palace catchment area). 'This is what we want… the more local boys the happier everyone will be.' This echoed the days when he sought-out young talent from the Tottenham area. During the 1970s the South East Counties' [youth] League would make a presentation to mark Rowe's 15 years' service to that league. Nine of his Spurs' 'push-and-run' side, including Danny Blanchflower, were present to mark the occasion and pay their respects to 'The Boss'.

SEASON 1969-70 Despite the daunting challenge of survival at the top level, not one player with top level experience arrived in pre-season. Whereas at Spurs Rowe had been unable to buy his top-rank targets, the likes of a Lofthouse or Robledo, at Palace it was manager Bert Head's fixation on bargain buys which would hold First Division progress back.

At the beginning of August journalist and Palace supporter Roy Peskett sat in the old 'main' stand at Selhurst Park, opposite the almost completed new one, describing the desperate efforts to make it ready for the First Division opener on August 9th: 'Underneath the grime and dust on his silver hair beamed the serene face of Arthur Rowe, the Assistant Manager. Improvisation is the order of the day, and will be until the alterations are complete. Which meant Sue Head, her father's secretary, yelling from the open window, above the roar of the concrete mixer: "MR ROWE, YOU ARE WANTED ON THE PHONE." A few minutes later he appeared in the office, looking like a rescued victim of a wartime bomb incident, and holding the phone receiver with the end of two dirt-smeared fingers, then carried on a highly intelligent conversation about football tactics, before resuming his stint with a shovel!' Rowe had far more to gain from the completion of the stand than most — his now postponed testimonial match having been scheduled as an enticing overture to the opening Division One game. The delay instead saw his testimonial re-scheduled for cold, dark November, thus hitting his pocket hard. The testimonial was designed to honour his entire contribution to English football and particularly to recognise his masterminding that all-important first step toward the premier division and his discovery and nurturing of a catalogue of talented young Palace first-teamers.

Having waited 64 years for this moment, Crystal Palace fully deserved the visit of mighty Manchester United for the season opener, in front of a record attendance of 48,610. The press were keen to point out to Bert Head that of Palace's first seven top-flight opponents five comprised Manchester United, Everton, Spurs, Liverpool and Chelsea, to which the manager dryly responded: 'We reckon if we can win the first ten games, we can take the title.' On the big day the sight of Denis Law, George Best and Bobby Charlton striding out onto the Selhurst Park turf had many locals rubbing their disbelieving eyes. Now back in the big time, Rowe's own, personal treat was to welcome wartime pal Sir Matt Busby to Selhurst Park, still managing United after 24 years. Author Peter Morris described Rowe '…meeting people in that impressive Selhurst entrance hall; standing quietly in a corner, smiling rather self-consciously, always glad to see you and to chat with an old friend.'

As for the action on that great day, Crystal Palace took a fairytale 1-0 lead before none other than Bobby Charlton equalised. Rowe himself will have thrilled

In the late 1970s Rowe was honoured for services to the South East Counties youth league. Present for the occasion were (back row, l-r): *Keith Burkinshaw (then Spurs' Manager), Eddie Baily, Bill Nicholson, Harry Clarke, Len Duquemin, Arthur Richardson (Spurs' Chairman), Ron Burgess, and* (front): *Jim Joyce, Arthur Willis, Les Bennett, Rowe, Danny Blanchflower and Ted Ditchburn.*

to Palace's second goal, by Queen. Not so much for the finish, slightly scuffed in-off a defender, but for two first-time passes, first by Cliff Jackson on halfway — with one touch he both killed and perfectly directed a vertically descending clearance into Steve Kember's path, Kember then first-timing a defence-splitting pass putting debutant striker Queen clear on goal. A respectable final score of 2-2 was a riposte to those who had forecast a drubbing. The following 2-0 home victory over Sunderland then set a club record of 18 consecutive games without defeat. Of Palace's first five First Division goals, Cliff Jackson had scored one himself and created three of the others, confirming his rightful place at the top level but, slight of build, he was then injured and Palace began to struggle. However on August 23rd Rowe enjoyed his adopted South London club welcoming his beloved 'Lillywhites'. Despite Spurs' 2-0 victory, Jimmy Hill forecast that Rowe's discovery, 'keeper 'Jacko' Jackson, would be included in the England party for the following summer's World Cup Finals in Mexico. Of Rowe's other two discoveries, Kember soon excelled at the top level but the cultured Payne had been sorely missed, having suffered a pre-season injury keeping him out of all 13 initial top-flight League games. Without him Palace began to struggle and, by early October, they were just a point clear of last place. The much-missed Payne finally returned at Burnley on October 11th when a comfortable 2-0 interval lead crumbled to a 4-2 defeat.

When Palace welcomed Leeds a week later Don Revie, overwhelmed by Palace's hospitality, said he wished more clubs did the same, adding, somewhat ironically, 'Perhaps then the game would not be played in such a ruthless atmosphere.' This from the man Rowe blamed as the prime architect of 'ruthless' football. Rowe may have felt slightly more disposed toward the Leeds manager had he known of Revie's admiration for Payne and Kember. The increasing spectre of relegation saw Queen receiving less-and-less support up front. When only a point was collected at relegation-rivals Sheffield Wednesday, Head admitted that the focus had changed: 'We would far sooner play one that is not a classic and win a point than be lauded to the skies and get nothing. We have one thing in mind this season and that is to consolidate.' 'Consolidation' translated into some dire results including a 5-1 home defeat by Arsenal. A rare victory over Wolves on November 22nd, was then followed by 13 League games without a win, and crisis talks began, Wait speaking of '…doing everything humanly possible to stop going down.'

Some relief, however, was provided by Rowe's all-star testimonial match on November 26th 1969. Palace had just enjoyed a rare victory, boosting the gate a little, only 10,369 resisting a chilly night. Sir Alf Ramsey officially opened the new 'Arthur Wait Stand' (named as such by Wait's co-directors, to his personal embarrassment), and at least three further contributors to Rowe's golden Tottenham years enjoyed this celebration of their old boss: Bill Nicholson, Eddie Baily and Vic Buckingham. Nicholson said: 'It is common knowledge at testimonial matches these days to hear the saying: "Football has been good to me", but here's a chance to applaud a man who has genuinely been "good for football."' For Spurs fans it seemed inconceivable that Rowe's career should be celebrated south of the Thames and not at White Hart Lane, his spiritual home. Sadly, at the time of writing, no adequate memorial to the first man to take Spurs to English football's highest peak (and in grand style) has been forthcoming, either at White Hart Lane or the Tottenham Hotspur Stadium. Rowe is, after all, Tottenham's equivalent to Arsenal's Herbert Chapman, whose statue greets visitors to the Emirates Stadium.

Arthur would surely have appreciated the event more had it been organised by the club he had devoted nearly half a century to (as fan, player and manager). Back in the 1950s unappreciative directors may have put a stop to such recognition, but one might have thought the travesty would have been rectified in later years, particularly during Bill Nicholson's long period in charge. Nicholson would himself be honoured with not just one, but *two* testimonials, one under the chairmanship of Irving Scholar, the other under Daniel Levy.

At least Rowe's 11 years at Selhurst Park were recognised after his prediction had been fulfilled that Palace would reach Division One before the end of the decade. Chairman Wait made it clear that the idea for a testimonial came not from Rowe himself but manager Head, who had by then come to know the great man well enough to state: 'Arthur is a great believer in football, but like all people at the top, has sometimes been hurt when the game has been cruel to him,' adding 'One of his weaknesses, if you can call it such, is that he is principally a kind man.'

Despite a tough baptism at football's top table, Crystal Palace Football Club was bathed in waves of positivity that night, thousands recognizing the life of a true great. The main event saw the Palace first-team confront an International XI including World Cup-winning trio Bobby Moore, Martin Peters and Geoff Hurst, plus Jimmy Greaves, Dave Mackay, Alan Mullery, Peter Osgood and, in goal, Rowe's own discovery, England Under-23 'keeper Bill Glazier while Alan Stephenson appeared as a second-half substitute. Guesting on the right-wing was popular singer and actor Tommy Steele, a pal of Greaves'. Steele had only recently just performed alongside Fred Astaire in the movie version of *Finian's Rainbow*. Once the match was under way, fans began to ignore the star players, wanting the ball passed to Steele as often as possible. No mean player, the star of stage and screen dribbled through to score at one point, before collapsing in mock shock before being doused with a bucket of water from the bench. Poor weather restricted the attendance to just 10,369 but those who did attend were treated to eight goals, Palace going down 5-3. After opening the stand Sir Alf Ramsey, in his customary,

In November 1969 Crystal Palace organised a testimonial for Rowe, the Palace side facing an all-star XI including Jimmy Greaves, Geoff Hurst and Bobby Moore. Here Rowe signs a ball with Alan Mullery (left), Greaves and Hurst.

Ken Jones of the Daily Mirror contributed this article to Goal magazine at the time of Rowe's testimonial.

faux upper-class accent, delivered a speech and Peter Morris recalled the moment: 'So while the crowd cheered Sir Alf as he performed the ceremony, Arthur Rowe, quietly dressed, a little more white haired if anything, softly and gently spoken, stood on one side. He had been 40 years in football — "it don't seem a day too much, mate" — and understandably, it was to the past rather than the future where his private thoughts wandered.'

Rowe's testimonial was the cue for deserved tributes. Sir Matt Busby said he was honoured to call Arthur Rowe a friend, saying: 'He is a great thinker, a great judge and a great manager' while Danny Blanchflower called Rowe '…one of the great preachers as well as practitioners of football', adding, 'he has made a major contribution to the game.' In recognition of the testimonial, a Ken Jones article began: 'Where he was once the most influential figure in British football, Arthur Rowe now presides with fatherly concern over the development of young players at Crystal Palace. The picture is one of calm respectability, of elder statesmanship, the silver hair and the worn face reflecting a lifetime in the game, its triumphs and its disasters.'

Rowe had wanted one particular player to appear that night, young Wolves' striker Peter Knowles, who had abruptly turned his back on football to become a disciple for the Jehovah's Witness religion. He had grown uncomfortable with the idolatry of fans and how it was affecting his behaviour. Knowles was in the George Best mould: long-hair, skills to die for and a pin-up for young female fans. Rowe said he had written to ask Knowles if he regretted turning his back on the game. 'If he wants to try again in a game that will be played in the best spirit, then I would be delighted to see him. If not, then good luck to him. He showed a lot of courage in what he did. But I feel it is a tragedy that such a talented young man should be out of football. It is a tragedy for the game, because it is the game's fault.' Interestingly, Rowe continued: 'I think I know the frustrations he has felt and the anger he has talked about. There are times when I wish I could put boots on again and go out and do something about it.' He added: 'And yet the great players can still come through. They still prove that character can overcome some of the bad things we see. If Peter has the strength of character to do what he has done—to give up a lucrative career—then I am positive he is the type of player we desperately need in football.' Sadly, Knowles failed to take up Rowe's well-intended invitation. Had he done so and reignited his enthusiasm, then little else could have capped Rowe's emotional and memorable evening.

A few days later, 27-year-old centre-forward Alex Ferguson of Glasgow Rangers, a longtime target of Head and Rowe's, was finally set to sign for Palace but his wife was not happy to come to London, 'Fergie' instead signing for Falkirk. The first mention of another exceptional Glaswegian came in a match report on December 6th, this was 16-year-old centre-half Jim Cannon, who tried out for Palace's Under-18s following several Rowe scouting missions to Scotland that season. Immediately identified as a player of huge potential, he would ultimately bypass Terry Long's lengthy Palace appearance record, finishing on 660. For now Blyth and McCormick remained the centre-back pairing for the following two seasons. Although the two were physically similar in build, the blonde Blyth, coached by Rowe, was the stronger ball-player, better able to bring the ball constructively out of defence.

Returning to that debut season, misjudgments saw over-cautious away performances and a lack of players with First Division experience. Also, Bobby Woodruff and Cliff Jackson were denied a decent run together up-front. Head had adopted a cautious approach, often fielding no fewer than three or four established centre-halves in the same eleven (McCormick, Blyth, Hynd and Hoy), this at the expense of players whose vision and skill might have kept the opposition more occupied. Ultimately it looked like being the '…brief season of ignominy' that one pessimistic fan had forecast. The final three fixtures of the season saw visits to Highbury and Anfield before a home date with Manchester City. Palace went down 2-0 against Arsenal and 3-0 to Liverpool to leave them third bottom of the table on the same points (25) as Sunderland and one ahead of Sheffield Wednesday, yet both clubs had two games remaining, Palace just one. All of which made Palace's last game of the season on April 6th a must win. Palace included four players who Rowe had brought to the club ('Jacko' Jackson, Hoadley, Payne and Kember) and played as if their lives depended on it. Even Cliff Jackson had been restored, his creative talent deemed necessary for this 'must-win' occasion. A Roger Hoy winner delivered both points for Palace but they had to wait another sixteen days to learn their fate. Sunderland drew before losing to Liverpool which saw them relegated while Wednesday drew at Old Trafford before losing to Manchester City leaving a relieved Palace to spend the summer planning for their second First Division season.

The absence of Payne and Kember for long spells during the season had cost Palace points which might have prevented such end-of-season anxiety, while the overworked 'Jacko' Jackson in goal confessed to me that it was when guarding the Palace goal in First Division football that he first resorted to swearing!

SEASON 1970-71   Extra income from the new stand allowed Palace to finally make a significant signing, Rowe travelling north to clinch a deal with Liverpool's Bill Shankly for 25-year-old full back Peter Wall. £40,000 was a more reassuring amount of money to adequately reinforce the side, as proved by Wall's eventual 208 appearances for Palace. Meanwhile, talking to *The Times*, Rowe enthusiastically summed-up Palace's rollercoaster First Division experience: 'Every match is an adventure', while in August he said the current crop of 15 year-olds at the club were '...the best we have had for some years', significantly adding, 'I would not be surprised in five years if we had our own team. It is what you have to aim at.' Indeed, four seasons' later the Palace first team contained six home-grown players, some, if not all, drawn from the group Rowe referred to in the summer of 1970:

Jim CANNON (aged 16 in 1970) 660 appearances — still a Palace club record

Nick CHATTERTON (also aged 16 in 1970) 181 appearances [plus 264 League appearances for Millwall and 49 for Colchester United]

Martin HINSHELWOOD (aged 18 in 1970) — from an earlier crop of Rowe juniors, he made 82 appearances before retiring injured at just 24

Paul HINSHELWOOD (aged 14 in 1970) [plus 187 combined League appearances for Oxford United, Millwall and Colchester United and also represented England Under-21s]

Bill ROFFEY (aged 16 in 1970) 25 appearances [plus 378 total appearances for Leyton Orient, Brentford and Millwall]

Dave SWINDLEHURST (aged 14 in 1970) 237 appearances [plus 276 total League appearances for Derby County, West Ham United, Sunderland, Wimbledon, Colchester United and Peterborough]

Significantly, no fewer than four of these, Cannon, Chatterton, Paul Hinshelwood and Swindlehurst, contributed to two promotions, helping the club bounce back from dropping into Division Three under the management of Malcolm Allison.

Season 1970-71 saw Palace lose just three of the first 11 games before winning at Old Trafford, dampening home celebrations for Bobby Charlton's 500th appearance. Charlton had needed one goal to break United's individual scoring record but was kept in check by Payne, while Blyth took care of George Best. For those fans who could still recall a (pre-Rowe) 7-1 Fourth Division defeat at Notts

"All my Christmasses have come at once," considered teenage striker Dave Swindlehurst when his parents received a visit from Rowe, leading to his signing as a Crystal Palace apprentice and thereafter a long career in the game, his later clubs including Derby and West Ham. He also represented England at Under-21 level.

County, this result seemed like a fairy tale. After hitting three in the following home win over West Brom, Palace had accumulated a healthy 17 from 26 points. But a cautious approach crept in once again, only five further victories being recorded from the remaining 29 games.

At least Rowe will have enjoyed watching Kember star for the England Under-23 side against West Germany, creating two goals in a 3-1 victory. Meanwhile, Petchey had been working with new signing Alan Birchenall, recently arrived from Chelsea. With previous clubs Birchenall had been accustomed to running forward once his side won possession but Petchey made him wait for the ball to be played to feet. Birchenall grew to regard Petchey as one of the finest coaches in football. Palace then became the only side in Arsenal's famous 'Double'-winning season to win at Highbury, this in a League Cup replay, a result achieved despite missing Kember and Blyth and then losing Sewell, injured early on. Then, in mid-January, Palace added Liverpool's scalp to Arsenal's.

However, this result was tempered by the news that Arthur Rowe was to leave. He was departing a few months' ahead of his official retirement date having been offered the role of Chief Host for the new *Football Hall of Fame* museum in London's West End (see Chapter 22), finally departing Selhurst Park on Saturday February 27th 1971.

His 12 years with Crystal Palace had been double the time he had spent managing Tottenham Hotspur.

CRYSTAL PALACE FOLLOWING ROWE'S DEPARTURE With his departure Crystal Palace began a steady decline. Tony Taylor, who would one day briefly coach the Canadian national side, felt that Rowe-disciple Petchey was 'stifled somewhat [at Palace], as Bert Head wasn't really into tactics and teamwork.' Wanting to put his ideas fully into practice, Petchey became manager of Orient that summer where he spent six years before later managing Millwall and, briefly, Brighton. He would also later work for Newcastle under both Sir Bobby Robson and Ruud Gullit. Without Petchey's Rowe-inspired talents Palace's plight worsened, the club finishing third from bottom in season 1971-72 despite a spending spree on six players. Sadly the cash for this came from Palace's record sale of a single player, captain Steve Kember, who joined Chelsea for £170,000. Late in his career Kember would return, playing a big role in returning Palace to the top level in 1979.

Chairman Arthur Wait outlasted Rowe at Selhurst Park by a little less than three years. But before his sad and bitter departure, he had overseen more realistic investment in players, beginning with Chelsea's Irish international full-back Paddy Mulligan and creative Scottish international midfielder Charlie Cooke. Their price tags will have made the chairman wince but Palace were, after all, in the big time now. Wait then ceded a 51% stake in the club to Raymond Bloye and assumed the title of 'Life President'. However soon after this Wait travelled with Head to Swindon to oversee the purchase of superb wing star Don Rogers. Wait's involvement in this deal led to a sharp confrontation with Bloye, and he walked away for good. Aside from the Rogers dispute, Wait was being excluded from board meetings and told he needed ID to gain admittance to a boardroom he still considered his own, and he eventually asked to be relieved of his financial commitments to the club. Without his wise counsel and with the likes of Kember, Petchey, and Rowe no longer around, Palace completely hit the skids, dropping back almost to the level Rowe had extricated them from twelve years earlier.

On his debut Rogers scored a breathtaking winner against Everton and also inspired Palace to an extravagant 5-0 win over a struggling, post-Busby Manchester United and the 14 games which followed (including the last, a defeat of Chelsea at home, watched by a new manager appointed by Bloye a day earlier) produced a points return which had staved-off relegation in the past. But Bloye, a man with little knowledge of the game, had by then appointed the flamboyant Malcolm Allison, with Bert Head pushed 'upstairs' as General Manager. After the defeat of Chelsea, which he had no more than watched, Allison's abrupt change of style led to defeats in five of his first six games, Palace crashing back into Division Two. It is notable that Allison's greatest successes had taken place at Manchester City, where he had shared managerial duties with the level-headed Joe Mercer. Working alone, he floundered for three disastrous seasons, taking Palace rapidly back to Division 3.

I have continued the Crystal Palace story beyond Rowe's departure both to complete the story of his honourable friend Arthur Wait, and as a painful example of how a stable football club can so rapidly be brought to its knees when placed in the care of the wrong individuals. Extraordinary, too, that despite Allison's weakness for the high life, he and Rowe were otherwise kindred spirits when it came to the art of soccer. The strong suspicion is that Allison took the Palace job to be within reach of London's nightlife and, a matter of months before arriving he had ominously said he would like to '…work at a smaller club …and have a quieter life.' His 'quieter life' entailed late arrivals for training and Bloye and Allison rapidly took Crystal Palace back down to the third tier of English football. Just two years earlier Arthur Rowe had confidently prophesied: 'I see [Crystal Palace] now as an established First Division side and with the power and ambition behind them you can only see them progressing'. However, in winning just 12 of 49 League games after taking over, Allison seemed to be crushing all the progress achieved by Rowe, Graham, Petchey and Head.

But maybe not. It was Arthur Rowe who initially gave everyone connected with the club the ambition and confidence to rise from the depths of England's fourth tier. That 1973 demotion proved to be a relatively short-lived setback as a result and, as I write this, the Crystal Palace club, with Rowe's ambition embedded in its thinking, have just spent a decade among the giants of the Premiership.

Giants who include another club Arthur set on their way back in 1949: his beloved 'Lillywhites'.

ROWE AND CRYSTAL PALACE: A SUMMARY Arthur Rowe's kindly and sympathetic approach gave Crystal Palace a big advantage when attracting young talent, and his common courtesies impressed and assured parents. On this theme John Matthews once wrote that Rowe's manner '…often tipped the scales in Palace's favour—boys who used to think only of joining Manchester United or Arsenal now look to Palace.' Striker Dave Swindlehurst recalled Arthur and Eddie Firmani (who had joined as Chief Scout) coming to his parents' house in Cricklewood: 'My dad was a train driver. Arthur and Eddie Firmani came in and we had these legends sitting together in our front room, talking to me and I am thinking "…all my Christmasses have come at once because I am going to be signing for Crystal Palace".' An earlier Rowe discovery, Steve Kember, said: 'To any young boy with any football talent who comes to the Palace, he soon finds Mr Rowe the father-figure, always ready to help.' 'Jacko' Jackson recalled Rowe going to his parents' house: 'Arthur had a great ability to be able to gently persuade you around to his point of view,' adding that he '…did everything the right way and conducted himself in the correct manner.' As for his message to young would-be professional footballers, Rowe would say: 'Work hard, look at it, study it. It's the only way, as the great ones are few and far between.'

Rowe passionately believed that the future of Crystal Palace depended on its youth programme. 'Lots of things have given me great personal pleasure since I have been at the club. Several of my boys have played for various England sides.' Rowe's other major gift to the club was his successful introduction of 'push-and-run'. That exhilarating football, laden with goals, attracted fans who became devoted for a lifetime. Both of his immediate successors, particularly, of course, Graham, were judged against the yardstick of the quality of football Rowe had introduced in 1960.

Returning to Allison, there can be no doubting his deep love for the game and I happily close this review of Rowe's Palace career in his own words: 'There is no logical explanation for the eminence of some football people. There are others, with infinitely more knowledge, instinct, and perhaps even courage, who are ultimately broken by the game. I'm thinking particularly of the seven men with whom I would have most liked to work had Joe Mercer not taken me on one side in the summer of 1965. Some of them have shown extraordinary ability in organising and developing teams, some of them have reached out to astonishing moments of success. But all of them have finished looking desperately for answers, their life's work spread by the erratic winds which blow through the game.' It was no surprise to find Arthur Rowe was foremost in his list and I end this chapter with Allison's own, perceptive 1975 tribute to Arthur:

> *'Rowe, a man of great charm and easy personality, launched the push-and-run Spurs, a team of subtlety and bite who opened the fifties with a flash of brilliance. He did his work with shrewdness and flair. He showed how he could organise and how he could bring to a team that crucial touch of inspiration. Now, when the game languishes, when the First Division can boast of no more than two or three genuinely inventive teams and when the overall standard lags appallingly, there is no place for Rowe. There is, apparently, no place for one of the great pioneers of modern English football. Yet he remains spry and healthy, and as deeply involved in the theory of the game as he was when he went to Hungary before the war. It is a strange waste'*

22

When Others Were Blind

FOREVER AN INSPIRATION

'It was adventurous stuff, a new art, like Surrealism, having its specially defined period. This method has never been used as expressively since.'
JOHN MOYNIHAN ON ARTHUR ROWE'S 'PUSH-AND-RUN'

'That lad's no coward. He can take it. You mark my words.'
ARTHUR ROWE ON THE YOUNG LAURIE CUNNINGHAM, IN RESPONSE TO
THE SUGGESTION THAT BLACK PLAYERS LACKED 'BOTTLE' 1976

On departing Crystal Palace in March 1971, the club presented Arthur Rowe with a 400-day clock and, recognising his work with youth players, the youngest professional, Keith Walley, had the honour of making the presentation. The staff also clubbed together to present him with a silver tray inscribed with the signatures of players he had discovered, some of whom were now competing with the greatest names in British football. Peter Burridge neatly summed Rowe up: 'Arthur Rowe was a quiet, inoffensive man with a purist idea of how the game should be played. He would never have had the team playing like Dick [Graham]. I remember Arthur asking me one day, when under Graham we had climbed to about 9th or 10th in the League, something to the effect that "You don't really want to play like that, do you?"' For Rowe, football could never be a mere physical coming-together of 22 players chasing after an inflated bladder, but as something capable of triggering involuntary gasps of wonder from the spectator.

Moving ahead to 2019 and considering Rowe's 12 years of devotion to the South London club, how serendipitous it turned out to be that Spurs' first opponents at their new 'Tottenham Hotspur Stadium' should have been Crystal Palace! Before summing-up Rowe's personal legacy to the sport and reviewing his opinions on the future of the game, I'll briefly review his final, post-Palace working years:

The Football Hall Of Fame opened with Rowe as Chief Host on March 29th 1971, with exhibits including trophies, memorabilia, club shirts, still photos and wax dummies of big stars, as well as movie clips illustrating the growth and history of the sport. An enthusiastic Rowe commented: 'It will be good for the game and can give it the dignity and lustre that has perhaps not been too obvious in recent weeks.' Rowe may have been referring to the uproar caused by an October 1970 TV interview when Leeds' centre-half Jack Charlton told the world that he kept a book in which he noted names of players he planned 'to do' and 'make suffer' before himself retiring from the game. A further blemish on Revie's Leeds.

Life-sized wax effigies of twelve British footballing personalities from throughout the decades would initially be displayed, selected by a distinguished panel including

Sir Alf Ramsey, Sir Matt Busby and Bobby Charlton. These were Steve Bloomer, Dixie Dean, Duncan Edwards, Tom Finney, Alex James, Sir Stanley Matthews, Billy Meredith, Frank Swift and Billy Wright. A *Movietone* clip shows Rowe holding the opening ribbon as wartime pal Sir Matt Busby cuts it. In this less-pressured environment he was able to enjoy the respect and affection of the public, telling tales of his career and experiences. The museum was housed in London's Newman Street, off Oxford Street. At the time it was inaugurated, jazz musician, critic and author Benny Green wrote a somewhat unflattering review in *The Spectator*, although he did enthuse about its location, it being the continuation of Cleveland Street, where he had grown up. Had it existed during his childhood, he wrote, '…we should have haunted its portals day and night' and '…speedily devised a thousand foolproof ways of bunking in.'

Green described a hoarding in the foyer on which Rowe stated that the game of football is every British schoolboy's birthright, which prompted Green to sardonically suggest that '…during Rowe's own playing career that birthright was worth no more than £8 per week… .' However, as Green moved through the exhibits he became irritated by loud sound effects which included the '…chanting of a Cup-tie crowd' and '…idiotic' club songs' which created a '…burning desire to do its organisers some permanent physical injury'. One suspects the sounds were none too pleasurable for Rowe, experiencing them on a daily basis, but lunch breaks occasionally spent chatting with reporters Norman Giller and Steve Richards may have provided welcome relief.

Green was more charitable when listing some exhibits, including a movie clip showing Sir Matt Busby embracing fellow Munich Air Disaster survivor Bobby Charlton at the moment of European Cup triumph in 1968, an early balance sheet showing Aston Villa had made an £1,876 18s 3d annual profit, or a photo of besuited West Bromwich Albion players walking down a rutted Victorian road as part of their training. As a 'man of the people' however, Green was offended about what was *not* on show: he suggested a photo of Jimmy Logie, Arsenal superstar of

Rowe holds the tape as Sir Matt Busby, his old wartime colleague, cuts the tape to open The Football Hall of Fame *in 1971. Behind Rowe is Gordon Taylor's predecessor as Secretary of the Professional Footballers' Association, Cliff Lloyd.*

the 1940s and 50s, eventually reduced to selling newspapers in Piccadilly Circus; or the lack of a graph to compare the considerable earnings of the-then Secretary of the Football League, Alan Hardaker, with football superstar Tommy Lawton who, despite talent which drew thousands to pass through the turnstiles, ended up sending begging letters to friends as he contemplated suicide. One can imagine Rowe himself resigned to agree particularly with this final concern of Green's.

The *Daily Mirror*'s Frank Taylor asked Rowe for his favourite recollections from 49 years in soccer. Modesty prevented him from choosing his own Spurs' side of 1951 as 'best team', so he selected instead Matt Busby's 1948 Manchester United side. Asked for his comments on the modern [1970s] game, he managed to summon-up a 'just great', but added, 'I would like to see more of the old one-two passes in midfield instead of so many crossfield passes. Spurs did it in '51. Why not now?' Asked whose fans were the best in London he gave Crystal Palace a pat on the back: 'Crystal Palace, Spurs and Arsenal cheer their own sides; at Palace they are [also] not afraid to applaud the other team.' Taylor did not ask who he considered were the outstanding players in his lifetime but Rowe selected the following when asked on another occasion:

'At wing forward [George] Best number one, with Matthews and Finney equal second; at centre-forward, Tommy Lawton and Di Stéfano with Budgie Byrne (at his best) not far out of the running; at wing half, the Hungarian Bozsik, Burgess, Blanchflower and Matt Busby (whose passing had an elegant certainty about it, later echoed by Bobby Charlton in his salad days).' Among Rowe's memorabilia I encountered a handwritten list of his own, probably prepared for a 1950s' interview, which also included Raich Carter, Jimmy Hagan, Alex James, Willie Hall, Dixie Dean, Peter Doherty and Len Goulden. Returning to Best, Tony Pawson once quoted Joe Mercer on the Best-versus-Finney argument. Mercer had asked Rowe to agree that Best (then at his peak) was the finest player there had ever been, to which Arthur responded with another question: 'But will [Best] last like Tom Finney?' Which of course, ultimately, he didn't, going AWOL several times in his last season or two. Rowe considered it important to recognise super-talented young players

A photo capturing perhaps the finest two players ever managed by Rowe, Johnny Byrne (by then with West Ham) and Spurs' Danny Blanchflower, both looking on as Spurs' 'keeper Bill Brown dives to save.

Rowe reunited with several former Palace staff members at Leyton Orient in 1972. Left-to-right: George Petchey, Phil Hoadley, David Payne, Rowe, Secretary Peter Barnes, and Gerry Queen.

who '...should be left alone to develop,' i.e. that in the rare instance of a naturally-gifted young player, coaching could have an adverse affect. As Rowe said, players like Best, '...are the diamonds. They don't need polishing'. Staying on the subject of Best, Ken Jones prised a quintessential quote out of Rowe. Jones asked what Rowe would do if he found a young player with Best's talents.

Rowe's reply, 'You say "Good morning ...have you got any brothers?"'

The *Daily Mirror*'s Frank Taylor suggested the *Hall of Fame* should have kept a niche available for another top class soccer man. 'For the son of an upholsterer, who left an indelible mark on this great game of soccer... a chap called Arthur Rowe.'

Sadly, however, the *Hall of Fame* had a very short life. With public interest disappointing it closed down barely nine months later in January 1972. Rowe commented: 'It was very sad. The game should be big enough to cater for something like this, yet for various reasons it did not work out. At first it went like a bomb and in the school holidays attendances reached 10,000 a week.' However the privately-run *Hall of Fame* had suffered financial constraints from the outset.

LEYTON ORIENT AND MILLWALL Within days of the closure, on January 24th, 1972, Rowe received an offer of employment from his old 'comrade-in-arms' George Petchey who, after six months, was still a novice manager at Leyton Orient. Rowe would do some scouting, spy on future opponents, help young players through personal or footballing difficulties, and act as an experienced 'sounding-board' for Petchey. Aside from Highbury, Orient was the nearest professional club to White Hart Lane so after over a decade in South London, Rowe was back in more familiar territory. His early spying dossier on Chelsea contributed to Orient's elimination of a side including the likes of Bonetti, Harris, Cooke, Hollins, Hudson and Osgood from the FA Cup in February 1972. By 1974 Rowe was enjoying how Petchey had the first-team playing, saying 'It's like watching my personal beliefs reborn'. Among players developed by the Petchey/Rowe duo were tigerish midfielder Tony Grealish and two Arsenal rejects, classy defender Glenn Roeder and the soon-to-be world-class Laurie Cunningham. Petchey had offered Cunningham a try-out in a practice match, this despite a warning that the boy needed 'a lot of help'. Richard Lewis, in his *England's Eastenders: from Bobby Moore to David Beckham*, writes of Petchey's request for Arthur to keep a close watch on Cunningham during the trial. Not long after the first whistle Rowe walked across to the otherwise occupied Petchey, suggesting he should get hold of the boy fast, because, said Rowe, '...he is bloody brilliant.' Orient quickly signed him up and Petchey and Rowe with, as Lewis puts it, 'plenty of [necessary] care and patience', ensured Cunningham, a rare black player at that time, was not lost to the game. Of course he eventually represented England and starred for Real Madrid. But Rowe felt that the exceptionally naturally-gifted Cunningham was better to play outside of a structure such as 'push-and-run': 'You don't tell him how to play, it would just clutter his brain. You say "Go out there and get on with it".' Rowe would continue scouting and spying for Orient after Petchey's departure in August 1977, when Jimmy Bloomfield took over. Indeed, *The Times* credited Arthur with the successful plan to stifle England's Ray Wilkins when Orient again knocked Chelsea out of the Cup in January 1978.

Standing in the middle of Cold Blow Lane on an inhospitable October night in 1976, Fleet Street's Brian Scovell met up with the now 70-year-old Arthur Rowe after a Cup tie. They had witnessed a typical encounter of the time: a lot of effort, few shots, little entertainment. However Rowe, wrote Scovell, 'who sees 100 matches a year and never gets bored, saw things we failed to see. He was happy about the game. "You never saw matches like that in the old days," he said. "All that effort. They are so much fitter today. Directly you get the ball someone is breathing down your neck. You've got to be a good player to compete with that. Tactically it's a different game to what it was in my day."' When Scovell doubted there were any great players still around, aside from George Best, Rowe said Cunningham was 'The best since Best.' High praise indeed, especially as Scovell had not been overly impressed by Cunningham's performance, sensing that an early tough tackle from behind had intimidated the boy for most of the rest of the game, at least until the late stages when Scovell suggested it was only due to tiring defenders that Cunningham was getting opportunities. Scovell wrote: 'The common belief about coloured players is that they lack heart. The phrase in football is "bottle".'

When George Petchey trialled the then young and rather naive Laurie Cunningham at Orient, he asked Rowe to check the boy out in action. In no time Arthur told Petchey to urgently snap him up.

In 1979 Cunningham would become only the second black player to represent England, the same year that he became the first Englishman to sign for Real Madrid.

Right: *In the early 1980s Rowe returned to Selhurst Park to make a special presentation to one of his many discoveries, full-back Paul Hinshelwood, who had completed 200 appearances as well as representing England at Under-21 level.*

Left: *Helping grandson Duncan ride his new bike.*

Rowe promptly rose to the bait: 'That lad's no coward. He can take it. You mark my words. He'll be a good player.'

On August 20th 1977, Rowe traveled the short distance from his South London home to see Terry Venables' Palace beat Millwall 3-0 at the Den. It appears he made the short trip from home to enjoy seeing three of his Palace protégés in action, Jim Cannon, Nick Chatterton and Paul Hinshelwood. However, Hinshelwood was on a one-match ban so 17-year-old midfielder Peter Nicholas made his debut out of position at right-back. Another rising black winger with great flair, Vince Hilaire, also made his first full Palace debut that same afternoon and scored. But on this occasion Rowe was impressed by the more workmanlike Nicholas: 'He is going to be a fine player. He is what I term "a natural". He knows what is going on around him all the time and takes up excellent positions.' Nicholas later moved on to Arsenal and in time received more than double the Welsh caps Ron Burgess had collected. With Venables' side moving the ball about swiftly and sweetly that afternoon, Rowe clearly enjoyed the game, 'I don't think anyone who paid to see it could complain.'

During the 1970s Rowe and wife Pom took time out to cross the Atlantic, visiting eldest son Derek and family in Toronto in 1975 and, two years later, second son Graham and wife in Los Angeles.

Five months after leaving Leyton Orient, George Petchey became manager of Millwall and once again took Rowe on board. By then 71 this proved to be Rowe's final role in football. Rowe and Petchey remained at Cold Blow Lane nearly three years, until November 30th 1980. Rowe could not have wished for more than to finish his career alongside Petchey.

COMPARING ROWE'S AND NICHOLSON'S SPURS When asked in 1961 how his 1951 League Championship-winning Spurs' side compared to Nicholson's of a decade later, Rowe first clarified that any comparison of performance in soccer was an inexact science, largely based on opinion, unlike, for example in athletics or swimming, where the measure of time or distance is incontrovertible but he did point out two clear similarities between the two Spurs sides: excellent half-back lines (Nicholson/Clarke/Burgess and Blanchflower/Norman/Mackay) and good leadership on the field (Burgess and Blanchflower). Then he highlighted the

Photographed by the author, Graham Rowe (right, with charming and lovely wife Louise), bears an uncanny resemblance to his father (left).

essential parallel: the mentality of both sides: to 'try to win' rather than 'try not to lose': 'I have always believed that football is basically an entertainment business, and that goalscoring is entertainment with universal appeal.' The great Johan Cruyff later echoed that sentiment: 'The spectators had been working all week; we had to entertain them on their day off with fine football, and at the same time, get a good result.'

Nicholson felt that had Rowe's Spurs and his own Spurs met each other, there would not have been much between them. But in a 1960 article Rowe didn't hesitate to emphasise that paramount difference that gave Nicholson such a huge advantage: Nicholson's budding 'Double' side was comprised of '...expensively bought players, and all stars in their own right,' whilst his own side, from a decade earlier, was 'Tottenham-trained as a collective unit—bought at a total cost of less than £20,000.' This is the only instance I have uncovered of Rowe himself emphasising the gross financial imbalance between the sides. It can't be stressed enough just how heavily the success of Chapman's Arsenal and Nicholson's Spurs depended on the sizeable financial input Rowe had to go without.

England manager Walter Winterbottom felt that Nicholson, like Rowe, encouraged his more gifted players to control their individualistic inclinations to better blend with their less talented companions. Winterbottom also emphasised that Nicholson was fortunate to have a larger number of outstandingly talented players at his disposal than had his predecessor but that he had also harnessed them to rigorous team-work. Rowe himself reflected that his side depended less on individual skill, his 'good players' concentrating on '...making the others more efficient.' Renowned, pioneering journalist Julie Welch, a Spurs' fan from childhood but too young to see Rowe's side in action, once admitted to reaching adulthood before realising that Nicholson's side were not the first Tottenham side to, as she put it, '...achieve enduring greatness.' Thereafter, she correctly identified that Spurs' reputation derived not from Nicholson's side but from Rowe's, having initiated the Tottenham approach that winning alone was not enough.

Rowe was asked on various occasions to select a best eleven from his and Nicholson's Championship-winning sides. He chose Ditchburn in goal and Ramsey ('a truly great player') at right-back. At left-back he chose Withers or Henry. When comparing the wing-halves he praised Burgess but felt Blanchflower could match him (although on another occasion gave Burgess the nod over Blanchflower on the grounds the Irishman could be too individualistic). He chose Mackay over Nicholson, considering him more constructive. He felt both Clarke and Norman at centre-half 'lacked a little' (perhaps subconsciously believing he could have done better himself)! As wide-right attackers he felt Walters compared well with Dyson or Medwin and, as far as creative inside forwards were concerned, both White and Baily were fine players, but selected Baily over White '…because I understood the pungency of [Baily's] football' (he used the term 'pungency' frequently, his intended meaning being 'intensity' or 'vitality'). At centre-forward Bobby Smith won his vote over Len Duquemin, who Rowe dismissed as merely 'able' whilst considering Smith 'more positive' in front of goal (the very category of striker Rowe himself had tried to add to his Spurs' side). With Greaves yet to join Spurs at that time, he chose Les Bennett for the striking inside-forward role over Les Allen, believing Bennett was '…a better all-round player' and also thought he would have picked-up more goals if accompanied by Smith. At outside-left he chose Cliff Jones over Medley, but only on grounds of consistency — he felt Medley scored higher on '…pure football ability.' On other occasions Rowe preferred the Baily/Medley combination, thinking Jones too much the individual. By the time of a later interview with Geoffrey Green, Rowe selected Jones at right-wing (instead of left) and the newly-added and truly world-class Greaves over Bennett. This allowed him to install Medley on the left. From Rowe's changing opinions it can be seen that there was little to separate the two great sides. The huge gulf between Nicholson's and Rowe's elevens, and by a margin, was cost!

'Push-and-run' spread the goalscoring across the five-man forward line, and the even spread of goals across the 'Double' side's attack is a further indication of continuity between the Rowe and Nicholson approach: in 1960-61, for example, the Spurs' wingers scored 32 League goals (averaging 16 per winger), the inside-forwards 35 (averaging 17), and centre-forward Bobby Smith 28, which was the kind of total Rowe will have wished from Duquemin, hence his frustrated search for a replacement. Yet despite the enormous difference in financial investment, Rowe still believed his 1950 side would have defeated the 1960 side. Distinguished philosopher and Spurs fanatic A J ('Freddie') Ayer also compared Rowe's and Nicholson's sides, pointing out that in 1961 Nicholson's side had fielded almost an unchanged side for two seasons due to good fortune with injuries, the result being a high-level of understanding between the players but interestingly, and in favour of Nicholson's Spurs, he felt the additional, occasional use of the long-ball reduced the energy burnt with constant 'push-and-run'. Ayer's observation was that Nicholson's side conserved their energy '…between bouts of pressure' whereas Rowe always insisted on maintaining the same pace throughout.

Incidentally Ayer, who had occasionally watched Spurs in the 1930s and 1940s, only became a regular fan once he had witnessed Rowe's first season in charge (Ben Rogers, in his biography of Ayer, writes: 'The speed and energy the [Spurs'] game took on naturally appealed to [Ayer]; Rowe's motto, "Make it simple, make it quick", could have been his own'). When once accompanying her husband at a game, Ayer's wife Dee recalled him pointing out the patterns the players made on the field, saying, "Pretty, aren't they?"

WOULD BYGONE STARS EXCEL IN MODERN TIMES? When asked in the 1970s if he thought Stanley Matthews would still have been effective with so many defenders covering and denying him space, Rowe admitted that before the war full backs were comparatively unfit and there was little defensive tactical awareness. Indeed, Rowe considered Matthews at 50 was a better player than when he had started out in 1932 — he simply had to be, as by the 1960s defenders were being taught to hold off rather than dive into the tackle. Rowe believed too that had the old stars reappeared in 1970s football they would have been sure to reach the new fitness levels required: 'There is no doubt in my mind that they would succeed, that they would be as influential as they were in their own time.'

REVIE'S LEEDS UNITED AND NEGATIVE TRENDS As for the destructive approach of the otherwise extremely talented Leeds United team of the 60s and 70s, Rowe apportioned some of the blame to society in general: 'Discipline …takes it's lead from our way of life. The law is more benevolent. We have abolished the death penalty and wrongdoers are treated differently. This shows itself in football. Excuses for bad behaviour are always at hand. It is the world of the psychiatrist rather than that of the stern judge.'

Rowe conceded that 'push-and-run' was harder to execute during that era because defensive coaching had advanced and whilst admitting there had always been dirty players, he felt 'a destructive attitude was creeping in at team level.' He will have had Revie's Leeds in mind again, as well as Dick Graham's Crystal Palace. Most 1970s sides had at least one 'destroyer' in their side, such as Ron Harris at Chelsea, Peter Storey at Arsenal, Nobby Stiles at Manchester United and Tommy Smith at Liverpool.

Rowe was appalled by the underhand tactics and aggression of the Leeds United side under Manager Don Revie. Here Rowe's fine midfield discovery for Palace, David Payne, accelerates away despite Leeds' Irish international Johnny Giles trying to pull him back, with England international full-back Paul Reaney looking on. Giles, a superb midfielder, later became a TV pundit and excellent newspaper columnist.

In 1973 Rowe said a '…return to our Tottenham 'push-and-run' of 20 years ago would be healthiest for all concerned, especially with techniques so much better all-round now than then. We saw flashes of ['push-and-run'] from Netzer, Beckenbauer and Müller in the European side ('The Six') at Wembley the other night [a 1973 exhibition match marking the UK's entry into the European Union]. When it works it lifts the game and the crowd.' He added: 'I believe that the game's just come through a very dark age. And I've got to say it, Leeds are the team that led us into that age. They set the pattern. What they did was to show people you could win things by bending the rules. Instead of being a question of how much you could contribute, it became a matter of how much you could get away with. They disgusted me.' This statement more than confirms just how uncomfortable Rowe will have been to work under Dick Graham at Crystal Palace, when his exquisite 'push-and-run' was tossed aside to achieve tarnished, disfigured success. When Leeds did belatedly begin playing truly inspiring, slick-passing football, it only made one wonder why they hadn't chosen that path before.

Rowe appreciated the Leeds' improvement but believed no club needed to change more than they did: 'They could have given the game, what shall I say, greater glory. But they cheapened it. It was a tragedy.' Journalist and broadcaster Steve Tongue recalled interviewing Rowe on this subject and how the great man regretted he had used the actual word 'cheating', so Tongue printed a letter from Arthur stating that by 'cheating' he had meant 'exploiting the rules'. But this did not diminish Rowe's fury when Revie was later selected to sit on the committee of the Football League Secretaries and Managers Association: 'I missed that meeting,' said Rowe, adding that if he had been there, '…there'd have been a row!' Astonishingly, despite the mud attached to his name Don Revie replaced Sir Alf Ramsey as England manager in July 1974, drawing a typically succinct comment from Rowe: 'It's like giving the gamekeeper's job to the leading poacher.' (Incidentally, having told Steve Tongue Revie's methods were 'cheating', Rowe later said he had really meant to say 'exploiting the rules')! With the greatest irony of all, however, when Revie was asked which of the two Spurs Championship-winning sides he rated the highest (Rowe's or the 'Double' side), Revie chose Rowe's, saying their fast inter-passing '…cut through teams like a knife through butter.'

But overall Arthur Rowe insisted he was *not* a pessimist, simply wishing kids had not seen '…things on television it would have been better not to have seen' (i.e. primarily games involving Leeds). Speaking of up-and-coming players, he said '…some of them have got so much talent that it's heartwarming. I suppose that's the nicest part of my job at Orient.' When Rowe wished kids had not seen certain things on television it brings to mind Vince Hilaire's admiration for his Crystal Palace youth coach in the 1970s, former Rowe player John Cartwright. He advised Hilaire and his colleagues not to watch the multitude of workmanlike but uninspiring players then regularly witnessed on *Match of the Day* but to instead watch 'great players from abroad' and read *World Soccer* magazine!

Reflecting on his time in charge at Tottenham, Arthur Rowe admitted to one particular frustration. He ruminated on how children played football for the love of it, something he felt was also essential in the make-up of the professional player, but, '…when you become a paid performer, I found in my experience …that the hardest thing to get them to do was to go out happily and willingly and try to improve on the weaknesses of their game. There seemed to be a latent resentment or shyness to try to do something which they couldn't, in case their team-mates laughed at them. They would sooner reserve it for a Saturday afternoon and show 50,000 spectators that they couldn't do it!' Rowe pondered the possibility that a wage scale for players might enable a manager to entice an individual to develop or improve his skills, by offering another '£5 a week' to equal the rate of pay for a team-mate who, for example, was not solely reliant on the use of one foot. This theme turned his thoughts to the diminutive Tommy Harmer, who, he recalled wistfully, '…could flick the ball on to his head, nod it back to his foot and keep it balanced one way or another, just as long as you were prepared to stand and watch him. But it never evoked any kind of ambition in any other player on my staff to do something similar.'

In 1975, when repeating his belief that players had become more athletic and had improved through coaching, he back-tracked mid-sentence: 'I look at a game like Newcastle against Spurs on telly [Terry Neill had replaced Nicholson by this point] and I think what is this? — Third Division football or First?'. Rowe suggested that individual skills needed improving but this, he emphasised needed to be started at an early age. In modern times fewer and fewer children arrive at adulthood having naturally developed the basic skills Rowe and his pals picked-up kicking around under the street lamps. Even as early as 1960 Rowe himself had said: 'Remember …that the cinema and television have claimed many of the boys who would have been players in our own floodlight football.' In his wildest nightmares Rowe will not have imagined all the additional impediments which would arrive within the next half-century. Parked cars and heavier road traffic keeping ball play off the streets; the increase in sedentary ways for children to pass the time of day (computer games, smartphones etc); the planting of signs reading: 'NO BALL GAMES' on more-and-more of the diminishing green spaces to be found in urban locations: and, worst of all, the selling-off of school playing fields. The *Daily Telegraph* claimed that more than 10,000 playing fields were sold off for commercial development under the 1979-1997 Conservative governments, an initiative started under Margaret Thatcher and continued under John Major. In 2009 John Cartwright painted the even grimmer picture, for those who still had playing fields to play on, of young players now confined to playing competitive 11-a-side games under the demanding watchful eyes of parents and coaches, the pressure on winning creating an emphasis on negative tactics: '…the offside trap, squeezing-up, physical commitment and so on — at the expense of imaginative and experimental play.'

SOCCER UNDER THE LIGHTS AND UNDER THE SUN Back in the 1950s, Arthur Rowe had been a great advocate of floodlighting (previously outlawed by the football authorities), both to enable backlogged games to be played in midweek and at an hour when nine-to-five workers could attend. For Rowe, floodlights recalled those street games under lampposts and he once eloquently described the pleasure many football fans experience with night games: 'With vision fixed to the pitch (that

Rowe followed the international game when reading World Soccer *and contributed to the magazine too. Right: What great insight into soccer is he expressing here?*

alone is illuminated) there can be no distraction at all to disturb or frustrate attention. There is an accentuated feeling of expectation and excitement, and the speed of the players and of the game itself is, or seems to be, increased. The flash of bright-coloured jerseys against the bright green of the grass combine in one 'Vistavision' panorama, but with the added reality of live people seen in the flesh.' Rowe had been impressed when a Third Division North game played under lights at Carlisle in November 1955 attracted approximately three times the daytime gate.

However, Rowe's early attempts to bring in extra revenue by persuading his Tottenham directors to arrange floodlit challenge games at White Hart Lane (see Chapter 14), fell on deaf ears. Later, in 1960, Rowe wrote enthusiastically about the prospect of a future 'Grand European Floodlight League' with '…all the matches played in mid-week,' adding, 'without question some great games would be certain.' Here he was 32 years ahead of his time, anticipating the 1992 launch of the Champions' League. Such was Rowe's enthusiasm for floodlit football that he even suggested ways clubs might pay for installation, including interest-free loans to be repaid by a percentage of the gates forthcoming from floodlit fixtures; income from pre-season exhibition games, and a share of the profits earned by super-rich pools companies.

Another long-standing hope of Rowe's was for summer football because he believed that the annual break should take place during the three worst months for weather, not in the summer. His season would start at the beginning of March to the end of November, playing all games during midweek evenings (to avoid the heat of mid-summer afternoons), '…leaving the weekends clear for families to drive to the sea or countryside in an affluent society where nearly everyone owns a car.' Yet he overlooked lost revenue due to fewer travelling fans attending evening fixtures. Also, for many fans, football in deep mid-winter was one of the few pleasurable diversions after a long working week but Rowe also considered the comfort of the spectator.

Most stadiums in the 1950s and 1960s had at least two completely unsheltered sides and portions of the banked, uncovered standing-only areas were merely grassed. Rowe had witnessed the improvements to comfort in cinemas etc., with no similar progress at Saturday afternoon football, which he put down to football still being regarded '…by too many people as the "poor man's" sport, and its progress has been in line with this attitude.'

ROWE AND DIMINISHING TECHNICAL SKILLS   In the early 1980s Rowe said that in the previous decade 'skill and intelligence' had been '…squeezed out of the game by an increase in physical fitness. There has been a 50% increase in fitness and it is that which now dominates the game.' The taciturn Ron Saunders, who won a League title with Aston Villa in 1980-81, once famously stated that he 'didn't like ball-players in the middle of the park'. Which prompts the obvious question - where would he like them if not where they can most damage the opposition? Given the chance, many English managers of those times would have preferred to acquire a Peter Storey or a Vinnie Jones rather than a Hoddle, Zidane or de Bruyne!

Over the years John Cartwright has done Rowe proud with his emphasis on the passing game and the acquisition of technical skills at an early age. When coaching the nation's best 14 year-olds at Lilleshall just a few years before Arthur Rowe's death, Cartwright was shocked to find 'the nation's best' lacked basic skills. Many were one-footed and had only experienced the hurly-burly of eleven-a-side football (probably on adult-size pitches which increased their physical endurance but at the expense of developing close ball-control): 'It was basically about knocking the ball forward and scrapping for it in midfield. It was as though these young players saw football as a kind of combat sport,' sighed Cartwright. David Miller wrote that 1970s football had increasingly become '…no more than "industrial" football' and Rowe, with the spectator in mind, concisely summed-up: 'There is not too much these days in the game which allows you to go home happy.'

PUSH-AND-RUN IN ROWE'S TWILIGHT YEARS AND BEYOND   In 1969 Arthur Rowe told Ken Jones that he saw the football of the late '60s as a reflection of society and its compulsions: mass production, efficiency and speed, time and action. 'Leisure time,' he said, '…has been impregnated with this sense of urgency. There is this constant need for stimulation. Football has become caught up in this.' He continued: 'It has become more efficient. There is a more physical effort.' On the positive side he saw teams such as Mercer and Allison's Manchester City, as well as [Rowe-admirer] Harry Catterick's Everton, with its outstanding midfield trio of Ball, Harvey and Kendall, and even Revie's Leeds (on occasion) employing '…the same basic principle as I did,' but conceded that 'push-and-run' was made more difficult due to the greater concentration on preventing a loss, as opposed to trying to win.

'It is the team which reacts to change of possession which succeeds. If they are slow to recognise that they are in a position to counter-attack they will find that opponents have settled in on them' and likewise, 'if they are quick to regroup when they have lost the ball they will kill the threat of counter-attack at source.' Here

Rowe was a forerunner of the likes of Pochettino, Guardiola, Klopp and Arteta. Everton's legendary manager Harry Catterick, who brought two League titles and an FA Cup to Goodison, said of Rowe: 'I admired what he did at Tottenham. The Spurs of those days were so entertaining to watch. They were also highly effective, and this, after all, is what the game is all about.'

Although believing few coaches favoured his 'push-and-run' approach (at any rate, those who utilised it for 90 minutes), in a 1974 article headlining him as a 'soccer idealist', Rowe said he still saw 'push-and-run' used periodically in games, most teams achieving it at some stage during a match:

'I go to a game and a side suddenly strings a few passes together; short, quick passes with people moving intelligently to give-and-take them. It's as if the game suddenly got a little electric shock. The crowd catches its breath, and when it's over everyone claps because it's been a lovely moment.'

Surely, that description is right up there with the most pleasurable evocations of a soccer ideal ever expressed.

Even at the grand age of 80 years Arthur Rowe was still promoting 'push-and-run'. The occasion was the 100th League meeting between Spurs and Arsenal in 1987 which Rowe watched on TV at his Norbury home where he was interviewed by Brian Scovell. Spurs' then striker Clive Allen also spoke with Scovell, telling him that Spurs' manager David Pleat '…admires Spurs' traditions, especially Arthur Rowe's push-and-run style and is trying to put that back into our play.' Three years' later, in January 1990, Brian Clough's double-European Cup winning team were playing Tottenham in the League Cup and the *Guardian*'s David Lacey wrote: 'There was nothing complicated about Forest's performance. It was the old Spurs push-and-run set in a modern context and given extra speed and vision.' Moving further ahead toward the third decade of the twenty-first century, the Premier League has been lit up by the likes of Wenger's Arsenal, Klopp's Liverpool and, perhaps more than any other, Guardiola's Manchester City, delighting us with rapid, sharp, pass-and-move football, so often ending with a tap into an empty net.

FROM ROWE TO GUARDIOLA In 2013, Jonathan Wilson, in his remarkable study of soccer tactics, *Inverting the Pyramid*, considered Pep Guardiola's Barcelona as the '…greatest side the world has known for at least two decades.' Wilson highlighted a progression through the ages starting (as mentioned in Chapter 2) with Scotland's Queen's Park, followed by the Spurs of McWilliam, Rowe's Championship-winning side, then Rinus Michels taking the helm at Ajax from previous incumbent (and former Rowe sidekick) Vic Buckingham (who had given Cruyff his Ajax debut at 17). It has already been seen that Buckingham took his pal's 'push-and-run' to Pegasus and West Bromwich Albion (albeit adding the occasional pinpoint, long pass). James Corrigan of the *Telegraph* pointed out that Rowe had been Buckingham's mentor and added that Buckingham had '…eschewed the "hoof it" mentality and instead called for the ball to be played out of trouble.'

Left: Manager Rowe with player Vic Buckingham at Tottenham (left). Right: Buckingham in his later role as manager of Ajax of Amsterdam. The young man second from left is future all-time Dutch great Johann Cruyff and it was Buckingham who gave him his League debut in Holland and later played a role in Cruyff's eventual move to Barcelona.

In the late 1960s and early 70s Michels adding 'pressing' to curb opponents' attacking intentions, took Ajax to three consecutive European Cup victories and then coached the greatest-ever Dutch national side to consecutive World Cup Finals in 1974 and 1978. The epitome of 'Total Football' performance is often considered that displayed in the opening minutes of the 1974 World Cup Final, not by eventual victors West Germany but by losers Holland. Just 80 seconds after Referee Jack Taylor's first peep on the whistle the ball had already been passed 14 times between the ever-circulating Dutch players by the time captain Cruyff, with a sudden burst into the area, was brought crashing down and a penalty awarded. The first touch of the ball by a West German came when goalkeeper Sepp Maier retrieved Johan Neeskens' penalty from his net.

Vic Buckingham took over at Barcelona in January 1970 with the Catalan club down in tenth but by spring they in fourth. He had told his players to forget the opposition once they themselves were in possession. As for defending, he considered the last player to lose the ball was the first line of defence. In admiration Barça player Charly Rexach described Buckingham as the first coach at Barcelona who provided discipline and 'a game plan'. A back problem cut short Buckingham's successful stay in the Barça hot seat and, for the second time, the man who took over the reins from him (as at Ajax), was the man most commonly regarded as the inventor of 'Total Football', Rinus Michels. Ferenc Puskás later claimed that Hungary's play at the 1952 Olympics was 'the prototype' of 'Total Football', saying 'When we attacked, everyone attacked. In defence, it was just the same.'

Of course, the common denominator between 1970s Ajax, 1970s Barcelona and 1950s' Hungary was Arthur Rowe.

During his tenure at the Nou Camp Buckingham twice travelled covertly to Amsterdam to set-up the transfer of Cruyff to Barcelona, and Cruyff and Michels then inspired the Catalans to win La Liga in 1974. The Rowe-Buckingham-Michels-

Cruyff link continued when Cruyff himself coached Barça to 11 trophies (including the 1992 European Cup) between 1988 to 1996. Cruyff's Barça side became known as the 'Dream Team' and included a young Pep Guardiola who has since taken the same style with him (with great success) from Barcelona to Bayern Munich and finally Manchester City.

As has been seen Rowe believed strongly in 'footballers' rather then 'centre-forwards', 'half-backs' or 'full-backs', a factor inherent in the concepts of 'Total Football' decades later. Cruyff would describe members of Michel's 1974 World Cup side as '...footballers who could think in terms of the overall game. They were positionally sound and technically even better.' Fourteen years earlier Rowe had said, 'Our football has suffered, I think, in the last twenty-five years through our players being "typed". We have had "types" of players for full-backs; "types" for wing-halves; "types" for centre-halves and centre-forwards, tall enough and big enough to bash the daylights out of each other; your inside-forwards have got to supply the craft; the wing-forwards have got to be able to run; full backs have got to be strong and be able to kick. All of which, of course, is quite wrong. They are all "footballers"; they should all be able to put up a good performance whether at right-back or outside-left. It would be difficult, I know, to reach that point of perfection, but we should try to get eleven footballers, largely interchangeable, who could play together as a team.' In 1961 he took England captain Johnny Haynes as an example: 'This boy has the lot as far as I'm concerned. You could play Johnny at centre-forward and he would bring you goals through his accuracy in finishing and his sheer skill as a footballer. He would also succeed anywhere in the half-back line or at back.'

Dr Rogan Taylor, Director of the Football Industry Group at Liverpool University, considers the 1950s' Hungary team as the forerunners of 'Total Football' rather than Dutch team of two decades later. If he is correct, and comparisons are made with the 1951 Championship-winning Spurs, thoughts turn once again to Arthur Rowe. In 1936 the father of Ferenc Puskás [also Ferenc], became coach of the Budapest side which eventually became Honvéd. He will almost certainly have attended some of Rowe's coaching sessions in 1939. The case for Rowe's influence on the superb Hungarian national side of the 1950s is perhaps reinforced with this quote by Puskás himself (taken from 'Puskás on Puskás' by Rogan Taylor and Klara Jamrich): 'In a sense, we were unknowingly developing a very modern training routine: lots of one- or two-touch five-a-sides; shooting practice; rehearsals of set-pieces and so on.' (Rowe, of course, had come-up with various, innovative dead-ball plays at Spurs).

Former Real Madrid coach Jorge Valdano made the significant point that it is more often the entertaining, exciting football teams from history which remain in the public's memory than those who have picked up trophies in uninspiring fashion. For example, Arrigo Sacchi's late twentieth century AC Milan and those exciting Netherlands' sides who only finished second in successive World Cups in 1974 and 1978. Many in Britain forgave Arsène Wenger the relative paucity of trophies Arsenal picked up after he became manager in 1996, as in the eyes of a neutral, the 'Gunners's football could be breathtaking to witness, particularly the Thierry

Henry/Dennis Bergkamp side of the early twenty-first century with accurate, fast, first-time passing in 'push-and-run' fashion. Backing up Valdano's opinion, Terry Venables posed an apt question following that 1974 World Cup Final: 'Would you rather be remembered as the coach of the team that played a stubborn, strong game [winners West Germany], or the coach of the team that lost [Holland] but created dreams for the world's youth and those who watched the game?'

There is little doubt Rowe was working toward what today would be called 'Total Football' in the 1940s, as were the Hungarians in the early 1950s. Rowe wanted his players to feel free to 'give-and-go' as they moved up-field, with no fear, in the knowledge a team-mate would cover them, possession being of the essence. Possession, allied to speed, was difficult for any traditional defence to deal with. As Julian Holland wrote of Rowe's Spurs': 'The opposition had no opportunity to tackle; they could only hope to intercept the ball on its way from one Spur to another.'

'Total Football' keeps Rowe's flag flying in the 21st Century.

ON THE PITCH IT'S DOWN TO THE PLAYERS Unlike many of today's self-aggrandising, egotistical managers, Rowe very much believed that results on the field were due more to the player than the manager: 'Success or failure depends on the split-second decisions of the eleven men in the team.' He felt that no other business was so reliant on quickness of thought as was football. Writing in 1961 he had this to say: 'In the end, the blokes you talk to and kid a bit and prod a bit have to go out there and do it. That is why they must be given that feeling of personal responsibility.' With the modern day custom of managers remaining on their feet, gesticulating and shouting instructions for 90 minutes, you might be forgiven for thinking that an individual player's sense of responsibility hardly exists. 'Push-and-run' (or the 'Barça way') demands that players take risks and think throughout the game, the players constantly moving both themselves and the ball at speed and guidance from the bench thus becoming irrelevant.

As a player under Rowe at Spurs Bill Nicholson absorbs his manager's instructions.

Aside from adopting 'push-and-run' for his own Spurs' side when managing them to multiple successes in the early 1960s, one wonders just how much Nicholson's success owed to Rowe's influence and ideas?

DEVOTED TO HIS 'LILLYWHITES' In a 1982 BBC documentary on the history of Tottenham Hotspur Football Club presented by John Motson, Arthur Rowe struggled to contain his emotions when asked 'What does Tottenham Hotspur mean to you?' In earlier clips from the same interview he had appeared in jaunty mood, but his disposition had dramatically altered by the time Motson asked the considered question 'Looking back over all the years you've been associated with Spurs, whether as player, manager, supporter, what do you think the club really means to you?' Hesitating to answer, Rowe tries to smile, lets out a sigh, draws a breath, gasps, grits his teeth, and, almost inaudibly says, 'A lot.' He manages a brief smile before tightening his jaw again. He finally composes himself, and, with a steadying hand to his chin, calmly says 'They are a great club and to be associated with them, was nice.' The director cuts to a sound bite of Spurs' fans singing 'Glory, Glory Hallelujah', which overlays a series of historical clips of Spurs, bringing the programme to a fitting close. It has been a little disconcerting to view and one wonders if Arthur still dwelled on the treatment he had suffered at White Hart Lane all those years' earlier?

A FINE EPITAPH 'In the bad years since the war only three football managers have scaled the heights of greatness. They are Matt Busby, the canny Scot who runs Manchester United, Stan Cullis, the tough realist who bosses Wolves and… Arthur Rowe, late of Tottenham Hotspur.' So wrote *Sunday Express* journalist Alan Hoby on October 2nd 1955, before adding: 'All these famous men I count as friends—but none more than Rowe'. Norman Giller recalls Rowe as 'A gentle, kindly man,' adding, '…easy to talk to.' In 2017, a series entitled *The Men Who Made Modern Football* on the *The Educated Left Foot* website considered Rowe '…had become a forgotten man, remembered only by those privileged to see his [Spurs] team play in a pre-television era'.

It added: 'This proved to be a fleeting glimpse of what English football might have become.'

Around the turn of the millennium Brian Glanville, who described 'push-and-run' as Rowe's 'exhilarating creation', selected a top ten of football managers in the English game. Naturally he included Rowe in the ten, alongside such as Chapman, Busby, Clough, Ferguson, Shankly, Paisley and Wenger. Ken Jones, in *Goal* magazine, wrote how '…only Matt Busby has matched [Rowe] for vision, outlasting him as a manager because of a less sensitive reaction to pressure.' Rowe's erudite former goalkeeper Ron Reynolds said: 'I can't speak highly enough about Arthur in every sense, but especially as a theorist on the game. He was a very nice man as well as a very good tactician and coach.' Bobby and Jack Charlton, when boys, would stand on the terraces at Newcastle's St James' Park and when later reflecting on his life, Sir Bobby would name only one club side which particularly impressed him: Rowe's Championship-winning side of 1951. The renowned journalist John Moynihan said of 'push-and-run': 'It was adventurous stuff, a new art, like Surrealism, having its specially defined period. This method has never been used as expressively since.' Sir Alf Ramsey once said 'Rowe was the most brilliant manager of the time and I gained a great deal of satisfaction from playing in his team.' Yet Eamonn

Dunphy considered Ramsey-the-manager became a risk-averse realist, quoting him as saying: 'I'm employed to win football matches. That's all.' Dunphy continued: '[Ramsey had] concluded that there was no point in trying to emulate the great Spurs' team he'd played in when his dressing room at Ipswich was populated by journeymen, and with England, the same pragmatism applied.' Perhaps Ramsey, having witnessed how Rowe's health suffered from the maintenance of his ideals, preferred reliance on a more guaranteed, workmanlike route to successful results.

Johnny Byrne said of his mentor that he '…would have been one of the great managers of all time had he not been hampered by ill-health,' and continued: 'I rate him one of the kindest and sincerest men I have ever come across in football. He was always approachable and helpful when he was the manager behind the desk. If a player had a problem he did not worry about whether or not he should mention it to Arthur. He had a nice way of putting a player at his ease.' On another occasion Byrne said he trusted Rowe so completely that '…he could tell me black was white and I would believe it,' and in further tribute said Rowe was 'One hell of a good guy… one of the greatest. Arthur Rowe was football. He was everybody's friend.' That final sentence is now regarded as a weakness in modern football. Byrne's great pal, Palace team-mate Vic Rouse, told me: 'Arthur was a lovely man and I never saw him lose his temper once. He was a one-off', while George Petchey considered his 20-plus years with Rowe as 'the happiest days I have experienced in football.'

Sir Stanley Rous, as President of FIFA, regarded Arthur as a '…man I am pleased to count among my friends', while Sir Matt Busby considered him a '…great thinker, a great judge and a great manager.' Rowe discovery Steve Kember, a member of two Palace sides that achieved promotion to Division One, considered Rowe (along with Petchey) as the biggest influence on his career, as did David Payne who would coach Millwall to FA Youth Cup triumph, sharing the acclaim with scout Bob Pearson and with Arthur Rowe (who at that time was working behind the scenes at the Den). Payne particularly recalled Rowe talking about football '…but talking about life at the same time.'

One of Arthur's final discoveries for Crystal Palace, Dave Swindlehurst, scorer of 132 League goals for Palace, Derby, West Ham and Sunderland, told me 'Arthur was a lovely man, a gentlemen, steeped in history and great tradition.' Another of Rowe's Palace discoveries, John Holsgrove, spoke with the *Daily Mail* about English football's insularity, exposed so savagely by Hungary in the 1950s, pitying the fact that no other English club nor the national team had '…ever tried to emulate Rowe's style.' Holsgrove considered that only Chapman, Rowe and Ramsey had introduced 'revolutionary change' to the English game. In 1993 Geoffrey Green commended the radical changes brought to soccer by all three of those men, but when summarising the changes created by each, concluded that Chapman's had '…in the long term harmed football', Ramsey's had '…cast a blight on entertainment' and only Rowe's initiative had '…brought a bloom of beauty and excitement' to the game. Esteemed manager Alec Stock once talked-up his own managerial achievements but was compelled to add 'but I have left no telling footprints in the sand like Herbert Chapman, Arthur Rowe, or Alf Ramsey, all of whom did something original.'

Rowe's obituary in *The Times* read: '[Rowe's] precepts have influenced, directly or indirectly, most of the more progressive club sides of the last three decades, with the great Liverpool sides of the late 1970s and 1980s embodying his fundamental principles,' and described 'push-and-run' simply as '…a gust of fresh air in the stereotyped postwar game.' As late as 2019 James Corrigan in *The Daily Telegraph*, when talking of Vic Buckingham breaking 'the mould' with success coaching in Europe, made it clear he owed it all to his mentor, 'the great Arthur Rowe.'

THE FINAL YEARS During the decade following that poignant TV interview with John Motson, Rowe became a patient of Warlingham Park Hospital in Surrey. George Petchey, who regarded Rowe, Godfather to one of his children, as a 'friend for life', would visit his old boss to reminisce until such time as he former boss no longer recognised him. In 1991, two years before his passing, Rowe received a visit from son Derek and 26-year-old grandson Duncan, over from Canada. On this same trip Duncan, a Spurs' fan to this day, was proud to meet Bill Nicholson.

With the Premier League just a year old, Arthur Sydney Rowe passed away on November 5th 1993, aged 87. Having moved away from his North London roots when managing Crystal Palace, Rowe's funeral took place at The South London Crematorium in Streatham, just three miles from Rowe's second football 'home', Selhurst Park. Many of his former players and colleagues were in attendance.

All the major national newspapers would carry lengthy obituaries, headlines including:

'MANAGER OF VISION' *The Daily Telegraph*
'PASSING ON HIS VISION' *The Guardian*
'ROWE'S 'PUSH-AND-RUN' OPENED NEW HORIZONS' *Evening Standard*

Reg Drury of *The Independent* wrote that Rowe's story was '…one of triumph and tragedy,' adding 'English football could do with a young Arthur Rowe.' *The Times* described Rowe as '…one of the most perceptive theorists in modern professional football.

A FITTING TRIBUTE Norman Giller believes a statue of Rowe should be erected alongside the bust of Bill Nicholson at Tottenham, '…in memory of the man who pumped pride and passion back into the Club.' Others likewise ponder why his 'pupil' (Nicholson) and not Rowe himself, should have had a street named after him. Surely something similar should enshrine forever that first-ever Spurs' Championship success and the style with which it was won. It is an anomaly which can and should still be rectified. In 1994, even Spurs' Argentinian manager Ossie Ardiles, answering a question from new signing Ilie Dumitrescu, was informed enough to point out that it was Rowe who won Spurs' first-ever League title.

One former comrade-in-arms of Rowe's sadly outlived him by just 34 days. Danny Blanchflower, nearly 20 years Rowe's junior, passed away from Alzheimer's. It is sadly ironic to think that had they met in their last few years, these two sharp-witted, eloquent, intelligent football men would have struggled to engage in the activity they both enjoyed so much: incisive, intelligent and humorous conversation.

ROWE'S LASTING LEGACY It is undeniable that Arthur Rowe improved the entertainment level and brought success to all three clubs he managed. He oversaw Chelmsford City's 'double'-winning season of 1945-46 and their runners-up spot in 1948-49, achieved successive championships in his first two years at Spurs and took Crystal Palace to promotion in his first season, presiding over the club's all-time record goals' total. A promotion which triggered Palace's ambition to become the established top flight club it is today.

Players uniformly enjoyed playing 'push-and-run'. In the 1970s Peter Allen experienced it playing under Petchey and Rowe at Leyton Orient: 'It was terrific, such an easy way to play. When you're playing it, and it's going well, you wonder 'why isn't everyone playing this way?' Give it to the first team-mate you see and keep moving.' Eddie Baily said: '[Playing 'push-and-run'] you felt that you were helping to lift the tone of the game and so you got that respect from the crowds as well.' Late in his career Rowe modestly put his Spurs success with 'push-and-run' down to having the players who could best practice it, not so much that it was a new invention of his. Further modesty can be seen in a statement he made on his pet subject of 'players' rather than 'centre-forwards' or 'midfield-generals': 'Don't get the idea from this that I am laying any fancy claims to being a great thinker. A manager, and let us all remember it, is only as good as his current players allow him to be.' In later life he reflected just how much pleasure he had gained from watching his own Spurs side in action, sometimes becoming 'transfixed' by what he had created. He felt the game would have benefitted had all teams played like his. Rowe once said something which could be echoed by anyone unfortunate not to witness his 'push-and-run' side in action: 'It would have been great to have had all those wonderful games on tape so you could take them out when you wanted and enjoy them all over again.' For Rowe there was only one downside when watching his side play: 'I was jealous for them, anxious that they should do justice to themselves. That was the only pressure, the rest was sheer pleasure.'

Unlike his managerial successors of today, Rowe would sit high in the stand. As Tony Marchi told me, 'Before the game, every manager in those days would go in the dressing room, give their instructions and then they'd say 'Good luck, lads' and then go and sit in the stand. Sit and watch the game. They were up there and could see all that was happening. You don't get one manager now that goes up in the stand. They're all on the bench, ranting and raving.' As previously mentioned, today's players enter the field of play with a reduced sense of individual responsibility, knowing that if they suffer a lapse in concentration or take a breather, someone will harangue them back into action from the touchline. As for the team captain, Tony Marchi dismissively says: 'Nowadays the captain is just tossing up the coin.' Gone are the inspirational Burgesses or Blanchflowers to take control and direct operations on the field, as Rowe believed should be the case.

In the late 1960s, author Peter Morris recalled Rowe's great gift to football: 'It has been over 20 years now since we first saw the old 'push-and-run' played. The youngsters have barely heard of it but for those of us who marvelled, it is like remembering a [Glenn] Miller or a [Benny] Goodman orchestration – the melody, sweet and mellow, lingers on.' Ken Jones too, wrote admiringly: '[Rowe] has known his triumphs, suffered his disappointments. He is part of, and yet, somehow, apart from football. But the history of it will never be complete without total recognition of his wisdom. He has won and lost. Punished himself beyond all reasonable need. But he could see when others were blind. He did when others didn't. In the final reckoning he and Busby will stand as men apart.'

Then there is the question: 'Would Nicholson's 'Double' Spurs of 1960-61 have so triumphed had they not based their play on Rowe's 'push-and-run'? A playing colleague of Nicholson's, Derek Castle, once said Rowe had greatly influenced Nicholson, while 'Double' star Les Allen said Nicholson wanted 'one-touch' right through the team, telling his men to: 'Give it and go'. Sir Walter Winterbottom said of 'push-and-run': 'That was Arthur's contribution, welding a team who could play this style of football which was so attractive to watch. It was silky stuff.' Eamonn Dunphy wrote that [Rowe]'s convictions about a game based on passing and movement '…were mocked as a Continental fad by the reactionary forces still dominant in the English game,' adding that Rowe '…thought soccer was about guile and technical skills, brain rather than brawn. And even as the Hungarians and Real Madrid emerged from the despised 'Continent' in the fifties to prove that brawn was a lesser virtue, Rowe remained a prophet without honour – or respect – in his own land.'

Writing about a Spurs' challenge for the Premiership title in 2016, the *Independent* newspaper wrote that '…the Argentine boss [Pochettino] may be set to join Arthur Rowe and Bill Nicholson in Tottenham lore.' Sadly Pochettino didn't quite make it but he did remarkably take Spurs to the Champions' League Final for the very first time. In April 2017, when Spurs were breathing down Chelsea's necks in an attempt to win the Premier League, Alasdair Gold wrote: 'In recent decades the phrase 'The Tottenham Way' has become an almost derogatory term — one signifying a pretty but ultimately unsatisfying experience. It wasn't always that way. First, Arthur Rowe's 'push-and-run' side in the 50s and then Bill Nicholson's double-winners the following decade gave Spurs their identity and 'The Tottenham Way' was born — a thrilling, vibrant, attacking form of football that delivered results as well as eye-catching performances.' Sacked by Spurs in April 2021, Pochettino's successor José Mourinho failed to absorb the fact that it is Rowe and Nicholson who any new Tottenham boss should aim to emulate.

There is little doubt Arthur Rowe's work was taken to another level by Nicholson, but largely due to huge financial investment in quality players. The combined period of Rowe and Nicholson rule at White Hart Lane (disregarding the three 'lost' years under Anderson) was the most productive, trophy-winning time in the club's history. The years between joining the Football League in 1908 until Rowe's arrival as manager in 1949, if deducting the 11 seasons lost to war, saw Spurs win a trophy, on average, once every ten seasons. Skipping then to the period from the end of Nicholson's reign until 2021, Spurs won a trophy only every five to six seasons. The 21 seasons in between (again disregarding the Anderson period, which produced nothing), stretching from Rowe's introduction of 'push-and-run' in 1949, to 1955, then from 1958 to 1974 (the Nicholson years), astonishingly produced a trophy, on average, every one-and-a-half seasons.

ARTHUR 'PUSH-AND-RUN' ROWE

Spurs celebrate their capture of the 1963 European Cup Winners' Cup in Rotterdam. The side based their playing style on 'push-and-run' and included five players Rowe brought to the Club: Baker, Dyson, Henry, Marchi and, of course, Blanchflower. Greaves would have been too, had he not been tempted away from joining Rowe's Spurs as a boy (see Chapter 15).

Further confirmation that Nicholson's success was built heavily on Rowe's 'push-and-run' can be found in two quotes from Spurs' captain Alan Mullery: 'It wasn't enough for [Nicholson's] teams to win: they had to win in style and entertain the public. That philosophy came from Arthur Rowe's "push and run" Spurs team'. Mullery also wrote that Nicholson followed '…training routines used by Arthur Rowe and his push-and-run Spurs. Bill Nick and Eddie Baily were both part of that team and believed in Rowe's methods'.

It is sad but hardly surprising that innovative Continental coaches who came into the unenterprising English game, such as Arsène Wenger, suffered much criticism. Wenger's predecessor, interim manager Bruce Rioch, had spent a season trying to play more enterprising football than that of George Graham, whose Arsenal teams had tasted success by sticking to the traditional Chapman virtues of a tight defence and swift, long ball counter-attacks. Wenger took Rioch's progress further when bringing in players who could engage in breathtaking one- or two-touch interchanges at pace. A prime example was a move involving five one-touch passes which was voted the *Match of the Day* 'Goal of the Season' in 2013-14 (Jack Wilshere the scorer). The Wilshere goal, which ended in his passing the ball into the net, beat long-distance blasts from the likes of Luis Suárez by a considerable margin — proof of the appeal of a 'push-and-run' style in the present century.

The second decade of the century saw the arrival in English football of Pep Guardiola, whose 'Total Football' inevitably made jaws drop the length and breadth of the country. At the time of writing, more managers are absorbing his influence. As for the England international side, at the time of writing progress has been made under Gareth Southgate, his players having upped their game to compete with the skills of foreign players entering the English top flight.

A NEW GENERATION Meanwhile a 17-year-old all-action Canadian midfielder named Amy fulfilled her ambition to win a soccer scholarship in the USA, at the University of Louisiana-Monroe, where she was majoring in pharmacy studies whilst playing for the Louisiana Warhawks in the NCAA's Division 1 Sun Belt Conference.

Returning to study in Canada she then played for the St. Francis Xavier University side in Nova Scotia. Amy is the daughter of Arthur's grandson Duncan, whose father Derek never left Canada while her uncle Graham was tempted south to the warmer climes of California and lives there to this day. Duncan was once President of the local Spurs Supporters' Club and in 2005 took Amy and the rest of his family to White Hart Lane where they visited the 'Arthur Rowe Room'. It was then that Amy realised just how significant her great-grandfather was in the history of the club and soccer in general. Amy told a local Aurora newspaper: 'Sometimes my dad (Duncan) would talk about [his grandfather Arthur]. He says soccer is in my blood. It has been a big part of my life.' How proud great-grandfather Arthur would have been to witness Amy's progress in the very sport which was his own life and legacy. Meanwhile 'Uncle Arthur' is still remembered warmly by niece Carol and nephew David. 'You don't need me to tell you that Arthur was a really lovely man,' Carol told me, adding, '...gentle and unostentatious. A real gentleman.'

Talking with those who worked under him at both Spurs and Crystal Palace, one bathes in the warmth of their admiration for Rowe, for example Peter Burridge, telling me: 'He was a nice bloke, Arthur. He was a genuine man, he really was.' But, as Terry Long has said, he was also a worrier, often due to his concern for others. He would always help his players and ask after their families. A typical example: at a time when few players, let alone their wives, had their own transport and Palace player Stewart Imlach was in hospital having knee surgery, Rowe, aware how difficult it was for his wife to visit her husband, would come by in his car to take them all to see Stewart at visiting time. His sincerity was total. Unlike so many administrators and businessmen in contemporary football, Rowe was smart enough to know that a happy staff, with a secure and contented life outside the game, translates into success.

Returning to the game itself, in 2015, Norman Giller wrote of the pressure he felt from the 'younger generation' to declare Pochettino's Spurs as the best in his lifetime. 'But — sorry,' responded Giller, '...I must keep faith with my old heroes, ...and I repeat [Pochettino's side] cannot be held up as superior to Arthur Rowe's push-and-run champions and Bill Nicholson's dynamic 'Double' team. Better to

Arthur's great-granddaughter Amy Rowe won a soccer scholarship to the University of Lousiana-Monroe and later signed for Glen Shields FC.

In 2014 a group of Arthur Rowe's descendants attended a game at Toronto FC's BMO field during Spurs' 2014 summer tour. From left-to-right: Barbara Rowe (widow of Arthur's son Derek), Amy Rowe (great-granddaughter of Arthur), Duncan Rowe (Arthur's grandson), Graham Rowe (Arthur's son), Kurt Felker, Louise Rowe (Graham's wife), Julia Juszczuk (Arthur's great-granddaughter), Jessica Bourque (niece of Louise Rowe), Melanie Rowe (Duncan's wife) and Tracey Rowe (Arthur's granddaughter).

watch? You obviously never saw Sonny Walters and Les Medley hurtling down the touchline and having their crosses smashed into the net by Len Duquemin and Les Bennett.'

Who knows if Rowe might not have taken Tottenham Hotspur to even greater glories than those Nicholson achieved in the 1960s had he, instead of Anderson and Nicholson, been presented with the gushing flow of cash which attracted the likes of Mackay, Norman, Jones, White, Smith and others?

During the celebrations following the final match at the original White Hart Lane in May 2017, a rainbow appeared over the stadium. Norman Giller grasped the moment to reel off the names of all the Spurs' greats no longer 'with us', making sure he included 'the beloved' Rowe. 'The final whistle has sounded for the Lane,' wrote Giller, 'but Glory Glory Hallelujah, the spirit of Spurs will march on into the new ground bathed in the promise of that beautiful rainbow that was like a signpost for great things to come.'

Epilogue

An article on the 'Spurs-Web.com forum', penned by 'Borodin', had this to say of Rowe: 'I wonder if this guy is looking down and hoping we win the League…' and continued: '…without Rowe, the English game would have stayed isolated for far longer than it did. And Spurs would certainly not be the force they are today. As English football once again considers its role in the world, it's time for a new assessment of Arthur Rowe's quiet revolution.' I hope this book can be viewed as a contribution to a fresh assessment of Arthur Rowe's contribution to the game. I close with a collection of six 'afterwords'.

Rowe, at the age of 55: *'Often I go to watch schoolboys play in the same way a motorist goes to have his batteries charged. They recharge you and all you believe in. They show you the one essential truth… that football is really a very simple game. Eleven against eleven, all using the same equipment and the same ball; all working to the same principles of time and space.'*

> **Rowe again:** *'There was no thuggery in our game. You played football and you won the ball by positional sense. You played them out of the game. We did it in style.'*
>
> **Rowe's response to reporter Reg Drury when asking for an explanation of 'push-and-run':** *In fact, mate, it's just a case of doing the obvious.'*
>
> **Rowe's ultimate quote:** *'Football's a simple game, it's the players who make it difficult.'*
>
> **Johnny Byrne, 1962:** *'Arthur Rowe? He's forgotten more about football than most blokes will ever know.'*

In 1960 Rowe reflected, as eloquently as ever, on one particular game he managed at Tottenham, a game played on March 26th 1952, mentioned in Chapter 11.

Rowe was a master wordsmith and when one thinks that his Tottenham predecessor Joe Hulme ended his managerial career so disillusioned that he turned instead to journalism, one regrets Rowe didn't follow a similar course, either when he left Tottenham or when again struck down by stress at Crystal Palace. In his description of that 1952 game Rowe began by stating that it would: '…surely be my lasting memory of all soccer.' He continued with the following passionate, lyrical evocation:

'A floodlight game in Brussels, Tottenham v F.C. Austria; a brilliantly played match, fought at tremendous speed and ending in a draw of two goals each. This whole rousing, thrilling panorama of soccer skill and fierce endeavour, against a background of gently falling snow, was a strange but beautiful picture that I shall never forget.'

How heartwarming it is to imagine Arthur, having passed to the other side, looking down for eternity at that *'thrilling panorama'* still unfolding below.

Bibliography and Acknowledgements

INDIVIDUALS (to whom I am particularly grateful):

Zsofia Bachman and **Andrea Petroczi**, for their kind help with Hungarian translations.

Norman Giller (author and journalist) for his Foreword, his general encouragement and sharing his personal recollections of Rowe.

Gary Mixture For supplying excerpts from the 1947-48 Chelmsford City Handbook.

Hy Money (legendary, crusading photographer) for her consistent encouragement when I was putting this biography together. Her 'HY ON PALACE', a groundbreaking photographic study of all aspects of a professional football club, must not be missed.

David Payne (player, Crystal Palace and Leyton Orient; FA Youth Cup-winning coach at Millwall) for his tremendous and unfailing support during the creation of this book, aside from his unforgettable performances on the pitch as Crystal Palace fulfilled Rowe's ambition to reach the First Division for the first time in the Club's history.

Clare Stephens (Archivist) and Valerie Crosby (Archives Assistant), at Bruce Castle Museum (Haringey Culture, Libraries and Learning).

Steve Tongue (writer and broadcaster) for his support of this project.

PARTICULAR THANKS TO THOSE WHO GAVE UP THEIR TIME FOR INTERVIEWS:

Peter Barnes (Club Secretary at Leyton Orient, West Ham United and Tottenham Hotspur)

Peter Burridge (who turned out for Spurs' youth team under Rowe and later played under him at Crystal Palace)

Gilbert 'Dickie' Dowsett (who worked with Rowe at both Tottenham Hotspur and Crystal Palace)

John 'Jacko' Jackson (discovered by Rowe at Crystal Palace and strongly challenged for an England World Cup place in 1970)

Danny Light (who came through the juniors under Rowe at Crystal Palace)

Terry Long (regular first-teamer under Rowe's management at Crystal Palace and second in the club's all-time appearance record)

McClelland, David (retired sports journalist at the Croydon Advertiser) — interviewed by telephone

Tony Marchi (played under Rowe but left Anderson's Spurs to play in Italy, only to return when Bill Nicholson took over)

David Payne (discovered by and played under Rowe at Crystal Palace)

George Petchey (played under Rowe at Crystal Palace and later also worked with him at both Leyton Orient and Millwall)

Vic Rouse (played under Rowe at Palace)

Graham Rowe (son of Arthur Rowe)

John Sewell (played under Rowe at Palace)

Roy Summersby (played under Rowe at Palace — since his sad passing his widow Betty has continued to provide the author with encouragement)

Dave Swindlehurst (discovered by Rowe at Crystal Palace and top scorer in Crystal Palace's Second Division Championship-winning side 1979)

Dr Rogan Taylor (former Director of the Football Industry Group at the University of Liverpool, also writer and broadcaster) — interviewed by telephone

Brian Wait (son of the late Crystal Palace Chairman Arthur Wait) — by telephone

Ralph Wetton (played under Rowe at Tottenham Hotspur FC)

Bobby Woodruff (joined Palace when Rowe was scouting as Assistant Manager under Bert Head and proceeded to find the net 36 times in his first 81 League appearances)

OTHERS WHO SHARED RECOLLECTIONS OF ROWE WITH THE AUTHOR:

Mel Blyth (Crystal Palace defender who benefitted from ex-centre-half Rowe's advice when converting supremely well to that role)

Frank Parsons (goalkeeper discovered by Rowe at Crystal Palace)

Carol Rowe (niece of Arthur Rowe)

David Rowe (nephew of Arthur Rowe)

Duncan Rowe (grandson of Arthur Rowe)

Alan Stephenson (discovered by Rowe at Crystal Palace, represented England at Under-23 level and later shared central defence duties with the great Bobby Moore at West Ham United)

Tony Taylor (started out with Celtic but as a Crystal Palace player during Rowe's spell as General Manager he was a significant member of the 1969 promotion side. His coaching career included a spell as the national team manager of Canada)

ALSO:

Grateful thanks to **Brimsdown FC** [for help in arranging my interview with the late Ralph Wetton]

BOOKS:

Allen, Matt: *Four Four Two Great Footballers: Jimmy Greaves* (Virgin Publishing 2001)

Allison, Malcolm with Lawton, James: *Colours of My Life* (Everest Books 1975)

Arlott, John: *Basingstoke Boy* (Guild Publishing 1990)

Armfield, Jimmy: *Jimmy Armfield: The Autobiography* (Headline 2004)

Arnold, Peter and Davis, Christopher: *The Hamlyn Book of World Soccer* (The Hamlyn Publishing Group 1973)

Ashby, Sydney R: *Crystal Palace Supporters' Club Handbook* 1967-68, 1969-70

Bale, Bernard: *Bremner! The Legend of Billy Bremner* (André Deutsch 1998)

Ball, Peter and Shaw, Phil: *The Book of Football Quotations* (Stanley Paul & Company 1984)

Barclay, Patrick: *The Life and Times of Herbert Chapman* (Wiedenfeld & Nicholson 2014)

Barrett, Norman S: *Purnell's Encyclopedia of Association Football* (Purnell & Sons 1972)

Batt, Peter: *Mick Channon: The Authorised Biography* (Highdown, an imprint of Raceform 2004)

Belton, Brian: *Burn Budgie Byrne: Football Inferno* (Breedon Books Publishing Company 2004)

Belton, Brian: *The First and Last Englishman* (Breedon Books Publishing Company 1998)

Belton, Brian: *The Men of '64* (Tempus Publishing 2005)

Betts, Graham: *England: Player by Player* (Green Umbrella Publishing 2006)

Blanchflower, Danny: *The Double and Before* (Nicholas Kaye 1961)

Blows, Kirk and Hogg, Tony: *The Essential History of West Ham United* (Headline Book Publishing 2000)

Bolchover, David: *The Greatest Comeback* (Biteback Publishing 2017)

Bower, Tom: *Broken Dreams: Vanity, Greed and the Souring of British Football* (Simon & Schuster UK 2003)

Bowler, Dave and Reynolds, David: *Ron Reynolds: The Life of a 1950s' Footballer* (Orion Books 2003)

Bowler, Dave: *Danny Blanchflower: A Biography of a Visionary* (Victor Gollancz 1997)

Bowler, Dave: *Three Lions on the Shirt* (Victor Gollancz 1999)

Brazier, Roy: *Tottenham Hotspur Football Club 100 Greats* (Stadia, an imprint of Tempus Publishing 2006)

Brown, Deryk: *The Tottenham Hotspur Story* (Arthur Barker 1971)

Buchan, Charles: *A Lifetime in Football* (Mainstream Publishing 2010, originally published 1955)

Burgess, Ron: *Football—My Life* (Souvenir Press 1952)

Burns, Jimmy: *Barça: A People's Passion* (Bloomsbury Publishing PLC revised edition 2009)

Butler, Bryon: *The Football League 1888-1988: The Official Illustrated History* (Macdonald / Queen Anne Press 1987)

Byrne, Johnny: *The Strategy of Soccer* (Pelham Books 1965)

Carter, Neil: *Meet the New Boss; Same as the Old Boss: A Social History of the Football Manager 1880—c.1966* (University of Warwick thesis 2002)

Carter, Neil: *The Football Manager: A History* (Sport in the Global Society) (Routledge 2006)

Charlton, Sir Bobby: *My England Years: The Autobiography* (Headline Book Publishing 2007)

Cohen, George: *My Autobiography* (Headline Book Publishing 2003)

Crane, Tim: *They Played with Bobby Moore: The West Ham Years* (Tim Crane 2014)

Crystal Palace FC official Arthur Rowe testimonial programme (November 1969)

Crystal Palace FC Supporters' Club Handbook 1969-70

Crystal Palace FC Supporters' Club Handbook 1970-71

Daly, James: *Power to the Palace* (Crystal Palace fans' publication 1969)

Daniels, Phil: *Moore Than a Legend: From Barking to Bogota* (Goal! Publications 1997)

Davies, Hunter: *The Glory Game* (Mainstream Publishing 2001, originally published 1972)

Davies, Hunter: *My Life in Football* (Mainstream Publishing 1990)

BIBLIOGRAPHY AND ACKNOWLEDGEMENTS

Dickinson, Matt: *Bobby Moore: The Man in Full* (Penguin Random House Group 2014)

Doherty, Peter: *Spotlight on Football* (Art & Educational Publishers 1947)

Dubé, Stephen: *Palace* (Crystal Palace Supporters' Magazine) November 1969

Dunphy, Eamonn: *A Strange Kind of Glory* (William Heinemann 1991)

Dunphy, Eamonn: *The Rocky Road* (Penguin Books 2014)

Fabian, A. H. and Green, Geoffrey (Editors): *Association Football*, Volumes 1-4 (The Caxton Publishing Company, 1960)

Ferris, Ken: *The Double: The Inside Story of Spurs' Triumphant 1960-61 Season* (Mainstream Publishing 1999)

Fifield, Dominic and Fifield, Andrew: *Crystal Palace FC Centenary Book* (Publications UK 2005)

Finney, Tom: *My Autobiography* (Headline Book Publishing 2003)

Gardiner, Susan: *The Wanderer — the Story of Frank Soo* (Electric Blue Publishing 2016)

Giles, John with Lynch, Declan: *A Football Man: The Autobiography* (Hachette Books Ireland 2010)

Giller, Norman: *The Lane of Dreams* (NMG Enterprises 2009)

Glanville, Brian: *The Footballer's Companion* (Eyre & Spottiswoode Publishers 1962)

Goldblatt, David: *The Ball is Round* (Viking 2006)

Golesworthy, Maurice: *Soccer Who's Who* (Robert Hale 1964)

Greaves, Jimmy and Giller, Norman: *Don't Shoot the Manager* (Boxtree 1993)

Greaves, Jimmy and Giller, Norman: *This One's on Me* (Arthur Barker 1979)

Greaves, Jimmy and St John, Ian: *Football is Still a Funny Game* (Stanley Paul 1988)

Green, Geoffrey: Pardon Me for Living (George Allen & Unwin 1985)

Green, Geoffrey: Soccer in the Fifties (Ian Allan 1974)

Greenwood, Ron with Butler, Bryon: *Yours Sincerely* (Willow Books Collins 1984)

Harrison, Paul: *Images of Sport: Gravesend & Northfleet FC* (NPI Media Group 2006)

Haynes, Johnny: *It's All in the Game* (Arthur Barker 1962)

Henderson, Michael: *50 People Who Fouled Up Football* (Constable, an imprint of Constable & Robinson 2009)

Hilaire, Vince: *The Autobiography of Vince Hilaire* (Biteback Publishing 2018)

Hill, Jimmy: *The Jimmy Hill Story* (Hodder & Stoughton 1998)

Holden, Jim: *Stan Cullis: The Iron Manager, A Biography* (The Breedon Books Publishing Company 2000)

Holland, Julian: *Spurs: A History of Tottenham Hotspur Football Club* (Phoenix Sports Books 1956)

Holland, Julian: *Spurs—'The Double'*, (William Heinemann, in association with the Naldrett Press 1961)

Hopcraft, Arthur: *The Football Man—People and Passions in Soccer* (Aurum Press reissue 2013)

Hopkinson, Tim: *When Football Was Football: Crystal Palace. A Nostalgic Look at a Century of the Club* (Haynes Publishing 2014)

Hughes, Charles: *Soccer Skills: Tactics and Teamwork* (Parragon Books 1990)

Hunter, Norman: *Biting Talk* (Hodder and Stoughton 2005)

Hurst, Geoff: *1966 And All That* (Headline Book Publishing 2001)

Hurst, Geoff with Hart, Michael: *1966 World Champions: Relive the Glorious Summer with Those Who Were There* (Headline Book Publishing 2006)

Hurst, Geoff: *World Champions* (Headline Book Publishing 2006)

Hutchinson, Roger: *66! The Inside Story of England's World Cup Triumph* (Mainstream Publishing 1995)

Hylton, Stuart: *From Rationing to Rock: The 1950s Revisited* (Sutton Publishing 1998)

Imlach, Gary: *My Father and Other Working-Class Football Heroes* (Yellow Jersey Press 2006)

Inglis, Simon (editor): *The Best of Charles Buchan's Football Monthly* (English Heritage 2006)

James, Gary: *Football with a Smile: The Authorised Biography of Joe Mercer OBE* (ACL Colour Print & Polar Publishing UK 1993)

Joy, Bernard: *Soccer Tactics: A New Appraisal* (Phoenix House 1957, revised and reset 1962)

Kavanagh, Dermot: *Different Class: The Story of Laurie Cunningham* (Mainstream Publishing 2002)

Kelly, Stephen F (edited by): *A Game of Two Halves* (first published by The Kingswood Press 1992 as '*The Kingswood Book of Football*')

King, Ian: *Crystal Palace The Complete Record* (DB Books 2011)

Kuper, Simon and Szymanski, Stefan: *Soccernomics* (HarperSport, an imprint of HarperCollins Publishers 2012)

Lawton, Tommy: *My Twenty Years of Soccer* (Heirloom Modern World Library 1955)

Lewis, Richard: *England's Eastenders from Bobby Moore to David Beckham* (Mainstream Publishing 2002)

Madgwick, Don: *Palace Heroes and Legends* (Legends Publishing 2009)

Marquis, Max: *Anatomy of a Football Manager: Sir Alf Ramsey* (Arthur Barker 1970)

Matthews, Stanley: *The Way It Was: My Autobiography* (Headline Book Publishing 2000)

Matthews, Tony with Ellis, John and Axell, J: *We All Follow the Palace: Supporters Guide to Crystal Palace Football Club* (Eagle Eye Publications, 1993)

McKinstry, Leo: *Jack and Bobby* (Collins Willow 2002)

McKinstry, Leo: *Sir Alf* (HarperSport 2006)

Meisl, Willy: *Soccer Revolution* (Phoenix Sports Books 1955)

Miller, David: *Stanley Matthews: The Authorised Biography* (Pavilion Books 1989)

Moore, Tina: *Bobby Moore By The Person Who Knew Him Best* (Harper Collins 2005)

Morris, Peter: *The Team Makers: A Gallery of the Great Soccer Managers* (Pelham Books 1971)

Morse, Graham: *Sir Walter Winterbottom: The Father of Modern Football* (John Blake Publishing 2013)

Motson, John: *Forty Years in the Commentary Box* (Virgin Books 2009)

Moynihan, John: *The Soccer Syndrome* (MacGibbon & Kee 1966)

Mullery, Alan and Trevilion, Paul: *Double Bill: The Bill Nicholson Story* (Mainstream Publishing 2005)

Mullery, Alan: *The Autobiography* (Headline Publishing Group 2006)

Multiple contributors: *We All Follow the Palace* (Eagle Eye Publications 1993)

Nicholson, Bill: *My Life with Spurs* (Macmillan 1984)

Pawson, Tony (editor): *The Observer on Soccer: An Anthology of the Best Soccer Writing* (Unwin & Hyman 1989)

Pawson, Tony: *Runs and Catches* (Faber and Faber 1980)

Pawson, Tony: *The Goalscorers from Bloomer to Keegan*, (Cassell & Company 1978)

Peskett, Roy: *The Crystal Palace Story* (A Roy Peskett Publication 1969)

Peters, Ian: *PALACE* (Crystal Palace Supporters' Magazine August 1969)

Peters, Martin: *The Ghost of '66*, (Orion Books 2006)

Powell, Jeff: *Bobby Moore: The Life and Times of a Sporting Hero* (Robson Books 1993)

Prole, David: *Football In London* (Robert Hale 1964)

Pullin, Jack: *Soccer at War* (Headline Book Publishing 2005)

Purkiss, Mike with the Reverend Nigel Sands: *Crystal Palace - A Complete Record 1905-1989* (Breedon Books 1989)

Raath, Peter: *First Official History of South African Soccer* (Peter Raath 2002)

Ramsey, Alf: *Talking Football* (Stanley Paul and Company 1952)

Rippon, Anton: *Gas Masks for Goalposts: Football in Britain During the Second World War* (Sutton Publishing 2005)

Robson, Bobby with Harris, Bob: *My Autobiography: An Englishman Abroad* (Pan Books 1999)

Rogers, Ben: *A.J. Ayer, A Life* (Chatto & Windus 1999)

Rollin, Jack: *Soccer at War 1939-45: The Complete Record of British Football and Footballers During the Second World War* (Headline Book Publishing 2005)

Rowlinson, John: *Boys of 66: The Unseen Story Behind England's World Cup Glory* (Virgin Books, an imprint of Ebury Publishing, Penguin Random House 2016)

Sands, Reverend Nigel: *Crystal Palace: The Complete Record* (Breedon Books Publishing Company 1989)

Sands, Reverend Nigel: *Crystal Palace: The History of the Club 1905-1997* (Sporting and Leisure Press 1997)

Sands, Reverend Nigel: *The Men Who Made Crystal Palace Football Club* (Tempus Publishing 2004)

Scovell, Brian: *Bill Nicholson: Football's Perfectionist* (John Blake Publishing 2010)

Shearwood, Ken: *Pegasus* (Oxford Illustrated Press 1975)

Signy, Dennis: *The Tottenham Hotspur Football Book* (Stanley Paul and Company)

Smallbone, Kevin: *Brushes with the Greats: The Story of a Footballer/Cricketer* (sportingmemoriesonline.com 2001)

Smith, Rory: *Mister: The Men Who Gave the World the Game* (Simon & Schuster 2016)

Soar, Phil and Tyler, Martin: *Official History Arsenal FC 1886-1995* (Hamlyn 1995)

Soar, Phil: *The Hamlyn A-Z of British Football Records* (The Hamlyn Group 1981)

Soar, Phil: *Tottenham Hotspur: The Official Illustrated History 1882-1996* (Hamlyn 1996)

Swan, Peter with Johnson, Nick: *Setting the Record Straight* (Tempus Publishing 2006)

Swift, Frank (edited by Peskett, Roy): *Football from the Goalmouth* (Sporting Handbooks 1948)

Szöllösi, György: *Puskás* (Freight Books, Glasgow 2015)

Taylor, Rogan P and Ward, Andrew: *Kicking and Screaming: An Oral History of Football in England* (Robson Books 1998)

Taylor, Rogan P and Klara Jamrich [editors and translators]: *Puskás on Puskás: The Life and Times of a Footballing Legend* (Robson Books 1998)

Tossell, David: *Bertie Mee: Arsenal's Officer and Gentleman* (Mainstream Publishing 2005)

Tossell, David: *Big Mal: The High Life and Hard Times of Malcolm Allison, Football Legend* (Mainstream Publishing 2008)

Tottenham Hotspur Football Club *Official Handbook 1949-50*

Turk, Nigel: *PALACE* (Crystal Palace Supporters' Magazine November 1969)

Various contributors: *Saturday's Boys: The Football Experience* (Willow Books, William Collins Sons & Company 1990)

BIBLIOGRAPHY AND ACKNOWLEDGEMENTS

Venables, Terry and Montgomery, Alex and Nottage, Jane: *Terry Venables' Football Heroes* (Ebury Press 2001)

Venables, Terry with Montgomery, Alex: *Terry Venables: Born to Manage* (Simon & Schuster 2014)

Ward, Andrew and Williams, John: *Football Nation: Sixty Years of the Beautiful Game* (Bloomsbury, 2009)

Welch, Julie and Inglis, Simon: *Charles Buchan's Football Monthly Spurs Gift Book* (Malavan Media and Football Monthly 2008)

Weller, Ian: quoted from *PALACE* (Crystal Palace Supporters' Magazine January 1969)

White, Rob and Welch, Julie: *The Ghost: In Search of My Father the Football Legend* (Yellow Jersey Press, Random House 2012)

Wilson, Jonathan: *Inverting the Pyramid* (Orion Publishing Group 2013)

Wilson, Jonathan: *Nobody Ever Says Thank You: Brian Clough* (Orion 2011)

Wolstenholme, Kenneth: *They Think It's All Over… Memories of the Greatest Day in English Football* (Robson Books 1996)

SOCCER ANNUALS:
Bert Williams All-Star Football Book 1951
Billy Wright's Football Album 1954
Charles Buchan's Soccer Gift Book 1956-57
Charles Buchan's Soccer Gift Book 1958-59
FA Book for Boys 4 1951
FA Book for Boys 7 1954
FA Book for Boys 9 1956
FA Book for Boys 15 1962
FA Year Book 1951, 1961, 1962, 1963, 1964, 1965, 1967, 1968
Football Parade Annual 1951
International Football Book No. 4 1962
Playfair Football Annual 1950, 1951
Tommy Lawton's All-Star Football Book 1950
Topical Times 1962

MAGAZINES:
Backpass
Charles Buchan's Football Monthly
FA News November 1969
Football Association Bulletin August 1951 (Push and Run article by Rowe)
Football Digest Monthly
Four Four Two
Goal
Illustrated Magazine (September 2nd 1950)
Inside Football
Jimmy Hill's Football Weekly
Palace Echo (fan magazine)
Soccer Star
The Blizzard
Time Out
West Ham Retro Magazine (especially Terry Roper)
World Soccer
World Sports

NEWSPAPERS:
Croydon Times
Daily Post [North Wales newspaper]
Evening Standard [now *London Evening Standard*]
Irish Independent
Manchester Evening News
News of the World
Sunday Despatch
Sunday Express
Sunday Mirror
The Croydon Advertiser
The Daily Express
The Daily Graphic
The Daily Mail
The Daily Mirror
The Daily Sketch
The Essex Newsman-Herald
The Evening News
The Guardian
The Malay Mail
The People
The Sun
The Times
Tottenham Weekly Herald
Watford Observer
Western Morning News

SPECIAL HELP AND ADVICE:

Ian King, Official Club Historian, Crystal Palace FC

Andy Porter (the late), Official Club Historian, Tottenham Hotspur FC

Graham Rowe kindly and generously allowed me access to press cuttings and memorabilia from his father's personal collection. Grateful thanks too for he and his wife Louise's extraordinary hospitality when I was their guest in Los Angeles.

WEBSITES:
www.archive.spectator.co.uk
www.arsenal.com
www.bbc.co.uk/sport/
www.englandfootballonline.com
www.fifa.com
www.football.london/tottenham-hotspur
www.footballfancast.com
www.hitc.com

www.hotspurhq.com
www.indiaspurs.com
www.margatefchistory.com
www.metro.co.uk
www.myfootballfacts.com
www.planetfootball.com
www.soccer-history.co.uk
www.spartacus-educational.com
www.spursodyssey.com
www.spursweb.com
www.thedaisycutter.co.uk
www.thehardtackle.com
www.tottenhamhotspur.com
www.uefa.com
www.walesonline.co.uk
www.world-football-legends.co.uk
www.worldsoccer.com
www.educatedleftfoot.blogspot.com.
www.uk.sports.yahoo.com
www.westham.wordpress.com
uttonfromuddersfield.blogspot.com
www.soccerbase.com
www.superhotspur.com
www.theblizzard.co.uk
www.vavel.com
www.90min.com

ILLUSTRATIONS AND PHOTO CREDITS

p. 126 Cartoon is reproduced with kind permission of Tottenham Hotspur Football and Athletic Company Limited

From private collections of:

(Those uncredited here are taken from the personal collections of Arthur Rowe and Norman Turpin.)

PETER BURRIDGE:
p. 303 Players competing to head the ball
p. 332 Rowe watches Burridge shoot left-footed
p. 336 Burridge scoring against Nottingham Forest
p. 336 Celebrating his goal

JOHNNY BYRNE:
p.253 Vic Rouse with a young Byrne
p.274 Byrne admires football cake
p. 280 Byrne in army uniform
p. 281 Rowe, Byrne's wife (and others) with Player of Year award

CHRIS HASSELL:
p. 273 Rowe and Byrne at 5-a-side youth competition
p. 273 Hassell portrait

PETER HURN (pete@petespicturepalace.co.uk):
p. 274 Byrne scores v West Germany U-23s
p. 295 Alan Stephenson portrait

p. 300 Byrne in action versus Real Madrid

HY MONEY
p. 364 Rowe discovery Dave Swindlehurst in action for Crystal Palace

DAVID PAYNE
p. 335 Letter from Rowe to Payne's parents
p. 371 Six former Palace men at Leyton Orient

MICHAEL PUDNEY
p. 278 Rowe pouring champagne at Selhurst Park

DUNCAN ROWE
p. 373 Duncan Rowe getting helping hand on bicycle from grandfather Arthur Rowe
p. 391 Amy Rowe photos
p. 392 Duncan and Graham Rowe family group

ALAN STEPHENSON
p. 301 Crystal Palace tour group, Bermuda
p. 317 Dick Graham monitoring pitchside stretching exercises
p. 340 Smiling, muddied Burridge and Stephenson

ROY SUMMERSBY
p. 268 Summersby scores against Workington
p. 285 Byrne scoring v Swindon 1961
p. 289 Summersby scores against Newport County

IAN WELLER
p. 262 Rowe addressing new players on pitch
p. 295 Byrne signs for West Ham
p. 394 Portrait of young Rowe in Spurs' shirt

From photo agencies:

ALAMY STOCK PHOTO
p. 226 Marchi and Blanchflower in action

GETTY IMAGES
p. 19 Herbert Chapman with Alex James
p. 61 United Services team, Belfast
p. 99 Rowe addressing players seated in shade
p. 122 Burgess and Medley in new showers
p. 151 Rowe with director Fred Wale in stands
p. 152 Rowe with Ramsey on treatment table
p. 162 Duquemin scoring v Blackpool
p. 205 Rowe with four directors reading book
p. 209 Anderson sitting on Rowe's desk
p. 376 David Payne of Crystal Palace outwitting Johnny Giles
p. 382 Rowe addressing Vic Buckingham on training ground

SHUTTERSTOCK
p. 193 Rowe at FA meeting table

COLORSPORT
p. 224 Team group at Burnley

BRITISH PATHÉ
p. 159 Rowe as fashion model (newsreel still)

Index

AC Milan 383
Accrington Stanley FC 263-4, 270, 278, 292
Adams, Chris 81, 149, 165
Airdrieonians FC [Airdrie] 355
Ajax (AFC Ajax) 80, 100, 137, 237, 353, 381-382
Alberta, Canada 155
Aldershot Barracks (British Army base) 57-58
Aldershot FC 85, 273-275, 278
Allardyce, Sam x, 100
Allen, Clive (son of Les Allen) 381
Allen, Les 232, 248, 375, 389
Allen, Peter 388
Allen, Reg 124
Allen, Ronnie 159, 166, 198, 208, 253, 282-294, 296-297, 301, 303-308, 310-312, 318-320, 322-323, 328, 332, 335, 350
Allison, George 30, 55
Allison, Malcolm 105, 186, 188, 196, 201, 261, 267, 283, 335, 341, 358, 364, 366-367, 380
Ames, Percy 323
Amsterdam, Netherlands 300, 382
Ancona, Italy 61
Anderson, Jimmy 16, 75-80, 128, 136, 204-205, 208-212, 215, 230-233, 236-238, 241, 244, 246-249, 270, 307, 343, 389, 392
Andrasi, Béla 53
Andrews, Eamonn (radio and TV presenter) 158
Andrews, Jimmy 188
Araquistáin, José 299-300
Ardiles, Ossie 249, 387
Argentina (national team) 180
Arlott, John (journalist and broadcaster) 107, 135, 158
Army Physical Training Course, Aldershot 57-58
Army Representative side 57,143
Arsenal FC 1, 6-7, 10, 13, 17-21, 25, 28-30, 34, 36-38, 43, 47, 55, 59, 61, 75, 82-83, 96, 99, 102, 107, 118, 120, 122-123, 125-128, 130, 133, 135, 140, 143-144, 146-153, 160, 167-168, 175, 177, 179, 183, 198-200, 202, 207, 215-222, 224-225, 229, 240-241, 246, 253, 256, 266, 270, 294, 320, 326, 351, 360-361, 363, 365-366, 369-371, 373-374, 376, 381, 383, 390
Arteta, Mikel 100, 381
Arthur Rowe Room (White Hart Lane) 391
Ashford Town FC (now Ashford United) 255
Astle, Jeff 309
Astley, Dai 24, 33
Aston Villa FC 24, 28, 33, 36, 45, 124, 128, 142, 149, 164, 174, 179, 202, 207, 215, 218, 220-224, 244, 249, 291-293, 302, 315, 369, 380
Atlético Madrid 247
Attlee, Clement (Prime Minister of Great Britain 1945-51) 115, 127
Austria (nation) 182, 193, 212, 233, 238
Austria (national team) 18, 26-27, 40, 181, 187, 190, 193, 212, 233
Austria FC Wien (Austrian football club, now FK Austria Wien) 136, 149, 193, 238, 394
Ayer, A.J. (philosopher) 153, 375-376
Ayer, Dee 376
Ayre, Bobby 217

Bacuzzi, Joe 60
Baily, Eddie 1-2, 77-78, 81, 85-87, 93, 95, 97, 105, 107-108, 110-111, 116, 119-122, 124-129, 132-133, 135-136, 138-139, 141, 144, 146, 148-150, 152, 154-155, 160-162, 164, 166-168, 170-174, 190, 199-202, 204, 209-211, 215-217, 219, 224-227, 229, 231, 239, 250, 263, 286, 302, 360, 375, 388, 390
Baker, Gerry 342
Baker, Peter 77, 159, 161, 170, 174, 201-203, 215, 219, 227, 230-231, 233, 239, 249
Balderstone, Chris 346
Ball, Alan 380
Banks, Gordon 273, 335-336, 338
Bannister, Jack 338
Bannister, Roger (athlete) 158
Barcelona 80, 91, 102, 118, 137, 180, 194, 237, 270, 274, 381-383
Barcs, Sándor (President, Hungarian Football Association) 191, 195
Barking, Essex 81
Barnes, Walley 59, 123
Barnett, Tom 276-278
Barnsley FC 39-40, 78, 83, 88, 92, 124, 179, 183, 243, 287, 293, 306-307, 333
Barrow AFC 257, 266, 274
Barry AFC 73
Bartram, Sam 21, 146
Basingstoke 141
Bastin, Cliff 20, 29, 35
Bath City FC 65
Batson, Brendon 347
Battersby, John (Secretary, Chelsea FC) 273
Battle Hymn of the Republic ('Glory, Glory, Hallelujah') 385
Baxter, Bill 342
Bayern Munich 383
Beal, Phil 100
Bearman, Fred (Chairman, Tottenham Hotspur FC) 73, 94, 96, 217, 242
Beattie, Andy 192
Beckenbauer, Franz 243, 377
Bedford Town FC 65, 70
Belgian representative team 59
Belgium (army XI) 256
Belgium (nation) 59, 96, 150
Belgrade 191
Bell, Colin 346
Belmont School 8
Benfica 52, 201, 235

401

Bennett, Les 1, 2, 16, 77, 82, 86, 88, 91, 94, 96, 108, 113, 123-125, 129-130, 136, 139-144, 146, 148-150, 153, 156, 160-161, 163-164, 166-173, 197-198, 200-205, 208-210, 213-217, 224, 375, 392
Bentley, Roy 137
Bergkamp, Dennis 384
Bermuda 284, 296, 300-301
Berry, Johnny 146, 163
Best, George 243, 359, 362, 364, 370-372
Beverley Sisters, The (popular female singing trio) 136
Bidewell, Sid 72
Birch, Billy 326
Birchenall, Alan 183, 365
Birmingham (City) 178, 2344
Birmingham City FC 59, 169, 178, 346, 353-354
Birmingham University 178
Bishop Auckland FC 131, 251
Blackburn Rovers FC 22, 33, 41, 87, 209, 351-352, 355-356
Blackman, Jack (Crystal Palace trainer) 258
Blackpool FC 59, 69, 97, 111, 122-123, 126, 128, 130, 143, 152, 161-162, 169-173, 202, 211, 216, 226-228, 250, 354
Blanchflower, Danny 88, 102, 104, 106, 135, 142, 153, 164, 174, 179-180, 201-202, 215, 218, 231, 233-234, 236-244, 246-250, 257, 261, 265, 267, 270, 277, 294, 302, 328, 337, 355, 358, 362, 370, 373-375, 387
Bliss, Bert 12
Bloomer, Steve 369
Bloomfield, Jimmy 372
Bloye, Raymond 365-366
Bly, Terry 265, 294
Blyth, Mel 353-354, 363-365
Blythe, Arthur (referee) 229
Boleyn Castle Ground (Upton Park) 9
Bolton, J. T. (author) 111
Bolton Wanderers FC 60, 123-124, 137, 139, 146, 163, 171, 174, 200, 210, 224, 286, 354
Bond, Derek (actor) 158
Bonetti, Peter 371
Bournemouth (town) 245
Bournemouth & Boscombe Athletic Football Club [now AFC Bournemouth] 215, 300, 310-311, 318, 322, 333, 336
Bowden, Ray 28-29
Bowers, Jack 24
Bowler, Dave (author) 237
Bozsik, József 52, 189, 370
Bradford City FC 22, 26, 38, 228
Bradford Park Avenue FC 24, 39, 41, 69, 88, 92, 137, 255, 261, 266, 274, 280, 295-296, 311, 323-324
Branagan, Ken 277
Brazil (nation) 96, 182
Brazil (national side) 182-183
Brennan, Frank 3, 146
Brentford FC 59, 72, 86, 297, 331, 333, 364

Brett, Ronnie 295, 297-299, 304, 327
Bridges, Barry 353
Brighton (town) 271
Brighton and Hove Albion 256, 304-305, 321, 365
Bristol City FC 59, 290, 300, 324-325, 331, 342
Bristol Rovers FC 303, 332
British Army XI 58, 256
British Columbia, Canada 155
British Liberation Army (Italy) 60
Brittan, Colin 1, 86, 124, 166, 174, 199, 201-202, 213, 215
Britton, Cliff 60
Broadis, Ivor 91
Broadstairs 320
Brook, Eric 32
Brooking, Trevor 115, 350
Brooks, Johnny 167-168, 174, 197-198, 201, 204, 210-211, 213, 217, 219, 224-225, 229, 231, 233, 243, 247, 297, 331
Brown, Bill 248
Brown, Deryk (author, *The Tottenham Hotspur Story*) 45, 105
Browning, Robert (*Home Thoughts from Abroad*) 90
Bruce, Steve 89
Bruce Grove, Tottenham 168
Bruce Grove Station 5, 33
Brussels 59, 149, 163, 193, 394
Buchan, Charles 18-19, 21, 24, 29, 31-32, 110, 135, 186, 191
Buckingham, Vic 16, 38, 42, 80, 91, 103, 108, 110, 128, 130-131, 137, 165, 180, 192, 198, 208, 211, 233, 237-238, 251-252, 268, 282, 289, 360, 381-382, 387
Budai, László 189
Budapest (Hungary) 4, 47, 49-50, 53-56, 184-185, 191-192, 195-196, 213, 383
Burgess, Ron 1, 3-4, 14, 16, 43, 45-46, 57, 60, 77-78, 80-81, 83-89, 91, 95, 107, 110-114, 122-124, 126-128, 131-135, 138, 142, 148-149, 153, 156, 160-61, 163, 165-167, 169-170, 197, 199-205, 210-211, 214-215, 217-218, 222, 242, 244, 247, 257, 266, 270, 282, 294, 370, 373, 375
Burkinshaw, Keith 87, 249-250
Burley, Ben 66, 72, 74
Burnley FC 23-24, 38, 40, 124, 128, 139, 151, 161, 194, 198, 219, 233, 248, 295, 354, 360
Burnside, David 336, 339, 345-346, 348
Burridge, Peter 240, 243, 262, 276-277, 302-303, 305, 307-313, 316-317, 319-321, 324, 327-328, 331-332, 336-337, 339, 341, 347, 368, 391
Burrows, Frank 353
Burrows, Harry 292-293
Bury FC 22, 91, 339, 345
Busby, Matt 57-62, 75, 96, 99, 103, 111, 124, 130, 134, 138, 140, 146, 149-150, 152, 163-164, 172-173, 192, 207, 209, 216, 243, 253, 306,

359, 362, 366, 369-370, 385-386, 389
Busby Babes 111, 164, 209, 216
Byrne, Johnny 'Budgie' 115, 252-261, 263-267, 269, 271-296, 298-304, 307, 309-312, 315-316, 326, 334, 338, 349-352, 355, 358, 370, 386, 393
Byrne, Kevin (eldest of Johnny's three sons) 271-272
Byrne, Margaret (wife of Johnny) 271
Byrne, Roger 111
Byrne, Tommy 72

Cambridge Town FC 68
Cambridge University 131, 219, 251
Camsell, George 18, 24, 32, 40
Canada (nation) 85, 151, 155, 163, 175, 230, 314, 320, 331, 387, 391
Canada (national side) 365
Canadian/New York tour 1952 151-156
Cannon, Jim 363-364, 373
Cantrell, Jimmy 12
Cardiff (city) 60
Cardiff City 65, 75, 128, 159-160, 167-168, 201, 219, 231, 233, 247, 340, 353
Carlin, Willie 346
Carlisle United 256, 271, 273, 305-306, 340, 346, 379
Carter, Dr Neil (Senior Lecturer, De Montfort University) 242
Carter, Raich 58-60, 94, 370
Cartwright, John 103, 179, 283, 292, 303-304, 307-308, 319, 324, 377-378, 380
Casado, Pedro 300
Castle, Derek 389
Catterick, Harry 130, 380-381
Catton, J.A.H. (journalist) 35
Celtic (Glasgow Celtic) 354-355
Champions' League Final 2019 ix, 249-250, 379, 389
Channell, Fred 30
Chaplin, Alec 16
Chapman, Herbert 3, 12, 17-21, 27, 29-30, 32-34, 40, 48-49, 76, 80, 82-83, 98-99, 102, 107, 133, 135-136, 183-184, 235, 240-241, 246, 254, 361, 374, 385-386, 390
Chapman, Roy 312
Charles, John 91, 204, 306
Charlton Athletic FC 21, 25, 59, 127, 145-146, 165, 173, 175, 197-198, 217, 229, 238, 265, 283, 302, 327, 329, 335, 347, 351
Charlton, Bobby 111, 188, 284, 290, 328, 334, 338, 364, 369-370, 386
Charlton, Jack 263, 306, 350, 354, 359, 368, 385
Chatterton, Nick 364, 373
Chelmsford City ix, 57, 62-76, 78-79, 87, 93-94, 103, 124, 134, 140, 154, 159, 279, 295, 334, 347, 388
Chelsea FC 24, 30, 33, 81, 124, 128, 137, 143, 150, 152, 162, 167-170, 190-191, 193, 198, 202, 210-211, 219, 228, 231-232, 235, 238-239, 243, 246, 254, 258, 272-273, 294,

INDEX

328, 347, 353, 359, 365-366, 371-372, 376, 389
Cheltenham Town FC 64, 66
Cheshunt FC (Athenian League) 12
Cheshunt (Spurs' training ground acquired by Rowe) 157
Chester City FC (ceased to be in 2010) 257, 272, 283, 292
Chesterfield FC 27, 44-45
Childerley Street Central School, Fulham 9-10
Chile (nation) 219
Chingford, Essex 81
Choules, Len 264, 266, 276, 285
Christ's College, Finchley 145, 175
Churchill, Winston (Prime Minister of Great Britain 1940-45 and 1951-55) 58, 190
Clapton 121
Clapton Orient FC 65
Clarke, Harry 78, 82, 86, 92, 95, 109-110, 125, 127-128, 130, 133, 138-140, 146-147, 159, 169-172, 200-201, 213-216, 225, 227, 233, 239, 373, 375
Clarke, Ray 100
Clarke, Roy 160
Clay, Tommy 11-12, 33
Clemence, Ray 351
Cloake, Martin (author) 207
Clough, Brian 100, 177, 241, 354, 381, 385
Coates, Ralph 242
Cohen, George 338
Colchester United FC 63-64, 68-69, 71-72, 309, 322, 333-334, 344, 364
Colfar, Ray 254, 276-277
Colquhoun, Davie 25, 33
Coluna, Mário 334
Combined Services Representative sides 58-59
Communism 45, 190
Compton, Dennis (cricketer & footballer) 158
Cook, Billy 42
Cook, Bobby 82, 90
Cooke, Charlie 347, 365, 371
Corinthian-Casuals 309
Corinthian Shield (London Under-15s competition) 10
Corrigan, James (journalist) 381, 387
Coulter, Jackie 42
Coventry City 88, 119, 290, 297, 302, 322, 325-326, 328-329, 333-335, 347, 350-351
Crawford, Ray 290
Crayston, Jack (Arsenal manager) 253
Crewe Alexandra FC 254, 279, 329, 338
Cricklewood, North London 367
Crowe, Vic 292
Crowther, Stan 272
Croydon 268, 290, 294, 355, 358
Croydon Chamber of Commerce 294
Cruyff, Johan 103, 106, 109, 180, 240, 243, 374, 382-383
Crystal Palace fans 370
Crystal Palace FC vii, ix, 38, 55, 69, 100, 103-104, 109, 115-116, 206,
215, 236-237, 239, 243 [note: beyond page 251 Crystal Palace references are too frequent to index]
Cullis, Stan 57, 96, 101-102, 124, 164, 192, 194, 207-208, 385
Cunliffe, Jimmy 42
Cunningham, Laurie 347, 371-372
Cunningham, Willie 218
Cutler, Paul 342
Czechoslovakia 103
Czibor, Zoltán 188-189

Dagenham 78-79, 81, 232
Darlington FC 203-204, 264-265
Darnell, A.J.K. (President, Southern League) 66
Dartford FC 68
Davies, Hunter (journalist and author) 100, 114, 234
Davies, Reg 167
Davies, Willie 25
Day, Alf 15
Deacock, Tom (Director, Tottenham Hotspur FC) 12
Deakin, Alan 293
Deakin, Mike 256-257, 259, 278
Dean, Dixie 18, 24, 40-42, 369-370
De Bruyne, Kevin 380
Del Sol, Luis 297, 300
Denmark 136
Dennis, Mick (journalist) 178
Derby County 24, 100, 103, 126-127, 130, 141, 148, 161, 170, 334, 336, 340, 354, 364, 386
Dewar Shield (London Schools' Championship) 8, 9, 11-12
Dewhurst-Hornsby, E. (Director, Tottenham Hotspur FC) 154, 203, 206, 208, 231, 234, 244, 246
Dick, John 176, 243
Dicker, Les 159, 164, 166
Dickinson, Jimmy 189, 287, 289
Dietz, Dr Károly (Coach, Hungary, World Cup 1938) 50, 52
Dimmock, Jimmy 7, 11-12
Di Stéfano, Alfredo 293-294, 297-300, 370
Ditchburn, Ted 2, 16, 46, 78, 80, 86-87, 95- 96, 100, 108, 113, 119-120, 123, 125, 130, 132-133, 139-140, 146-148, 155, 158, 160-161, 163-164, 167-171, 173, 190, 198-200, 202, 208, 211, 213, 215-219, 224, 239, 263, 273, 302, 374
Docherty, Tommy 347
Dodge, Bill 302, 305, 319
Dodgin, Bill 79
Doherty, Peter 59, 103, 179, 187, 325, 370
Doncaster Rovers FC 38, 258, 264, 272
Double, The (Spurs' 1960-61 season) ix, 219, 246-247, 249, 279, 349, 374-375, 377, 389, 392
Dougan, Derek 292-293
Downsborough, Peter 303
Dowsett, Gilbert (*Dickie*) 154, 215, 243, 300, 310-311, 315, 318, 320-321, 324, 326
Doyle, Mike 342
Drake, Ted 20, 25, 169, 184, 191-192, 194, 258
Drewry, Arthur (President, Football League) 95, 134, 192
Drury, Reg (journalist) 387, 393
Dulwich Hamlet FC 182, 306
Dumitrescu, Ilie 387
Duncan, Andy 64, 66, 70
Dunmore, Dave 204, 209-213, 215, 217-219, 223-225, 228-230, 242-243, 247
Dunphy, Eamonn (player, author and journalist) 98, 135, 243, 386, 389
Dunster, John (Director, Crystal Palace FC) 289, 296, 339-340, 343
Duquemin, Len 1-2, 65, 76, 86-87, 91, 96, 102, 105, 108, 110, 120, 124-127, 129, 131-134, 136, 139-140, 142-143, 146,148-151, 155, 160-162, 164, 166-170, 174, 198, 200-202, 204, 210, 213, 215-216, 225-226, 228-229, 231, 239, 247, 320, 375, 392
Dwight, Roy 297
Dyson, Terry 219, 231, 248-250, 261, 375

Eaton, Clifford 64-66
Edelston, Maurice 59-60
Edmonton, London 89, 120, 327, 331
Edwards, Duncan 111, 369
Eintracht Frankfurt 182, 193, 262, 298
Elektromos (Hungarian club) 51
Elliott, Billy 60
Ellis, Arthur 171
England (nation) x, 5, 14, 27,35, 39, 48, 51-56, 60-62, 100, 103, 135, 141, 151, 153, 163, xxx 212, 219, 232, 245, 269-270, 279
England (national side, full, under-23, under-21) 1-2, 4, 9, 12, 21-23, 26, 29, 32-33, 50-52, 58-60, 62, 68, 70, 76, 80-81, 83, 89, 91, 96-97, 102-103, 110-111, 118, 120, 122, 124, 126, 130, 142, 145-146, 149, 154-155, 158-159, 161, 166-167, 174, 176-196 [England v Hungary 1953 and 1954), 202, 204, 207, 216, 220, 222, 227, 232, 239-240, 246, 251, 263, 267, 272-275, 279, 282-283, 287, 290, 294, 296-297, 306-309, 326-327, 334, 336, 338-339, 341, 343, 345-346, 349, 351-354, 360-361, 364-367, 372, 374, 377, 383, 386, 390
Epping Forest 83, 121, 138
Epsom 257
Europe XI (football team) 51, 180
Eusébio da Silva Ferreira 334
Euston Station, London 340-341
Evans, Godfrey (cricketer) 158
Evans, Gwyn 263-264, 288, 306, 319, 321-322
Evans, Willie 23-27, 31
Everton FC 18, 24, 33-34, 41-42, 58, 92, 119, 125, 130, 219, 233, 248, 273, 359, 366, 380-381
Exeter City FC 69, 259, 274

403

FA representative side 143, 284
FA Youth Cup 329, 352-353, 386
Fairbrother, Jack 1, 2, 125
Falkirk FC 363
Farley, Brian *Jake* 64, 66, 74, 139
Farm, George 152, 170
FC Austria 136, 149, 193, 394
Feleki, László *Lotzi* (Hungarian journalist) 47-50, 53-56
Feleki, Szendi (Lotzi's wife) 47
Felton, Billy 24-27, 29-30, 37
Fenton, Micky 24
Fenton, Ted 120, 176, 179, 188, 192
Ferencváros 50-52
Ferguson, Alex x, 239, 354, 363, 385
Ferris, Ken (author) 249
Festival of Britain (1951) 127, 129, 136
FIFA 182, 386
Finch, Jack 27
Finchley FC 12, 145, 160-161, 219
Finland (nation) 181-182
Finn, Ralph L 177, 190
Finney, Alan 216
Finney, Tom 62, 94, 104, 167, 186-188, 190, 211, 218, 229, 369-370
Fiorentina, ACF 283
Firmani, Eddie 366-367
Florence, Italy 61
Folkestone FC 15
Follows, Dennis (Secretary, Football Association) 180
Foot, Miss Amy Lilian [maiden name of Rowe's wife *Pom*] 37
Football Hall of Fame 368, 371
Forbes, Alex 147, 200
Ford, Trevor 125, 128, 149, 164, 218, 244
Foreman, *Denny* 63, 65-66, 68
Forster, Stan 307-308
Foulkes, Bill 147, 200
Francis, Tom 72
France (nation) 136, 233, 238, 349
France (national side) 31-32, 62, 182, 233, 238, 349
Franco, Francisco (Spanish general and dictator) 297
Franklin, Neil 59-60, 91
Freedman, Dougie 263
Froggatt, Jack 150
Fulham FC 9, 27, 118, 120-21, 139, 179, 193, 286, 352, 355-356

Gallacher, Hughie 24, 30, 33, 40
Gateshead United FC [now *Gateshead FC*] 225
Gavin, Johnny 218-219, 224-228, 231, 238, 256, 259, 263, 267, 270, 274, 276, 280
Gento, Francisco 297-300
George V, King 11, 38
George VI, King 61, 147
Germany (nation) 54-57, 63, 96, 103, 193, 212
Germany (national side) 182
Germany (West, national side) 182, 192, 213, 275, 365, 382, 384
Giller, Norman (journalist) vii, 85, 107, 195, 247, 249, 345, 369, 385, 387, 391-392
Gillingham FC 72-74, 257, 266, 274

Gillman, Peter (journalist) 351
Glanville, Brian (journalist and author) x, 98, 139, 192, 205-207, 244, 385
Glasgow 98, 176
Glasgow Rangers 199, 354-355, 363
Glazier, Bill 271, 293-294, 298-301, 305, 310-312, 316, 320, 322, 328-329, 334-335, 358, 361
Glazzard, Jimmy 130
Gloucester City FC 68
Gold, Alasdair (journalist) 389
Goodall, Roy 32
Goodman, Benny (music of) 388
Goring, Peter 160
Goulden, Len 370
Graham, Anne (wife of Dick) 343
Graham, Dick 268-270, 273, 275, 279, 287-288, 292, 296, 305-307, 311-334, 336-350, 352-355, 366-368, 373, 376-377
Graham, George 390
Graham, Mark (son of Dick) 312
Gravesend and Northfleet FC 15, 73
Grays Athletic FC 12
Graydon, John (journalist) 195
Grayson, Edward (sports barrister) 23, 118, 254
Grealish, Tony 371
Great Britain 1936 Olympics football team 39
Great Britain football team 180
Greaves, Jimmy vii, 23, 106, 177, 218-219, 231-232, 242, 249, 306, 308, 328, 334, 361, 375
Green, Benny (jazz musician, critic and author) 369-370
Green, Geoffrey (journalist) 4, 186, 190, 192, 194, 196, 232, 236, 257, 375, 386
Green, Tony 354
Greenfield, George 'Nobby' 24-27, 112
Greenwood, Ron 68, 102, 115-116, 179, 186, 188, 190, 195-196, 240, 275, 283, 294-295, 326, 334, 350-351
Grimsby Town FC 89, 95, 290, 297
Grimsdell, Arthur 6, 11, 41, 89, 131
Grosics, Gyula 187
Grosvenor, Tom 32
Groves, Vic 159-160, 166, 175, 198, 201, 217
Grubb, Alan 159-160
Guardiola, Pep x, 100, 102, 106, 109, 129, 239, 381, 383, 390
Guernsey 87
Gullit, Ruud 365
Gunner, Ron 69
Gurney, Bobby 24
Guildford City FC 66, 229
Gustafsson, Karl 183
Guttmann, Béla 52, 201, 234, 240

Hackett, Desmond (journalist) x, 190, 279, 299, 337
Hagan, Jimmy 370
Halifax Town FC 168, 293, 303, 320
Hall, Jack 41-42, 63-64
Hall, Willie 23, 25, 27, 29, 31-32, 37, 62, 65, 112, 245, 370

Halsey, Stanley (journalist) 42-43
Hamburg 193
Hancocks, Johnny 202
Hardaker, Alan (Secretary, The Football League) 193, 370
Hardwick, George 59-60
Hardy, George (Spurs' trainer during Rowe's playing days) 37, 115
Harland, Stan 346
Harmer, Tommy 70, 86, 139-141, 145-146, 148, 160, 164, 167, 174-175, 198, 200-201, 211, 216, 223-224, 226, 229, 239, 247, 261, 270, 289, 326
Harper, Ted 22-23
Harris, George 311
Harris, John 143
Harris Lebus [furniture makers] 10
Harris, Ron 231, 371, 376
Harrogate 227
Hartlepool United FC 265, 272
Harvey, Colin 380
Harvey, Joe 1-3
Harwich and Parkeston FC 174, 251
Hassall, Harold 163, 200
Hassell, Chris (Secretary, Crystal Palace FC) 257, 272-274, 330, 355
Hawksworth, Derek 202
Haynes, Johnny 106, 118, 120-121, 141, 186-188, 191, 193, 220, 232, 255, 284, 290, 306, 383
Hayward, Eric 152-153
Head, Bert 239, 306, 329, 348, 350, 352-353, 358, 359, 365-366
Head, Sue (daughter of Bert Head) 356, 359
Headlam & Sims (manufacturers of *Arthur Rowe* and *Danny Blanchflower* brand football boots) 222, 252
Heart of Midlothian FC (*Hearts*) 248
Heckman, Ron 261, 263, 270, 277, 287, 289-292, 298-299, 307, 318-319, 322
Hector, Kevin 354
Helsinki (city) 56
Helsinki Olympics (1940, cancelled) 53, 56, 185
Helsinki Olympics (1952) 158, 185, 382
Hendon FC 251
Henry, Ron 170, 219, 225, 227, 233, 239, 249, 261, 374, 384
Henry, Thierry 383-384
Henty, *Tex* 81
Hereford United FC 65-66, 72, 310
Herod, Dennis 91
Herrera, Helenio 194
Heryet, W. J. Bill (Director, Tottenham Hotspur FC) 154, 203, 206, 231, 234, 246
Hewie, John 217
Hibernian FC 131, 175, 197, 199
Hidegkuti, Nándor 49, 189
Hilaire, Vince 373, 377
Hill, Jimmy 267, 271, 322, 325-326, 328-329, 333, 335, 350, 360
Hinshelwood, Martin 364
Hinshelwood, Paul 364, 373
Hitchens, Gerry 283
Hoadley, Phil 352-353, 363

INDEX

Hoby, Alan (journalist) 241, 245, 252, 385
Hoddle, Glenn 380
Hogan, Jimmy 47-48, 182, 184, 195
Holden, Jim (author) 207
Holland / Netherlands (nation) 13, 183, 353, 357
Holland / Netherlands (national side) 183, 240, 382, 384
Holland, Julian (author of *Spurs: A History of Tottenham Hotspur Football Club*) 82, 84, 107, 118, 208, 242, 384
Hollins, John 371
Hollis, Roy 165, 242
Holsgrove, John 109, 327, 329, 358, 386
Holton, Cliff 140, 143, 164, 168, 225, 243, 257, 285, 307, 320-321, 323, 326, 331-334, 336-337, 341, 347
Hóman, Bálint (Hungarian Minister of Culture, 1939) 49
Honvéd 49, 194, 256, 383
Hopcraft, Arthur (sports journalist, TV scriptwriter) 236, 240
Hopkins, Mel 138, 154, 161, 166, 201, 204, 214, 216-219, 224, 227, 229, 233, 249, 354
Hopkinson, Eddie 354
Horobin, Roy 336
Horthy, Miklós 54
Houghton, Eric 222
Howe Bert 308, 320-322, 345-346
Howe, Les 14, 25
Hoy, Roger 354, 363
Huddersfield Town FC 12, 22, 38, 60, 69, 126-127, 130, 132, 143, 149-150, 202, 211, 233, 247, 252, 347, 355
Hudson, Alan 371
Hudson, George 288, 294, 306
Hughes, Billy 59
Hughes, Charles (Director of Coaching, Football Association) 101-102, 178
Hughes, Emlyn 351
Hull City FC 94, 209, 291, 296, 301, 306, 324, 350
Hulme, Joe 20, 35, 72, 75-76, 78, 80, 82, 87, 90, 137-138, 170, 236, 242, 394
Hungária (Hungarian football club which later became 'MTK Budapest') 50
Hungary (nation) 47, 49, 50-56, 180, 195-196, 233, 238, 367
Hungary (national side) 4, 21, 49, 51-52, 103, 158, 177-178, 180, 182, 184-185, 186-192, 195-196, 202, 283, 287, 382-383, 386
HungaryHunt, Doug 60
Hunt, George 22-31, 33-34, 37-39, 43, 266
Hunter, Norman 306, 350
Hurst, Charlie 65, 68, 70, 334
Hurst, Geoff 68, 70, 295-296, 334, 349-350, 352, 356, 361
Hutchinson, George 175, 197, 199
Hylton, Stuart (author) 190, 192
Hynd, Roger 363

Iley, Jim 248
Illingworth, Jack 15
Imlach, Gary (author and broadcaster) 302, 321, 349
Imlach, Stewart 290, 297, 302-303, 306-308, 310-312, 319, 321, 329, 332, 347, 349, 391
Ingham, Jack (journalist) 40
Ipswich Town FC 246, 279, 290, 309, 341-342, 345-347, 386
Italy (nation) 54, 60, 208, 239, 279
Italy (national side) 50, 52, 182, 220

Jack, David 19-20, 29, 177-178
Jackson, Cliff 350, 353-356, 360, 363
Jackson, John *Jacko* 103, 273, 310, 317, 322, 325, 335, 337, 339, 341-343, 345, 350, 354, 356, 358, 363, 367
Jackson, Barry 281
James, Alex 19-20, 29, 99, 369-370
Jamrich, Klara (co-author of *Puskás on Puskás*) 383
Jennings, Pat 80, 242
Jewell, Jimmy (comedian) 121
Jones, Bryn 61
Jones, Cliff 248-249, 275, 308, 375, 392
Jones, Ernie 79
Jones, Ken (journalist, brother of Cliff) 195, 362, 371, 380, 385, 388
Jones, Vinnie 380
Joy, Bernard (Arsenal player, journalist and author) 1, 20, 59, 83, 106, 116, 131, 168, 178, 182-183, 186, 194, 198, 240, 255
Jubilee Park (Edmonton) 119
Juventus 204, 247

Kane, Harry x, 270
Kellard, Bobby 327, 331-333, 339, 341, 343, 347
Kember, Steve 329, 339, 342, 345-347, 349-351, 354, 356, 358, 360, 363, 365-366, 386
Kendall, Howard 380
Kerrins, Pat 261
Kevan, Derek 338-340, 342, 346, 348
Kidderminster Harriers FC 72
Kiernan, Billy 146
King, Derek 139, 174, 199, 201, 216
Kispest (former name of Hungarian club Honvéd) 49
Klopp, Jurgen 89, 100, 381
Knowles, Peter 362-363
Kocsis, Sándor 191
Korányi, Lajos (Hungarian international defender) 52

La Liga (Spanish First Division) 382
Lacey, Arthur (golfer) 158
Lacey, David (journalist) 249, 381
Lambert, Jack 47-48
Langton, Alderman, Vice Chairman of Chelmsford City 64, 66-67, 74
Law, Dennis 359
Lawson, Ian 338-339, 342, 348
Lawton, Tommy 24, 40, 42, 57-62, 106, 183, 200, 216, 225, 290, 351, 370

Lazarus, Mark 353
Leeds United 59, 91, 204-205, 207-208, 306, 337, 343-344, 350, 353-354, 360, 368, 376-377, 380
Leicester City FC 28, 37, 55, 88, 92, 204, 219, 233, 237, 268, 336-337
Levy, Daniel (Chairman, Tottenham Hotspur FC) ix, 361
Lewis, Brian 287, 298, 307, 310, 316, 324
Lewis, Richard (author) 371-372
Leyton Orient / Orient 217, 261-262, 290, 302, 308, 344, 346, 352, 364-365, 371-373, 377, 388
Leytonstone FC 159
Liberation of Paris (1944) 59
Liddell, Billy 143, 151-152
Liège (Belgium) 59
Light, Danny 350-351, 353
Lille Olympic 215
Lilleshall (former training centre for English national side) 179, 196, 380
Lilywhite (Spurs' Supporters' Club journal) 239
Lincoln City FC 288
Lisbon (Portugal) 96, 283, 334
Lishman, Doug 123, 168, 216
Little, Roy 283-284, 298, 309, 329
Liverpool FC 11, 30, 109, 133, 143, 150-151, 155, 160, 166-167, 177, 190, 198, 204, 208, 212, 234, 323, 359, 363, 365, 376, 381, 383, 387
Lofthouse, Nat 124, 137, 146, 163-164, 176, 200, 243, 358
Logie, Jimmy 160, 168, 200, 216, 369
London Five-a-Side Tournament (1969) 356
London Football Coaches' Association 326
London Schools representative side 8-9, 11-12, 218, 255, 290
London Society of Referees 117
Long, Terry 254-255, 260-261, 263-266, 275-276, 279, 281-282, 284-285, 290, 298-299, 306, 308, 312-313, 316, 318-321, 324, 328-329, 342-343, 345-346, 350-351, 353, 356, 363, 391
Lorenzo, Peter (journalist/broadcaster) 337
Los Angeles 252
Loughlan, John 354
Lovell's Athletic FC 72, 78
Lowe, Eddie 328
Lucas, Fred 329
Lunnis, Roy 261, 308, 319
Luton Town FC 15, 70, 88, 92, 333
Lutz, Lajos (Hungarian player and coach) 52

McAuley, Bob 33
McClellan, Syd 68, 70, 72, 74, 124, 127-128, 139, 141, 143, 151, 155, 159-160, 167, 170-171, 174, 199, 201, 212, 216-219, 243, 288
McClelland, David (journalist) 288
McCormick, Jimmy *Boy* 23, 27-28, 41, 63, 204
McCormick, John 349, 352, 354, 363

405

McDermott, Clancy 71-72
McFarland, Roy 354
McIntosh, Dave 132
McMichael, Alf 2
McNichol, Johnny 162, 211, 231, 254, 259, 263, 267, 271, 277, 279, 285, 291-292, 298, 308-309, 319, 324, 356
McParland, Peter 292-293
McWilliam, Peter 6-7, 11-14, 38, 45-46, 62, 115, 125, 130, 138, 141, 184, 235, 381
Macauley, Archie 208
Mackay, Dave 242, 248, 308, 354, 361, 373, 375, 392
Madgwick, Don (author) 254
Maidstone United FC 15, 306
Maier, Sepp 382
Major, John (Prime Minister of Great Britain 1990-97) 378
Manager of the Year 96, 122, 144, 279
Manchester (city) 208, 357
Manchester City x, 32, 58-59, 102-103, 105, 105, 129, 141, 148, 159-160, 201, 208-210, 220, 229, 246-247, 283, 338-339, 341, 348, 351, 363, 366, 380-381, 383
Manchester Schools representative side 218
Manchester United 25, 27, 48, 58, 75, 96, 111, 118, 124, 127-130, 132-134, 140, 146-149, 151, 155-156, 167, 199, 207, 235, 243, 247, 306, 351, 354, 359, 366, 370, 376, 385
Mandela, Nelson 352
Manitoba, Canada 155
Mannion, Wilf 126, 130, 166
Mansfield Town FC 100, 274, 280, 311-313, 315, 318, 324, 329-330
Maple & Company Limited (furniture manufacturers and retailers) 10
Mapson, Johnny 149
Marchi, Tony 10, 77, 89, 110, 113, 119-120, 123, 125, 141, 157, 159, 174-175, 178-179, 197-198, 201, 204, 206, 210, 213, 215, 217, 219, 224-225, 227-228, 231, 233, 239, 242-243, 246-249, 388
Marconi Company 63
Marquess of Londonderry 97, 137
Marquis, Max (author) 187, 204, 206
Marquitos (Marcos Alonso Imaz) 300
Martin, Jack 60
Match of the Day, BBC TV 21, 339, 343, 377, 390
Matthews, John (journalist) 263, 275, 285, 287-288, 296, 305, 309-313, 315, 320, 332-323, 331, 347, 366
Matthews, Stanley 27, 34, 59-60, 69-70, 85, 97, 104, 111, 122, 126, 143, 161, 169-171, 177, 188, 190, 202, 227, 275, 369-370, 376
Mattler, Étienne 31
Maximum wage 121, 258, 267, 270, 272
Maynard, Michael (*Chick*) 347
Meadows, Jimmy 160
Meads, Tommy 25

Medley, Les 1-2, 16, 77, 83, 85-87, 89, 93-94, 96, 107-108, 111, 123-124, 126, 128, 130, 132-134, 136, 140, 142-146, 148, 150-153, 160-164, 166-167, 170, 172-173, 175, 197, 210, 375, 392
Medwin, Terry 246, 375
Mee, Bertie 179, 326
Meek, Joe 42
Meisl, Hugo (coach of Austrian national team, brother of journalist Willy) 18, 21, 26-27, 40
Meisl, Willy (journalist and author, particularly known for *Soccer Revolution*) 18-21, 82-83, 99, 145, 181-185, 187, 192, 195, 325
Joe Mercer 42, 57-60, 62, 123, 207, 341, 366-367, 370, 380
Meredith, Billy 369
Merrick, Gil 170, 189
Merthyr Town FC 73
Messer, Alf 24
Michels, Rinus 109, 381-382
Middlesbrough FC 13, 18, 24, 59, 126-128, 130, 139, 144, 166, 198, 204, 212, 347
Miera, Vicente 300
Milburn, Jackie 1-3, 130, 140, 167, 180
Millard, Lance 278
Miller, David (journalist) 26, 112, 114, 196, 240, 252, 380
Miller, Glenn (music of) 388
Miller, Les 42
Milligan, Jack (journalist) 4
Mills, Freddie (World Champion boxer) 144
Millwall FC 55, 262-263, 276-277, 302, 320, 324, 364-365, 371, 373
Millwall (FA Youth Cup winners under coach David Payne and Chief Scout Bob Pearson) 386
Milton, Arthur 160, 168, 200
Minter, Billy (Spurs' player, trainer and manager) 12-13, 16, 22, 25, 236
Misángyi, Professor Otto (Hungarian Council of Physical Education) 52, 54
Mitcham (town in South London) 283, 314
Mitcham Wanderers FC 12
Mochan, Neil 139
Monte Cassino, Italy 61
Montgomery, Bernard (Field Marshall of Alamein) 146
Moore, Bobby 227, 273, 283, 290, 296, 334, 338, 350, 356, 361
Morris, Peter (journalist) 263, 359, 362, 388
Morrison, Angus 161
Morrison, Johnny 38, 41-43
Morrison, Lord (President, Tottenham Hotspur FC) 93-94, 122-123
Morse, Graham (author) 82
Mortensen, Stan 59, 143, 170, 189-190
Morton FC (now Greenock Morton FC) 154, 355

Moscow Dynamos (FC Dynamo Moscow) 67, 98
Moss, Arthur 70
Motson, John (BBC commentator) 11, 82, 385, 387
Mourinho, José x, 87, 228, 239, 389
Moynihan, John (journalist) 96, 126, 180, 385
Mudie, Jackie 171, 331
Mullen, Jimmy 59-60, 202
Mullery, Alan 361, 390
Mulligan, Paddy 365
Munich air disaster 164, 369
Murdoch, Richard *Stinker* (actor and entertainer) 158
Murphy, Marcus *Spud* 70
Murphy, Peter 119, 123-124, 127, 129-130, 133-134, 136, 139-140, 144-146, 175, 243

Naples, Italy 60-62
Napoleon Bonaparte 56, 111
National Health Service (birth of) 62
Neeskens, Johan 382
Neill, Terry 378
Netzer, Günther 377
New York 155-156
Newcastle Boys side 10
Newcastle United FC ix, 1-4, 6-7, 10, 17, 31, 34, 41, 98, 125-126, 128, 130, 139-140, 146-148, 153, 160-161, 166-167, 199, 209, 218, 228, 238, 338, 365, 378, 385
Newman, Ron 308, 319
Newport County 289, 296
Newton, Frank 27
Newton, Isaac 18
Nicholas, Peter 373
Nicholls, Joe 25, 27
Nicholls, Johnny 198
Nicholson, Bill ix, 16, 41, 46, 78, 80, 85-87, 92, 95-97, 100, 104, 112-114, 116, 120, 123, 125-126, 129, 132-133, 136, 138, 140, 143, 146-147, 149, 153-155, 158-160, 163-164, 166, 169-170, 175-176, 179, 190, 194-195, 197, 199-204, 210-212, 215, 217, 220, 222, 232-233, 237, 239-240, 246-250, 260-261, 269, 272, 276-277, 279, 282, 294, 326, 349, 360-361, 373-375, 378, 387, 389-392
Noakes, Alf 263, 266, 274
Norbury (district of south London) 381
Norman, Barry (journalist, TV presenter) 348
Norman, Maurice 227, 246-247, 249, 373, 375, 392
Northampton Town FC 64-65, 247-248, 257, 259, 267, 274-275, 278, 280, 285, 307-308, 318, 320
Northern Ireland (nation) 181
Northern Ireland (national side) 218, 222, 290
Northfleet United FC 14-17, 24, 38, 46, 76, 80
Norway (nation) 181-182
Norwich City FC 165, 218, 227, 242, 246, 339, 347-348, 353

INDEX

Nottingham Forest FC 57, 100, 177, 302, 336-337, 347, 381
Notts County FC 24, 27, 57, 258, 284, 309, 328, 332, 364-365
O'Callaghan, Eugene *Taffy* 14, 23, 25, 27
O'Neill, Liam 71-72, 74
Offside Law change (1925) 12, 14, 17-21, 35, 80, 98, 122, 135
Oldham Athletic FC 24-25, 64, 269, 276-277, 328, 333-334
Olympic Games: 1928 (Amsterdam) 182; 1936 (Berlin) 39; 1940 (Helsinki - cancelled due to WW2) 53, 56, 185; 1948 (London) 180; 1952 (Helsinki) 56, 158, 185, 382; Ontario, Canada 155, 230
Orient — see 'Leyton Orient'
Orr, Tommy 155
Osgood, Peter 347, 351, 361, 371
Oxford United FC 12, 364
Oxford University 131, 251

Pachin, Enrique Pérez Diaz 300
Paisley, Bob 385
Paris 59
Parkhurst Road School (Rowe's school), Tottenham 7-11
Parry, Bill 64
Pawson, Tony (Pegasus player, journalist and author) 145-146, 187, 250-252, 370
Payne, David 309, 320, 328-330, 335-336, 338-339, 342, 345-346, 350-352, 354, 356-358, 360, 363-364, 386
Pearce, Cyril 25
Pegasus AFC 114, 131, 137, 145, 174, 251-252, 381
Pelé, Edson Arantes do Nascimento 243, 336
Peñarol (Uruguay) 182
Pennington, Bob (journalist) 253, 260, 265, 284, 296
Pepillo, José García Castro 300
Perry, Bill 170
Perryman, Steve 116
Peskett, Roy (journalist, author) 313, 358
Petchey, George 261-264, 270, 272, 274-278, 284, 290-292, 296, 298, 302-304, 306-309, 311, 315-318, 320, 324-325, 328-330, 333, 337-339, 341-352, 355-358, 365-366, 371-373, 386-388
Peterborough United FC 265-266, 270-275, 277, 279, 281, 288, 294, 306, 312, 324, 347, 364
Peters, Martin 242, 296, 327, 334, 350, 356, 361
PFA (Professional Footballers' Association) 179, 258, 267, 270-271, 322
Phöbus (Hungarian football club) 51-52
Pleat, David 249, 381
Plunkett, Sid 72
Plymouth Argyle FC 41, 70, 76, 87, 335, 350

Pochettino, Mauricio ix, 87, 136, 153, 249, 381, 389, 391
Poland, 1936 Olympic football team 39
Poland, German invasion of (1939) 55
POMO [Positions of Maximum Opportunity] 178
Pompeii, Italy 61
Pope, E.A. (Headmaster, Parkhurst Road School) 7, 9
Pope Pius XII 61
Poplühár, Jan 294
Port Vale FC 24, 27, 38, 225-226, 290, 300, 318-319, 324, 331
Portsmouth FC [Pompey] 31, 34, 41, 69, 125, 143, 146, 148, 150, 163, 173, 203, 216, 226-228, 259, 287, 289, 294, 301, 326, 354
Portugal (national side) 279, 334
Powell, Aubrey 59
Poynton, Cecil 80, 83, 152, 180, 205, 208
Preston North End FC 22, 25, 43, 62, 89, 94, 148, 150-151, 161, 167-169, 173, 211, 218, 229-230, 242, 273, 339, 347
Priestley, Gerry 255
Prince, H.M. (Army Football Association) 73
Prole, David (journalist) 249, 266, 316
Pulis, Tony 100
Puskás, Ferenc 49, 52, 107,179, 184, 186, 188-189, 191-192, 265, 293, 297-300, 382-383
Puskás, Ferenc (Senior) 383
Pyle, Leslie 67, 72

Quebec, Canada 154
Queen, Gerry 354, 360
Queen's Park FC 6, 98, 381
Queen's Park Rangers FC [QPR] 15, 89, 93, 261, 263, 286, 288, 293, 305-306, 342, 351
Quizball (BBC TV quiz show) 349

Racing Club de Paris 136, 153, 193, 200, 229
Radcliffe, Chelmsford City goalkeeper 66
RAF 57, 59, 85, 302
RAF Representative side 59, 101
Ramsey, Alf 2, 23, 78-79, 81-87, 89-90, 95-97, 102, 107-108, 110, 113-114, 122-124, 126-128, 130-131, 133, 138-140, 142-143, 146-147, 149-155, 159-164, 168, 170-175, 185, 187, 189-190, 193, 197-202, 204, 208-213, 215, 217-218, 224-225, 230-231, 233, 237-239, 241, 243, 246, 249-251, 279, 282, 290, 302, 309, 315, 326, 329, 338-339, 343, 349, 351, 360-361, 369, 374, 377, 385-386
Ray, Ted (comedian) 137
Raynor, George 48, 180
Reading FC 59, 168, 284, 296, 314-315, 324
Real Madrid 112, 182, 262, 270, 293, 296-301, 372, 384, 389
Redknapp, Harry 87, 118, 249

Reep, Charles 101-102
Rees, Billy 82, 119
Reg Hayter Sports Agency 230
Regis, Cyrille 347
Reid, Duggie 216
Reilly, Lawrie 197, 243
Republic of Ireland (nation) 181
Rest of Europe (select side versus England, 1938) 51
Rest of the World XI (versus England, 1953) 184-187
Revell, Charlie 322
Revie, Don 229, 306, 337, 344, 350, 354, 360, 368, 376-377, 380
Rexach, Charly 382
Reynolds, Ron 85, 113, 119, 159, 201, 211, 219, 224-225, 228, 231, 233-234, 237, 239, 248, 385
Rhodes, Brian 304
Rhodesia [today's Zimbabwe] 238
Richards, Steve (journalist) 369
Richardson, W. G. *Billy* 129
Ridding, Bill 192
Rimini, Italy 61
Ringstead, Alf 202
Rioch, Bruce 390
Robb, George 145, 160-161, 163, 175, 186, 197-202, 209-210, 212, 216-217, 219-220, 224-225, 227-228, 231, 233, 245, 247
Roberts, Herbert *Herbie* 18, 28
Roberts, Jack 65-66
Robertson, Max (BBC TV presenter) 121
Robinson, Patrick (journalist and novelist) 346
Robledo, George 1, 139, 146-147, 161, 164, 176, 219, 243, 358
Robson, Sir Bobby 179, 269, 290, 352, 365
Robson, Bryan 118
Rochdale AFC 258, 274
Roe, Tommy 14
Roeder, Glenn 371
Roffey, Bill 364
Rogers, Ben (author of *A J Ayer: A Life*) 375
Rogers, Don 365-366
Romania (army) 54
Romania (nation) 182
Romania national side 181
Rome 17, 61
Roper, Don 147
Rotherham United 339, 346
Rous, Sir Stanley (Secretary, The Football Association and President of FIFA) 39, 48, 54, 57, 91, 186, 282, 386
Rouse, Vic 252, 261, 263, 270, 276-278, 285, 287, 291-293, 298-299, 305, 309-310, 313, 315, 319, 321-322, 386
Route One (term originating from TV football quiz *Quizball*) 99, 349
Rowe, Amy (Arthur's great-granddaughter) 390-391
Rowe, Amy *Pom* (Arthur's wife) 37, 39, 43, 53-56, 62, 75, 156, 226, 230, 246, 282, 319, 321, 345, 355, 373

407

Rowe, Arthur: Testimonial Match, Selhurst Park 116, 359-362
Rowe, Carol (daughter of Arthur's brother, Frank) 391
Rowe, Charlotte (Arthur's mother 'Lottie') 5, 41
Rowe, Daisy Charlotte (Arthur's eldest sister) 5
Rowe, David (son of Arthur's brother, Frank) 391
Rowe, Derek (Arthur's elder son) 39, 55, 230, 373, 387, 391
Rowe, Duncan (Arthur's grandson) 387, 391
Rowe, Frank (Arthur's younger brother) 5, 62
Rowe, Graham (Arthur's younger son) iv, vii, x, 43-44, 55, 125, 207, 230, 234, 252, 373, 391
Rowe, Sydney (Arthur's father) 5, 7
Rowe, Violet (Arthur's younger sister) 5
Rowland Hill School, Tottenham 138
Rowley, Arthur 288
Rowley, Jack 58, 60, 127, 140
Ruiz, Félix 300
Russia, nation 54-56, 117
Ryan, Reg 166

Sacchi, Arrigo 383
Sadler, David 306
Sagar, Ted 41-42
Salonika, Greece 62
Sánchez, Isidro 299-300
Sanders, Jim 129, 217
Sanders, *Mr* (disciple of Rowe and coach of the schoolboy Johnny Haynes) 120
Santamaría, José 297, 300
Sargent, Freddie 38, 65-66, 70-72, 75
Sárosi, Béla 51, 53
Sárosi, György 49, 51, 53, 191
Saskatchewan, Canada 155
Saunders, Ron 380
Scarth, Jimmy 90, 139
Scholar, Irving (Chairman, Tottenham Hotspur FC) 361
Scotland (nation) 92-93, 175, 181, 199, 204, 212, 243, 353, 363
Scotland (national side) 6, 12, 59, 98, 274-275, 338
Scotland (schoolboys) 119
Scott, George (journalist) 93-94
Scott, Laurie 59-60
Scovell, Brian (journalist) 203, 354, 372, 381
Scunthorpe & Lindsey United / Scunthorpe United FC 144, 146, 353
Sebes, Gusztáv 49, 52, 184-186, 189-190, 192, 195-196
Seccombe, Arthur 15
Secretaries and Managers Association 377
Seed, Angus 179
Seed, Jimmy 11-12, 192
Service of Youth scheme 70
Sewell, Jackie 216-217, 225, 243
Sewell, John 329, 341, 343, 351-353, 356, 365

Sexton, Dave 186, 188, 196, 256-258, 261, 272, 282, 292
Seymour, Stan (Director, Newcastle United FC) 2
Shackleton, Len 91, 149
Shalcross, Tom 74
Shankly, Bill 363, 385
Sharpe, Ivan (amateur footballer, journalist and author) 12, 91, 135
Sharratt, Harry 162
Shaw, Jack 216
Shearwood, Ken 131, 171, 251-252
Sheffield United FC 18, 28, 38-39, 45, 89, 92, 95, 175, 202, 207, 211, 218, 230-231
Sheffield Wednesday FC 24, 79, 87, 95-96, 131, 133, 160, 167, 180, 197, 202, 216-217, 225, 233, 243, 277, 363
Sheppey United FC 15
Shilton, Peter 349
Shrewsbury Town FC 288, 294, 303-304, 308
Sidey, Norman 10
Sidlow, Cyril 60
Sillett, Peter 231
Simpson, John 274
Simpson, Peter 268
Simpson, Robert (U.S. hurdler) 50-51
Simpson, Ronnie 160, 167
Sims, Nigel 292
Singer, Jimmy 310
Sittingbourne FC 15-16
Slater, Bill 101, 103
Sliman, Alan 63
Slovan Bratislava 293-294, 301
Smillie, Andy 283-286, 290-291, 294, 296-300, 307-310, 312, 318-319, 324
Smith, Bobby 198, 246-249, 283, 375, 390
Smith, George 58-60, 253-260, 266, 268, 282-283, 287, 289, 326
Smith, Keith 336, 339, 343, 345, 347-348
Smith, Leslie 59
Smith, Maurice (journalist) 96
Smith, Percy 16, 22-25, 27, 30, 37-38, 214, 236
Smith, Tommy 376
Smyth McColl, Robert (Newcastle United manager) 6
Soar, Phil (author) 223
Somerfield, Alf *Slim* 65-66
Soo, Frank 59, 70-72, 74, 76
South Africa 175, 352
South America 141, 180, 184, 194, 290
South East Counties' [youth] League 358
South Korea (national side) 213
Southampton FC 25, 79, 81-82, 92, 126, 141, 242, 337, 339, 353
Southend United FC 64, 74, 287, 294, 308, 327
Southern League [The] 64, 66 (Chelmsford Southern League Champions and Cup winners 1946) 74 (Chelmsford finish runners-up in Rowe's last season)

Southgate, Gareth 390
Southport FC 266, 279
Spain (nation) 102, 194, 284
Spain (national side) 97, 181-182, 267
Sparta Prague 102
Spiers, Cyril 168, 253
Spivey, Douglas 121
SportKlub Wacker (Austrian side) 218
Sports Magazine BBC TV 121
Sports Special BBC TV 276
Sprake, Gary 306
Sproston, Bert 59-60
Spuhler, Johnny 130
Spurs/Tottenham Hotspur [only from page 251 onwards — occurrences are too frequent prior to that] 251-253, 255, 256-257, 260-261, 265, 269-270, 272, 274, 276-277, 279, 282, 284-288, 292-293, 300, 302, 305, 307-308, 313, 315-316, 319-320, 326-327, 346, 349, 353-354, 357-361, 365, 367-368, 370, 373-375, 377-379, 381, 383-392
St Albans City FC 74
Steele, Tommy (singer and actor) 361
Stephenson, Alan 290, 294, 297, 300-301, 304, 316, 319, 329, 335, 337-338, 341-343, 345-347, 349-350, 352, 356, 358, 361
Stephenson, Clem 12
Stevenson, Alex 41
Stiles, Nobby 239, 338, 376
Stock, Alec 217, 386
Stockport County FC 266, 273, 279-280
Stoke City FC 27, 36-37, 59, 70, 90-91, 119, 125, 129-130, 140, 146, 168, 173-174
Stokes, Alf 174
Stokoe, Bob 238, 347
Storey, Peter 376, 380
Storrie, Jim 306
Strange, Alf 32
Stratton Smith, Tony (sports journalist and rock music promoter) 235
Stringer, Mary Ann (Arthur's aunt) 5
Stuttgart 193
Suárez, Luis 390
Summerbee, Mike 291
Summersby, Roy 103, 254-255, 257, 259, 261-264, 266, 268, 272, 274-278, 280-281, 283-286, 288-289, 292, 294, 297-299, 306-310, 312, 318-319, 321-322, 324, 326, 329
Sunderland FC 24, 30-31, 44, 59, 91, 119, 124-125, 128, 142, 149, 164, 167, 174, 198, 202, 211, 215, 218, 225, 244, 360, 363-364, 386
Sutcliffe, C.E. (English football administrator) 177
Sutton United FC 12, 253-254
Swansea 351
Swansea Town FC 24, 26, 69, 95, 214, 248
Sweden (national side) 48, 180, 182
Swedish Football Association 180
Swift, Frank 58-60, 62, 351, 369
Swindin, George 126, 140, 253, 266
Swindlehurst, Dave 364, 366, 386

INDEX

Swindon Town FC 65, 88, 101, 113, 285, 291, 306, 321, 348
Swindon (town) 60, 365
Switzerland (nation) 183, 185
Switzerland (national side) 326
Szeder, György 53

Tambling, Bobby 347
Taylor, Allan 23
Taylor, Carl 278
Taylor, Dr Rogan (co-author of *Puskás on Puskás*) 383
Taylor, Ernie 1, 171, 189, 202
Taylor, Frank (journalist) 370-371
Taylor, Graham 102
Taylor, H.E. (Director, Tottenham Hotspur FC) 203
Taylor, Jack (referee) 382
Taylor, Peter 290
Taylor, Tommy 111, 243
Taylor, Tony, 354, 365
Tejada, Justo 298, 300
Terry, Pat 285
Thatcher, Margaret (student of Dr Harold Thompson, Prime Minister of Great Britain 1979-90) 251, 378
This is Your Life (long-running TV show) 253
Thompson, George 167
Thompson, Harold *Tommy* (Pegasus founder, later FA Chairman) 251-252
Thompson, Jimmy (agent, aka *Mr Pope*) 232
Thompson, John 190
Thornton Heath (suburb of Croydon) 309
Thorpe, Jimmy 31
Three Degrees, The (Batson, Cunningham, Regis) 347
Timpson, John (BBC correspondent) 297-298
Tongue, Steve (journalist and broadcaster) 377
Torino (air crash) 96
Toronto, Canada 155, 373
Torquay United FC 73-74, 258, 260, 284, 291
Torres, José 334
Total Football 100, 102,107,109, 240, 269, 354, 382-384, 390
Tottenham Schools' Football Cup Final 8
Tottenham Schools' Representative side 8
Townsend, Andy 302
Townsend, Don 302, 306, 308, 320
Tranmere Rovers FC 167
Trautmann, Bert 148, 160, 201, 224
Tresadern, Jack 38, 40-41, 43-45, 81, 236
Tripartite Act (Germany, Italy and Japan) 54

Ugolini, Rolando 130, 166
Újpest FC 50-52
Uphill, Dennis 124, 148, 163, 257, 266, 268, 270-272, 274-278, 286, 288-292, 296, 305, 307-308, 312, 319, 321-322
Uruguay (national side) 182, 84, 334
USA (nation) vii, 390
USA (national side) 97, 182

Vághy, Kálmán 50, 53
Valdano, Jorge (coach, Real Madrid) 383-384
Valmontone, Italy 61
Vardy, Jamie 89
Veinante, Émile 31
Venables, Terry 87, 118, 168, 180, 188, 192, 218, 232, 243, 249, 327, 373, 384
Vicente, José 300
Victoria and Albert Museum 158-159
Vries, Jacob de (BBC radio presenter) 286

Wager, Len 72
Wagstaff, Ken 312
Wagstaffe Simmons, Greville (Director, Tottenham Hotspur FC) 203
Wait, Arthur (Chairman, Crystal Palace FC) 206, 237, 253-255, 258-261, 264-265, 267-268, 271-272, 278-279, 281-284, 287, 290, 293-298, 305, 308, 311-315, 319, 321-322, 324, 326-327, 332-334, 339-345, 347, 350-355, 358, 360-361, 365-366
Wait, Brian (son of Crystal Palace Chairman Arthur) 206, 235, 253, 262, 268, 305, 313-314, 341
Walden, Fanny 12
Wale, Fred (Director, Tottenham Hotspur FC) 203, 248
Wales (nation) 24, 81-82, 181, 212
Wales (national side including Under-23s) 59-60, 77, 222, 273, 351
Wall, Peter 363
Walley, Ernie 210
Walley, Keith 368
Walsall FC 255, 258, 333, 344
Walters, Charlie 12
Walters, William *Sonny* 2, 82, 85-86, 89-91, 94, 96, 108, 113, 123-128, 130, 133-134, 136, 138-140, 142-143, 145-150, 158, 160-161, 163-164, 166, 169-170, 175, 197-199, 201-202, 204, 209-210, 212-213, 215-216, 228, 239, 375, 392
Waring, Tom *Pongo* 24, 33
Watford FC 69, 102, 257, 266, 270, 288, 311, 328, 333
Watson, Willie 60
Wayman, Charlie 242-243
Weeks, Alan (BBC TV sports commentator) 276
Welch, Julie 374
Welfare State (birth of) 62
Welham, Benny (Chelmsford City trainer) 66
Wembley Stadium 12, 49, 62, 98, 119, 130-131, 153-154, 170-172, 174, 176, 178, 180, 182, 184-188, 190, 192, 194-196, 202, 222, 227, 251, 267, 290, 334, 338, 377.
Wembley Wizards, the (1928) 12, 98

Wenger, Arsène x, 107, 144, 240, 249, 253, 351, 381, 383, 385, 390
Werge, Eddie 283-285, 296, 307-309, 312, 320, 328
West Bromwich Albion 60, 71, 129-130, 139, 144, 152, 159, 165, 198, 208 [documentary *The Saturday Men*], 210, 217, 229, 238, 252, 254, 268-269, 275, 282-283, 287, 293, 305, 307, 309, 318, 326, 329, 336, 338, 347, 365, 369, 381.
West Germany schoolboy XI 182
West Germany (national side) 192, 213, 275, 365, 382, 384
West Ham boys side 10
West Ham United FC 5, 9, 27, 40, 59, 68, 92, 100, 115, 121, 174, 176, 188, 224, 232, 247, 261, 263, 283, 294-296, 301, 304, 334, 347, 349-350, 352-353, 356, 364, 366
Wetton, Ralph 77, 81, 83, 86, 104, 106-107, 112-113, 122, 136, 141-144, 148, 153, 155-157, 159, 162-163, 166-167, 188, 193, 197, 199, 201, 204, 206-207, 210, 213, 215-216, 224, 230, 232, 234, 237-238, 244
Weymouth FC 72
Whatley, Bill 25
Whittaker, Tom 96, 120, 207, 220-221, 229
White, John 242, 248, 308, 349, 375, 392
White, Tommy (brother of John) 349-350, 352
Whitehouse, Brian 329, 333, 343, 346-347
Wignall, Trevor (journalist) 20, 35
Wilkins, Ray 372
Willard, Jess 356
Williams, Bert 59-60, 128, 142
Willis, Arthur 86, 95, 110, 113, 123, 125-127, 133, 142, 160-162, 167-168, 170, 201, 204, 212-214
Wilshere, Jack 390
Wilson, Jonathan (journalist and author) 102, 110, 184, 190, 381
Wilson, Ray 338
Wilson, Tom (1920s' England defender) 12
Wimbledon FC (now AFC Wimbledon) 344, 364
Windsor & Eton FC 12
Winter, Danny 60
Winterbottom, Walter (Football Association Director of Coaching and England Manager) 47-48, 82, 89, 102, 115, 177, 180, 183, 187-189, 275, 290, 326, 374, 389
Withers, Charlie 77, 86, 95, 122-123, 140, 150, 159-161, 167, 170, 201, 213, 215-216, 224, 239, 374
Woan, Alan 257, 263, 265-266, 270-273, 275, 278
Wolverhampton Wanderers FC [Wolves] 11, 24, 28, 59-60, 65, 96, 101-103, 124, 127-128, 142, 149, 164-165, 167, 173, 175, 183, 194, 202, 207-208, 212, 215-216,

409

229, 248, 335, 339, 349-350, 360, 362, 385
Wood, Brian 283, 291-293, 296, 298, 300-301, 304-305, 312, 315, 320, 324, 329, 345-346
Woodruff, Bobby 349-351, 353-354, 363, 398
Woods, Alan 216, 233
Woods, Charlie 336, 342, 345
Wooller, Wilfred (rugby international) 158-159
Worcester City FC 65-66, 69, 73
Workington A.F.C. 255, 258, 269, 277
World Cup Finals:
1930 (Uruguay) 31
1934 (Italy) 50, 182
1938 (France) 50, 52
1950 (Brazil) 96-97, 181-182
1954 (Switzerland) 185, 192, 213
1958 (Sweden) 48, 182
1962 (Chile) 290, 294, 301, 309, 335, 338, 343, 349
1966 (England) 68, 193, 309, 339, 349
1970 (México) 239, 336, 360
1974 (West Germany) 382-384
1978 (Argentina) 382-383

World Soccer magazine x, 56, 182, 190, 196, 377
World War One 6-7, 15, 54, 76
World War Two 47, 56-62, 77, 98, 188
Wrexham AFC 265, 272, 333

Wright, Alex 124
Wright, Billy 113, 142-143, 183, 189-190, 351, 369

Yankee Stadium, New York 155-156
Yard, Ernie 338-339, 342, 345
Yeovil Town FC 329
York City 203-204, 226-229, 233, 238-239, 270, 273, 277-278, 280-281
Yorkshire County Cricket Club 273, 330
Young, Alf 38
Yugoslavia 191

Zidane, Zinedine 380
Zsengellér, Gyula 51, 53, 191